MARKETING
REAL PEOPLE, REAL DECISIONS

STUDENT ACCESS KIT – DON'T THROW IT AWAY!

With your purchase of this textbook, you received a Student Access Kit for MyMarketingLab: an online learning environment that produces a personalised Study Plan for each student.

When you see this icon in the margin of the text, go to www.pearsoned.co.uk/solomon. There you will find a quiz, the results of which will indicate your understanding of each key concept. MyMarketingLab uses your results to diagnose your individual strengths and weaknesses, and builds a customised Study Plan to help improve your grades.

MYMARKETINGLAB PUTS YOU IN CONTROL!

MyMarketingLab gives you access to an unrivalled suite of online resources:

- Practice tests for each key concept in Marketing that assess your understanding
- A Personalised Study Plan, which adapts to your strengths and weaknesses
- Interactive exercises that break key concepts into component steps, allowing you to actively engage with each issue.
- Pages from an e-book version of this book, allowing for convenient study on the go!
- A wealth of video clips demonstrate how top Marketing Managers from a wide range of companies (including IKEA, Land Rover, HSBC, VSO and many more) refer to Marketing theory in their day-to-day lives.
- Audio MP3 clips, recorded by a Marketing professional, outlining how a key concept relates to contemporary practice.
- An online Glossary defines key terms and provides examples
- Learn and save! We've devised several exercises for you to learn about sales promotion. If you complete the online exercises and use the vouchers we mention, then you should easily save more than our book cost. The only marketing book ever published that pays for itself!

To activate your pre-paid subscription go to www.pearsoned.co.uk/solomon and follow the instructions on-screen to register as a new user, and see your grades improve.

Praise for the first European edition of *Marketing: Real People, Real Decisions*

"Seen through the lens of real-life situations and people, it captures the mood, direction and reality of marketing today . . . it is very much a text of the noughties; modern, youthful with a particular emphasis on the technologically-enabled times in which we live. It is a feet-on-the-ground text, which comprehensively covers all the standard marketing theories, updates them to modern living, but, MOST IMPORTANTLY acknowledges that despite all the theory, reality is different and challenging. It reflects the fact that studying marketing is much more than learning theories and rules, that there is a requirement to make decisions, that there are always a number of choices available, and that a key element of implementing marketing is accountability, measurement and learning from the practical outcome, whether or not that was as intended. It is a text which brings marketing to life and brings life to marketing."

Marilyn Hunt, University of Worcester

"A treasure trove of information and insight"

Yvonne McGivern, Market Research Society

"The way the real cases are used in this text is an innovative attempt to engage and inspire students"

Fiona Syson, Edgehill University

"How refreshing to see a text that combines real life views of practitioners with those of academics and students"

Janet Hull, Institute of Practioners of Advertising

"A highly engaging marketing textbook with up-to-date coverage of marketing concepts, a broad range of European marketing applications and lots of opportunities for student discussion and problem-solving."

Sally McKechnie, Nottingham University

"Up-to-date, interesting and relevant cases and scenarios which challenge students to put themselves in the shoes of modern marketing decision makers."

Matthew Wood, University of Brighton

"Engages students with real world business issues and challenges them to come to decisions"

Colin Mason, University of Strathclyde

First European Edition

Solomon • Marshall • Stuart • Barnes • Mitchell

MARKETING

Real People, Real Decisions

 FT Prentice Hall

FINANCIAL TIMES

An imprint of **Pearson Education**

Harlow, England • London • New York • Boston • San Francisco • Toronto • Sydney • Singapore • Hong Kong
Tokyo • Seoul • Taipei • New Delhi • Cape Town • Madrid • Mexico City • Amsterdam • Munich • Paris • Milan

Pearson Education Limited

Edinburgh Gate
Harlow
Essex CM20 2JE
England

and Associated Companies throughout the world

Visit us on the World Wide Web at:
www.pearsoned.co.uk

Authorised adaptation from the United States edition, entitled *Marketing: Real People, Real Choices*, fifth edition, ISBN: 0-13-229920-8 by Michael R. Solomon, Greg W. Marshall and Elnora W. Stuart, published by Pearson Education, Inc., publishing as Prentice Hall, copyright © 2008.

First published 2009

© Pearson Eduction Limited 2009

ISBN: 978-0-273-70880-3

British Library Cataloguing-in-Publication Data
A catalogue record for this book is available from the British Library

Library of Congress Cataloging-in-Publication Data
Marketing : real people, real decisions / Michael R. Solomon . . . [et al.]. — 1st European ed.
   p. cm.
 Previous ed. entered under: Solomon, Michael R.
 ISBN 978-0-273-70880-3
 1. Marketing—Vocational guidance. I. Solomon, Michael R.
 HF5415.35.S65 2009
 658.8—dc22

                                 2008055087

10 9 8 7 6 5 4 3
11 10

Typeset in 10/12.5 Goudy by 73
Printed and bound by Rotolito Lombarda, Italy

*To Gail, Amanda, Zachary, Alexandra, Orly, Squishy,
and Kelbie Rae—my favourite market segment*

M.S.

To Patti and Justin

G.M.

To Sonny, Patrick, Gabriela, and Marge

E.S.

*This book is dedicated to my mother, Elizabeth Mitchell, who
died 1 July 1988, for her unfailing belief in and support
for me during my academic studies*

V.M.

*To my wife Sophavy, children Isabelle and Edouard and our
late grandfather, Eddie, who we all loved so much!*

B.B.

FOREWORD

Marketing is a wonderful career that offers an amazing variety of work while also being intellectually stimulating and creative. It is about understanding people and what motivates them, which means we must understand marketing's role in the wider context of business. *Marketing: Real People, Real Decisions* is a stimulating book that is easy to read and relates directly to the day-to-day experiences of the reader and is applicable to issues met every day in a consumer society.

Marketing is a discipline which is based on practical experience. While academics have summarised 'best practice' into frameworks, theories and concepts, marketing is still more an art than a science, and as an applied discipline professional marketers need to understand that the application varies in different situations and industries. No two jobs are the same and the practice of marketing requires a balance between science and subjectivity, and recognition of when to apply the science and when it will not be suitable. This book avoids the sterile discussions found in some texts and instead uses the material to illustrate the complex intellectual challenge found in solving particular dilemmas and choosing between options.

The wealth of examples and case studies means the ideas and concepts can be directly related to work and life experiences, giving them more meaning, and hence making them more easily understood. The marketing exercises are a good way of stimulating debate as to the 'best' solution and will allow application of the concepts and issues discussed in the chapters.

All marketers should be professionally qualified and this book gives a very good introduction to the real experiences met by professional marketers. I hope it stimulates its readers to follow marketing as a career and to continue their professional development.

Professor Keith Fletcher
Director of Education at the Chartered Institute of Marketing

Brief contents

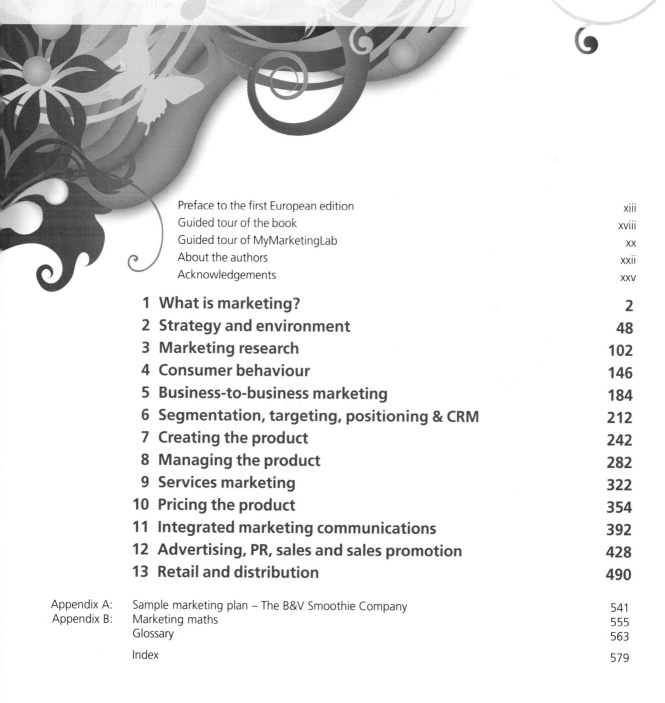

Contents

1 What is marketing?   2

2   Strategy and environment   **48**

3   Marketing research   **102**

4   Consumer behaviour   **146**

8 Managing the product   282

9 Services marketing   322

10 Pricing the product   354

Preface to the first European edition

Whether you are a student, a managing practitioner, or marketing lecturer, what is interesting to know about this marketing text book is that it is the only one that presents marketing from the perspective of the people who actually do marketing and make real decisions. In the text, you will meet real marketers, i.e. those who make marketing decisions every day in industry. We have carefully focused on specific case scenarios to broaden learning and help students consider more real-to-life situations, in addition to providing the core essentials relating to the themes of each chapter.

This book has been developed for those who aspire to work in marketing roles, as well as those who don't. If you fall into the first category, you'll soon learn the basics so that you can understand how marketers contribute to the creation of value. If you fall into the second category, then hopefully by the time you have worked your way through this text, we will have been able to persuade you to move into the first category. Even if we don't persuade you, the text will highlight how the principles of marketing apply to many fields of business, everything from sports to accounting. Regardless of your reasons for studying marketing, we have worked hard to develop lively material in an attempt to stimulate your thinking and allow you to consider the options and make decisions. You don't just read about it, you are actively involved in decisions.

Real Marketing Topics and Events

This European text reflects what's happening right now in the world of marketing. You'll start by learning the most recent definition of just what marketing is. You'll learn that marketing focuses on creating and transferring value from providers to consumers, and ensuring that all parties in any marketing transaction are satisfied (making it more likely they'll continue to do business in the future). These steps in the book include:

- Making Marketing Value Decisions
- Understanding Consumers' Value Needs
- Creating the Value Proposition
- Communicating the Value Proposition
- Delivering the Value Proposition

To keep you on top of the world of marketing, we've updated our coverage. Here's just a sample of what's new:

- 12 new and wide-ranging Real Voice case studies open and close each chapter to give you a taste of what it is to be a marketer today. Watch video interviews with a selection of these, and other marketers in case studies exclusive to the website, online.
- Marketing Ethics, a new and unique feature to this book provides topical coverage on ethical issues and an opportunity to debate ethical dilemmas from the headlines.
- There are many more Marketing Metrics insights throughout the book and real decision support spreadsheets for you to do on the website.
- Expanded coverage of e-marketing, especially on our website, gives you insight into this rapidly evolving area.
- MyMarketingLab is the brand new online learning environment that diagnoses your individual strengths and weaknesses before building you a customized study plan. You'll watch Real Voice interviews and YouTube clips about marketing, hear Podcasts and audio bulletins, access an e-book version of your textbook and engage with interactive challenges, before tracking your own progress within the online gradebook. This icon in the text will tell you when there is material on the website to support your learning.

www.pearsoned.co.uk/Solomon

Acknowledgements

We feature many talented marketers and successful companies in this book. In developing it, we also were fortunate to work with a team of exceptionally talented and creative people at Pearson Education. David Cox and Sarah Busby were instrumental in helping us stay on track and meet deadlines, and provided invaluable support when it was most needed – many thanks, as without them this book would not have made it.

A special note of appreciation goes to Hanah Iqbal Mirza and Katherine Johnson of Kent Business School and Adam Szuts, Sabrina Gottschalk and Maximilian Link at Cass Business School for their great support in helping assemble chapter material and photographs to ensure this text is as fresh and timely as possible. No book is complete without a solid supplements package. We extend out thanks to our dedicated supplement authors, particularly Professor Bob Shaw for his work on marketing metrics. Finally, our utmost thanks and appreciation go to our friends and families for their continued support and encouragement. Without them this project would not be possible.

Many people have worked to make this text a success. The guidance and recommendations of the following participants have helped us update and improve the chapters and the supplements:

 # Review Board

These reviewers consistently gave thorough and considered feedback throughout the writing process which proved invaluable in the development of the chapters.

Andrea Beetles, Cardiff University
Anne Hampton, University of Buckingham
Associate Professor Jacob Aabroe Hansen, Roskilde Business College, Denmark
Dr Els Breugelmans, Maastricht University, The Netherlands
Dr Elisabeth Brüggen, Maastricht University, The Netherlands
Fiona Syson, Edge Hill University
Marilyn Hunt, University of Worcester
Dr Anthony Willis, University of Surrey
Tarja Saarinen, Haaga-Helia University of Applied Sciences, Finland

 # Executives Featured in 'Real People, Real Decisions'

These opening case studies with a broad range of real marketing executives will allow you to explore what it is to be a marketer and the day-to-day decisions they must make.

Chapter 1:   Keith Edelman, former Managing Director of Arsenal Football Club.
Chapter 2:   Philippe Garnier, Senior Director of Distribution and Sales at Hilton Hotels.
Chapter 3:   Helen Armstrong, Client Services Director of Research International in London.
Chapter 4:   Richard Sells, Chief Innovation Officer, Electrolux, Sweden.
Chapter 5:   Brian Oxley, Commercial Director at SASH UK.
Chapter 6:   Ken Moss, Sheffield Chamber of Commerce and Industry.
Chapter 7:   Ben Tisdall, Director of SpeedBreaks.
Chapter 8:   Jamie Mitchell, former MD, Innocent Drinks, Fruit Towers, London.
Chapter 9:   Patricia Vaz, former MD of UK Customer Service for BT.
Chapter 10:   Phil Byrne, Chief Executive at BR Pharmaceuticals.

Chapter 11:   Ian Bruce, Director of the Centre for Charity Effectiveness and former chief
of the RNIB.
Chapter 12:   Rick Goings, Tupperware, Brands Corporation.
Chapter 13:   Jill Carter and Kate Crapper-Reardon, Partners at The Holiday Shop Ltd.

Contributions to the 'Marketing in Action' case studies

These academics have contributed some of their most interesting and thought-provoking case studies, providing you with examples of real marketing decisions in practice.

Chapter 4:   Written by Dr Paul Harborne, Cass Business School.
Chapter 6:   Written by Dr Stan Maklan, Cranfield School of Management.
Chapter 9:   Written by Professor Leyland Pitt, Segal Graduate School of Business,
Simon Fraser University.
Chapter 10:   Written by Dr Ben Lowe, Kent Business School.
Chapter 12:   Written by Frederick Thomson, Kent Business School, based on contributions
by Cameron Thomson.

Contributions to the 'Across the Hall' boxes

These reflections on the opening marketing dilemma will give you an invaluable insight into how marketing practitioners and people in overlapping disciplines might approach a marketing problem.

Professor Keith Fletcher is Director of Education at the Chartered Institute of Marketing.
Yvonne McGivern is Joint Chief Examiner for the MRS Advanced Certificate in Market and Social Research Practice and author of *The Practice of Market Research*.
Professor Cary L. Cooper CBE is an expert and author in organisational psychology and founder of leading business psychology company Robertson Cooper Limited.
Shane Redding is founder of Think Direct, experts in business-to-business marketing, and Chair of the Institute of Direct Marketing's B2B Council.
Professor Merlin Stone is a leading expert and author on direct and relationship marketing and Fellow of the Chartered Institute of Marketing and the Institute of Direct Marketing.
Colin Mason is Professor of Entrepreneurship in the Hunter Centre for Entrepreneurship, University of Strathclyde.
Marcel Knobil is a leading expert, author and consultant on branding, founder of Superbrands and chair of Creative and Commercial.
Alan Griffiths is Reader in Economics at the Ashcroft International Business School of Anglia Ruskin University and co-author of *Economics for Business and Management*, published by Financial Times/Prentice Hall.
Janet Hull is Consultant Head of Marketing at the Institute of Practitioners in Advertising and has been a judge of the IPA Effectiveness Awards and the CIM Effectiveness Awards.
Tom Beaumont-Griffin is Strategy Director at Sledge Integrated, a leading brand experience agency in the UK.
Dr Adrian Haberberg, Principal Lecturer in Strategic Management and MBA Director at the University of East London and co-author of *Strategic Management: Theory and Application*.
Derek Williams, Managing Director of The WOW! Awards at www.TheWowAwards.co.uk.
Don Hales, World of Customer Service founder and Chairman of Judges for the National Customer Service Awards.

Academics featured in the 'Real People, Other Voices' boxes

These marketing academics' analysis of the Real Voices case studies offer you a broad variety of interpretations and solutions to the dilemmas encountered.

Jocelyn Hayes, University of York
David Chalcraft, University of Westminster
Tony Garry, De Montfort University
Michael Howley, University of Surrey
Stephen Brown, University of Ulster
Nnamdi O. Madichie, University of East London
Jenny Lloyd, University of the West of England
Deborah Roberts, Nottingham University
John Desmond, University of St Andrews
Carol Kelleher, University College Cork
Adrian Palmer, Swansea University
Matthew Wood, University of Brighton
Zubin Sethna, University of Westminster
Peter Rudduck, University of Central Lancashire
Nigel Bradley, University of Westminster (photo by Chris Haydon)
Philip Warwick, University of York
Fiona Cheetham, University of Salford
Bill Barlow, University of Abertay, Dundee
Sally McKechnie, Nottingham University
Fiona Ellis-Chadwick, Loughborough University
Laurent Muzellec, Dublin City University

Students featured in the 'Real People, Other Voices' boxes

It's also interesting for you to hear other students' perspectives on these marketing dilemmas and here you can read their thoughts and suggestions.

Christian Grønlund, Roskilde Business College, Denmark
Richard Victor, University of East London
Hannah Geddes, University of Surrey
Tony Bqain, University of Worcester
Toby Wade, University of York
Eliska Janackova, University of Surrey
Christina Hansen, Roskilde Business College, Denmark

Guided tour of the book

Real Voices open each chapter by introducing a real marketer and a genuine dilemma they've faced, along with three possible solutions. Hear stories from companies as diverse and innovative as Innocent, Electrolux and Arsenal, and think about which option you would choose, if you were in their shoes.

In **Real People, Other Voices** you'll hear a range of opinions from marketing academics and students who discuss the options and offer their own advice on which solution to adopt.

In **Across the Hall** hear practitioners and academics from related disciplines offer a fresh perspective on the dilemma.

At the end of each chapter, you'll discover the marketer's 'real decision' in **How it Worked Out** which will explore why the decision was made, the benefits and problems, and the marketing metrics used to measure the outcome's success. This unique feature gives you an invaluable insight into how marketing works in practice.

Marketing Metrics in every chapter provide real-world examples of the calculations marketers use to inform good decisions. Just how do marketers add value to a company and can that value be quantified? More and more, businesses demand accountability, and marketers have responded by developing a variety of "scorecards" that show how specific marketing activities directly affect their company's ROI—return on investment. In real life, the decisions that marketers make increasingly come from data and calculations and less from instinct.

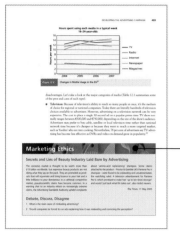

As the role of ethics in business and in marketing is so important, coverage of ethics appears throughout the book, and ***Marketing Ethics*** boxes explore topical issues from the headlines, encouraging you to "discuss, debate or disagree"

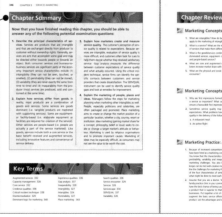

At the end of the every chapter you can revise and extend your knowledge of the topic using the ***Chapter Summary*** and list of ***Key Terms***, the ***Chapter Review*** which includes a variety of questions and projects including ***Real People, Real Surfers***, a feature using the web, and finally a ***Marketing Plan exercise*** to put your learning into practice.

Each chapter also concludes with an exciting ***Marketing in Action*** case about a real company or real issue facing marketers. Questions at the end let you "make the decision" to get the company on the right track, or consider the problem in greater depth.

Guided tour of MyMarketingLab

New to this European Edition is **MyMarketingLab** which puts you in control of your learning by testing your knowledge, identifying the areas you need to study further and creating a personalised Study Plan.

Within selected chapters of MyMarketingLab, watch **video interviews** with the marketers you've read about in the book talking in-depth about their marketing dilemma with the authors. There are also brand new **Real Voice** case studies, exclusive to MyMarketingLab.

The **interactive marketing plan** breaks down this essential aspect of marketing planning into a series of simple steps and shows you how to use the book to guide you. Click on each step in the marketing plan to see the questions that you should be answering and where in the text you'll find these issues discussed.

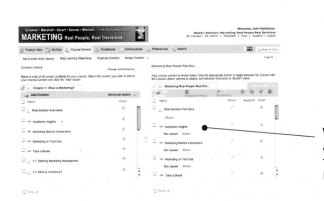

We've asked **renowned marketing academics** from around the world to discuss their area of expertise for each chapter. Click on this section MyMarketingLab to read their advice.

Robert Shaw and David Merrick have created **Marketing Metrics Interactions** exclusively for the web, for you to test your skills and make real marketing decisions, based on your calculations.

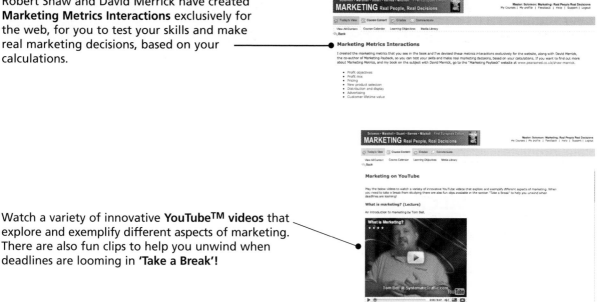

Watch a variety of innovative **YouTube™ videos** that explore and exemplify different aspects of marketing. There are also fun clips to help you unwind when deadlines are looming in **'Take a Break'!**

4321-9237

NeoReader, a unit of NeoMedia Technologies, has created software that links you directly from your mobile phone to pages on the web using brand names, barcodes and smartcodes as hyperlinks. Just go to www.neoreader.com, click on 'get neoreader' to download the software and scan this qode with your camera phone to go direct to our website! NeoReader's software is a demonstration of how new technologies, consumer trends and innovative marketing come together to create something exciting – and just one example of the cutting-edge marketing that you'll be introduced to throughout this book. Read more about the company in the Marketing in Action case study at the end of Chapter 3, *Marketing Research*.

For Lecturers

A full suite of lecturer support material is provided with this textbook including:

- Extensive **Instructor's Manual**, with sample answers for all the question material in the book, detailed lecture outlines, potential exam questions and marketing plan assignments and 'marketing moments' which offer ideas for class activities.

- A **Testbank** of over 500 multiple choice questions.

- Media-rich **PowerPoint slides** including figures and tables from the book.

- **Additional Real Voice case studies**, exclusive to the website, some of which have accompanying interview footage.

- A range of **international Real Voice case studies** from the US, Canada and Australia.

- New **Marketing in Action** case studies that explore the latest trends.

- A wealth of **YouTube™ video clips**, about marketing, for each chapter.

Contact your local Pearson Education sales consultant to obtain more details about these resources or to arrange a demonstration. Sales consultant details can be found at www.pearsoned.co.uk/replocator.

About the authors

MICHAEL R. SOLOMON

MICHAEL R. SOLOMON, Ph.D., joined the Haub School of Business at Saint Joseph's University in Philadelphia as Professor of Marketing in 2006, where he also serves as Director of the Center for Consumer Research. From 1995 to 2006, he was the Human Sciences Professor of Consumer Behavior at Auburn University. Prior to joining Auburn in 1995, he was Chairman of the Department of Marketing in the School of Business at Rutgers University, New Brunswick, New Jersey. Professor Solomon's primary research interests include consumer behavior and lifestyle issues, branding strategy, the symbolic aspects of products, the psychology of fashion, decoration and image, services marketing, and the development of visually oriented online research methodologies. He currently sits on the Editorial Boards of the *Journal of Consumer Behaviour*, the *European Business Review*, and the *Journal of Retailing*, and he recently completed a six-year term on the Board of Governors of the Academy of Marketing Science. In addition to other books, he is also the author of Prentice Hall's text *Consumer Behavior: Buying, Having, and Being*, which is widely used in universities throughout the world. Professor Solomon frequently appears on television and radio shows such as The Today Show, Good Morning America, Channel One, The Wall Street Journal Radio Network and National Public Radio to comment on consumer behaviour and marketing issues.

GREG W. MARSHALL

GREG W. MARSHALL, Ph.D., is the Charles Harwood Professor of Marketing and Strategy in the Crummer Graduate School of Business at Rollins College, Winter Park, Florida. Prior to joining Rollins, he served on the faculties of Oklahoma State University, the University of South Florida and Texas Christian University. He earned a BSBA in Marketing and an MBA from the University of Tulsa and a Ph.D. in Marketing from Oklahoma State University. Professor Marshall's research interests center on issues surrounding sales force and sales manager perform-ance, decision making by marketing managers and intraorganisational relationships. He currently serves on the Editorial Boards of the *Journal of the Academy of Marketing Science*, *Journal of Business Research* and *Industrial Marketing Management*, and he is Editor of the *Journal of Marketing Theory and Practice* and former editor of the *Journal of Personal Selling & Sales Management*. Professor Marshall is President-Elect of the Academy of Marketing Science, Past-President of the American Marketing Association Academic Division and a Fellow and Past-President of the Society for Marketing Advances. His industry experience prior to entering academe includes product management, field sales management and retail management positions with firms such as Warner-Lambert, the Mennen Company and Target Corporation.

ELNORA W. STUART

ELNORA W. STUART, Ph.D., is Professor of Marketing at the University of South Carolina Upstate. Prior to joining USC Upstate in 2008, she was Professor of Marketing and the BP Egypt Oil Professor of Management Studies at The American University in Cairo, Professor of Marketing at Winthrop University in Rock Hill, South Carolina, and on the faculty of the University of South Carolina. She is also a regular visiting professor at Instituto de Empresa in Madrid, Spain. She earned a B.A. degree in Theatre/Speech from the University of North Carolina at Greensboro and both a Master of Arts in Journalism and Mass Communication and a Ph.D. in Marketing from the University of South Carolina. Professor Stuart's research has been published in major academic journals including the *Journal of Consumer Research*, *Journal of Advertising*, *Journal of Business Research*, and *Journal of Public Policy and Marketing*. For over 25 years she has served as a consultant for numerous businesses and not-for-profit organisations in the United States and in Egypt.

BRADLEY R. BARNES

BRADLEY R. BARNES, Ph.D., is the Hong Kong Alumni Endowed Chair Professor of International Management at Kent Business School, University of Kent, United Kingdom. Prior to becoming an academic, he worked extensively in export, services and business-to-business marketing. He obtained his BA in Business at Sheffield Business School, his M.Sc in Marketing from the University of Huddersfield and his Ph.D from the University of Leeds. Professor Barnes researches in the area of Anglo-Chinese Business, building on much of his practitioner expertise in the areas of international (export) marketing in a business-to-business marketing context. He currently serves on the Editorial Boards of *Industrial Marketing Management*, *International Journal of Advertising* and *Journal of Medical Marketing*. His research has appeared in a number of academic as well as practitioner led journals including *Industrial Marketing Management*, *European Journal of Marketing*, *Journal of Marketing Management*, *International Journal of Advertising*, and *Journal of Business-to-Business Marketing* among others.

VINCENT-WAYNE MITCHELL

VINCENT-WAYNE MITCHELL, Ph.D., is the Sir John E Cohen Professor of Consumer Marketing Cass Business School, City University London. Prior to Cass, he was Professor of Marketing at University of Manchester Institute of Science and Technology where he did his MSc and Ph.D. His research focuses on consumer behavior, with particular focus on consumer problems such as complaining and risk taking. He has won 8 Best Paper Awards and has published over 200 academic and practitioner papers in journals such as *Harvard Business Review*, *Journal of Business Research*, *Journal of Economic Psychology*, *Journal of Consumer Affairs*, *Journal of Business Ethics*, *Services Industries Journal*. He sits on the Editorial Boards of six international journals, is associate editor of the *International Journal of Management Reviews* as well as being an Expert Adviser for the Office of Fair Trading and Head of Marketing at Cass. He has undertaken work for numerous organisations and received research funding and support from; the DTI, Lancashire County Council, Early Learning Centre, Cooperative Bank, British Brandowners Group, Coca Cola, Boots, KPMG, Safeway, Viatel, and Tesco. His research has been extensively reported in the *Financial Times*, *Times*, *Guardian*, *The Daily Telegraph*, in THES, Radios 1 and 4, Granada TV, BBC's Inside Story, Ten O'clock News, Working Lunch and Channel 5.

ROBERT SHAW

ROBERT SHAW, BA, MA, MSc, PhD, FCIM, FRSA. Consultant, businessman and author of the international best-sellers Marketing Payback, Improving Marketing Effectiveness and Database Marketing, Professor Robert Shaw has a global reputation as a leading authority on finance and marketing, including Value Based Marketing and Customer Relationship Management. Robert has worked as strategic adviser to Lou Gerstner and Sam Palmisano on IBM's entry into the global services market and as head of the Marketing Practice at Accenture (under its previous name Andersen Consulting). He has also consulted for many major companies and advised professional bodies all over the world including Barclays, BP, CIMA, Diageo, IBM, IPA, Manchester United, Nestlé, Scottish Widows, Unilever and Universal Music.

Currently Professor of Marketing Metrics at Cass Business School, London, Robert is also director of the Value Based Marketing Forum, a consulting firm that offers strategic reviews, analysis and modelling best-practice processes for finance and marketing. Having authored of over 100 books and papers, Robert is in demand both in the UK and overseas as a conference chairman and keynote speaker. He has been invited to speak at over 250 events in addition to teaching on in-company executive education programmes and MBAs.

Acknowledgements

We are grateful to the following for permission to reproduce copyright material:

Table 2.1 from the CIA world factbook (2008) http://www.cia.gov/library/publications/the-world-factbook; Table 2.2 material used in this table is licensed under the GNU Free Documentation License (http://www.gnu.org/copyleft/fdl.html) and it also includes material from the article http://en.wikipedia.org/wiki/European_Community_competition_law, and material from Europa © European Communities 1995–2008; Table 2.3 © European Parliament 2000–2005 and © European Communities, 1995–2008; Table 6.1 reprinted by permission of Harvard Business Review from Don Peppers, Martha Rogers and Bob Dorf, 'Is your company ready for one-to-one marketing?', *Harvard Business Review* (Jan–Feb), pp. 151–60 (1999), copyright © 1999 by the Harvard Business School Publishing Corporation, all rights reserved; Table 8.1 'The EFQM Excellence Award', from http://www.efqm.org/uploads/Press/documents/PR2007EEA_Winners_Announced.pdf; Figure 8.7 from Kevin Lane Keller, 'Building Customer-Based Brand Equity: A Blueprint for Creating Strong Brands', Working Paper Series (2001) Report 01-107, p. 7; Figure 9.2 reproduced with permission of Emerald Group Publishing Ltd from G. Lynn Shostack, 'How to design a service', *European Journal of Marketing*, 16(1), p. 52 © 1982, permission conveyed through the Copyright Clearance Center, Inc.; Table 11.3 'Word of mouth 101; an introduction to word of mouth marketing' from www.womma.org/wom101.htm; Figure 13.2 reprinted with the permission of the Free Press, a Division of Simon & Schuster, Inc., from *Competitive Advantage: Creating and Sustaining Superior Performance* by Michael E. Porter, copyright © 1985, 1998 by Michael E. Porter, all rights reserved; Figure B3 from R. Shaw and D. Merrick, *Marketing Payback*, © 2005, Pearson Education Ltd.

Chapter 1, p. 17, from 'Make it green and keep them keen . . . ', *Guardian*, 21 January 2008, copyright Guardian News and Media Ltd 2008; Chapter 1, p. 18, from 'The ASA sees red about "green" claims in ads', *Marketing Week* (6 December 2007), published by Sarah Bromley; Chapter 1, pp. 38 from 'Furious vicar clears shelves at local shop of Playboy stationery "targeted at children"', Chris Brooke, Mail Online, 20 May 2008, © Daily Mail; Chapter 3, p. 113, from 'Supermarkets use loyalty cards to kill off local stores', *The Daily Telegraph*, 8 June 2007; Chapter 4, pp. 160 from 'Cruel consumer cost of the human egg trade', *The Observer*, 20 April 2006, © Helena Smith; Chapter 6, pp. 224, from 'Half of all children don't know their own name – but two thirds of three-year-olds can recognise the McDonald's golden arches', *Guardian*, 25 October 2005, copyright Guardian News and Media Ltd 2005; Chapter 7, pp. 271, 'Bottled water or tap water? Which is better?', from Consumers International – Press Briefing: International Bad Product Awards 2007, December 2007, Consumers International; Chapter 8, p. 308, from 'Unexpected bitter taste', *Marketing Week*, 5 April 2007, published by Sarah Bromley; Chapter 9, pp. 339, from 'Co-op bank develops ethical financial products, but at a cost of £9m', © The Independent (London), 25 July 2005; Chapter 10, pp. 383, from 'Pricing gas causes sparks', *Utility Week*, 27(16), p. 5, reproduced from *Utility Week* 13 July 2007; Chapter 12, pp. 439, 'Secrets and lies of beauty industry laid bare by advertising', *The Times*, 11 May 2005; Chapter 12 p. 451, from 'Drug firms a danger to health – international research exposes flaws in £33bn marketing budget', *Guardian*, 26 June 2006, copyright Guardian News and Media Ltd 2006.

We are grateful to the Financial Times Limited for permission to reprint the following material:

Chapter 5 'Many GreenPac products hang on the shelves of top retailers', © *FT Your Business*, 12 May 2007.

We are grateful to the following for permission to reproduce photographs:

The Absolut Company for: 4.1 (p. 158); The Advertising Archives for: 1.2 (p. 17); 1.3 (p. 28); 1.4 (p. 40); 2.1 (p. 56); 2.3 (p. 64); 3.1 (p. 107); 4.2 (p. 163); 4.3 (p. 165); 4.4 (p. 166); 4.5 (p. 167); 4.6 (p. 172); 6.1 (p. 217); 6.2 (p. 219); 6.3 (p. 221); 6.5 (p. 228); 7.1 (p. 242); 7.2 (p. 257); 7.3 (p. 269); 7.4 (p. 272); 8.2 (p. 287); 8.3 (p. 298); 8.4 (p. 306); 8.5 (p. 309); 9.2 (p. 327); 9.3 (p. 343); 9.4 (p. 343); 10.1 (p. 359); 10.2 (p. 370); 10.3 (p. 372); 10.4 (p. 381); 11.2 (p. 397); 11.3 (p. 400); 11.5 (p. 414); 12.1 (p. 431); 12.2 (p. 432); 12.3 (p. 433); 12.4 (p. 437); 12.5 (p. 441); 12.9 (p. 461); and 31.2 (p. 501); BMW Group (Germany) for: 3.3 (p. 120); 8.1 (p. 286); and 13.3 (p. 508); Borders for: 13.4 (p. 516); BP plc for: 11.1 (p. 395); BT Image Library for: 9.5 (p. 345); Centre for Consumer Freedom for: 1.5 (p. 33); Christians Against Poverty for: 2.5 (p. 81); DHL (Germany) for: 5.1 (p. 187); 5.2 (p. 194); 12.7 (p. 455); and 12.8 (p. 455); easyJet Airline Company for: 2.4 (p. 75); Electrolux for: 4.7 (p. 175); Getty Images/Yoshikazu for: 13.5 (p. 519); Greenpeace UK for: 9.1 (p. 325); Holiday Shop for: 13.8 (p. 530); IPA for: 3.4 (p. 126); Keith Edelman for: 1.6 (p. 39) and 1.7 (p. 40); Linden Research Ltd for: 1.1 (p. 11); Philippe Garnier for 2.6 (p. 91) and 2.7 (p. 91); Tesco Image Library for 2.2 (p. 57); Trendwatching.com for: 3.2 (p. 118); Tupperware Ltd for: 12.11 (p. 477); Volvo Group UK Ltd for: 5.3 (p. 200); and the World Gold Council for 3.5 (p. 136).

In some instances we have been unable to trace the owners of copyright material, and we would appreciate any information that would enable us to do so.

Chapter 1
What is Marketing?

Meet Keith Edelman,
Former Managing Director of Arsenal Football Club

**Q & A with
Keith Edelman**

Career high?
Opening the Emirates Stadium

Best business book you've read?
The Coke Wars

Motto to live by?
Explore your own boundaries

**My management
style is . . .**
Direct and tough; don't sell it, tell it!

**Don't do this when interviewing
me . . .**
Ask me about my personal life

Favourite drink?
Red wine

Best holiday?
Alaska

Keith graduated from the University of Manchester Institute of Science and Technology in 1968 where he studied Management Sciences. He then held a number of financial positions in blue chip companies including IBM, Xerox and Grand Metropolitan. He joined Ladbroke Group in 1985 as a Corporate Planner and joined the Board in 1986. At Ladbrokes he was responsible for all M&A activity culminating in the acquisition of Hilton International in 1987. At that time he also took up the role of Chairman of Texas Homecare. In 1991 he took up the position of Managing Director of Carlton Communications and then became Chief Executive of Storehouse in 1993. The Storehouse Group included BHS, Mothercare, One Up and Blazer. The two latter brands were sold and Keith drove the profitability of the group from £49 million to £128 million in 1998. He then joined Arsenal Football Club where he oversaw the successful development of the Emirates Stadium which was completed on time and budget alongside the commercial development of the business.

Real People, Real Decisions
Decision time at Arsenal

Arsenal Football Club began life when a group of workers at the Woolwich Arsenal Armament Factory decided to form a football team in late 1886. Major successes on the field for over a century, such as in 2004 when they went 49 league matches without defeat and in 2006 when they were the first English club to win at Real Madrid, resulted in a loyal and growing fan base. Part of their success was the sheer talent of star players such as Gunners captain and the club's record goalscorer, Thierry Henry, who in 2006 committed his future to Arsenal before going on to help France reach the World Cup final in Germany. The old, hallowed and art deco Highbury stadium which had opened in 1936 and had a seating capacity of 38,000 was no longer big enough for the ever-increasing fan base. Arsenal had 22,000 season ticket holders and a base of 25,000 fans who could buy a matchday ticket (of which there were only 12,000 for each match) and a long waiting time for both lists.

It was decided that a new stadium had to be built to cater for the increasing number of fans, to better serve their needs and to fully explore the potential business opportunities for the Gunners. The total cost of the entire project including the construction of Emirates Stadium, a new waste and recycling centre and relocation of local businesses and statutory services was £430 million, which left Arsenal with a big debt to pay off despite gaining major sponsorship deals with companies such as Emirates airlines. The main issue for Arsenal after it moved to the new Emirates Stadium in 2006 was how to fill the stadium's capacity, which had increased from 38,000 seats to 60,000 seats and the daunting task for Keith Edelman and his team prior to the move was: How do you expand your core business by 40 per cent in 12 months? Key to this was how the tickets were allocated and the decision between season ticket holders and one-off matchday ticket holders.

Keith and his team came up with three options of different complexity and cost.

Keith considers his options . . .

Option 1 Keep the old system.

The simplest option was to keep with the existing paper ticket system and stay with the same system with respect to season ticket holders' rights. There were 22,000 season ticket holders and 25,000 on a matchday ticket scheme for which there were only ever 12,000 matchday tickets. For both types of tickets, the waiting list was free to join. Keeping the waiting list where anyone could join to become either a season ticket holder or have matchday ticket rights had the advantage that it was simple to operate and fans knew what to expect and how the system worked, and the 'open door' policy had a welcoming feel about it. It also did not disadvantage those who did not have access to the internet and it required no additional investment. However, the disadvantages were the cost of running security for paper tickets which are much more easily copied and open to ticket tout abuse. The open waiting list for tickets was subject to abuse from people who put down several entries and addresses and was often abused by ticket touts. It was also applicable only to UK fans, which – given the international makeup of the Gunners team – disadvantaged the growing international fan base.

Option 2 Get everyone involved.

Get everyone who is interested in the club to be a member and sign up on an electronic database. They could still keep season ticket holders and the separate list for matchday tickets, but they would separate membership of the club from these match ticket rights. This would have the advantage of enabling everyone who had an interest in Arsenal to be a member and allow the club to 'know' and be connected with their wider fan base. It would also allow for cheaper e-communication with individuals and thus everyone might receive some benefits such as email updates and a magazine. The simple email list would be very cheap to operate. However, the disadvantages would be that it might raise the expectation of fans that in becoming a club member and being on the email list they would get match tickets, which would not be the case. Also, the marketing data from the email database would not be driven by or linked to any transactional database such as match-going or Arsenal purchases made so would not be very useful.

Option 3 To have separate levels of membership.

This option was the most complicated and involved separating all the fans into different types of membership with different types of costs and membership benefits. For example, the entry level would be Red level members who would have access to match tickets after Silver members had had the chance to buy them; they would receive an access-all-areas membership pack including annual membership DVD, bottle opener and iconic club drink coasters and could watch the players training at Emirates Stadium for free. In addition, as the Arsenal website improved, Red level members might have access to monthly e-newsletters, messageboards, blogs, wallpapers, screensavers and exclusive use of online match ticket booking. The next level up, Silver members would have all of the above but could also purchase matchday tickets. Gold members would have all of the above, but would be season ticket holders. Finally, Platinum club level season ticket holders might enjoy a premium matchday experience with outstanding views of the action and superb hospitality in a range of luxurious bars, lounges and restaurants as well as the ability to entertain clients, family and friends, and free half-time drinks. The advantages of this option were that is recognised different fans' level of financial commitment to the club and rewarded them accordingly. However, the system was very complicated and difficult to manage as well as being extremely costly and would be a major departure from what the fans were used to. At a time of great change for the club anyway, could the fans and Keith's staff manage such a major upheaval? Now put yourself in Keith's shoes, which option would you choose and why?

Objectives

When you finish reading this chapter, you will be able to understand:

1 Who marketers are, where they work, and marketing's role in the firm

2 What marketing is and how it provides value to people involved in the marketing process

3 The evolution of the marketing concept

4 The range of services and goods that are marketed.

5 How value is created from the perspectives of customers, producers and society

6 The basics of marketing planning and the marketing mix tools used in the marketing process

Welcome to a Branded World

I'm imagining myself on television, in a commercial for a new product – wine cooler? tanning lotion? sugarless gum? – and I'm moving in jump-cut, walking along a beach, the film is black-and-white, purposefully scratched, eerie vague pop music from the mid-1960s accompanies the footage, it echoes, sounds as if it's coming from a calliope. Now I'm looking into the camera, now I'm holding up the product – a new mousse? tennis shoes? – now my hair is windblown then it's day then night then day again and then it's night.

(from Bret Easton Ellis'
American Psycho (1991), p. 327)

Alex wakes up with a groan as the latest iTunes blares from the next bedroom. Why does her housemate have to download these loud ringtones onto her mobile and then leave it on so early in the morning? She throws back the IKEA sheets and rolls off of her new Sealy mattress. As Alex stumbles across the room in her pyjamas from H&M, her senses are further assaulted as she catches wafts of her housemate's favourite perfume from Gaultier. She pours herself a steaming cup of Illy coffee from the Krups coffeemaker and stirs in a spoonful of Splenda. As she starts to grab a Yoplait from the Electrolux fridge, she checks her Blackberry and suddenly remembers: big job interview with P&G today! Good thing she texted her friends last night to get advice about what to wear so she wouldn't have to think about it this morning. Alex does a quick scan of *The Financial Times* online, checks the forecast on weather.com, and for one last time Googles the executive who will be interviewing her. Hopefully he won't remember to check out her page on MySpace; those photos she posted from her trip to Ibiza don't exactly communicate a professional image! Well, he'll be more impressed by the volunteer work she's doing with Amnesty International to build a buzz about horrific labour conditions in developing countries. Just in case, she glances down at her wrist to be sure she's wearing her turquoise advocacy bracelet (which new cause was that for, anyway?).

Alex slips into her sleek new TM Lewin suit, slides on her Prada shoes, grabs her Louis Vuitton briefcase that was a graduation present from her parents, and climbs into her Peugeot 207.

While listening to the Coke ad blaring over her Sony radio, Alex finds herself looking forward to tomorrow. The pressure will be off, and she can put on the new casual outfit she picked up at Zara. Then, it'll be out to that hot new bar to look for Mr. Right – or maybe a few Mr. Wrongs.

Welcome to Brand You

Marketing is all around us. Indeed, some might say we live in a branded world. Like Alex, you have encounters with many marketers even before you leave for the day. Ads. Products. TV. The web. Charitable causes.

What's more, like Alex: YOU are a **product**. That may sound weird, but companies like P&G couldn't exist if you weren't. After all, you have 'market value' as a person – you have qualities that set you apart from others and abilities other people want and need. After you finish this course, you'll have even more **value** because you'll know about the field of marketing and how this field relates to you both as a future businessperson and as a **consumer**. In addition to learning about how marketing influences each of us, you'll have a better understanding of what it means to be 'Brand You'.

Although it may seem strange to think about the marketing of people, in reality we often talk about ourselves and others in marketing terms. It is common for us to speak of 'positioning' ourselves for job interviews or to tell our friends not to 'sell themselves short'. Some people who are looking to find love even refer to themselves as 'being in the market for love'. In addition, many consumers hire personal image consultants to devise a 'marketing strategy' for them, while others undergo plastic surgery or makeovers to improve their 'product images'. The desire to package and promote ourselves is the reason for personal goods and services markets ranging from cosmetics and exercise equipment to CV specialists and dating agencies.[1] So, the principles of marketing apply to people, just as they apply to coffee, convertibles and computer microprocessors. Of course, there are differences in how we go about marketing each of these, but the general idea remains the same: marketing is a fundamental part of our lives both as consumers and as participants in the business world. We'll tell you why throughout this book. But first, we need to answer the basic questions of marketing: Who? Where? What? When? and Why? Let's start with Who and Where.

Market Ethics

Researching yourself . . .

When is the last time you were on Facebook? In fact so many people check their Facebook profile regularly that by 2009 it was one of the top ten websites in the world according to Alexa.com. Despite Facebook's success in the early stages of its existence, there are still many questions and concerns that could limit its long-term future. Up to 35 per cent of US companies now routinely check out a job applicant's Facebook posting and can reject him or her if they find unacceptable material there: www.msnbc.msn.com/id/20202935.

Debate, Discuss, Disagree

1 Do you think companies checking up on applicants' personal lives is right?

2 What do you think of the development of websites such as Facebook and Bebo?

The Who and Where of Marketing

Objective

1

Who marketers
are, where they
work, and
marketing's role
in the firm

Marketers come from many different backgrounds. Although many have earned marketing degrees, others have backgrounds in areas such as engineering or agriculture. Retailers and fashion marketers may have training in merchandising or design. Advertising copywriters often have degrees in their native language, such as English, French or Spanish. **E-marketers** who do business over the internet might have studied computer science.

Marketers work in a variety of locations. They work in **consumer goods** companies such as Burger King or Black & Decker or at service companies like Universal Studios or British Airways. You'll see them in retail organisations like Zara and at companies that manufacture products for other companies to use like Hewlett-Packard. You'll see them at new media companies like squarefruit.co.uk, mobilemedia.com and at 'buzz-building' public relations organisations like vbma.net.

And, although you may assume that the typical marketing job is in a large, consumer-oriented company such as Gillette or Benetton, marketers work in other types of organisations too, including charities, health care, universities and railway companies.

No matter where they work, all marketers are real people who make choices that affect themselves, their companies, and very often thousands or even millions of consumers. That's why at the beginning of each chapter we'll introduce you to marketing professionals like Keith Edelman in a feature called 'Real People, Real Decisions'.

 ## Marketing's Role in the Firm: Working Cross-Functionally

What role do marketers play in a firm? The importance organisations assign to marketing activities varies a lot. Top management in some firms is very marketing-oriented, like Sir Richard Branson at Virgin or Sir Stelios Haji-Ioannou at easyJet (especially when the chief executive officer comes from the marketing ranks), whereas in other companies marketing is an afterthought. However, analysts estimate that for some countries one-third of chief executives come from marketing backgrounds, so it's worth knowing about marketing.

Sometimes the company uses the term marketing when what it really means is sales or advertising. In some organisations, particularly small not-for-profit ones, there may not be anyone in the company specifically designated as 'the marketing person'. In contrast, some firms such as professional service firms, e.g. legal firms, where people are the product, realise that marketing is a part of virtually everyone's job.

No matter what size the firm, a marketer's decisions affect – and are affected by – the firm's other operations. Marketing managers must work with financial and accounting officers to figure out whether products are profitable, to set marketing budgets, and to determine prices. They must work with people in manufacturing to be sure that products are produced on time and in the right quantities. Marketers also must work with research-and-development specialists to create products that meet consumers' **needs**.

 ## Where do YOU Fit in? Careers in Marketing

Marketing is an incredibly exciting, diverse discipline brimming with opportunities. There are many paths to a marketing career; we've tried to summarise the most typical ones here. Look at Table 1.1 and think about which path might interest you. Now that you've had a glimpse of who marketers are and where they work, it's time to dig into what marketing really is.

Marketing Field	Where Can I Work?	What Entry-Level Position Can I Get?	What Course Work Do I Need?
Advertising	**Advertising agency:** Media research and creative departments; account work. **Large corporation:** Advertising department; brand/product management. **Media:** Magazine, newspaper, radio and television selling; management consulting; marketing research.	Account coordinator (traffic department); assistant account executive; assistant media buyer; research assistant; assistant brand manager.	Undergraduate business degree.
Brand Management	**Any size corporation:** Coordinate the activities of specialists in production, sales, advertising, promotion, R&D, marketing research, purchasing, distribution, package development and finance.	Associate brand manager.	MBA preferred but a few companies recruit undergraduates. Expect a sales training programme in the field from one to four months and in-house classes and seminars.
Business-to-Business Marketing	**Any size corporation:** Only a few companies recruit on campus, so be prepared to search out job opportunities on your own, as well as interview on campus.	Sales representative; market research administrator; product manager; pricing administrator; product administrator; assistant marketing manager; sales administrator; assistant sales manager; sales service administrator.	Undergraduate business degree. A broad background of subjects is generally better than concentrating on just one area. A technical degree may be important or even required in high-technology areas. Courses in industrial marketing and marketing strategy are very helpful.
Direct-Response Marketing	**Any size corporation:** Marketing-oriented firms, including those offering consumer goods, industrial products, financial institutions and other types of service establishments. Entrepreneurs seeking to enter business for themselves.	Direct-response marketing is expanding rapidly and includes direct mail, print and broadcast media, telephone marketing, catalogues, in-home presentations, and door-to-door marketing. Seek counsel from officers and directors of the Direct Marketing Association and the Direct Selling Association.	Undergraduate business degree. Supplemental work in communications, psychology, and/or computer systems is recommended.
Distribution Channel Management	**Any size corporation, including transportation corporations:** The analysis, planning and control of activities concerned with the procurement and distribution of goods. The activities include transportation, warehousing, forecasting, order processing, inventory control, production planning, site selection and customer service.	Physical distribution manager; inventory control manager; traffic manager; distribution centre manager; distribution planning analyst; customer service manager; transportation marketing and operations management.	Undergraduate business degree and MBA. Broad background in the core functional areas of business, with particular emphasis on distribution-related topics such as logistics, transportation, purchasing and negotiation.
International Marketing	**Large corporations:** Marketing department at corporate headquarters.	Domestic sales position with an international firm may be the best first step towards international opportunities.	MBA. A broadly based background in marketing is recommended, with some emphasis on sales management and market research.

Table 1.1   Careers in Marketing

Marketing Field	Where Can I Work?	What Entry-Level Position Can I Get?	What Course Work Do I Need?
Marketing Models and Systems Analysis	**Large corporations:** Consult managers who are having difficulty with marketing problems.	Undergraduate: few positions available unless you have prior work experience. Graduate: market analyst, market research specialist and management scientist.	MBA. Preparation in statistics, mathematics and the behavioural sciences.
Marketing Research	**Any size corporation:** Provide management with information about consumers, the marketing environment and the competition.	Assistant market analyst or assistant product analyst level.	MBA, although prior experience and training may improve an undergraduate's chances.
New Product Planning	**Any size corporation:** Marketing of consumer products, consumer industries, advertising agencies, consulting firms, public agencies, medical agencies, retailing management.	Assistant manager or director of product planning or new product development.	MBA.
Retail Management	Retail corporations	Assistant buyer positions; department manager positions	Undergraduate business degree
Sales and Sales Management	**Profit and non-profit organisations:** Financial, insurance, consulting and government.	Trade sales representative who sells to a wholesaler or retailer. Missionary sales representative in manufacturing who sells to retailers or decision makers. Pharmaceutical representative is an example. Technical sales representative who sells to specified accounts within a designated geographic area.	Undergraduate business degree. MBA. *Helpful courses:* consumer behaviour psychology; sociology; economics; anthropology; cost accounting; computer science; statistical analysis; communications; drama; creative writing. Language courses, if you're interested in international marketing. Engineering or physical science courses if you're interested in technical selling.
Services Marketing	**Any size corporations:** Banking and financial service institutions, health care organisations, leisure-oriented businesses, and in various other service settings.	Assistant brand manager; assistant sales manager.	Undergraduate business degree. MBA. Additional coursework in management policy, research, advertising and promotion, quantitative analysis, consumer behaviour, and the behavioural sciences should prove useful.

Table 1.1   Careers in Marketing *(continued)*

Source: This information was adapted from an excellent compilation prepared by the Marketing faculty of the Marshall School of Business, University of Southern California: http://www.marshall.usc.edu/web/marketing.cfm?doc_id=2890. For recent salary figures broken down by job type and region, visit *Marketing Week*/Ball & Hoolahan, Marketing Salary Survey 2008, www.marketingweek.co.uk.

The Value of Marketing

Marketing. Lots of people talk about it, but what is it? When you ask people to define marketing, you get many answers. Some people say, 'That's what happens when a pushy salesman tries to sell me something I don't want.' Other people say, 'Oh, that's simple – TV commercials.' Students might answer, 'That's a course I have to take before I can get my business degree.' Each of these responses has a grain of truth in it, but the official definition of marketing according to the UK's Chartered Institute of Marketing, is 'the management process responsible for identifying, anticipating and satisfying customer requirements profitably'.[2] In September 2007 a new definition of marketing was proposed by the institution to reflect the changes that had occurred during the past 30 years since the old definition was introduced in 1976.

The proposed new definition reads:

> The strategic business function that creates value by stimulating, facilitating and fulfilling customer demand.
> It does this by building brands, nurturing innovation, developing relationships, creating good customer service and communicating benefits.
> By operating customer-centrically, marketing brings positive returns on investment, satisfies shareholders and **stakeholders** from business and the community, and contributes to positive behavioural change and a sustainable business future.[3]

The basic idea of this somewhat complicated definition is that marketing is all about delivering value to everyone who is affected by a transaction. Let's take a closer look at the different parts of this definition.

Marketing Is About Meeting Needs

One aspect is that marketing is about meeting the **needs** of diverse stakeholders including buyers, sellers, investors in a company, community residents, and even citizens of the nations where goods and services are made or sold – in other words, any person or organisation that has a 'stake' in the marketing exchange.

One important stakeholder is the consumer. A consumer is the ultimate user of a good or service. Consumers can be individuals or organisations, whether a company, government, student association, or charity. We like to say that the consumer is king (or queen), but it's important not to lose sight of the fact that the seller also has needs – to make a profit, to remain in business, and even to take pride in selling the highest quality products possible. This is particularly true for artistic products. Madonna is a good example of someone who constantly tries to create an ever-changing high quality artistic product.

A need is the difference between a consumer's actual state and some ideal or desired state. When the difference is big enough, the consumer is motivated to take action to satisfy the need. When you're hungry, you buy a snack. If you're not happy with your hair, you get a new hairstyle.

Needs are related to physical functions (such as eating) or to psychological ones (such as wanting to look good). Levi Strauss & Company is one company that tries to meet needs of consumers to look good as well as their basic need to be clothed. The company's research indicates that people wear Levi's jeans to signal things about themselves and their desired image. So much so that sometimes the company even receives a worn-out, handed-down pair in the mail, with a letter from the owner requesting that the jeans be given a proper burial, such was the psychological attachment to their jeans![4]

A **want** is a desire for a particular product to satisfy a need in specific ways that depends on an individual's history, learning experiences, and cultural environment. For example, two classmates' stomachs rumble during a lunchtime lecture, and both need food. However, as they are different individuals with different personal histories and experiences, one student may be a health nut who wants a fruit smoothie, while the other wants a greasy cheeseburger and fries.

A product delivers a **benefit** when it satisfies a need or want. For marketers to be success-ful, they must develop products that provide one or more benefits that are important to con-sumers while also convincing consumers that their product is better than a competitor's product. As management expert Peter Drucker observed, 'The aim of marketing is to make selling superfluous.'[5]

Everyone can want your product, but that doesn't ensure sales unless they have the means to obtain it. When you couple desire with the buying power or resources to satisfy a want, the result is **demand**. So, the potential customers for a snappy, red BMW convertible are the peo-ple who want the car minus those who can't afford to buy or lease one. A **market** consists of all the consumers who share a common need that can be satisfied by a specific product and who have the resources, willingness and authority to make the purchase.

A **marketplace** used to be only a location where buying and selling occurs face to face such as a street corner or an open-air market where people sell fruits and vegetables much as they have done for thousands of years. However in today's 'wired' world buyers and sellers might not even see each other. The modern marketplace may take the form of a glitzy shopping centre, a mail-order catalogue, a television shopping network like QVC, an eBay auction, or an **e-commerce** website like Amazon. Indeed, a marketplace may not even exist in the physi-cal world – as players of online games will tell you. Residents of cyberworlds like the Sims, SecondLife.com and Project Entropia buy and sell virtual real estate – with real money. One Project Entropian recently paid over €75,000 (that's in real money) for a space resort he calls Club Neverdie. He plans to develop the station's facilities and sell homes for game dollars, which the project's developer converts into US dollars at a 10:1 exchange rate.[6]

 ## Marketing Is About Creating Utility and Value

Marketing activities play a major role in the creation of utility; the term refers to all the bene-fits we receive from using a product or service. When reading this section, begin to think about how much value might be created for consumers for each of the options Keith Edelman at Arsenal Football Club is considering. By working to ensure that people have the type of prod-uct they want and where and when they want it, marketing develops **utility**, which is what cre-ates value. Value can be seen as the perceived utility minus the perceived sacrifice the consumer has to make in order to obtain the utility the product or service offers. Marketing can provide several different kinds of utility in order to generate value for consumers:

- Form utility is the benefit marketing provides by transforming raw materials into finished products, as when a dress manufacturer combines silk, thread and zips to create a brides-maid's dress, i.e. doing something you can't or don't want to do for yourself.

- Place utility is the benefit marketing provides by making products available where cus-tomers want them. The most sophisticated evening gown sewn in a chic Paris designer's studio is of little use to a bridesmaid in Copenhagen if it isn't shipped to her in time.

- Time utility is the benefit marketing provides by storing products until they are needed. For example, having your wedding dress ready the day after the wedding is not providing time utility.

- Possession utility is the benefit marketing provides by enabling the consumer to own and use the product or store it for future use. For example, a bride can hire or buy her wedding dress.

Marketers provide utility in many ways; now, let's see how customers 'take delivery' of this added value.

Marketing Is About Exchange Relationships

At the heart of every marketing act – big or small – is something referred to as an 'exchange relationship'. An **exchange** occurs when something is obtained for something else in return. The buyer receives an object, service or idea that satisfies a need and the seller receives something he or she feels is of equivalent value. For example, a politician can agree to work towards certain goals in exchange for your vote, or a minister can offer you salvation in return for your faith. As Christian Gronroos from Sweden puts it: 'Marketing is to establish, maintain and enhance long-term customer relationships at a profit, so that the objectives of the parties involved are met. This is done by mutual exchange and fulfilment of promises.'[7]

For an exchange to occur, at least two people or organisations must be willing to make a trade, and each must have something the other wants. Think about eBay. The two parties must be able to communicate with each other, like on eBay. Both parties must agree on the value of the thing to be exchanged on eBay and how it will be carried out, usually by post. Each party also must be free to accept or reject the other's terms for the exchange. Underlying these conditions are expectations that all aspects of the exchange will be ethical and honest, i.e. the money will arrive and whatever was bought will be sent. In addition, not being able to return faulty goods for example does not constitute a valid exchange. Think also about music piracy, where music labels claim they lose millions of euros a year when consumers download songs without paying for them. However, a lot of people who download music don't feel that they are participating in an unfair exchange and say it is the fault of record companies that charge way too much for new songs. What do you think?

The debate over music downloading reminds us that an agreed-on transfer of value must occur for an exchange to take place.

Photo 1.1 Some transactions today, like those in the online world of Second Life, are virtual exchanges.
Source: Linden Research, Inc.

Real People, Other Voices

Advice for Keith Edelman

Jocelyn Hayes,
University of York

I would choose option 3. The move for Arsenal Football club presents a real opportunity to enable the customers' perceptions of the club to be heightened and strengthened by any new strategies introduced and enable its brand image to grow. The club's concerns about not alienating its core loyal fans (e.g. by ensuring their access to tickets) means that the planning of new developments to attract in new fans should not to be at the detriment of existing ones. But finding the right balance to satisfy its different target groups of fans (customers) is key to its future success. Maintaining and growing customer satisfaction is at the core of marketing strategies and operations. Tapping into customer needs will enable this. Multiple customer audiences require tailored schemes to make their marketing activities effective and meaningful.

The introduction of four separate levels of membership of Red, Silver, Gold and Platinum offers major benefits to both the fans and the club; the scheme is easy and clear to understand, the introduction of web/communication via e-newsletters and message boards will allow greater interaction between club members, direct instant updates, data capture on the fans and the new online booking facility will provide efficient and up-to-date manageable procedures and may be cheaper to operate (after the initial set-up costs). New and younger fans would be accommodated by a scheme that is simple and clear to use.

Planned growth could be facilitated by the introduction of a more efficient ticketing system (e.g. buying online facilities) and the strong, clear branding of these new schemes should certainly help both in terms of minimising costs and in increasing operationability in business terms.

The downside of option 3 is that some fans without easy online access could be disadvantaged. There could also be increased costs associated with the Platinum Club level (special offer). Instead, three levels could be tested out first and then a move to introduce the fourth Platinum level if required/or revision of the benefits. Slow phasing in of online ticketing by still providing some purchase outlets may be necessary. Overall, option 3 allows faster, more relevant, cost-effective operations with better communication facilities.

David Chalcraft,
University of Westminster

I would choose option 3. The opening of the Emirates Stadium offers Arsenal an opportunity to grow the fan base and increase revenue to the club. Also, soccer is a global sport and Arsenal needs to cater for a global fan base. Although the most complex (and presumably expensive) option, option 3 offers the most scope for growth – both to meet the immediate need of a 40 per cent increase in core business within 12 months and to drive continued growth thereafter.

The tiered membership scheme offers 'something for everyone', enabling all interested fans to become actively involved, yet it retains the strengths of the current system by respecting the rights and loyalty of existing fans. An internet-based solution has the capability to enable this and, once set up, is likely to be less expensive to operate than a paper-based system. Being driven by electronic activity, there is great potential for data collection about the fan base. This will enable Arsenal to learn more about fans and their interests, and use this information for better recruitment campaigns and to develop the 'offer' made to the fans.

A key aspect of modern marketing is the desire to develop a relationship with and retain customers. This scheme allows fans to 'progress' in their relationship with the club, for instance by moving from Red to Silver to Gold memberships. Also, email can be used to develop two-way communication with fans and offers possibilities such as fan-to-fan communication through blogs, encouraging them to feel that they have a real stake in 'their' club. The flexibility and immediacy of email and the internet can also be used tactically, for instance to enable Arsenal to react quickly to opportunities or needs, such as driving up ticket sales for particular games.

Richard Victor,
a student at the University of East London

My obvious choice would be option 3 'to have separate levels of membership' – this is a clear market segmentation strategy with a lot of promise. The main segments on membership levels – (i) Red level membership; (ii) Silver member; (iii) Gold level members; and (iv) Platinum Club Level season ticket holders with premium matchday experience – have been well tested and applied in a variety of retail sectors. From gym memberships, through professional car wash experiences, to auto breakdown services provided by the likes of AA and RAC to maximum effect. Similar strategies have also been adopted in the airline industry with its different classes of travel – economy, business and first – with outstanding results. However, this is the first time such a strategy has been suggested in the case of professional sports – notably football. It also strikes a balance between the competing needs of key stakeholder groups.

Objective

3

The evolution of
the marketing
concept

When Did Marketing Begin?
The Evolution of a Concept

Although it sounds like good old common sense to us, believe it or not the notion that businesses and other organisations succeed when they satisfy customers' needs actually is a recent idea. Before the 1950s, marketing was basically a means of making production more efficient. Let's take a quick look at how the marketing discipline has developed. Table 1.2 tells us about some of the more recent events in this marketing history.

Table 1.2
Marketing History

1954–55	Three volumes of *The Lord of Rings* is published in Britain
1956	The first self-service Tesco supermarket opens in a converted cinema in Maldon, UK
1958	The British era of Formula 1 begins when Mike Hawthorn becomes a champion in a Ferrari 246
1961	Mattel introduces the Barbie doll in Europe
1962	Ford's first ever rear-wheel-drive car, the Cortina model, goes on sale in Britain The Beatles record their 'Please Please Me' single which reaches number 2 in the official UK chart
1963	The Pepsi Generation kicks off the cola wars
1965	All TV commercials for cigarettes are banned in the UK
1968	The famous *Hair* musical opens at Shaftesbury Theatre in London, one day after the abolition of theatre censorship
1970	Following the birth of the mass package holiday business, British European Airways (today British Airways) establishes its own charter airline
1971	First European McDonald's outlet opens in Zaandam, Netherlands
1972	The Swedish band ABBA is formed and wins the Eurovision contest two years later with the song 'Waterloo'
1974	DHL opens its first office in London
1978	The band Queen releases the *Jazz* album featuring hit singles such as 'Fat Bottomed Girls' and 'Bicycle Race'
1979	Sony introduces the first Walkman
1980	Ted Turner creates CNN
1983	Microsoft Windows is announced and sells for £100
1985	Nike releases the Air Jordan, Michael Jordan's signature shoe New Coke is launched, Old Coke is brought back 79 days later
1986	Launch of *The Independent* newspaper in Britain
1987	MTV Europe launches First GAP store opens outside the US, in London
1991	Nokia equipment is used to make the world's first GSM call
1992	EuroDisney opens in Paris
1995	eBay is founded by Pierre Omidyar in his California living room
1998	Germany's Daimler-Benz acquires America's Chrysler Corporation for more than $38 billion in stock to create a new global auto-making giant called Daimler-Chrysler
2003	Amazon debuts its 'Search Inside the Book' feature that allows users to search the full text of more than 33 million pages from over 120,000 printed books

The Production Era Up Until 1930

The classic example of this era is Henry Ford's Model T. Even from the start in 1908, when the 'Tin Lizzie', or 'flivver' as the T was known, sold for $825, Henry Ford continued to make improvements in production. By 1912, Ford got so efficient that the car sold for $575, a price even the Ford employees who made the car could afford.[8] As the price continued to drop, Ford sold even more flivvers. By 1921, the Model T Ford had 60 per cent of the new car market. In 1924, the ten-millionth Model T rolled off the assembly line. This was about getting the price right for customers and the way to achieve that was through steamlining the production process. Henry Ford actually got his production ideas of letting the car move through a factory and each worker doing a selected set of jobs by watching the process in a slaughterhouse!

Ford's focus illustrates a **production orientation**, which works best in a seller's market when demand is greater than supply because it focuses on the most efficient ways to produce products. On top of this, there weren't a lot of other cars competing for drivers in the 1920s so consumers had to take whatever was available. Firms that focus on a production orientation tend to view the market as a homogeneous group that will be satisfied with the basic function of a product. Sometimes this view is too narrow. For example, in a classic article Levitt talks about how Procter & Gamble's Ivory soap had been in decline for some time in the 1960s because the company viewed the brand as plain old soap, not as a cleansing product that could provide other benefits as well. Ivory soap lost business to newer deodorant and 'beauty' soaps containing cold cream that exploited this market.[9]

The Selling Era, 1920–64

This **selling orientation** is a company-centred, rather than a client-centred approach to conducting business which means that management tends to ignore what customers really want or need; in the case of a goods producer the company tries to move products out of warehouses so that inventories don't pile up. When a product's availability exceeds demand in a buyer's market, businesses may engage in the 'hard sell' where salespeople aggressively push their products. For example, when a salesperson tries to give buyers the impression that the product would be available for only a short period of time, that the deal might be withdrawn at any time and that they would not be offered the opportunity to think the decision over. During the Great Depression in the 1930s, when money was scarce for most people, firms shifted their focus from a product orientation to selling their goods in any way they could.

The selling orientation regained popularity after the Second World War in the UK. This was because the UK had dramatically increased its industrial capacity to manufacture tanks, combat boots, parachutes and countless other wartime goods. After the war, this industrial capacity was converted to producing consumer goods.

However, once consumers had bought all the things they couldn't get during the war years, and their initial needs and wants were satisfied, they became more selective. The race for consumers was on and prevailed well into the 1950s. But consumers as a rule don't like to be forced into buying, and the hard sell gave marketing a bad image. Think about the days of the travelling salesman selling encylopaedia or vacuum cleaners and applying high pressure doorstep selling techniques. Companies that still follow a selling orientation tend to be more successful at making one-time sales rather than building repeat business. This focus is most likely to be found among companies that sell unsought goods – products that people don't tend to buy without some prodding. For example, most of us aren't keen to shop for life insurance, so some encouragement may be necessary to splurge out on something that will one day pay for your final resting place.

The Consumer Era, 1957–98

> The marketing world came to terms with the fact that **return on investment** depended upon brand equity, and brand equity depends upon brand loyalty . . . Marketers have come to realise that it is better to first find out what the customer wants and then offer a suitable product rather than make a product first and then try to find a customer.

As the world's most successful firms began to adopt a **consumer orientation**, marketers had a way to outdo the competition – and marketing's importance was also elevated in the firm. Marketers did research to understand the needs of different consumers, assisted in tailoring products to the needs of these various groups, and did an even better job of designing marketing messages than in the days of the selling orientation. To assist marketing to deliver consistently good quality products to meet consumers' needs and do this repeatedly better than the competition, **Total Quality Management** (TQM) was widely followed in the marketing community which involves all employees from the assembly line onward in continuous product quality improvement. When Italian fashion giant Diesel opened its new flagship store in Mayfair, London, in spring 2006, the company took an unusual approach to recruiting staff by holding an out-of-the-ordinary themed recruitment day, where applicants were given a welcome pack that included an application form and a questionnaire to test what they would do in certain situations when serving consumers. Diesel head of retail Ruth Dangerfield explains: 'We need social beings who can engage quite comfortably with people. We are also looking for a good cross-section of people to reflect our mix of customers.'[10] Diesel took this approach to recruitment because of the importance and personality of this shop, to express its brand and because potential staff members were also customers who needed to be treated with respect. Diesel has found that it pays to have a consumer orientation that satisfies customers' needs and wants.

Another example of a company thinking about customers who are also its employees is Google. It offers its engineers a '20 per cent time' which means that they can take a day off each week to work on anything they are passionate about, and it does not have to be related to their daily jobs. Google News, Google Suggest, Orkut and Google Mail are products of the 20 per cent projects among many other Google services which have been born out of allowing employees to act as customers.[11]

The New Era: Make Money and Act Ethically, 1988 to the Present

Over time, many forward-thinking organisations began to see their commitment to quality and to 'just' satisfying consumers' needs during a single transaction as being insufficient. Instead, they began to focus on a **New Era orientation** that meant building long-term bonds with customers and acknowledging the role of business within society.

Within this approach the concept of **customer relationship management** (CRM) was developed which involves systematically tracking consumers' preferences and behaviours over time in order to tailor the **value proposition** as closely as possible to each individual's unique wants and needs. With the advent of the web, a CRM approach became easier to implement as more and more firms started to rely heavily on the web to connect with consumers to personalise its messages and products to meet the needs of each individual consumer better. For example, Marks & Spencer has implemented the CRM approach to make sure the company can respond quickly and effectively to customers. Before an agent answers a call they can check the customer's previous M&S orders in the system.

During the early 2000s, dot-com companies took a beating in the marketplace because of reduced business spending, market correction and outsourcing. Though many analysts believe

Marketing Ethics

The environment as a customer?

Take M&S as an example of a New Era firm that assumes a position of environmental stewardship when it makes socially responsible business decisions that also protect the environment. A green marketing strategy describes efforts to choose packages, product designs, and other aspects of the marketing mix that are earth-friendly but still profitable. Green marketing practices can indeed result in black ink for a firm's bottom line. Credit card companies are finding that their bottom line is benefiting from a recent 'green' innovation – corn-based plastic.[12] The corn-based products are biodegradable, renewable and reasonably priced, whereas the price of oil and thus of plastic cards made from oil byproducts has skyrocketed in recent years. Wal-Mart has also used the less expensive corn-based plastic to package fresh produce and baked goods – 114 million packages in all in 2005. Other organisations are using corn-based plastic cups for their cold beverages.

Debate, Discuss, Disagree?

1   Discuss the advantages and disadvantages of companies being green.

2   What are the main things you think every company should do?

---

that this was just a preliminary shakeout and that the heyday of the internet is yet to come. Indeed, some marketing analysts suggest that the web has created a paradigm shift for business, meaning that companies must adhere to a new model or pattern of how to profit in a wired world. They argue that we are moving towards an attention economy, where a company's success will be measured by its share of mind rather than share of market. This means that companies must find new and innovative ways to stand out from the crowd and become an integral part of consumers' lives rather than just being a dry distraction from it. For example, in 2007 Apple released the iPhone, which not only can play movies and music but also functions as a mobile phone so that people use it a lot more during their everyday lives than if it could only entertain them. Some of the ways of integrating with consumers' lives are focusing on business ethics, social benefits and accountability.

Focusing on Social Benefits

Another result of this new way of long-term thinking was the social **marketing concept**, which maintains that marketers must satisfy customers' needs in ways that are not only profitable for the firm but also benefit society.

Many firms practise this philosophy by satisfying society's environmental and social needs for a cleaner, safer environment by developing recyclable packaging, adding extra safety features such as car air bags, voluntarily modifying a manufacturing process to reduce pollution, and sponsoring campaigns to address social problems. By doing these, the company improves its brand image and reputation among customers and potential customers which ultimately results in a larger market share and improved profits for the firm. Today, New Era companies have abandoned this one-shot approach and instead make a long-term commitment to tackle a social problem, such as illiteracy or child abuse. New Era firms believe that cause marketing activities, when done right, yield a double benefit: they address a pressing social need and sales of their products increase as a result. Safeway grocery chain believes customers are more likely to respond to cause marketing activities that help charities in their own backyards. Safeway will donate up to $1 million in its 'Shop and Care' programme that lets US customers designate up to 10 per cent of their purchases to the charity of their choice from a list of local non-profit organisations.

The Avon Breast Cancer Crusade is a well-known example of cause marketing. In 2005, the programme reached $450 million worldwide for access to care and finding a cure. The money has

Timberland Earthkeepers:
Lightweight. Organic. Recycled.
Worship the ground you walk on.

The new lightweight Timberland® Earthkeepers boot. Made from 100% organic cotton canvas, a water repellent waxed upper and a 30% recycled rubber outsole. Gentle on you, gentle on the earth beneath your feet.

Timberland Make it better.
www.timberlandonline.co.uk

Photo 1.2	In a new era of making money and acting ethically, companies are promoting the ethical credentials. Source: The Advertising Archives

been raised in part by Avon independent sales representatives, who sell a variety of pink-ribbon products, as well as by Avon Foundation events such as the Avon Walk for Breast Cancer series. The Avon Breast Cancer Crusade has supported programmes in 50 countries around the world, each of which undertakes its own fundraising and awareness initiatives.

One of the biggest UK retailing companies, Marks & Spencer, is one of the firms that believes social and cause-related marketing is good for its customers and good for the company, in terms of reputation and profit. In 2006 the company was named for the second time as Company of the Year at Business in the Community's Awards for Excellence. In his laudation, HRH Prince of Wales said: 'M&S had a hugely successful year on the high street and has not only almost reinvented itself but in doing so has never sacrificed its commitment to responsible business practice – indeed it has continued to lead the way.'[13] M&S engages in social issues, such as animal welfare, non-GM foods, improved labour standards, fish sourcing and pesticides.

Within just one year, M&S was the first retailer in the UK to introduce a range of Fairtrade cotton clothing and convert all tea and coffee to Fairtrade; it removed additives from hydrogenated fats from over 700 prepared products; it provided 2500 people – including homeless and disabled – with work experience; it converted sandwich packaging to cardboard sourced from well managed forests; besides its support of Breakthrough Breast Cancer.

Marketing Ethics

Make it green and keep them keen . . .

Everyone seems to be embracing the green marketing trend – from fast-moving consumer goods giant such as Procter & Gamble, with a campaign for Ariel detergent encouraging consumers to wash their clothes at 30°C instead of 40°C, to boutique brands such as smoothie maker Innocent Drinks' campaign emphasising the good provenance of its ingredients and the fact that its bottles are now made from 100 per cent recycled plastic. Tesco's Green Clubcard offered users points incentives for buying and using environmentally friendly products. Charlotte Mullen, human resources and marketing director at a recruitment agency, says companies are interested in green marketing not only as a consumer-facing communication, but also as a way of presenting themselves to potential candidates as a desirable place to work.

The Guardian, 21 January 2008

Debate, Discuss, Disagree

1 How much does a greener product make you keener to buy?

2 How much does a greener company make you keener to work for them?

Marketing Ethics

The ASA sees red about on 'green' claims in ads

However, not everything is as green as it seems. The Advertising Standards Authority (ASA) in the UK has pledged to crack down on the so-called 'greenwash' in advertising in a bid to quell growing public concern. For example, it upheld a complaint concerning Boeing UK, after a press ad about the yet-to-launch 746-8 said that it produced 'less than 75 grams of CO_2 per passenger km'. The ad was found to be misleading because Boeing had based its figures on the aircraft being 100 per cent full and not on the UK government standards figure of 79.7 per cent when calculating CO_2 emissions. Joel Makower, co-founder and executive editor of Greener World Media, says that consumers are becoming increasingly wary of so-called greenwash and view it as a sales tactic.

Marketing Week, 6 December 2007

Debate, Discuss, Disagree

1 What is your opinion about greenwashing general?

2 How much do you think consumers are sceptical of companies' green credentials?

Business Ethics

A slew of corporate scandals in recent years have rocked the business world. Some of the major ones include:

- In autumn 2001, Enron revealed a massive accounting fraud. The US energy company had hidden hundreds of millions of dollars of debt through unethical and illegal accounting practices with the assistance of the nationally renowned accounting firm Arthur Anderson. Former Enron chief executive Ken Lay was on trial in 2006 for using off-the-books partnerships to manipulate Enron's finances and defraud investors. He maintained his innocence of conspiracy but he was found guilty in June 2006 and sentenced to jail.

- In 2002, when the US telecommunications company WorldCom collapsed into bankruptcy after revealing it had falsified its financial statements by roughly $11 billion, the US General Services Administration banned government contracts with the company, stating that WorldCom 'lacked internal controls and business ethics'. In July 2005, chief executive Bernard Ebbers was sentenced to 25 years in prison.

- In late 2003, Italian dairy-foods giant Parmalat went into bankruptcy and its founder landed in jail when the company failed to account for at least €8 billion.

The fallout from these and other cases raises the issue of how damaging unethical practices can be to society at large. The business press is filled with articles about accountability, corporate accounting practices and government regulation as the public and corporate world reassess what we define as ethical behaviour. When major companies defraud the public, everyone suffers. Thousands of people lose their jobs, and in many cases the pensions they counted on to support them in retirement vanish overnight. Other stakeholders are punished as well, including stockholders who lose their investments and consumers who end up paying for worthless merchandise or services. All taxpayers may wind up paying a penalty as well, if governments decide to 'bail out' an industry or company such as Northern Rock in the UK or the US savings-and-loan industry and Chrysler some years ago.

We think ethics are so important we've made a feature of them throughout this book in the inserts, 'Debate, Discuss, Disagree'. Ethics are rules of conduct – how most people in a culture judge what is right and what is wrong. Business ethics are basic values that guide a firm's

Marketing Ethics

Be good, do good and make more money

The practice of corporate social responsibility is not new. In the mid-nineteenth century, English textile manufacturer Sir Titus Sale built a model community for his workers. He had both a selfless and a selfish interest in doing so; he believed that well-housed and cared-for workers would be healthier and more productive. Henry Ford held a similar philosophy; he paid his assembly line workers extremely well to be sure they had enough money to buy his cars! Today, social responsibility activities are likely to go beyond humanely treating one's employees; they are also likely to include promoting environmental stewardship, engaging in cause marketing and promoting cultural diversity.

Firms that believe in social responsibility possess a value system that goes beyond the short-term bottom line. Instead, they consider the short- and long-term effects of decisions on the company, its employees, consumers, the community and the world at large. Who are the current corporate leaders in social responsibility? *Business Ethics* magazine in the US annually rates companies and lists the top 100 corporate citizens. In 2007, the top five companies were Cummins, Green Mountain Coffee Roasters, Advanced Micro Devices, Nike, Motorola and Intel Corporation.

Debate, Discuss, Disagree

1 Discuss the pros and cons of there being a law on forcing companies to be socially responsible.

behaviour. These values govern decisions managers make about what goes into their products, how they are advertised and sold, and how they are disposed of. Developing good business ethics is the first step towards creating social profit, which is the firm's normal profit plus or minus any externalities that occur during the transactions. In other words, when firms want to determine their social profit they have to take into account any benefit or harm they cause to other parties during their business activities. Good business ethics are very important for companies because this ensures that customers will trust them in the short and long term and that they can retain honest staff who won't carry out questionable business practices. The Chartered Institute of Marketing in the UK created its code of ethics (www.cim.co.uk).

Because each culture has its own set of values, beliefs and customs, ethical business behaviour varies in different parts of the world. Take bribery and extortion, for example. Bribery occurs when someone voluntarily offers payment to get an illegal advantage. Extortion occurs when someone in authority extracts payment under duress.[14] Some businesspeople give bribes to speed up required work, secure a contract, or avoid having a contract cancelled. Such payments are a way of life in many countries because many people consider them as natural as giving a waiter a tip for good service. In European countries, however, paying bribes is perceived as both illegal and unethical.

Codes of Ethics

With so many rules – written and unwritten – floating around, how do business managers know what upper management and investors expect of them? Many firms develop their own codes of ethics – written standards of behaviour to which everyone in the organisation must subscribe. These documents eliminate confusion about what the firm considers to be ethically acceptable behaviour for employees. For example, the Dow Chemical Company's Code of Business Conduct, available through its website at www.dow.com in 16 languages, is based on Dow's stated corporate values of integrity and respect for people. The code deals with issues of diversity, the environment, financial integrity, accurate company records, conflicts of interest, obligations to customers, competitors and regulators, computer systems and telecommunications security, safeguarding important information, interactions with the public and corporate social responsibility.

Marketing Ethics

False beauty claims

One place where ethical business practices can be on show is the beauty industry. Only months after a L'Oreal mascara advert was criticised for featuring the actress Penelope Cruz in false eyelashes, Rimmel's promotion starring the Croydon-born model Kate Moss similarly incurred the wrath of the Advertising Standards Authority. The agency behind Rimmel's television and magazine campaigns denied that Moss wore false lashes during the shoot but produced no evidence to prove it, the authority said. Rimmel's 'Magnif eyes mascara' adverts broke the rules by using images that might have exaggerated the product's benefits, it added. The television advert's claim that the mascara gave '70 per cent more lash lift' could have misled viewers because it referred to a change in appearance, not actual lash length.

Debate, Discuss, Disagree

1 What do you think?

2 Is this reasonable exaggeration which most consumers understand or a misleading way to generate sales?

 ## People Fighting Back: Consumerism

Organised activities that bring about social and political change are not new to developed nations. Women's right to vote, child labour laws, the minimum wage, equal employment opportunities and the ban on nuclear weapons testing all have resulted from social movements where citizens, public and private organisations, and businesses worked to change society. Consumerism is the social movement directed towards protecting consumers from harmful business practices.

In the US, the modern consumerism movement began in the 1960s, when bestselling books – such as Rachel Carson's *Silent Spring*, which attacked the irresponsible use of pesticides, and Ralph Nader's *Unsafe at any Speed*, which exposed safety defects in General Motors' Corvair cars – put pressure on businesses to mend their ways. Consumers organised to call for safer products and honest information, and they boycotted companies that did not comply with their demands.

In his 1961 inaugural speech, US President John F. Kennedy outlined what became known as the Consumer Bill of Rights, which includes the following:

● The right to be safe: products should not be dangerous when used as intended. Organisations such as the Consumer Products Safety Board and *Consumer Reports* magazine regularly identify products they find to be unsafe.

● The right to be informed: businesses should provide consumers with adequate information to make intelligent product choices. This right means that product information provided by advertising, packaging and salespeople should be honest and complete.

● The right to be heard: consumers should have the means to complain or express their displeasure in order to obtain redress or retribution from companies. Government agencies and industry self-regulatory groups should respond to every customer complaint.

● The right to choose freely: consumers should be able to choose from a variety of products. No one business should be allowed to control the price, quality, or availability of goods and services.

In the EU there are ten principles governing consumer protection. See Table 1.3.

Table 1.3
EU Consumer
Rights

1. Buy what you want, where you want
   EU law entitles you to 'shop until you drop' without having to worry about paying customs duty or additional VAT when you return home.

2. If it doesn't work, send it back
   What if you buy a new television set and it immediately breaks down? Under EU law, if a product you buy does not confirm to the agreement you made with the seller at the time of purchase, you can take it back and have it repaired or replaced. Alternatively, you can ask for a price reduction, or a complete refund of your money.

3. High safety standards for food and consumer goods
   Look around your local supermarket – you will see products from across the whole of Europe. Are they all safe? Yes, they have to be. Though no system of regulation can guarantee consumers zero risk, or 100 per cent safety, EU countries have among the highest safety standards in the world.

4. Know what you are eating
   How can you find out what's in your food? EU food labelling enables you to know what you are eating. Full details of the ingredients used to make a food product must be given on the label, along with details of any colouring, preservatives, sweeteners and other chemical additives used.

5. Contracts should be fair to customers
   Have you ever signed a contract without reading all the small print? What if that small print says the deposit you just paid is non-refundable – even if the company fails to deliver its side of the bargain? EU law says these types of unfair contact terms are prohibited.

6. Sometimes consumers can change their mind
   What if a salesman turns up unexpectedly at your home and somehow persuades you to sign a contract to have double glazing installed, or new carpets, costing hundreds of euros?
   EU law protects you against this sort of doorstep selling. As a general principle, you can cancel such a contract within seven days.

7. Making it easier to compare prices
   How do you compare the price of two different brands of breakfast cereal when one comes in a 375g box and the other in a 500g box? EU law requires supermarkets to give you the 'unit price' of products – for example, how much they cost per kilo or per litre – to help make it easier for you to decide which one is cheaper by weight.

8. Consumers should not be misled
   You receive a letter from a mail order company congratulating you on having won first prize in a lottery they have organised. It turns out, however, to be no more than a scam to get you to contact them so they can try to talk you into placing an order with them. You have not, in fact, won a prize. Is this kind of marketing legal? No. Advertising that misleads or deceives consumers is prohibited under EU law. In addition, when you are dealing with telesales, mail-order or online retailers, sellers must be open and honest with you. EU law requires them to give you full details of who they are, what they are selling, how much it costs (including taxes and delivery charges) and how long it will take for them to deliver it.

9. Protection while you are on holiday
   What if you go on a package holiday and the tour operator goes bankrupt? What if the package holiday brochure promised you a luxury hotel and what you get is a building site? In both these cases EU law offers you protection. Package tour operators must have arrangements in place to get you home should they go bankrupt while you are on holiday. They must also offer you compensation if your holiday does not correspond to what they promised in their brochure.

10. Effective redress for cross-border issues
    The European Consumer Centres Network (EEC-Net) is an EU-wide network to promote consumer confidence by advising citizens on their rights as consumers in the EU and helping them to solve disputes. These centres can advise you about your rights when you shop across borders and help you seek redress if you have a dispute with a trader in another EU country.

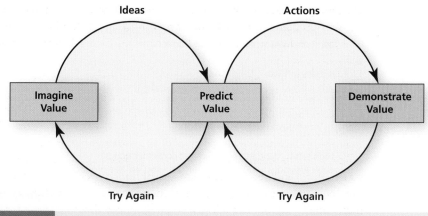

Figure 1.1	The Infinity Model of Accountable Marketing
	How to Imagine Value

Focusing on Accountability

New Era firms place a much greater emphasis on accountability. This means demonstrating that marketing creates more financial value than it costs, and that marketing resources have been applied with the maximum possible effect. To do this, you must adopt and align three working practices, as illustrated in Figure 1.1, the Infinity Model (so called because of the figure's resemblance to the symbol for infinity).

How to imagine value   Imagination is fundamental to marketing, creating value by finding better ways of spending marketing money. Old ideas wear out, markets evolve, customers and competitors change, campaigns slow down, so old marketing spending patterns must constantly change to drive value.

Don't misunderstand it. It is not just a matter of artistic sensibility or superior customer empathy, more than anything it's an ability to recognise and respond to failure, particularly rejection of ideas by customers. Every marketer faces this rejection and the good ones respond with ingenuity, with deliberate, even obsessive reflection on customer rejection and a search for new solutions. Prediction holds up a mirror to the marketing imagination, and usually the response is 'try again' because customers don't like the idea.

You need to generate a stream of ideas to create value at three levels:

Strategic marketing investment;

Value proposition;

Marketing mix.

Strategic marketing investment ideas are needed at the top of every organisation. Distribute marketing funding strategically, putting money where it will have the maximum impact and taking it away when its impact is marginal. Don't assume that marketing's funding should necessarily go up or down in proportion to the growth or decline in the sales for the product or market. All strategic marketing investment ideas should be subjected to predictive evaluation and you should manage your marketing resource allocation as a strategic portfolio, with one unifying model guiding the distribution of marketing funds.

Value proposition ideas are at the heart of imaginative marketing spending. The aim here is to deliver value to customers, and to the company, by delivering the right product (or service) at the right price. You do this by inventing a stream of ideas to keep your proposition appealing: re-packaging, re-pricing, new varieties, coordinated price and feature changes, big new product ideas. All value proposition ideas should be subjected to predictive tests, and the totality of ideas should be managed as a balanced portfolio taking into account risks and rewards.

Marketing mix ideas are the most commonplace, and they often dominate marketing spending. The mix is a marketing term for the multitude of activities that encourage customers to buy more products, more often, for more money. The mix includes press advertising, radio, outdoor, TV, direct, database and email marketing, banner advertising, blogs and search engines, new product development, packaging, consumer promotions, trade promotions, sponsorship, public relations, corporate hospitality, gifts, literature and brochures, events, call centres, personal selling and key account management. Every year hundreds, or even thousands, of ideas may be created to make these elementary marketing activities better. You must ensure too many small ideas are not allowed to proliferate without adequate scrutiny, to ensure that they are effectively screened and selected.

How to predict value   You need to predict how marketing ideas will generate value before choosing to implement them. This is different from the forecasts that are done during annual budgeting, as the aim here is to predict the value likely to be contributed by a new marketing idea or campaign (although similar methods may be employed).

You must choose an appropriate method of predictive modelling to suit the idea that is being assessed. Your choice depends on the degree of novelty of the idea, the time horizon and availability and quality of data. There are three main approaches to choose from:

Extrapolations from the past;

Simulations of the future;

Analogies and scenarios.

Extrapolations of the past are a good choice when the new idea is similar to something you have already done and historical data is readily available. There are numerous techniques available for analysing historical data, from simple univariate analysis to sophisticated multivariate models. Multivariate models are more powerful than univariate ones, as they take account of more factors, but they require the employment of a skilled statistician, and there are many situations when simple univariate methods are the most appropriate.

Simulations of the future mostly rely on canvassing the views of customers, and are used when the new idea is significantly different from existing ideas. There are numerous powerful techniques available, from test marketing, simulated test marketing and surveying the intentions of customer. Conjoint (or trade-off) analysis seeks to predict demand for new products or services by simulating purchase intentions in terms of product features, price, level of service, design, etc. When skilfully executed these simulation methods have an excellent potential.

Analogies with existing situations can also provide powerful evidence with which to evaluate a new idea. You need to make a systematic comparison between your new idea and some existing product or campaign. It is sometimes helpful to combine the insights from analogies into a range of future scenarios, incorporating a range of forecasting assumptions at the same time: for example, best-case and worst-case scenarios.

Prediction is never perfect, so don't dismiss it for this reason. By using systematic methods to screen and select marketing ideas, you have a level playing field for comparing ideas, you enforce a disciplined selection process, and you provide food for thought when the ideas are getting refined and made workable.

Marketing Metrics

Diageo's Activity Evaluator

Global drinks company Diageo has introduced a new decision-analysis procedure called the Activity Evaluator, which is used as a control on all marketing proposals. Managers have to forecast, before they run any new activity, what will be its effects. They must also determine how the effects are to be measured. Often there is a requirement for research – before/during/after – to measure the incremental effects. Expenditure and resources for the activity evaluator are set aside as a routine component of every marketing activity budget.

How to demonstrate value   Think of this as detective work, not as accounting; it involves gathering a chain of evidence as illustrated in Figure 1.2.

First, find out exactly how and why marketing money is being used. Find out how marketing activities are funded, what each one costs, whether it was procured effectively, and what was the thinking process that led to the particular cost deployment. Analyse the patterns of marketing activity too, by region, product or brand. Don't just settle for the total spend figure, dig into the logic behind the numbers.

Second, find out how customers responded to marketing activities. Get into as much detail as possible, compare responses to different marketing activities, compare products, regions, brands, look at customer activity over time and compare it with marketing activity, and discover what causes strong customer responses and what is weak. Don't assume that any old customer data is adequate; insist on getting customer data that can be linked back to marketing activity.

Third, investigate the patterns of revenues and profits. You must look for clues about the factors that shape your revenue and profit patterns. Once again, compare products, regions and brands, look at customer activity and revenue responses, and track it right back to marketing activity. Sometimes evidence is strong, other times you will have to use your judgement, but usually there are enough clues to answer the above questions.

Finally, gather data from outside your own firm. You are looking for external factors that have influenced your revenue and profit patterns. These will include competitor activity, economic trends and daily and seasonal customer habitual activity patterns.

When you've completed this analysis, don't just look at it as a yes or no answer to the question 'has marketing added value?' Learn from your findings and use them to refine your ideas and calibrate your predictions. Learning to select new ideas more reliably is the biggest benefit of demonstrating marketing's value.

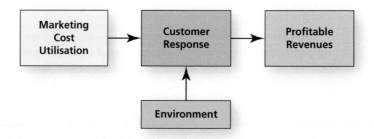

| Figure 1.2 | The Marketing Value Chain |

Marketing Metrics

Kraft

Consumer food manufacturer Kraft routinely uses modelling methods to extract insights about the effectiveness of its marketing activities. Tom Lloyd holds the post of Group Market Analytics Manager. His role is to ensure that the response to every element of the marketing mix is understood by decision makers – advertising, consumer promotion, trade promotion, pricing, new product development. He offers the following advice to anyone who is planning to establish their own modelling capabilities:

1 Start with the problem, not the tool (avoid the man with the model, if all you have is a hammer, every problem looks like a nail).

2 Don't get sidetracked by black-box debates (steer clear of anybody who says that you just feed raw data in, press a button and the answers come out).

3 Choose your modeller carefully – buy in the quality of work you need.

4 Model-fits are just the starting point (ask about the forecasting strength of the model).

5 Use your logic and ask stupid questions (if it doesn't feel right, say so).

Marketing can drive substantial financial value that far exceeds its costs. The practices that support this are described by the Infinity Model. These practices can, and should, be adopted by all marketing organisations, whatever their size or sector. There are many choices of technique to support each practice area, and they can be chosen to suit the needs and resources of each organisation. By adopting these practices, marketing will be more accountable for the value created by the money it spends, and it will have a better reputation and more influence in the boardroom.

Have you ever considered that your employer is your customer and needs to measure return on investment in you and your effectiveness? Employers have needs just like every other consumer.

Across the Hall

Advice for Keith Edelman

Professor Keith Fletcher

is Director of Education at the Chartered Institute of Marketing

I would choose option 3. Option 1 is the most democratic, inclusive and participative – three important values for the universal appeal of football. However, the paper-based system uses old technology which may restrict creative marketing activities, resulting in under-utilisation of the stadium. Option 2 allows ease of access and allows Arsenal to collect data on all people interested in the club but is unable to differentiate the fans. This may limit the opportunity to implement a successful CRM strategy. With broad support for a game which spans age, class, culture, and gender, it should be possible for anyone to see a game if they wish and a CRM strategy should facilitate this. Option 3 is again aimed at everyone, not just season ticket holders, but has many attractions as it offers a range of services at different levels. This would seem to be the best bet, assuming the technology and software can deliver what is promised. It is important that implementation of the strategy does not prioritise short-term profitability at the expense of the ardent, loyal fan, who will tirelessly support their heroes through good times and bad. Norwich City Football Club has adopted a similar approach, aimed at loyal season ticket holders, which has proved to be very successful.

Objective

4

The range of
services and goods
that are marketed

What can be Marketed?

Marketing applies to more than just canned peas or cola drinks. Some of the best marketers come from the ranks of services companies such as Group 4 Securicor (a security firm) or **not-for-profit organisations** such as Greenpeace. In this book, we'll refer to any good, service, idea, place or person that can be marketed as a product, even though what is being sold may not take a physical form. Is there any limit to what marketers can market? The basic answer is no, so long as the rules of exchange apply.

Consumer Goods and Services

Consumer goods are the tangible products that individual consumers purchase for personal or family use. **Services** are intangible products that we pay for and use but never own. Service transactions contribute on average more than 70 per cent to the gross national product of the EU and present special challenges to marketers.[15]

In both cases, though, keep in mind that the consumer is looking to obtain some underlying value, such as convenience, security or status, from a marketing exchange which can come from different competing sources. For example, both a new CD and a ticket to a local concert may cost about the same, and each provides the benefit of musical enjoyment, but one is a consumer good and the latter a service.

Business-to-Business Goods and Services

Business-to-business marketing is the marketing of goods and services from one organisation to another for further processing or for use in their business operations. Although we usually relate marketing to consumers, more goods are sold to businesses and other organisations than to consumers. For example, car makers buy tons of steel to use in the manufacturing process, and they buy computer systems to track manufacturing costs and other information essential to operations.

Not-for-Profit Marketing

As noted earlier, you don't have to be a businessperson to use marketing principles. Many not-for-profit organisations, including museums, zoos, charities and even churches, practise the marketing concept. The WWF has just undergone a major global rebranding with a new strap line 'for a living planet' and Medicins Sans Frontiers (Doctors without Borders) has heart-wrenching ads on TV and even sends out junior doctors on the streets to collect donations. Local governments are getting into the act as they adopt marketing techniques to create more effective taxpayer services and to attract new businesses and industries to their counties and cities.

Idea, Place and People Marketing

Marketing principles also get people to endorse ideas or to improve their behaviour. Many organisations work hard to convince consumers to use seat belts, not to drop litter, to engage in safe sex, or to believe that one political system (democracy, totalitarianism) is preferable to another, religion (Christianity, Islam), and art (realism, abstract) also compete for acceptance in a 'marketplace'. We are all familiar with tourism marketing that promotes exotic resorts like Monaco or Ibiza. For many developing countries like Thailand, tourism may be the best opportunity available for economic growth. Even cities are getting into the act: the UK's capital with

Marketing Ethics

The Politics in marketing

'Gordon wants to be like Maggie. But he doesn't want to be like Tony. Tony also wanted to be like Maggie. But Maggie only wanted to be like Ronnie. Now Dave, he wants to be like Tony. But he doesn't want to be like William, or Iain, or Michael. And certainly not like Maggie either.' One thing is clear: most people don't want to be like any of them! Marketing politics, marketing personality, marketing toothpaste, marketing a football club: they're all converging on the same game of market positioning, the trick of finding out where your audience would like you to be, and locating yourself there. The electorate might be unnerved by too much of this. It starts them asking what you're really for, and where the real you is to be found. They do not look to political leadership for a mirror image of themselves alone. So the first dilemma is if politicians just find out what people want and then try and do it, why don't we just have a market research company like MORI-NOP run the country? The second issue is that, as we apply marketing communication techniques to politicians, the party with the biggest budget will have the greatest impact. Think Coca-Cola! Is this right?

Debate, Discuss, Disagree

1   Should politics be determined by pounds?

2   What do you think of these dilemmas?

the Visit London campaign, using www.londontown.com. Recently, Glasgow has joined the city race and will spend £1.7 million on a new advertising and marketing campaign with the Slogan 'Glasgow, Scotland with Style'.[16] Other European cities, such as Amsterdam, Barcelona, Berlin, Copenhagen and Stockholm are following suit. Finally, politicians, athletes, performers use marketing to their advantage (just think about the spin doctors around Gordon Brown or Formula 1 legend Lewis Hamilton as a brand).

You may have heard the expression, 'Stars are made, not born'. There's a lot of truth to that. Beyonce Knowles may be a great voice and David Beckham may be a superb shot, but talent alone doesn't make thousands or even millions of people buy CDs or stadium seats. Whether a concert or a football match, they and their managers developed a 'product' that they hoped would appeal to some segment of the population.

Some of the same principles that go into 'creating' a celebrity apply to you. An entertainer – whether a busker or Pavarotti – must 'package' his or her talents, identify a **target market** that is likely to be interested, and work hard to gain exposure to these potential customers by appearing in the right musical venues. In the same way, everyday people like Alex, who you met at the start of the chapter, 'package' themselves by summing up their accomplishments on a CV and distributing it at venues like Monster.com to attract potential buyers.

'Something of Value' to Whom?

Objective

5

How value is created from the perspectives of customers, producers, and society

So far, we've talked a lot about marketing delivering value to customers and we said that value is the perceived benefits minus the perceived costs in terms of time, money, or emotion. But here's the tricky part: value is in the eye of the beholder. Your mother may believe that you are the greatest person on the planet, but a prospective employer may form a different conclusion. A big part of marketing is to communicate these benefits as the value proposition to the customer that fairly and accurately sums up the value that the customer will realise if he or she purchases the product or service. Let's look at value from the different perspectives of the parties that are involved in an exchange: the customers, the sellers and society.

| Photo 1.3 | Evian hopes to build demand for water as an alternative to other stylish beverage options.
Source: The Advertising Archives |

 ## Value from the Customer's Perspective

Think about buying a new pair of shoes. You have narrowed the choice down to several options. Your purchase decision no doubt will be affected by the ratio of costs versus benefits for each type of shoe. Remember, the value proposition includes the whole bundle of benefits the firm promises to deliver, not just the benefits of the product itself. For example, although most people probably couldn't run faster or jump higher if they were wearing Adidas versus Puma, many die-hard loyalists swear by their favorite brand. These archrivals are largely marketed in terms of their images – meanings that have been carefully crafted with the help of legions of athletes, slickly produced commercials and millions of euros. When you buy a pair of Microrides made by Adidas, you may be doing more than choosing shoes to wear – you may also be making a statement about the type of person you are or wish you were. You can probably think of possessions you own with which you've 'bonded' in some way – that is, their value to you goes beyond their function, for example your favourite sweatshirt or piece of jewellery.

 ## Value from the Seller's Perspective

We've seen that marketing transactions produce value for buyers, but how do sellers experience value, and how do they decide whether a transaction is valuable? One answer is obvious: they determine whether the exchange is profitable to them. Another is prestige among rivals or pride in doing what they do well. Some firms by definition don't even care about making money; non-profit organisations like Greenpeace, or children.org regard value in terms of their ability to motivate and educate the public, or to increase the living standards of impoverished children.

Now more than ever marketers are searching for new and better ways to accurately measure just what kind of value they are delivering, how this stacks up to the competition, and – as we'll see next – in some cases even whether the relationship they have with a customer possesses enough value for them to continue it.

Calculating the Value of a Customer

Intelligent companies today understand that making money from a single transaction doesn't provide the kind of value they desire. Instead, their goal is to satisfy the customer over and over again so that they can build a long-term relationship rather than just having a 'one-night stand'.

In recent years many firms have transformed the way they do business and have begun to regard consumers as partners in the transaction rather than as passive 'recipients'. That explains why it's becoming more common for companies to develop loyalty schemes such as Tesco's club card and Scandinavan Airlines' Eurobonus card which reward customers for using the company.

Tesco's decision to reward its customers means the company has learned an important secret: it often is more expensive to attract new customers than it is to retain current ones. In fact, it doesn't always hold. In recent years, companies have been asking, 'How much is this customer really worth to us?' This way of thinking is similar to how we may decide which friends are 'worth keeping'.

Companies that calculate the **lifetime value of a customer** look at how much profit they expect to make from a particular customer, including each and every purchase he or she will make from them now and in the future.

Providing Value to Stakeholders by Creating a Competitive Advantage

All things being equal, a firm creates value for stakeholders when it convinces customers that they will acquire greater value by buying its products rather than those of competitors. Companies are able to accomplish this goal because underlying all marketing strategies is the desire to create a **competitive advantage** for the firm. A firm has a competitive advantage when it is able to provide customers with a benefit the competition can't, thus giving consumers a reason to choose one product over another.

How does a firm go about creating a competitive advantage? The first step is to identify what it does really well. A **distinctive competency** is a firm's capability that is superior to that of its competition. For example, Coca-Cola's success in global markets – Coke commands 50 per cent of the world's soft-drink business – is related to its distinctive competencies in distribution and marketing communications.

Coke's distribution system got a jump on the competition during the Second World War. To enable US soldiers fighting overseas to enjoy a five-cent Coke, the US government assisted Coca-Cola in building 64 overseas bottling plants. Coke's skilful marketing communications programme, a second distinctive competency, has contributed to its global success. In addition to its television commercials, Coke has blanketed less developed countries such as Tanzania with its print advertisements so that even people without televisions will think of Coke when they get thirsty.

The second step in developing a competitive advantage is to turn a distinctive competency into a **differential benefit** – one that is important to customers. Differential benefits set products apart from competitors' products by providing either something unique, or more of something that customers want. Unique benefits provide reasons for customers to pay a premium for

Maclean's Whitening toothpaste is not an instant fix. It won't change the colour of your teeth overnight, and for good reason.

Instead of relying on harsh abrasives, its unique, patented formula* is clinically proven to break down stains gently over time, to help restore and then maintain the natural whiteness of your teeth.

It is the only whitening toothpaste accredited by the British Dental Association. It also provides all the benefits of a regular toothpaste with fluoride – protecting against cavities, helping to fight plaque and freshening breath. Commit to using it twice a day and you can expect results after just 28 days.

No White Lies

macleans Whitening

| Photo 1.4 | Marketers try to show us how their products will create value. Source: The Advertising Archives |

a firm's products and exhibit a strong brand preference. For many years, loyal Apple computer users benefited from superior graphics compared with their PC-using counterparts. When PC manufacturers caught up with this competitive advantage, Apple relied on its inventive product designers to create another differential benefit – futuristic looking computers in a multitude of colours. This competitive advantage even caused many loyal PC users to take a bite of the Apple.

Note that a differential benefit does not necessarily mean simply offering something different. For example, Apple created a 'Hockey Puck' USB mouse which was differentiated by a revolutionary design, but as far as ergonomics go it was possibly the worst-designed mouse. Many iMac users complained that it was literally painful to use it for extended periods of time. It quickly fell out of favour and generated a market for third-party input devices that functioned with the iMac.[17] The moral: effective product benefits must be both different from the competition and wanted by customers because they have utility.

Adding Value through the Value Chain

One approach to understanding the delivery of value and satisfaction is the **value chain**. This term refers to a series of activities involved in designing, producing, marketing, delivering and supporting any product.[18]

This concept reminds us that every product starts with raw materials that are of relatively limited value to the end customer. Each link in the chain has the potential to either add or remove value from the product the customer eventually buys. The successful firm is the one that can perform one or more of these activities better than other firms – this is its competitive advantage. The main activities of value chain members include the following:

- Bringing in materials to make the product, referred to as inbound logistics;
- Converting the materials into the final product, referred to as operations;
- Shipping out the final product, referred to as outbound logistics;
- Marketing the final product, where marketing and sales come into play;
- Servicing the product/customer, referred to as service.

For example, you buy a new Apple iPod at your shop. Have you ever thought about all the people and steps involved in designing, manufacturing and delivering that product to the shop – not to mention other people who create brand advertising, conduct consumer research to figure out what people like or dislike about their mobile music players or even make the box it comes in or those little plastic peanuts that keep the unit from being damaged in shipment?

As Figure 1.3 shows, all these companies (and more) belong to Apple's value chain. This means that Apple must make a lot of decisions. What electronic components will go into its

Inbound Logistics	Operations	Outbound Logistics	Marketing and Sales	Service
• Planar lithium battery (Sony) • Hard drive (Toshiba) • MP3 decoder and controller chip (PortalPlayer) • Flash memory chip (Sharp Electronics) • Stereo digital-to-analogue converter (Wolfson Microelectronics) • Firewire interface controller (Texas Instruments)	• Consumer research • New-product-development team • Engineering and production	• Transport companies • Wholesalers • Retailers	• Advertising • Sales force	• Computer technicians

Figure 1.3   A Value Chain for the Apple iPod

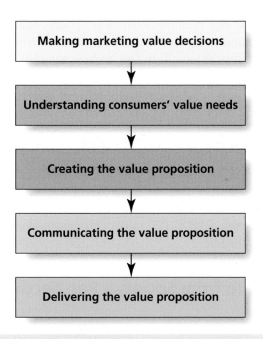

Figure 1.4   Making and Delivering Value

music players? What accessories will be included in the package? What transport companies, wholesalers, and retailers will deliver the iPods to shops? What service will it provide to customers after the sale? And what marketing strategies will it use? In some cases, members of a value chain will work together to coordinate their activities to be more efficient and thus create a competitive advantage.

This book is organised around the sequence of steps necessary to ensure that the appropriate value exchange occurs and that both parties to the transaction are satisfied. Figure 1.4

shows these steps. Basically, this involves learning about what marketers do as a product makes its way through the value chain from manufacturers into your hands. We'll start with a focus on how companies decide what to make, how and where to sell it, and whom to sell it to. Then we'll take a look at how they decide to 'position' the product in the marketplace, including choices about what it should look like, how its value should be communicated to customers, and how much to charge for it. As we reach the end of our marketing journey, we'll talk about how the product actually gets delivered to consumers.

Consumer-Generated Value: From Audience to Community

One of the most exciting new developments in the marketing world is the evolution of how consumers interact with marketers. In particular, we're seeing everyday people actually generating value instead of just buying it – consumers are becoming advertising directors, retailers and new product development consultants. They are creating their own ads (some flattering, some not) for products and posting them on sites like YouTube.com. They are buying and selling merchandise ranging from Beatles memorabilia to washing machines (to body parts, but that's another story) on eBay. They are sharing ideas for new styles with fashion designers, and customising their own unique versions of products on websites. These changes mean that marketers need to adjust their thinking about customers: they need to stop thinking of buyers as a passive audience and start thinking of them as a brand community that is motivated to participate in both the production and the consumption of what companies sell. In fact we have sampled a few of these videos related to marketing and at the end of each chapter in our Real People Real Surfers section will be giving you ones to look at which illustrate various points in the chapter. We'll talk more about this phenomenon later, but for now think about these recent examples of consumer-generated value.

Companies like LEGO and BMW are harnessing the creativity of their consumers, and sometimes they are even encouraging consumers to produce consumer generated media content (CGM). MasterCard also asked consumers to play a role in their 'Priceless' advertising campaign. The company showed two vague storylines – in one of them a man sitting in a field with a typewriter – and asked consumers to complete the ads by filling in blanks that appeared on the screen. Over 32,000 videos were submitted in the first few months and the winner ad was aired on TV.[19]

Value from Society's Perspective

We must also consider how marketing transactions add or subtract value from society. In many ways, we are at the mercy of marketers because we trust them: to sell us products that are safe and perform as promised, to price and distribute these products fairly. Conflicts often arise in business when the pressure to succeed in the marketplace provokes dishonest business practices – the 'NatWest Three', a trio of three businessmen who skimmed off £3.7 million in profits through a fraudulent deal between NatWest and Enron in 2000, were jailed for 37 months.[20] Enron filed for bankruptcy in 2001 after a scandal revealed the firm's irregular accounting practices that did not report many of the debts and losses of Enron in its financial statements. As the scandal was revealed the company's shares dropped from $90 to 50¢ before it went bankrupt.

Companies usually find that stressing ethics and social responsibility is also good business, at least in the long run. Some find out the hard way. For example, the Chrysler Corporation was accused of resetting the odometers of new cars that managers had actually driven prior to sale. The company admitted the practice only after some managers tried to get out of paying speeding tickets by claiming that their speedometers – and odometers – didn't work because the cables were disconnected.[21] These actions caused the company great embarrassment, and it took years of hard work to restore the public's trust.

In contrast, in 2007 after salmonella was found in two of the Marks & Spencer houmous range the company voluntarily removed all other unaffected houmous products from the shelves as a precaution. The company reported the incident to the Food Standards Agency and the Food Safety Authority of Ireland and started a thorough investigation with the suppliers to find out what exactly had happened. The recall cost the firm millions of pounds in revenues.[22]

The Dark Side of Marketing and Consumer Behaviour

Intentionally or not, some marketers do violate their bond of trust with consumers, and unfortunately the 'dark side' of marketing often is the subject of harsh criticism.[23] In some cases, these violations are illegal, such as when a retailer adopts a 'bait-and-switch' selling strategy, luring consumers into the shop with promises of inexpensive products with the sole intent of getting them to switch to higher-priced goods. In other cases, marketing practices have detrimental effects on society even though they are not actually illegal. Some alcohol and tobacco companies advertise in low-income areas where abuse of these products is a big problem. Others sponsor commercials depicting groups of people in an unfavourable light or sell products that encourage antisocial behaviour.

Sometimes consumers' worst enemies are themselves, and their desires, choices and actions result in negative consequences to individuals and the society in which they live. Some harmful consumer behaviours such as excessive drinking or cigarette smoking stem from social pressures, and the cultural value placed on money encourages activities such as shoplifting or insurance fraud. Exposure to unattainable ideals of beauty and success can create dissatisfaction with the self. 'The dark side' of consumer behaviour includes:

Addictive consumption: Consumer addiction is a physiological or psychological dependency on products or services. These problems include alcoholism, drug addiction and cigarettes – and many companies profit from addictive products or by selling solutions. Also 'shopaholics' turn to shopping in much the same way addicted people turn to drugs or alcohol which can result in massive credit card debt, loan consolidations and even bankruptcy.[24]

Exploited people: Sometimes people are used or exploited, willingly or not, for commercial gain in the marketplace; these situations range from travelling road shows

Did you hear the one about the fat guy suing the restaurants?

It's no joke.
He claims the food was too cheap so he ate too much!

Learn more about the erosion of personal responsibility and common sense. Go to:

ConsumerFreedom.com

Photo 1.5	Some people feel that marketers manipulate consumers, while others argue that people should be responsible for their own choices. This ad is critical of the current trend of lawsuits brought against fast food companies by people who blame their eating problems on the fast food industry. What do you think?
	Source: The Centre for Consumer Freedom

Marketing Ethics

Ethical voices on marketing's value creation

Whereas marketers often emphasise that marketing is about satisfying needs, critics of marketing sometimes argue on behalf of consumers that marketing just satisfies needs marketers themselves have created and imposed on consumers – sometimes even by applying manipulating strategies and techniques. Is it ethical for diet manufacturers to play on women's fear of becoming fat? Is it ethical for marketers to create a market for Nintendo which didn't exist or to introduct SMS and text messaging to teenagers? Some of these activities have contributed to marketers' sometimes poor reputation.

However, in order to answer these questions we have to resort to what criteria are being used to measure the ethics involved. Marketers operate within a legal framework they should abide by. Second, they also operate within the standards of other regulatory bodies such as the Advertising Standards Authority and codes of conduct from the Chartered Institute of Marketing and Direct Marketing. Third, they also take note of powerful lobbying groups on issues of marketing to children and alcohol advertising. Fourth, they would be foolish to ignore the ethics of their own customers who might desert them if they behaved unethically in their eyes. The question is whose ethical standards should marketers adhere to? The second point to note is that marketers can be responsible for creating people's perceived needs. It is true that, if you need a cold drink, marketers can influence you to think you want Coca-Cola. However, even if they exert this influence, they still can't make you buy it! This would be truly unethical, but it is almost never the case. Thus consumers purchase products of their own free will. Moreover, nowadays, the average consumer is more marketing savvy and well aware of the fact that marketing is not only conducted in order to satisfy his or her needs. As stated at the beginning of the book, marketing is not a one-way, but a two-way road.

Debate, Discuss, Disagree

1   What's your opinion on how much marketers create or simply serve needs?

that feature dwarfs and midgets to the selling of body parts and babies on eBay. Consumed consumers are people who themselves become commodities.

Illegal activities: The cost of crimes committed against business has been estimated at around £4 billion per year.[25] This includes attempts to put false items on an insurance bill to cover the amount deducted because the item was old, to sneeking into a theatre to avoid paying admission or to download music files from illegal file sharing systems on the internet.[26]

Shrinkage: A retail theft is committed every five seconds. Shrinkage is the industry term for inventory and cash losses from shoplifting and employee theft. This is a massive problem for businesses that is passed on to consumers in the form of higher prices. However, 40 per cent of the losses can be attributed to employees rather than shoppers.

Marketing as a Process

Our definition of marketing refers to processes. This means that marketing is not a one-shot operation. When it's done right, marketing is a decision process in which marketing managers determine the strategies that will help the firm meet its long-term objectives and then execute those strategies using the tools they have at their disposal. In this section, we'll look at how marketers make business decisions and plan actions and the tools they use to execute their plans.

Marketing Planning

Objective

6

The basics of marketing planning and the marketing mix tools used in the marketing process

A big part of the marketing process is to engage in what is called marketing planning. The first phase of marketing planning is analysing the marketing environment. This means understanding the firm's current strengths and weaknesses by assessing factors that might help or hinder the development and marketing of products. The analysis must also take into account the opportunities and threats the firm will encounter in the marketplace, such as the actions of competitors, cultural and technological changes, and the economy.

Firms (or individuals) engaging in marketing planning ask questions such as the following:

- What product benefits will our customers be looking for in three to five years in for example chocolate consumption?
- What capabilities does our firm have that set it apart from the competition, e.g. Cadbury has established brand and chocolate making expertise?
- What additional customer groups might provide important **market segment**s for us in the future, e.g. would older consumers prefer less sweet chocolate?
- How will changes in technology affect our production process, our communication strategy, and our distribution strategy, e.g. to produce the fine bubbles in Cadbury's Wispa a new procedure was invented.
- What changes in social and cultural values are occurring that will affect our market in the next few years, e.g. will people be more health conscious about chocolate snacks?
- How will customers' awareness of environmental issues affect their attitudes towards our manufacturing facilities, e.g. how will Cadbury's disposal of factory waste have to alter?
- What legal and regulatory issues may affect our business in both domestic and global markets, e.g. might the government add restrictions on the sale of chocolate to young children like banning it in schools?

Answers to these and other questions provide the foundation for developing an organisation's **marketing plan**. This is a document that describes the marketing environment, outlines the marketing objectives and strategy, and identifies who will be responsible for carrying out each part of the marketing strategy. A major marketing decision for most organisations is which products to market to which consumers without turning off other consumers at the same time. Some firms choose to reach as many customers as possible by offering their goods or services to a **mass market** that consists of all possible customers in a market regardless of the differences in their specific needs and wants. Marketing planning then becomes a matter of developing a basic product and a single strategy for reaching everyone.

Although this approach can be cost effective, the firm risks losing potential customers to competitors whose marketing plans are directed at meeting the needs of specific groups within the market. A market segment is a distinct group of customers within a larger market who are similar to one another in some way and whose needs differ from other customers in the larger market. Car makers such as Rover, Fiat and Volvo offer different automobiles for different market segments. Depending on its goals and resources, a firm may choose to focus on one segment. A product's **market position** is how the target market perceives the product in comparison to competitor's brands.

Marketing's Tools: The Marketing Mix

In determining the best way to present a good or service for consumers' consideration, marketers have a toolbox called the **marketing mix**. The elements of the marketing mix are commonly known as the Four Ps: product, price, promotion and place. However, for services there are three more Ps as we shall see in later chapters. As Figure 1.5 shows, each P is a piece of the puzzle that must be combined with other pieces. Just as a radio DJ puts together a collection of separate songs (a musical mix) to create a certain mood, the idea of a mix in this context reminds us that no single marketing activity is sufficient to accomplish the organisation's objectives.

Although we talk about the Four Ps as separate parts of a firm's marketing strategy, in reality, product, price, promotion and place decisions are totally interdependent. Decisions about any single one of the four are affected by and affect every other marketing mix decision. For example, assume that a firm is introducing a superior quality product, one that is more expensive to produce than its existing line of products. The price the firm charges for this new product must cover these higher costs, but in addition the firm must create advertising and other promotional strategies to convey a top-quality image. At the same time, the price of the product must cover not only the costs of production but also the cost of advertising. Furthermore,

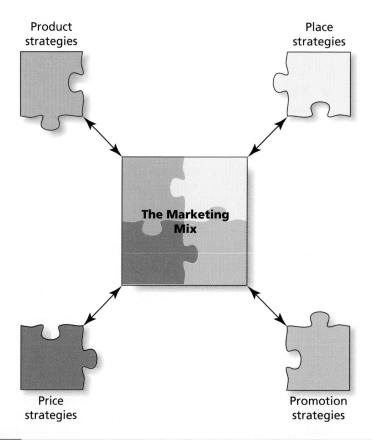

Figure 1.5	**The Marketing Mix**
	What marketing is all about! The Marketing Mix is a combination of the Four Ps – product, price, place and promotion – all used together to satisfy customer needs. However, throughout this book we will refer to the 7 Ps model you'll find in Chapter 9.

the firm must include up-market retailers in its distribution strategy. The elements of the marketing mix therefore work hand in hand.

We'll examine these components of the marketing mix in detail later in this book. For now, let's briefly look at each P to gain some insight into its meaning and role in the marketing mix.

Product

We've already seen that the **product** is a good, a service, an idea, a place, a person – whatever is offered for sale in the exchange. This aspect of the marketing mix includes the design and packaging of a good, as well as its physical features and any associated services, such as free delivery. So we can see that the product is a combination of many different elements, all of which are important to the product's success. For example, when the UK firm Virgin introduced Virgin Cola in the United States, the company attempted to make the product stand out from the competition through its distinctive packaging. Advertising that introduced the brand told customers about the curved squeezable bottles. 'If all you got is Va Va, You got to get some Voom; It's in the curvy bottle, Yeah, Virgin Drinks' got Voom. . . . Virgin puts the Voom in your Va Va'.[27] We're not quite sure what that means, but it does get your attention. Whether the focus is on the bottle or some other element, the product is an important part of the marketing mix.

Price

Price is the amount the consumer must exchange to receive the offering. A price is often used as a way to increase consumers' interest in a product, for example when an item is put on sale, but in other cases marketers try to sell a product with a higher price than people are used to if they want to communicate that it's high quality or cutting edge. For example, the Adidas 1 computerised running shoe got a lot of attention in the media. Some of the fuss was that the shoe was billed as the first 'smart shoe' because it contained a computer chip that adapted its cushioning level to a runner's size and stride. But a lot of the press coverage also revolved around the hefty price tag of €195 per pair, which made the shoe a status symbol for the hardcore runner.[28]

Promotion

Promotion includes all the activities marketers undertake to inform consumers about their products and to encourage potential customers to buy these products. Promotions can take many forms, including for example personal selling, direct marketing, buzz and viral marketing, television advertising, sponsorship, shop coupons, billboards, magazine ads and publicity releases. Marketing messages often communicate **myths**, stories containing symbolic elements that express the shared emotions and ideals of a culture.[29] Consider, for example, how McDonald's takes on mythical qualities. To some, the golden arches are virtually synonymous with American culture. They offer sanctuary to Europeans in foreign lands who are grateful to know exactly what to expect once they enter. Basic struggles of good versus evil are played out in the fantasy world of McDonald's advertising, as when Ronald McDonald confounds the Hamburglar. McDonald's even runs Hamburger University, where fast-food students learn how to make the perfect burger.

Place

Place refers to the availability of the product to the customer at the desired time and location. This P is related to a channel of distribution – the set of firms working together to get a

Marketing Ethics

Playboy using play toys for children

A furious vicar took direct action against Playboy stationery products aimed at children – by sweeping them off the shelves.

He was appalled when he found items carrying Playboy's bunny logo on the shelves at his local Stationery Box shop in York next to Winnie-the-Pooh and Mickey Mouse products. 'Playboy's target audience is 18- to 34-year-olds, so we clearly did not authorise or approve the placement of our product next to such well-known children's characters. We will be reviewing this situation immediately.'

Catherine Hanly, editor of the parents website raisingkids.co.uk said many mothers had condemned the sale of Playboy products in WH Smith shops on a recent discussion forum. 'They are perceived as targeting children,' she added.

Playboy's stationery range, which is widely sold in High Street shops, includes pink pencil cases, notebooks, folders, diaries, gel pens and ring binders. Playboy claims that all its products are aimed at adults only. Three years ago, WH Smith was attacked for selling the same Playboy range to children. Argos sells the Playboy stationery range in the section of its catalogue which includes 'toys and gifts'. But WH Smith defended the sale of the Playboy items, saying it aimed to strike the right balance to meet the needs of all its customers 'whilst not acting as a censor'.

'Furious vicar clears shelves at local shop of Playboy stationery "targeted" at children', Chris Brooke, Mail online, 20 May 2008

Debate, Discuss, Disagree

1　Do you think this is ethical or unethical to distribute these products in these shops?

2　Who is more in the right? The vicar? Playboy? The shops?

---

product from a producer to a consumer. For clothing or electronics, this channel includes local retailers as well as other outlets, such as retail websites that strive to offer the right quantity of products in the right styles at the right time, for example Amazon's next day delivery.

Now that you've read the chapter on how marketers create value for customers and heard the advice read 'Real People, Real Decisions' to see which strategy Keith selected to maximise the value created for fans and the revenue of Arsenal FC.

Real People, Real Decisions

How it worked out at Arsenal. . . .

Option 3 To have separate levels of membership was chosen because:

t is inclusive of everyone who has an interest in the club. The number of people registered at entry level was an astonishing 180,000. All these Red members get a yearly membership pack and e-card which allows for e-ticketing at the turnstyles; this helps to reduce the ticket tout problem because each e-card is photo-identified. As a result of the data collected during the registration process, the club now knows more about its wider fan base and can therefore market to them more easily, e.g. with cross-promotions for some of the club's sponsors such as O$_2$. The new database has been cleaned up and it's more difficult to give your e-ticket to someone else. The club can communicate more clearly different messages to each different level of membership rather than one message for all the fans and can target higher value services such as restaurant promotions to the right type of fan while at the same time it can send out unifying messages called 'all Arsenal' as a rallying call to the whole fan base when needed.

If a match doesn't sell out, the club can have quick email promotions to stimulate late demand. It can also set attendance criteria for high-profile matches. For example, it can insist you must attend a set number of matches if you want a ticket for the final and can accurately monitor this using the e-membership card which allows access to the stadium. Members can also access all their records online. Finally, the club can run promotions using the membership database, for example each month club members will be entered into special access-all-areas competitions including watching the first team squad training and lunch at their Hertfordshire HQ.

However, the system is very expensive to set up and run. Implementation is complicated and has created much greater expectations in the fan base for customer service. Although the club has engaged the 180,000 strong Red membership in the club's activities, it has raised their expectations of seeing a match which it still cannot deliver because there are not enough tickets.

> # The club can communicate different messages to each different level

| Photo 1.6 | Arsenal Emirates Stadium.
Source: Keith Edelman |

Marketing Metrics

Measuring Arsenal's success

Membership went from 44,000 to 180,000 in one year and the stadium is full for nearly every game. Moreover the club is making much more money from non-ticket items. Retail sales have increased 30–45 per cent and online sales have increased by 30 per cent. In addition, on a typical match day, 2000 meals are bought by Platinum members. The club has also seen a massive increase in engagement with other services which it offers. For example, Arsenal TV started with 1000 fans and now has over 40,000 paying subscribers and the website is used by over 2.5 million people interested in the Gunners prestigious past, the present and activities of stars such as Thierry Henri and the future of one of the world's greatest football clubs.

| Photo 1.7 | Keith at the Emirates Stadium. Source: Keith Edelman |

Chapter Summary

Now that you have finished reading this chapter, you should be able to understand:

1. **Who marketers are, where they work and marketing's role in the firm.** Marketers come from many different backgrounds and work in a variety of locations, from consumer goods companies to non-profit organisations to financial institutions to advertising and public relations agencies. Marketing's role in the firm depends on the organisation. Some firms are very marketing oriented, whereas others do not focus on marketing. Therefore, no matter what firm marketers work in, their decisions affect and are affected by the firm's other operations.

2. **What marketing is and how it provides value to everyone involved in the marketing process.** Marketing is an organisational function and a set of processes for creating, communicating and delivering value to customers, and for managing customer relationships in ways that benefit the organisation and its stakeholders. Therefore, marketing is all about delivering value to everyone who is affected by a transaction (stakeholders).

3. **The range of services and goods that are marketed.** Any good, service, idea that can be marketed is a product, even though what is being sold may not take a physical form. Consumer goods are the tangible products that consumers purchase for personal or family use. Services are intangible products that we pay for and use but never own. **Industrial goods** are those goods sold to businesses and other organisations for further processing or for use in their business operations. Not-for-profit organisations, places and people can also be marketed.

4. **Value from the perspectives of the customers, producers and society.** Value is the benefits a customer receives from buying a product or service. Marketing communicates these benefits as the value proposition to the customer. For customers, the value proposition includes the whole bundle of benefits the product promises to deliver, not just the benefits of the product itself. Sellers determine value by assessing whether its transactions are profitable, whether it is providing value to stakeholders by creating a competitive advantage, and whether it is providing value through its value chain. Society receives value from marketing activities when producers and consumers engage in ethical, profitable and environmentally friendly exchange relationships. One of the newest developments in marketing is that consumers themselves are playing an increasingly greater role in generating value on behalf of marketers in addition to consuming it.

5. **The basics of marketing planning and the marketing mix tools used in the marketing process.** The strategic process of marketing planning begins with an assessment of factors within the organisation and in the external environment that could help or hinder the development and marketing of products. On the basis of this analysis, marketers set objectives and develop strategies. Many firms use a target marketing strategy in which they divide the overall market into segments and then target the most attractive one. Then they design the marketing mix to gain a competitive position in the target market. The marketing mix includes product, price, place and promotion. The product is what satisfies customer needs. The price reflects the customer assigned value or amount to be exchanged for the product. The place or channel of distribution gets the product to the customer. Promotion is the organisation's efforts to persuade customers to buy the product.

6. **The evolution of the marketing concept.** Early in the twentieth century, firms followed a production orientation in which they focused on the most efficient ways to produce and distribute products. Beginning in the 1930s, some firms adopted a selling orientation that encouraged salespeople to aggressively sell products to customers. In the 1950s, organisations adopted a consumer orientation that focused on customer satisfaction. This led to the development of the marketing concept. Today, many firms are moving toward a New Era orientation that includes not only a commitment to quality and value, but also a concern for both economic and social profit.

Key Terms

Benefit 10	Market position 35	Product 37
Business-to-business marketing 26	Market segment 35	Product 5
Competitive advantage 29	Marketing 5	Production orientation 14
Consumer 5	Marketing concept 16	Promotion 37
Consumer goods 6	Marketing mix 36	Return on investment 15
Consumer orientation 15	Marketing plan 35	Selling orientation 14
Customer relationship management 15	Market position 35	Services 26
Demand 10	Marketplace 10	Stakeholders 9
Differential benefit 29	Mass market 35	Target market 27
Distinctive competency 29	Myths 37	Total Quality Management 15
E-commerce 10	Needs 9	Utility 10
E-marketers 6	Needs 6	Value 5
Exchange 11	New Era orientation 15	Value chain 30
Industrial goods 41	Not-for-profit organisations 26	Value proposition 15
Lifetime value of a customer 29	Place 37	Want 9
Market 10	Price 37	

Chapter Review

Marketing Concepts: Testing Your Knowledge

1. Where do marketers work, and what role does marketing have in a company?

2. Briefly explain what marketing is.

3. Explain needs, wants and demands. What is the role of marketing in each of these?

4. What is utility? How does marketing create different forms of utility?

5. Define the terms consumer goods, services and industrial goods.

6. What does the lifetime value of the customer refer to, and how is it calculated?

7. What does it mean for a firm to have a competitive advantage? What gives a firm a competitive advantage?

8. What is involved in marketing planning?

9. List and describe the elements of the marketing mix.

10. Trace the evolution of the marketing concept.

Marketing Concepts: Discussing Choices and Ethical Issues

1. Have you ever pirated software? How about music? Is it ethical to give or receive software instead of paying for it? Does the answer depend on the person's motivation and/or if he or she could otherwise afford to buy the product?

2. The marketing concept focuses on the ability of marketing to satisfy customer needs. As a typical college student, how does marketing satisfy your needs? What areas of your life are affected by marketing? What areas of your life (if any) are not affected by marketing?

3. In both developed and developing countries, not all firms have implemented programmes that follow the marketing concept. Can you think of firms that still operate with a production orientation? A selling orientation? What changes would you recommend for these firms?

4. Successful firms have a competitive advantage because they are able to identify distinctive competencies and use these to create differential benefits for their customers. Consider your business school or your university. What distinctive competencies does it have? What differential benefits does it provide for students? What is its competitive advantage? What are your ideas as to how your university could improve its competitive position? Write an outline of your ideas.

5. Ideally, each member of a value chain adds value to a product before someone buys it. Thinking about a music CD you might buy in a shop, what kind of value does the music retailer add? How about the label that signs the artist? The public relations firm that arranges a tour by the artist to promote the new CD? The production company that shoots a music video to go along with the cut?

6. User-generated commercials seem to be part of a broader trend towards user generated content of all sorts. Examples include MySpace.com, Flickr.com (where users post photos and comment on others' pictures), blogging and video sharing sites like YouTube.com. Do you think this is a passing fad or an important trend? How (if at all) should marketers be dealing with these activities?

7. Some marketing or consumption activities involve the (literal) consumption of people – voluntarily or not. In one recent controversial incident, a man in Germany advertised on the internet to find someone who wanted to be killed and eaten (we are not making this up). He actually found a willing volunteer and did just what he promised – and was jailed for manslaughter. If a person consents to be 'consumed' in some way, is this still an ethical problem? What of value is being exchanged here? Would it be different if a person ate part of themselves?

 ## Marketing Practice: Applying What You've Learned

1. An old friend of yours has been making and selling vitamin-fortified smoothies to acquaintances and friends of friends for some time. He is now thinking about opening a shop in a small city with a university, but he is worried about whether he'll have enough customers to keep a business going. Knowing that you are a marketing student, he's asked you for some advice. What can you tell him about product, price, promotion and place (distribution) strategies that will help him get his business off the ground?

2. Assume that you are employed by your city's chamber of commerce. One major focus of the chamber is to get industries to move to your city. As a former marketing student, you know that there are issues involving product, price, promotion and place (distribution) that can attract business. Next week you have an opportunity to speak to the members of the chamber, and your topic will be 'Marketing a City'. Develop an outline for that presentation.

3. As a marketing professional, you have been asked to write a short piece for a local business newsletter about the state of marketing today. You think the best way to address this topic is to review how the marketing concept has evolved and to discuss the New Era orientation. Write a short article to submit to the editor of the newsletter.

4. As university students, you and your friends sometimes discuss the various courses you are taking. One of your friends says to you, 'Marketing's not important. It's just dumb advertising.' Another friend says, 'Marketing doesn't really affect people's lives in any way.' As a role-playing exercise, present your arguments against these statements to your class.

Marketing Miniproject: Learning by Doing

The purpose of this miniproject is to develop an understanding of the importance of marketing to different organisations.

1. Work as a team with two or three other students in your class to select an organisation in your community that practises marketing. It may be a manufacturer, a service provider, a retailer, a not-for-profit organisation – almost any organisation will do. Then schedule a visit with someone within the organisation who is involved in the marketing activities. Arrange for a short visit in which the person can give your group a tour of the facilities and explain the organisation's marketing activities.

    Divide the following list of topics among your team and ask each person to be responsible for developing a set of questions to ask during the interview to learn about the company's programme:

   ● What customer segments the company targets;

   ● How it determines needs and wants;

   ● What products it offers, including features, benefits and goals for customer satisfaction;

   ● What its pricing strategies are, including any discounting policies it has;

   ● What promotional strategies it uses and what these emphasise to position the product(s);

   ● How it distributes products and whether it has encountered any problems;

   ● How marketing planning is done and who does it;

   ● Whether social responsibility is part of the marketing programme and, if so, in what ways.

2. Develop a team report of your findings. In each section of the report, describe what you learned that is new or surprising to you compared with what you expected.

3. Develop a team presentation for your class that summarises your findings. Conclude your presentation with comments on what your team believes the company was doing that was particularly good and what was not so good.

Real People, Real Surfers

Exploring the Web

H&M sells clothing and other merchandise both in its shops and on its website (www.H&M.com). Visit its website, and also identify the website of a competitor. *Hint*: You can do this by Googling the term 'fashion clothing'. Follow the links to find out as much as you can about the companies. Then on the basis of your experience, answer the following questions:

1. Which firm has the better website? What makes it better?

2. Do you think the firms are targeting specific market segments? If so, what market segments? What features of the website give you that idea?

3. What are your major criticisms of each of the websites? What would you do to improve each site?

Now, take a look at the website at www.pearsoned.co.uk/solomon to see some videos from YouTube relating to aspects of this chapter.

Marketing Plan Exercise

A key to long-term business success lies in a firm's ability to offer value to customers through its product offerings. The task of communicating that value proposition rests largely with the company's marketers. A marketing plan not only must clarify the sources of value, but also must specify how the value message gets out.

Pick a product or service you like – one that you believe has a strong value proposition. Identify the specific source(s) of value.

That is, what leads you to conclude the product or service offers value?

How is that value communicated? What other sources of value might be developed for the product or service you identified? How might these new value-adding properties be communicated to customers?

Marketing in Action Case

Real decisions at Virgin Galactic

Would you like to travel to outer space? Unless you are an astronaut or scientist conducting experiments in the weightlessness of space, is there any reason for you to undertake the risk of space travel? Sir Richard Branson, one of Britain's best-known entrepreneurs, thinks there are a lot of consumers who see outer space as the ultimate adventure holiday. In fact, up to 40 per cent of people in one survey said they would like to travel to space. Branson thinks this kind of enthusiasm could lead to thousands of passengers per year hoping to boldly go where few have gone before.

Richard Branson is not new to creating successful businesses. He has created a number of companies under the 'Virgin' brand name, including the Virgin Atlantic airline, Virgin Records, Virgin Megastores and the Virgin Mobile phone service. To capitalise on the growing interest in space tourism that one day may be a multi-billion-pound industry, Branson created Virgin Galactic after watching Spaceship One, the first spacecraft designed and built by a private citizen, reach space in 2004.

The product that Virgin Galactic hopes to offer to satisfy the demand for space tourism is a ride on Spaceship Two, a successor space vehicle to the original Spaceship One. The new space vehicle will be larger than the original with seating for six passengers and two pilots and will be launched from an airplane at an altitude of 55,000 feet. Once released from the airplane, Spaceship Two will fire rocket engines and will climb, almost vertically, to the edge of space, or roughly 70 miles above the Earth. At this altitude, passengers can experience the effects of weightlessness and view the darkness of space and the curvature of the Earth. After spending 15 minutes at this altitude, the spaceship will descend and land like an ordinary jet.

Being a space tourist will not be cheap. However, despite a fare of £100,000 per flight, more than 250 people had paid deposits or the full ticket price to Virgin Galactic by the summer of 2008. In addition, a core group of 100 tourists has paid the full £100,000 up front. Those numbers result in total revenue for the company of £390 million, a sizeable amount for a start-up company to take in. And passengers won't begin flying until 2010 at the earliest.

Obviously, space travel is not available from any existing airport. To satisfy the place, or distribution, element of its marketing mix, the company struck a deal with the state of New Mexico. Officials from the state agreed to build a £112 million spaceport from which Virgin Galactic can launch its space tourist flights. Virgin Galactic chose New Mexico as the site because of its steady climate, high altitude, free airspace and overall low population density. The spaceport will be built just 25 miles south of the town Truth or Consequences, which is likely to see a rise in tourism spending once the space flights begin.

A final element of the marketing mix Virgin Galactic addresses is its promotion. Aside from having a well-developed website (virgingalactic.com) the company has not had to engage in much promotion yet. Because the entire space tourism industry is so new, almost any development receives extensive (and free) coverage from major news outlets such as broadcast and cable TV news, newspapers, and magazines. Promotion is one element of the marketing mix that may require greater development as the space tourism business matures.

Certainly it seems that space tourism has a promising, even if somewhat uncertain, future. Still, there is no guarantee that Virgin Galactic will be a success. While there appears to be a large untapped market for space tourism, that could easily change. For instance, what might happen to the industry if an accident occurs and perhaps an entire spaceship, with its passengers and crew, is lost? Such an incident could easily lead to a drop in consumer demand and increased government regulation. And, despite the somewhat limited number of people who are willing to be space tourists and who actually can afford the price, there's growing competition. Space Adventures, Rocketplane Kistler and PlanetSpace are companies planning to begin space flights for tourists in the near future. Space Adventures plans to price its flights at only £50,000, just half of what Virgin Galactic charges (will they serve more than a bag of peanuts?), and Rocketplane Kistler hopes to begin flights in 2009.

While most of Branson's Virgin businesses have been successful, there have been failures. Virgin Cola was a flop in the US market. Virgin Galactic's management has made initial decisions about the four Ps – product, price, place and promotion. But are these basic marketing decisions enough? What else is needed to ensure a smooth take-off for Virgin Galactic?

> **Branson created Virgin Galactic after watching Spaceship One, the first spacecraft designed and built by a private citizen, reach space in 2004**

Things to Think About

1. What is the decision facing Virgin Galactic?

2. What factors are important in understanding this decision situation?

3. What are the options?

4. What decision(s) do you recommend?

5. What are some ways to implement your recommendations?

Source: Agence France Presse, 'Space Tourism Lures a Rising Number of US Entrepreneurs', 22 March 2006; Jane Wardell, 'Virgin Spaceport to be Built in N.M.' Associated Press, 13 December 2005; and Ben Webster, 'Space Tourists Prepare for Lift-Off 2008', *The Times*, 30 March 2006.

References

1. John W. Schouten, 'Selves in Transition: Symbolic Consumption in Personal Rites of Passage and Identity Reconstruction', *Journal of Consumer Research*, 17 March 1991, 412–25; Michael R. Solomon, 'The Wardrobe Consultant: Exploring the Role of a New Retailing Partner', *Journal of Retailing* 63 (1987), 110–28; Michael R. Solomon and Susan P. Douglas, 'Diversity in Product Symbolism: The Case of Female Executive Clothing', *Psychology & Marketing* 4 (1987), 189–212; Joseph Z. Wisenblit, 'Person Positioning: Empirical Evidence and a New Paradigm', *Journal of Professional Services Marketing* 4, no. 2 (1989), 51–82.

2. www.cim.co.uk, 2006.

3. www.cim.co.uk/NewsAndEvents/MediaCentre/NewsRelease/ Leading%20body%20calls%20for%20a%20new%20 definition%20.aspx, 2007.

4. Michael R. Solomon, 'Deep-Seated Materialism: The Case of Levi's 501 Jeans', in *Advances in Consumer Research*, ed. Richard Lutz (Las Vegas, NV: Association for Consumer Research, 1986), 13, 619–22.

5. Peter F. Drucker, *Management: Tasks, Responsibilities, Practices* (New York: Harper & Row, 1972), 64–5.

6. Evan Shannon, '3BR w/VU of Asteroid Belt', *Wired* (April 2006), 130.

7. Ch. Gronroos, 'Marketing redefined,' *Management Decisions,* 28 (8) (1990), 5–9.

8. 'Henry Ford and The Model T', in *Forbes Greatest Business Stories* (New York: John Wiley & Sons, 1996), www.wiley. com/legacy/products/subject/business/forbes/ford.html.

9. Theodore Levitt, 'Marketing Myopia', *Harvard Business Review*, July–August 1960, 45–56.

10. Liz Morrell, 'Your retailer needs you', *Retail Week*, 24 March 2006.

11. www.google.com/support/jobs/bin/static.py?page=about. html&about=eng.

12. *Promo*, January 2006, www.promomagazine.com/premiums/ corn_card_012506/index.html.

13. PR Newswire Europe, 'M&S – Fashioning Change and Changing Fashion', 13 July 2006.

14. Philip R. Cateora, *Strategic International Marketing* (Homewood, IL: Dow Jones-Irwin, 1985).

15. Lee D. Dahringer, 'Marketing Services Internationally: Barriers and Management Strategies', *Journal of Service Marketing* 5 (1991), 5–17.

16. Paul Beckett, 'Picking side in Scotland's battle of the buzz', *The Wall Street Journal*, 11 August 2006.

17. http://blogs.pcworld.com/staffblog/archives/001763.html.

18. Michael E. Porter, *Competitive Advantage: Creating and Sustaining Superior Performance* (New York: Free Press, 1985).

19. http://blog.searchenginewatch.com/blog/061013-100808; http://blogs.guardian.co.uk/organgrinder/2007/06/cannes_ the_impact_of_consumer.html; http://current.com/s/news/ news_usatoday032706.htm.

20. http://www.guardian.co.uk/business/enron.

21. 'Dear Chrysler: Outsiders' Advice on Handling the Odometer Charge', *Wall Street Journal*, 26 June 1987, 19.

22. http://news.bbc.co.uk/1/hi/uk/6367331.stm.

23. Parts of this section are adapted from Michael R. Solomon, *Consumer Behavior: Buying, Having, and Being,* 7th ed. (Upper Saddle River, NJ: Prentice Hall, 2007).

24. Thomas C. O'Guinn and Ronald J. Faber, 'Compulsive Buying: A Phenomenological Explanation', *Journal of Consumer Research* 16 (September 1989), 154.

25. www.chamberonline.co.uk/policy/issues/businesscrime/crimereport.pdf.

26. 'Advertisers Face up to the New Morality: Making the Pitch', *Bloomberg*, 8 July 1997.

27. Gerry Khermouch, 'Virgin's "Va Va" Bottle Has "Voom": First Ads via Long Haymes Carr', *Brandweek*, 10 July 2000, 13.

28. http://abclocal.go.com/kgo/business/050704ap_business_adidas.html.

29. Sal Randazzo, 'Advertising as Myth-Maker; Brands as Gods and Heroes', *Advertising Age*, 8 November 1993, 32.

Chapter 2
Strategy and Environment

Meet Philippe Garnier,
Senior Director of Distribution and Sales at Hilton Hotels

Q & A With Philippe Garnier

What do you do when not working?
Spend time with my children

First job out of university?
Selling vitamins to animal feed companies

Career high?
Still ahead of me I hope!

My management style is
Listen, Inspire, Measure

My pet peeve
Spelling mistakes

Best holiday?
Interrailing in Eastern Europe in 1991

Philippe is Senior Director, Distribution Sales with Hilton Hotels' International Division. He is in charge of the business with Global Distribution Systems, third-party online distributors and standardising sales contracts. Philippe has been with Hilton for five years and prior to that he was in management consulting with KPMG and PwC. He is married and has three children.

Real People, Real Decisions
Decision time at Hilton Hotels

Hilton Hotels was founded in 1919 by Conrad Hilton when he opened his first hotel in Texas after fighting in the First World War. The founding principle was to 'share the light and warmth of hospitality with the world' and in 1943 you paid only $20 for a room. The first hotel outside the US was in Puerto Rico, but it soon expanded to many countries around the world including Holland, and it was in the Amsterdam Hilton in the 1960s that John and Yoko held their 'bed in'. Although the international hotels and US hotels were separated for 40 years, in 2006 the American-owned Hilton Hotels Corporation (HHC) US bought the lodging assets of Hilton Group PLC, Hilton International, and reunited the two brands under one branding roof. In October 2007, the hotel group was bought by the Blackstone Group and delisted from the New York Stock Exchange.

The hotel environment is very competitive and there had been significant changes to the way hotel rooms were sold, with many more customers taking control of their own holiday and leisure planning by booking direct and searching on the web. In addition, third-party web distributors, such as Expedia, were bringing together many independent and smaller chains of hotels and making it easy for consumers to search and book these. This was eroding one of Hilton's natural strategic competitive advantages as an industry leader with over 400 hotels in 76 countries which gave customers ease and reliability of booking around the world. The booking process behind the scenes is not as simple as it appears to consumers because Hilton distributed its product (hotel rooms) through many different channels. It had its own websites, people could call the hotel direct, or even pop in off the street or call one of Hilton's reservation numbers. Hilton also sold its rooms through a series of distributors such as:

- Global Distribution Systems which supplies travel agencies and tends to deal with corporate bookings;
- Tour operators, such as Thomas Cook;
- Hotel wholesalers such as Miki Travel, which supplies the tour operators;
- Third-party websites such as Expedia.

This was quite a complicated distribution network with each player having different business models, margins and ways of interacting with Hilton.

The precipitating event which led to the problem happened in 2004, when Hilton took the major step of going over to 'floating' prices which meant that its rooms were priced according to demand in real time – a much more efficient way of pricing rooms which results in increased returns. This was a problem for many existing distributors, such as tour operators or hotel wholesalers for several reasons. First, they were not electronically connected to the Hilton reservation system. Second, their traditional way of buying was costly for Hilton as a large proportion of Hilton hotel rooms were allocated to them many months in advance at pre-agreed prices and, once allocated, Hilton had no control over them even if they were eventually unoccupied. Often rooms were sold to tour operators or wholesalers at large discounts allowing the tour operators to mark up the hotel room and cream off the profit. As a result, they were a high-cost route to market. In addition, having lots of hotel rooms already allocated prevented individual hotels from being able to maximise revenue from their stock. The challenge facing Philippe and his team was how to get all distributors to use the floating price booking system which would reduce the cost of hotel room distribution and result in increased return on each room sold. In addition, given the changes in consumer behaviour in booking their own hotels, Philippe wanted to increase the number of people who might consider Hilton as a hotel option. Not an easy task.

Philippe considers his options . . .

Option 1 Keep the existing system and contracts but negotiate better terms with the distributors to improve the return to Hilton

The status quo is often an option when choices are problematic. The pros of this option are continuity of the existing business and maintenance of the good and long relationship with existing distributors which had worked for the past 30 years. Another plus was that each hotel manager felt they knew their own market and ways to maximise revenue better than the central Hilton organisation and central interference was generally not appreciated. However, if they continued as they were, one practical problem they faced was that most of these existing channels still worked with paper, faxing bookings to the hotel which were then manually entered into the Hilton system. This was manpower intensive and had the potential to lead to more errors. Another disadvantage was that Hilton would not meet its stated goals of increased reach and would retain a less profitable distribution system.

Option 2 Get all suppliers to sign new standard contracts

This option would involve the distributors connecting to Hilton's central reservation system and stop the practice of bulk pre-allocation of rooms to distributors. Instead, distributors could make rooms available to consumers at the floating price and they could see the inventory Hilton had in real time. This would mean a massive communication and persuasion exercise to all distributors about Hilton's goal of increasing reach and decreasing cost of delivering inventory. Potential advantages of this option are that Hilton would be seen as an industry leader, sticking to its new business principles which would deliver greater shareholder value and give a signal both within Hilton and externally to competitors and other suppliers that Hilton meant business. It would also see an immediate increase to the profitability of each room sold. The disadvantages were that this would undoubtedly be resisted by some distributors who might choose not to buy rooms from Hilton because they felt their margins would be decreased, and therefore there would be a dip in sales. Also, telling individual hotel managers that you can't do business with a certain tour operator you've been working with for years was not an easy message to deliver. There was also the problem some distributors were not technologically advanced enough to connect to Hilton's online booking system. Finally, it would require a major mindset shift on the part of distributors to go from the standard advanced bulk room pre-allocation system of buying rooms to a floating price real time system.

Option 3 Engage with new distributors in the market such as Expedia, Lastminute.com and Opodo

This option involved beginning selling rooms through these intermediary websites via the online floating price mechanism with no pre-allocations, while at the same time continuing to issue pre-allocation of rooms to some of the powerful traditional distributors, such as Thomas Cook, to allow business continuity. However, for most distributors, Hilton would take a tough stance and try and convince them to move to the new contracts using the real time reservations and floating pricing system or not deal with Hilton. The advantages are that there would be less confrontation with existing distributors and it would allow Hilton to build up trust and familiarity with the new online players. Also, there were fewer practical technology hurdles as all of the new distributors were online businesses. This 'staged' approach might allow Hilton to see how these websites might work and give them some way of replacing the potential lost business from other distributors. Like option 2, however, some individual hotels might suffer badly from distributors who gave them lots of business declining to move over to the new contracts and head office would be accused of not listening to hotel managers. Finally, this was clearly a compromise in implementing Hilton's new distribution strategy of trying to decrease distribution costs and increase profits.

Now put yourself in Philippe's shoes. Which option would you chose and why?

Objectives

When you finish reading this chapter, you will be able to:

1 Describe the steps in marketing planning

2 Explain the strategic planning process

3 Discuss some of the important aspects of an organisation's internal environment and understand how factors in the external business environment influence marketing strategies and outcomes

4 Understand the big picture of international marketing, including trade flows, market scope and global competitive advantage

5 Explain the role of implementation and control in marketing planning

6 Explain operational planning

7 Explain the strategies that a firm can use to enter global markets

Business Planning: Composing the Big Picture

Objective

1

Describe the steps in marketing planning

Philippe Garnier at Hilton Hotels understands that planning is everything. Part of Philippe's role as a planner is to help define his product's distinctive identity and purpose. Careful planning enables a firm to speak in a clear voice in the marketplace so that customers understand what the firm is and what it has to offer that competitors don't – especially as it decides how to create value for customers, shareholders, employees and society. We think this process is so important that we're launching into our exploration of marketing with a discussion about what planners do and the questions they (both Hiltion and marketers in general) need to ask to be sure they keep their companies and products on course. Then, we'll come full circle and see how Hilton Hotels answers these questions to maintain its advantage.

Whether a firm is a well-established industrial company like Electrolux (which we'll feature in later chapters) or a services-based group like Hilton Hotels, planning for the future is key to prosperity. Sure, it's true that a firm can be successful even if it makes some mistakes in planning and there are times when even the best planning cannot anticipate the future accurately. It's also true that some seat-of-the-pants businesses are successful. But without good planning for the future, firms will be less successful than they could be. In the worst-case scenario, a lack of planning can be fatal for both large and small businesses. So, like a Boy Scout, it's always better to be prepared.

Business planning is an ongoing process of making decisions that guide the firm both in the short term and for the long haul. Planning identifies and builds on a firm's strengths, and it helps managers at all levels make informed decisions in a changing business environment. Planning means that an organisation develops objectives before it takes action. In large firms like Sony and Kodak that operate in many markets, planning is a complex process involving many people from different areas of the company's operations. At a small business like Jim's Diner, however, planning is quite different. Jim himself is chief cook, occasional dishwasher, and the sole company planner. With entrepreneurial firms like Innocent drinks, the planning process falls somewhere in between, depending on the size of the firm and the complexity of its operations.

Hilton Hotels' business model is analogous to capturing the right information in the lens of your mobile phone camera, positioning the image correctly and snapping the picture you'll need to set things in motion. A business plan is a lot like that. In this chapter, we'll look at the different steps in an organisation's planning. First, we'll see how managers develop a **business plan** which includes the decisions that guide the entire organisation or its business units. Then we'll examine the entire marketing planning process and the stages in that process that lead to the development and implementation of a **marketing plan** – a document that describes the marketing environment, outlines the marketing objectives and strategies, and identifies how the strategies imbedded in the plan will be implemented and controlled.

The Three Levels of Business Planning

We all know what planning is – we plan a vacation or a great Saturday night party. Some of us even plan how we're going to study and get our assignments completed. When businesses plan, the process is more complex. As Figure 2.1 shows, planning occurs at three levels: strategic, functional and operational.

● **Strategic planning** is the managerial decision process that matches the firm's resources (such as its financial assets and workforce) and capabilities (the things it is able to do well because of its expertise and experience) to its market opportunities for long-term growth. In a strategic plan, top management – usually the chief executive or managing director, chairman and other top executives – define the firm's purpose and specify what the firm hopes to achieve over the next five or so years. For example, a firm's strategic plan may set an objective of increasing the firm's total revenues by 20 per cent in the next five years. For large firms such as the Walt Disney Company that have a number of self-contained divisions or strategic business units (such as the theme park, movie, television network and cruise line divisions), strategic planning occurs both at the overall corporate level (Disney headquarters planning for the whole corporation) and at the individual business unit level (at the theme park, movie studios, television networks and cruise line level). We'll discuss these two levels later in the chapter.

What It Is	Strategic Planning	Functional Planning (In Marketing Department, called Marketing Planning)	Operational Planning
Who Does It	Planning done by top-level corporate management	Planning done by top functional-level management such as the firm's marketing director.	Planning done by supervisory managers
What They Do	1. Define the mission 2. Evaluate the internal and external environment 3. Set organisational or business unit objectives 4. Establish the business portfolio (if applicable) 5. Develop growth strategies	1. Perform a situation analysis 2. Set marketing objectives 3. Develop marketing strategies 4. Implement marketing strategies 5. Monitor and control marketing strategies	1. Develop action plans to implement the marketing plan 2. Use marketing metrics to monitor how the plan is working

Figure 2.1   Levels of Planning

During planning, an organisation determines its objectives and then develops courses of action to accomplish them. In larger firms, planning takes place at the strategic, functional and operational levels.

- The next level of planning is **functional planning** (sometimes called 'tactical planning'). This level gets its name because it is accomplished by the various functional areas of the firm, such as marketing, finance and human resources. Functional directors usually do this. The functional planning the marketing department conducts is referred to as *marketing planning*. The person in charge of such planning may have the title of Director of Marketing, or Chief Marketing Officer. Marketers like Philippe Garnier at Hilton might set an objective to gain 40 per cent of a particular market by introducing three distribution outlets during the coming year. This objective would be part of a *functional area plan*. Functional planning typically includes both a broad five-year plan to support the firm's strategic plan and a detailed annual plan for the coming year.

- Still further down the planning ladder are the first-line managers. In the marketing department, first-line managers include people such as sales managers, marketing communications managers and marketing research managers. These managers are responsible for planning at a third level called **operational planning**. This level of planning focuses on the day-to-day execution of the functional plans and includes detailed annual, semi-annual or quarterly plans. Operational plans might show exactly how many units of a product a salesperson needs to sell per month or how many television commercials the firm will place on certain channels during a season. At the operational planning level for Hilton Hotels, the marketing communications manager may develop plans to promote the new products to potential customers, while the sales manager may develop a quarterly plan for the company's sales force. Both of these activities are forms of operational planning.

Of course, marketing managers don't just sit in their offices dreaming up plans without any concern for the rest of the organisation. Even though we've described each layer separately, *all business planning is an integrated activity*. This means that the organisation's strategic, functional and operational plans must work together for the benefit of the whole. So, planners at all levels must consider good principles of accounting, the value of the company to its stockholders, and

Marketing Metrics

Norwich Union's Marketing Resource Management system

The UK's biggest insurer, Norwich Union, part of Aviva, uses Marketing Resource Management technology from Aprimo to plan and control marketing strategies, drive down costs, track results and enhance the customer experience. Historically, staff managed marketing ideas, plans and finances using a myriad of different methods such as spreadsheets, databases and documents. The company's acquisition of motoring organisation RAC prompted it to rethink this approach. The system establishes standardised processes and a central repository of relevant data and a full archive history of past marketing that will aid internal governance and regulatory compliance.

the requirements for staffing and human resource management – that is, they must keep the 'big picture' in mind even as they plan for their corner of the organisation's world.

In short, the different functional- and operational-level planners within an organisation have to make sure that their plans support the organisation's overall mission and objectives and that they work well together. A marketer like Philippe Garnier at Hilton Hotels can't go off and develop a successful plan for the marketing side of the firm without fully understanding how what he's doing fits with the whole organisation's direction and resources. In the case of Hilton Hotels, this means Philippe's plan must fit in with the overall strategic direction of Hilton Hotels. In the next sections, we'll further explore planning at each of these three levels: strategic, functional and operational.

Strategic Planning: Framing the Picture

Objective

2

Explain the strategic planning process

Many large firms realise that relying on only one product can be risky, so they have become multiproduct companies with self-contained divisions organised around products or brands. As mentioned earlier, firms such as Disney operate several distinctly different businesses. These self-contained divisions are called **strategic business units** (SBUs) – individual units representing different areas of business within the firm that are each different enough to have their own mission, business objectives, resources, managers and competitors. As we pointed out earlier, Disney's SBUs include its theme parks, movie studios, television networks and cruise line.

In firms with many SBUs, the first step in strategic planning is for top management to establish a mission for the entire corporation. Top managers then evaluate the internal and external environment of the business and set corporate-level objectives that guide decision making within each individual SBU. In small firms that are not large enough to have separate SBUs, strategic planning simply takes place at the overall firm level. Whether or not a firm has SBUs, the process of strategic planning is basically the same. Let's look at the planning steps in a bit more detail.

 ## Step 1: Define the Mission

Theoretically, top management's first step in the strategic planning stage is to answer such questions as, What business are we in? What customers should we serve? How should we develop the firm's capabilities and focus its efforts? In many firms, the answers to questions such as these become the lead items in the organisation's strategic plan. The answers become part of a **mission statement** – a formal document that describes the organisation's overall purpose and what it hopes to achieve in terms of its customers, products and resources. For example, the mission of Mothers Against Drunk Driving (MADD) is 'to stop drunk driving, support the victims of this violent crime and prevent underage drinking'.[1]

The ideal mission statement is not too broad, too narrow, or too shortsighted. A mission that is too broad will not provide adequate focus for the organisation. It doesn't do much good to claim, 'We are in the business of making high-quality products', as it's hard to find a firm that doesn't make this claim.

However, a mission statement that is too narrow may inhibit managers' ability to visualise possible growth opportunities. If, for example, a firm sees itself in terms of its product only, consumer trends or technology can make that product obsolete – and the firm is left with no future. If Xerox had continued to define its mission in terms of just producing copy machines instead of providing 'document solutions', the shift to electronic documents would have left the company in the dust the way the Model T Ford replaced the horse and cart. It's important to remember that the need for a clear mission statement applies to virtually any type of organisation, even those like MADD, whose objective is to serve society rather than to sell goods or services.

Step 2: Evaluate the Internal and External Environment

Objective

3

Discuss some of the important aspects of an organisation's internal environment and understand how factors in the external business environment influence marketing strategies and outcomes

The second step in strategic planning is to assess the firm's internal and external environments. This process is referred to as a situation analysis, *environmental analysis*, or sometimes a *business review*. The analysis includes a discussion of the firm's internal environment, which can identify a firm's strengths and weaknesses, as well as the external environment in which the firm does business so the firm can identify opportunities and threats.

By internal environment, we mean all the controllable elements inside a firm that influence how well the firm operates. Internal strengths may lie in the firm's technologies. What is the firm able to do well that other firms would find difficult to duplicate? What patents does it hold? A firm's physical facilities can be an important strength or weakness, as can its level of financial stability, its relationships with suppliers, its corporate reputation, its ability to produce consistently high-quality products and its ownership of strong brands in the marketplace.

Internal strengths and weaknesses often reside in the firm's employees – the firm's human and intellectual capital. What skills do the employees have? What kind of training have they had? Are they loyal to the firm? Do they feel a sense of ownership? Has the firm been able to attract top researchers and good decision makers? Pret A Manger has always been very focused on hiring and developing employees who reflect the 'Pret Spirit' to customers.

The external environment consists of elements outside the firm that may affect it either positively or negatively. The external environment for today's businesses is global, so managers/marketers must consider elements such as the Political, Economic and competitive, Sociocultural, Technology, Legal and Environmental trends sometimes known as a PESTLE analysis. Unlike elements of the internal environment that management can control to a large degree, the firm can't directly control these external factors, so management must respond to them through its planning process.

The Global Marketing Environment

Once a marketer makes the initial decision about whether or not to go global and about what country or countries provide attractive opportunities, the company must gain a good understanding of the local conditions in the targeted country or region. As we saw earlier in this chapter, successful planning depends upon a clear understanding of the environment. In this section, we'll see how economic, competitive, technological, political and cultural factors affect marketers' global strategies.

The Economic Environment

Objective

4

Understand the big picture of international marketing, including trade flows, market scope and global competitive advantage

Understanding the economy of a country in which a firm does business is vital to the success of marketing plans. Marketers need to understand the state of the economy from two different perspectives: the overall economic health and level of development of a country and the current stage of its business cycle.

Indicators of Economic Health

One way to gauge the market potential for a product is to look at a country's economic health. The most commonly used measure of economic health of a country is the **gross domestic product (GDP)**; the total value of goods and services a country produces within its borders in a year. A similar but less frequently used measure of economic health is the **gross national product (GNP)**, which measures the value of all goods and services produced by a country's individuals or organisations, whether located within the country's borders or not. Table 2.1 shows the GDP and other economic and demographic characteristics of a sampling of countries. In addition to total GDP, marketers may also compare countries on the basis of *per capita GDP*: the total GDP divided by the number of people (population) in a country.

Still, such comparisons may not tell the whole story. Per capita GDP can be deceptive because the wealth of a country may be concentrated in the hands of a few. Furthermore, the costs of the same goods and services are much lower in some global markets. For example, goods and services valued at €30,000 in say Belgium would cost only €5100 in Uganda. Of course, GDP alone does not provide the information needed by marketers in deciding if a

	Sweden	Netherlands	UK	European Union	United States	China
Total GDP	$333.1 billion	$638.9 billion	$2.15 trillion	$14.45 trillion	$13.86 trillion	$7.04 trillion
Per capita GDP	$36,900	$38,600	$35,300	$32,900	$46,000	$5,300
Population below poverty line	NA	10.5%	14%	See individual member state entries	12%	8%
Inflation rate	2%	1.6%	2.4%	1.8%	2.7%	4.7%
Unemployment rate	4.5%	4.1%	5.4%	8.5%	4.6%	4%
Population	9.05 million	16.65 million	60.94 million	491.02 million	303.82 million	1.33 billion
Birth rate per 1000 population	10.15	10.53	10.65	9.97	14.18	13.71
Population aged 0–14	16%	17.6%	16.9%	15.7%	20.1%	20.1%
Population aged 15–64	65.6%	67.8%	67.1%	67.2%	67.1%	71.9%
Population aged 65 and over	18.3%	14.6%	16%	17.1%	12.7%	8%

Table 2.1 Comparisons of Several Countries on Economic and Demographic Characteristics

Source: CIA World Factbook 2008, https://www.cia.gov/library/publications/the-world-factbook/.

country's economic environment makes for an attractive market. Marketers also need to consider whether they can conduct 'business as usual' in another country. The **economic infrastructure** is the quality of a country's distribution, financial and communications systems.

Level of Economic Development

These are just some of the issues a marketer must think about when determining whether a country will be a good prospect. However, there are other economic conditions that marketers must understand as well, including the broader economic picture of a country, called its **level of economic development**.

When marketers travel around the world to seek opportunities, it helps if they consider a country's level of economic development to understand the needs of people who live there and the infrastructural conditions with which they must contend. Economists look past simple facts such as growth in GDP to decide this; they also look at what steps are being taken to reduce poverty, inequality and unemployment. Economists describe the following three basic levels of development.

A country at the lowest stage of economic development is a **less developed country (LDC)**. In most cases, its economic base is agricultural. Many nations in Africa and South Asia are considered LDCs. A country's **standard of living** is an indicator of the average quality and quantity of goods and services a country consumes. In these countries, the standard of living is low, as are literacy levels. Opportunities to sell many products, especially luxury items such as diamonds and caviar, are minimal because most people don't have enough spending money. They grow what they need and barter for the rest. These countries are attractive markets for inexpensive items.

All the flavours of Asian cuisine in *one* melting pot.

Journey through Asia and a gastronomical feast awaits you, satisfying your palate with a variety of flavours. Mouth-watering Malay satay. Delectable Chinese noodles. Spicy Indian curries. Irresistible desserts and many more. There is only one country where you can taste all of Asia's culinary heritage. Colourful Malaysia. Where Asia's greatest cultures – Malay, Chinese, Indian and other ethnic groups – give you an irresistible banquet for all your senses.

TOURISM MALAYSIA *Kuala Lumpur (Head Office): 17th Floor, Menara Dato' Onn, Putra World Trade Centre, 45, Jalan Tun Ismail, 50480 Kuala Lumpur, Malaysia. Tel: (60-3) 2693-5188. Fax: (60-3) 2693 3884. United Kingdom: 57 Trafalgar Square, London WC2N 5DU, United Kingdom. Tel: (020) 7930 7932 Fax: (020) 7930 9015 E-mail: mtpb.london@tourism.gov.my Website: www.tourismmalaysia.gov.my*

Photo 2.1 Many developing countries rely heavily on tourism to build their economies.
Source: The Advertising Archives

They may export important raw materials such as minerals or rubber to industrial nations.

When an economy shifts its emphasis from agriculture to industry, standards of living, education and the use of technology rise. These are **developing countries**, and in such markets there may be a viable middle class, often largely composed of entrepreneurs working hard to run successful small businesses.

Because over three-quarters of the world's population lives in developing countries, the number of potential customers and the presence of a skilled labour force attracts many firms to these areas. Eastern Europe, with its more than 300 million consumers, is an important region that includes a number of developing countries. Similarly, the countries of Latin America are emerging from decades of state control, and their economies are opening to foreign business.[2] Finally, the Pacific Rim countries of China, South Korea, Malaysia, Indonesia, Thailand, Singapore and Hong Kong are nicknamed the 'Tigers of Asia' because of their tremendous economic growth. For example, in China, consumer spending on products such as mobile phones is encouraging economic growth. Nokia estimates that more than 70 per cent of Beijing residents and more than 60 per cent of Shanghai residents have mobile phone subscriptions.[3]

A **developed country** boasts sophisticated marketing systems, strong private enterprise, and market potential for many goods and services. Such countries are economically advanced, and they offer a wide range of opportunities for international marketers. The United Kingdom, France and Germany are among the most economically developed countries in the EU and the world.

The Business Cycle

The overall pattern of changes or fluctuations of an economy is called the **business cycle**. All economies go through cycles of prosperity (high levels of demand, employment and income), recession (falling demand, employment and income) and recovery (gradual improvement in production, lowering unemployment and increasing income).

A severe recession is a depression, a period in which prices fall but there is little demand because few people have money to spend and many are out of work. Inflation occurs when prices and the cost of living rise while money loses its purchasing power because the cost of goods escalates. During inflationary periods, incomes may increase, but real income – what your currency will buy – decreases because goods and services cost more.

The business cycle is especially important to marketers because of its effect on consumer buyer behaviour. During times of prosperity, consumers buy more goods and services. Marketers are busy trying to grow their business, maintain inventory levels and develop new products to meet demands of customers with the willingness to spend. During periods of recession, consumers simply buy less. The challenge to most marketers is to maintain their firm's level of sales by convincing customers who are buying to select their firm's product over

| Photo 2.2 | Rapidly developing countries like China provide great opportunities for European retailers such as Tesco to expand. |
| | Source: Tesco Image Library |

the competitors' offerings. Of course, even recessions aren't bad for all businesses. Although it may be harder to sell luxury items, firms that make basic necessities are not likely to suffer significant losses.

It is important to note that when firms assess the economic environment, they evaluate all factors that influence consumer and business buying patterns, including the amount of confidence people have in the health of the economy. This 'crystal ball' must be a global one because events in one country can affect the economic health of other countries. For instance, the economic damage from the US subprime mortgage crisis in 2008 affected the fortunes of businesses around the world. The financial services industry is just starting to recover now as people regain their confidence in the banking system.

 # The Competitive Environment

A second important element of a firm's external environment is the competitive environment. For all products, firms must keep abreast of what the competition is doing so they can develop new product features, new pricing schedules, or new advertising to maintain or gain market share.

Analysing the Market and the Competition

Before a firm can begin to develop strategies that will create a competitive advantage in the marketplace, it has to know who its competitors are and what they're doing. Marketing managers size up competitors according to their strengths and weaknesses, monitor their marketing strategies and try to predict their moves.

An increasing number of firms around the globe engage in **competitive intelligence (CI)** activities, the process of gathering and analysing publicly available information about rivals. Most of the information that companies need to know about their competitors is available from rather mundane sources, including the news media, the internet, and publicly available governmental documents. Successful CI implies that a firm learns about a competitor's new products, its manufacturing, or the management styles of its executives. Then the firm uses this information to develop superior marketing strategies.

Competition in the Micro-environment

To be successful in a competitive marketplace, marketers must have a clear understanding of exactly who their competition is. Competition in the micro-environment means the product alternatives from which members of a target market may choose. We can think of these choices at three different levels.

At a broad level, many marketers compete for consumers' **disposable income**; the amount of money people have left after paying for necessities such as housing, utilities, food and clothing. Few consumers are wealthy enough to buy anything and everything, so each of us is constantly faced with choices: do we plough 'leftover' money into a new MP3 player, donate it to charity, or turn over a new leaf and lose those extra pounds by investing in a healthy lifestyle? Thus, the first part of understanding who the competition is means understanding all the alternatives that consumers consider for their discretionary income – not just the brands against which we directly compete within a product category.

A second type of choice is **product competition**, in which competitors offering different products attempt to satisfy the same consumers' needs and wants. So, for example, if a couch potato decides to use some of his discretionary income to get fit, he may join a health club or buy equipment/machinery in order to exercise at home. Starbucks is successfully competing against tea in England. In a country known as much for its afternoon tea as for Manchester United, there are already close to 500 Starbucks outlets (more in London than New York),

Marketing Ethics

Wal-Mart gets smart

Giant retailers such as Wal-Mart and Tesco are increasingly criticised for forcing scores of independent competitors to go out of business. But Wal-Mart has begun a programme to help its smaller rivals. The US-based programme offers hardware shops, dress shops and bakeries near its new urban shops financial grants, training on how to survive with Wal-Mart in town, and even free advertising in Wal-Mart shops. Of course, Wal-Mart hopes to benefit from the programme in cities like Los Angeles and New York where its plan to build new shops in urban neighbourhoods has met high resistance.[4]

Debate, Discuss, Disagree

1　What do you think about Wal-Mart's motives?

2　How would such a strategy work in the UK (where Wal-Mart controls Asda) and Scandinavia?

as well as fast-growing local chains such as Café Nero and Coffee Republic. As a consequence, tea sales in the United Kingdom fell 12 per cent from 2000 to 2005.[5]

The third type of choice is **brand competition**, in which competitors offering similar goods or services fight for a share of the consumer's wallet. So, if our flabby friend decides to join a gym, he still must choose among competitors within this industry. He may forgo the exercise thing altogether and count on a Greek sea food diet to work its magic.

Competition in the Macro-environment

When we talk about examining competition in the macro-environment, we mean that marketers need to understand the big picture, that is, the overall structure of their industry. This structure can range from one firm having total control to numerous firms that compete on an even playing field.

Four structures describe differing amounts of competition. Let's review each structure, beginning with total control by one organisation.

1. It's not just a board game, but a **monopoly** exists when one seller controls a market. Because the seller is the only player in town, it feels little pressure to keep prices low or to produce quality goods or services. In the old days, the state-run postal service had a monopoly on the delivery of documents. Nowadays, the monopoly status has been eroded, as postal services must now compete with couriers such as FedEx and DHL, as well as electronic mail for a share of the market.

2. In an **oligopoly** market there is a relatively small number of sellers, each holding substantial market share in a market consisting of many buyers. Because there are few sellers, each is very conscious of the others' actions. Oligopolies most often exist in industries requiring substantial investment in equipment or technology to produce a product. This means that only a few competitors have the resources to enter. The airline industry is an oligopoly. It is pretty hard for an entrepreneur with little start-up cash to be successful entering the airline industry. It's left to billionaires like Richard Branson who have the resources to launch a new entry like Virgin Atlantic.

3. In a state of *monopolistic competition*, there are many sellers who compete for buyers in a market. Each firm however, offers a slightly different product, and each has only a

small share of the market. For example, many sports shoe manufacturers, like Nike, Reebok and Adidas, vigorously compete with one another to offer consumers some unique benefit.

4. Finally, *perfect competition* exists when there are many small sellers, each offering basically the same good or service. In such industries, no single firm has a significant impact on quality, price or supply. Although true conditions of perfect competition are rare, agricultural markets in which there are many individual farmers each offering the same produce come the closest. Even in the case of food commodities, there are opportunities for marketers to distinguish their offerings on quality, service and delivery.

The Technological Environment

Firms today see technology as an investment they can't afford not to make, it provides firms with important competitive advantages. Many technological developments profoundly affect marketing activities. Free phone numbers, easy computer access to customer databases and, of course, the web have made it possible for people to buy almost anything they want without ever leaving their homes. Distribution has also improved because of automated stock control as a direct result of such advancements.

Changes in technology can dramatically transform an industry. Successful marketers continuously scan the external business environment in search of ideas and trends to spark their own research efforts. They also monitor ongoing research projects in government and private organisations. When inventors feel they have come across something exciting, they usually want to protect their exclusive right to produce and sell the invention by applying for a patent. A **patent** is a legal document issued from a country's patent office that gives inventors or individuals and firms the exclusive rights to produce and sell a particular invention in a country (or countries). Marketers monitor government patent applications to discover innovative products they can purchase from the inventor.

The Political and Legal Environment

The political and legal environment refers to the local, state, national and global laws and regulations that affect businesses. Legal and regulatory controls can be prime motivators for many business decisions. While firms that choose to remain at home have to worry about only local regulations, global marketers must understand more complex political issues that can affect how they do business and their potential for success.

Table 2.2 outlines some of the major EU legislation that protects and serves the rights of consumers within the European Union member states. Several legal institutions also exist within the European Union that monitor business activity and enforce how laws are practised throughout the EU (see Table 2.3).

Sometimes firms learn the hard way that government watchdog activities can put a stop to their marketing plans. Warner-Lambert, the manufacturer of Listerine antiseptic, went on US television in the 1970s with advertising claims that its germ-killing properties help reduce the incidence and severity of the common cold. Unfortunately, the firm lacked data to substantiate the claim. The company stopped making this claim in its advertising only after it was forced to do so. However, Warner-Lambert learned from its mistake, as a few years later the company funded medical research that resulted in new claims based on scientific evidence that Listerine was effective against such gum and dental problems like plaque and gingivitis. These claims continue to be a cornerstone of Listerine's advertising message to this day.

Competition Law

Four main policies of the antitrust law include:

Cartels, or control of collusion in other anti-competitive practices which has an effect on the EU. This is covered under Article 81 of the Treaty of the European Community.

Monopolies, or preventing the abuse of firms' dominant market positions. This is governed by Article 82 of the EC Treaty.

Mergers, control of proposed mergers, acquisitions and joint ventures involving companies which have a certain, defined amount of turnover. This is governed by the Council Regulation 139/2004 of the EC Treaty (the EC Merger Regulation).

State aid, control of direct and indirect aid given by EU member states to companies. Covered under Article 87 of the EC Treaty.

Consumers

The European policy in favour of consumers aims to safeguard the health, safety and interests of consumers, as set out in Articles 153 and 95 of the Treaty establishing the European Community, by promoting openness, fairness and transparency in the internal market.

Culture

The Maastricht Treaty (1993) enabled the European Union, which is historically geared towards the economy and trade, to take action in the field of culture in order to safeguard, disseminate and develop culture in Europe. However, the EU's role is limited to promoting cooperation between the cultural operators of the different member states or to complementing their activities in order to contribute to the flowering of the cultures of the member states, while respecting their national and regional diversity, with a view to highlighting the shared cultural heritage. With this aim in mind, the EU implements measures in support of cultural initiatives such as the Culture Programme and the European Capital of Culture initiative.

Employment and Social Policy

In the Treaty of Rome, social and employment policy was practically neglected. In fact, most of the provisions in this field related to the creation of freedom of movement for workers and freedom of establishment for the purpose of the common market. In contrast, the Treaty of Amsterdam attached importance to social policy in the fight against all types of discrimination, and the policy for the promotion of employment finally moved to the top of the agenda, becoming a 'matter of common interest'. Given the need for a Europe capable of sustainable economic growth accompanied by a quantitative and qualitative improvement in employment and greater social cohesion, the interlinking of employment, social affairs and equal opportunities is evident today. In this respect, the European Union provides major impetus for the convergence of Community and national policies through the 'open coordination method'.

Enterprise

Under Article 157 of the Treaty establishing the European Community, the European Union has set itself the goal of creating the best possible conditions for competitiveness.

Maintaining competitiveness is a constant challenge. This is why the EU aims to encourage an environment favourable to initiative, to the development of businesses, to industrial cooperation and to improving the exploitation of the industrial potential of innovation, research and technological development policies. These policies are of vital importance in the context of global competition.

Environment

Since the early 1970s Europe has been firmly committed to the environment: protection of air and water quality, conservation of resources and protection of biodiversity, waste management and control of activities which have an adverse environmental impact are just some of the areas in which the EU is active, at both member state level and internationally. Whether through corrective measures relating to specific environmental problems or cross-cutting measures integrated within other policy areas, European environment policy, based on Article 174 of the Treaty establishing the European Community, aims to ensure the sustainable development of the European model of society.

Food Safety

The objective of the European Union's food safety policy is to protect consumer health and interests while guaranteeing the smooth operation of the single market. In order to achieve this objective, the EU ensures that control standards are established and adhered to as regards food and food product hygiene, animal health and welfare, plant health and preventing the risk of contamination from external substances. It also lays down rules on appropriate labelling for these foodstuffs and food products.

This policy underwent reform in the early 2000s, in line with the approach 'From the Farm to the Fork', thereby guaranteeing a high level of safety for foodstuffs and food products marketed within the EU, at all stages of the production and distribution chains. This approach involves both food products produced within the European Union and those imported from third countries.

Table 2.2 Areas of EU activities concerning businesses

Product Labelling and Packaging

The objective of foodstuff labelling is to guarantee that consumers have access to complete information on the content and composition of products, in order to protect their health and their interests. Other information may provide details on a particular aspect of the product, such as its origin or production method. Some foodstuffs, such as genetically modified organisms, allergenic foods, foods intended for infants or even various beverages, are also subject to specific regulations.

Labelling of certain non-food products must also contain particular information, in order to guarantee their safe use and allow consumers to exercise real choice. In addition, the packaging of foodstuffs must adhere to production criteria in order to avoid contaminating food products.

Fight against fraud

Protecting the financial interests of the European Community is a priority for the European institutions. It is estimated that nearly a billion euros out of an annual budget of more than €100 billion is misappropriated. The European Union combats fraud with a series of regulations to fight currency counterfeiting, violations of intellectual property rights and corruption both in Europe and internationally. The legal basis for the fight against fraud is Article 280 of the Treaty establishing the European Community.

Taxation

Tax policy in the European Union consists of two components: direct taxation, which remains the sole responsibility of member states, and indirect taxation, which affects free movement of goods and the freedom to provide services. With regard to direct taxation, member states have taken measures to prevent tax avoidance and double taxation. Tax policy ensures that competition between member states on the internal market is not distorted by differences in indirect taxation rates and systems. Measures have also been adopted to prevent the adverse effects of tax competition if companies transfer money between European Union member states.

Table 2.2   Areas of EU activities concerning businesses (*continued*)

Sources: Competition Law summary, http://en.wikipedia.org/wiki/European_Community_competition_law; all other summaries, http://europa.eu/index_en.htm.

European Parliament

The European Parliament is the only directly elected body of the European Union. The 785 members of the European Parliament are there to represent you, the citizen. They are elected once every five years by voters right across the 27 member states of the European Union on behalf of its 492 million citizens.

Each revision of the Treaties has seen an increase in the power of the European Parliament in relation to the other institutions. Today the European Parliament is firmly established as a co-legislator, has budgetary powers and exercises democratic controls over all the European institutions.

Council of the EU

The acts of the Council can take the form of regulations, directives, decisions, common actions or common positions, recommendations or opinions. The Council can also adopt conclusions, declarations or resolutions.

European Commission

The European Commission represents and upholds the interests of Europe as a whole. It is independent of national governments. It drafts proposals for new European laws, which it presents to the European Parliament and the Council. It manages the day-to-day business of implementing EU policies and spending EU funds. The Commission also keeps an eye out to see that everyone abides by the European treaties and laws. It can act against rule breakers, taking them to the Court of Justice if necessary.

The Court of Justice

The job of the Court of Justice is to make sure that EU law is interpreted and applied in the same way in all EU countries, thereby ensuring that the law is equal for everyone. It ensures, for example, that national courts do not give different rulings on the same issue. The Court also makes sure that EU member states and institutions do what the law requires them to do.

The European Economic and Social Committee

The 344 members of the European Economic and Social Committee represent a wide range of interests: from employers to trade unionists, from consumers to ecologists. The Committee is an advisory body which must give its opinion on proposed EU decisions about employment, social spending, vocational training, etc.

The European Central Bank

Based in Frankfurt, the Central Bank is responsible for managing the euro – for example, by setting interest rates. Its prime concern is ensuring price stability so that the European economy is not damaged by inflation. The Bank takes it decisions independently of governments and other bodies.

Table 2.3   EU Institutions (relevant for businesses)

Sources: EU Parliament, http://www.europarl.europa.eu/parliament/public/staticDisplay.do?language=EN&id=146; Council of the EU, http://www.consilium.europa.eu/showPage.ASP?lang=en; rest, http://europa.eu/abc/panorama/howorganised/index_en.htm#commission.

Political Constraints on Trade

Global firms know that political actions taken by a government can drastically affect the business operations of outsiders. At the extreme, of course, it goes without saying that when two countries go to war, the business environment changes dramatically. Often people overseas dislike the actions of another country. This was the case when the United Kingdom sent troops to Iraq. Short of war, a country may impose economic sanctions that prohibit trade with another country so access to some markets may be cut off.

In some situations, the government may decide to take over the operations of foreign companies doing business within its borders. It is called **nationalisation** when the domestic government reimburses a foreign company (often not for the full value) for its assets after taking it over. Think about the way the UK bailed out banks during the credit crunch. It is called **expropriation** when a domestic government seizes a foreign company's assets. To keep track of the level of political stability or instability in foreign countries, firms often engage in formal or informal analyses of the potential political risk in various countries.

Regulatory Constraints on Trade

Governments and economic communities impose numerous regulations about what products should be made of, how they should be made, and what can be said about them. For example, sometimes a company has no choice but to alter product content to comply with local laws. Heinz sauce tastes quite different in Europe simply because of different legal restrictions on preservatives and colour additives.[6]

Other regulations are more focused on ensuring that the host country gets a piece of the action. **Local content rules** are a form of protectionism stipulating that a certain proportion of a product must consist of components supplied by industries in the host country or economic community. For example, under NAFTA (North American Free Trade Agreement) rules, cars built by Mercedes-Benz in the US must have 62.5 per cent of their components made in North America to be able to enter Mexico and Canada duty free.[7] These types of rules also help to explain why Japanese car producers such as Toyota and Nissan have heightened their local presence by opening manufacturing plants within the EU.

The Socio-Cultural Environment

Another element of a firm's external environment is the socio-cultural environment. This term refers to the characteristics of the society, the people who live in that society, and the culture that reflects the values and beliefs of the society. Whether at home or in global markets, marketers need to understand and adapt to the customs, characteristics and practices of its citizens. Basic beliefs about such cultural priorities as the role of family or proper relations between the sexes affect people's responses to products and promotional messages in any market.

Disney learned the hard way about the importance of being sensitive to local cultures after it opened Disneyland Resort Paris in 1992. The company was criticised for creating an entertainment venue that re-created its American locations without catering to local customs. More recently, the company applied the lessons it learned in cultural sensitivity to its new Hong Kong Disneyland. Executives decided to shift the angle of the front gate by 12 degrees after consulting a *feng shui* specialist, who said the change would ensure prosperity for the park. Disney also put a bend in the walkway from the train station to the gate, to make sure the flow of positive energy, or *chi*, did not slip past the entrance and out to the China Sea. Cash registers are close to corners or along walls to increase prosperity. And, since the Chinese consider

BUY FAIRTRADE?

BUY ORGANIC?

BUY FREE RANGE?

BUY LOCAL PRODUCE?

RECYCLE?

If you do any of this green stuff, then why not move over to Ecover? Based on plant and mineral ingredients, our range cleans effectively and has a minimal impact on the environment.

IT'S ECOLOGICAL

ECOVER

www.its-ecological.com

| Photo 2.3 | This brand's emphasis on sustainability, fair trade, local and organic products, is in step with a sociocultural trend. Source: The Advertising Archives |

the number four to be bad luck, you won't find any fourth-floor buttons in hotel lifts.[8] Disney eventually discovered that understanding consumer attitudes, beliefs and ways of doing things in different parts of the world is especially important to firms when developing a marketing strategy.

Demographics

The first step towards understanding the characteristics of a society is to look at its **demographics**. These are statistics that measure observable aspects of a population, such as size, age, gender, ethnic group, income, education, occupation and family structure. Demographic studies can be of great value to marketers in helping to predict the size of markets for many products.

Values

More than 8.2 million women in 50 countries read versions of *Cosmopolitan* in 28 different languages. However, because of local norms about modesty, some women have to hide the magazine from their husbands. Adapting the *Cosmo* credo of a 'Fun, Fearless Female' in some cultures may be tricky. Different cultures emphasise varying belief systems that define what it means to be female, feminine, appealing, and what is considered appropriate to see in print on these matters. For example, whilst in India and China *Cosmo* may have articles relating to sex replaced with stories about youthful dedication, there isn't much of this material in the Swedish edition either – because the culture is so open about this topic that it doesn't grab readers' attention.[9]

As this example shows, every society has a set of **cultural values**, or deeply held beliefs about right and wrong ways to live, that it imparts to its members.[10] Those beliefs influence virtually every aspect of our lives, even the way we mark the time we live them. For example, in Hong Kong time is a core value. Indeed, time is money, and business meetings tend to be precise and start promptly. In other countries, like Latin America, this is not at all the case. If you schedule a business meeting at 10 a.m. you can be assured most people will not arrive until around 10.30 or later.

These differences in values often explain why marketing efforts that are a big hit in one country can flop in another. For example, Italian housewives spend about five times as many hours per week than do their US counterparts on household chores. This dedication should make them perfect customers for cleaning products, but when Unilever launched an all-purpose spray cleaner about six years ago, the product failed. The reason is that the company did not realise that the benefit of labour-saving convenience is a huge turnoff to Italian women, who want products that are tough cleaners, not timesavers. As a result, Unilever had to make big adjustments in order to clean up in the Italian market, including making the bottles 50 per cent bigger because Italians clean so frequently.[11]

One important dimension on which cultures differ is their emphasis on collectivism versus individualism. In **collectivist cultures**, such as those found in Turkey, Greece and Portugal, people tend to subordinate their personal goals to those of a stable community. In contrast, consumers in **individualist cultures**, such as Great Britain and the Netherlands, tend to attach more importance to personal goals, and people are more likely to change memberships when the demands of the group become too costly.[12] This difference can be important to marketers who are appealing to one extreme or the other. For example, try selling a garment that is 'sure to stand out' to consumers who would much prefer to 'fit in'.

Norms and Customs

Values are general ideas about good and bad behaviours. From these values flow **norms**, or specific rules dictating what is right or wrong, acceptable or unacceptable. Some specific types of norms include the following:[13]

- A **custom** is a norm handed down from the past that controls basic behaviours, such as division of labour in a household.

- **Mores** are customs with a strong moral overtone. Mores often involve a taboo, or forbidden behaviour, such as incest or cannibalism. Violation of mores often meets with strong punishment from other members of a society.

- **Conventions** are norms regarding the conduct of everyday life. These rules deal with the subtleties of consumer behaviour, including the 'correct' way to furnish one's house, wear one's clothes, host a dinner party, and so on.

All three types of norms may determine what behaviours are appropriate in different countries. For example, mores may tell us what kind of food it is permissible to eat. For example, whilst Hindus would turn down a steak, Muslims avoid pork products. Local customs also dictate the appropriate hour at which a meal should be served. In some European countries, and in the Middle East, dinner tends not to be served until around 9 p.m. or later. People in such countries are amused by British visitors whose stomachs are rumbling around 7 p.m. Conventions tell us how to eat the meal, including such details as the utensils, table etiquette and even the appropriate clothes to wear for dining.

Conflicting customs can be a problem when Western marketers try to conduct business in other countries where executives have different ideas about what is proper or expected. These difficulties even include body language. People in Latin countries tend to stand much closer to each other than do Anglo-Saxons, and are often insulted if their counterpart tries to stand further away. Understanding such customs as these may be the difference between a firm's success and failure on the global stage.

Language

The language barrier is one obvious problem confronting marketers who wish to break into foreign markets. Travellers abroad commonly encounter signs in poor, yet often humorous English – such as a note to guests at a Tokyo hotel saying, 'You are invited to take advantage of the chambermaid', a notice at a hotel in Acapulco reassuring people that 'The manager has personally passed all the water served here', or a dry cleaner in Majorca who urged passing customers to 'drop your pants here for best results'.

These barriers are not just potentially embarrassing; they can affect product labelling and usage instructions, advertising and personal selling. It's vital for marketers to work with local people who understand the subtleties of language so as to avoid the confusion that may result. For example, the meaning of a brand name, one of the most important signals a marketer can send about the character and quality of a product can get mangled as it travels around the world. Local product names often raise eyebrows of visitors who may be surprised to stumble on a Japanese coffee creamer called Creap, a Spanish bread named Bimbo, or even a Scandinavian product that unfreezes car locks called Super Piss.[14]

Ethnocentrism

Even if a firm succeeds in getting its products to a foreign market, there's no guarantee that local consumers will be interested. Sometimes a willingness to try products made elsewhere comes slowly. In marketing, the tendency to prefer products or people of one's own culture over those from other countries is called **ethnocentrism**. For example, the French tend to have strong preference for their own cuisine, and they evaluate food products from other countries critically. Despite this, the upscale British department store Marks & Spencer had moderate success in France selling English-style sandwiches like egg and watercress on wholemeal bread.

For now, it is important for you to be aware that opportunities and threats can come from any part of the external environment. On the one hand, trends or currently unserved customer needs may provide opportunities for growth. On the other hand, if changing customer needs or buying patterns mean customers are turning away from a firm's products, it's a signal of possible danger or threats down the road.

What is the outcome of an analysis of a firm's internal and external environments? Managers often synthesise the results of a situation analysis into a format called a **SWOT analysis**. A SWOT analysis allows managers to focus clearly on the meaningful strengths (S) and weaknesses (W) in the firm's internal environment and opportunities (O) and threats (T) coming from outside the firm (the external environment). A SWOT analysis enables a firm to develop strategies that make use of what the firm does best in seizing opportunities for growth while at the same time avoiding external threats that might hurt the firm's sales and profits. Table 2.4 shows an example of a partial SWOT analysis for McDonald's.

Step 3: Set Organisational or SBU Objectives

After constructing a mission statement, top management translates that mission statement into organisational or SBU objectives. These goals are derived from the mission statement and broadly identify what the firm hopes to accomplish within the general time frame of its long-range business plan. If the firm is big enough to have separate SBUs, each SBU will have its own objectives relevant to its operations.

To be effective, objectives need to be SMART, *Specific*, *Measurable* (so firms can tell whether they've met them or not). To ensure measurability, objectives are often stated in

Table 2.4
SWOT Analysis for McDonald's

Strengths	• World-class research and product development.
	• Global franchise system that is second to none.
	• Strong cash position.
	• Consistency of product and service quality around the globe.
Weaknesses	• Until recently, slow to react to consumer trends and preferences.
Opportunities	• Changing consumer tastes and dining preferences signals opportunity to remake some of the locations into more upmarket bistro formats.
	• Reconnecting with Baby Boomers and Gen X while cultivating Gen Y and younger provides opportunity for product innovation and more flexibility by market area.
	• Rising cost of petrol means more people want to eat closer to home.
Threats	• The general degeneration of the image of Americans globally, especially in Europe, may affect sales.
	• Strongly negative PR surrounding unhealthy eating has tarnished the brand.
	• Burger King has emerged as an edgy innovator, especially with the younger crowd.

Source: Compilation of research by the authors.

numerical terms. For example, a firm might have as an objective a 10 per cent increase in profitability. It could reach this objective by increasing productivity, by reducing costs or by selling off an unprofitable division. Or it might meet this 10 per cent objective by developing new products, investing in new technologies, or entering a new market. They also need to be *Attainable*. Attainability is especially important – firms that establish 'pie in the sky' objectives they can't realistically obtain can create frustration for their employees (who work hard but get no satisfaction of accomplishment) and other stakeholders in the firm, such as vendors and shareholders who are affected when the firm doesn't meet its objectives. Objectives also need to be *Relevant* to the company's objective and may relate to revenue and sales, profitability, the firm's standing in the market, return on investment, productivity, product development, customer relations and satisfaction, and social responsibility. Finally, objectives are best if they are *Time* bound, for example to increase sales by 10 per cent over a one-year period.

For many years, Procter & Gamble (P&G) had an objective of having a number one brand in every product category in which it competed. This objective was specific and clearly it was attainable, since P&G could boast of such market leaders as Crest in the toothpaste category, Folgers in coffee, Pampers in nappies, and Head & Shoulders in shampoo. It was also measurable in terms of the share of market of P&G's products versus those sold by competitors. However, in the long run such an objective is very difficult to sustain because of competitive activity and ever-changing consumer tastes. Sure enough, over time, some P&G brands continued to hold a respectable market share, but they dropped from the number one position. Should P&G not sell in a product category simply because its brand is not number one? Management realised the answer to this question was clearly 'no', and the objective moved from category leadership into one focused on profitability for each brand.

 ## Step 4: Establish the Business Portfolio

For companies with several different SBUs, strategic planning includes making decisions about how best to allocate resources across these businesses to ensure growth for the whole organisation. As Figure 2.2 illustrates, each SBU has its own focus within the firm's overall strategic plan, and each has its own target market and strategies for reaching its objectives. Just like an independent business, each SBU is a separate *profit centre* within the larger corporation – that is, each SBU within the firm is responsible for its own costs, revenues and profits.

Marketing Metrics

Who uses metrics most?

A survey of leading marketing firms in five countries (United States, United Kingdom, France, Germany and Japan) found that market share is the metric that managers are most likely to report to the company's board of directors. Other commonly used metrics include the following:

- Perceived product/service quality;
- Customer loyalty/retention;
- Customer/segment profitability;
- Relative price.

Across the five countries, German companies are the heaviest users of metrics and Japanese firms the lightest. Of the companies surveyed, 97 per cent of German firms said they reported their market share to their boards compared with 79 per cent of American firms and only 57 per cent of Japanese firms. Overall, firms that do business in several countries and those that have above-average marketing budgets are more likely to rely on metrics.[15]

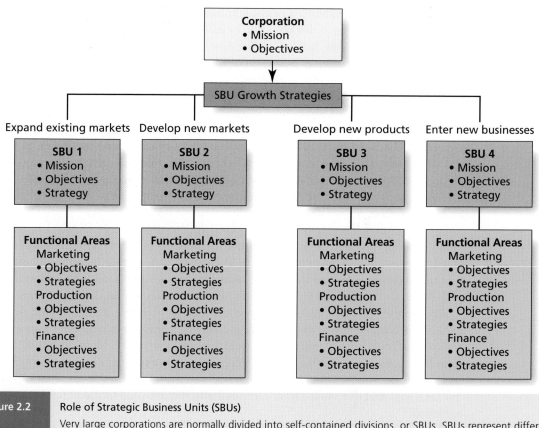

Role of Strategic Business Units (SBUs)

Very large corporations are normally divided into self-contained divisions, or SBUs. SBUs represent different major areas of the overall firm's business. For example, General Electric has a jet engine division, a lighting division, an appliance division and numerous other divisions. At GE, as with most corporations, each SBU operates as an independent business with its own mission and objectives – and its own marketing strategy.

Just as the collection of different stocks an investor owns is called a portfolio, the range of different businesses that a large firm operates is called its **business portfolio**. These different businesses usually represent very different product lines, each of which operates with its own budget and management. Having a diversified business portfolio reduces the firm's dependence on one product line or one group of customers. For example, if travel suffers and Disney has a bad year in theme park attendance and cruises, its managers hope that the sales will be made up by stay-at-homers who go to Disney movies and watch Disney's television networks.

Portfolio analysis is a tool management uses to assess the potential of a firm's businesses portfolio. It helps management decide which of its current SBUs should receive more – or less – of the firm's resources, and which of its SBUs are most consistent with the firm's overall mission. Several models are available to assist management in the portfolio analysis process. Let's examine one popular model the Boston Consulting Group (BCG) developed: the **BCG growth–market share matrix**.

The BCG model focuses on determining the potential of a firm's existing successful SBUs to generate cash that the firm can then use to invest in other businesses. In the BCG matrix, as Figure 2.3 shows, the vertical axis represents the attractiveness of the market, the *market growth rate*. Even though the figure shows 'high' and 'low' as measurements, marketers might ask whether the total market for the SBU's products is growing 10, 50, 100 or 200 per cent annually.

The horizontal axis in Figure 2.3 shows the SBU's current strength in the market through its *relative market share*. Here, marketers might ask whether the SBU's share is 5, 25, or perhaps 75 per cent of the current market. Combining the two axes creates four quadrants

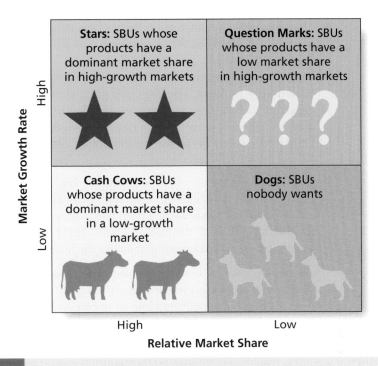

Figure 2.3	BCG Growth-Market Share Matrix
	The Boston Consulting Group's (BCG) growth–market share matrix is one way a firm can examine its portfolio of different products or SBUs. By categorising SBUs as stars, cash cows, question marks, or dogs, the matrix helps managers make good decisions about how the firm should grow.

representing four different types of SBUs. Each quadrant of the BCG grid uses a symbol to designate business units that fall within a certain range for market growth rate and market share. Let's take a closer look at each cell in the grid:

- **Stars** are SBUs with products that have a dominant market share in high-growth markets. Because the SBU has a dominant share of the market, stars generate large revenues, but they also require large amounts of funding to keep up with production and promotion demands. Because the market has a large growth potential, managers design strategies to maximise market share in the face of increasing competition. The firm aims at getting the largest share of loyal customers so that the SBU will generate profits that can then be put into other parts of the company. For example, in recent years Disney has viewed its movie brand for grown-ups, Touchstone Studios, as a star. Its strategy of investing in expanding that brand is based on the huge market potential of adult cinemagoers.

- **Cash cows** have a dominant market share in a low-growth potential market. Because there's not much opportunity for new companies, competitors don't often enter the market. At the same time, the SBU is well established and enjoys a high market share that the firm can sustain with minimal funding. Firms usually milk cash cows of their profits to fund the growth of other SBUs. Of course, if the firm's objective is to increase revenues, having too many cash cows with little or no growth potential can become a liability. For Disney, its Disney Pictures unit, which focuses on family films and animated features, fits into the cash cow category. In fact, Disney periodically recycles even its oldest animated films such as *Snow White* back into the cinemas to delight another generation of fans.

- **Question marks** – sometimes called *problem children* – are SBUs with low market shares in fast-growth markets. When a business unit is a question mark, it suggests that the firm has failed to compete successfully. Perhaps the SBU's products offer fewer benefits than competing products. Or maybe its prices are too high, its distributors are ineffective, or its advertising is too weak. The firm could pump more money into marketing the product and hope that market share will improve. But the firm may find itself 'throwing good money after bad', gaining nothing but a negative cash flow and disappointment. For Disney, its Disney Stores may be in the question mark category, as their performance has lagged behind the overall speciality retail market in recent years.

- **Dogs** have a small share of a slow-growth market. They are businesses that offer specialised products in limited markets that are not likely to grow quickly. When possible, large firms may sell off their dogs to smaller firms that may be able to nurture them – or they may take the SBU's products off the market. Disney, being a very savvy strategic planner, does not appear to have any businesses that are currently in the dog house (so to speak).

Like Disney, Philippe Garnier at Hilton Hotels may use the BCG matrix to evaluate his product lines to understand which ones are primarily cash generators and which are primarily cash users. This analysis will lead him to important decisions about where to invest for the future growth of his business.

Step 5: Develop Growth Strategies

Although the BCG matrix can help managers decide which SBUs they should invest in for growth, it doesn't tell them much about *how* to make that growth happen. Should the growth of an SBU come from finding new customers, from developing new variations of the product, or from some other growth strategy? Part of the strategic planning at the SBU level entails evaluating growth strategies.

Marketers use the product–market growth matrix shown in Figure 2.4 to analyse different growth strategies. The vertical axis in Figure 2.4 represents opportunities for growth, either in

	Product Emphasis	
	Existing Products	**New Products**
Existing Markets	**Market penetration strategy** • Seek to increase sales of existing products to existing markets	**Product development strategy** • Create growth by selling new products in existing markets
New Markets	**Market development strategy** • Introduce existing products to new markets	**Diversification strategy** • Emphasise both new products and new markets to achieve growth

Market Emphasis (label on left axis)

Figure 2.4   Growth Strategies

existing markets or in new markets. The horizontal axis considers whether the firm would be better off putting its resources into existing products or if it should acquire new products. The matrix provides four different fundamental marketing strategies: market penetration, market development, product development and diversification:

- **Market penetration strategies** seek to increase sales of existing products to existing markets such as current users, non-users, and users of competing brands within a market. For example, Campbell's can advertise new uses for soup in lunches and dinners, encourage current customers to eat more soup, and prod non-users to find reasons to buy soup. The firm might try to increase sales by cutting prices, improving distribution or conducting promotions aimed at attracting users of competing soup brands.

- **Market development strategies** introduce existing products to new markets. This strategy can mean expanding into a new geographic area, or it may mean reaching new customer segments within an existing geographic market. For example, Red Bull, the 'energy' drink that had its beginnings in the 1990s as a cult favourite among the emerging young club crowd, is trying to move up the generational chain to attract older users as well. To do this, Red Bull has recently switched some of its marketing efforts from edgy ads to more mainstream messages. Founder and largest shareholder Dietrich Mateschitz understands the monetary power of the older generation, and to appeal to them he has broadened Red Bull's distribution into shops, restaurants and clubs they frequent. Mateschitz is betting on the vast numbers of clubbers' parents to prop up sales, especially now that the heavyweights like Coca-Cola, Pepsi and Anheuser-Busch are trying to make inroads into fans of energy drinks.[16]

- **Product development strategies** create growth by selling new products in existing markets. Product development may mean extending the firm's product line by developing new variations of the item, or it may mean altering or improving the product to provide enhanced performance. Take the humble mattress for example. US business class hotels like Sheraton, Wyndham and Marriott have engaged in something of a 'mattress war'. That is, each one is trying to convince the traveller that its bed is softer, more comfortable and more inviting than the competition (and in some cases if you fall in love with the bed

Marketing Ethics

Back to basics . . .

McDonald's is the largest operator in the UK fast food market, and has 1225 outlets. Customers can choose from a variety of burgers. The Big Mac is a double beef burger in a bun with melted cheese and a calorie content of almost 500. Another popular product on the menu, a Double Quarter Pounder with Cheese, contains 710 calories, more than a third of the recommended daily energy intake for women. In 2004, due to heavy criticism of the menu, McDonald's decided on a new strategy and launched a number of what it described as healthier options, such as salads with low-fat dressings, fruit bags containing pieces of fresh fruit, organic milk and a range of toasted sandwiches. However, as part of its 'back-to-basics' policy, the fast food giant launched a new burger in June 2006 that is 40 per cent bigger than a Big Mac.

Debate, Discuss, Disagree

1 Who do you think should regulate the food sector and how?

2 Is it fair to communicate a healthier strategy to the customers and launch unhealthy products at the same time?

Real People, Other Voices

Advice for Philippe Garnier

Dr Els Breugelmans,
Maastricht University, The Netherlands

I would advise Hilton Hotel to select option 3. At the time of the decision, it was apparent that it could no longer ignore the changing environment it was facing. The online environment empowered customers that were planning their own holiday and leisure activities and new web-based intermediaries were there to stay. This would argue against options 1 and 2 where Hilton ignores the changing environment and these new entrants. In addition, in order to reach its objective to gain better control and implement 'floating' prices, it was forced to change the current strategy. Although this might cause some resistance, it has been shown that, in industries with perishable products (like hotels, tickets, rental cars . . .), revenue management pays off. This would argue against option 1 where Hilton would continue in the old way. In option 3, however, Hilton pays careful attention to both strategic issues. So, instead of ignoring the threat of empowered customers and the new web-based entrants, I believe it should indeed engage with the new players in the market and force them to use the floating price mechanism. Yet I would advise Hilton to give all existing distributors the choice not to deal with Hilton or to collaborate via the new strategy, instead of making exceptions for some more powerful distributors.

Although this might be a risky strategy and probably needs a gradual implementation, I believe it could work in Hilton's case: it has a strong leadership position in the industry, and the competition among distributors is quite severe. In addition, the freed distribution costs as well as the increased control would give it the opportunity to steer more potential customers to its own website where it can sell rooms with the floating price mechanism and gain an increased piece of the growing online consumer travelling segment.

Dr Tony Garry,
De Montfort University

I would choose option 3. Hilton has a high level of brand awareness among potential customers and through appropriate communication and promotional techniques these customers may be enticed or 'pulled' to Hilton's own website or third-party websites such as Expedia. This reduces the need for other higher margin intermediaries and allows a more market-driven approach whereby 'real time' customer demand determines room allocation and room pricing hence optimising resource utilisation.

The market that Hilton is competing in is extremely intense. As with other markets, the process of 'disintermediation' (whereby the functions and 'value adding' opportunities for intermediaries are being increasingly concentrated with fewer and fewer members of the channel) is becoming commonplace particularly within service industries where margins are increasingly being pressurised. An example of this is easyJet where the customer is able to purchase direct from the service provider using online facilities. Certainly, the leisure industry is seeing huge changes in organisational 'routes to market'. More and more individuals are designing and booking short and long holiday breaks online direct with service providers or through third-party web distributors often viewing this process as an integral part of the 'holiday experience'.

This option will also avoid direct confrontation with those existing intermediaries reluctant to adopt the necessary processes and systems required for Hilton to achieve its objectives. Instead, a more collaborative relationship between Hilton and its intermediaries should ensue whilst they are brought 'on board'. Also, with an incremental rolling out of the new model, potential teething problems should be ironed out satisfactorily thus avoiding a potential 'T5' scenario that British Airways faced on the implementation of a number of new systems simultaneously at Heathrow.

Sabrina Gottschalk,
student at Cass Business School

I would choose option 3. More and more consumers want the freedom of planning their holidays and searching for hotels on the internet on their own. This trend in consumer behaviour must not be ignored and it would be a mistake to underestimate the growing importance of websites like Expedia or Opodo. If Hilton wants to remain industry leader, the company needs to engage with those third-party web players and include them in their strategy. On the other hand, the traditional distributors also continue to play an important role. Certain customer segments, such as older guests, might prefer to carry out their booking in a more conventional way. It is therefore a sensible move for Hilton to continue its relationship with existing powerful distributors, but also going one step further and bonding with new players. This option allows Hilton to strengthen its distribution system and at the same time helps to replace possible lost business from other, weaker distributors.

you can actually buy it and take it home!) This 'sleeper' strategy appears to be effective: Radisson Hotels' research with guests told it that the mere fact that a bed was 'upgraded' would allow the chain to charge an additional €7.5 more per room. These new-age beds even carry their own brand names – 'Heavenly Bed' at Westin, 'The Revive Collection' at Marriott and 'Sweet Sleeper' at Sheraton. Radisson's 'Sleep Number' beds even allow each occupant to adjust the firmness of each side with a remote control device.[17] Such a product development strategy is waking up the hotel industry, as the major players (and some smaller luxury hotels) now are scrambling to turn other room elements such as toiletries into products that can be sold.

- **Diversification strategies** emphasise both new products and new markets to achieve growth. After a long period of sluggish performance in the fast food market, McDonald's has re-energised itself over the past few years through successful strategic planning. For example, feeling that there was little growth potential in the hamburger business in the late 1990s, McDonald's sought to attract different customers with lines of business to diversify its portfolio of food offerings. Among those are Donatos Pizza, Boston Market and a controlling interest in Chipotle Mexican Grills. Interestingly, now that their core business has been back on track, McDonald's has begun to divest some of these other brands and is shifting from diversification back to more of a product development strategy around the core McDonald's brand.[18]

For Philippe Garnier at Hilton Hotels, using the product–market growth matrix can be a very important way to analyse where his future opportunities lie. To what degree does he want to focus on increasing current customers with Hilton Hotels's existing product line, taking share away from potential competitors and solidifying his position in his core market space? Or will he quickly expand the product line, perhaps into new markets? These are fundamental issues in planning for future growth.

To review what we've learned so far, strategic planning includes developing the mission statement, assessing the internal and external environment (resulting in a SWOT analysis), setting objectives, establishing the business portfolio and developing growth strategies. In the next section, we'll look at marketers' functional plans – marketing planning.

Marketing Planning: Selecting the Camera Setting

Up until now, we have focused on strategic plans. The strategic plan, however, does not provide details about how to reach the objectives that have been set. Strategic plans 'talk the talk' but put the pressure on lower-level functional area managers, such as the marketing manager, production manager and finance manager, to 'walk the walk' by developing the functional plans – the nuts and bolts – to achieve organisational and SBU objectives. Thus, marketers develop functional plans (for example, marketing plans) – the next step in planning as Figure 2.1 showed.

The Four Ps of the marketing mix we discussed in Chapter 1 remind us that successful firms must have viable *products* at *prices* consumers are willing to pay, the means to get the products to the *place* consumers want to buy, and a way to *promote* the products to the right consumers. Making this happen requires a tremendous amount of planning by the marketer. The steps in this marketing planning process are quite similar to the steps at the strategic planning level. An important distinction between strategic planning and marketing planning, however, is that marketing professionals focus much of their planning efforts on issues related to the firm's product, its price, promotional approach and distribution (place) methods. In the end, as you learned in Chapter 1, marketing focuses on customer value and customer relationships, and marketing planning plays a central role in making these critical components of marketing successful. Let's look at the steps involved in the marketing planning process in a bit more detail.

Step 1: Perform a Situation Analysis

The first step in developing a marketing plan is for marketing managers to conduct an analysis of the *marketing* environment. To do this, managers build on the company's SWOT analysis by searching out information about the environment that specifically affects the marketing plan. For example, for Philippe Garnier at Hilton Hotels to develop an effective marketing communications programme, it's not enough for him to have a general understanding of the target market. He needs to know specifically what media potential customers connect with, what messages about the product are most likely to make them buy, and how they prefer to communicate with his firm about upgrades, new services and customer care issues. Philippe also must know how his competitors are marketing to customers so that he can plan effectively.

Step 2: Set Marketing Objectives

Once marketing managers have a thorough understanding of the marketing environment, the next step is to develop specific marketing objectives. How are marketing objectives different from corporate objectives? Generally, marketing objectives are more specific to the firm's brands, sizes, product features, and other marketing mix-related elements. Think of the connection between business objectives and marketing objectives this way: business objectives guide the entire firm's operations, while marketing objectives state what the marketing function must accomplish if the firm is ultimately to achieve these overall business objectives. So, for Philippe Garnier at Hilton Hotels, setting marketing objectives means deciding what he wants to accomplish in terms of marketing mix-related elements, such as the development of distribution channels or specific sales figures.

Step 3: Develop Marketing Strategies

In the next stage of the marketing planning process, marketing managers develop their actual marketing strategies. That is, they make decisions about what activities they must accomplish to achieve the marketing objectives. Usually this means deciding which markets to target and actually developing the marketing mix strategies (product, price, promotion and distribution) to support how the product is positioned in the market. At this stage, marketers must figure out how they want consumers to think of their product compared to competing products.

Selecting a Target Market

The target market is the market segment selected because of the firm's belief that its offerings are most suited to winning those customers. The firm assesses the potential demand – the number of consumers it believes are willing and able to pay for its products – and decides it has the distinctive competencies that will create a competitive advantage in the marketplace among target consumers. The mission statement for Hilton Hotels provides insight about what businesses it is in. From this mission statement, Philippe Garnier can rest assured that he is responsible for focusing resources on developing target markets for Hilton's products.

Get an Eiffel of this...

Luton to
Paris
from
£24.99
single inc. taxes

easyJet.com
Flights · Hotels · Cars · Holidays

We fly to Paris, Charles de Gaulle

Hurry, book now

Price correct as of 07/07/2008 – Base on summer flying July to October

Photo 2.4 EasyJet's adverts reinforce its image as a low-priced airline in the market.
Source: easyJet Airline Company Ltd

Developing Marketing Mix Strategies

Marketing mix decisions identify how marketing will accomplish its objectives in the firm's target markets by using product, price, promotion and place.

- Because the product is the most fundamental part of the marketing mix – firms simply can't make a profit without something to sell – carefully developed *product strategies* are essential to achieving marketing objectives. Product strategies include decisions such as product design, packaging, branding, support services (such as maintenance), if there will be variations of the product, and what product features will provide the unique benefits targeted customers want. For example, product planners for Virgin Atlantic decided to include in-seat video games and television as a key product feature during the flight. Their planes get you from point A to point B just as fast (or slow) as the other airlines – that is, the basic product is the same – but the flight seems shorter because there is more to do while you are in the air.

- The *pricing strategy* determines how much a firm charges for a product. Of course, that price has to be one that customers are willing to pay. If not, all the other marketing efforts are futile. In addition to setting prices for the final consumer, pricing strategies usually establish prices that will be charged to wholesalers and retailers. A firm's pricing strategies may be based on costs, demand or the prices of competing products. EasyJet uses a pricing strategy to successfully target customers who could not previously afford air travel. It does not compete solely on price. However, consumers do perceive easyJet as a low-priced airline compared to others, and the airline reinforces this theme regularly in its ads.

- A *promotion strategy* is how marketers communicate product benefits and features to the target market. Marketers use promotion strategies to develop the product's message and the mix of advertising, sales promotion, public relations and publicity, direct marketing and personal selling that will deliver the message. Many firms use all these elements to communicate their message to consumers. British Airways strives to portray an image of quality and luxury for the serious business traveller. To do so, it combines television ads focused on that target with sales promotion in the form of the BA's loyalty programme, personal selling to companies and conventions to promote usage of British Airways as the 'official carrier' for the groups, direct marketing via mail and email providing information to loyal users, and, its managers hope, positive publicity through word of mouth about the airline's good service and dependability.

- *Distribution strategies* outline how, when and where the firm will make the product available to targeted customers (the place component). In developing a distribution strategy, marketers must decide whether to sell the product directly to the final customer or whether to sell through retailers and wholesalers. And the choice of which retailers should be involved depends on the product, pricing and promotion decisions. For example, if the firm is producing a luxury good, it may wish to avoid being seen on the shelves of 'discount shops' for fear that it will cheapen the brand image. In recent years, the airline industry has made major changes in its distribution strategy. For many years, most customers bought their airline tickets through travel agencies or at ticket counters of the major airlines. Today, many airlines such as easyJet actually penalise customers who don't opt for online purchase of 'ticketless' flight reservations by charging them a 'ticketing fee' or forcing them to call a premium rate helpline. This strategy has moulded the behaviour of many consumers to go online 24/7 to save money as well as experience the convenience of scheduling the flight they want.

Step 4: Implement and Control the Marketing Plan

Objective

5

Explain the role of implementation and control in marketing planning

Once the plan is developed, it's time to get to work and make it successful. In practice, marketers spend much of their time managing the various elements of the marketing plan. For Hilton Hotels, once Philippe Garnier and his group understand the marketing environment, determine the most appropriate objectives and strategies, and get their ideas organised and on paper in the formal plan, the plan really begins to gain traction. Like all firms, how Hilton Hotels implements its plan is usually what makes or breaks the success of the firm in the marketplace.

During the implementation phase, marketers must have some means to determine to what degree they are actually meeting their stated marketing objectives. Often called **control**, this formal process of monitoring progress entails the three steps of (1) measuring actual performance, (2) comparing this performance to the established marketing objectives or strategies, and then (3) making adjustments to the objectives or strategies on the basis of this analysis. This issue of making adjustments brings up one of the most important aspects of successful marketing planning: marketing plans aren't written in stone, and marketers must be flexible enough to make such changes when changes are warranted.

Effective control requires appropriate *marketing metrics*, which, as we discussed in Chapter 1, are concrete measures of various aspects of marketing performance. You will note throughout the book a strong emphasis on metrics within each chapter. Today's CEOs are keen on quantifying just how an investment in marketing affects the firm's success, financially and otherwise. Think of this overall notion as **return on marketing investment (ROMI)**. Considering marketing as an investment rather than an expense is critical because this distinction drives firms to use marketing more strategically to enhance the business. The ROMI concept heightens the importance of identifying and tracking appropriate marketing metrics.[19] Table 2.5 provides some example metrics that are applied across an array of marketing planning situations including all the marketing mix variables.

Philippe Garnier at Hilton Hotels has to establish appropriate metrics related to his marketing objectives and then track those metrics to know how successful his marketing strategy is, as well as whether he needs to make changes in the strategy along the way. For example, what happens if Hilton Hotels sets an objective to increase market share in the youth market by 25 per cent in a given year but after the first quarter sales in this market are only even with the previous year? The control process means that Philippe and his crew would have to look carefully at why they were not meeting their objectives. Is it due to internal factors, external factors, or a combination of both? Depending on the cause, Philippe would then have to either adjust the marketing plan's strategies (such as to increase advertising or implement product alterations) or adjust the marketing objective so that it reflects realistic goals. This scenario illustrates the important point made earlier in our discussion of strategic planning that objectives must be specific and measurable, but also *attainable* in the sense that if an objective is not realistic it can become very demotivating for everyone involved in the marketing plan.

Action Plans

How does the implementation and control step acually manifest itself within a marketing plan? One very convenient way is through the inclusion of a series of **action plans** in support

Table 2.5
Example Marketing
Metrics

Cost of a prospect
Value of a prospect
Return on investment of a campaign
Value of telesales
Conversion rates of users of competitor products
Long-term value of a customer
Customer commitment to relationship/partnership
Referral rate
Response rates to direct marketing
Perceived product quality
Perceived service quality
Customer loyalty/retention
Customer turnover
Customer/segment profitability
Customer mindset/customer orientation
Customer satisfaction
Company/product reputation
Customer word-of-mouth (buzz) activity
Salesperson perceived self-efficacy
Timeliness and accuracy of competitive intelligence
Usage rates of technology in customer initiatives
Reach and frequency of advertising
Recognition and recall of message
Sales calls per day/week/month
Order fulfilment efficiency/stock-outs
Timeliness of sales promotion support

of the various marketing objectives and strategies within the plan. Action plans are also sometimes referred to as *marketing programmes*. The best way to utilise action plans is by including a separate action plan for each important element involved in implementing the marketing plan. Table 2.6 provides a template for an action plan.

For example, let's consider the use of action plans in the context of supporting Philippe at Hilton Hotels in increasing Hilton's share of the youth market by 25 per cent this year. To accomplish this, the marketing plan would probably include a variety of strategies related to how he will employ the marketing mix elements to accomplish this. Important questions will be: Who is his target market? How will the product be positioned against this market? What will be his product and branding strategies? What will be his pricing strategy for this group? How will the product be promoted to them? And what is the best distribution strategy to access the youth market? Any one of these important strategic issues may require several action plans to implement.

Table 2.6
Action Plan
Template

Title of action plan Give the action plan a relevant name.
Purpose of action plan What do you hope to accomplish by the action plan? That is, what specific marketing objective and strategy within the marketing plan does it support?
Description of action plan Be succinct, but still thorough, in explaining the action plan. What are the steps involved? This is the core of the action plan. It describes what must be done in order to accomplish the intended purpose of the action plan.
Responsibility for the action plan What person(s) or organisational unit(s) are responsible for carrying out the action plan? What external parties are needed to make it happen? Most importantly, who specifically has final 'ownership' of the action plan – that is, who is accountable for it?
Time line for the action plan Provide a specific timetable of events leading to the completion of the plan. If different people are responsible for different elements of the time line, provide that information.
Budget for the action plan How much will implementation of the action plan cost? This may be direct costs only, or may also include indirect costs depending on the situation. The sum of all the individual action plan budget items will ultimately be aggregated by category to create the overall budget for the marketing plan.
Measurement and control of the action plan Indicate the appropriate metrics, how and when they will be measured, and who will measure them.

Action plans provide an additional convenience for developing assignment of responsibilities, time lines, budgets, and measurement and control processes for marketing planning. Notice in Table 2.6 that these four elements are the final four items to be documented in an action plan. Sometimes when a marketing plan is viewed in total it can seem daunting and nearly impossible to actually implement. Like most big projects, implementation of a marketing plan is best done one step at a time, paying attention to maximising the quality of that step. In practice, what happens is that the input from these last four elements of each action plan can be aggregated to form the overall implementation and control portion of the marketing plan. Let's examine each a bit further.

Responsibility

A marketing plan can't be implemented without people and not everybody who will be involved in implementing a marketing plan is a marketer. Truth is, marketing plans touch most areas of an organisation. Upper management and the human resource department will need to be involved in deploying the necessary human resources to accomplish the plan's objectives. Reviewing the various action plans needed for implementation is a great way to develop an overall human resource deployment strategy for accomplishing the marketing plan. You learned in Chapter 1 that marketing isn't just the responsibility of a marketing department. Nowhere is that idea more vivid than in marketing plan implementation. Sales, production, quality control, shipping, customer service, finance, information technology – the list goes on – all will probably have a part in making the plan successful.

Time line

Notice that each action plan requires a *time line* for accomplishment of the various tasks. This is essential to include in the overall marketing plan. Most marketing plans portray the timing of tasks in flow chart form so that it is easy to visualise when the pieces of the plan will come together. Marketers often use workflow tools such as *Gantt charts* or *PERT charts*, popular in operations management, and the same type of tools might be used to map out the different elements of building a house from the ground up. Ultimately, budgets and the financial management of the marketing plan are developed around the time line so that managers know when cash outlays are required.

Budget

Each action plan carries a budget item, assuming there are costs involved in carrying it out. Forecasting the needed expenditures related to a marketing plan is difficult, but one way to improve accuracy in the budgeting process overall is to ensure as accurate as possible estimates of the individual action plans. At the overall marketing plan level, a master budget is created and tracked throughout the market planning process. Variances from the budget are reported to the parties responsible for each budget item throughout the process. For example, a firm's director of sales might receive a weekly or monthly report showing each sales area's performance against their budget allocation. The director would note patterns of budget and contact affected sales managers to determine what, if any action, should be taken to get the budget back on track. The same approach would be repeated across all the different functional areas of the firm affected by the budget. In this manner, the budget itself becomes a critical element of control.

Measurement and Control

Earlier we described the concept of control as a formal process of monitoring progress through measuring actual performance, comparing the performance to the established marketing objectives or strategies, and making adjustments to the objectives or strategies on the basis of this analysis. The metric(s) a marketer uses to monitor and control individual action plans

---

Across the Hall

Advice for Philippe Garnier

Dr Adrian Haberberg,
Principal Lecturer in Strategic Management and MBA Director at the University of East London, and co-author of *Strategic Management: Theory and Application*

Philippe Garnier is confronting a very modern strategy dilemma. Hilton's well-developed competencies in running hotels have given it a good reputation – but this is not enough to guarantee competitive advantage. Its competitiveness depends on the way it manages partnerships with other firms – distributors, tour operators, wholesalers – but new technology is disrupting the way in which those relationships function. Hilton has to decide how quickly it responds; I would look closely at option 2, but advise adopting option 3.

Option 1 can be excluded. It could be fatal to tie Hilton to a high-cost distribution system, and to slow-moving, technologically backward partners. Customers, and firms such as

Expedia that are fast becoming a major force in the travel industry, would turn quite quickly to other hoteliers. With option 3, Hilton positions itself as a progressive force in the industry, but also as a good partner, willing to work with distributors to update their systems. Moreover, it allows itself time to manage the internal disruption that the change will trigger – by not forcing its hotel managers to break established relationships with tour operators – and to learn how best to use the new technology. With radical strategic change it is important to manage implementation risks carefully, and Hilton's strong market position means it does not have to move too hastily. However, if Hilton has faith in its systems and can convince its hotel managers of the need to change, then option 2 deserves serious consideration. By 2004, it was clear that traditional distributors and tour operators were being 'disintermediated' by the internet, so breaking with weaker ones and grabbing technological leadership would send the right signal to customers, distributors, competitors and staff. This option would be particularly attractive if Philippe felt that Hilton's corporate culture was complacent and needed shaking up.

ultimately forms the overall control process for the marketing plan. It is an unfortunate fact that many marketers do not consistently do a good job of measurement and control, which of course compromises their marketing planning. Pay close attention throughout the remainder of the book to highlights on marketing metrics and how they are used to assess the effectiveness of the different components of marketing. Learning these metrics will help you make good choices as a marketer and move up the corporate ladder.

Creating and Working with a Marketing Plan: Snapping the Picture

A marketing plan should provide the best possible guide for the firm to successfully market its products. In large firms, top management often requires such a written plan because putting the ideas on paper encourages marketing managers to formulate concrete objectives and strategies. In small entrepreneurial firms, a well-thought-out marketing plan is often a key factor in attracting investors who will help turn the firm's dreams into reality.

Make Your Life Easier!: Use the Marketing Planning Template

Ultimately, the planning process we've described in this section gets documented into a formal written marketing plan. You'll find a handy template for a marketing plan to download at the book's website (www.pearsoned.co.uk/solomon). The template will come in handy as you make your way through the book, as each chapter will give you information you can use to 'fill in the blanks' of a marketing plan. You will note that the template is cross-referenced with the questions you must answer in each section of the plan and that it also provides you with a general road map of the topics covered in each chapter. By the time you've finished, we hope that all these pieces will come together and you'll understand how real marketers make real decisions.

Operational Planning: Day-to-Day Execution of Marketing Plans

Objective

6

Explain operational planning

In the previous section, we discussed marketing planning – the process by which marketing planners perform a situation analysis, set marketing objectives, and develop, implement and control marketing strategies. But talk is cheap: the best plan ever written is useless if it's not properly carried out. That's what **operational plans** are for. They really make it happen by focusing on the day-to-day execution of the marketing plan. The task falls to the first-line supervisors we discussed earlier, such as sales managers, marketing communications managers and marketing research managers. Operational plans generally cover a shorter period of time than either strategic plans or marketing plans – perhaps only one or two months – and they include detailed directions for the specific activities to be carried out, who will be responsible for them, and timelines for accomplishing the tasks. In reality, the action plan template we provide in Table 2.6 is most likely to be applied at the operational level.

Importantly, many of the marketing metrics managers employ to gauge the success of plans actually get used at the operational planning level. Sales managers in many firms are charged with the responsibility of tracking a wide range of metrics related to the firm–customer relationship such as number of new customers, sales calls per month, customer turnover, and customer loyalty. The data are collected at the operational level, then sent to management for use in planning at the functional level and above.

The Value of a Marketing Culture

A central issue for marketers is gaining a good understanding of the environment in which their planning must take place. That is, how well marketers understand the situation, or environment, in which their firm operates is central to the success of marketing planning.

Earlier in the chapter, we defined the internal environment as being the controllable elements inside an organisation that influence how well the organisation operates. We also mentioned that internal strengths and weaknesses may lie in the firm's technologies, physical facilities, financial stability, reputation, quality of its products and services, and employees. Marketers must analyse and document all these elements in the SWOT analysis part of the marketing plan.

Ultimately, a firm's **corporate culture** determines much of its internal environment. By this we mean the values, norms and beliefs that influence the behaviour of everyone in the organisation. Corporate culture may dictate whether new ideas are welcomed or discouraged, the importance of individual ethical behaviour, and even the appropriate dress code for work.

For many years, IBM was known as 'the white shirt company' because of its unwritten rule that all employees must wear white shirts to look the part of an 'IBMer'. Fortunately, corporate cultures do evolve over time, and even radical changes such as blue shirts are now tolerated at 'Big Blue'. In contrast, Microsoft has always prided itself on having a more casual dress code, reflecting its roots as an entrepreneurial upstart (at least compared with IBM). If you visit Microsoft's US headquarters in Redmond, Washington, you will notice everyone's informal attire right away. However, don't make the mistake of equating informal dress with low work productivity. Microsoft hasn't evolved into the corporate giant it is today by hiring slackers.

Some corporate cultures are more inclined to take risks than others. These firms value individuality and creativity; they recognise that by nurturing these characteristics their employees are more likely to create important competitive advantages. A risk-taking culture is especially important to the marketing function because firms must continually improve their products, their distribution channels, and their promotion programmes to remain successful in a competitive environment. In firms with more traditional corporate cultures, getting managers to buy into a new way of doing things is like inviting the board of directors to go on a skydiving mission.

If a firm is totally focused on economic profit – increasing revenues and decreasing costs – management attitudes will be profit-centred, often at the expense of employee morale. Firms that harbour a concern for employees, customers and society, as well as shareholder profits, produce a corporate culture that is much more appealing for employees and other stakeholders in the business. In which corporate culture would *you* rather work?

The Sunday Times publishes an annual list of the best companies to work for based on a variety of criteria, including company philosophy and practices, employee trust in management, pride in work and the company,

Photo 2.5 Employees at CAP, a Christian debt counselling charity that operates through a network of 72 church-based centres, voted it the best small company to work for in a *Sunday Times* 2008 survey.
Source: Christians Against Poverty

and camaraderie. In 2007, Goldman Sachs International was the best company to work for according to the Times Best Companies Survey. What keeps employees happy is strong leadership, close teamwork, being stretched professionally and the buzz of working for the leading company in its field. Among the top 20 big companies Goldman Sachs staff returned the highest positive scores for 34 of the 70 points that make up the employee survey. These include having pride in working for the firm (88 per cent), happiness with pay and benefits (76 per cent), having a job that is good for personal growth (84 per cent), having confidence in the leadership skills of senior management (83 per cent) and confidence in the abilities of team-mates (84 per cent). In 2008, Bradford-based Christians Against Poverty won the Best Small Company to work for. Chief executive Matt Barlow looks after the Bradford head office and the 72 church-based centres in the UK and, along with founder John Kirkby, provides inspiring leadership, which resulted in the charity's employees giving them a top and near perfect positive score of 98 per cent for leadership. Employees love working for CAP (95 per cent) and have confidence in the leadership of senior managers (98 per cent), another top score. Every day in the Bradford office begins with a staff meeting to pray and discuss company news.

Playing on an International Stage: The Complicated World of Global Marketing

Objective

7

Explain the strategies that a firm can use to enter global markets

The global marketing game is exciting, the stakes are high – and it's easy to make mistakes. Competition comes from both local and foreign firms, and differences in national laws, custom and consumer preferences can make life difficult. The successful global business needs to set its sights on diverse markets around the world, but it needs to act locally by being willing to adapt business practices to unique conditions in other parts of the globe.

For example, in the mid-1990s, Nike had to adjust its global strategy to increase its business in foreign markets. The company attempted to appeal to football fans worldwide and actively pursued new customers in Europe, the Far East and South America. This was a major change for a company that had made its mark in sports such as basketball and American football. Nike's president claimed that in order to be a global company, there was a need to focus on football.[20] With the acquisition of Reebok by Adidas in 2006, Nike had to work even harder to achieve its goal. Perhaps that's why Nike won a bidding war with Adidas in 2006 for the sponsorship of the Indian national cricket team, in a five-year deal worth around €50 million.[21]

 ## World Trade

World trade refers to the flow of goods and services among different countries – the value of all the exports and imports of the world's nations. World trade activity is steadily increasing year by year. In 2004, merchandise exports of all countries totalled €9.15 trillion, up 9 per cent from 2003. Similarly, world exports of commercial services totalled €2.13 trillion, up 17 per cent.[22] This growth was the largest in nearly 10 years and was the second year of growth since the world economy was sent into a tailspin by the US terrorist attacks in 2001.[23] Of course, not all countries participate equally in the trade flows among nations. Understanding the 'big picture' of who does business with whom is important to marketers when they devise global trade strategies.

Having customers in far-away places is important, but it requires some flexibility since business must be done differently to adapt to local social and economic conditions. For example, firms engaged in global marketing must be able to accommodate the needs of trading partners when those foreign firms can't pay cash for the products they want to purchase. Believe it or not, the currency for as many as 70 per cent of all countries is not convertible. This implies it cannot be spent or exchanged outside the country's borders. In other countries, because sufficient cash or credit is simply not available, trading firms work out elaborate deals in which they trade (or barter) their products with each other, or even supply goods in return for tax breaks from the local government. This **counter trade** accounts for about 25 per cent of all world trade. For instance, the Philippine International Trading Corporation agreed to import Vietnamese rice which was paid for with fertiliser, coconuts and coconut by-products produced in the Philippines.[24]

 ## Making the Decision to Go Global

When firms consider 'going global', they must make a number of decisions. As you can see in Figure 2.5 the first two highly related decisions are (1) 'go' or 'no go' – whether it is in the best interest of the firm to remain in its home market or to go where there are good opportunities – and (2) which global markets are most attractive. Although the prospect of millions of consumers purchasing your goods in other countries is very tempting, not all firms can or should go global, and not all markets around the world are alike. In making these decisions, firms need to consider a number of factors that may enhance or detract from their possible success abroad.

One key factor, and it's a fairly broad one, is domestic and foreign market conditions, particularly those that affect a firm's ability to develop a competitive advantage in foreign markets. A second key factor is identifying which markets are attractive given the firm's unique capabilities. Finally, the company must consider the extent to which opportunities for success may be hampered by regulations or other constraints on trade that local governments or international bodies impose.

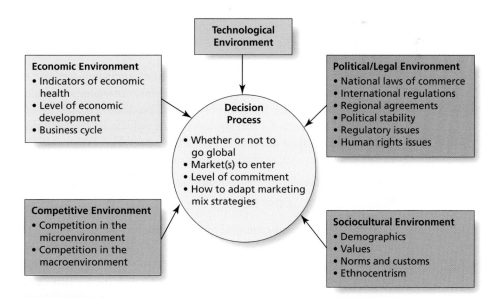

Figure 2.5	Decision Model for Entering Foreign Markets

Entering foreign markets involves a complex decision process. Marketers must fully understand market conditions and environmental factors in order to determine the best strategy for entering the market and to create a successful marketing mix.

Market Conditions

Many times, a firm makes a decision to go global because domestic demand is declining while demand in foreign markets is growing. For example, the market for personal computers has matured in Europe, where more sales come from people replacing old or obsolete machines than from those buying a new personal computer for the first time. In examining the market potential abroad for computers, the demand is much greater in some other parts of the world where consumers and businesses are only now beginning to tune into the power of the web. So, it's no coincidence that in 2005 IBM sold its entire personal computing business to Lenovo, a Chinese company.

Of course, it isn't only Western countries that are going global. Countries such as China that have been a vast market for Western firms to expand in are now fighting to win a larger share of business in the global market place. Dozens of Chinese companies have global ambitions, including Chery Automobile, which plans to export 250,000 low-priced cars a year to North America. Chery, founded in 1997, realises that growth in its home Chinese market has slowed down while competition has increased. The company sees the US as an attractive new market. Other Chinese car makers such as Great Wall and Geely are also looking in the same direction.[25]

Competitive Advantage

In Chapter 1, we saw how firms seek to create competitive advantage, a means to outperform the competition. When firms compete in a global marketplace, this challenge is even greater because there are more players involved and typically some of these local firms have home advantage. In practice, firms need to capitalise on their home country's assets and avoid competing in areas in which they are at a disadvantage. For example, German firms have trouble keeping production costs down because of the high wages, relatively short working weeks and long vacations that their skilled factory workers enjoy. As a result, they are obliged to compete on high quality rather than on low price. Developing countries typically have a large labour force and low wage rates, but have relatively little in the way of highly trained workers or high-tech facilities. In response they tend to compete better for handmade goods and low-cost manufacturing.

Some of the most significant European exports include healthcare equipment, food, industrial supplies and services – including tourism and entertainment, industries where consumers around the world value European brands and products. The success of these industries shows that a firm's prospects for success depend not only on its own abilities, but also on its home country's competitive advantage. As we'll see next, barriers to trade and membership in economic communities also affect a firm's success overseas.

Trading Blocks at the Borders

Even the best of competitive advantages may not allow a firm to be successful in foreign markets if the opportunities for success are not available. People like to think of it as one large, open marketplace where companies from every country are free to compete for business by meeting customers' needs better than the next. Although countries seem to be moving towards such an ideal of free trade, they're not quite there yet. Often a company's efforts to expand into foreign markets are hindered by trade blocs designed to favour local businesses over outsiders.[26]

Of course, marketers who operate in a global environment must consider not only the legal, regulatory and political environments in their own, but other individual countries as well. In recent years a number of initiatives have had a major impact on how marketers do business in markets around the globe. The World Trade Organization has made significant strides in creating a single open world market, while economic communities encourage regional groups of countries to trade among themselves.

Global Trade Agreements: GATT and the WTO   Established under the United Nations after the Second World War, the **General Agreement on Tariffs and Trade (GATT)** did a lot to reduce the problems that protectionism creates. This regulatory group is now known as the **World Trade Organization (WTO)**. The WTO was established during GATT's 1986–94 Uruguay Round and effectively replaced GATT in 1995. During the 50-plus years of GATT/WTO, world trade exports increased by 6 per cent annually. With nearly 150 members (and around 30 more negotiating membership), the WTO member nations account for over 97 per cent of world trade. The WTO's decisions are made by their entire membership, and all participating governments must ratify agreements.

Through a series of trade negotiations (known as rounds) that set standards for how much countries are allowed to favour their own goods and services, the WTO has become a global referee for trade.[27] The objective of the WTO is to 'help trade flow smoothly, freely, fairly, and predictably'. With over three-quarters of its membership drawn from the world's poorer countries, negotiations in recent years have largely focused on issues concerning economic development.[28]

One important issue that the WTO tackles is the protection of copyright and patent rights. This protection will help firms prevent copied versions of software, books and music CDs from being sold in other countries. *Pirating* is a serious problem for many companies, as their profits are eroded by illegal sales. According to a senior Microsoft executive based in Asia, 'Piracy is clearly our number one competitor, and not only Microsoft's number one competitor but also a big impediment to the growth of the local software industry'.[29]

Groups of countries may also band together to promote trade among themselves and make it easier for member nations to compete elsewhere. These **economic communities** coordinate trade policies and ease restrictions on the flow of products and capital across their borders. Economic communities are important to marketers because they set policies in such areas as product content, package labelling and advertising regulations that influence strategic decisions when doing business in these areas (see Table 2.7).

An even larger American free trade zone may be in the making. While talks stalled in November 2005, there is still hope that the Free Trade Area of the Americas (FTAA) will eventually be a reality. If and when the parties reach an agreement, FTAA will include

Table 2.7
Economic communities that have now been created around the world; each economic community includes a number of countries.

- **South America** includes two economic communities: 1) Mercado Común del Sur, known as the Southern Common Market (MERCOSUR) and includes five countries; and 2) the Andean Community, which includes Bolivia, Columbia, Ecuador, Peru and Venezuela.
- **Central America** has the Central American Free Trade Agreement (CAFTA) that includes Costa Rica, the Dominican Republic, El Salvador, Guatemala, Honduras, Nicaragua, and the United States.
- **Africa** has the Common Market for Eastern and Southern Africa (COMESA), which includes 20 African countries.
- **Asia** has three groups: the Asia-Pacific Economy Cooperation (APEC) includes 22 countries, the Association of Southeast Asian Nations (ASEAN) includes 10 nations, and the South Asia Association for Regional Cooperation (SAPTA) includes seven countries.
- **Europe** has two economic communities: the Central European Free Trade Agreement (CEFTA) includes seven countries, and the European Union (EU) includes 27 members. The EU now represents 450 million consumers, 300 of whom use the euro as their currency.
- **North America** has the North American Free Trade Agreement (NAFTA), which includes the United States, Canada, and Mexico.

34 countries in North, Central, and South America with a population of 800 million and a combined output of equivalent to around €11 trillion.[30]

Protected Trade: Quotas, Embargoes and Tariffs

In some cases, a government adopts a policy of **protectionism** in which it enforces rules on foreign firms designed to give home companies an advantage. Many governments set **import quotas** on foreign goods to reduce competition for their domestic industries. Quotas are limitations on the amount of a product allowed to enter or leave a country. Quotas can make goods more expensive to a country's citizens because the absence of cheaper foreign goods reduces pressure on domestic firms to lower their prices. For example, Russia placed import quotas on meat products to protect its own meat production industry.[31]

An **embargo** is an extreme quota that prohibits specified foreign goods completely. In the 1990s many of the UK's trading partners in Europe placed an embargo on British beef due to the fear of contracting 'mad cow' disease (bovine spongiform encephalopathy – BSE). Governments also use **tariffs**, or taxes on imported goods, to give domestic competitors an advantage in the marketplace by making foreign competitors' goods more expensive than their own goods.

How Global Should a Global Marketing Strategy be?

Going global is not a simple task. As you have seen, understanding all the economic, legal and cultural differences around the world can be a difficult task. However, if a firm decides to expand beyond its home country, it must make important decisions about how to structure its business and whether to adapt its product marketing strategy to accommodate local needs. First, the company must decide on the nature of its commitment, including whether the company will partner with another firm or go it alone. Then it must make specific decisions about the marketing mix for a particular product or service. In this final section, we'll consider issues related to global strategy at these two levels: the company and the product.

Choosing a Market-Entry Strategy

Just like a romantic relationship, a firm deciding to go global must determine the level of commitment it is willing to make to operate in another country. This commitment can range from a casual involvement to a full-scale 'marriage'. At one extreme, the firm can simply export its products, while at the other extreme it can directly invest in another country by buying a foreign subsidiary or opening its own shops. The decision about the extent of commitment entails a trade-off between control and risk. Direct involvement gives the firm more control over what happens in the country, but risk also increases if the operation is not successful.

Let's review four strategies representing increased levels of involvement: exporting, contractual arrangements, strategic alliances and direct investment. Figure 2.6 summarises these.

Exporting

If a firm chooses to export, it must decide whether it will attempt to sell its products on its own or rely on intermediaries to represent it in the target country. These representatives are

Figure 2.6	Market-Entry Strategies
	Choosing a market-entry strategy is a critical decision for companies that want to go global. Choosing whether to operate the new venture versus sharing responsibility with organisations in the local market involves a trade-off between control and risk

specialists known as export merchants (including agents/distributors) who understand the local market and who can find buyers and negotiate terms.[32] An exporting strategy allows a firm to sell its products in global markets and cushions the firm against downturns in its domestic market. Because the firm actually makes the products at home, it is able to maintain control over design and production decisions.[33]

Sometimes, exporting is the best way to be successful in a foreign market. Frontier Foods Ltd has developed a thriving business exporting cheese to China, where wealthy Chinese consumers are developing an unprecedented taste for it. Because there is so little open farmland in China for large herds of dairy cows, China can't produce enough milk to sustain a domestic cheese industry. Hence, it is easier to import cheese than to make it in China.[34]

Contractual Agreements

The next level of commitment a firm can make to a foreign market is a contractual agreement with a company in that country to conduct some or all of its business there. These agreements can take several forms. Two of the most common are licensing and franchising.

In a **licensing** agreement, a firm (the licenser) gives another firm (the licensee) the right to produce and market its product in a specific country or region in return for royalties. Because the licensee produces the product in its home market, it can avoid many of the barriers to entry that the licenser would have encountered. However, the licenser also loses control over how the product is produced and marketed, so if the licensee does a poor job, this may tarnish the company's reputation. Licensers also have to accept the possibility that local licensees will alter its product to suit local tastes.

Franchising is a form of licensing that gives the franchisee the right to adapt an entire way of doing business in the host country. Again, there is a risk to the parent company if the franchisee does not use the same quality ingredients or procedures, so firms monitor these operations carefully. For example, in India, where Hindus do not eat beef, all McDonald's have vegetarian and non-vegetarian burger cooking lines and offer customers such vegetarian specialities as Pizza McPuff and McAloo Tikki (a spiced-potato burger).[35]

Strategic Alliances

Firms seeking an even deeper commitment to a foreign market can develop a **strategic alliance** with one or more domestic firms in the target country. These relationships often take the form of a **joint venture** whereby two or more firms create a new entity to allow the partners to pool their resources for common goals. Strategic alliances also allow companies easy access to new markets, especially because these partnerships often bring with them preferential treatment in the partner's home country.

Direct Investment

An even deeper level of commitment occurs when a firm expands internationally by buying a business outright in the host country. Instead of starting from scratch in its quest to become multinational, direct investment allows a foreign firm to take advantage of a domestic company's political know-how and market position in the host country. The Chinese appliance maker Haier recently chose this route when it became the first Chinese company to set up facilities in the United States to manufacture some of its 96 product lines ranging from refrigerators and water heaters to mobile phones and flat screen TVs.[36] Ownership gives a firm maximum freedom and control, and it can also overcome import restrictions. Direct investment also carries greater risk. Firms that own businesses in foreign countries could suffer losses of their investment if economic conditions deteriorate or if political instability leads to nationalisation or expropriation.

Born-Global Firms

The appeal of catering to a global market is so strong that it's even spawning a breed of start-up companies called **born-global firms**.[37] These are companies that deliberately try to sell their products in several countries from the moment they're created rather than taking the usual path of developing business in their local market and then slowly expanding into other countries. For example, Logitech International is a Swiss company that quite possibly made your computer mouse. In addition to having a US base the company has local subsidiaries in Switzerland, Taiwan and Hong Kong. The company has offices throughout major cities in Europe, Asia and North America, and subsidiaries in Switzerland, Taiwan and Hong Kong. In total the company employs over 4500 people worldwide. It's truly a 'born global' company.

Product-Level Decisions: Choosing a Marketing Mix Strategy

In addition to 'big picture' decisions about how a company will operate in other countries, managers must decide how to market the product in each country. The famous Four Ps – product, price, promotion and place – may need to be modified to suit local conditions. To what extent will the company need to adapt its marketing communications to the specific styles and tastes of each local market? Will the same product appeal to people there? Will it have to be priced differently? How does the company get the product into people's hands? Let's consider each of these questions in turn.

Standardisation versus Localisation

When top management makes a company-level decision to expand internationally, the firm's marketers have to answer a crucial question: How necessary is it to develop a customised marketing mix for each country – a localisation strategy? Gillette decided to offer the same products in all its markets – a standardisation strategy. In contrast, Procter & Gamble (P&G) adopted a localised strategy in Asia, where consumers like to experiment with different brands of shampoo. Most of P&G's shampoos sold in Asia are now packaged in single-use sachets to encourage people to try different kinds.[38]

So, which strategy is right? Advocates of standardisation argue that the world has become so small with tastes so homogenised that basic needs and wants are the same everywhere.[39] A focus on the similarities among cultures certainly is appealing. After all, if a firm didn't have to make any changes to its marketing strategy to compete in foreign countries, it would realise large economies of scale because it could spread the costs of product development and promotional materials over many markets. Reebok, realising this, created a new centralised product development centre to develop shoe designs that can easily cross borders.[40] Widespread, consistent exposure also helps create a global brand by forging a strong, unified image all over the world – Coca-Cola signs are visible on billboards throughout London or on metal roofs deep in the forests of Thailand.

In contrast, those in favour of localisation feel that the world is not that small and that products and promotional messages should be tailored to local environments. These marketers feel that each culture is unique and that each country has a national character – a distinctive set of behavioural and personality characteristics.[41]

Product Decisions

A firm seeking to sell a product in a foreign market has three choices: sell the same product in the new market, modify it for that market, or develop a brand-new product to sell there. Let's take a closer look at each possibility:

A **straight extension strategy** retains the same product for domestic and foreign markets. For generations, proper etiquette in Japan was for girls to bow and never raise their eyes to a man.[42] However, the new generation of Japanese women wants to look straight at you, showing their eyes and eyelashes. Japanese eyelashes are very short, so they have to be curled to show. To meet this need, L'Oréal introduced its Maybelline brand Wonder Curl that dramatically thickens and curls lashes as it is applied. The launch was such a success in Japan that local television news showed Japanese girls standing in queues to buy the product.

A **product adaptation strategy** recognises that in many cases people in different cultures do have strong and different product preferences. Sometimes these differences can be subtle yet important.

A **product invention strategy** means a company develops a new product as it expands to foreign markets. For example, firms that wish to market household appliances in Japan where apartments are very small by Western standards must design and manufacture smaller products. In some cases, a product invention strategy takes the form of *backward invention*. A firm may find it needs to offer a less complex product than it sells elsewhere, such as a manually operated sewing machine or a hand-powered clothes washer for people without access to a reliable source of electricity.

Promotion Decisions

Marketers must also decide whether it's necessary to modify their product promotions in a foreign market. Some firms endorse the idea that the same message will appeal to everyone around the world, while others feel the need to customise it. The 2006 FIFA World Cup was broadcast in 189 countries to one of the biggest global television audiences ever. This major event illustrates how different marketers make different decisions – even when they're creating ads to be run during the same game. MasterCard ran ads that appeared in 39 countries, so its ad agency came up with a spot called 'Fever', in which 100-odd fans from 30 countries appear cheering. There's no dialogue so it works in any language. At the end, the words 'Football fever. Priceless' appeared under the MasterCard logo. Gillette, in contrast, ran an ad in over 20 countries that it digitally altered to reflect local differences. The spot shows cheering fans, wearing the colours and carrying the flags of their national team. The colours were changed depending on the country where the ad was shown.[43]

Price Decisions

Costs associated with transportation, tariffs, differences in currency exchange rates and even bribes paid to local officials often make the product more expensive for the company to manufacture for foreign markets than in its home country. To ease the financial burden of tariffs on companies that import goods, some countries have established free trade zones. These are designated areas where foreign companies can store goods without paying taxes or customs duties until the goods are moved into the marketplace.

One danger of pricing too high is that competitors will find ways to offer their product at a lower price, even if they do this illegally. **Grey market goods** are items that are imported without the consent of the trademark holder. While grey market goods are not counterfeits, they may be different from authorised products in warranty coverage and compliance with local regulatory requirements.[44]

Another unethical and often illegal practice is **dumping**, in which a company prices its products lower than they are offered at home – often removing excess supply from home markets and keeping prices high there.

Distribution Decisions

Getting the product to consumers in a remote location is half the battle. Thus, establishing a reliable distribution system is essential if a marketer is to succeed in a foreign market. Marketers used to dealing with a handful of large wholesalers or retailers may have to rely instead on thousands of small shops or distributors, some of whom transport goods to remote rural areas in a primitive fashion. In less developed countries, marketers may run into problems finding a way to package, refrigerate or store goods for long periods of time.

Even the retailing giant Wal-Mart has occasionally stumbled at going global. When Wal-Mart attempted to ease its entry into the German market by buying local retailers, it underestimated the problems it would face in dealing with local distributors. When the chain tried to force the distributors to switch from supplying individual shops to utilising Wal-Mart's new centralised warehouse system, the distributors refused and left Wal-Mart with empty shelves. Wal-Mart has had to work hard to understand local business cultures and to work more closely with suppliers.[45]

To summarise what we've discussed in this chapter, business planning, a key element of a firm's success, occurs in several different stages. Strategic planning takes place at both the corporate and the SBU level in large firms and in a single stage in smaller businesses. Marketing planning, one of the functional planning areas, comes next. Operational planning ensures proper implementation and control of the marketing plan.

Now that you've learned the basics of marketing strategy and read the advice, read 'Real People, Real Decisions' to see which strategy Philippe Garnier selected to develop the business for Hilton Hotels.

Real People, Real Decisions

How it worked out at Hilton

Option 3, engage with new distributors in the market such as Expedia, Lastminute.com and Opodo, was selected. This was because there had been significant growth in new website providers such as Expedia, Lastminute.com, Orbitz, Opodo and HRS over the last decade which were all signed up by Hilton. As they started to deliver volume, it allowed Hilton to be more forceful with existing distributors in moving over to the new contracts. In addition, the refusal of Hilton to do business with a handful of operators soon became known in the industry and this had the effect of making other distributors more amenable to Hilton's new contract. By adopting a two-pronged

| Photo 2.6 | The Hilton in Manchester city centre. Source: Philippe Garnier |

| Photo 2.7 | The Hilton at Canary Wharf. Source: Philippe Garnier |

approach, it allowed Hilton to stagger the process and manage any lost booking for their hotels more effectively which resulted in fewer complaints from them.

create their own full package. In particular, the fact that Hilton has fewer rooms pre-allocated to distributors means that it has more rooms which it can control and

The change has capitalised on the increasing consumer preference to use third party travel websites and given guests more choice in how they purchase a Hilton stay

The change has capitalised on the increasing consumer preference to use third party travel websites and given guests more choice in how they purchase a Hilton stay which is especially important for those who want to

manage revenue with its floating pricing strategy to make more money. In addition, Hilton now sells its rooms through more outlets thus achieving increased reach, which was another goal of the strategy.

Marketing Metrics

Measuring success: the marketing metrics Hilton used

The most important metric was the increase in traffic to Hilton's own website which has increased year on year by 48 per cent. The business they are now doing with the likes of Expedia is increasing 60 per cent year on year. Because most of the bookings are now done in real time via the central online booking system, there are fewer errors, it takes less time and therefore offers better customer service. The shift from faxing to e-booking has also freed up manpower which used to be used to enter

data manually from distributors to the Hilton system. Crucially, there has been an increase of 50 per cent in the profitability of Hilton's new distribution channels over the traditional distribution networks. Finally, as Hilton is now on every major online travel site, there has been a large increase in awareness of the brand, which achieves its goal of reaching a wider audience to be seen and booked.

Chapter Summary

Now that you have finished reading this chapter, you should be able to:

1. **Explain the strategic planning process.** Strategic planning is the managerial decision process in which top management defines the firm's purpose and specifies what the firm hopes to achieve over the next five or so years. For large firms that have a number of self-contained business units, the first step in strategic planning is for top management to establish a mission for the entire corporation. Top managers then evaluate the internal and external environment of the business and set corporate-level objectives that guide decision making within each individual SBU. In small firms that are not large enough to have separate SBUs, strategic planning simply takes place at the overall firm level. For companies with several different SBUs, strategic planning also includes making decisions about how to allocate resources across these businesses to ensure growth for the whole organisation and developing growth strategies.

2. **Describe the steps in marketing planning.** Marketing planning is one type of functional planning. Marketing planning begins with an evaluation of the internal and external environments. Marketing managers then set marketing objectives usually related to the firm's brands, sizes, product features, and other marketing mix-related elements. Next, marketing managers select the target market(s) for the organisation and decide what marketing mix strategies they will use. Product strategies include decisions about products and product characteristics that will appeal to the target market. Pricing strategies state the specific prices to be charged to channel members and final consumers. Promotion strategies include plans for advertising, sales promotion, public relations, publicity, personal selling and direct marketing used to reach the target market. Distribution strategies outline how the product will be made available to targeted customers when and where they want it. Once the marketing strategies are developed, they must be implemented. Control is the measurement of actual performance and comparison with planned performance. Maintaining control implies the need for concrete measures of marketing performance called *marketing metrics*.

3. **Understand how factors in the external business environment influence marketing strategies and outcomes.** The economic environment refers to the economic health of a country that may be gauged by its gross domestic product and its economic infrastructure, its level of economic development, and its stage in the business cycle. Marketers use competitive intelligence to examine brand, product and discretionary income competition in the micro-environment and in the structure of the industry within the macro-environment. A country's political and legal environment includes laws and regulations of individual countries that affect business, international regulations developed by the World Trade Organization (WTO) and regional agreements among countries that form economic communities. In addition, marketers must understand the local political situation, the prospects for nationalisation or expropriation of foreign holdings, regulations such as local content rules, and labour and human rights regulations. Marketers also examine a country's socio-cultural environment including demographics, values, norms and customs, language and ethnocentricity.

4. **Explain operational planning.** Operational planning is done by first-line supervisors such as sales managers, marketing communication managers, and marketing research managers and focuses on the day-to-day execution of the marketing plan. Operational plans generally cover a shorter period of time and include detailed directions for the specific activities to be carried out, who will be responsible for them, and time lines for accomplishing the tasks.

5. **Explain the key role of implementation and control in marketing planning.** Any plan is only as good as its ability to actually be implemented. To ensure effective implementation, a marketing plan must include individual action plans, or programmes, that support the plan at the operational level. A template for documenting action plans

within a marketing plan is included as Table 2.6. Each action plan necessitates providing a budget estimate, schedule or timeline for its implementation, and appropriate metrics so that the marketer can monitor progress and act on discrepancies or variation from the plan. Sometimes variance from a plan requires shifting or increasing resources to make the plan work; other times, it requires changing the objectives of the plan to recognise changing conditions. The key is that marketing plans aren't written in stone, and marketers must be flexible enough to make such changes when warranted.

6. **Discuss some of the important aspects of an organisation's internal environment.** The internal environment includes the controllable elements inside an organisation that influence how well the organisation operates, including the firm's technologies, its physical facilities, its financial stability, its reputation, the quality of its products and services, and its employees. Ultimately, much of the internal environment of a firm is related to its corporate culture.

7. **Explain how countries seek to protect local industries by establishing roadblocks to foreign companies and by bonding together into economic communities.** Some governments adopt policies of protectionism with rules designed to give home companies an advantage. Such policies may include trade quotas, embargoes, or tariffs that increase the costs of foreign goods. The World Trade Organization works to reduce such protectionism and encourage free trade. Many countries have come together to form economic communities to promote free trade.

8. **Explain how factors in the external business environment influence marketing strategies and outcomes.** The economic environment refers to the economic health of a country that may be gauged by its gross domestic product and its economic infrastructure, its level of economic development, and its stage in the business cycle. Marketers use competitive intelligence to examine brand, product and disposable income competition in the micro-environment and in the structure of the industry within the macro-environment. A country's political and legal environment includes laws and regulations of individual countries that affect business, international regulations developed by the World Trade Organization and regional agreements among countries that form economic communities. In addition, marketers must understand the local political situation, the prospects for nationalisation or expropriation of foreign holdings, regulations such as local content rules, and labour and human rights regulations. Marketers also examine a country's socio-cultural environment including demographics, values, norms and customs, language and ethnocentricity.

9. **Explain the strategies that a firm can use to enter global markets.** Different foreign market – entry strategies represent varying levels of commitment for a firm. Exporting of goods entails little commitment but allows little control over how products are sold. Contractual agreements such as licensing or franchising allow greater control. With strategic alliances through joint ventures, commitment increases. Finally, the firm can choose to invest directly by buying an existing company or starting a foreign subsidiary in the host country.

10. **What are the arguments for standardisation versus localisation of marketing strategies in global markets?** Firms that operate in two or more countries can choose to standardise their marketing strategies by using the same approach in all countries or choose to localise by adopting different strategies for each market. The firm needs to decide whether to sell an existing product, change an existing product, or develop a new product. In many cases, the promotional strategy must be tailored to fit the needs of consumers in another country. The product may need to be priced differently, especially if income levels are not the same in the new market. Finally, different methods of distribution may be needed, especially in countries lacking a solid infrastructure that provides adequate transportation, communications, and storage facilities.

Key Terms

Chapter Review

 ## Marketing Concepts: Testing Your Knowledge

1. What is strategic functional and operational planning? How does strategic planning differ at the corporate and the SBU levels?

2. What is a mission statement? What is a SWOT analysis? What role do these play in the planning process?

3. What is a strategic business unit (SBU)? How do firms use the Boston Consulting Group model for portfolio analysis in planning for their SBUs?

4. Describe the four business growth strategies: market penetration, product development, market development and diversification.

5. Explain the steps in the marketing planning process.

6. How does operational planning support the marketing plan?

7. What are the elements of a formal marketing plan?

8. What is an action plan? Why are action plans such an important part of marketing planning? Why is it so important for marketers to break the implementation of a marketing plan down into individual elements through action plans?

9. What is return on marketing investment (ROMI)? How does considering marketing as an investment instead of an expense affect a firm?

10. Give several examples of marketing metrics. How might a marketer use each metric to track progress of some important element of a marketing plan?

11. What is corporate culture? What are some ways that the corporate culture of one organisation might differ from that of another? How does corporate culture affect marketing decision making?

12. Describe the market conditions that influence a firm's decision to enter foreign markets.

13. What is protectionism? Explain import quotas, embargoes and tariffs.

14. Explain how GDP, the categories of economic development and the business cycle influence marketers' decisions in entering global markets.

15. What are a monopoly, an oligopoly, monopolistic competition and pure competition?

16. What aspects of the political and legal environment influence a firm's decision to enter a foreign market?

17. Why do marketers need to understand these environments in a global marketplace?

18. What is ethnocentricity? How does ethnocentricity affect a firm that seeks to enter a foreign market?

19. How is a firm's level of commitment related to its level of control in a foreign market? Describe the four levels of involvement that are options for a firm: exporting, contractual agreements, strategic alliances and direct investment.

20. What are the arguments for standardisation of marketing strategies in the global marketplace? What are the arguments for localisation? What are some ways a firm can standardise or localise its marketing mix?

Marketing Concepts: Discussing Choices and Ethical Issues

1. The Boston Consulting Group matrix identifies products as stars, cash cows, question marks and dogs. Do you think this is a useful way for organisations to examine their businesses? What are some examples of product lines that fit in each category?

2. In this chapter we talked about how firms do strategic, functional and operational planning. Yet some firms are successful without formal planning. Do you think planning is essential to a firm's success? Can planning ever hurt an organisation?

3. Most planning involves strategies for growth. But is growth always the right direction to pursue? Can you think of some organisations that should have contraction rather than expansion as their objective? Do you know of any organisations that have planned to get smaller rather than larger in order to be successful?

4. When most people think of successful marketing, internal firm culture doesn't immediately come to mind as a contributing factor. What are some reasons a firm's corporate culture is important to the capability to do good marketing? Give some examples of what you consider to be a good corporate culture for marketing.

5. Most marketers today feel pressure to measure (quantify) their level of success in marketing planning. Is it easy to measure marketing's success (compared with, say, measuring the success of a firm's financial management or production quality)? Explain your viewpoint.

6. The World Trade Organization seeks to eventually remove all barriers to world trade. Do you think this will ever be a reality? What do you think are the positive and negative aspects of a totally free marketplace? Which countries will win and which will lose in such a world?

7. In recent years, terrorism and other types of violent activities around the globe have made the global marketplace seem very unsafe. How concerned should firms with international operations be about such activities? Should these firms consider abandoning some global markets? How should firms weigh their concerns about terrorism against the need to help the economies of developing countries? Would avoiding countries such as those in the Middle East make good sense in terms of economic profit? What about in terms of social profit?

Marketing Practice: Applying What You've Learned

1. Assume that you are the marketing director for a small firm that manufactures educational toys for children. Your boss, the company president, has decided to develop a mission statement. He's admitted that he doesn't know much about developing a mission statement and has asked that you help guide him in this process. Write a memo outlining what exactly a mission statement is, why firms develop such statements, how firms use mission statements, and your thoughts on what the firm's mission statement might be.

2. As a marketing student, you know that large firms often organise their operations into a number of strategic business units (SBUs). A university might develop a similar structure in which different academic schools or departments are seen as separate businesses. Working with a group of four to six classmates, consider how your university might divide its total academic units into separate SBUs. What would be the problems with implementing such a plan? What would be the advantages and disadvantages for students and for faculty? Present your analysis of university SBUs to your class.

3. An important part of planning is a SWOT analysis, understanding an organisation's strengths, weaknesses, opportunities and threats. Choose a business in your community with which you are familiar. Develop a brief SWOT analysis for that business.

4. As an employee of a business consulting firm that specialises in helping people who want to start small businesses, you have been assigned a client who is interested in introducing a new concept in health clubs – one that offers its customers both the usual exercise and weight training opportunities and certain related types of medical assistance such as physical therapy, a weight loss physician and diagnostic testing. As you begin thinking about the potential for success for this client, you realise that developing a marketing plan is going to be essential. In a role-playing situation, present your argument to the client as to why she needs to invest in formal marketing planning.

5. Assume that your firm is interested in the global market potential for a chain of coffee shops in the following countries: Italy, the UK and the Netherlands. You recognise that an understanding of the external environments in each of these potential markets is essential. First, decide which environmental factors are most important to your business. Then, use your library to gather information about the environments of each of these countries. Finally, tell how the differences among the environments might affect marketing strategies for coffee shops.

6. Although most large firms have already made the decision to go global, many small to medium-sized firms are

only now considering such a move. Consider a small firm that manufactures gas barbecue grills.

a. What type of market entry strategy (exporting, contractual agreement, strategic alliance or direct investment) do you feel would be best for the firm? Why?

b. How would you recommend that the firm implement the strategy? That is, what type of product, price, promotion and distribution strategies would you suggest? What role can the internet play?

 # Marketing Miniprojects: Learning by Doing

The purpose of this miniproject is to gain an understanding of marketing planning through actual experience.

1. Select one of the following for your marketing planning project:
   - yourself (in your search for a career);
   - your university;
   - a specific department in your university.
2. Next, develop the following elements of the marketing planning process:
   - a mission statement;
   - a SWOT analysis;
   - objectives;
   - a description of the target market(s);
   - a positioning strategy;
   - a brief outline of the marketing mix strategies – the product, pricing, distribution, and promotion strategies – that satisfy the objectives and address the target market.
3. Prepare a brief outline of a marketing plan using the template provided on the book's website as a guide.

The purpose of this second mini-project is to begin to develop an understanding of a culture other than your own and how customer differences lead to changes in the ways marketing strategies and socially responsible decision making can be implemented in that culture.

1. As part of a small group, select a country you would like to know more about and a product you think could be successful in that market. As a first step, gather information about the country. Many campuses have international students from different countries. If possible, find a fellow student from the country and talk with him or her about the country. You will probably also wish to investigate other sources of information, such as books and magazines found in your library, or access information from the web.

2. Prepare a summary of your findings that includes the following:
   a. An overall description of the country, including such factors as its history, economy, religions, and so on, that might affect marketing of the product you have selected;
   b. A description of the cultural values and business ethics dominant in the country;
   c. The current status of this product in the country;
   d. Your recommendations for a product strategy (product design, packaging, brand name, price and so on);
   e. Your recommendations for promotional strategies.
   f. A discussion of the ethical and social responsibility issues present in the recommendations you have made.

Real People, Real Surfers

Exploring the Web

Visit the home pages of one or more firms you are interested in. Follow the links to find out about the company's products, pricing, distribution, and marketing communications strategies. Do a search of the web for other information about the company. Based on your findings, answer the following questions:

1. What is the organisation's business? What is the overall purpose of the organisation? What does the organisation hope to achieve?

2. What customers does the business want to serve?

3. What elements of the web page specifically reflect the business of the organisation? How is the web page designed to attract the organisation's customers?

4. Do you think the marketing strategies and other activities of the firm are consistent with its mission? Why do you feel this way?

5. Develop a report based on your findings and conclusions about the firm. Present your report to your class.

Assume that you are the director of marketing for a firm that manufactures small household appliances such as mixers, coffee makers, toasters and so forth. You are considering entering _____ (the country you have selected). You recognise that businesses must carefully weigh up opportunities for global marketing. Use the internet to gather information that would be useful in your firm's decision.

Write a report that answers the following questions:

1. What are the physical characteristics of the country (geography, weather, natural resources and so forth)?

2. Describe the economy of the country.

3. What is the country's investment climate?

4. What trade regulations will your firm face in entering the country?

5. What is the country's political climate? Are there obvious political risks?

6. Based on this information, what overall strategy do you recommend for your firm – exporting, a contractual agreement, a strategic alliance or direct investment?

7. What are your specific recommendations for implementing the strategy?

As a final part of your report, describe the websites you used to gather this information. Which sites were most useful and why?

Now, take a look at the website at www.pearsoned.co.uk/solomon to see some videos from YouTube relating to aspects of this chapter.

Also at www.pearsoned.co.uk/solomon, try some analysis and calculations yourself by looking up the marketing metrics exercise called Profit Objectives to learn how to model the financial effects of marketing investments across any industry.

Marketing Plan Exercise

The airline industry has experienced a lot of turbulence in recent years that inhibits its ability to plan for the future. Pick your favourite airline and help it plan by doing the following:

1. See if you can locate its mission statement, then develop a few marketing objectives that you believe would nicely support it.

2. Take a look at Figure 2.4, the product – market growth matrix, and the accompanying discussion. How might your chosen airline go about developing some strategies in each of the boxes: penetration, market development, product development and diversification. (Hint: Remember that airlines are in

the business of providing a service. The strategies you come up with will probably entail adding new or modified services in their targeted markets.)

3. Considering the strategies you identified in question 2, identify some specific marketing metrics that are appropriate for use in control.

4. What are some important global marketing issues that one must be mindful of when developing a marketing plan? Why do these issues need to be considered separately from a firm's domestic plan?

Marketing in Action Case

Real decisions for the Apple iPhone

*T*ime magazine named it the Invention of the Year. Experts and consumers alike called it 'revolutionary'. Introduced in June 2007, the iPhone is Apple's internet-enabled multimedia mobile phone. In the first six months after Steve Jobs announced the planned launch of the iPhone at the Macworld Expo in January 2007, the invention was the subject of 11,000 print articles and 69 million hits on Google.

So why is the iPhone revolutionary? For starters, the iPhone is a quad-band mobile phone, thus having international calling capability. It is a portable media player or iPod and a web browser, thus accessing owners' email. It does text messaging, visual voice-mail and has local Wi-Fi connectivity. It's sleek, slim and has a multi-touch screen with virtual keyboard. The multi-touch screen technique means owners can expand or shrink the screen image by sliding the finger and the thumb apart or together. The iPhone offers owners three types of radio: mobile, Wi-Fi and Bluetooth. As an added benefit, one iPhone battery charge provides 8 hours of calls, 7 hours of video or 24 hours of music.

Indeed, the iPhone was the year's most desired gadget. Customers stood in line to be the first to own one. In fact, some more entrepreneurially minded customers bought more than one, convinced they could sell one at a profit and make enough to pay for the second!

Apple made the iPhone available to UK consumers through an alliance that made O_2 the exclusive carrier and under which O_2 subsidised the cost of the iPhone. To use an iPhone, customers had to sign an 18-month contract with O_2 for mobile and internet service. The price of the phone itself was £99 for the eight-gigabyte model.

> **The iPhone was the year's most desired gadget. Customers stood in line to be first to own one**

But in the US, consumers' love affair with the iPhone soon faced trouble. Just two months after the iPhone introduction, Apple dropped the price from $600 to $399, angering customers who had paid top price only two months before. And those customers immediately let Apple know of their dissatisfaction by phone, by email and on blogs. In response, Steve Jobs admitted that the company had abused its core customers and offered a $100 shop credit to early iPhone buyers.

Furthermore, UK consumers were not happy that they were restricted to O_2 with their iPhones. Soon after introduction, hackers posted directions on the internet for consumers to unlock the mobile service feature of their phone, allowing them to use the iPhone with any mobile service provider. Even though Apple was quick to warn consumers that unlocking the phone might damage the iPhone software, eventually making downloading with upgraded software impossible, unlocked phones continued to be available.

To make matters worse, various European countries have laws to protect consumers from being forced to buy something as a condition of buying a product, thus creating barriers for the global iPhone business. The courts in both France and Germany have refused to allow Apple to sell the iPhone locked to a long-term contract with a single mobile service supplier.

For Apple, the iPhone is the product of the future with plans for introducing software upgrades and newer versions to stimulate increased world sales. Steve Jobs is betting that the iPhone will enjoy the same success he has had with the iPod and with Apple computers. But for that success to materialise, Apple must carefully consider what long-term strategies are necessary to make the iPhone both popular and profitable.

Things to Think About

1. What are Apple's growth options in your country?
2. What factors are important in developing demand for the iPhone in your country?
3. What are the pros and cons of alternative growth strategies?
4. What decision(s) do you recommend?
5. What are some ways to implement your recommendation?

Sources: Katie Hafner and Brad Stone, 'iPhone Owners Crying Foul Over Price Cut', *New York Times*, 7 September 2007, http://www.nytimes.com/2007/09/07/technology/07apple.html; Times Topics, iPhone, http://topics.nytimes.com/top/reference/timestopics/subjects/i/iphone/index.html?8qa&scp=1-spot&sq=iphone&st=nyt; The Associated Press, 'Altered iPhones at Risk of Failure', *New York Times*, 25 September 2007, http://www.nytimes.com/2007/09/25/technology/25iphone.html?sq=iphone%20unlocked&st=nyt&scp=6&pagewanted=print; Victoria Shannon, 'Iphone Must Be offered Without Contract Restrictions, German Court Rules', *New York Times*, 21 November 2007, http://www.nytimes.com/2007/11/21/technology/21iphone.html?scp=3&sq=iphone+unlocked&st=nyt; David Pogue, 'The iPhone Matches Most of Its Hype', *New York Times*, 27 June 2007, http://www.nytimes.com/2007/06/27/technology/circuits/27pogue.html.

References

1. www.madd.org (accessed 30 May 2006).
2. 'Peru: Privatization Is Principal Policy for Attracting Foreign Investment', *Wall Street Journal*, 27 October, 1993, B7.
3. Keith Bradsher, 'Consumerism Grows in China, with Beijing's Blessing', *New York Times*, 1 December, 2003 www.bdachina.com/content/about/pressquotes/P1070443598/en?portal_skin=printable.
4. Michael Barbaro, 'Wal-Mart Offers Aid to Rivals', *New York Times*, 5 April 2006, Section C, page 1 at http://web.lexis-nexis.com/universe/document?_m=a65b59dd05c3bc4cd6408663bf954224&_docnum=5&wchp=dGLbVzb-zSkVb&_md5=9d53d563cc5228449eebb4a230887f3f
5. Deborah Ball, 'Lattes Lure Brits to Coffee; Tea Sales Fall as Starbucks Draws the Young', *The Wall Street Journal*, 20 October 2005, B1.
6. Sara Hope Franks, 'Overseas, It's What's Inside That Sells', *Washington Post National Weekly Edition*, 5–11 December 1994, 21.
7. William C. Symonds, 'Border Crossings,' *Business Week*, 22 November 1993, 40.
8. Adapted from Michael R. Solomon, *Consumer Behavior: Buying, Having, and Being* 7th ed. (Upper Saddle River, NJ: Prentice Hall, 2007).
9. David Carr, 'Romance, In *Cosmo*'s World, Is Translated in Many Ways', 26 May 2002, *New York Times*, sec. 1, p. 1, adapted from Michael R. Solomon, *Consumer Behavior: Buying, Having, and Being*, 6th ed. (Upper Saddle River, NJ: Prentice Hall, 2003).
10. Richard W. Pollay, 'Measuring the Cultural Values Manifest in Advertising', *Current Issues and Research in Advertising* 6 (1983), 71–92.
11. Deborah Ball, 'Women in Italy Like To Clean but Shun the Quick and Easy', *Wall Street Journal*, 25 April 2006, A1.
12. Daniel Goleman, 'The Group and the Self: New Focus on a Cultural Rift', 25 December 1990, at www.nyt.com, 37; Harry C. Triandis, 'The Self and Social Behavior in Differing Cultural Contexts', *Psychological Review* 96 (July 1989), 506; Harry C. Triandis *et al.*, 'Individualism and Collectivism: Cross-Cultural Perspectives on Self-Ingroup Relationships', *Journal of Personality and Social Psychology* 54 (February 1988), 323.
13. George J. McCall and J.L. Simmons, *Social Psychology: A Sociological Approach* (New York: Free Press, 1982).
14. Adapted from Solomon, *Consumer Behavior: Buying, Having, and Being,* 7th ed.
15. Patrick Barwise and John U. Farley, 'Which Marketing Metrics Are Used and Where?', *Working Paper Series*, Report No. 03-111 (Cambridge, MA: Marketing Science Institute, 2003).
16. Kerry A. Dolan, 'The Soda with Buzz', *Forbes*, 28 March 2005, 126.
17. Christina Binkley, 'Hotels "Go to the Matresses"; Marriott is Latest to Make Huge Bet on Better Bedding', *Wall Street Journal*, 25 January 2005, D1.
18. Pallovi Gogoi, 'Chipolte's IPO: One Hot Tamale', *Business Week Online,* 23 September 2005.

19. Gordon A. Wyner, 'Beyond ROI: Make Sure the Analytics Address Strategic Issues', *Marketing Management* 15 (May/June 2006), 8–9.

20. Nike, 'Nike Reports Second Quarter Earnings Up Nine Percent; Worldwide Futures Orders Increase Eight Percent', press release, 20 December 2001, www.nikebiz.com/media/n_q202.shtml.

21. Michael Barbaro, 'Cricket Anyone? Sneaker Makers on Fresh Turf', *The New York Times Online*, 28 January 2006.

22. 'World Trade in 2004 – Overview', www.wto.org/english/res_e/ststis_e/its2005_e/its05_overvoew_e.pdf.

23. World Trade Organization, 'Stronger Than Expected Growth Spurs Modest Trade Recovery', press release, 5 April 2004, at www.wto.org/english/news_e/pres04_e/pr373_e.htm.

24. 'Phillippines Implements Countertrade Program for Vietnamese Rice', *Asia Pulse*, 27 April 2005, at http://web.lexis-nexis.com/universe/document?_m=39eaf11285f8163c2b36a2ad0a15af9f&_docnum=3&wchp=dGLbVzb-zSkVb&_md5=8af529d535ea2a669565a8be3399ef0e.

25. www.usatoday.com/money/autos/2005-12-15-china-cars-usat5_x.htm.

26. Michael R. Czinkota and Masaaki Kotabe, 'America's New World Trade Order', *Marketing Management* 1 (3) (1992), 47–54.

27. World Trade Organization, 'The WTO in Brief' www.wto.org/english/thewto_e/whatis_e/inbrief_e/inbr02_e.htm.

28. Ibid.

29. Nic Hopkins, 'Software Piracy Microsoft's Big Threat', *CNN.com*, 7 February 2001 www.cnn.com/2001/WORLD/asiapcf/east/02/07/hongkong.microsoft.

30. Geri Smith, Elisabeth Malkin, Jonathan Wheatley, Paul Magnusson and Michael Arnds, 'Betting on Free Trade', *Business Week*, 23 April 2001, 60–62; Free Trade Area of the Americas, 'Antecedents of the FTAA Process' (accessed 20 March 2006), at www.ftaa-alca.org/View_e.asp#PREPARATORY; Johathan Wheatley, 'Bush and Lula Try to Paper Over Divisions Seen at Summit of Americas', *Financial Times*, 7 November 2005 http://web.lexis-nexis.com/universe/document?_m=621ddc7a6d8e970d0c1068f13f4da39b&_docnum=88&wchp=dGLbVzb-zSkVb&_md5=7dd29a69c250e36cf7a13cf6cf73539d.

31. 'Russia: Introduction of Mean Import Quotas' www.iet.ru/afe/english/apk/january03.pdf.

32. Alexander Hiam and Charles D. Schewe, *The Portable MBA in Marketing* (New York: John Wiley & Sons, 1992).

33. Harvey S. James Jr. and Murray Weidenbaum, *When Businesses Cross International Borders* (Westport, CT: Praeger, 1993).

34. Rebecca Buckman, 'China's Cheeseman Is No Longer Alone', 11 December 2003, at www.wsj.com.

35. Saritha Rai, 'Tastes of India in U.S. Wrappers', 29 April 2003, at www.nyt.com.

36. 'Haier's Global Ambitions Demand Flexible Advice', *Managing Intellectual Property*, February 2006, 1.

37. P.D. Harveston and P.S. Davis, 'Entrepreneurship and the Born Global Phenomenon: Theoretical Foundations and a Research Agenda', in *E-Commerce and Entrepreneurship: Research in Entrepreneurship and Management*, vol. 1, ed. John Butler (Information Age Publishing, 2001), 1–30; text adapted from www.campbell.berry.edu/faculty/pharveston/bornglobal.html.

38. Jeremy Kahn, 'The World's Most Admired Companies', *Fortune*, 26 October 1998, 206–16.

39. One of the most influential arguments for this perspective can be found in Theodore Levitt, 'The Globalization of Markets', *Harvard Business Review*, May–June 1983, 92–102.

40. Juliana Koranteng, 'Reebok Finds Its Second Wind as It Pursues Global Presence', *Advertising Age International*, January 1998, 18.

41. Terry Clark, 'International Marketing and National Character: A Review and Proposal for an Integrative Theory', *Journal of Marketing* 54 (October 1990), 66–79.

42. Richard C. Morais, 'The Color of Beauty', *Forbes*, 27 November 2000, 170–76.

43. Aaron O. Patrick, 'World Cup's Advertisers Hope One Size Fits All: Month-Long Tournament Sets Off Scramble to Reach Huge Global TV Audience', *The Wall Street Journal*, 28 March 2006, B7.

44. Better Business Bureau, 'Gray Market Goods' www.newyork.bbb.org/library/publications/subrep45.html.

45. Wendy Zellner, 'How Well Does Wal-Mart Travel?', *BusinessWeek*, 3 September 2001, 82(2), 82–4.

Chapter 3
Marketing Research

Meet Helen Armstrong,
Client Services Director of Research International in London

Q & A with Helen Armstrong

Career high?
Doing all the research for the global launch of Colgate's Total toothpaste

A job-related mistake you wish you hadn't made?
Travelling to Seville on a bank holiday to do ad testing work for Pepsi and the testing equipment broke

Your Hero?
No hero, but my anti-hero is Margaret Thatcher

Motto to live by?
Live for today

What drives me?
Curiosity

My management style is . . .
Inclusive and involving

Don't do this when interviewing me . . .
Tell me that women's purchase of luxury goods is not rational

A Client Services Director working across business sectors, Helen is highly experienced, having spent more than 20 years in product development, segmentation and brand strategy. She's worked both in the UK and internationally in a wide variety of areas including agricultural and construction equipment, IT, food service, FMCG, alcoholic beverages, finance and luxury goods.

Helen is experienced in both qualitative and quantitative research techniques with particular application in international markets. She has specialist experience in conducting and applying segmentation studies in an international context and will aid the effective management and analysis of segment solutions. She is a full member of the Market Research Society and heads RI UK's segmentation expert forum.

Real People, Real Decisions
Decision time at the World Gold Council

The World Gold Council (WGC) (www.gold.org) is a commercial marketing organisation funded by the world's leading gold mining companies with a remit to stimulate demand for gold in all its forms in regions around the world. The key gold jewellery markets are the United States, Italy, India, Saudi Arabia and China. However, prior to 2003 the gold market was in decline in most regions around the world, with gold jewellery commoditised and sold by length and gold investment seen as a short-term option.

In late 2001 WGC identified the need to do some in-depth fundamental market research to understand what consumers thought about gold in general and specifically to understand the functional and emotional benefits of owning gold and what were the barriers to buying more gold. This research was also designed to help to define what makes gold different in the eyes of consumers, i.e. its unique selling propositions (USPs). The research was to be used to segment gold consumers and subsequently to develop more appropriate and targeted communications campaigns around gold. Helen Armstrong, who was then working for GfK Roper Consulting, met with the World Gold Council (WGC) to understand the organisation's needs and explore the market research options. Helen suggested a combination of qualitative interviews and focus groups followed by a large quantitative survey in all the major markets. There were challenges with qualitative research in these markets, such as multi-language requirements when researching in India and issues with interviewing females in Saudi Arabia which requires an all-female research team. However, the main issue, and far more important than any local research issues, was deciding who should actually be interviewed, which had many implications for the study. Should the study be limited to buyers and receivers of gold, or should it encompass all women whether they buy or not?

Helen Considers her Options . . .

Option 1 Focus on existing purchasers of gold only

In this option, the qualitative personal interviews would focus only on women who had purchased gold in the past year. Six personal interviews and accompanied shops were proposed and four two-hour focus groups per country

(United States, Italy, India, Saudi Arabia and China). Personal interviews were important as some of the motivations for purchasing gold are very personal and women might not feel comfortable talking about these in a focus group, hence the need to use both approaches. Focusing on existing gold purchases also allowed some accompanied shopping interviews to be done to look at their decision-making processes when shopping for gold. This was to be followed in each country by 750 face-to-face in-home questionnaire surveys of about one hour to get a quantitative assessment of the functional and emotional benefits of buying or receiving gold. The advantages of this option and only researching gold users is that there was thought to be more potential in getting existing purchasers, who already like gold, to purchase more. It would provide a deeper understanding of existing users' perception and allow a more in-depth segmentation of them. The time and cost was also much less than alternative options, coming in at around £350,000.

Option 2 Include stakeholders and opinion leaders in the sample as well as gold purchasers

In this option, the idea was to research a broader sample of consumers to include everyone who was involved in buying or receiving jewellery, whether gold or not. In addition to focusing on purchasers, it was felt that the views of internal industry stakeholders such as WGC heads from their important markets and opinion leaders who were experts from the fashion industry, design and fashion media would be important to the overall learning and success of the study. This involved nine one-hour telephone interviews with internal stakeholders and five face-to-face one-hour interviews with opinion leaders in the five markets. The advantages of this option were that it provided information about other competing forms of luxury goods from the main competitive set. In addition, understanding non-buyers' perceptions of gold might uncover some of the barriers as to why they were not buying. However it had significant implications for the research design and the outcome. It was not possible to mix buyers and non-buyers of gold in the same focus group because strong preferences for buying or not buying gold can influence participants. The disadvantage of this option was that it would mean an increase in the number of personal interviews to 12 and 8 focus groups per country and you cannot do accompanied shopping trips with non-buyers.

There were also potential implications for the sample size and the length of interviews. It may increase the number of interviewees for the quantitative part, (from 750 to 1000–1250) in order to have sufficient numbers for a segmentation study involving the additional non-buyers. This would add considerable time and expense to the tune of £400,000.

Option 3 Broaden the study to include all luxury goods consumers whether they buy jewellery or not

In this option, the stakeholder and opinion leader interviews would be retained, but the consumer population to be studied would include everyone, *whether they bought jewellery or not*. The advantage to this option is that it would allow the research to examine the total market of buyers and potential buyers, which was particularly important in China where gold jewellery purchasing at that time was very limited. The option would provide a better understanding as to why and where consumers currently got some of the emotional and functional benefits from buying competing products to gold, such as holidays, fashion accessories, electronics or other luxury items. It would also explore barriers to buying jewellery as a category and thus tap into consumers who might be in the market, but did not yet buy gold. However, this would mean that many people in the sample might not have experience of buying or receiving gold and thus the research could potentially focus on the perceptions of the majority of non-buyers. Also sample sizes needed to be increased (from 750 to 1000–1250) to provide sufficient numbers of buyers and non-buyers to do a quantitative segmentation study and thus the cost of this approach was in the region of £500,000. Another potential disadvantage of this broader sample structure was that with a wider sample definition of the target population, many more segments might be identified which might lead to complex and more expensive communication programmes to meet the needs of each segment.

Put yourself in Helen's shoes. Which option do you think is best and why?

Objectives

When you finish reading this chapter, you will understand and be able to identify and evaluate:

1 The role of the marketing information system and the marketing decision support system in marketing decision making

2 The marketing research process

3 The differences among exploratory, descriptive and causal research techniques available to marketers

4 The different types of data-collection methods and types of consumer samples that researchers use

5 The growing use of online research

Knowledge Is Power

In Chapter 1, we talked about how marketing is a decision process in which marketing managers determine the strategies that will help the organisation meet its long-term objectives. In Chapter 2, we said that successful planning meant that managers made good decisions for guiding the organisation. But how do marketers make good decisions? How do they go about developing marketing objectives, selecting a target market, positioning (or repositioning) their product, and developing product, price, promotion and place strategies?

The answer is *information*. Information is the fuel that runs the marketing engine. To make good decisions, marketers must have information that is collectable and accessible as well as accurate, up to date and relevant. Information is also indispensable for effective Customer Relationship Management (CRM). Only with access to the best possible information are companies able to identify truly valuable customers and satisfy them on a long-term basis. As you'll see in Figure 3.1, we are now in the second section of the book, 'Understanding Consumers' Value Needs'. Part of the marketer's role in understanding these needs is to conduct *marketing research* in order to identify them. In this chapter, we will discuss some of the tools that marketers use to get that information. In the chapters that follow, we will look at consumer behaviour, at how and why organisations buy, and then at how marketers sharpen their focus through target marketing strategies. But first, let's talk about the marketing information system.

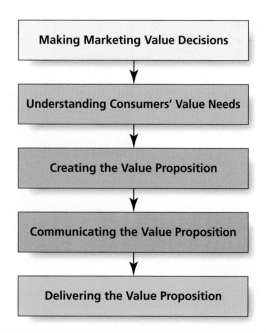

Making Marketing Value Decisions
↓
Understanding Consumers' Value Needs
↓
Creating the Value Proposition
↓
Communicating the Value Proposition
↓
Delivering the Value Proposition

Figure 3.1   Making and Delivering Value

 ## The Marketing Information System

www.pearsoned.co.uk/solomon

Objective

1

The role of the marketing information system and the marketing decision support system in marketing decision making

One of the ways in which firms collect information is through a **marketing information system (MkIS)**. The MkIS is a process that first determines what information marketing managers need and then gathers, sorts, analyses, stores and distributes relevant and timely marketing information to system users. Another possible definition comes from the American Marketing Association, which describes an MkIS as 'a set of procedures and methods for the regular, planned collection, analysis, and presentation of information for use in making marketing decisions'.[1] As you can see in Figure 3.2, the MkIS system includes three important components:

- Four types of data;
- Computer hardware and software to analyse that data and to create reports;
- Information and the decision makers who use it.

Where exactly do all the data come from? Information to feed the system comes from four major sources: these are internal company data, marketing intelligence data on competition and other elements in the firm's business environment, information gathered through marketing research and acquired databases.

The data are stored and accessed through computer hardware and software. Based on an understanding of managers' needs, MkIS personnel generate a series of regular reports for various system users. For example, supermarket chain Tesco gains most of the market insights through information from its Tesco Clubcard loyalty scheme. The research specialist firm Dunnhumby, which is responsible for Tesco's database management, receives five billion bits of information per week through the Clubcards and is able to convert the data into regular, valuable reports about sales figures, customer preferences and shopping patterns.

Let's take a closer look at each of the four different data sources for the MkIS.

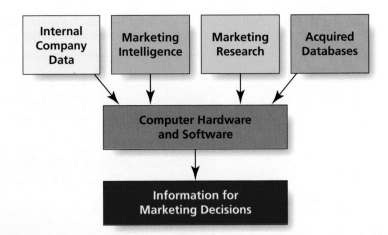

Figure 3.2	The Marketing Information System
	A firm's marketing information system (MkIS) stores and analyses data from a variety of sources and turns the data into information for making marketing decisions.

1. Internal Company Data

The internal company data system uses information from within the company to produce reports on the results of sales and marketing activities. Internal company data consists of a firm's internal records of sales, basic information which every company possesses – information such as which customers buy which products in what quantities and at what intervals, what items are in stock and which ones are back-ordered because they are out of stock, when items were shipped to the customer, and what items have been returned because they are defective.

Often, an MkIS allows salespeople and sales managers in the field to access internal records through a company intranet. An **intranet** is an internal corporate communications network that uses internet technology to link company departments, employees and databases. Intranets are secured so that only authorised employees have access. When the MkIS is made available to managers, they can serve their customers better by having immediate access to information on pricing, inventory levels, production schedules, shipping dates, and the customer's sales history.

Marketing Metrics

BP Lubricants intranet-based data repository

Global oil company BP has a lubricants division active in 60 countries. Maintaining an accurate picture of these markets is challenging. Historically, marketing data had been manually transcribed onto spreadsheets and then manually consolidated into one master spreadsheet, often with the need for re-keying of data or cutting and pasting. The company decided to standardise its global marketing data and as a first step defined and agreed a set of data standards. Next it created a standard data collection system that could be used by all 60 countries. Then a set of macro programs was written that loaded the country data into a master spreadsheet that was hosted on the corporate intranet. Users globally can access a set of reports from their web browsers that enable them to compare and rank their performance against that in the 59 other countries; they can also press a button that automatically generates a PowerPoint slide show with the latest figures.

But equally important – because salespeople and sales managers are the ones in daily direct contact with customers – their reports are entered directly into the system via the company intranet. This means the reports can provide an important source of information to upper management on changes in sales patterns or new sales opportunities.

From the internal company data system, marketing managers can get daily or weekly sales data for a brand or product line. They can also get monthly sales reports which help them to measure progress toward sales goals and market share objectives. For example, managers and buyers at many large retailers use up-to-the-minute sales information obtained from shop cash registers around the country so they can detect problems with products, promotions, and even the firm's distribution system.

2. Marketing Intelligence

As we saw in Chapter 2, to make good decisions marketers need to have information about the marketing environment. Possessing up-to-date and relevant information is absolutely crucial for successful knowledge management which is seen as a vital tool for achieving competitive advantage. Thus, a second important element of the MkIS is the **marketing intelligence system**, a method by which marketers get information about everyday happenings in the marketing environment. The name intelligence may suggest cloak-and-dagger spy activities, in reality nearly all the information companies need about their environment – including the competitive environment – is available by monitoring everyday sources: newspapers, trade publications, or simple observations of the marketplace. And because salespeople are the ones 'in the trenches' every day, talking with customers, distributors and prospective customers, they can provide valuable information as well.

In recent years, the web has become a major source of marketing intelligence. Tremendous amounts of information are available on company web pages, including those of competitors, through news sources from around the globe, through government reports, and on trade association sites. The ease of accessing and searching the web and individual sites makes the internet an attractive source of marketing intelligence.

Sometimes companies engage in specific activities to gain intelligence. For example, retailers often hire 'mystery shoppers' to visit their shops and those of their competitors posing as customers to see how people are treated. (Imagine being paid to shop for a living!) When McDonald's set up a quality improvement scheme, its managers sent mystery shoppers to visit restaurants on a regular basis to collect information about the shop environments and service. Other information may come from speaking to organisational buyers about competing products, attending trade shows, or simply purchasing competitors' products.

Marketing managers may use marketing intelligence data to predict fluctuations in sales due to economic conditions, political issues, and events that heighten consumer awareness or to forecast the future so that they will be on top of developing trends. For example, knowledge

| Photo 3.1 | L'Oreal was able to forecast the popularity of skincare products for men.
Source: The Advertising Archives |

Marketing Metrics

Nokia Consumer Insights

World leader in mobile communications, Nokia, has a Consumer Insights division of 30 people. It was established in 2001, and absorbed the old Market Research function. Its remit includes product conception and design and interpreting attitudes and behaviour of consumers. They try to track and forecast changes in long-term consumer motivation. Their aim is to provide internal consultancy to Nokia's managers. Market research firms are retained for their data collection and tabulation roles, but are not expected to provide added value. 'They lack real understanding of Nokia's business needs and where the company is heading' comments Jane Hanford, head of brand and customer understanding.

of trends in consumer preferences, driven by the younger teen generation, prompted Avon to create an entirely new brand of cosmetics called Mark. While traditional Avon salesladies (and buyers) are 30+, Mark is sold and bought by tweens, teens and 20-somethings. The cosmetic industry, for example, is currently experiencing a new trend concerning beauty and skincare products for men. Firms like Biotherm or L'Oréal which were able to forecast this trend gained an extraordinary advantage as they could launch profitable product lines and attract customers before the competition became aware of the trend.

Indeed, some marketing researchers, known as *futurists*, specialise in predicting consumer trends to come. They try to forecast changes in lifestyles that will affect the wants and needs of customers in the coming years by engaging in scenario planning. Futurists try to imagine different **scenarios**, or possible future situations, that might occur and assign a level of probability to each.

A scenario can be shaped by a number of key outcomes. For example, deregulation laws could shape the future of the banking or telecommunications industries. In those cases, a futurist might develop different scenarios for different levels of deregulation, including forecasts assuming no deregulation, moderate deregulation, and complete deregulation. Each scenario allows marketers to consider the impact of different marketing strategies and to come up with plans based on which outcomes they consider are most likely to happen. No one can predict the future with certainty, but it's better to make an educated guess than no guess at all and be caught totally unprepared. Even something as seemingly simple as accurately predicting the price of a gallon of petrol next year greatly affects business success.

In some cases, companies are enlisting consumers' help to predict the success or failure of different products. The online stock exchange Ball Street (http://ball-street.ftd.de/view/) is a virtual project from the *Financial Times Germany* and Dresdner Bank which was launched for the world cup in 2006, where football fans could trade stocks, for example of national teams, and by doing so forecast the results of the tournament. The predictions of Ball Street turned out to be quite precise and were of great interest for sponsors and investors. The stock exchange game was so popular that it was kept alive after the world cup and now predicts the German premier league.[3]

Of course, collecting marketing intelligence data is just the beginning. An effective MkIS must include procedures to ensure that the marketing intelligence data are translated and combined with internal company data and other marketing data to create useful reports for marketing managers.

3. Marketing research

Marketing research refers to the process of collecting, analysing and interpreting data about customers, competitors, and the business environment to improve marketing effectiveness. It is defined by the American Marketing Association (AMA) as the function that links consumer, customer and public to the marketer through information. Although marketing intelligence data are collected continuously to keep managers abreast of happenings in the marketplace, marketing research is called for when unique information is needed for specific decisions. Whether their business is selling cool clothes to teens or coolant to factories, firms succeed by knowing what customers want, when they want it, where they want it – and what competing firms are doing about it. In other words, the better a firm is at obtaining valid marketing information, the more successful it will be. Therefore, virtually all companies rely on some form of marketing research, though the amount and type of research they conduct varies dramatically. Although marketing research offers many potential benefits, a firm must not lose sight of the costs involved. Conducting effective marketing research can be very expensive and time consuming and therefore should not be undertaken in every case. If a company faces serious budget deficits, if managers cannot agree what information they need for decision making, or if poor timing would result in irrelevant research results, it is very likely that costs of the research outweigh its benefits. A careful cost-benefit analysis will therefore help the company to find out whether marketing research can be beneficial in a certain situation or not. In general, marketing research available in an MkIS include syndicated research reports and custom research reports.

Syndicated research is general research collected by firms on a regular basis, then sold to other firms. The QScores Company, for instance, reports on the familiarity and appeal of over 1700 celebrity performers and provides information about how they are being perceived by customers. The obtained research can serve as a decision basis for companies that are interested in using a performer in their advertising. The services of the QScores Company include ratings of cartoon characters, sports stars and even deceased celebrities, so that the client could, for example, gain insights into the demographic appeal of Elvis Presley and Marilyn Monroe and determine whether they would be a valuable input for an advertising campaign.[4] The Broadcasters' Audience Research Board (BARB), for example, conducts research on the estimated number of people watching certain television shows and sells this audience data to the TV channels and advertisers.[5] Another example is the British Marketing Research Bureau (BMRB), which conducts a variety of syndicated research ranging from social policy and public interest research, environmental and climate change research to reports on in-store advertising, giving information about customer perceptions, shopping behaviours and the most useful media to use for advertising.

Alternative examples of syndicated research techniques are consumer panels, where members receive periodic invitations to participate in a survey, or retail audits, which are the continuous monitoring of product flows from supplier to consumer. As valuable as it may be, syndicated research doesn't provide all the answers to marketing questions because the information collected typically is broad but shallow; it gives good insights about general trends, such as who is watching what television shows or what brand of perfume is hot this year.

Often firms need to undertake custom marketing research. **Custom research** is research conducted for a single firm to provide answers to specific questions. This kind of research is especially helpful for firms when they need to know more about why certain trends have surfaced.

Some firms maintain an in-house research department that conducts studies on its behalf. Many firms, however, hire outside research companies that specialise in designing and conducting projects based on the needs of the client. These custom research reports are another kind of information that is included in the MkIS.

Marketers may use marketing research to identify opportunities for new products, to promote existing ones, or to provide data about the quality of their products, who uses them and how. Sometimes a company will even do research to counter a competitor's claim. Procter & Gamble (P&G), for example, challenged rival Revlon's claim that its ColorStay line of cosmetics wouldn't rub off. P&G researchers wanted to answer a specific question: was

ColorStay's claim true? Because that kind of question can't be answered by buying a syndicated report, P&G commissioned 270 women to provide the specific information needed to support its case against Revlon. The women rubbed their cheeks against their shirts while wearing ColorStay and reported that, in fact, most of the shirts did get stained. Revlon, however, countered that P&G's test was flawed because the women might have been encouraged to rub too hard. Revlon did its own test on 293 women who were told to use 'the pressure they use when caressing someone else's face'. This time the women found few stains. To avoid further controversy, Revlon now says that ColorStay won't rub off under 'normal circumstances'.[6] (Aren't you relieved?)

4. Acquired databases

A large amount of information that can be useful in marketing decision making is available in the form of external databases. Firms may acquire databases from any number of sources. For example, some companies are willing to sell their customer database to non-competing firms. Government databases, including the massive amounts of economic and demographic information compiled by the statistics offices of the respective country, are available at little or no cost.

Recently, the use of such databases for marketing purposes has come under increased government scrutiny. Using the data for analysing consumer trends and product planning is one thing – using it for outbound mailings and unsolicited phone calls and emails has evoked a backlash resulting in 'do-not-call' lists and anti-spam laws. Maybe you have noticed that when you sign up for a credit card or have other occasion to give a seller your contact information, you receive an invitation to 'opt out' of receiving promotional mailings from them or from others who may acquire your contact information from them later. By law, if you decide to opt out, companies cannot use your information for marketing purposes.

Marketing Decision Support Systems

A firm's marketing information system generates regular reports for decision makers on what is going on in the internal and external environment. But sometimes these reports are inadequate. Different managers may want different information, and in some cases, the problem that must be addressed is too vague or unusual to be easily answered by the MkIS process. As a result, many firms take the vital step to beef up their MkIS with a **marketing decision support system (MDSS)**. An MDSS includes analysis and interactive software that allows marketing managers, even those who are not computer experts, to access MkIS data and conduct their own analyses, often over the company intranet. Figure 3.3 shows the elements of an MDSS.

Marketing Metrics

Deciding Which Ice Cream

Famous ice cream producer Ben & Jerry's, owned by consumer product giant Unilever, was looking for a technology system which would give managers and marketing executives easy access to customer information collected by the different departments. The IT (information technology) department chose a business intelligence software called BusinessObjects which offered the possibility to easily and quickly receive, analyse and act on consumer information data. This made it a lot easier for the company to discover buying patterns and taste preferences and react to customer comments. Any cream and chocolate sprinkles with your data?[7]

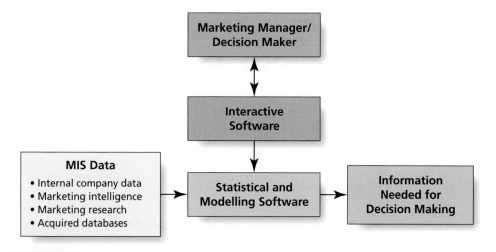

Figure 3.3	The Marketing Decision Support System
	Although an MkIS provides many reports managers need for decision making, it doesn't answer all their information needs. The marketing decision support system (MDSS) is an enhancement to the MkIS that makes it easy for marketing managers to access the system and find answers to their questions.

Modelling Software, 'Perceptual Maps' and 'What-If' Questions

Typically, an MDSS includes sophisticated statistical and modelling software tools. Statistical software allows managers to examine complex relationships among factors in the marketplace. For example, a marketing manager who wants to know how consumers perceive her company's brand in relation to the competition's brand might use a sophisticated statistical technique called multidimensional scaling to create a 'perceptual map', or a graphic presentation of the various brands in relationship to each other. You'll see an example of a perceptual map in Chapter 6 on segmentation and positioning.

Modelling software can be used for scenario planning, as mentioned before, and helps decision makers to examine possible or preconceived ideas about correlations in the data – to ask cause and effect questions. For example, media modelling software allows marketers to see what would happen if they made certain decisions about where to place their advertising. A manager may be able to use sales data and a model to find out how many consumers stay with his brand and how many switch, thus developing projections of market share over time. *Contingency planning* is the sister tool of scenario planning and is especially concerned with developing alternatives for the main plan in case of threats or emergencies – events which are foreseen but unlikely to occur. Table 3.1 gives some examples of the different marketing questions that an MkIS and an MDSS might answer.

Searching for Gold: Data Mining

As we have explained, most MkIS systems include internal customer transaction databases and many include acquired databases. Often these databases are extremely large. To take advantage of the massive amount of data now available, sophisticated analysis techniques called data mining are becoming a priority for many firms. **Data mining** is a process in which analysts sift through data (often measured in terabytes – much larger than kilobytes or even gigabytes) to identify unique patterns of behaviour among different customer groups. This

Questions Answered with an MkIS	Questions Answered with an MDSS
What were our company sales of each product during the past month and the past year?	Have our sales declines simply reflected changes in overall industry sales, or is there some portion of the decline that cannot be explained by industry changes?
What changes are happening in sales in our industry, and what are the demographic characteristics of consumers whose purchase patterns are changing the most?	Are the same trends seen in our different product categories? Are the changes in consumer trends very similar among all our products? What are the demographic characteristics of consumers who seem to be the most and the least loyal?
What are the best media for reaching a large proportion of heavy, medium, or light users of our product?	If we change our media schedule by adding or deleting certain media buying, will we reach fewer users of our product?

allows the company to get to know its customers inside out and aids successful and tailored customer relationship management.

British Airways, for example, uses data mining to create customised services for its travellers. The company receives a lot of information through customers who sign up for a frequent traveller programme or for newsletters as they have to fill out some questionnaires before joining. Through data mining the company can segment its customer base into different groups of interest concerning price, destination and dates of flights. Those customers can then receive specific promotional offers tailored to their needs.[8]

Data mining uses supercomputers that run sophisticated programs so that analysts can combine different databases to understand relationships among buying decisions, exposure to marketing messages and in-store promotions. These operations are so complex that companies often need to build a data warehouse (sometimes costing more than £5 million) simply to store and process the data.[9]

What Marketers can do with Data Mining

Data mining has four important applications for marketers:[10]

1. **Customer acquisition:** Many firms work hard to include demographic and other information about customers in their database. For example, a number of supermarkets offer weekly special price discounts for shop loyalty card holders. These shops' membership application forms require that customers indicate their age, family size, address and so on. With this information, the supermarket can determine which of its current customers respond best to specific offers and then send the same offers to non-customers who share the same demographic characteristics.

2. **Customer retention and loyalty:** The firm can identify big-spending customers and then target them for special offers and inducements other customers won't receive. Keeping the most profitable customers coming back is a great way to build business success because keeping good customers is less expensive than constantly finding new ones.[11]

3. **Customer abandonment:** Strange as it may sound, sometimes a firm wants customers to take their business elsewhere because servicing them actually costs the firm too much. Today, this is popularly called 'firing a customer'. For example, a department store may use data mining to identify unprofitable customers – those who are not spending enough or who return most of what they buy. Top luxury fashion brand Burberry has experienced a major crisis since its well-known checked products became highly demanded by a new customer segment – the so-called 'chavs', who are associated with tracksuits, fake jewellery

Marketing Ethics

Supermarkets 'use loyalty cards to kill off local shops'

Supermarkets have been accused of using information gleaned form loyalty cards to drive small local retailers out of business. The use of loyalty card schemes came under the spotlight during the Commons home affairs select committee's latest hearing into Britain's surveillance society. For example, Loyalty Management Group (LMG), which operates the

Nectar card on behalf of Sainsbury's, confirmed that the chain could access data on where its customers lived, where and when they shopped and how much they spent.

The Daily Telegraph, 8 June 2007

Debate, Discuss, Disagree

1 Is it a legitimate business practice for big retail companies to use their databases to gain competitive advantage over other retailers?

and rowdy behaviour. Football hooligans and unpopular ex-reality soap stars wearing Burberry hats and outfits were regarded as a nightmare by Burberry, whose real desired target customers are the rich and famous. Throughout the last few years Burberry has been fighting rigorously to 'fire' its unwanted customers and re-establish its luxury image. Measures of customer abandonment undertaken by the company included removing baseball caps, which were extremely popular among the chavs, from its product line and replacing items with the eye-catching checked pattern by ones with a more 'classy' and plain design.[12]

4. **Market basket analysis:** Firms can develop focused promotional strategies based on their records of which customers have bought certain products. Hewlett-Packard, for example, carefully analyses which of its customers have recently bought new printers and targets them to receive emails about specials on ink cartridges and tips on getting the most out of their machines.

So far, we have looked at the MkIS and the MDSS, the overall systems that provide the information marketers need to make good decisions. We've seen how the data included in the MkIS and MDSS include internal company data, marketing intelligence data gathered by monitoring everyday sources, acquired databases and information gathered to address specific marketing decisions through the marketing research process. In the rest of the chapter, we'll look at the steps that marketers must take when they conduct marketing research.

Marketing Metrics

How to measure car capabilities

Companies like BMW often use a market research concept called 'car clinics' in which customers can spend a day driving, testing and evaluating not only the car of the specific company but also the ones of their competitors. Several questionnaires, interviews and group discussions are being carried out in order to find out as much valuable information as possible. To avoid biases and make the research more reliable, the

company often uses an independent agency which invites the customers to the clinic and all the cars are made unrecognisable so that the customers do not actually know which company is carrying out the research. If, for example, the research reveals that the perception of the car is better than the competitor's car, it can be used in advertising against competitors and in order to counter their claims.

Steps in the Marketing Research Process

Objective

2

The marketing
research process

The collection and interpretation of strategic information is hardly a one-shot deal that managers engage in 'just out of curiosity'. Ideally, marketing research is a continual process, a series of steps marketers take to learn about the marketplace. Whether a company conducts the research itself or hires another firm to do it, the goal is the same: to help managers make informed marketing decisions and reduce risks of taking actions which could harm the business. Figure 3.4 shows the steps in the research process, and we'll go over each of these now.

Step 1: Define the Research Problem

The first step in the marketing research process is to clearly understand what information managers need. This step is referred to as defining the research problem. You should note that the word 'problem' here does not necessarily refer to 'something that is wrong' but instead to the overall questions for which the firm needs answers. Defining the problem has three components:

1. **Specifying the research objectives:** What questions will the research attempt to answer?

2. **Identifying the consumer population of interest:** What are the characteristics of the consumer groups of interest?

3. **Placing the problem in an environmental context:** What factors in the firm's internal and external business environment might be influencing the situation?

Providing the right kind of information for each of these pieces of the problem is not as simple as it seems. For example, suppose a luxury car manufacturer wants to find out why its sales have fallen off dramatically over the past year. The research objective could revolve around any number of possible questions: Is the firm's advertising failing to reach the right consumers? Is the right message being sent? Do the firm's cars have a particular feature (or lack of one) that's turning customers away? Is there a problem with the firm's reputation for providing quality service? Do consumers believe the price is right for the value they get? The particular objective chosen depends on a variety of factors, such as the feedback the firm is getting from its customers, the information it receives from the marketplace, and sometimes even the intuition of the people designing the research.

Often the focus of a research question is driven by feedback from the marketplace that identifies a possible problem. Mercedes-Benz is a great example of a firm that, for years, has continually monitored drivers' perceptions of its cars. When the company started getting reports from its dealers in the 1990s that more and more people were viewing Mercedes products as 'arrogant' and 'unapproachable', even to the point at which they were reluctant to sit in showroom models, the company undertook a research project to understand the reasons for this perception.

The research objective determines the consumer population the company will study. In Mercedes' case, the research could have focused on current owners to find out what they especially liked about the car. Or it could have been directed at non-owners to understand their lifestyles, what they looked for in a luxury automobile, or their beliefs about the company itself that kept them from choosing its cars. So what did Mercedes find out? Research showed that although people rated its cars very highly on engineering quality and status, many were too intimidated by the elitist Mercedes image to consider buying one. Mercedes dealers reported that a common question from visitors to showrooms was, 'May I actually sit in the car?'[13] Based on these findings, Mercedes has in recent years worked hard to adjust perceptions by projecting a slightly more down-to-earth image in its advertising, and it ultimately created new downsized classes of vehicles to appeal to consumers who wanted something a little less ostentatious.[14]

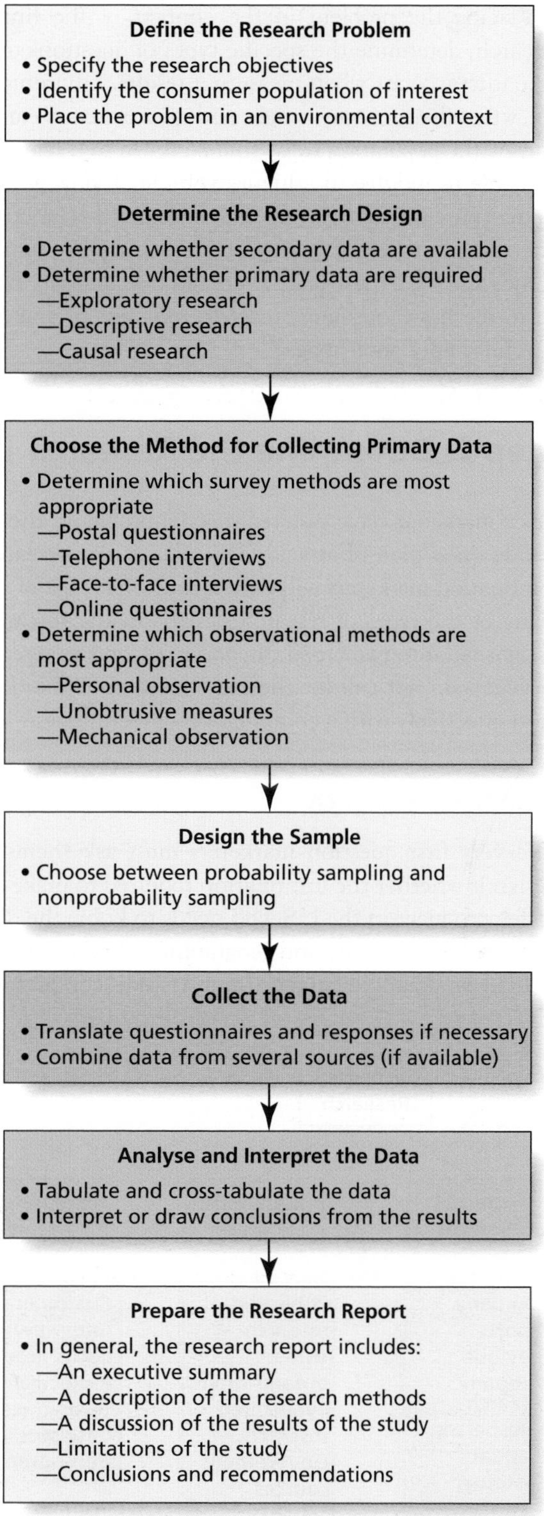

Define the Research Problem

- Specify the research objectives
- Identify the consumer population of interest
- Place the problem in an environmental context

Determine the Research Design

- Determine whether secondary data are available
- Determine whether primary data are required
  —Exploratory research
  —Descriptive research
  —Causal research

Choose the Method for Collecting Primary Data

- Determine which survey methods are most appropriate
  —Postal questionnaires
  —Telephone interviews
  —Face-to-face interviews
  —Online questionnaires
- Determine which observational methods are most appropriate
  —Personal observation
  —Unobtrusive measures
  —Mechanical observation

Design the Sample

- Choose between probability sampling and nonprobability sampling

Collect the Data

- Translate questionnaires and responses if necessary
- Combine data from several sources (if available)

Analyse and Interpret the Data

- Tabulate and cross-tabulate the data
- Interpret or draw conclusions from the results

Prepare the Research Report

- In general, the research report includes:
  —An executive summary
  —A description of the research methods
  —A discussion of the results of the study
  —Limitations of the study
  —Conclusions and recommendations

Figure 3.4   Steps in the Marketing Research Process

The marketing research process includes a series of steps that begins with defining the problem or the information needed and that ends with the finished research report for managers.

Placing the problem in the context of the firm's environment helps to structure the research, determine the specific types of questions to ask, and identify factors it will need to take into account when measuring results. Environmental conditions also matter. For example, when the economy is tight and sales of luxury cars are generally declining, researchers may narrow the population to be studied down to a select group of consumers who are still willing and able to indulge in a luxury vehicle. Today, many car consumers are moving away from status-conscious materialism and more towards functionality. In addition, as petrol prices have skyrocketed in recent years, drivers' sensitivity to miles per gallon translates even to luxury brands and huge sport-utility vehicles like a mighty BMW X5. Thus, a research question might be to see how consumers react to different promotional strategies for luxury goods that go beyond simply 'snob appeal'.

 # Step 2: Determine the Research Design

Once marketers have isolated specific problems, the second step of the research process is to decide on a 'plan of attack'. This plan is the **research design**, which specifies exactly what information marketers will collect and what type of study they will do. Figure 3.5 summarises many of the types of research designs in the researcher's arsenal. As you can see, research designs fall into two broad categories: secondary research and primary research. All marketing problems do not call for the same research techniques, and marketers solve many problems most effectively with a combination of techniques.

Secondary Research

The very first question marketers must ask themselves when determining their research design is whether the information required to make a decision already exists. For example, a coffee producer in the US who needs to know the differences in coffee consumption among different demographic and geographic segments of the market may find that the information needed is already available from a study conducted by the National Coffee Association.

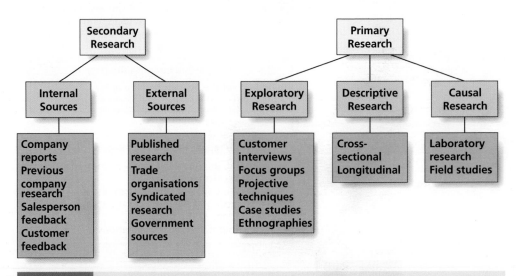

Figure 3.5	Marketing Research Design
	For some research problems, the secondary research may provide the information needed. At other times, one of the primary research methods may be needed.

Data that have been collected for some purpose other than the problem at hand are called **secondary data**.

Many marketers thrive on going out and collecting new, 'fresh' data from consumers. However, if secondary data are available, it saves the firm time and money because the expense of designing and implementing a study has already been incurred. It is often helpful to start off with secondary research as a first step in the research process. Even if it does not lead to the actual solution, it may give a better understanding of the research problem or aid in the design of further primary research. Sometimes the data that marketers need may even be 'hiding' right under the organisation's nose in the form of company reports; previous company research studies; feedback received from customers, salespeople or shops; or even in the memories of long-time employees. More typically, though, researchers need to look elsewhere for secondary data. They may obtain reports published in the popular and business press, studies that private research organisations or government agencies conduct, and published research on the state of the industry from trade organisations.

For example, many companies gain market and consumer knowledge by subscribing to reports from the Mintel International group which researches many different business problems ranging from 'opportunities for retailing in emerging markets' to 'new trends in the health food sector'.[15]

Another very effective way of acquiring useful secondary data, which gives the company new ideas, is to partner up with an academic institution such as a well-known university. Both sides benefit from this partnership as the university improves its reputation and importance and the company receives a useful, scientifically backed insight into the market and business problems. An example is the creation of the 'Audi Lab for Market Research' where German car manufacturer Audi partnered up with the prestigious Swiss university St. Gallen to create a leading research centre for customer needs, product improvement and development into new markets.[16]

On the downside, however, secondary research data may be outdated, inaccurate or not available for specialised markets and products. Before relying on secondary information, the researcher needs to assess its usefulness and the trustworthiness of the source, as well as filter out the truly relevant sources from an overload of data.

Table 3.2 lists a number of websites helpful to marketers looking for secondary research topics.

Table 3.2
Helpful websites for
Marketing Research

URL	Description
www.statistics.gov.uk	The Office for National Statistics (ONS) collects and publishes official statistics about the UK's society and economy.
www.gfk.com/group/index.en.html	The GfK group is one of the world's largest market research organisations, specialising in custom retail, retail and technology, consumer tracking, and media and healthcare.
www.mintel.co.uk	The Mintel International Group is a global supplier of consumer, media and market research and publishes reports on various business topics.
www.bmrb.co.uk	The British Marketing Research Bureau (BMRB) provides different kinds of research solutions such as syndicated and proprietary research.
www.lexis-nexis.co.uk	Lexis-Nexis is a large database featuring information from all major newspapers, trade journals and magazines and reports.

Objective

3

The differences
among
exploratory,
descriptive and
causal research
techniques
available to
marketers

Primary Research

Of course, secondary research is not always the answer. When a company needs to make a specific decision, it often needs to conduct research to collect **primary data** – that is, information collected directly from respondents to specifically address the question at hand. Primary data include demographic and psychological information about customers and prospective customers, customers' attitudes and opinions about products and competing products, as well as their awareness or knowledge about a product and their beliefs about the people who use those products. In the next few sections, we'll talk briefly about the various designs useful in conducting primary research.

Exploratory (Qualitative) Research

Marketers use **exploratory research** to generate topics for future, more rigorous studies to come up with ideas for new strategies and opportunities or perhaps just to get a better handle on a problem they are currently experiencing with a product. Besides, exploratory research also plays an assisting role in designing subsequent research. The studies are usually carried out on a small scale, are less costly than other techniques and often provide a deep insight into consumer behaviour. Quantitative research, by contrast, is rather concerned with testing hypotheses, for example with the help of large-scale surveys and other quantifiable methods. This explains why marketers may use exploratory research to test their hunches about what's going on without too much risk. Think about Helen Armstrong's decision.

Exploratory studies often involve in-depth probing of a few consumers who fit the profile of the 'typical' customer. Researchers may interview consumers, salespeople or other employees about products, services, ads or shops. They may simply 'hang out' and watch what people do when choosing among competing brands in a shop aisle. Or they may locate places where the consumers of interest tend to be and ask questions in these settings. For example, some researchers find that members of Generation Y – those born between 1977 and 1994 – are too suspicious or sceptical in traditional research settings, so they may interview young people queueing to buy concert tickets or in clubs.[17] Firms like the trendy sportswear manufacturer Puma employ so-called 'coolhunters', young people who observe and record crowds in metropolitan areas with cameras and try to forecast upcoming trends. By doing so, Puma hopes to always stay one step ahead of competition and gain a leadership position regarding trends and style.[18]

Most exploratory research is referred to as qualitative in nature: that is, the results of the research project tend to be non-numeric and instead might be detailed verbal or visual information about consumers' attitudes, feelings and buying behaviours in the form of words rather than in numbers. For example, when Beiersdorf, producer of the well-known Nivea product range, wanted to introduce a new deodorant, it conducted a 'blind test' where people used the Nivea deodorant on one armpit and a conventional deodorant on the other without knowing which was which. The tested people were being questioned about the comfort and smell of the deodorant and this made it possible for Beiersdorf to improve the product.[19]

Exploratory research can take many forms, as Helen Armstrong from Research International at the start of the chapter knows, and she has to choose how to advise the World Gold Council on which would be most appropriate. **Consumer interviews** are one-on-one discussions in which an individual shares his or her thoughts in person with a researcher. The mobile phone maker Nokia has

Photo 3.2   Trendwatching.com, one of the world's leading trend firms, has 8,000+ trend spotters scanning the globe for emerging consumer trends.
Source: Trendwatching.com

used consumer interviews in the past to identify important changes in consumer behaviour. They were able to spot a trend in customers wanting to move away from fixed line phones towards using a wireless headset service for all calls. With this new knowledge it became easier for Nokia to develop innovative product lines and stay ahead of the competition.[20]

Nestlé used personal interviews to find out reasons for the decline in sales of the Maggi brand. The interviews revealed that consumers perceived both the design of the bottle and the flavour of the product as uninteresting and old-fashioned. When consumers explained that they were longing for fresher ingredients and a younger design, Nestlé was able to reposition its Maggi brand and add 'more natural qualities in terms of taste, smell, look and texture'.[21]

The **focus group** is the technique that marketing researchers use most often for collecting exploratory data. Focus groups typically consist of five to nine consumers who have been recruited because they share certain characteristics. These people sit together to discuss a product, ad, or some other marketing topic introduced by a discussion leader. Focus group facilitation is a real art that requires discipline, patience and a strong sense of when to sit back and listen and when to jump in and direct discussion. Typically, the leader video- or audiotapes these group discussions, which may be held at special interviewing facilities that allow for observation by the client, who watches from behind a one-way mirror.

In addition to getting insights from what the participants say about a product, a good moderator can sometimes learn by carefully observing other things such as body language. While conducting focus groups on bras, an analyst noted that small-chested women typically reacted with hostility when discussing the subject. The participants would unconsciously cover their chests with their arms as they spoke and complained that they were ignored by the fashion industry. To meet this overlooked need, the company introduced a line of A-cup bras called 'A-OK' that depicted these women in a positive light.[22]

Researchers use **projective techniques** to get at people's underlying feelings, especially when they think that people will be unable or unwilling to express their true reactions. A projective test asks the participant to respond to some object, often by telling a story about it. For example, Georgia-Pacific, a manufacturer of paper kitchen towels, was locked in a struggle with ScotTowels (made by Kimberly-Clark) for the number two position in the US behind leading seller Bounty (made by Procter & Gamble). The company decided to re-examine its brand identity, which was personified by a 60-foot character named Brawny who held an axe. Georgia-Pacific managers were afraid that their brand was too old-fashioned or that women were confused about why a man was selling paper towels in the first place. Researchers asked women in the focus groups questions such as, 'What kind of woman would he go out with?' and 'What is his home life like?' Then the researchers asked the women to imagine how he would act in different situations and even to guess what would happen if they were locked in a lift with him for 20 minutes.

Responses were reassuring: the women saw the Georgia-Pacific kitchen towel as a knight in shining armour who would get them out of the elevator – a good spokesman for a product that's supposed to be reliable and able to get the job done. The character kept his job and in fact since he was originally introduced in 1975 he has had two makeovers to keep his look modern.

The idea of creating brand personalities and finding out what customers think about the character was taken to a new level with the 'Volcanicity' campaign of bottled water producer Volvic. The company created a profile for the TV ad character 'Mr. Volcano' in the virtual community MSN Live Spaces (volcanogeorge.spaces.live.com). Just like a real person, 'Mr. Volcano' published pictures, blogs and news about himself, and by the reactions which he received from other Live Space users the company could gain information about how the brand was perceived by customers.[23]

The **case study** is a comprehensive examination of a particular firm or organisation. In business-to-business marketing research in which the customers are other firms, for example,

| Photo 3.3 | This is the 'Mini United' festival where Mini owners and fans come together to socialise. Source: BMW Group (Germany) |

researchers may try to learn how one particular company makes its purchases. The goal is to identify the key decision makers, to learn what criteria they emphasise when choosing among suppliers and perhaps to learn something about any conflicts and rivalries among these decision makers that may influence their choices.

An **ethnography** is a different kind of in-depth report. It is a technique borrowed from anthropologists who go to 'live with the natives' for months or even years. This approach has been adapted by some marketing researchers who visit people's homes or participate in real life consumer activities to get a handle on how they really use products. Imagine having a researcher follow you around while you shop and then while you use the products you bought to see what kind of consumer you are.

Of course, unlike anthropologists living with indigenous tribes, marketing researchers usually don't have months or years to devote to a project, so they devise shortcuts to get the information they need. For example, when Nissan was preparing for the $60 million launch of its first full-size truck, the Titan, its ad agency (TBWA/Chiat/Day) deployed researchers in the field to understand the psyche of such US truck owners. Team members hung out for several months at hunting expos, gun shows, cross-country events and even fishing spots – places that target consumers frequented. Results from the observations, supported by results from focus groups and interviews, provided strong ammunition for Nissan to communicate its message of what the Titan could do. Ultimately, to portray a rough-and-tumble image the ads showed dirty Titans in action, sloshing through mud and driving up inclines.[24] Another example is the 'Mini United 2007' festival which took place in June 2007 in Zandfoort, Holland. True to the motto 'Friends. Festival. Challenge', thousands of Mini fans and Mini Classic fans from all over the world came together to party, socialise and exchange experiences about their favourite car. Apart from being a great PR event, this festival gave the car manufacturer excellent opportunities to mingle among the fans, conduct market research and spot trends in customer behaviour.[25]

Descriptive (Quantitative) Research

We've seen that marketers have many tools in their arsenal, including focus groups and observational techniques, to help them better define a problem or opportunity. These are usually modest studies of a small number of people, enough to get some indication of what is going on but not enough for the marketer to feel confident about generalising what he or she observes to the rest of the population.

The next step in marketing research, then, often is to conduct **descriptive research**, which probes systematically into the marketing problem and bases its conclusions on a large sample of participants. Descriptive research is typically expressed in quantitative terms – averages, percentages or other statistics summarising results from a large set of measurements. In such quantitative approaches to research, the project can be as simple as counting the number of Listerine bottles sold in a month in different regions of the country or as complex as statistical analyses of responses to a survey mailed to thousands of consumers. In each case, marketers conduct the descriptive research to answer a specific question in contrast to the 'fishing expedition' that may occur in exploratory research.

Marketing researchers who employ descriptive techniques most often use a **cross-sectional design**. This approach usually involves the systematic collection of responses to a consumer survey instrument, such as a questionnaire, from one or more samples of respondents at one point in time. The data may be collected on more than one occasion but generally not from the same pool of respondents.

In contrast to these one-shot studies, a **longitudinal design** tracks the responses of the same sample of respondents over time. Market researchers sometimes create consumer panels to get information; in this case a sample of respondents representative of a larger market agrees to provide information about purchases on a weekly or monthly basis. Procter & Gamble, for instance, recruits consumer advisory panels on a market-by-market basis to keep its finger on the pulse of local shoppers. Since P&G acquired the Gillette line of razors and blades, for the first time it had to recruit special all-male consumer panels to contribute to the development of new products such as the Fusion line of razors.[26]

Causal Research

It's a fact that purchases of both nappies and beer peak between 5.00 and 7.00 p.m. Can we say that purchasing one of these products caused shoppers to purchase the other as well – and, if so, which caused which? Or is the answer simply that this happens to be the time that young fathers stop at the shop on their way home from work to pick up some brew and Pampers?[27]

The descriptive techniques we've examined do a good job of providing valuable information about what is happening in the marketplace, but descriptive research, by its very nature, can only *describe* a marketplace phenomenon – it cannot tell us why. Sometimes marketers need to know if something they've done has brought about some change in behaviour. For example, does placing one product next to another in a shop mean that people will buy more of each? We can't answer this question through simple observation or description.

Causal research attempts to understand cause-and-effect relationships. Marketers use causal research techniques when they want to know if a change in something (for example, placing cases of beer next to a nappy display) is responsible for a change in something else (for example, a big increase in nappy sales). They call the factors that might cause such a change independent variables and the outcomes dependent variables. The independent variable(s) cause some change in the dependent variable(s). In our example, then, the beer display is an independent variable, and sales data for the nappies are a dependent variable. That is, the study would investigate whether an increase in nappy sales 'depends' on the proximity of beer. Another example for the use of causal research would be to examine a rise in sales after the implementation of a 'buy-one-get-one-free' offer. Did sales really go up because of this offer or was the rise caused by some other, external, factors? Researchers can gather data and test the causal relationship statistically.

To rule out alternative explanations, researchers must carefully design **experiments** that test predicted relationships among variables in a controlled environment. Because this approach tries to eliminate competing explanations for the outcome, respondents may be brought to a laboratory so that the researcher can control precisely what respondents should see. For example, a study testing whether the placement of nappies in a supermarket influences the likelihood that male shoppers will buy them might bring a group of men into a testing facility and show them a 'virtual store' on a computer screen. Researchers would ask the men to fill a grocery trolley as they click through the 'aisles'. The experiment might vary the placement of the nappies – next to shelves of beer in one scenario, near paper goods in a different scenario. The objective is to see which placement gets the men to put nappies into their carts.

Although a laboratory allows researchers to exert control over what test subjects see and do, marketers don't always have the luxury of conducting this kind of 'pure' research. But it is possible to conduct field studies in the real world, as long as the researchers can control the independent variables.

For example, a nappy company might choose two supermarkets that have similar customer bases in terms of age, income and so on. With the cooperation of the supermarket's management, the company might place its nappy display next to the beer in one shop and next to the paper goods in the other and then record nappy purchases made by men over a two-week period. If a lot more nappies were bought by guys in the first shop than in the second (and the company was sure that nothing else was different between the two shops, such as a money-off coupon for nappies being distributed in one shop and not the other), the nappy manufacturer might conclude that the presence of beer in the background does indeed result in increased nappy sales.

Step 3: Choose the Method for Collecting Primary Data

Objective

4

The different types of data-collection methods and types of consumer samples that researchers use

When the researcher decides to collect primary data, the next step in the marketing research process is to figure out just how to collect it. Primary data collection methods can be broadly described as either survey or observation. There are many ways to collect data, and marketers are trying new ones all the time. Today, a few marketing researchers are even turning to sophisticated brain scans to directly measure our brains' reactions to various advertisements or products. These 'neuromarketers' hope to be able to tell companies how people will react to their brands by scanning consumers' brains rather than collecting data the old-fashioned way – by asking them.[28] These techniques are still in their infancy, so for now we'll still rely on other methods to collect primary data.

Survey Methods

Survey methods involve some kind of interview or other direct contact with respondents who answer questions. Questionnaires can be administered on the phone, in person, through the mail, or over the internet. Table 3.3 summarises the advantages and disadvantages of different methods for collecting data.

Questionnaires

Questionnaires differ in their degree of structure. With a totally unstructured questionnaire, the researcher loosely determines the questions in advance. Questions may evolve from what the respondent says to previous questions. At the other extreme, the researcher uses a completely structured questionnaire. He or she asks every respondent exactly the same questions and each participant responds to the same set of fixed choices. You have probably experienced this kind of questionnaire, where you might have had to respond to a statement by saying if you 'strongly agree', 'somewhat agree', and so on. Moderately structured questionnaires ask each respondent the same questions, but the respondent is allowed to answer the questions in his or her own words.

Mail questionnaires are easy to administer and offer a high degree of anonymity to respondents. This removes the interviewer bias and lowers the social desirability bias. Respondents are given the opportunity to answer the questions at their own pace. On the downside, because the questionnaire is printed and mailed, researchers have little flexibility in the types of questions they can ask and little control over the circumstances under which the respondent is answering them. The researcher cannot ask any probing questions or clarify responses. Mail questionnaires also take a long time to get back to the company and are likely to have a much lower response rate than other types of data collection methods because people tend to ignore them. In addition, because they use paper, they may be perceived as being less environmentally friendly.

Telephone interviews usually consist of a brief phone conversation in which an interviewer reads a short list of questions to the respondent. Although telephone interviews are relatively

Date-Collection Method	Advantages	Disadvantages
Mail questionnaires	• Respondents feel anonymous • Low cost • Good for ongoing research	• May take a long time for questionnaires to be returned • Low rate of response; many may not return questionnaires • Inflexible questionnaire • Length of questionnaire limited by respondent interest in the topic • Unclear whether respondents understand the questions • Unclear who is responding • No assurance that respondents are being honest
Telephone interviews	• Fast • High flexibility in questioning • Low cost • Limited by interviewer	• Decreasing levels of respondent cooperation • Limited questionnaire length • High likelihood of respondent misunderstanding • Respondents cannot view materials • Cannot survey households without phones • Consumers screen calls with answering machines and caller ID • Do-not-call lists allow many research subjects to opt out of participation
Face-to-face interviews	• Flexibility of questioning • Can use long questionnaires • Can determine whether respondents have trouble understanding questions • Can use visuals or other materials	• High cost • Interviewer bias a problem • Take a lot of time
Online questionnaires	• Instantaneous data collection and analysis • Questioning very flexible • Low cost • No interviewer bias • No geographic restrictions • Can use visuals or other materials	• Unclear who is responding • No assurance that respondents are being honest • Limited questionnaire length • Unable to determine whether respondent is understanding the question • Self-selected samples

cheap, reach a large number of people quite easily, and a random sample can be generated by using random digital dialling, there are several problems with this data collection method. One problem with this method is that the growth of **telemarketing**, where businesses sell directly to consumers over the phone, has eroded consumers' willingness to participate in phone surveys (especially during dinnertime!). In addition to aggravating people by barraging them with telephone sales messages, some unscrupulous telemarketers have 'poisoned the well' for legitimate marketing researchers by hiding their pitches behind an illusion of doing research. They contact consumers under the pretence of doing a research study when in fact their real intent is to sell the respondent something or to solicit funds for some cause. In the US, the act of selling under the guise of doing market research is called 'sugging', and 'frugging' is the practice of fundraising under the pretence of doing market research (see Marketing Ethics box). The respondent also may not feel comfortable speaking directly to an interviewer, especially if the survey is about a sensitive subject and the researcher cannot use any visual aids during the interview or try building up a rapport with the interviewee. Besides, body language and non-verbal clues cannot be observed. Collectable information therefore often stays limited and it only makes sense to use a short questionnaire. Of course, increasing numbers of people use voicemail and caller ID to screen calls, further reducing the response rate. Besides, some numbers may not be listed, which can lead to an unrepresentative sample. And, as noted earlier, do-not-call lists allow many would-be research subjects to opt out of participation both in legitimate marketing research and unscrupulous telemarketing.[29]

Using *face-to-face interviews*, a live interviewer asks questions of one respondent at a time. Although in 'the old days' researchers often went door to door to ask questions, which allowed the interviewer to adapt questions to the specific situation and possibly gain deeper insights, that's much less common today because of fears about security and because the large numbers of dual income families make it less likely to find people at home during the day. Other disadvantages are that this research method is very time-consuming, expensive, slow to complete and that there is a high likelihood of bias, for example that the respondent will answer in a socially desirable way. Typically, today's face-to-face interviews occur in a shopping centre intercept study in which researchers recruit shoppers in shopping centres or other public areas. You've probably seen this going on in your local shopping centre where a smiling person holding a clipboard stops shoppers to see if they are willing to answer a few questions.

Shopping centre intercepts offer good opportunities to get feedback about new package designs, styles or even reactions to new foods or fragrances. Besides, this method is easy to supervise and less time-consuming than for example in-house interviews. However, because only certain groups of the population frequently shop at shopping centres, a shopping centre intercept study does not provide the researcher with a representative sample of the population (unless the population of interest is shopping centre shoppers). In addition to being more expensive than mail or phone surveys, respondents may be reluctant to answer questions of a personal nature in a face-to-face context.

Online questionnaires are growing in popularity, mainly due to their ability to reach a large number of people, speed of distribution and collection and low cost. However, the use of such questionnaires is not without concerns. Many researchers question the quality of responses they will receive – particularly because (as with mail and phone interviews) no one can be really sure who is typing in the responses on the computer. In addition, it's uncertain whether savvy online consumers are truly representative of the general population.[30] Response rates are often rather low since consumers might perceive them as spam, have technical problems or are worried about data security issues. As a result it can be argued that although online surveys become easier to do, good online surveys become increasingly harder to do.[31] However, these concerns are rapidly evaporating as research firms devise new ways to verify identities; present surveys in novel formats, including the use of images, sound and animation; and recruit more diverse respondents.[32] The importance and impact of online surveys will be covered in more depth later on in this chapter.

Observational Methods

The second major primary data collection method is observation. Observation is a type of data collection that uses a passive instrument in which the researcher simply records the consumer's behaviour – often without their knowledge. On the one hand, observational research offers

Marketing Ethics

Have you ever been Sugged or Frugged?

The Labour Party and some charities have been accused of 'selling under guise' or 'sugging'. Sugging is something that appears to be market research questionnaires at first, and actually is little more than direct marketing forms soliciting the names, addresses and ideally cash from participants. It relies on the fact that there are plenty of people who are willing to cooperate with market research, but who don't want to get involved in a sales approach. Frugging is fund raising under the guise of doing market research. So a cancer charity might ask people about their perceptions on the risks of getting cancer and end up by asking for a donation. Ultimately, the important thing is not to mislead the consumer. If you haven't, it's up to the consumer whether they want to fill out a questionnaire and give money.

Debate, Discuss, Disagree

1 Have you ever been sugged or frugged?

2 Should sugging and frugging activities be allowed?

3 If so, when in the direct mail, e-mail or street interview should the respondent be told they will be asked for money?

the advantage of being able to measure behaviour in a direct and flexible way. On the other hand, however, it can be rather difficult to interpret and generalise the observed patterns. Researchers might tend to 'see what they want to see' in the observed behaviours. Besides, disguised research, for example with hidden cameras, might cause some difficulties regarding legal issues. Researchers do this through personal observation, unobtrusive measures and mechanical observation.

When researchers use *personal observation*, they simply watch consumers in action to understand how they react to marketing activities. Household goods manufacturer Vileda gained insight into customer behaviour by sending researchers into their homes and observing their cleaning techniques. It was discovered that there is a large customer group with a rather easygoing attitude towards cleaning which helped the company develop its Magic Mop which makes cleaning fast and convenient.

A shopping centre in Texas became a laboratory for the workplace of the future when it put a 'Connection Court' in the middle of the shopping centre. In an observational project sponsored by the internet Home Alliance, a group of mostly high-tech companies including Cisco Systems, Microsoft, and IBM, workers installed chairs and couches; set up desks with laptops, flat-panel monitors and printers; and hooked up a high-speed wireless internet network. This space is free for use by people who want to work in a more casual – and public – setting. The motivation: to understand if and how people want to work outside their homes and offices. With the spread of wireless internet by companies like McDonald's and Starbucks that are setting up networks to let their customers work, these companies are doing observational research to understand just how to structure the physical environment that will let them do that more comfortably.[33]

Researchers use **unobtrusive measures** that measure traces of physical evidence that remain after some action has been taken when they suspect that people will probably alter their behaviour if they know they are being observed. For example, instead of asking a person to report on the alcohol products which they currently stock at home, the researcher might go to the house and perform a 'pantry check' by actually counting the bottles in the drinks cabinet. Another option for collecting primary data is to sift through garbage, searching for clues about each family's consumption habits. The 'garbologists' can tell, for example, which soft drink accompanied what kind of food. As one garbologist noted, 'The people in this study don't know that we are studying their garbage so the information is totally objective'.[34] Smelly, too!

Mechanical observation is a primary data-collection method that relies on non-human devices to record behaviour. For example, one well-known application of mechanical observation is A.C. Nielsen's famous use of 'people meters' – boxes attached to the television sets of selected viewers, to record patterns of television watching. Data obtained from these devices indicate who is watching which shows. These 'television ratings' help the networks determine how much to charge advertisers for commercials and which shows to cancel or renew, although critics claim that there are problems of under-counting minorities, Arbitron has recently deployed thousands of 'portable people meters', or PPMs. PPMs resemble pagers and automatically record the wearer's exposure to any media that has inserted an inaudible code into its promotion (TV ad, shelf display, and so on). Thus, when the consumer is exposed to a broadcast commercial, cinema ad, internet banner ad or other form of commercial exposure, the PPM registers, records and time-stamps the signal. At day's end, the media history is downloaded by a home docking station that simultaneously recharges the PPM. Portability ensures that all exposures register, eliminating obtrusive people meters and written diaries that participants often forget to fill out.[35] The Institute of Practitioners in Advertising developed 'IPA Touchpoints' which measure the exposure of an individual to media streams with a PDA (personal digital assistant) in combination with a self-completion questionnaire. The Touchpoint project is designed to get an insight into how consumers move through the media jungle and to improve overall industry media research. This form of market research helps with answering questions like 'is TV still the dominant form of media?' or 'how much time do consumers in the Greater London area spend shopping on the internet?'[36]

Of course, many research firms are developing techniques to measure which websites are being visited and by whom. As we'll see shortly, there are ways for companies to tell where you've travelled in virtual space, so be careful about the sites you surf!

Photo 3.4   IPA TouchPoints is a relatively new survey. IPA TouchPoints 1 was published in 2006 followed by IPA TouchPoints 2 in 2008. The hub survey is conducted by TNS who questioned 5,000 people for both surveys using a substantial self-completion questionnaire and a PDA time-based diary that collected data every half hour for a week on how they were spending their time, their opinions, and the role of the media in their lives.
Source: IPA

Data Quality: Garbage In, Garbage Out

We've seen that a firm can collect data in many ways, including focus groups, ethnographic approaches, observational studies, and controlled experiments. But how much faith should marketing managers place in what they find out from the research?

All too often, marketers who have commissioned a study assume that because they have a massive report full of impressive-looking numbers and tables, they must have the 'truth'. Unfortunately, there are times when this 'truth' is really just one person's interpretation of the facts. At other times, the data used to generate recommendations are flawed. As the expression goes, 'garbage in, garbage out!'[37] That is, bad data mean bad managerial decisions. Typically, three factors influence the quality of research results – validity, reliability and representativeness.

Validity is the extent to which the research actually measures what it was intended to measure. This was part of the problem underlying the famous New Coke fiasco in the 1980s in which Coca-Cola underestimated people's loyalty to its flagship soft drink after it replaced 'Old Coke' with a new, sweeter formula. In a blind taste test, the company assumed testers' preferences for one anonymous cola over another was a valid measure of consumers' preferences for a cola brand. Coca-Cola found out the hard way that measuring taste only is not the same as measuring people's deep allegiances to their favourite soft drinks. After all, Coke is a brand that elicits strong consumer loyalty and is nothing short of a cultural icon. Tampering with the flavours was like assaulting Mum and her Sunday roast. Sales eventually recovered after the company brought back the old version as 'Coca-Cola Classic'.[38]

Reliability is the extent to which the research measurement techniques are free of errors. Sometimes, for example, the way a researcher asks a question creates error by biasing people's responses. Imagine that an attractive female interviewer working for Trojans condoms stopped male college students on campus and asked them if they used contraceptive products. Do you think their answers might change if they were asked the same questions on an anonymous survey they received in the mail? Most likely, their answers would be different because people are reluctant to disclose what they actually do when their responses are not anonymous. Researchers try to maximise reliability by thinking of several different ways to ask the same questions, by asking these questions on several occasions, or by using several analysts to interpret the responses. Thus, they can compare responses and look for consistency and stability.

Reliability is a problem when the researchers can't be sure that the consumer population they're studying even understands the questions. For example, kids are difficult subjects for market researchers because they tend to be undependable reporters of their own behaviour, they have poor recall, and they often do not understand abstract questions. In many cases, the children cannot explain why they prefer one item over another (or they're not willing to share these secrets with grown-ups).[39] For these reasons, researchers have had to be especially creative when designing studies on younger consumers. Figure 3.6 shows part of a completion test used to measure children's preferences for television programming in Japan.

Representativeness is the extent to which consumers in the study are similar to a larger group in which the organisation has an interest. This criterion for evaluating research underscores the importance of **sampling**, the process of selecting respondents for a study. The issue then becomes how large or small the sample should be and how these people are chosen. The requirements regarding representativeness have to be adapted slightly depending on what type of research the marketers use. When a large-scale survey is being conducted as part of a quantitative research project, representativeness is absolutely crucial. When dealing with qualitative research, such as a focus group, marketers will much rather look for in-depth information about this small group of consumers than for representativeness across the whole population. In order to ensure representativeness, it is important to select an experiment group, which receives a certain stimulus, as well as a control group, which does not receive any stimulus. Afterwards, the results can be compared. We'll talk more about sampling in the next section.

Figure 3.6	Completion Test
	It can be especially difficult to get accurate information from children. Researchers often use visuals such as this Japanese completion test to encourage children to express their feelings. The test asked boys to write in the empty balloon what they think the boy in the drawing will answer when the girl asks, 'What programme do you want to watch next?'

Online Research

www.pearsoned.co.uk/solomon

Objective

5

The growing use of online research

The growth of the internet is rewriting some of the rules of the marketing research process. As more and more people have access to the web, many companies are finding that the internet is a superior way to collect data – it's fast, it's relatively cheap and it lends itself well to forms of research from simple questionnaires to focus groups.

Fifty per cent of European researchers state that they have replaced face-to-face interviews with online research.[40] Seventy-five per cent of research decisions makers in the US have tried online research and expect to use it again in the future. In 2005, some researchers predicted that within two years, online surveys would have an average predicted share of business of 39.6 per cent, more than telephone (30.7 per cent), face-to-face (23.9 per cent) or mail surveys (5.7 per cent).[41]

Developments in online research are happening quickly, so let's take some time now to see where things are heading.

The web is revolutionising the way many companies collect data and use them to guide marketing decisions. There are two major types of online research. One type is information gathered by tracking consumers while they are surfing. The second type is information gathered through questionnaires on websites, through e-mail or from moderated focus groups conducted in chat rooms.

The internet offers an unprecedented ability to track consumers as they search for information. Marketers can better understand where people go to look when they want to learn about products and services – and which advertisements they stop to browse along the way. How can marketers do this? One way is by the use of cookies. Beware the Cookie Monster! **Cookies** are text files inserted by a website sponsor into a user's hard drive when the user connects with the site. Cookies remember details of a visit to a website, typically tracking which pages the user visits. Some sites request or require that visitors 'register' on the site by answering questions

Real People, Other Voices

Advice for Helen Armstrong

Mr Michael Howley,
University of Surrey

I would choose option 2, sample everyone who was involved in the purchasing or receiving of jewellery whether gold or not. In this way you would focus on those who had purchased gold jewellery or received it, and thereby establish their motivations for doing so, while also studying those who had purchased jewellery which was not gold. This second group must constitute a prime target market for the WGC because as they have shown a willingness to purchase or receive jewellery of some sort it should be a relatively easy step to convert them to the concept of gold jewellery. By contrast, option 3 would, to my mind, involve spreading the net too broadly. By extending the population to be studied to include everyone, whether they buy jewellery or not, the researcher runs the risk of including large numbers of respondents who are highly unlikely ever to purchase gold jewellery and thereby wasting resources in studying them. The difference between the size of the budgets involved, £350,000 for option 1 and £500,000 for both options 2 and 3, is not really significant compared with the huge potential returns that would accrue from a successful communications strategy inaugurated by the WGC and its partners.

Associate Professor Jacob Aabroe,
Roskilde Business College, Denmark

If there are no financial constraints, I would choose to examine the broadest possible population (option 3). It is of little use to know the habits of existing gold customers when the purpose is to find out why people are NOT buying gold for jewellery. Using a sample that includes the entire population for the marketplace is the best choice for the World Gold Council, as it can help to Identify new potential customers, as well as to understand existing

customers better. The expectation that this type of study will most likely find more segments, leading to higher communication expenses, is not a valid reason to exclude it as an option. Consumers are acting in a more complex way today than ever before and companies should take this into account when they perform their marketing research.

Professor Stephen Brown,
University of Ulster

They say that if Thomas Edison had held focus groups he'd have invented bigger candles, not light bulbs. And Alexander Graham Bell, analogously, would've built a better bullhorn. My preferred option therefore is none of the above. It is almost impossible to grasp the meaning of gold using market research techniques as vapid as focus groups and tick-box questionnaires. Such meanings, I suspect, are very deeply embedded in the consumer psyche. They cannot be adequately accessed by methods that scratch the surface, at most. Even much-lauded methodologies like ethnography, projective research and metaphor elicitation are incapable of cracking the code of something as tantalisingly mysterious as gold. Can focus groups really get a handle on 'gold fever'? I very much doubt it.

Gfk Roper Consulting might be better off initiating a programme of cultural market research, which attempts to grasp underlying meanings by examining the artefacts of popular culture – for example, movies like *The Gold Rush* or *The Treasure of the Sierra Madre* or *Diamonds Are Forever* – which better express the essence of consumer motivation than the pie-charted results of 1250 survey interviews. This is not to say that questionnaire surveys and focus groups are pointless. All market research information, if judiciously evaluated, can help creative managers make better decisions, but market research findings must always be taken with a sizeable pinch of salt. Indeed, even if sales subsequently soar in the markets that have received the research-led treatment, that doesn't necessarily mean the marketing made it happen. There's a world of difference between correlation and causality.

about themselves and their likes and dislikes. In such cases, cookies also allow the site to access these details about the customer.

This technology allows websites to customise services, such as when Amazon.co.uk recommends new books to users on the basis of what books they have ordered in the past. Most consumers have no idea that cookies allow websites to gather and store all this information. You can block cookies or curb them, although this can make life difficult if you are trying to log on to many sites, such as online newspapers or travel agencies that require this information to admit you.

This information generated from tracking consumers' online journeys has become a product as well – companies sell these consumer data to other companies that are trying to target prospects. But consumers have become increasingly concerned about the sharing of these data. In a study of 10,000 web users, 84 per cent objected to the reselling of their information to other companies. Although internet users can delete cookie files manually or install anti-cookie software on their computers, there are many people who feel there is a need for privacy regulation and for cookie regulation in order to limit potential abuses.

Online Research Applications

The internet offers a faster, less expensive alternative to traditional communication data collection methods. Here are some ways companies are using the internet to get feedback from consumers:

- **New-product development:** In the 1990s, Procter & Gamble spent more than five years testing products such as Febreze, Dryel and Fit Fruit & Vegetable Wash the old-fashioned way before launching in the US. Using online tests, its Crest MultiCare Flex & Clean toothbrush was launched in less than a year. General Motors and Nissan are two car makers that now gather online consumer reactions to forthcoming products. Such research allows manufacturers to learn what consumers want in future vehicles.[42]

- **Estimating market response:** A few cutting-edge companies are creating virtual worlds and using them to test consumers' responses to brands. Using 'There-bucks', people who sign up to join the virtual community at There.com can choose to 'buy' products like Levi's Type I jeans or Nike's high-end Zoom Celar shoes on the site. Companies can then analyse who chose to buy which brands and which activities they engaged in while on the site (for example, do people who select the Levi's style tend to spend a lot of time socialising in There clubs that are available on the site?).[43]

- **Exploratory research:** Online focus groups have mushroomed in popularity in recent years. Firms such as itracks.com offer complete focus group capabilities via the web, claiming that 'online research does not mean you lose the human touch. The online environment elicits honest responses, uninfluenced by peer pressure or group dominance'. To achieve this comfort level, all participants and the moderator log in anonymously using password protection. Of course, with online groups it is impossible to observe body language, facial expressions and vocal inflection. But marketers continue to develop new ways to talk to consumers in virtual space, including software that allows online focus group participants to indicate non-verbal responses. For example, an online participant can register an expression of disgust by clicking on the command to 'roll eyes'.[44]

- **Instant messaging:** A few forward-thinking marketers are starting to take advantage of the fact that 75 per cent of teens who go online use IM (instant messaging) and 48 per cent trade IM messages at least once a day. These researchers link IM to online focus groups: a moderator can conduct a chat with a respondent using IM technology in order to probe his or her answers more deeply in a separate conversation.[45]

Advantages and Disadvantages of Online Data Collection

Many marketing research companies are running, not walking, to the web to conduct studies for clients. Why? For one thing, replacing traditional mail consumer panels with internet panels allows marketers to collect the same amount of data in a weekend that used to take six to eight weeks. And consumers can complete surveys when it is convenient – even at 3 a.m. in their pyjamas. There are other advantages: companies can conduct large studies at low cost. International borders are not a problem either, since in many regions (such as Scandinavia) internet use is very high and it's easy to recruit respondents. web-based interviews eliminate interviewer bias or errors in data entry.

However, no data collection method is perfect, and online research is no exception – although many of the criticisms of online techniques also apply to offline techniques. One potential problem is the representativeness of the respondents. Although the number of internet users continues to grow, many segments of the consumer population, mainly the poor and elderly, do not have equal access to the internet. In addition, in many studies (just as with mail surveys or shopping centre intercepts) there is a self-selection bias in the sample in that respondents have agreed to receive invitations to take part in online studies, which means they tend to be the kind of people who like to participate in surveys. As with other kinds of research such as live focus groups, it's not unusual to encounter 'professional respondents' – people who just enjoy taking part in studies (and getting paid for it). Online firms such as Harris Interactive, Survey Sampling, or Greenfield online address this problem by monitoring their participants and regulating how often they are allowed to participate in different studies over a period of time.

There are other disadvantages of online research. Hackers can actually try to influence research results. Even more dangerous may be competitors who can learn about a firm's marketing plans, products, advertising and so forth by intercepting information used in research. Despite the potential drawbacks, online research has a bright future. This research has the potential to take off even faster as a result of the 2001 terrorist attacks since many Americans are more hesitant to answer questions from strangers, drive to focus group facilities, or open mail surveys from sources they don't recognise.

 ## Step 4: Design the Sample

Once the researcher has defined the problem, decided on a research design and determined how to collect the data, the next step is to decide from whom to obtain the needed data. This is Helen Armstrong's main problem in doing the World Gold Council's research project, namely, 'who should they interview?' Of course, she could collect the information from every single customer or prospective customer. But this collection, known as a consensus, would be extremely expensive and time-consuming, if possible at all. Instead, researchers collect most of their data from a sample of the population of interest. Based on the answers from this sample, researchers hope to generalise to the larger population. Whether such inferences are accurate or inaccurate depends on the type and quality of the study sample. There are two main types of samples: probability and non-probability samples.

Probability Sampling

With a **probability sample**, each member of the population has some known chance of being included in the sample. Using a probability sample ensures that the sample is representative of the population and that inferences about the population made from the sample are justified. For example, if a larger percentage of males than females in a probability sample say they prefer action movies to 'chick flicks', one can infer with confidence that a larger percentage of males than females in the general population also would rather see a character get sliced and diced.

Simple random sampling. The most basic type of probability sample is a simple random sample in which every member of a population has a known and equal chance of being included in the study. For example, if we simply take the names of all students in your class, let's assume there are 40 students for now, and put them in a hat and draw one out, each member of your class has a 1 in 40 chance of being included in the sample. In most studies, the population from which the sample will be drawn is too large for a hat, so marketers generate a random sample from a list of members of the population using a computer program.

Systematic sampling. Sometimes researchers use a systematic sampling procedure to select members of a population in which they select the nth member of a population after a random start. For example, if we want a sample of 10 members of your class, we might begin with the second person on the register and select every fourth name after that, that is, the 2nd, the 6th, the 10th, the 14th and so on. Researchers know that studies that use systematic samples are just as accurate as with simple random samples. Unless a list of members of the population of interest is already in a computer data file, it's a lot simpler to create a systematic sample.

Stratified sampling. Yet another type of probability sample is a stratified sample in which a researcher divides the population into segments that are related to the study's topic. For example, imagine that you are interested in studying what types of films are most liked by members of a population. You have learned from previous studies that men and women in the population differ in their attitudes toward different types of movies – men like action flicks and women like romances. To create a stratified sample, you would first divide the population into male and female segments. Then respondents from each of the two segments would be selected randomly in proportion to their percentage of the population. In this way, you have created a sample that is proportionate to the population on a characteristic that you know will make a difference in the study results.

Non-Probability Sampling

Sometimes researchers do not believe the time, effort and costs required to develop a probability sample are justified, perhaps because they need an answer quickly or they just want to get a general sense of how people feel about a topic. They may choose a **non-probability sample**, which entails the use of personal judgement in selecting respondents – in some cases just asking whomever they can find. With a non-probability sample, some members of the population have no chance at all of being included in the sample. Thus, there is no way to ensure that the sample is representative of the population. Results from non-probability studies can be generally suggestive of what is going on in the real world but not necessarily definitive.

A **convenience sample** is a non-probability sample composed of individuals who just happen to be available when and where the data are being collected. For example, if you simply stand in front of the student union and ask students who walk by to complete your questionnaire, that would be a convenience sample.

Quota sampling. Finally, researchers may also use a quota sample that includes the same proportion of individuals with certain characteristics as is found in the population. For example, if you are studying attitudes of students in your university, you might just go on campus and find bachelor, master and PhD students in proportion to the number of members of each class in the university. The quota sample is much like the stratified sample except that with a quota sample, the researcher uses his or her individual judgement to select respondents.

 ## Step 5: Collect the Data

At this point, the researcher has determined the nature of the problem that needs to be addressed. He or she has decided on a research design that will specify how to investigate the problem and what kinds of information (data) will be needed. The researcher has also selected the data collection and sampling methods. Once these decisions have been made, the next task is to actually collect the data.

Although collecting data may seem like a simple process, researchers are well aware of its critical importance to the accuracy of research. There are several criteria which affect how successful the chosen research collection method will be. A precise timescale can help, for example accurate decision making and the access to relevant skills and expertise can speed up the collection process. When interviewers are involved, researchers know that the quality of research results is only as good as the poorest interviewer collecting the data. Careless interviewers may not read questions exactly as written, or they may not record respondent answers correctly. So marketers must train and supervise interviewers to make sure they follow the research procedures exactly as outlined. In the next section, we'll talk about some of the problems in gathering data and some solutions.

Challenges to Gathering Data in Foreign Countries

Conducting market research around the world is big business for many firms. Remember Helen Armstrong and the World Gold Council project at the beginning of the chapter. However, market conditions and consumer preferences vary worldwide, and there are major differences in the sophistication of market research operations and the amount of data available to global marketers. In Mexico, for instance, because there are still large areas where native Indian tribes speak languages other than Spanish, researchers may bypass these groups in surveys.

Another example for 2003 (the last year for which figures are available), estimated expenditures for research by marketing research companies – $387 million – rank China number two in Asia Pacific markets, topped only by Japan. In fact, money spent on marketing research in China is growing faster than in any other country in the world, with increases of over 25 per cent a year. The reason for such expenditures is obvious: China is an emerging market of more than 1.3 billion potential consumers. Interestingly, however, there's an erroneous impression among foreign marketers that most of the population lives in large cities. Coupled with real infrastructure and transportation challenges, this demographic misconception has left large portions of the vast Chinese countryside virtually untouched by modern marketing – so far.[46]

For these and other reasons, choosing an appropriate data collection method is difficult. In some countries, many people may not have phones, or low literacy rates may interfere with mail surveys. *Local customs* can be a problem as well. Offering money for interviews is generally considered rude in Latin American countries.[47] Saudi Arabia bans gatherings of four or more people except for family or religious events, and it's illegal to stop strangers on the street or knock on the door of someone's house.[48]

Cultural differences also affect responses to survey items. Both Danish and British consumers, for example, agree that it is important to eat breakfast, but the Danish sample may be thinking of fruit and yogurt while the British sample is thinking of toast and tea. Sometimes marketers can overcome these problems by involving local researchers in decisions about the research design.

Another problem with conducting marketing research in global markets is *language*. Sometimes translations just don't come out right. In some cases entire subcultures within a country might be excluded from the research sample. In fact, this issue is becoming more and more prevalent inside the United States as non-English speakers increase as a percentage of the population.

To overcome language difficulties, researchers use a process called **back-translation**, which requires two steps. First, a native speaker translates the questionnaire into the language of the targeted respondents. Then this new version is translated back into the original language to ensure that the correct meanings survive the process. Even with precautions such as these, however, researchers must interpret data obtained from other cultures with care. The European Society for Opinion and Marketing Research (ESOMAR, www.esomar.org) is a world organisation which publishes codes and guidelines for conducting market research. Look at their website. Why is such an organisation useful? Which standards do you regard as most necessary?

Across the Hall

Advice for Helen Armstrong

Yvonne McGivern
is Joint Chief Examiner for the MRS Advanced Certificate in Market and Social Research Practice and author of *The Practice of Market Research*

I would advise Helen to choose option 3. As the case points out, a key element in the choice of research approach is the decision about who to interview – in other words, who should be the target population for the research? The value of the information produced by the research and its applicability to the client's business decisions rests on this. My reading of the case is that the client needs to have a clear and comprehensive picture not only of its current market (those who buy gold jewellery) but of its potential market. It needs to know how it can grow its business. Its remit is to market gold as a product and one of its key business objectives must be to increase sales. Thus the target population should not be confined to existing gold jewellery buyers – likely to deliver only a limited amount of sales growth – but should include all potential buyers, those who spend on competing products in the luxury sector and who could – with the right communications campaign – be enticed into buying gold.

So expanding the target population to those who are in the luxury spending/luxury item market – as only option 3 suggests – should ensure that the research delivers the information the client needs to develop its business.

The case states that a disadvantage of using a wider definition of the target population is that 'many more segments might be identified which might lead to complex and more expensive communication programmes to meet the needs of each segment'. This should not be seen as a disadvantage but as an opportunity: identifying segments can only be useful for the client. Knowing what type of consumers belong to each segment will help the client decide whether that segment is likely to yield a return on investment and so enable it to make a decision about whether or not to develop a communications campaign for that segment. An investment now in research among this wider population to uncover segments is likely to be a much more efficient approach, one that incurs a smaller degree of a risk/opportunity cost than using the narrower definition and failing to discover a potentially lucrative segment.

The qualitative research proposed will be useful in achieving in-depth insight into the luxury spending market. It will be useful in exploring and reaching some understanding of the motivations for spending on luxury items and of the decision-making processes involved in that spending, and in exploring thoughts and feelings prior to, during and after the purchase has been made. The insight from the qualitative research will be useful in designing the survey questionnaire. In particular, it will be useful in developing the attitude statements that will be key in segmenting the sample.

The sample size of 1000 to 1250 is likely to be necessary to run a robust segmentation analysis. The client will want to be reassured that the segments are credible, given that it plans to invest in a communications campaign targeted at those segments.

 ## Step 6: Analyse and Interpret the Data

To understand the important role of data analysis, let's take a look at a hypothetical research example. In our example, a company that markets frozen foods wishes to better understand consumers' preferences for varying levels of fat content in their diets. They have conducted a descriptive research study in which they collected primary data via telephone interviews. Because companies recognise that gender is related to dietary preferences, they have used a stratified sample that includes 175 males and 175 females.

Tabulating and Cross-Tabulating

Typically, marketers first tabulate the data as Table 3.4 shows – that is, they arrange the data in a table or other summary form so they can get a broad picture of the overall responses. The data in this table show that 43 per cent of the sample prefers a low-fat meal. In addition, there may be a desire to cross-classify or cross-tabulate the answers to questions by other variables. Cross-tabulation means that the data are examined by subgroups, in this case males and females

Table 3.4
Examples of Data
Tabulation and
Cross-Tabulation
Tables

Fat Content Preference (number and percentages of responses)		
Questionnaire Response	Number of Responses	Percentage of Responses
Do you prefer a meal with high fat content, medium fat content, or low fat content?		
High fat	21	6
Medium fat	179	51
Low fat	150	43
Total	350	100

Fat Content Preference by Gender (number and percentages of responses)						
Questionnaire	Number of Females	Percentage of Females	Number of Males	Percentage of Males	Total Number	Total Percentage
Do you prefer a meal with high fat content, medium fat content, or low fat content?						
High fat	4	2	17	10	21	6
Medium fat	68	39	111	64	179	51
Low fat	103	59	47	27	150	43
Total	175	100	175	100	350	100

separately, to see how results vary between categories. The cross-tabulation in Table 3.4 shows that 59 per cent of females versus only 27 per cent of males prefer a meal with low fat content. In addition, researchers may wish to apply additional statistical tests.

Based on the tabulation and cross-tabulations, the researcher must then interpret or draw conclusions from the results and make recommendations. For example, the study results shown in Table 3.4 may lead to the conclusion that females are more likely than males to be concerned about a low-fat diet. The researcher might then make a recommendation to a firm that it should target females in the introduction of a new line of low-fat foods.

Step 7: Prepare the Research Report

The final step is to prepare a report of the research results. In general, a research report must clearly and concisely tell the readers what they need to know in a way that they can understand. A typical report includes the followings:

● An executive summary of the report that covers the high points of the total report.

● An understandable description of the research methodology.

● A complete discussion of the results of the study, including the tabulations, cross-tabulations and additional statistical analyses.

● Limitations of the study (no study is perfect).

● Conclusions and recommendations for managerial action based on the results.

Now you've learned about marketing research, and read 'Real People, Real Decisions' advice to see which market research strategy Helen Armstrong chose for her client, the World Gold Council. Here's how it worked out.

Real People, Real Decisions

How it Worked out at the World Gold Council

World Gold Council went for option 3, to broaden the study to include all luxury goods consumers whether they buy jewellery or not. In the end, the qualitative exercise consisted of: nine one-hour telephone in-depth interviews with internal WGC stakeholders around the world, five one-hour face-to-face in-depth interviews with opinion leaders in key markets, six one-hour in-depth interviews and accompanied

It wanted the research to be as comprehensive and statistically robust as possible and to have confidence in the results

shopping trips were conducted with consumers by market.

All were buyers of luxury goods, split between those who included gold in their purchase and those who did not. Four two-hour focus groups were also conducted among buyers of luxury goods, *again divided between those who bought gold and those who did not.* The final quantitative research was conducted among 1000–1250 women, regardless of whether they bought gold or not, with a longer interview than in option 2.

Despite the potential issue with a large number of segments, it was felt that this final structure gave a better picture of the role and value of gold jewellery in consumers' lives. Including non-buyers was crucial for market development in the US, China and Italy where fewer people buy gold. As the WGC was not going to repeat this for a few years, yet was going to focus its worldwide marketing campaigns to target the key segments identified, it wanted the research to be as comprehensive and statistically robust as possible and to have confidence in the results. Being the most comprehensive option (which in fact involved spending the equivalent of 3.5 working years talking to consumers throughout the whole project), it also had the greatest credibility when talking to gold retail partners in each of its core countries.

The study has proved invaluable to World Gold Council, such that a major update was undertaken in 2005 to explore in detail the motivations behind the behaviours observed to give them even greater insight into the functional and emotional benefits of gold and the role gold jewellery plays in the everyday lives of consumers around the world.

| Photo 3.5 | An advert for gold jewellry from Temple St. Clair. Source: World Gold Council |

Marketing Metrics

Measuring success at the WCG

The study ultimately produced five global segments of gold purchasers all with differing attitudes towards and needs from gold jewellery. As a result of these segments, the WGC fine-tuned its communications strategy and messaging to more closely reflect the way target consumers perceive and purchase gold. The results speak for themselves. In the face of a consistently rising gold price, demand for gold jewellery has been robust and by the end of 2007 stood at its highest level, $54 billion. Since 2002, in the countries where the WGC worked with its partners and introduced the new communications strategy, the market has consistently outperformed those where WGC is not present. Also, gold jewellery sales outperformed GDP growth, retail sales indices and diamond and platinum jewellery sales in the target countries.

Chapter Summary

Now that you have finished reading this chapter, you should understand:

1. **The role of the marketing information system and the marketing decision support system in decision making.** A marketing information system (MkIS) is composed of internal data, marketing intelligence, marketing research data, acquired databases, and computer hardware and software. Firms use an MkIS to gather, sort, analyse, store and distribute information needed by managers for marketing decision making. The marketing decision support system (MDSS) allows managers to use analysis software and interactive software to access MkIS data and to conduct analyses and find the information they need.

2. **The marketing research process.** The research process begins by defining the problem and determining the research design or type of study. Next, researchers choose the data collection method, that is, whether there are secondary data available or if primary research with a communication study or through observation is necessary. Then researchers determine what type of sample is to be used for the study and then collect the data. The final steps in the research are to analyse and interpret the data and prepare a research report.

3. **The differences among exploratory, descriptive and causal research and some research techniques available to marketers.** Exploratory research typically uses qualitative data collected by individual interviews, focus groups or observational methods such as ethnography. Descriptive research includes cross-sectional and longitudinal studies. Causal research goes a step further by designing controlled experiments to understand cause-and-effect relationships between marketing independent variables, such as price changes, and dependent variables, such as sales.

4. **The different types of data-collection methods and types of samples that researchers use.** Researchers may choose to collect data via survey methods and observation approaches. Survey approaches include mail questionnaires, telephone interviews, face-to-face interviews or online questionnaires. A study may utilise a probability sample such as a simple random or stratified sample in which inferences can be made to a population on the basis of sample results. Non-probability sampling methods include a convenience sample and a quota sample. The research tries to ensure that the data are valid, reliable and representative. Validity is the extent to which the research actually measures what it was intended to measure. Reliability is the extent to which the research measurement techniques are free of errors. Representativeness is the extent to which consumers in the study are similar to a larger group in which the organisation has an interest.

5. **The growing use of online research.** Online research accounts for more than 25 per cent of all marketing research. Online tracking uses cookies to record where consumers go on a website. Consumers have become increasingly concerned about privacy and how this information is used and made available to other internet companies. The internet also provides an attractive alternative to traditional data collection methods because of its speed and low cost.

Key Terms

Chapter Review

Marketing Concepts: Testing Your Knowledge

1. What is a marketing information system (MkIS)? What types of information are included in a marketing information system? How does a marketing decision support system (MDSS) allow marketers to easily get the information they need?

2. What is data mining? How is it used by marketers?

3. What are the steps in the marketing research process? Why is defining the problem to be researched so important to ultimate success with the research project?

4. What techniques are used to gather data in exploratory research? How can exploratory research be useful to marketers?

5. What are some advantages and disadvantages of telephone interviews, postal questionnaires, face-to-face interviews and online interviews?

6. When considering data quality, what are the differences among validity, reliability and representativeness? How do you know data have high levels of these characteristics?

7. How do probability and non-probability samples differ? What are some types of probability samples? What are some types of non-probability samples?

8. What is a cross-tabulation? How are cross-tabulations useful in analysing and interpreting data?

9. What is a cookie? What ethical and privacy issues are related to cookies?

10. What important issues must researchers consider when planning to collect their data online?

Marketing Concepts: Discussing Choices and Ethical Issues

1. Some marketers attempt to disguise themselves as marketing researchers when their real intent is to sell something to the consumer. What is the impact of this practice on legitimate researchers? What do you think might be done about this practice?

2. Do you think marketers should be allowed to conduct market research with young children? Why or why not?

3. Are you willing to divulge personal information to marketing researchers? How much are you willing to tell, or where would you draw the line?

4. What is your overall attitude toward marketing research? Do you think it is a beneficial activity from a consumer's perspective? Or do you think it merely gives marketers new insights on how to convince consumers to buy something they really don't want or need?

5. Sometimes firms use data mining to identify and abandon customers who are not profitable because they don't spend enough to justify the service needed or because they return a large proportion of the items they buy. What do you think of such practices? Is it ethical for firms to prune out these customers?

6. Many consumers are concerned about online tracking studies and their privacy. Do consumers have the right to 'own' data about themselves? Should governments limit the use of the internet for data collection?

7. One unobtrusive measure mentioned in this chapter involved going through consumers' or competitors' garbage. Do you think marketers should have the right to do this? Is it ethical?

8. Consider the approach to tracking consumers' exposure to promotions via portable people meters, or PPMs. How would you feel about participating in a study that required you to use a PPM? What would be the advantage of a PPM approach versus keeping a written diary of television shows you watched and ads you saw?

 ## Marketing Practice: Applying What You've Learned

1. Your firm is planning to begin marketing a consumer product in several markets. You have been given the responsibility of developing plans for marketing research to be conducted in South Africa, in Spain, and in China. In a role-playing situation, present the difficulties you expect to encounter, if any, in conducting research in each of these areas.

2. As an account executive with a marketing research firm, you are responsible for deciding on the type of research to be used in various studies conducted for your clients. For each of the following client questions, list your choices of research approaches.

    a. Will television or magazine advertising be more effective for a local bank to use in its marketing communication plan?

    b. Could a new package design for breakfast cereal do a better job at satisfying the needs of buyers and thus increase sales?

    c. Are consumers more likely to buy brands that are labelled as environmentally friendly?

    d. How do female consumers determine if a particular perfume is right for them?

    e. What types of people read the local newspaper?

    f. How frequently do consumers switch brands of soft drinks?

    g. How will an increase in the price of a brand of laundry detergent affect sales?

    h. What are the effects of advertising and sales promotion in combination on sales of a brand of shampoo?

3. Your marketing research firm is planning to conduct surveys to gather information for a number of clients. Your boss has asked you and a few other new employees to do some preliminary work. He has asked each of you to choose three of the topics (from among those listed next) that will be included in the project and to prepare an analysis of the advantages and disadvantages of these communication methods of collecting data: mail questionnaires, telephone interviews, face-to-face interviews, and online questionnaires.

    a. The amount of sports nutrition drinks consumed in a city.

    b. Why a local bank has been losing customers.

    c. How heavily the company should invest in manufacturing and marketing home fax machines.

    d. The amount of money spent on euro lottery tickets in Denmark, Sweden, Holland and the UK.

    e. What local doctors would like to see changed in the hospitals in the city.

    f. Consumers' attitudes toward several sports celebrities.

4. For each of the topics you selected in item 3, how might a more passive (observation) approach be used to support the communication methods employed?

Marketing Miniproject: Learning by Doing

The purpose of this miniproject is to familiarise you with marketing research techniques and to help you apply these techniques to managerial decision making.

1. With three other students in your class, select a small retail business or fast-food restaurant to use as a 'client' for your project. (Be sure to get the manager's permission before conducting your research.) Then choose a topic from among the following possibilities to develop a study problem:

   ● Employee–customer interactions.
   ● The busiest periods of customer activity.
   ● Customer perceptions of service.
   ● Customer likes and dislikes about offerings.
   ● Customer likes and dislikes about the environment in the place of business.
   ● The benefits customers perceive to be important.
   ● The age groups that frequent the place of business.
   ● The buying habits of a particular age group.
   ● How customer complaints are handled.

2. Develop a plan for the research:
   a. Define the problem as you will study it;
   b. Choose the type of research you will use;
   c. Select the techniques you will use to gather data;
   d. Develop the mode and format for data collection.

3. Conduct the research.

4. Write a report (or develop a class presentation) that includes four parts:
   a. Introduction: a brief overview of the business and the problem studied;
   b. Methodology: the type of research used, the techniques used to gather data (and why they were chosen), the instruments and procedures used, the number of respondents, duration of the study, and other details that would allow someone to replicate your study;
   c. Results: a compilation of the results (perhaps in table form) and the conclusions drawn;
   d. Recommendations: a list of recommendations for actions management might take based on the conclusions drawn from the study.

Real People, Real Surfers

Exploring the Web

As discussed in this chapter, monitoring changes in demographics and other consumer trends is an important part of the marketing intelligence included in an MkIS. Today, much of this information is gathered by government research and is available on the internet.

The UK National Statistical Office provides tabled data for cities and counties across the nations at its site, www.statistics.gov.uk. Statistics Netherlands is a governmental institution which collects and provides data about the Netherlands at its site, www.cbs.nl/en-GB/default.htm. A similar statistics website exists for Denmark, at www.dst.dk/homeuk.aspx.

On the homepage, click on population. You should be able to locate the statistical data for your area by using a search engine such as Google, and entering something like 'Utrecht Statistical Abstract'. Using both state data and Statistics Netherlands data, develop a report on a city or county of your choice that answers these questions:

1. What is the total population of your city or town?

2. Describe the population of the area in terms of age, income, education, ethnic background, marital status, occupation and housing.

3. How does your city or town compare to the demographic characteristics of the entire UK or Dutch or Danish population?

4. What is your opinion of the different websites you used? How useful are they to marketers? How easy were they to navigate? Was there information that you wanted that was not available? Was there more or less information from the sites than you anticipated? Explain.

Now, take a look at the website at www.pearsoned.co.uk/solomon to see some videos from YouTube relating to aspects of this chapter.

Marketing Plan Exercise

Select a company that makes a product that you use and with which you are familiar. For the company to make decisions about developing new products and attracting new customers, it must rely on marketing research. These decisions feed into the company's marketing plan. For the firm you selected:

1. Undertake preliminary secondary research, for example by looking at company and market reports in order to get a better initial insight into the company. Try to identify problems which the company is facing and areas where performance could be improved. Now pick and define one specific problem they could address through marketing research.

2. What type of research design do you recommend for addressing that problem, and why?

3. What is the most appropriate way to collect the data? Justify your choice.

4. How will you ensure high validity, reliability, and representativeness of the data?

5. Design an appropriate sampling plan.

Marketing in Action Case

Real decisions at NeoMedia Technologies

A standard mobile phone lets you send and receive calls, shop numbers and addresses, and play games. Advanced mobile phones let you take and send digital photos, access the internet, and listen to music. With that in mind the question is, how many more features can manufacturers and service providers pack into a mobile phone? And when will the buying public say 'enough' about what they are willing to pay for all these features? The people at NeoMedia Technologies, designer of NeoReader software for mobile phones, hope the answer to the first question is 'at least one more', and the answer to the second question is 'hopefully, not for a long time'.

Mobile phone software launched by NeoMedia in late 2006 allows consumers to use the camera feature of their phone to look up information about virtually anything that has a UPC, or Universal Product Code. For example, a consumer in a beauty supply shop is considering buying a certain brand of shampoo but is not sure if the shampoo works well with her type of hair. Unfortunately, the package description doesn't answer her question. To gather more information about the product, the consumer can select the NeoMedia software from the icon already included on her mobile phone and take a picture of the UPC on the shampoo package. The software will read the UPC and link to the website for the product. Once the connection is made, the consumer can use her phone to browse the product's website to learn whether the shampoo is compatible with her hair.

Consider products that have bar codes on them – textbooks, music CDs, computers, MP3 players and cereal boxes – or could have bar codes – cars, paintings in museums, and buildings – and the possibilities for this latest addition to mobile phone software seem endless. What if a group of friends wants to see a film one evening but can't decide what to see? If you have a mobile phone with the right software, you can snap a picture of the bar codes on the promotional posters at the cinema and watch the film trailers. After everyone has viewed the ad for each film, the group can decide which film to see. Also, consider a tourist passing by Big Ben in London and wanting to know when it was built, who designed it and how much it cost. With the right mobile phone software he could take a picture of a unique product code attached to or near the building and pull up the Wikipedia.org entry for that building.

To successfully introduce this product, NeoMedia Technologies will need a detailed marketing plan that includes an examination of the external environment. In addition, there may be market research applications to the technology. For example, questionnaires could have a bar code in restaurants or bar and you could complete the survey online in real time while you are experiencing the event and the data would be aggregated instantaneously for the

You can snap a picture of the bar codes on promotional posters at the cinema and watch the film trailers

company. By allowing access to many more websites in real time, web tracking of what people do on the web will become more important and could give clues and to which type of information people want to see more of. There could be a code for the hotline or complaints line so you could take a picture or video of the problem and upload it onto the company's complaint pages.

NeoMedia Technologies' marketing planning must also consider who is its real customer? Is it the mobile phone manufacturers that can pre-install the software on the phones as they are produced or consumers who can select the software as an option to install when they purchase the phone from a phone service provider? Or could it be used by market research agencies alone as a data collection tool? To maximise the opportunities for success in the marketplace, NeoMedia Technologies must make good marketing planning decisions.

Things to Think About

1. What are the market research applications of NeoReader?

2. Which type of data do you think it would be best and worse at collecting?

3. What types of situations or companies might most be interested in these applications and why?

4. What course of action would you recommend for them to exploit these?

Source: Jessica E. Vascellaro, 'The Staid Bar Code Gets a Hip New Life', *Wall Street Journal*, 24 May 2006, D1, D11.

References

1. American Marketing Association Website. Accessed 24 January 2008. www.marketingpower.com/mg-dictionary.php?SearchFor=Marketing+Research&Searched=1.

2. Megan Dowd, 'Avon's Daughters Make their "Mark"'. Accessed 17 February 2006. www.foxnews.com/story/0,2933,136233,00.html.

3. 'Ball Street Börsenspiel', *Financial Times Deutschland*. Accessed 8 June 2007. http://ball-street.ftd.de/view/.

4. 'The Q Scores Company', Marketing Evaluations. Accessed 15 February 2006. www.qscores.com.

5. 'About BARB', Broadcasters' Audience Research Board. Accessed 13 June 2007. www.barb.co.uk/about.cfm?flag=about.

6. Yumiko Ono, 'An Ad for Smudge-Proof Makeup Rubs a Big Marketer Wrong Way,' *Wall Street Journal*, 12 April 1996, B1.

7. 'Consumer Products: Ben & Jerry's', Business Objects. Accessed 14 June 2007. www.businessobjects.com/company/customers/company.asp?industryid=2&productid=&companyid=83.

8. 'Privacy Policy', British Airways. Accessed 4 June 2007. www.britishairways.com/travel/fullpp/public/en_gb.

9. Pan-Ning Tan, Michael Steinbach and Vipin Kumar, *Introduction to Data Mining*, 1st ed. (New York: Addison Wesley, 2005).

10. Tan *et al.*, *Introduction to Data Mining*.

11. Frederich F. Reichheld, *Loyalty Rules! How leaders build lasting relationships in the digital age* (Cambridge, MA: Harvard Business School Press, 2001).

12. Claire Bothwell (2005): 'Burberry versus the chavs.' *BBC Money Programme*. Accessed 13 June 2007. http://news.bbc.co.uk/2/hi/business/4381140.stm.

13. Robert Baxter, Mercedes-Benz North America, personal communication, June 1996.

14. Hamilton Nolan, 'Mercedes Launches PR Push,' *PR Week*, 6 February 2006, 3.

15. Mintel International, 'Consumer Media and Market Research.' Accessed 5 June 2007. www.mintel.com/frontpage/.

16. Audi Deutschland Website Press Releases (2006): 'Audi Lab for Market research an der Universität St. Gallen gegründet.' Audi Website, Press Release 23 August 2006. Accessed 4 June 2007. www.audi.de/audi/de/de2/unternehmen/news/pressemitteilungen/_Audi_Lab_for_Market_Research__an_der_Universitaet_St__Gallen_gegruendet.html.

17. Michael R. Solomon, *Conquering Consumerspace: Marketing Strategies for a Branded World* (New York: Amacom Books, 2003).

18. English, Paul, 'So cool, it hurts: Paul English gets hip to the glamorous work of professional trendsetters.' *Daily Record*, 20 October 2001, 6-7. Hedley, Don (2007): 'Trendspotter: The uber-sexual man.' *Brand Strategy*, 8, 12 June 2007.

19. 'Nivea deodorant. How market research supports the new product development process.' *The Times* and MBA Publishing (eds). Edition 12. 105–108. www.thetimes100.co.uk/ downloads/nivea/nivea_12_full.pdf.

20. Nokia Website, 'Consumers increasingly giving up their fixed line phones' Press Release October 21, 2004. Accessed 6 June 2007. http://press.nokia.com/PR/200410/965166_5.html.

21. 'Nutrition, health and wellness: New product development at Nestlé.' *The Times* and MBA Publishing (eds). Edition 11, 113–116. www.thetimes100.co.uk/downloads/nestle/nestle_11_full.pdf.

22. Michael R. Solomon, *Consumer Behavior: Buying, Having and Being*, 5th ed. (Upper Saddle River, NJ: Prentice Hall, 2001).

23. 'Volvic puts TV ad character on MSN spaces.' *New Media Age*, 17 May 2007, 2.

24. Jean Halliday, 'Nissan Delves into Truck Owner Psyche,' *Advertising Age*, 1 December 2003, 11.

25. Mini (2007): 'Mini united: Friends challenge festival: Are you ready for Amsterdam' Accessed 14 June 2007. www.mini.de/de/de/mini_united/index.jsp?refType=teaserHomepage&refPage=/de/de/general/homepage/content_specials.jsp.

26. Jack Neff, 'Six-Blade Blitz,' *Advertising Age*, 19 September 2005, 3.

27. Srikumar Rao, 'Diaper–Beer Syndrome,' *Forbes*, 6 April 1998, 128(3).

28. Clive Thompson, 'There's a Sucker Born in Every Medial Prefrontal Cortex,' NYTimes.com, 26 October 2003. http://query.nytimes.com/gst/fullpage.html?res=9B07E1DE113EF935A15753C1A9659C8B63.

29. Direct Marketing Association, 'Where Marketers Can Obtain State Do-Not-Call Lists.' Accessed 7 February 2006. www.the-dma.org/government/donotcalllists.shtml.

30. Kim Bartel Sheehan, 'Online Research Methodology: Reflections and Speculations,' *Journal of Interactive Advertising*, 3:1 (Fall 2002). Accessed 7 February 2006. www.websm.org/index.php?fl=2&lact=1&bid= 631&cat= 351&p1=1123&p2=82&id=520&page=1&parent=12.

31. Cooper, Mick P., 'Web Surveys. A Review of Issues and Approaches.' *Public Opinion Quarterly*, 64(4) (2001).

32. Basil G. Englis and Michael R. Solomon, 'Life/Style OnLine: A Web-Based Methodology for Visually-Oriented Consumer Research,' *Journal of Interactive Marketing* 14(1) (2000), 2–14; Basil G. Englis, Michael R. Solomon, and Paula D. Harveston, 'Web-Based, Visually-Oriented Consumer Research Tools,' in *Online Consumer Psychology: Understanding How to Interact with Consumers in the Virtual World*, ed. Curt Haugtvedt, Karen Machleit, and Richard Yalch (Hillsdale, NJ: Lawrence Erlbaum Associates, in press).

33. Matt Richtel, 'A New On-the-Job Hazard: Turning into a Mall Rat,' NYTimes.com, 3 May 2004. Accessed 7 February 2006. www.internethomealliance.com/press_room/in_the_news/docs/NewYorkTimesMay32004.pdf.

34. Mike Galetto, 'Turning Trash to Research Treasure,' *Advertising Age*, 17 April 1995, 1–16.

35. Linda Dupree and John Bosarge, 'Media on the Move: How to Measure In- and Out-of-Home Media Consumption'. Accessed 16 February 2006. http://us.acnielsen.com/pubs/documents/media_000.pdf.

36. IPA. 'The IPA TouchPoints initiative.' Accessed 11 June 2007. www.ipa.co.uk/touchpoints.

37. Bruce L. Stern and Ray Ashmun, 'Methodological Disclosure: The Foundation for Effective Use of Survey Research,' *Journal of Applied Business Research* 7 (1991), 77–82.

38. Alan E. Wolf, 'Most Colas Branded Alike by Testy Magazine,' *Beverage World*, 31 August 1991, 8.

39. Gary Levin, 'New Adventures in Children's Research,' *Advertising Age*, 9 August 1993, 17.

40. Greenfield/Ciao Online Research Barometer 2005. www.greenfield-ciaosurveys.com/.

41. Nicolas Metzke and Katherine Allan (2005). 'Researching the researchers: the online barometer.' *Esomar Panel Conference Proceedings*, April 2005.

42. Jean Halliday, 'Automakers Involve Consumers,' *Advertising Age*, 31 January 2000, 82.

43. Tobi Elkin, 'Virtual Test Market,' *Advertising Age*, 27 October 2003, 6.

44. James Heckman, 'Turning the Focus Online,' *Marketing News*, 28 February 2000, 15; Judith Langer, ''On' and 'Offline' Focus Groups: Claims, Questions,' *Marketing News*, 5 June 2000, H38.

45. Deborah L. Vence, 'In an Instant: More Researchers Use IM for Fast, Reliable Results,' *Marketing News,* 1 March 2006: 55 (3).

46. 2004 Honomichl Top 50 Report, *Marketing News*, 15 June 2004, H4.

47. Jack Honomichl, 'Research Cultures Are Different in Mexico, Canada,' *Marketing News*, 10 May 1993, 12.

48. Esomar, Amsterdam, reported in *Marketing News*, 15 July 2005, 24.

Chapter 4
Consumer Behaviour

Meet Richard Sells,
Chief Innovation Officer,
Electrolux, Sweden

Richard Sells is married with two children. After his A levels he started his career in 1977 with Quaker Oats in fast-moving consumer goods (FMCG) sales, subsequently had a number of roles in FMCG companies in sales management before moving into marketing in consumer electronics. He was part of the team that built Alba, a resource and sell consumer electronics business through the late 1980s and early 1990s, including a period serving as a PLC main board director. Since then he has held various roles at Electrolux including Managing Director for UK and Eire, Vice president of the European refrigeration business and now Chief Innovation Officer.

Q & A with
Richard Sells

First job out of university?
Sales rep for Quaker Oats selling pet foods

Best business book you've read?
Blue Ocean Strategy

What drives me?
Seeing my team succeed

My management style is . . .
Consultative

My pet peeve
Negativity and people who always focus on the problem rather than the solution

Favourite drink?
Puilly-Fumé wine or Source sparkling water

Real People, Real Decisions
Decision time at Electrolux

Electrolux started in 1912 when it launched its first vacuum cleaner. Since those early days, it has grown to be an enormous multinational company through acquiring other companies and now owns brands such as Frigidaire, AEG, Zanussi, Electrohelios and Husqvarna (which, by the way, is the world's biggest supplier of chain saws and outdoor appliances such as Flymo). Electrolux turns over a staggering £10 billion a year by selling over 40 million electrical appliances in 150 countries, which makes it the number 2 in the world in domestic electrical appliances. The head office is in Stockholm, Sweden (where it has over 50 per cent of the retail electrical goods market) where Richard Sells, Chief Innovation Officer and his team reside. Richard's job is to lead several different teams to make Electrolux a consumer-focused innovative organisation. These teams focus separately on consumer insights, business processes, market optimisation strategies and new business ideas. Their main *raison d'être* is to make running a house and household chores easier.

Here we focus on one of the teams, the consumer insight team, and look at how they analyse consumers to generate insights. The research is conducted at several levels. First, is to look at macro-trends in the marketplace, which are the major changes in consumers' habits. This involves looking for secondary data on consumers' lifestyles which might affect the way they use Electrolux's products. For example, looking at figures which tell Electrolux what people are buying which might need refrigerating helps Electrolux know what consumers might want from their fridge. The next stage is microanalysis. Here, the consumer insight teams do observational work with consumers where a researcher goes and lives with consumers to see how they use electrical appliances and what problems they have. These visits are often captured on video as well as the researcher making notes. Indeed, Richard and his team spend many dinner parties in consumers' homes around the world talking about electrical appliances and consumers are happy to help and be listened to.

Before becoming Chief Innovation Officer, Richard headed up the refrigeration business and faced several challenges. He had seen in other consumer electronic markets, such as microwaves and vacuum cleaners, that commoditisation had occurred with many products being thought of as similar and with lots of price competition. For example, Tesco now sells vacuum cleaners for £14! It appeared that the refrigeration market was going the same way. This was partly because of new entrants into the market from manufacturers in Asia with cheaper cost bases which were driving down prices. Electolux's options were either to acquire more refrigeration companies, perhaps even some in Asia, and become the world's largest manufacturer of fridges and freezers. This would enable it to focus on economies of scale and drive down costs and compete on price. Alternatively it could follow a differentiation strategy which was driven by innovation that focused on consumer problems as well as increasing the allure of the Electrolux brand to maintain prices. The company opted for the second route and Richard and his team's task was to explore what consumer insights might lead to interesting innovations which consumers would value. They came up with three. The question is, which insight and solution would be likely to resonate most with consumers?

Richard considers his options . . .

Option 1 Source – on-tap refrigerated sparkling water

Macro-trend analysis suggested that bottled water consumption had exploded over the past decade and most consumers wanted their drinks to be chilled. Microanalysis while living with consumers uncovered the annoyance for consumers of having to physically get rid of bulky drinks bottles. In addition, many people, despite having an inbuilt fridge water dispenser, also had bottles of sparkling water as this was preferred by many consumers for its more refreshing taste, look and feeling of being more special and luxurious. Microanalysis also revealed the problem that traditional in-door dispensers were designed to place a glass underneath the tap and it was difficult to fill jugs that way. The solution was Source through the fridge door carbonated water dispenser. Check out www.electrolux.co.uk to see the invention. The push action was smooth and high quality and it had seductive blue lighting in the surround. The advantage was that it solved the consumers' bulky drinks bottle problem but initial feedback suggested that consumers also did not like having the bulky unit on the inside of the fridge door taking up space, so Electrolux designed a slimline version. The disadvantage of this option was that the reason sparkling water is special is sometimes because of the bottle. Think San Pellegrino for example. This option removed some of the specialness. It was also very expensive to produce, costing €1300 for a fridge.

Option 2 Chilled drinks express

Macro-trend analysis indicated that people were buying many more chilled drinks such as fruit juices, smoothies and fizzy drinks like cola and water. All these drinks had to be stored and consumed chilled, creating a massive cold storage problem for consumers. For many people, having a bigger fridge in their kitchen was not an option and chilling the drinks with ice alters and sometimes spoils the flavour. Microanalysis consumer insight research uncovered that there were embarrassing occasions when people were either disorganised or had unexpected visitors and needed chilled beverages, such as white wine, quickly. Serving warm white wine is a social faux pas. The solution was a quick chill zone in the bottom of the fridge which, using air from the freezer, chilled beverages six times faster than putting them in the freezer and once it had brought a bottle to temperature kept it there. The advantages of this option were that unlike the traditional distress method of putting a bottle in the freezer only to forget about it and have the bottle smash, this method prevented that. In addition, apart from the unexpected situations, it meant that not as many bottles, cans and cartons needed to be stored in the fridge, which freed up space for other things. The downside was that it took up the space of one salad drawer so that overall storage was reduced. The benefit was also seen very differently between men and women. Men liked the gadget appeal on the whole, while women generally were not impressed by the gadget appeal and preferred the practicality of the extra space. Another disadvantage was that it cost around €700.

Option 3 Brita

Consumers prefer the taste of bottled water, even though scientists say there is no taste difference. They like the purity and how clear the water is. No more floating scum in your tea! This has led to increasing bottled water consumption which was putting pressure on the space available in fridges. For the average family of three, drinking the recommended two litres per day, the problem is where to store six litres of water in the average fridge? Macro-trend analysis also indicated consumers were increasingly concern about the environment and issues of how to dispose of the plastic bottles in an environmentally sound way. In addition, there was some evidence that consumers were concerned about the carbon footprint of transporting bottled water from France to Denmark, for example. Microanalysis consumer insight work also suggested that people didn't like to have to carry 21 bottles of water home every week! The solution was an inbuilt Brita filtration system. The original flat design was inside the fridge, which replaced part of a shelf, but consumer research found people didn't like losing the space so the final solution was an upright version in the fridge door. The advantages of this option were: Brita was a well-established brand in this market and the co-branding helped both brands solve a consumer problem. It was particularly helpful on the shop floor when all the fridges look the same to have Brita on the front to make it stand out. Also, consumers said that one thing they disliked about their existing Brita jugs was having to constantly fill it up, and the inbuilt design had a capacity of four litres which is much bigger than any jug. The price of this alternative was attractive as well, at around €500. The disadvantage was that there was no jug to take to the table and what would you do with leftover water?

Now, put yourself in Richard's shoes: Which option would you choose to be a winner, and why?

Objectives

When you finish reading this chapter, you will be able to:

1 Define consumer behaviour and explain why consumers buy what they buy

2 Describe the pre-purchase, purchase and post-purchase activities that consumers engage in when making decisions

3 Explain how internal factors influence consumers' decision-making processes

4 Show how situational factors at the time and place of purchase influence consumer behaviour

5 Explain how consumers' relationships with other people influence their decision-making processes

6 Show how the internet offers consumers opportunities to participate in consumer-to-consumer marketing

Decisions, Decisions

Objective

1

Define consumer behaviour and explain why consumers buy what they buy

Compelling new products, clever packaging, and creative advertising surround us, clamouring for our attention – and our money. But each of us is unique, with our own reasons for choosing a product. Recall that the focus of the marketing concept is to satisfy consumers' wants and needs and therefore we need to understand what those wants and needs are. **Consumer behaviour** is the process individuals or groups go through to select, purchase, use and dispose of goods, services, ideas or experiences to satisfy their needs and desires.

Let's look at an example of consumer purchase which is probably very familiar to you: breakfast cereal.

Marketers need to understand why and where you buy your cereal. Do you go to a large hyper-market in order to buy big boxes of cereal at a cheaper price? Or do you just go to the local corner shop if you get the urge for cereal in the middle of the night? Then there is the decision of the type of cereal. Do you eat only low-fat, high-fibre bran cereals, or do you go for the sugar-coated varieties or maybe you like to vary between all of them?

Marketers also need to know how and when you consume their products. Do you eat cereal only for breakfast, or do you snack on it while sitting in front of the TV at night? Do you eat certain kinds of cereal only at certain times (like sugary 'kids' cereals' that serve as comfort food when you're staying up late)? What about storing the product? Do you have a kitchen pantry where you can store the super-size box, or is space an issue?

Actually, there's lots more marketers also need to understand such as factors at the time of purchase, how was it displayed and the social influences of people around us, who was with us at the time? In this chapter, we'll talk about how all these factors influence how and why consumers do what they do. But first we'll look at the types of decisions consumers make and the steps in the decision-making process.

Steps in the Consumer Decision Process

Extended Problem Solving Versus Habitual Decision Making

Objective

2

Describe the pre-purchase, purchase and post-purchase activities that consumers engage in when making decisions

Researchers realised that decision makers actually possess a set of approaches ranging from painstaking analysis to pure whim, depending on the importance of what they are buying and how much effort the person is willing to put into the decision. Marketers have found it convenient to think in terms of an 'effort' continuum that is anchored on one end by habitual decision making, such as deciding to purchase a box of cereal, and at the other end by extended problem solving, such as deciding to purchase a new car.

When consumers make very important decisions – such as buying a new house or a car – they engage in extended problem solving and carefully go through the steps. Figure 4.1 outlines problem recognition, information search, evaluation of alternatives, product choice and post-purchase evaluation.

When they make habitual decisions, however, consumers make little or no conscious effort, they don't search for information, and they don't compare alternatives. Rather, they make purchases automatically. For example, you may simply throw the same brand of cereal in your shopping trolley week after week without thinking about it. Consumers are also often tempted to make impulse purchases, for example when they are waiting in the queue for the supermarket checkout and grab, in a sudden impulse, a cereal bar or chewing gum from the till next to them. Figure 4.2 provides a summary of the differences between extended problem solving and habitual decision making. Many decisions fall somewhere in the middle and are characterised by limited problem solving, such as deciding on a new pair of running shoes. Two factors often dictate the type of decision-making process: these are involvement and perceived risk.

Knowing the Level of Involvement and Perceived Risk Involved

The answer to just how much effort we put into our buying decisions depends on our level of involvement – the importance of the perceived consequences of the purchase to the person and if we think the product is risky in some way. **Perceived risk** may be present if the product is expensive, complex and hard to understand, such as a new computer, or highly socially

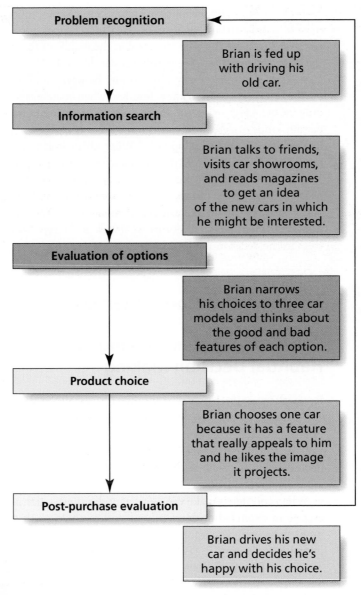

Problem recognition

Brian is fed up with driving his old car.

Information search

Brian talks to friends, visits car showrooms, and reads magazines to get an idea of the new cars in which he might be interested.

Evaluation of options

Brian narrows his choices to three car models and thinks about the good and bad features of each option.

Product choice

Brian chooses one car because it has a feature that really appeals to him and he likes the image it projects.

Post-purchase evaluation

Brian drives his new car and decides he's happy with his choice.

Figure 4.1 The Consumer Decision-Making Process
The consumer decision-making process involves the series of steps summarised here.

visible like some new trendy clothes where the risk of embarrassment or social rejection is present. For example, wearing a pair of Adidas trainers on a job interview may be fashion suicide and jeopardise the job, unless of course the job is with Adidas. In fact there are five main types of risk: time risk, i.e. the time needed to make the purchase; financial risk, i.e. the money required; social risk, i.e. what people think of us buying this; psychological risk, i.e. what we think of ourselves buying this; and physical risk, i.e. the risk to consumers' health or appearance.

When perceived risk is low, as in buying a box of cereal, consumers feel low **involvement** in the decision-making process and are often more influenced by environmental

	Extended Problem Solving	*Habitual Decision Making*
Product	New car	Box of cereal
Level of involvement	High (important decision)	Low (unimportant decision)
Perceived risk	High (expensive, complex product)	Low (simple, low-cost product)
Information processing	Careful processing of information (search advertising, magazines, car dealers, websites)	Respond to environmental cues (shop signage or displays)
Learning model	Cognitive learning (use insight and creativity to use information found in environment)	Behavioural learning (ad shows product in beautiful setting, creating positive attitude)
Needed marketing actions	Provide information via advertising, salespeople, brochures, websites. Educate consumers to product benefits, risks of wrong decisions, etc.	Provide environmental cues at point of purchase, such as product display

Figure 4.2   Extended Problem Solving versus Habitual Decision Making

cues, such as in special offers or whether the cereal is prominently displayed at the end of the supermarket aisle. Knowing this, a cereal marketer may decide to spend extra money to be sure its cereal stands out at a shop display or to change the packaging so consumers notice it.

For high-involvement purchases, such as buying a new TV or a car, a consumer will spend a lot of time thinking about the decision and evaluating the alternatives as the consequences of a bad decision may result in significant financial losses, aggravation, or embarrassment. Therefore, managers must start to reduce perceived risk by educating the consumer about why their product is the best choice well in advance of the time that the consumer is ready to make a decision.

To understand each of the steps in the decision-making process better, in the next section we'll follow the fortunes of a consumer named Brian, who, as Figure 4.1 shows, is in the market for a new car – a highly involving purchase decision, to say the least.

 ## Step 1: What's My Problem?

Problem recognition occurs whenever a consumer sees a significant difference between their current state of affairs and some desired or ideal state. For example, you like your car, but it eats up too much petrol and is not economical or eco friendly or a man might think that he would have a better chance with women if he drove a sports car rather than his current Skoda. Brian falls into the latter category – his old Skoda runs okay, but he wants some sporty wheels that will get him more admiring stares instead of laughs.

So do marketers have a role in consumers' problem recognition? Well, although most problem recognition occurs spontaneously or when a true need arises, marketers often develop creative advertising messages that stimulate consumers to recognise that their current state – that old car – just doesn't equal their desired state – a shiny, new sports convertible. Figure 4.3 provides examples of marketers' responses to consumers' problem recognition and the other steps in the consumer decision-making process.

Stage in the Decision Process	Marketing Strategy	Example
Problem recognition	Encourage consumers to see that existing state does not equal desired state	• Create TV commercials showing the excitement of owning a new car
Information search	Provide information when and where consumers are likely to search	• Book advertising around TV programmes with high target-market viewership • Provide sales training that ensures knowledgeable salespeople • Make new-car brochures available in dealer showrooms • Design exciting, easy-to-navigate, and informative websites
Evaluation of alternatives	Understand the criteria consumers use in comparing brands and communicate own brand superiority	• Conduct research to identify most important evaluative criteria • Create advertising that includes reliable data on superiority of a brand (e.g., miles per litre, safety, comfort)
Product choice	Understand choice heuristics used by consumers and provide communication that encourages brand decision	• Advertise "Made in Germany" (country of origin) • Stress long history of the brand (brand loyalty)
Post-purchase evaluation	Encourage accurate consumer expectations	• Provide honest advertising and sales presentations

Figure 4.3   Marketer's Responses to Decision-Making Stages

Step 2: What Information Is There About Alternative Solutions?

Once Brian recognises his problem (that he wants a new sports car), he needs information to resolve it. **Information search** is the step of the decision-making process in which the consumer checks his memory and surveys the environment to identify what options are out there that might solve his problem. Brian's evoked set of alternatives consists of all the car brands and models which come immediately to his mind. For most of the brands, he will have some form of specific associations and possess some information about them. However, this form of internal information search might not be enough and Brian then needs to turn to external sources. Advertisements in newspapers, on TV or the radio, in the Yellow Pages or on the internet often provide valuable guidance during this step. Brian might rely on television ads about different

Marketing Metrics

Measuring Web Stickiness

Conventional internet metrics have relied on counting the number of people viewing a website. Research has shown, however, that conversion rates and average order value are better measures for a website's success. A new method allows companies to conduct funnel-based analysis of where revenue is lost when consumers drop-off. One such method is **clickstream analysis**, which helps companies analyse where customers enter their websites and where they exit. The managers at some companies are using clickstream data to increase site subscription and convert free visitors into paying members. They can now examine exactly where on the website customers are converted and where they lose them by tracking each user's movements around the website. The company receives reports from the clickstream provider about how traffic comes in from other websites, how the site compares with competitors and where conversions are failing.

cars, recommendations from his friends, and additional information he finds in media reports, at www.whatcar.co.uk, in brochures from car dealerships, or on the manufacturers' websites.

The Internet as a Search Tool

Increasingly, consumers are using web search engines, portals, or 'shopping robots' to find information. Search engines, sites such as Google (www.google.co.uk) and Excite (www.shopping.net), help consumers locate useful information by searching millions of web pages for key words and returning a list of sites that contain those key words. Shopping portals such as Yahoo! (www.yahoo.co.uk) simplify searches by organising information from many websites into topics or categories. Shopping robots, also called 'shopbots', are software programs some websites use to find internet retailers selling a particular product (e.g. www.pricerunner.co.uk or www.kelkoo.co.uk). The programs trawl the web for information and then report it back to the host site. Some sites also provide information on competitors' prices and ask customers to rate the retailers that they have listed on their site; this enables consumers to view both positive and negative feedback from other consumers (e.g. www.reviewcentre.com).

The role of marketers during the information search step of the consumer decision-making process is to make the information consumers want and need about their product easily accessible. For example, car manufacturers make sure that information about their newest models is on the web, in magazines, radio and TV, and, of course, are available in dealer showrooms. To fine-tune this, some marketers have started to experiment with so-called **behavioural targeting** techniques; Amazon is a good example. The basis for this approach is that by watching what you do online, marketers can deliver advertisements for products and services you are actually looking for. So, for example, if you are surfing at several motoring sites you might start to notice pop-up ads on your monitor for a new car model.[1] What a coincidence!

 ## Step 3: How do I Evaluate all the Options?

Once Brian has identified his options, it's time to decide on a few true contenders. First, armed with information, a consumer identifies a small number of products in which he is interested. Second, he narrows down the choices by deciding which of all the options are feasible and by comparing the pros and cons of each remaining option.

Brian has always wanted a red Ferrari, but knows that, realistically, he couldn't afford one right now. As he looks around, he decides that the cars he and his friends like in his price range are the Renault Clio Sport, Ford Focus and Honda Civic. He's narrowed down his options by considering the criteria of affordability and what his friends suggest.

Evaluative Criteria

Now Brian has to choose. It's time for him to look more systematically at each of the three possibilities and identify the important characteristics, or **evaluative criteria**, he will use to decide among them. The criteria may be power, space, comfort and price, as well as the style of the car, insurance costs, safety and especially the driving experience. Keep in mind that marketers often play a role in educating consumers about which product characteristics they should use as evaluative criteria – usually, they will emphasise the dimensions on which their product excels. Understanding what criteria consumers use and which are more or less important helps sales and advertising professionals to point out a brand's superiority on the most important criteria. After Brian has examined his alternatives and gone on a few test drives, it's time to make a decision.

Step 4: Making the Final Choice

Deciding on one product and acting on this choice is the next step in the decision-making process. Choices such as Brian's are often difficult because it's hard to juggle all the product characteristics in your head. One car may be more eco-friendly, another is €1000 cheaper, while another boasts a better safety record or a better driving experience. So how do we make sense of all these characteristics and arrive at a decision?

Heuristics

Consumers often rely on decision guidelines when weighing the claims that companies make. These **heuristics**, or rules, help simplify the decision-making process. One such heuristic is 'price = quality', so many people willingly buy the more expensive brand because they assume that if it costs more, it must be better.

Perhaps the most common heuristic is **brand loyalty**, where people buy from the same company over and over because they believe that the company makes superior products. Consumers who have strong brand loyalty feel that it's not worth the effort to consider competing options. Creating this allegiance is a prized goal for marketers because once some people form preferences for a favourite brand, they may never change their minds in the course of a lifetime, making it extremely difficult for rivals to persuade them to switch. That explains why many companies are working harder to woo consumers early on. For example, it's hard to find an adult in Helsinki, home to the Finnish company Nokia, who doesn't have a mobile phone – 92 per cent of its households have at least one, if not several. But while the phones have been an accepted part of daily life for grown-ups and teenagers for over a decade, the latest boom in phone use is occurring among young children. Many of them get their first phone around the age of seven when they start to engage in activities like soccer practice where their parents aren't present. Now there's an expanding market for accessories like phone covers decorated with pictures of Donald Duck or Star Wars characters.[2] Another good example would be how designer clothes companies try to create a bond with customers from early age by offering exclusive child collections (e.g. D&G Junior or Prada Kidswear).

Still another heuristic is based on *country of origin*. We assume that a product has certain characteristics if it comes from a certain country. For example, Brian assumed that the Japanese-made Honda Civic would be a bit more reliable than the Ford Focus or Renault Clio Sport, so he factored that into his decision. Sometimes a marketer wants to encourage a country association even when none exists. Anheuser-Busch, for example, introduced a new beer brand into the US that it hopes customers will think of as an import, even though it's not. Anheuser World Select comes in a Heineken-style green bottle and a tagline that reads: 'Ten Brew masters. Four Continents. One Beer.' The label on the neck of the bottle lists the home countries of the brewmasters

Marketing Metrics

AC Nielsen Homescan

Nielsen Homescan provides key consumer insights in 27 countries, based on consumer purchase information from over 260,000 households globally. Each household provides daily information on their purchases of consumer goods for in-home use. Collected on a continuous basis, it is possible to measure the ongoing changes and interactions of households' purchasing behaviour across all grocery and fresh foods products. Each panel is demographically representative and it is also possible to filter purchasing behaviour by discrete demographic groups. Homescan information is granular in detail. Its depth can produce revealing analysis and help answer questions such as:

- How many households purchased my product on a trial basis? Did they return later to purchase again?
- What did my buyers purchase before my marketing campaign, what did they purchase subsequently?
- Where did buyers of my brand come from?
- What else do my buyers purchase?
- Where else do my buyers shop?
- How store loyal are my shoppers?
- What is the demographic composition of my buyers?

involved in the beer's production, such as Japan, Ireland, Canada and Spain, but the reality is that the beer is actually made in the US.[3] Marketers must not forget that there is often a further pre-purchase evaluation step involved in the decision-making process. This step concerns thoughts about the possible disposal or recyclability of the product. If the consumer wants to buy a soft drink, he might choose an environmentally friendly glass bottle, which is easily recyclable. This also applies to Brian's decision-making process. Thinking ahead, he will ask himself how easy will it be to re-sell or recycle the car once he has driven it for several years.

After agonising over his choice, Brian decides that even though the Renault Clio Sport and the Honda Civic have attractive qualities, the Ford Focus has the affordability he needs and its carefree image is the way he wants others to think about him. All this thinking about cars was 'driving' him crazy, and he's relieved to make a decision to buy the Ford Focus and get on with driving his new car and seeing what others think.

Step 5: Using and Evaluating the Purchase

In the last step of the decision-making process, the consumer evaluates just how good a choice it was. The evaluation of the product results in a level of **consumer satisfaction/dissatisfaction**, which is determined by the overall feelings, or attitude, a person has about a product after purchasing and using it.

How do consumers decide if they're satisfied with their purchases? When we buy a product, we have some expectations of product performance created by a mixture of information from marketing communications, informal information sources such as friends and family, and their own experience with the product category. Consumers then judge the product performance against these expectations. That's why it's very important that marketers create accurate expectations of their product in advertising and other communications. However, everyone has experienced regret after making a purchase ('what *was* I thinking?') and this is called cognitive dissonance. Reducing this dissonance between what you wanted to happen and what the product actually does for you is in consumers' as well as the marketers' interests. If the consumer comes to the conclusion that his purchase was a mistake, he is not only very unlikely to return to the company, but might also engage in negative word of mouth. This highlights the crucial importance of the post-evaluation stage. The marketer needs to gain as many insights

Real People, Other Voices

Dr Nnamdi O. Madichie,
University of East London

'My preferred option would be Option 3 – the inbuilt filtration system. My reasons are four-fold and quite simple. First, it is consistent with the company's adopted differentiation strategy – 'driven by innovation and focusing on consumer problems' and increasing the allure of the Electrolux brand to maintain prices. Second, it is healthy – recent media reports have suggested that tap water was more purified and comes at no cost to the consumer, to the extent that in 2008 even London's Mayor Ken Livingstone encouraged a consumer boycott of bottled water consumption in the capital. Third, it provides solutions to not only consumers' but also governments' increasing concern for the environment – especially on how to dispose of the plastic bottles in an environmentally sound way. Indeed, the revised upright version of the inbuilt Brita filtration system also benefits from a co-branding with Brita – itself a well-established brand in this market – in what has been highlighted as 'a collective effort to solve a consumer problem'. It even goes one step further by solving a problem at the heart of global public policy. Finally, it is cheap – comes at a third of the cost of going with option 1 – at only €500 it is value for money! Life couldn't come any better than being able to filter and chill tap water in an environmentally friendly manner and at no extra cost.

Dr Jenny Lloyd,
University of the West of England

As a general principle, in situations such as these when low-cost producers put pressure on margins, a strategy of adding value through consumer-driven innovation is definitely the most appropriate response. However, saying that, it is interesting that Electrolux has chosen to pursue a research strategy that is potentially limiting its scope for innovation.

In this case, the focus of the research appears to be on purely functional attributes (i.e. *how* people use refrigeration products) and this is reflected in the innovations it has produced. However, the acknowledgement of the growing importance of aesthetics in kitchen design suggests that consumers may also seek to satisfy needs other than purely utilitarian ones when choosing a refrigerator and these too offer potential opportunities for innovation.

I believe a widening of the research brief to consider *why* consumers choose one product or brand in preference to another would offer Electrolux a quality of insight that would better support their innovation programme on three counts. Firstly, it would highlight the variety of types of consumer need that influence the decision-making process, for example, the hedonic need for beauty or the psychological need to minimise risk or to support self-esteem. In addition, researchers at Electrolux would be able to probe the choice criteria used by consumers to identify the most important factors when selecting a refrigeration appliance and, finally, they would be able to map the consumer decision-making process to identify key points of influence. This achieved, innovation at Electrolux need not be limited to the functionality of the product, but instead could be used to add value by enhancing its market position through innovation in product aesthetics, brand enhancement and all other aspects of the marketing and promotional mixes.

Christina Hansen,
Student at Roskilde Business College, Denmark

I would choose option 1, Source, through the fridge door carbonated water dispenser. Consumers like to feel special, so they do not drink water directly from the tap any more. They want to have it ice cold. The consumers buy bottled water instead but the focus on environmental protection puts people in a dilemma, between being either modern or being good towards the environment. I think that Source can solve this dilemma. People can have their special carbonated water but without all the empty bottles. It is about making it easy for the consumers, who do not have a lot of time to carry around bottles, they choose the easy solution. Electrolux is a well-known brand, therefore I believe consumers are willing to pay €1300 to get a new and unique fridge, which also can express their personality.

as possible about how the consumer feels after the purchase and try to reinforce his feeling of having made the right decision. Cognitive dissonance can often occur when two alternatives are similarly attractive, but you can only buy one. Hence, you often feel regret at not buying the other. So, even though Brian's new Ford Focus is not exactly as powerful as a Ferrari, he's still happy with the car because he never really expected a fun little car to streak up the motorway like a high-performance sports car which costs 10 times as much.

Influences on Consumers' Decisions

Apart from understanding the mechanics of the consumer decision-making process, marketers also try to ascertain what influences in consumers' lives affect this process. There are three main categories: internal, situational and social influences. In Brian's case, the evaluative criteria which he used to compare cars and his feelings about each car were influenced by internal factors such as the connection he learned to make between a name like Ford Focus and an image of 'slightly hip yet safe and solid', situational factors such as the way he was treated by the Ford salesperson, and social influences such as his prediction of his friends would say when they saw him cruising down the road in his new wheels.

Figure 4.4 shows the influences in the decision-making process and emphasises that all these factors work together to affect the ultimate choice each person makes. Let's consider how each of these three types of influences work, starting with internal factors.

Internal Influences on Consumers' Decisions

Objective

3

Explain how internal factors influence consumers' decision-making processes

Car manufacturers know that one consumer's ideal car can be quite different from that of another consumer. You may think the ideal car is a sporty Porsche, while your best friend dreams of a classic Mercedes and your father is set on owning a big BMW. Some of these differences are due to the way in which consumers internalise information about the outside world such as perception, exposure, attention and interpretation.

Perception

Perception is the process by which people select, organise and interpret information from the outside world. We receive information in the form of sensations, the immediate response of our sensory receptors – eyes, ears, nose, mouth and fingers – to such basic stimuli as light, colour

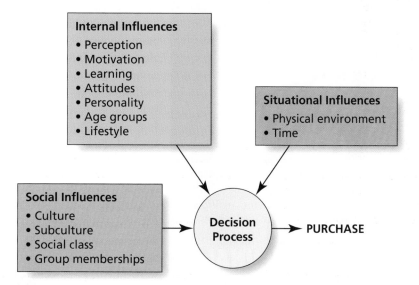

Figure 4.4	Influences on Consumer Decision Making

A number of different factors in consumers' lives influence the consumer decision-making process. Marketers need to understand these influences and which ones are important in the purchase process to make effective marketing decisions.

and sound. Our impressions about products are often based on their physical qualities. We try to make sense of the sensations we receive by interpreting them in light of our past experiences. For example, people associate the textures of fabrics and other surfaces with product qualities, and some new plastic containers for household beauty items incorporate 'soft touch' resins that provide a soft, friction-like resistance when held. US focus group members who tested one such package for Clairol's Daily Defense shampoo described the sensations as 'almost sexy' and were actually reluctant to let go of the containers![4] That's a powerful impact for a piece of plastic.

Consumers are bombarded with information on products – thousands of ads, in-store displays, special offers, opinions of their friends, and on and on have led to some consumers becoming confused by either too much information, too similar information (e.g. look-alike products), or ambiguous or conflicting information such as what's healthy to eat. Therefore, some consumers see all brands within a category as similar even when they are not. The perception process has implications for marketers because, as consumers absorb and make sense of the vast quantities of information competing for their attention, the odds are that any single message will get lost in the clutter. And, if they do notice it, there's no guarantee that the meaning they give it will be the same one the marketer intended. The issues that marketers need to understand during this process include exposure, attention and interpretation.

The stimulus must be within range of people's sensory receptors to be noticed; in other words, people must be physically able to see, hear, taste, smell or feel the stimulus. For example, the lettering on a hoarding by the motorway must be big enough for a passing motorist to read easily, or the message will be lost. **Exposure** is the extent to which a stimulus is capable of being registered by a person's sensory receptors.

| Photo 4.1 | One company's play on subliminal advertising. If you look hard enough you can see Absolute Vodka in the ice cubes. Source: www.absolutad.com |

Many people believe that even messages they can't see will persuade them to buy advertised products. Claims about **subliminal advertising**, which means that messages are hidden in advertisements in order to affect consumers in their subconsciousness have been surfacing since the 1950s. Coca Cola tried using subliminal advertising by very quickly flashing pictures of a Coke bottle during films shown in a cinema, hoping that this would result in a sudden craving for the drink among the cinema-goers. A survey of US consumers found that almost two-thirds believed in the existence of subliminal advertising, and over one-half were convinced that this technique could get them to buy things they did not really want.[5] In 2007, the American Food Network show *Iron Chef* apparently mistakenly aired a single frame of the McDonald's logo and the 'I'm lovin it' slogan during the final few moments of a show which was captured on video by two boys and exposed. The network denies it was an attempt at subliminal advertising.

In 2006 in the US, ABC rejected a commercial for KFC that invited viewers to slowly replay the ad to find a secret message, citing the network's longstanding policy against subliminal advertising. The ad (which other networks aired), was a seemingly ordinary pitch for KFC's 99-cent Buffalo Snacker chicken sandwich. But if replayed slowly on a digital video recorder or VCR, it revealed a message that viewers could visit KFC's website to receive a coupon for a free sandwich. Ironically, this technique was really the *opposite* of subliminal advertising because instead of secretly placing words or images in the ad, KFC blatantly publicised its campaign by informing viewers that it contained a message and how to find it.[6] But stunts like this certainly can make consumers pay more attention to an ad, which is the second crucial element.

As you drive down the road, you pass hundreds of other cars. But how many do you pay attention to? Probably only one or two – the bright pink and purple VW and the Honda with the broken rear light that cut you off at the motorway exit. **Attention** is the extent to which mental processing activity is devoted to a particular stimulus. Consumers are more likely to pay attention to messages that speak to their current needs. For example, you're far more likely to notice an ad for a fast-food restaurant when you're hungry, while smokers are more likely than non-smokers to block out messages about the health hazards of smoking.

Grabbing consumers' attention is getting harder than ever, because people's attention spans are shorter than ever. Now that people are accustomed to *multitasking*, flitting back and forth between their emails, TV, Instant Messenger, SMS, mobile, Blackberry, iPod and so on, advertisers have to be more creative in the mix and type of messages they send. That's why we're seeing on the one hand long (60 second) commercials that almost feel like miniature movies and, on the other hand, short (some as brief as five seconds) messages that are meant to have surprise value: they are usually over before commercial-haters can zap or zip past them. Indeed, brief blurbs that are just long enough to tantalise viewers but just short enough not to bore them are becoming commonplace – in contrast to the old days when most commercials on US television networks were 30-second spots, today more than a third run for only 15 seconds.[7]

Another cutting-edge strategy to grab attention by increasing the relevance of ads is to actually customise them to the audience that's viewing them. Uniquely for now, in the US a TV station called Fox plans to offer *tweakable ads* – spots that can be digitally altered to contain elements relevant to particular viewers at the time they are seen. By changing voiceovers, scripts, graphic elements or other images, for instance, advertisers could make an ad appeal to teens in one instance and retired people in another. As this approach is refined, for example, a cola company could have actors refer to the particular teams in a sporting event. Or a soup company could direct viewers' attention to a snowstorm brewing outside to encourage people to stock up on soup.[8] However, all these techniques rely on the consumer interpreting the message in the way the company wants.

Interpretation is the process of assigning meaning to a stimulus based upon prior associations a person has with it and assumptions he or she makes about it. A Pepsi drink called 'Pepsi Blue' flopped despite heavy marketing and advertising campaigns. Consumers didn't associate its blue colour with a fruity and refreshing beverage (as the marketing department hoped) but rather with too many artificial ingredients and chemicals. Another example would be the BMW C1, which is a motorcycle with a roof and the possibility for the driver to wear a seatbelt which made it much safer than other motorcycles and reduced the risk of severe injury in accidents. BMW therefore specifically stressed this safety aspect in all of its marketing and advertising approaches. However, the company did not consider that many consumers who drive motorcycles are rather looking for fun and speed than for protection and thought that the C1 was a boring vehicle. If we don't interpret the product the way it was intended because of other experiences, the best marketing ideas will be 'wasted'.

Motivation

Motivation is an internal state that drives us to satisfy needs. Once we activate a need, a state of tension exists that drives the consumer toward some goal that will reduce this tension by eliminating the need.

For example, think about Brian and his old car. Brian began to experience a gap between his present state (owning an old car) and a desired state (having a car that gets him noticed and is

Marketing Ethics

Cruel consumer cost of the human egg trade

One of the most basic needs is the need to procreate and British women who desperately want to have babies are being sent to Eastern Europe and Cyprus. There, clinics are thriving on the profits of fertility tourism. But donors in this egg harvest run hidden health risks. Women from countries like the Ukraine are told that the process of donating eggs is straightforward and that they will be given $300. But the process is not a straightforward matter like donating sperm. It can be a lengthy, painful and potentially dangerous procedure involving the injection of a powerful drug, follicle stimulating hormone. In today's global market, a healthy human egg from a young white European woman is more valuable than gold. The human need to reproduce and to have mothering and fathering needs met is very powerful. While there is no denying the joy of an infertile woman who has been able to have a baby using an overseas donor, there can be an unsavoury underside to the process where poor young women are exploited, injected with potentially dangerous hormones and treated like 'battery hens' being farmed for their eggs.

The Observer, 20 April 2006

Debate, Discuss, Disagree

1   Who should be responsible/ blamed for the situation?

2   What would you suggest to put a stop to the illegal human egg trade?

fun to drive). The need for a new car is activated, motivating Brian to test different models, to talk with friends about different makes, and finally to buy a new car.

Psychologist Abraham Maslow developed an influential approach to motivation.[9] He formulated a **hierarchy of needs** that categorises motives according to five levels of importance, the more basic needs being on the bottom of the hierarchy and more sophisticate needs at the top. The hierarchy suggests that before a person can meet needs at a given level, he must first meet the lower level's needs – somehow those hot new Diesel jeans don't seem so enticing when you don't have enough money to buy food.

As you can see from Figure 4.5, people start at the lowest level with basic physiological needs for food and sleep and then progress to higher levels to satisfy more complex needs, such as the need to be accepted by others or to feel a sense of accomplishment. Ultimately, people can reach the highest level such as self-fulfilment. Brian's need for a new car would be an example of the fourth level of Maslow's hierarchy, referring to esteem needs. Brian hopes to gain prestige and to be admired while taking a ride in his new car. If marketers understand the level of needs relevant to consumers in their target market, they can tailor their products and messages to them. Now think about Richard Sells at Electrolux and ask yourself which of the motivations the three fridge ideas satisfy.

Learning

Learning is a change in behaviour caused by information or experience. Learning about products can occur deliberately, as when we set out to gather information about different MP3 players before buying one brand. We also learn even when we are not trying. Consumers recognise many brand names and can hum many product jingles, for example, even for products they themselves do not use. Learning theories to explain the learning process are important because a major goal for marketers is to 'teach' consumers to prefer their products. Let's briefly review the most important perspectives on how people learn.

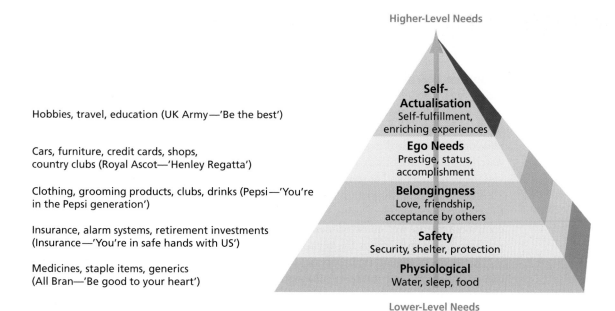

Higher-Level Needs

Hobbies, travel, education (UK Army—'Be the best')

Cars, furniture, credit cards, shops,
country clubs (Royal Ascot—'Henley Regatta')

Clothing, grooming products, clubs, drinks (Pepsi—'You're
in the Pepsi generation')

Insurance, alarm systems, retirement investments
(Insurance—'You're in safe hands with US')

Medicines, staple items, generics
(All Bran—'Be good to your heart')

Self-Actualisation
Self-fulfillment,
enriching experiences

Ego Needs
Prestige, status,
accomplishment

Belongingness
Love, friendship,
acceptance by others

Safety
Security, shelter, protection

Physiological
Water, sleep, food

Lower-Level Needs

Figure 4.5 Maslow's Hierarchy of Needs and Related Products

Abraham Maslow's proposed hierarchy of needs that categorises motives. Savvy marketers know they need to understand the level of needs that motivates a consumer to buy a particular product or brand.

Behavioural Learning **Behavioural learning theories** assume that learning takes place as the result of connections that form between events that we perceive. In the first type of behavioural learning, **classical conditioning**, a person perceives two stimuli at about the same time. After a while, the person transfers his response from one stimulus to the other. This theory was primarily developed by Ivan Pavlov, a Russian scientist who executed an experiment in which his dog received two stimuli in the form of dog food and the ringing sound of a bell at the same time. After a while the dog did indeed transfer his response from one stimuli to the other, because he started salivating when the bell was ringing, even when there was no food in sight. Marketers also try to make use of this phenomenon. For example, an ad shows a product and a breathtakingly beautiful scene so that (the marketer hopes) you will transfer the positive feelings you get from looking at the scene to the advertised product. (Did you ever notice that ads often show a new car on a beautiful beach at sunset or speeding down a mountain road with brightly coloured leaves blowing across the pavement?)

Another common form of behavioural learning is called **operant conditioning**, which occurs when people learn that their actions result in rewards or punishments. This influences how they will respond in similar situations in the future. Just as a rat in a maze learns the route to a piece of cheese, consumers who receive a reward, such as a prize in the bottom of a box of cereal, will be more likely to buy that brand again. We don't like to think that marketers can train us like lab mice, but that kind of prize feedback does reward us for our behaviour.

These acquired associations in classical and operant conditioning have a tendency to transfer to similar things in a process called **stimulus generalisation**. This means that the good or bad feelings associated with a product will 'rub off' on other products that resemble it. For example, some marketers create *product line extensions* in which new products share the name of an established brand so that people's good feelings about the current product will transfer to the new one. Dove, which is associated with gentle soap, was able to also establish itself as a producer of body lotions and moisturisers without great difficulties. The consumer already trusted the product and mentally connected it with soothing body care. More on this in Chapter 7.

Cognitive Learning In contrast to behavioural theories of learning, **cognitive learning theory** views people as problem solvers who do more than passively react to associations between stimuli. Supporters of this point of view stress the role of creativity and insight during the learning process. Cognitive learning occurs when consumers make a connection between ideas or by observing things in their environment. **Observational learning** occurs when people watch the actions of others and note what happens to them as a result. They store these observations in memory and at some later point use the information to guide their own behaviour. Marketers often use this process to create advertising and other messages that allow consumers to observe the benefits of using their products. Health clubs and manufacturers of exercise equipment feature well-muscled men and women using their products, while mouthwash makers show that fresh breath is the key to romance.

The results of the internal processes of perception, motivation and learning influence how consumers absorb and interpret information. This also depends on some unique consumer characteristics. Let's talk next about some of these characteristics: existing consumer attitudes, the personality of the consumer and consumer age groups.

Attitudes

An **attitude** is someone's lasting evaluation of a person, object, or issue.[10] Consumers have attitudes towards brands, such as whether McDonald's or Burger King has the best beefburgers, as well as towards more general consumption-related behaviours, for example, whether high-fat foods including beefburgers are a no-no in a healthy diet. A person's attitude has three components: affect, cognition and behaviour:

Affect refers to the overall emotional response a person has to a product. Affect, the feeling component, is usually dominant for expressive products such as perfume. In this case, our attitude towards the product is simply determined by our immediate reaction of whether we like the smell of the perfume or not. Some marketing researchers are trying to understand how consumers' emotional reactions influence how they feel about products. A company called Sensory Logic, for example, studies videotape of people's facial reactions – to products and commercials – in increments as fleeting as 1/30th of a second. Staffers look for the difference between a so-called true smile (which includes a relaxation of the upper eyelid) and a social smile (which occurs only around the mouth). Whirlpool hired the company to test consumers' emotional reactions to a yet-to-be-launched generation of its Duet washers and dryers. Its perhaps ambitious goal was to design appliances that would actually make people happy. The research led Whirlpool to change some design options on the Duet products, including geometric patterns and certain colour combinations.[11] Research has also concluded that while smiling has little effect in service encounters, employees displaying authentic emotions does affect consumers' emotional states.[12]

Cognition, the knowing component, is the beliefs or knowledge a person has about a product and its important characteristics. You may believe that a Mercedes is built better than most cars or that a Volvo is very safe. Cognition is especially important for complex products, such as computers, where we may develop beliefs on the basis of technical information.

Behaviour, the doing component, involves a consumer's intention to do something, such as the intention to purchase or use a certain product. For products such as cereal, consumers purchase and try the product on the basis of limited information and then form an evaluation of the product simply on the basis of how the product tastes or performs.

LIVE LIFE ON
CENTRE STAGE.

BE FABULOUS★

MOËT & CHANDON
CHAMPAGNE

| Photo 4.2 | Observational learning means we learn by observing the behaviour of others. In this ad, Moet and Chandon want to encourage observational learning by showing by whom and how their drink can be consumed. Source: The Advertising Archives |

Depending on the nature of the product, one of these three components – feeling, knowing, or doing – will be the dominant influence in creating an attitude towards a product. Marketers need to decide which part of an attitude is the most important driver of consumers' preferences. For example, Pepsi's advertising focus changed from its typical emotional emphasis on celebrities, jingles and music to an attempt which offers rational reasons to drink the beverage. The new campaign portrayed the soft drink as the perfect accompaniment to foods and social situations like football matches and dates.[13]

Personality

Personality is the set of unique psychological characteristics that consistently influence the way a person responds to situations in the environment. One adventure-seeking consumer may always be on the lookout for new experiences and cutting-edge products, while a different consumer may prefer familiar surroundings, and wants to use the same brands over and over again. The German brewery Beck's, for example, tries to position its product as a beer for thrill-seeking consumers. Its commercials always show young, outgoing people who are looking for the ultimate adventure in exotic locations and the slogan invites consumers to join the 'Beck's Experience'[14]. A contrasting example would be Nivea, which puts its main focus on pointing out the long tradition, experience and expertise with skin care products. Nivea tries to create a very close bond with its customers and consumers voted it to be one of the most-trusted brands in the "European Trusted Brand" studies 2006.[15]

For marketers, differences in *personality traits* such as thrill seeking underscore the potential value of considering personality when they are crafting their marketing strategies. The following are some specific personality traits relevant to marketing strategies:

- *Innovativeness:* The degree to which a person likes to try new things. Cutting-edge products such as radical new fashions or the latest iPhone might appeal to innovative women.

- *Materialism:* The amount of emphasis placed on owning products. Materialistic consumers focus on owning products simply for the sake of ownership. For example, many people buy D&G designer handbags not because they urgently need a place to store keys and wallet, but much rather for the mere sake of owning them and showing off.

- *Self-confidence:* The degree to which a person has a positive evaluation of her abilities, including the ability to make good decisions. People who don't have much self-confidence are good candidates for services like image consultants, who help clients select the right outfit for a job interview. People who do have a lot of self-confidence are more likely to travel alone or go on independent holidays.

- *Sociability:* The degree to which a person enjoys social interaction. Sociable people might respond to entertainment-related products, like pub quiz nights or group outing to the cinema that claim to bring people together or make parties more fun.

Marketing Ethics

Frenzied footwear

When a new product is hot, it's hot – but the burning desire to get hold of it can make it too hot to handle. Athletic shoe manufacturers compete fiercely to produce dynamically continuous innovations that children want. For example, Puma, Nike, Reebok and other manufacturers introduce new models every year, and with each new version the products become more and more desirable to young children. News of new model's arrival date in shops sometimes causes frenzy. Children go so far as to gamble for money with their friends or try with all means to beg their parents to be the first to buy the latest shoe.

Debate, Discuss, Disagree

1   Do you think marketers should feel good or bad about kids being so anxious to buy their new products?

● *Need for cognition*: The degree to which a person likes to think about things and expend the necessary effort to process brand information.[16] Such people are likely to buy *Which? Guides* or *What Car* magazine when purchasing products to get as much information as possible about them.

The Self: Are You what You Buy?   It makes sense to assume that consumers buy products that are extensions of their personalities. That's why marketers try to create brand personalities that will appeal to different types of people. For example, consider the different 'personalities' invented by fragrance marketers: a brand with a 'wholesome, girl-next-door' image such as Clinique's Happy would be hard to confuse with the sophisticated image of Christian Dior's Dolce Vita. We'll talk more about this in Chapter 8.

A person's **self-concept** is his attitude towards the self and is composed of a mixture of beliefs about one's abilities and observations. This includes, for example, behaviour and feelings (both positive and negative) about one's personal attributes, such as body type or facial features. The extent to which a person's self-concept is positive or negative can strongly influence his buying decision.

Dove, a marketer for body and skincare products, recognised that many girls and women suffer from a lack of self-confidence because they feel they cannot compete with the trend of those perfect size-zero supermodels which they see in magazines and on TV. The company therefore launched a global marketing campaign called 'Campaign for Real Beauty' which aims to help women to gain more self-esteem and make them feel beautiful the way they are.[17] This technique is also used in ads for Clairol ('You're not getting older, you're getting better'), Budweiser in the US ('For all you do, this Bud's for you'), and L'Oréal ('Because you're worth it').

Age Group

A person's age is another internal influence on purchasing behaviour. Many of us feel that we have a closer connection with people of our own age because we share a common set of experiences and memories about cultural events, whether these involve the student revolts in the 1960s or the introduction of the euro.

As people are attracted to products that remind them of past experiences, marketers of products from cereals to cars are banking on nostalgia to draw in customers. Audi, for example,

Marketing Ethics

An unhealthy need for the beauty industry

The rise of an image-conscious, celebrity-obsessed society has led to massive growth in the health and beauty industries, and cosmetic surgery is reaping the benefits. The cosmetic surgery industry was worth £359 million in the UK in 2005 and it was expected to top £1 billion by 2010. As consumer attitudes change and procedures become less invasive, cosmetic surgery providers have shifted their positioning to become more holistic. Bupa Cosmetic Surgery and Transform Medical Group, the largest provider of cosmetic surgery in the UK, has been promoting its services as 'enhancements' that improve self-esteem and confidence.

Debate, Discuss, Disagree

1   What do you think?

2   How great a role should plastic surgery have in promoting better self-esteem and confidence?

---

created a commercial for its model Audi A6, which showed a short, humorous remake of the classic film *The Graduate*. The commercial was very popular among consumers who were reminded of their 'old favourite classic movie'.[18]

Goods and services often appeal to a specific age group. Although there are exceptions, most buyers of Mika CDs are younger than those who buy Elton John discs. Thus, many marketing strategies appeal to the needs of such different age groups as children, teenagers, the middle-aged and the elderly.

Young people are among the most enthusiastic users of the internet. In fact, teens spend over €1 billion online each year using their own or their parents' cards, so many firms are working hard to develop websites that will capture their interest. What do teens do online? Approximately three out of four teens do research, and nearly two out of three use the internet for e-mail, while far fewer use it for finding or buying products. For marketers, this means that the web may be a great way to get information about their goods and services to teens but not so good for sales.

Make the earth move.
Not your dentures.

Even well fitting dentures can still slip or wobble at inconvenient times. And the mere thought of it can be enough to restrict your confidence *and* your fun. When that happens it's time to get a grip. Poli-Grip® Ultra holds dentures firmly in place and reduces wobble. So you can forget all about them and concentrate on your knees wobbling instead.

Get a grip with **Poli-Grip** Ultra

www.dentura.co.uk

Photo 4.3 This ad targets an older generation, later in the family life cycle.
Source: The Advertising Archives

The Family Life Cycle

Marketers know that the process of change continues throughout consumers' lives. Interestingly, the purchase of goods and services may depend more on consumers' current position in the **family life cycle** – the stages through which family members pass as they grow older – than on chronological age. Singles of any age are more likely to spend money on expensive cars, entertainment and recreation than married people. Couples with small children purchase baby furniture, insurance and a larger house, while older couples whose children have 'left the nest' are more likely to buy a retirement home in the south of France.

Lifestyle

A **lifestyle** is a pattern of living that determines how people choose to spend their time, money and energy and that reflects their values, tastes and preferences. Lifestyles are expressed in a person's preferences for activities such as sports, interests such as music, and opinions on politics and religion. Consumers often choose goods, services and activities that are associated with a certain lifestyle. Brian may drive a Ford Focus, hang out in internet cafés and go snowboarding during the Easter holidays because he views these choices as part of a cool university student lifestyle.

Marketers often develop marketing strategies which recognise that people can be grouped into market segments based on similarities in lifestyle preferences.[19] Many kids happily fork out €20 for T-shirts and more than €50 for skate shoes in addition to the hundreds they may spend on the latest skate boards. In fact, kids spend well over €3 billion a year on skateboard 'soft goods', like T-shirts, shorts and sunglasses, while actual skateboarding equipment 'only' sells over €600 million.[20]

If lifestyles are so important, how do marketers identify them? How can they reach consumers who share preferences for products they associate with a certain lifestyle? Demographic characteristics, such as age and income, tell marketers what products people buy, but they don't reveal why. Two consumers can share the same demographic characteristics yet be completely different from each other – all 20-year-old male university students are hardly identical. That's why it is often important to further profile consumers in terms of their passions and how they spend their leisure time.

We'll look further at how marketers identify and find these kinds of specialised consumer groups in Chapter 6.

Psychographics   To breathe life into demographic analyses, marketers turn to **psychographics**, which groups consumers according to psychological and behavioural similarities. One way to do this is to describe people in terms of their activities, interests and opinions (known as **AIOs**). These AIOs are based on preferences for holiday destinations, club memberships, hobbies, political and social attitudes, tastes in food and fashion, and so on. Using data from large samples, marketers create profiles of customers who resemble each other in terms of their activities and patterns of product use.[21]

For example, US marketers looking at people who wanted walking shoes assumed that all recreational walkers were just burned-out joggers. Subsequent psychographic research that examined the AIOs of these walkers showed that there were actually several psychographic segments within the larger group who engaged in the activity for very different reasons, including walking for fun, walking to save money and walking for exercise. This research resulted in the creation of walking shoes aimed at different segments, from Footjoy Walkers to Nike Healthwalkers.

| Photo 4.4 | Our choices of clothing, furniture and other products often reflect our commitment to a consistent lifestyle. Source: The Advertising Archives |

Situational Influences on Consumers' Decisions

www.pearsoned.co.uk/Solomon

Objective

4

Show how situational factors at the time and place of purchase influence consumer behaviour.

We've seen that internal factors such as how people perceive marketing messages, their motivation to acquire products, and their unique personalities influence the decisions they make. In addition, when, where and how consumers shop – what we call *situational influences* – shape their purchase choices. Some important situational cues are our physical surroundings and time pressures.

Marketers know that dimensions of the physical environment, including such factors as decor, smells, lighting, music and even temperature, can significantly influence consumption. If you don't believe this, consider that one study found that pumping certain odours into a Las Vegas casino actually increased the amount of money patrons fed into slot machines.[22] Let's see how situational factors influence the consumer decision-making process.

The Physical Environment

It's no secret that people's moods and behaviours are strongly influenced by their physical surroundings. Despite all their efforts to sway consumers through advertising, marketers know that the shop environment strongly influences many purchases. For example, consumers decide on about two out of every three of their supermarket product purchases while standing in the aisles (so always eat before you go to the supermarket). The messages they receive at the time and their feelings about being in the shop influence their decisions.[23]

Two dimensions, arousal and pleasure, determine whether a shopper will react positively or negatively to a shop environment. In other words, the person's surroundings can be either dull or exciting (arousing) and either pleasant or unpleasant. Just because the environment is arousing doesn't necessarily mean it will be pleasant – we've all been in crowded, loud, hot shops that are anything but pleasant. Maintaining an upbeat feeling in a pleasant context is one factor behind the success of theme parks such as Disney World, which tries to provide consistent doses of carefully calculated stimulation to visitors.[24]

The importance of these surroundings explains why many retailers focus on packing as much entertainment as possible into their shops. For example, IKEA creates its shops in such a way that they appeal to the whole family. Huge children's playgrounds, restaurants, special workshops or events such as visits from Santa Claus during Christmas time are only some of the features which make the shopping at IKEA a special experience.

Photo 4.5 As consumers are exposed to more and more advertising, advertisers must work harder than ever to get their attention. Place-based media, in this case one of the Orange mobile phone cinema adverts starring Spike Lee, offers a way to reach consumers when they are a 'captive audience'. Source: The Advertising Archives

Another example is the Easy Everything café in London, which welcomes about 5000 people every day, including backpackers who can check their email on the café's computers. This cyber-hangout is trying to increase traffic with computer game competitions, training seminars and wine tastings.[25] Whether through entertainment, email or information services, it increases sales if a company provides surroundings that consumers want.

In-store displays are a marketing communication tool that attracts attention. Although most displays consist of simple racks that dispense the product or related coupons, some marketers use elaborate performances and scenery to display their products. And advertisers are also being more aggressive about hitting consumers with their messages, wherever they may be. A **place-based media** strategy is a growing way to target consumers in non-traditional places. Today, messages can pop up in airports, doctors' offices, college cafeterias, and health clubs. An example of this would be the TV screens that you see at the checkout in a Tesco supermarket while waiting in the queue for the cashier.

Time

In addition to the physical environment, time is another situational factor. Marketers know that the time of day, the season of the year and how much time one has to make a purchase affect decision making. Time is one of consumers' most limited resources. We talk about 'making time' or 'spending time', and are frequently reminded that 'time is money'.

Indeed, many consumers believe that they are more pressed for time than ever before.[26] This sense of **time poverty** makes consumers responsive to marketing innovations that allow them to save time, including such services as one-hour photo processing, drive-through lanes at fast-food restaurants, and ordering products on the web.[27] Many websites, including Apple's iTunes, Virgin Digital and even Tesco, now offer consumers the speed and convenience of downloading music. These sites allow consumers to browse through thousands of titles, listen to selections, and order and pay for them – all without setting foot inside a shop. This saves the customer time, plus the 'shop' is always open.

Social Influences on Consumers' Decisions

Our discussion of consumer behaviour so far has focused on factors that influence us as individuals, such as the way we learn about products. Although we are all individuals, we are also members of many groups that influence our buying decisions. Families, friends and classmates often influence our decisions, as do larger groups with which we identify, such as ethnic groups and political parties. Now let's consider how social influences such as culture, social class, and influential friends and acquaintances affect the consumer decision-making process.

Culture

Objective

5

Explain how consumers' relationships with other people influence their decision-making processes

Think of **culture** as a society's personality. It is the values, beliefs, customs and tastes produced or practised by a group of people. However, what people in one culture find desirable or appropriate will not necessarily be appreciated in other cultures as well. The producers of the Middle Eastern version of the hit reality show *Big Brother* had to realise this when a male character kissed a female character on the cheek in the first few minutes of an episode. In conservative Bahrain, the Persian Gulf island where the show was filmed, a social kiss between a young man and a young woman meeting for the first time suggested rampant moral depravity. In the wake of street protests, the show was pulled.[28]

Rituals and Values

Thus, a consumer's culture influences buying decisions. For example, cultures have their own rituals, such as weddings and funerals that have specific activities and products associated with them. Some companies are more than happy to help us in these efforts. Consider the elaborate weddings Disney stages for couples who want to re-enact their own version of a popular fairy tale: at Disney World, the princess bride wears a tiara and rides to the park's lakeside wedding pavilion in a horse-drawn coach, complete with two footmen in grey wigs and gold lamé trousers. At the exchange of vows, trumpets blare as Major Domo (he helped the Duke in his quest for Cinderella) walks up the aisle with two wedding rings gently placed in a glass slipper on a velvet pillow. Disney stages about 2000 of these extravaganzas in the US each year.[29]

Even corporations sometimes have myths and legends as a part of their history, and some make a deliberate effort to be sure that newcomers to the organisation learn these. Nike designates senior executives as 'corporate storytellers' who explain the company's heritage to other employees, including the hourly workers at Nike shops. They tell stories about the founders of Nike, including the coach of the Oregon track team who poured rubber into his family waffle iron to make better shoes for his team – the origin of the Nike waffle sole. The stories emphasise the dedication of runners and coaches involved with the company to reinforce the importance of teamwork.

As we also saw in Chapter 2, cultural values are deeply held beliefs about right and wrong ways to live.[30] For example, one culture might feel that being a unique individual is preferable to subordinating one's identity to a group, whereas another culture may emphasise the importance of the group over individuality. That's not to say, however, that values can't change. A recent study showed that both baby-boomer women (born between 1946 and 1964) and Generation X men (born between 1965 and 1976) and Generation Y men (born after 1976) are more likely to seek balance than to seek only material success.[31]

Marketers who understand a culture's values can tailor their product offerings accordingly. For example, cigarette brands Salem Pianissimo and Virginia Slims One, which emit less smoke than other brands, flopped in the United States yet sell well in Japan. Why? Because the Japanese culture values the welfare of others more than it values individual pleasure. The cigarettes that emit less smoke won't offend others (especially non-smokers) quite as much, so the Japanese prefer to buy them. An industry executive observed: 'Japanese are much more concerned about people around them. If you develop a product which helps them address these concerns, then you have a good chance of developing a hit product.'[32]

 ## Subculture

A **subculture** is a group coexisting with other groups in a larger culture whose members share a distinctive set of beliefs or characteristics. Each of us belongs to many subcultures. These subcultures could be religious groups, ethnic groups or regional groups as well as those that form around music groups such as fans of the Rolling Stones, media creations such as Trekkies (*Star Trek* fans), or leisure activities such as extreme sports. The hip-hop subculture has had enormous influence as many marketers relied on young trendsetters to help decide what brands were off the hook (good) and which were wack (bad). Successful hip-hop artists like P. Diddy, Jay-Z, Nelly and Usher are slowly but surely becoming major players in the marketing world. Nelly has branched out into the beverage business by creating 'Pimp Juice', a hip-hop inspired energy drink, Usher has created his own fragrances and Gwen Stefani started her own clothing line.[33]

For marketers, some of the most important subcultures are racial and ethnic groups because many consumers identify strongly with their heritage and are influenced by products that appeal to this aspect of their identities. Some racial differences in consumption preferences can be subtle but important.

 ## Social Class

Social class is the overall rank of people in a society. People who are within the same class work in similar occupations, have similar income levels, and usually share tastes in clothing, decorating styles and leisure activities. These people also share many political and religious beliefs as well as ideas regarding valued activities and goals.

Many products and shops are designed to appeal to people in a specific social class.[34] Working class women often are less likely to experiment with new products or styles, such as modern furniture or coloured appliances, because they tend to prefer predictability to novelty.[35] Marketers need to understand these differences and develop product and communication strategies that appeal to the different groups.

Luxury goods often serve as **status symbols**, visible markers that provide a way for people to flaunt their membership in higher social classes (or at least to make others believe they are members). Marketers of high-end products often seek out rich people (or those who want others to think they are) to buy their brands. For example, Mercedes teamed up with designer Giorgio Armani to produce a line of products for the well-heeled, including a new car with sand-coloured leather seats, jet-black dashboard and brown leather steering wheel designed by Armani.[36]

However, it's important to note that, over time, the importance of different status symbols rises and falls. Today, wealthy consumers who want to let the world know of their success are far more likely to choose a Mercedes or Porsche. The 'in' car five years from now is anyone's guess.

In addition, traditional status symbols today are available to a much wider range of consumers around the world with rising incomes, so this change is fuelling demand for mass-consumed products that still offer some degree of panache or style. Think about the success of companies like Nokia, H&M, Zara, ING, Dell Computers, Gap, Nike, easyJet, or L'Oréal. They cater to a consumer segment that analysts have labelled **mass-class**; the hundreds of millions of global consumers who now enjoy a level of purchasing power that's sufficient to let them afford high-quality products – except for expensive items like college education, housing or luxury cars. The mass-class market, for example, has spawned several versions of affordable cars: Latin Americans had their Volkswagen Beetle (affectionately called *el huevito*, the little egg), Indian consumers have their Maruti 800 (selling for as little as US $4860), and the Fiat Palio, the company's 'world car', aimed at emerging countries such as Brazil, Argentina, India, China and Turkey. Today the Fiat Palio is marketed in 40 countries.[37]

Across the Hall

Advice for Richard Sells

Professor Cary L. Cooper CBE

is an expert and author in organisational psychology and founder of leading business psychology company Robertson Cooper Limited

I would choose either option 1 or option 3. I like option 3 from the point of the view of the business case, because of the partnership or co-branding arrangement with Brita, the low cost of the fridge, and the environmental issues. However, the design of the unit itself doesn't seem upmarket enough, given that bottled water is a quasi-luxury product. And indeed, the cost is in fact too low given the brand image of Electrolux in terms of innovative design. On these grounds I thought that option 1 was the best, because it combined an attractive design element (i.e. blue lighting in the surround), which conveys a 'cool' image, and the product was carbonated. This latter point is important because the middle-class consumer tends to prefer carbonated water. Obviously the downside of this is the price and the need to put it in jugs at dinner parties. In terms of the former, the market is clearly at the luxury end of the product range, which reinforces the design image and brand. Even though the consumer has to fill up the jug for a dinner party, the fact that it is carbonated and chilled implies to the recipient it is not simply tap water. As a lifestyle product, option 1 hits most of the buttons. The only concern I would have is the cutbacks that people will inevitably make during an economic downturn, where price and function may play a more important role.

Group Membership

Anyone who's ever 'gone along with the crowd' knows that people act differently in groups than they do on their own. There are several reasons for this phenomenon. With more people in a group, it becomes less likely that any one member will be singled out for attention, and normal restraints on behaviour may be reduced (think about the last wild party you attended). In many cases, group members show a greater willingness to consider riskier alternatives than they would if each member made the decision alone.[38]

Since many of the things we buy are consumed in the presence of others, group behaviours are important to marketers. Sometimes group activities create new business opportunities. Consider, for example, the football world cup which took place in Germany in summer 2006. This event gave ideal opportunities for companies to benefit from the huge popularity and immense media presence. Not only main sponsors made good profits but also smaller companies which sold fan articles such as banners, T-shirts and hats or souvenirs from Germany.

Reference Groups

A **reference group** is a set of people a consumer wants to please or imitate. Consumers 'refer to' these groups in evaluating their behaviour – what they wear, where they go, what brands they buy, and so on. Unlike a larger culture, the 'group' can be composed of one person, such as your significant other, or someone you've never met, such as a statesman like Winston Churchill, a star like Gwyneth Paltrow, or a sophisticated man of the world like James Bond. The group can be small, such as your immediate family, or it could be a large organisation, such as Greenpeace.

Conformity

Consumers often change their behaviour to gain acceptance into a particular reference group. **Conformity** is at work when a person changes as a reaction to real or imagined group pressure. For example, a student getting dressed to go to a college ball may choose to wear clothing similar to what he knows others will be wearing so that he's accepted by the group.

Home shopping parties, as epitomised by the Tupperware party that we will encounter in Chapter 12, capitalise on group pressures to boost sales. A company representative makes a sales presentation to a group of people who have gathered in the home of a friend or acquaintance. Participants model the behaviour of others who can provide them with information about how to use certain products, especially because the home party is likely to be attended by a relatively homogeneous group (for example, neighbourhood homemakers). Pressures to conform may be intense and may escalate as more group members begin to 'cave in' (this process is sometimes termed the *bandwagon effect*). Even though Tupperware has moved into new sales venues, including a website (www.tupperware.co.uk), the Home Shopping Network and kiosks in shopping centres, it hopes the shopping party remains a popular means of generating sales.[39]

Opinion Leaders

If, like Brian, you are in the market for a new car, is there someone you know you would seek out for advice? Some individuals are particularly likely to influence others' product decisions. An **opinion leader** is a person who influences others' attitudes or behaviours because others perceive them as possessing expertise about the product.[40] Opinion leaders usually exhibit high levels of interest in the product category and may continuously update their knowledge by reading, talking to salespeople, and so on. Because of this involvement, opinion leaders are valuable information sources, and, unlike commercial endorsers who are paid to represent the interests of just one company, they have no axe to grind and can impart both positive and negative information about the product. In addition, opinion leaders are often among the first to buy new products, so they absorb much of the risk, reducing uncertainty for others who are not as courageous.

Today, many shrewd marketers appreciate the value of coaxing opinion leaders – and especially celebrities – to be seen using or wearing their products so that others will follow suit. For example, the sport clothing company Puma used this approach in order to enhance the popularity of its products. It looked for opinion leaders such as popular DJs or barkeepers in clubs who generally have a big influence on young people and equipped them with Puma clothes and shoes. As a result, the brand image improved and suddenly everybody wanted to wear those hip 'Speedcat trainers'.

Gender Roles

Some of the strongest pressures to conform come from our **gender roles**, society's expectations regarding the appropriate attitudes, behaviours and appearance for men and women. These assumptions about the proper roles of men and women, flattering or not, are deeply ingrained in marketing communications.[41] For example, men are far less likely than women to see a doctor regularly, and 25 per cent say they would delay seeking help as long as possible. Experts suggest that this may be because boys playing sports are taught to 'ignore pain and not ask for help'.[42]

Many products take on masculine or feminine attributes, and consumers often associate them with one gender or another.[43] For example, many women downplay their femininity at work by wearing masculine clothing such as trouser suits. These women feel that feminine dress in the workplace hurts their chances of being promoted – that the corporate world still rewards men more than women. Trouser suits, in this case, take on a masculine attribute. A different example of how gender differences influence consumer behaviour is the insight that the female online population in the UK spends far more time surfing websites with health and beauty content than one would predict by simply looking at their share of the total population. Marketers can use such information to reach their target audience and tailor their marketing plan.[44]

'Sex-Typed' Products

Marketers play a part in teaching us how society expects us to act as men and women. As consumers, we see women and men portrayed differently in marketing communications and in products promoted to the two groups. And these influences teach us what the 'proper' role of women or men is and, in addition, which products are appropriate for each gender. Some of these 'sex-typed' products have come under fire from social groups. For example, feminists have criticised the Barbie doll for reinforcing unrealistic ideas about what women's bodies should look like – even though a newer version of the doll isn't quite as skinny and buxom. Other Barbie protests erupted when Mattel introduced a shopping-themed version called Cool Shoppin' Barbie. The doll comes with all the equipment kids need to pretend Barbie is shopping – including a

let's face it, firming the thighs
of a size 8 supermodel is no challenge.

There's not much point in testing a new firming lotion on size-eight supermodel thighs, is there? That's why Dove's Firming range was tested on ordinary women with real lives to live – and real, curvy thighs to firm. After using Dove's nourishing and effective combination of moisturisers and seaweed extracts, we asked if they'd go in front of the camera. What better way to show the unretouched, unairbrushed results?

new Dove Firming Range

| Photo 4.6 | In terms of gender roles, Dove's real beauty campaign challenges the conventional size zero model beauty which helps to define what is attractive in women. Source: The Advertising Archives |

Barbie-size MasterCard. When the card is pressed into the card scanner, her voice says, 'Credit approved!' Although Mattel includes a warning about sticking to a budget, some critics fear the doll sends the wrong message to girls about the desirability of shopping.[45]

Consumer-to-Consumer e-Commerce

Objective 6

Show how the internet offers consumers opportunities to participate in consumer-to-consumer marketing

Of course, not all consumer behaviour is related to marketers offering goods and services to consumers. **Consumer-to-consumer (C2C) e-commerce** refers to online communications and purchases that occur among individuals without directly involving the manufacturer or retailer. The most famous of such sites, eBay, provides an opportunity for consumers (and an increasing number of small businesses) to sell everything from comic books to a vintage trombone. In 2005, eBay ranked number 14 in Fortune's 100 Fastest-Growing Tech companies list, had websites in 23 countries and 8000 employees.[46]

Much of C2C e-commerce is far less sensational. It's more about groups of 'netizens' around the world with similar interests united through the internet by a shared passion. These virtual communities meet online and share their enthusiasm for a product, recording artist, art form, celebrity, and so on.[47] In fact, over 40 million people worldwide participate in such virtual communities. How many consumers actually visit these sites? Let's review the most popular online C2C formats:[48] gaming, chat rooms, boards and blogs.

Gaming   The emergence of gaming as an online, shared experience opens new vistas to marketers. Consider this: Toyota's digital racing game Tundra Madness attracts 8000 consumers who spend an average of eight minutes on the site daily. The company's research showed that the campaign raised brand awareness among consumers by 28 per cent and intent to purchase by 5 per cent. Heartened by the success of this experiment, Toyota launched games to promote other models. To target first-time car buyers the company created the Matrix Video Mixer game, which it promoted through sites like RollingStone.com, GetMusic.com and Launch.com. The effort was tied to a Gravity Games sponsorship and an in-cinema commercial campaign. About three in ten registered users forwarded videos created through the game to their friends.

The secret behind the appeal of this format is the huge chunks of time people spend immersed in these games. The average online player logs 17 hours per week, and firms like Sony, Microsoft and Sega are building their own virtual worlds to get a piece of the action. As one game company executive put it, 'This is not a genre of game but a break-through new medium. It provides a completely new social, collaborative shared experience. We're basically in the internet community business.'

Sony online's EverQuest is among the most successful of the Massively Multiplayer online Role-Player Games that allow people to live shadow lives. More than 430,000 registered players worldwide belong to 'guilds' in a never-ending journey to slay monsters and earn points. EverQuest combines the stunning graphics of advanced gaming with the social scene of a chat room. Like The Sims, players create a character as a virtual alter-ego, which may be a wise elf or a backstabbing rogue. Some players sell powerful characters on eBay for $1000 or more.

Chat rooms rings and lists   These include internet relay chat (IRC), otherwise known as chat rooms. Rings are organisations of related home pages, and lists are groups of people on a single mailing list who share information.

Boards   Online communities organised around interest-specific electronic bulletin boards. Active members read and post messages sorted by date and subject. There are boards devoted to musical groups, movies, wind, cigars, cars, comic strips, even fast-food restaurants.

The Japanese have embraced chat rooms as a way to express themselves bluntly in a society where face-to-face confrontation is avoided. Channel 2 is Japan's largest internet bulletin

Marketing Metrics

Electrolux

How did Electrolux know the Source was such a success? The first metric was volume of sales, for example, annualised sales equate to volume of 100,000 units over three years on this range of drinks-focused products.

Crucially, given the pressure to reduce prices, which was a trend in refrigeration, Electrolux was able to sell products at substantially above the market average prices and also without annual retail price deflation (as opposed to the 2–3 per cent that is common in this market). This enabled margin improvement even in a time of globally increasing raw material prices. On measures of brand perception such as familiarity, market share and likelihood of purchase, all showed improvements. Prior to these innovations Electrolux was in 5th or 6th place in its target segments in the €650–900 fridge freezer segment, it is now in 2nd or 3rd place in terms of value market share in these target segments.

board – the place where disgruntled employees leak information about their companies, journalists include tidbits they cannot get into the mainstream news media, and the average salaryman attacks with ferocity and language unacceptable in daily life. It is also the place where gays come out in a society in which they mostly remain in the closet. About 5.4 million people come to Channel 2 each month (www.2ch.net), many of them several times a day. Founded in 1999, *ni-channeru*, as the Japanese call it, has become part of Japan's everyday culture. News organisations follow it closely to gauge the public mood; big companies meticulously monitor how their products or companies are portrayed on it; and the police react immediately to threats posted on the site. As with any bulletin board, anonymous users start threads on myriad subjects and post comments. Unlike the real Japanese world, where language is calibrated according to one's social position, the wording on Channel 2 is often stripped of social indicators or purposefully manipulated to confuse readers. Language is also raw. 'Die!' is a favourite insult.

Blogs   The fastest-growing form of online community is the 'weblog', or blog. These online personal journals are building an avid following among people who like to dash off a few random thoughts, post them on a website, and read similar musings by others. Although these sites are similar to web pages offered by Geocities and other free services, they employ a different technology that lets people upload a few sentences without going through the process of updating a website built with conventional home page software. Bloggers can fire off thoughts on a whim, click a button, and quickly have them appear on a site. Weblogs frequently look like online diaries, with brief musings about the days' events, and perhaps a link or two of interest. This burgeoning **Blogosphere** (the name given to the universe of active weblogs) is starting to look like a force to be reckoned with.

At the start of the chapter, you met Richard Sells from Electrolux. He needs to work out which one of the fridges is going to be a winner in the market. Having read 'Real People, Other Voices' to learn how marketing professors and students advised Richard, now see how it worked out at Electrolux.

Real People, Real Decisions

How it worked out at Electrolux

Option 1, Source, the on-tap sparkling water dispenser, turned out to have the greatest splash in the marketplace. This was because it solved a set of real consumer issues which were practical and environmental, as well as the psychological aspect of feeling special by having on-tap chilled sparkling water. In particular, the design of the fridge hit upon a macro-

> ## It solved a set of real consumer issues which were practical and environmental, as well as the psychological aspect

trend that fridges are increasingly being seen as a design component of kitchens which can stand alone and be impressive rather than being hidden behind fitted cupboards. With its stainless steel finish and blue light in-door smooth action dispenser, it really looked stylish. Electrolux was first to market such a product, and there is still no competition. As a result of this uniqueness, the €400 increase on a normal fridge was considered reasonable value by consumers who saw the benefit of not have to carry and dispose of 400 bottles of sparkling water per year! The product was also successful because the salesforce liked having something new and innovative to talk about and they engaged with the credible consumer insight story which accompanied it. The whole company gained from it too as it was one of the first physical manifestations of the change in the business from being manufacturing led to being consumer and innovation led, with a feel-good factor for staff morale, giving them something to be proud of.

| Photo 4.7 | An Electrolux fridge with carbonated water and ice dispenser. Source: www.electrolux.com |

Chapter Summary

Now that you have finished reading this chapter, you should be able to

1. **Define consumer behaviour and explain why consumers buy what they buy.** Consumer behaviour is the process individuals or groups go through to select, purchase, use and dispose of goods, services, ideas or experiences to satisfy their needs and desires. Consumer decisions differ greatly ranging from habitual, repeat (low involvement) purchases to complex, extended problem-solving activities for important, risky (high involvement) purchases.

2. **Describe the pre-purchase, purchase and post-purchase activities that consumers engage in when making decisions.** When consumers make important purchasing decisions, they go through a set of five steps. First, they recognise there is a problem to be solved and search for information to make the best decision. They then evaluate a set of alternatives and judge them on the basis of various evaluative criteria. At this point, they are ready to make their purchasing decision. Following the purchase, consumers decide whether it matched their expectations.

3. **Explain how internal factors influence consumers' decision-making processes.** Several internal factors influence consumer decisions. Perception is how consumers select, organise and interpret stimuli. Motivation is an internal state that drives consumers to satisfy needs. Learning is a change in behaviour that results from information or experience. Behavioural learning results from external events, while cognitive learning refers to internal mental activity. An attitude is a lasting evaluation of a person, object or issue and includes three components: affect, cognition and behaviour. Personality traits such as innovativeness, materialism, self-confidence and sociability and the need for cognition may be used to develop market segments. Marketers seek to understand a consumer's self-concept in order to develop product attributes that match some aspect of the consumer's self-concept.

   The age of consumers and their lifestyle also are strongly related to consumption preferences.

Marketers may use psychographics to group people according to activities, interests, and opinions that may explain reasons for purchasing products.

4. **Show how situational factors at the time and place of purchase influence consumer behaviour.** Situational influences include our physical surroundings and time pressures. Dimensions of the physical environment including decor, smells, lighting, music, and even temperature can influence consumption. The time of day, the season of the year and how much time one has to make a purchase also affect decision making.

5. **Explain how consumers' relationships with other people influence their decision-making processes.** Consumers' overall preferences for products are determined by the culture in which they live and their membership in different subcultures. Social class, group memberships and opinion leaders are other types of social influences that affect consumer choices. A reference group is a set of people a consumer wants to please or imitate, and this affects the consumer's purchasing decisions. Purchases also often result from conformity to real or imagined group pressures. Another way social influence is felt is in the expectations of society regarding the proper roles for men and women. Such expectations have led to many sex-typed products.

6. **Show how the internet offers consumers opportunities to participate in consumer-to-consumer marketing.** Consumer-to-consumer (C2C) e-commerce includes marketing communication and purchases between individuals. C2C activities include virtual communities that allow consumers to do such things as share their enthusiasm or dislike for a product or company. Virtual communities and other C2C e-commerce activities provide both a source of information about the market and about competitors for marketers and an opportunity to communicate with consumers.

Key Terms

Chapter Review

 ## Marketing Concepts: Testing Your Knowledge

1. What is consumer behaviour? Why is it important for marketers to understand consumer behaviour?

2. Explain habitual decision making, limited problem solving and extended problem solving. What is the role of perceived risk in the decision process?

3. What are the steps in the consumer decision process?

4. What is perception? Explain the parts of the perception process: exposure, attention and interpretation. For marketers, what are the implications of each of these components?

5. What is motivation? What is the role of motivation in consumer behaviour?

6. What is behavioural learning? What is cognitive learning? How is an understanding of behavioural and cognitive learning useful to marketers?

7. What are the three components of attitudes? What is personality? What are some personality traits that may influence consumer behaviour?

8. Explain what is meant by lifestyle. What is the significance of family life cycle and lifestyle in understanding consumer behaviour and purchasing decisions?

9. How do culture and subculture influence consumer behaviour? What is the significance of social class to marketers?

10. What are reference groups, and how do they influence consumers? What are opinion leaders?

11. How does the physical environment influence consumer purchasing behaviour?

12. What is consumer-to-consumer (C2C) e-commerce? What are virtual communities, and how are they related to consumer behaviour?

Marketing Concepts: Discussing Choices and Issues

1. Demographic or cultural trends are important to marketers. What are some current trends that may affect the marketing of the following products?

   a. Housing

   b. Food

   c. Education

   d. Clothing

   e. Travel and tourism

   f. Cars

2. What are the core values of your culture? How do these core values affect your behaviour as a consumer? What are the implications for marketers?

3. Consumers often buy products because they feel pressure from reference groups to conform. Does conformity exert a positive or a negative influence on consumers? With what types of products is conformity more likely to occur?

4. Millions of consumers around the globe use eBay to supplement their incomes or as their primary source of income. What do you think of the future of sites such as eBay? What opportunities does eBay provide for twenty-first century entrepreneurs?

5. Retailers often place impulse purchase items such as magazines and chocolate bars near the entrance to the shop or near the checkout area. How would you describe the decision process for these products? Why are these locations effective?

6. In different cultures, perceptions about the proper roles for men and women, that is, sex roles, can vary greatly. What are some ways you think sex roles may differ in the following countries, and what are the implications for global marketers?

   a. UK

   b. Bahrain

   c. Japan

   d. Holland

7. We noted in the chapter that consumers often use country-of-origin as a heuristic to judge a product. Sometimes this tendency can backfire: While one study found that around the world 'the Golden Arches are now more widely recognised than the Christian cross', the strong link between McDonald's and the USA has been a liability for the food chain in recent years. As anti-war protests in many countries give vent to raw anti-US sentiment, the familiarity of McDonald's has made it a widespread target. In Quito, Ecuador, protesters burned a Ronald McDonald statue. In Paris, demonstrators smashed a McDonald's window. South Korean activists calling for an end to the war sought attention by climbing up a McDonald's sign. Other McDonald's outlets – in Karachi, in Buenos Aires – have been ringed with police officers to stave off trouble. Should a company that takes credit for its association with its country-of-origin in good times have to take its blame in bad times? What steps can marketers take to avoid these problems?[49]

8. Behavioural targeting involves tracking where people go online and then feeding them advertising information that's related to what they're looking for. While proponents of this approach argue that it's a very efficient and convenient way for people to conduct information search, others who are concerned about a potential invasion of privacy aren't so enthusiastic. What's your opinion – do you mind having marketers know what sites you visit in return for having a better sense of the competing products available while you're searching?

9. Online games like The Sims and EverQuest attract thousands of people around the world, many of whom spend virtually all of their free time hunched over their computer monitors. Advocates of online gaming point to the social benefits, including an outlet for creativity and the opportunity to interact (at least electronically) with other like-minded people. Critics argue that the games are antisocial because they reduce the amount of time gamers spend in 'the real world'. What do you think?

 Marketing Practice: Applying What You've Learned

1. Assume that you are the vice president of marketing for a car maker. You know that internal factors such as perception, motivation, learning, attitudes and personality influence consumers' decision making. Develop a report that describes these internal factors, why each is important in the purchase of a car and how you might use these factors in developing marketing strategies for your firm.

2. This chapter indicated that consumers go through a series of steps (from problem recognition to post-purchase evaluation) as they make purchases. Write a detailed report describing what you would do in each of these steps when deciding to choose one of the following products:

   a. Mobile telephone;

   b. A university;

   c. A fast-food lunch.

3. Using one of the products in question 2, what can marketers do to make sure that consumers going through each step in the consumer decision process move towards the purchase of their brand? Hint: think about product, place, price and promotion strategies.

4. Sometimes advertising or other marketing activities cause problem recognition to occur by showing consumers how much better off they would be with a new product or by pointing out problems with products they already own. For the following product categories, what are some ways marketers might try to stimulate problem recognition?

   a. Life insurance;

   b. Mouthwash;

   c. A new brand of laundry detergent;

   d. An airline.

5. Assume that you are a marketing manager for a large hotel chain with outlets in popular tourism sites around the world. You are concerned about the effects of current consumer trends, including changing ethnic populations, changing roles of men and women, increased concern for time and for the environment, and decreased emphasis on status goods. Others in your firm do not understand or care about these changes. They believe that the firm should continue to do business just as it always has. Develop a role-playing exercise with a classmate to discuss these two different points of view for your class. Each of you should be sure to include the importance of each of these trends to your firm and offer suggestions for marketing strategies to address these trends.

 ## Marketing Miniproject: Learning By Doing

The purpose of this miniproject is to increase your understanding of the roles of personal, social and situational factors in consumer behaviour.

1. With several other members of your class, select one of the following product categories (or some other product of your choice):

   ● Hairstyling;

   ● Large appliances such as refrigerators or washing machines;

   ● Children's clothing;

   ● Banking;

   ● Fine jewellery.

2. Visit three shops or locations where the product may be purchased. (Try to select three that are very different from each other.) Observe and make notes on all the elements of each retail environment.

3. At each of the three locations, observe people purchasing the product. Make notes about their characteristics (e.g. age, race, gender, and so on), their social class and their actions in the shop in relation to the product.

4. Prepare a report for your class describing the situational variables and individual consumer differences between the three shops and how they relate to the purchase of the product.

5. Present your findings to your class.

Real People, Real Surfers

Exploring the Web

Visit two or three virtual communities such as the ones listed in this chapter's discussion of C2C e-commerce. Based on your experience, answer the following questions for each site you visit:

1. What is the overall reason for the site's existence?

2. What is your opinion of the site?

3. What type of consumer do you think would be attracted to the site?

4. How easy or difficult is it to navigate each site?

Now, take a look at the website at www.pearsoned.co.uk/solomon to see some videos from YouTube relating to aspects of this chapter.

Marketing Plan Exercise

An important key to success for marketers is understanding consumers and how they go about selecting the products they buy. Pick a product, either a good or a service, that you like and that perhaps you've purchased in the past. As part of developing a marketing plan for this product, do the following;

1. Make a list of the many things you need to know about the consumers of your product and how they make the decision to purchase so that you can help to devise, where you should

sell your product, as well as how and what you should communicate to them.

2. What are some of the ways you might go about gathering the information?

3. Which consumer information is most useful in developing the marketing plan?

Marketing in Action Case

Real decisions at Net-a-Porter

Natalie Massenet, a former fashion editor of Tatler magazine, founded Net-a-Porter in 2000, having identified the potential of selling designer clothes online.

Net-A-Porter's site has been described as like a Hollywood film set from the 1930s or 1950s, creating a mood of sophistication and style. As well as describing the styles of the designers who sell through its shop, the website offers tips for achieving the right look, and previews from the fashion shows showing next season's styles. Careful attention is given to easy navigation – for example readers can click on the photographs as they browse and be routed through to the appropriate product page to purchase the item. Two special attractions are the exclusive online links with Jimmy Choo and Chloé, supporting easy switching between the Net-a-Porter, Choo and Chloé home pages, with each operating as an independent shop within a shop and maintaining a separate brand identity. Additionally, the site offers

features such as lists of gift suggestions put together by the editorial team, under four price brackets, and 'Tell Santa', which allows you to generate a personalised message to send to a friend, supplying details of what you would like from the site and how to buy it.

Since launching in June 2000, Net-a-Porter has successfully established itself as a luxury brand and is described as the premier online destination for women's designer fashion. It has achieved this through innovation as well as a highly developed offering. Net-a-Porter now sells over 150 top fashion labels, focusing on the latest must-have items from the international fashion collections. The company offers express delivery worldwide with same-day delivery in London and Manhattan. Additionally, in July 2007, Net-a-Porter mounted an online fashion show with the designer Roland Mouret revealing his new collection and being interviewed backstage. Customers watched the show online, including close-ups of hair and make-up, and details of all clothes and looks. They could then 'drag'

> ## Since June 2000, Net-a-Porter has successfully established itself as a luxury brand

whatever they wanted into a shopping basket and pre-order for delivery in November.

Supporting this scale of online operation has required attention to systems and processes. As the business had developed since its launch in 2000, Net-a-Porter used three types of emails to communicate and for sales promotion. Net-A-Porter was sending emails to some customers up to 10 times a week with information including generic updates, highlights from specific designers and details of new products. Not only was this a significant operation for the company but it also risked alienating its client base because of the sheer volume of emails, particularly where they were not seen as sufficiently personal or relevent. Net-a-Porter knew that it has to rationalise its communications whilst still satisfying its clients' wishes to have the most up-to-date information because fashion items can sell out within hours of becoming available. Furthermore, given the growth of the business, Net-a-Porter's management needed to review both communications strategy and technology for more than just the short term.

Things to Think About

1. What is the decision facing Net-a-Porter?

2. What factors are important in understanding the decision situation?

3. What are the options?

4. What decision(s) do you recommend?

5. What are some ways to implement your recommendation(s)?

References

1. David Kesmodel, "Marketers Push Online Ads Based on Your Surfing Habits," *The Wall Street Journal Interactive Edition* (5 April 2005).

2. Michael R. Solomon, *Consumer Behavior: Buying, Having, and Being,* 7th ed. (Upper Saddle River, NJ: Prentice Hall, 2007).

3. Christopher Lawton, 'Pushing Faux Foreign Beer in U.S.: Can Anheuser-Busch Tap Imports' Growth with Beers Produced in Land of Budweiser?', 27 June 2003, www.wsj.com.

4. 'Touch Looms Large as a Sense That Drives Sales', *Brand Packaging* (May/June 1999), 39–40.

5. Michael Lev, 'No Hidden Meaning Here: Survey Sees Subliminal Ads', *New York Times*, 3 May 1991, D7.

6. 'ABC Rejects KFC Commercial, Citing Subliminal Advertising', *The Wall Street Journal Interactive Edition* 2 March 2006.

7. Stuart Elliott, 'TV Commercials Adjust to a Shorter Attention Span', *The New York Times Online,* 8 April 2005.

8. Brian Sternberg, 'Next Up on Fox: Ads that can Change Pitch', *The Wall Street Journal,* 21 April 2005, B1.

9. Abraham H. Maslow, *Motivation and Personality*, 2nd ed. (New York: Harper & Row, 1970).

10. Robert A. Baron and Donn Byrne, *Social Psychology: Understanding Human Interaction*, 5th ed. (Boston: Allyn & Bacon, 1987).

11. Jeffrey Zaslow, "Happiness Inc.: Science is Exploring the Roots of Joy – and Companies are Putting the Findings to Work. How it's Changing your Appliances and Cheering up your Sales Clerks', *The Wall Street Journal,* 18 March 2006, P1.

12. Thorsten Hennig-Thurau, Markus Groth, Michael Paul and Dwayne D. Gremler, 'Are All Smiles Created Equal? How Emotional Contagion and Emotional Labor Affect Service Relationships', *Journal of Marketing*, 70(3) (2006), 58–73.

13. Stuart Elliott, 'Pepsi's New Campaign Leaves Left Brain for Right', 20 November 2003, at www.nyt.com.

14. www.becks.co.uk.

15. www.nivea.co.uk; www.rdtrustedbrands.com/TrustedBrands 2006.

16. Richard E. Petty and John T. Cacioppo, 'Need for Cognition and Advertising: Understanding the Role of Personality Variables in Consumer Behavior', *Journal of Consumer Psychology* 1(3) (1992), 239–60.

17. www.campaignforrealbeauty.com/press.asp?id=4737& section=news&target=press.

18. www.audiworld.com/news/05/hoffman/content.shtml.

19. Benjamin D. Zablocki and Rosabeth Moss Kanter, 'The Differentiation of Life-Styles', *Annual Review of Sociology* (1976), 269–97.

20. Damien Cave, 'Dogtown U.S.A.', *The New York Times Online* 12 June 2005.

21. Alfred S. Boote, 'Psychographics: Mind Over Matter', *American Demographics* (April 1980), 26–29; William D. Wells, 'Psychographics: A Critical Review', *Journal of Marketing Research* 12 (May 1975), 196–213.

22. Alan R. Hirsch, 'Effects of Ambient Odors on Slot-Machine Usage in a Las Vegas Casino', *Psychology & Marketing* 12(7) (October 1995), 585–94.

23. Marianne Meyer, 'Attention Shoppers!', *Marketing and Media Decisions* 23 (May 1988), 67.

24. See Eben Shapiro, 'Need a Little Fantasy? A Bevy of New Companies Can Help', *New York Times*, 10 March 1991, F4.

25. Stephanie Grunier, 'An Entrepreneur Chooses to Court Cafe Society (Cyber Version, Actually)', 24 September 1999, www.wsj.com.

26. John P. Robinson, 'Time Squeeze', *Advertising Age* (February 1990), 30–33.

27. Leonard L. Berry, 'Market to the Perception', *American Demographics* (February 1990), 32.

28. Neil MacFarquhar, 'A Kiss Is Not Just a Kiss to an Angry Arab TV Audience', 5 March 2004, www.nyt.com.

29. Adapted from Solomon, *Consumer Behavior: Buying, Having, and Being,* 7th ed.

30. Richard W. Pollay, 'Measuring the Cultural Values Manifest in Advertising', *Current Issues and Research in Advertising,* 2(1), (1983), 71–92.

31. Becky Ebenkamp, 'Chicks and Balances', *Brandweek*, 12 February 2001, 16.

32. Norihiko Shirouzu, 'Japanese "Hygiene Fanatics" Snap Up Low-Smoke Cigarette', 8 September 1997, www.wsj.com.

33. Adapted from Solomon, *Consumer Behavior: Buying, Having, and Being,* 7th ed.

34. J. Michael Munson and W. Austin Spivey, 'Product and Brand-User Stereotypes among Social Classes: Implications for Advertising Strategy', *Journal of Advertising Research* 21 (August 1981), 37–45.

35. Stuart U. Rich and Subhash C. Jain, 'Social Class and Life Cycle as Predictors of Shopping Behavior', *Journal of Marketing Research* 5 (February 1968), 41–49.

36. Alessandra Galloni, 'Armani, Mercedes to Form Marketing, Design Venture', 30 September 2003, www.wsj.com.

37. Adapted from Solomon, *Consumer Behavior: Buying, Having, and Being* , 7th ed.

38. Nathan Kogan and Michael A. Wallach, 'Risky Shift Phenomenon in Small Decision-Making Groups: A Test of the Information Exchange Hypothesis', *Journal of Experimental Social Psychology* 3 (January 1967), 75–84; Arch G. Woodside and M. Wayne DeLozier, 'Effects of Word-of-Mouth Advertising on Consumer Risk Taking', *Journal of Advertising* (Fall 1976), 12–19.

39. Jack Neff, 'Door-to-Door Sellers Join the Party Online', *Advertising Age*, 27 September 1999, www.adage.com/news.cms?newsld=1100.

40. Everett M. Rogers, *Diffusion of Innovations*, 3rd ed. (New York: Free Press, 1983).

41. Kathleen Debevec and Easwar Iyer, 'Sex Roles and Consumer Perceptions of Promotions, Products, and Self: What Do We Know and Where Should We Be Headed', in *Advances in Consumer Research*, vol. 13, ed. Richard J. Lutz (Provo, Utah: Association for Consumer Research, 1986), 210–14; Lynn J. Jaffe and Paul D. Berger, 'Impact on Purchase Intent of Sex-Role Identity and Product Positioning', *Psychology and Marketing* (Fall 1988), 259–71.

42. Becky Ebenkamp, 'Battle of the Sexes', Brandweek, 17 April 2000, www.findarticles.com/p/articles/mi_m0BDW/is_16_41/ai_61860406.

43. Debevec and Iyer, 'Sex Roles and Consumer Perceptions of Promotions, Products and Self'; Deborah E. S. Frable, 'Sex Typing and Gender Ideology: Two Facets of the Individual's Gender Psychology That Go Together', *Journal of Personality and Social Psychology* 56 (1989), 95–108; Jaffe and Berger, 'Impact on Purchase Intent of Sex-Role Identity and Product Positioning'; Keren A. Johnson, Mary R. Zimmer and Linda L. Golden, 'Object Relations Theory: Male and Female Differences in Visual Information Processing', in *Advances in Consumer Research*, vol. 14, ed. Melanie Wallendorf and Paul Anderson

(Provo, Utah: Association for Consumer Research, 1986), 83–7; Leila T. Worth, Jeanne Smith and Diane M. Mackie, 'Gender Schematicity and Preference for Gender-Typed Products', *Psychology & Marketing* 9 (January 1992), 17–30.

44. VITALSTATS (2008) 'Behaviourally targeted advertising,' *Media Week,* 4–11 March 2008, 15.

45. Kara K. Choquette, 'Not All Approve of Barbie's MasterCard', *USA Today*, 30 March 1998, 6B.

46. Adam Lashinsky, 'Meg and the Machine', *Fortune,* 11 August, 2–3, http://money.cnn.com/magazines/business2/b2fastestgrowing/ snapshots/457.html

47. This section adapted from Michael R. Solomon, *Consumer Behavior: Buying, Having and Being*, 7th ed. (Upper Saddle River, NJ: Prentice Hall, 2001).

48. This section adapted from Solomon, *Consumer Behavior: Buying, Having, and Being,* 7th ed.

49. Quoted in Rob Walker, 'McDonald's: When a Brand Becomes a Stand-In for a Nation', *The New York Times Online,* 30 March 2003.

Chapter 5
Business-to-Business Marketing

Meet Brian Oxley,
a Decision Maker at Sash UK

B rian Oxley is Commercial Director at Sash UK Ltd a supplier of PVCu industrial windows. The company was founded in 1965, then known as Bean & Morrell, and quickly established a reputation for traditional craftsmanship. During the initial ten years the company's business flourished, partly as a result of the buoyant housing market where the company had been highly successful in supplying to construction companies. During the next decade, the demand for replacement windows really took off, there was an emphasis on energy efficiency, with the introduction of double glazing at the forefront of governmental-led initiatives. The company moved into aluminium designs in the early 1980s. Following this period, the company launched its new range of PVCu windows, and managed to penetrate the UK market with remarkable speed. By continually monitoring the industrial and commercial markets, and through re-investing in the company in terms of innovation and design (and adding PVCu conservatories to its existing product range of high-quality windows and doors) – Sash enjoyed significant growth throughout the 1980s and 1990s. Brian joined the company some 23 years ago. He was appointed Commercial Director at Sash in 1999, where he holds responsibility for 70 per cent of the company's sales turnover. Brian's role is to nurture and develop business in various B2B markets including local government, housing associations, education authorities, other governmental bodies, and large private sector businesses.

Q & A with Brian Oxley

First job out of school:
Pattern Maker for loom manufacturing at Wilson & Longbottom, UK.

Career high:
I am still searching for it.

My hero:
Lance Armstrong. He's achieved his goals through adversity.

Don't do this when interviewing with me:
Tell lies. Be honest and truthful.

My pet peeve:
Irony in all shapes and forms.

Favourite TV programme:
House

Real People, Real Decisions
Decision Time at Sash

As a new millennium was looming, the company had to make some tough decisions. In the midst of the national success that the company had experienced in the industrial marketplace, competition was becoming more intense. A number of highly reputable suppliers that had traditionally operated in the residential consumer marketplace had decided to expand their operations by establishing a presence in the industrial market. The market was about to become more competitively intense, as those suppliers in the market were forced to react to these new entrants; at the same time, because of new EU regulations, several German suppliers were looking to enter at the high quality end of the market, and other suppliers from Southern Europe were aiming to take advantage of their 'low cost' base to spearhead further attacks.

Whilst several European players were planning to enter an already somewhat saturated and competitive UK market, board members of Sash were considering export themselves. For several years the company had received unsolicited enquiries from the US but because it did not have the skills and knowledge to consider export, nor the production capacity to fulfil potential demand, decided against such ventures.

Brian and his team had to consider that their UK market position was vulnerable, and needed to react accordingly, and at the same time think long and hard about investing heavily in a new manufacturing plant, aimed at serving both domestic orders and potential US demand.

Brian considers his options . . .

Option 1 Do nothing and continue with the current strategy of competing at the high end of the UK industrial market

There are several advantages to this: (1) the company has a well-established market share, and a good reputation. As a result it may be able to maintain a similar position. (2) Sash would not need to risk a commercial loan of about €5 million, and more investment could be placed on defending the company's market position.

(3) Because Sash is a privately run limited company, and would not be subject to the pressures from the London Stock Exchange for quarterly earnings and rapid expansion, there may be less constraints on the board members of the company, who could be happy for the company to make modest returns. (4) The uncertainty of venturing into the US for a company that has never exported makes staying at home less risky. Sash is comfortable with its current business model. Any change requires learning new business processes and positioning strategies with new customers. On the other hand, Sash is experiencing growing competition, and further developments within Europe suggest that depending on the home market will continue to be more and more difficult.

Option 2 Continue with the current strategy of competing at the high end of the UK industrial market, but outsource production that can serve the demand for the US market

The advantages of this option include all those discussed above for option 1, and the company has the potential to increase revenues further through using the production facilities of another company. Of course there would be much lower start-up risks compared with the construction of a new production site, and as a company Sash controls the marketing arm, and importantly manages the customer relationship. The downside to this option is that when dealing with a third-party producer, the management and control of quality is more difficult. Remember that Sash has established a reputation for quality and service. Put simply, an outsourced company may not be able to deliver to the standards and specification associated with Sash and this could tarnish the company's reputation and spoil the chance of breaking into the large potential US market.

The third-party manufacturing company would also be likely to become financially much stronger due to the US orders. Sash would of course live in fear of creating a competitor, that may even have the desire and drive to enter the US market itself. This may be an expensive option too, as profits need to be shared with the manufacturer which could otherwise be used for further investment at Sash.

Option 3 Go for the plant investment and use this to update production and serve the needs of US demand

This would allow Sash to enter the US and not have to share profits with third-party manufacturers. At the same time Sash would benefit in the medium and long term from the economies of scale which a larger and more efficient production base could offer. Choosing this option would result in higher capital investment and a commercial loan. Sash would be able to build on its experience in the UK to enter a similar market in terms of culture – a realistic expectation. On the other hand, there is no guarantee of success, but US demand appears huge.

Now, put yourself in Brian's shoes: Which option would you choose, and why?

Objectives

When you finish reading this chapter, you will be able to:

1 Describe the general characteristics of business-to-business markets

2 Explain the unique characteristics of business demand

3 Describe how business or organisational markets are classified

4 Explain the business buying situation and describe business buyers

5 Explain the roles in the business buying centre

6 Understand the stages in the business buying decision process

7 Understand the growing role of B2B e-commerce

Business Markets: Buying and Selling when the Stakes are High

Objective

1

Describe the general characteristics of business-to-business markets

You might think most marketers spend their days dreaming up the best way to promote cutting-edge web browsers or trendy shoes – not really. Many marketers know that the 'real action' more likely lies in industrial products like Sash offers, or in office supplies, work safety shoes, group medical insurance, machine components or construction products that other companies sell to businesses and organisations. In fact, some of the most interesting and lucrative jobs for young graduates are in industries you've probably never heard of because these businesses don't deal directly with consumers.

Like an end consumer, a business buyer makes decisions – but with an important difference: the purchase may be worth millions of euros, and both the buyer and the seller have a lot at stake. A consumer may decide to buy two or three T-shirts at one time, each showing a different design. Leading companies such as British Airways, Shell and Pizza Hut buy hundreds, even thousands of employee uniforms embroidered with their corporate logos in one single order.

Consider these transactions: IBM produces computer network servers to sell to its business customers. Unilever has contracts with several advertising agencies to promote its brands at home and around the globe. The London Theatre Company buys costumes, sets and programmes. The EU in Brussels places orders for thousands of new computers.

All these exchanges have one thing in common: they're part of **business-to-business (B2B) marketing**. This is the marketing of goods and services that businesses and other organisations buy for purposes other than personal consumption. Some firms resell these goods and services, so they are part of a channel of distribution. Other firms use the goods and services they buy to produce other goods and services that meet the needs of their customers or to support their own operations. These **business-to-business markets**, or *organisational markets*, include manufacturers, wholesalers, retailers and a variety of other organisations, such as hospitals, universities and governmental agencies.

To put the size and complexity of business markets into perspective, let's consider a single product – a pair of jeans. A consumer may browse through several racks of jeans and ultimately purchase a single pair, but the shop at which the consumer shops has purchased many pairs of jeans in various sizes, styles and brands from different manufacturers. Each of these manufacturers purchases fabrics, zips, buttons and cotton thread from other manufacturers – that in turn purchase the raw materials to make these components. In addition, all the firms in this chain need to purchase equipment, electricity, labour, computer systems, legal and accounting services, insurance, office supplies, packing materials and countless other goods and services. So even a single purchase of the latest style of Diesel jeans represents the culmination of a series of buying and selling activities among many organisations.

In this chapter, we'll look at the big picture of the business marketplace, a world in which the success of business buyers and sellers can hang in the balance of a single transaction. Then we'll examine how marketers categorise businesses and other organisations to develop effective business marketing strategies. We'll look at business buying behaviour and the business buying decision process. Finally, we'll talk about the important world of business-to-business e-commerce.

Characteristics that make a Difference in Business Markets

Objective

2

Explain the unique characteristics of business demand

In theory, the same basic marketing principles hold in both consumer and business markets – firms identify customer needs and develop a marketing mix to satisfy those needs. For example, take the company that made the desks and chairs at your university. Just like a firm that markets consumer goods, the furniture company that supplies university establishments first must create an important competitive advantage for its target market of universities. Next the firm develops a marketing mix strategy beginning with a product – the lecture/seminar room furniture that will withstand years of use by thousands of students while providing a level of comfort required for a good learning environment. The firm must offer the furniture at prices that universities can afford and that will allow the firm to make a reasonable profit. Then the firm must develop a sales force or other marketing communications strategy to make sure your university (and many others) consider, and hopefully choose its products when it furnishes classrooms.

Although marketing to business customers does have a lot in common with consumer marketing, there are differences that make this basic process more complex.[1] Figure 5.1 provides a quick look at some of these differences.

WE KEEP THINGS MOVING – AND AN EYE ON THE ENVIRONMENT. THAT'S HOW WE GO GREEN.

www.dhl-gogreen.com

GOGREEN
Climate Protection with DHL

DHL

Photo 5.1 With Go Green, DHL differentiates itself in the B2B marketplace.
Source: DHL (Germany)

Organisational Markets	Consumer Markets
• Purchases made for some purpose other than personal consumption	• Purchases for individual or household consumption
• Purchases made by someone other than the user of the product	• Purchases usually made by ultimate user of the product
• Decisions frequently made by several people	• Decisions usually made by individuals
• Purchases made according to precise technical specifications based on product expertise	• Purchases often based on brand reputation or personal recommendations with little or no product expertise
• Purchases made after careful weighing of alternatives	• Purchases frequently made on impulse
• Purchases based on rational criteria	• Purchases based on emotional responses to products or promotions
• Purchasers often engage in lengthy decision process	• Individual purchasers often make quick decisions
• Interdependencies between buyers and sellers; long-term relationships	• Buyers engage in limited-term or one-time-only relationships with many different sellers
• Purchases may involve competitive bidding, price negotiations, and complex financial arrangements	• Most purchases made at 'list price' with cash or credit cards
• Products frequently purchased directly from producer	• Products usually purchased from someone other than producer of the product
• Purchases frequently involve high risk and high cost	• Most purchases are low risk and low cost
• Limited number of large buyers	• Many individual or household customers
• Buyers often geographically concentrated in certain areas	• Buyers generally dispersed throughout total population
• Products often complex; classified based on how organisational customers use them	• Products: consumer goods and services for individual use
• Demand derived from demand for other goods and services, generally inelastic in the short run, subject to fluctuations, and may be joined to the demand for other goods and services	• Demand based on consumer needs and preferences, is generally price-elastic, steady over time and independent of demand for other products
• Promotion emphasises personal selling	• Promotion emphasises advertising

Figure 5.1   Differences between Organisational and Consumer Markets

There are many major and minor differences between organisational and consumer markets. To be successful, marketers must understand these differences and develop strategies that can be effective with organisational customers.

 ## Large Buyers

In business markets, products often have to do more than satisfy an individual's needs. They must meet the requirements of everyone involved in the company's purchase decision. If you decide to buy a new chair for your room or apartment, you're the only one who has to be satisfied. For the lecture/seminar room, the furniture must satisfy not only students but also faculty, administrators, campus planners, financial controllers and the people at your institution who actually do the purchasing. In some cases the furniture may also have to meet certain governmental and safety standards.

Number of Customers

Organisational customers are few and far between compared with end consumers. In Europe, there are several million consumer households but significantly fewer businesses or organisations. Dutch giant Philips Medical, which markets sophisticated electrical products to hospitals, health maintenance organisations and other medical groups, has a limited number of potential customers compared with its consumer electronics division. This means that business marketing strategies may be quite different from consumer marketing strategies. For example, in consumer markets Philips may use TV advertising, but in its business markets a strong sales force is vital for promoting the product.

Size of Purchases

Business-to-business products can influence consumer purchases, both in the quantity of items ordered and in the price of individual purchases. A company that hires out uniforms to other businesses, for example, buys huge volumes of washing detergent each year to clean its uniforms. In contrast, even a hard-core football mother dealing with piles of dirty socks and shorts is likely to use just one box every few weeks. Organisations purchase many products, such as highly sophisticated manufacturing equipment or computer-based marketing information systems that can cost millions of euros. Recognising such differences in the size of purchases allows marketers to develop effective marketing strategies. Although it makes perfect sense to use mass-media advertising to sell laundry detergent to consumers, selling laundry detergent worth thousands of euros or a million-euro machine tool is often best handled by a strong personal sales force.

Geographic Concentration

Another difference between business markets and consumer markets is geographic concentration. Business customers are often located in a small geographic area rather than being spread out across a country. Whether they live in the heart of Paris or in a small fishing village in Greece, consumers buy toothpaste and televisions. Business-to-business customers may be almost exclusively located in a single region of a country. Birmingham is home to a significant number of companies that supply steel and engineering components. For business-to-business marketers who wish to sell to these markets, this means that they can concentrate their sales efforts and perhaps even locate distribution centres nearby.

Business-to-Business Demand

Demand in business markets differs from consumer demand. Most demand for business-to-business products is derived, inelastic, fluctuating and joint. Understanding these differences in business-to-business demand is important for marketers in forecasting sales and in planning effective marketing strategies.

Derived Demand

Consumer demand is based on a direct connection between a need and the satisfaction of that need. However, business customers don't purchase goods and services to satisfy their own needs. Business-to-business demand is **derived demand** because a business's demand for goods and services comes either directly or indirectly from consumer demand.

Consider an airline carrier such as KLM (from the Netherlands). Demand for the purchase of aircraft (Boeing or Airbus orders) comes from the demand for air travel and holidays. Likewise, demand for a marketing textbook is likely to come from the demand for business and marketing education. As a result of derived demand, the success of one company may depend on another company, and it could be in a different industry. The derived nature of business demand means that marketers must be constantly alert to changes in consumer trends that ultimately will have an effect on business-to-business sales.

 ## Inelastic Demand

Inelastic demand means that it usually doesn't matter if the price of a business-to-business product goes up or down – business customers still buy the same quantity. Demand in business-to-business markets is mostly inelastic because what is being sold is often just one of many parts or materials that go into producing the consumer product. It is not unusual for a large increase in a business product's price to have little effect on the final consumer product's price.

For example, you may be able to buy a BMW Z4 Roadster 3.0i 'loaded' with options for about €60,000. To produce the car, BMW purchases thousands of different parts. If the price of tyres, batteries or stereos goes up or down, BMW will still buy enough to meet consumer demand for its cars. As you might imagine, increasing the price by €30, €40 or even €100 won't change consumer demand for this type of cars, so demand for parts remains the same (if you have to ask how much it costs, you probably can't afford one).

But business-to-business demand isn't always inelastic. Sometimes producing a consumer good or service relies on only one or a few materials or component parts. If the price of the part increases, demand may become elastic if the manufacturer of the consumer good passes the increase on to the consumer. Steel, for example, is a major component in cars. Vehicle manufacturers will need to pay a lot more for steel should its price rise. An increase in the price of steel can drive up the price of vehicles so greatly that consumer demand drops, and eventually decreases the demand for steel.

 ## Fluctuating Demand

Business demand is also subject to greater fluctuations than consumer demand. There are two reasons for this. First, even small changes in consumer demand can create large increases or decreases in business demand. Take for example air travel – and even a small increase in demand for air travel can cause airlines to order new equipment, creating a dramatic increase in demand for planes.

A product's life expectancy is another reason for fluctuating demand. Business customers tend to purchase certain products infrequently. Some types of large machinery may need to be replaced every 10 or 20 years. Thus, demand for such products fluctuates. It may be very high one year when a lot of customers' machinery is wearing out, but low the following year because everyone's old machinery is working fine. One solution for keeping production more constant is to use price reductions to encourage companies to order products *before* they actually need them.

 ## Joint Demand

Joint demand occurs when two or more goods are necessary to create a product. For example, the BMW Z4 needs tyres, batteries, and spark plugs (a range of products). If the supply of one of these parts decreases, BMW may find it difficult to manufacture as many vehicles, and the company may not buy as many of the other items either.

Types of Business-to-Business Markets

Objective

3

Describe how business or organisational markets are classified

As we noted earlier, many firms buy products in business markets so they can produce other goods. Other business-to-business customers resell, rent or lease goods and services. Still other customers, including governments and not-for-profit institutions such as the Red Cross or a local church, serve the public in some way. In this section, we'll look at the three major classes of business-to-business customers – producers, resellers and organisations (Figure 5.2). Then we'll look at how marketers classify specific industries.

Producers

Producers purchase products for the production of other goods and services that they in turn sell to make a profit. For this reason, they are customers for a vast number of products from raw materials to goods manufactured by still other producers. For example, in our introductory case, Sash buys PVCu and uses it to manufacture its windows. Airbus buys engines, high-tech navigation systems, passenger seats and a host of other component parts to put into its planes. The French hotel chain Accor purchases linens, furniture and food to produce the ambiance and meals its guests expect.

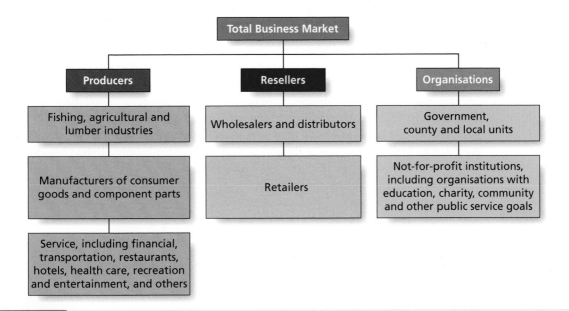

Figure 5.2	**The Business Marketplace**
	The business marketplace consists of three major categories of customers: producers, resellers and organisations. Business-to-business marketers need to understand the different needs of these customers if they are to build successful relationships.

Resellers

Resellers buy finished goods for the purpose of reselling, renting, or leasing to other businesses. Although resellers do not actually produce goods, they do provide their customers with the time, place and possession, by making goods available to consumers when and where they want them. For example, French supermarket chain Carrefour buys toothpaste, soft drinks, clothing and thousands of other product lines to sell in its retail shops.

Organisations

Governments may be the only customers for certain products – Tornado fighter jets for example. But much governmental expenditure is for more familiar and less expensive items. In any one year, the national government in any one of the largest EU countries is likely to purchase a range of goods and services, ranging from thousands of note pads and paintbrushes, to rail tickets, hotel rooms and the like.

To inform possible vendors about purchases they are about to make, governments regularly make information on forthcoming purchases available to potential bidders. The EU government provides information on business opportunities and tenders through the *Official Journal of the European Union*, and suppliers can easily seek opportunities through scanning the journal.

Not-for-profit institutions are organisations with educational, community and other public service goals, such as hospitals, churches, universities, museums and charitable and lobby groups. These institutions tend to operate on low budgets. Because non-professional part-time buyers who have other duties often make purchases, these customers may rely on marketers to provide more advice and assistance before and after the sale.

The Standard Industry Classification (SIC) System

In addition to looking at business-to-business markets within these three general categories, marketers can identify potential customers using the **Standard Industrial Classification system (SIC)**. This is a numerical coding system whereby companies that operate within specific industrial sectors (their SIC code) can be identified.

Firms may therefore use the SIC system to find new customers. A marketer might first determine the SIC industry classifications of his current customers and then evaluate the sales potential of other firms occupying these categories. For example, Brian at Sash may find that several of his large customers are in the commercial construction industry. To find new customers, he could contact other firms in the same industrial group.

www.pearsoned.co.uk/solomon

The Nature of Business Buying

Objective

4

Explain the business buying situation and describe business buyers

So far we've talked about how business-to-business markets are different from consumer markets and about the different types of customers that make up business markets. In this section, we'll discuss some of the important characteristics of business buying. This is important because just like companies that sell to end consumers, a successful business-to-business marketer needs to understand how his or her customers make decisions. Armed with this knowledge, the company is able to participate in the buyer's decision process from the start. Take a firm that sells equipment to hospitals. Understanding that doctors who practise at the hospital (rather than buyers who actually purchase medical supplies) often initiate new equipment purchases means that the firm's salespeople have to be sure that they establish solid relationships with such individuals as well as with the hospital's buyers – if they expect their products to be taken seriously.

 # The Buying Situation

Like end consumers, business buyers spend more time and effort on some purchases than on others. Devoting such effort to a purchase decision usually depends on the complexity of the product and how often the decision has to be made. A **buy class** framework identifies the degree of effort required by the firm's personnel to collect information and make a purchase decision. These classes, which apply to three different buying situations, are called straight re-buys, modified re-buys and new-task buys.

Straight Re-Buy

A **straight re-buy** is the routine purchase of items that a business-to-business customer regularly needs. The buyer has purchased the same items many times before and routinely reorders them when supplies are low, often from the same suppliers. Reordering takes little time. Buyers typically maintain a list of approved suppliers that have demonstrated their ability to meet the firm's criteria for pricing, quality, service and delivery. Such products for example could include paper or stationery.

Because straight re-buys often contribute the 'bread and butter' revenue a firm needs to maintain a steady stream of income, many business marketers go to great lengths to cultivate and maintain relationships with customers who submit reorders on a regular basis. Salespeople, for example, regularly call on these customers to handle orders personally and to see if there are additional products the customer needs. The goal is to be sure that the customer doesn't even think twice about just buying the same product every time he or she is running low. Re-buys keep a supplier's sales volume up and selling costs down.

Modified Re-Buy

Life would be sweet for companies whose customers automatically do straight re-buys. Unfortunately, these situations do not last forever. A **modified re-buy** occurs when a firm wants to shop around for suppliers with better prices, quality, or delivery times. This situation also can occur when the organisation has new needs for products it already buys. A buyer who has purchased many office printers in the past, for example, may have to evaluate several lines of printers if the firm has a new need for office equipment.

Modified re-buys require more time and effort than straight re-buys. The buyer generally knows the purchase requirements and a few potential suppliers. Marketers know that modified re-buys can mean that some vendors get added to a buyer's approved supplier list while others may be dropped. Astute marketers routinely call on buyers to detect and define problems that can lead to winning or losing in such situations.

New-Task Buy

A first-time purchase is a **new-task buy**. Uncertainty and risk characterise buying decisions in this classification, and they need the most effort because the buyer has no previous experience on which to base a decision.

Your university, for example, may decide (if it hasn't done so already) to go into the 'distance learning' business, which is delivering courses to off-site students. Buying the equipment to set up classrooms with two-way video transmission is an expensive and complex new-task

| Photo 5.2 | DHL aims to appeal to its routine business customers and discourage them from 'shopping around' through providing more reach.
Source: DHL (Germany) |

buy. The buyer has to start from scratch to gather information on purchase specifications that may be highly technical/complex and require detailed input from others. In new-task buying situations, not only do buyers lack experience with the product, but they also are often unfamiliar with firms that supply the product. Supplier choice is critical, and buyers gather much information about quality, pricing, delivery and service from several potential suppliers.

A prospective customer's new-task buying situation represents both a challenge and an opportunity. Although a new-task buy can be significant in itself, many times the chosen supplier gains the added advantage of becoming an 'in' supplier for more routine purchases that will follow. A growing business that needs an advertising agency for the first time, for example, may seek exhaustive information from several firms before selecting one, but then it may continue to use the chosen agency's services for future projects without exploring other alternatives. We can see through 'Marketing Metrics' how Dow Chemicals has invested in identifying ways of retaining business customers – trying to influence them to move towards a straight re-buy.

Marketers know that to get the order in a new-buy situation, they must develop a close working relationship with the business buyer. Keep in mind that these relationships aren't just important in industries like industrial glass. There are in fact many situations where marketers focus on selling their product or service through inspiring people to recommend their products – over and above the end consumers who actually buy them. To use an example, think about all of the products and services that make up the higher education industry. For instance, even though you are perhaps the one who paid the money for this textbook, your tutor was the one who made the wise decision to assign it. He or she may have made their choice only after carefully considering numerous textbooks and talking to several publishing sales representatives.

At the start of the chapter, you met Brian Oxley of Sash. He needs to figure out a strategy. Read the 'Real People, Other Voices' box on page 196 to learn how other people advise Brian.

 ## The Professional Buyer

Objective 5

Explain the roles in the business buying centre

Just as it is important for marketers of consumer goods and services to understand their customers, it is essential that business-to-business marketers understand who handles the buying for business customers. Trained professional buyers frequently carry out buying in business-to-business markets. These people typically have a title such as *purchasing manager, purchasing director* or *head of purchasing*.

While some consumers like to shop till they drop almost every day, most of us spend far less time roaming the aisles. However, professional purchasers do it all day, every day. These individuals focus on economic factors beyond the initial price of the product, including transportation and delivery charges, accessory products or supplies, maintenance, and other costs. They are responsible for selecting quality products and ensuring their timely delivery. They shop as if their jobs depend on it – and they do.

 ## The Buying Centre

Many times in business buying situations, several people work together to reach a decision. Depending on what they need to purchase, these participants may be production workers, supervisors, engineers, secretaries, shipping clerks or financial controllers. In a small organisation, everyone may have a voice in the decision. The group of people in the organisation who participate in the decision-making process is referred to as the **buying centre**. Although this term may conjure up an image of offices buzzing with purchasing activity, a buying centre is not a place at all. Instead, it is a cross-functional team of decision makers. Generally, the members of a buying centre have some expertise or interest in the particular decision, and as a group they are able to make the best decision.

Hospitals, for example, frequently make purchase decisions through a large buying centre. When making a decision to purchase disposable oxygen masks, one or more doctors, the director of nursing and purchasing personnel may work together to determine quantities and select the best products and suppliers. A separate decision regarding the types of pharmaceutical

Real People, Other Voices

Advice for Brian Oxley

Dr John Desmond,
University of St. Andrews

My suggestion is for option 3, but with certain caveats. In the short term, Sash should as a priority, adopt a defensive position in the UK.

Given the strong likelihood of declining UK margins it makes sense for Sash to consider establishing operations in the USA. However the directors should beware that this market is likely to have quite different dynamics to that of the UK. There is a lengthening list of UK companies that have tried to enter North America and failed, including Marks & Spencer and some of the biggest banks. Currently Tesco is engaged in a major retail development, following years of research. Sash does not have the resources of these larger companies and must be careful not to dilute its position. Option 2 is risky. Sash is a relatively small business and so will probably find it has little clout when it comes to negotiating with larger producers. It may also experience production time overruns and may experience difficulties in controlling quality, which would be disastrous for a company seeking entry to a new market.

Option 3 is potentially even more risky and would be unthinkable for a company of Sash's size, without some kind of tie-in to another party. Sash needs to be able to cushion the risk of entry into the US as far as possible, perhaps by seeking out a similar family-run US partner, which is seeking to add to its range. It needs to quickly come up to speed with US market intelligence – by buying industry reports and paying industry insiders for information about competition and the buying process. If that looks favourable, it should commission research to seek potential partners. The directors should consider setting up a separate company to focus on these developments.

Dr Deborah Roberts,
Nottingham University

Sash UK presents an interesting dilemma as its home market is becoming saturated yet it does not appear to have relevant expertise to venture into overseas markets. Although option 1 is the least risky option it is just an attempt to maintain the status quo. Making modest returns would not provide Sash UK with enough funds for reinvestment and is essentially a slow exit strategy. Similarly, option 2 bears less risk but may be regarded as a conventional supply chain arrangement. Here the company may lose the advantages of a close and direct relationship with its customers. Therefore, I would choose option 3. This would enable the company to be proactive in its strategy and approach to learning about the marketplace. Companies no longer necessarily follow the traditional staged models of internationalisation starting with exporting. By moving straightaway to a joint venture with companies operating in the American market, value can be created for all concerned. It is a strategy which recognises that value can be created through the development of relationships and networks and is not just product related. It will also enable Sash UK to learn about its new marketplace and adapt production accordingly.

---

supplies to stock might need a different cast of characters to advise the purchasing manager. Marketers must continually identify which employees in a firm take part in every purchase and develop relationships with them all.

Depending on the complexity of the purchase and the size of the buying centre, a participant may assume one, several, or all of the six roles (Figure 5.3).

- The *initiator* begins the buying process by first recognising that the firm needs to make a purchase. A production employee for example may notice that a piece of equipment is not working properly and notify a supervisor. At other times, the initiator may suggest purchasing a new product because it will improve the firm's operations. Depending on the initiator's position in the organisation and the type of purchase, the initiator may or may not influence the actual purchase decision. For marketers, it's important to make sure that individuals who might initiate a purchase are aware of improved products they offer.

- The *user* is the member of the buying centre who actually needs the product. The user's role in the buying centre varies. For example, an administrative assistant may give his

Role	*Potential Player*	*Responsibility*
• Initiator	• Production employees, sales manager, almost anyone	• Recognises that a purchase needs to be made
• User	• Production employees, secretaries, almost anyone	• Individual(s) who will ultimately use the product
• Gatekeeper	• Buyer/purchasing agent	• Controls flow of information to others in the organisation
• Influencer	• Engineers, quality control experts, technical specialists, outside consultants	• Affects decision by giving advice and sharing expertise
• Decider	• Purchasing agent, managers, chief executive	• Makes the final purchase decision
• Buyer	• Purchasing agent	• Executes the purchase decision

Figure 5.3	Roles in the Buying Centre

A buying centre is a group of individuals brought together for the purpose of making a purchasing decision. Marketers need to understand that the members of the buying centre play a variety of roles in the process.

input on the features needed in a new copier that he will be 'chained to' for several hours a day. Marketers need to inform users of their products' benefits, especially if the benefits outweigh those that competitors offer.

● The *gatekeeper* is the person who controls the flow of information to other members. Typically the gatekeeper is the purchasing agent who gathers information and materials from salespeople, schedules sales presentations and controls suppliers' access to other participants in the buying process. For salespeople, developing and maintaining strong personal relationships with gatekeepers is critical to being able to offer their products to the buying centre.

● An *influencer* affects the buying decision by dispensing advice or sharing expertise. By virtue of their expertise, engineers, quality control specialists and other technical experts in the firm generally have a great deal of influence in purchasing equipment, materials, and component parts used in production. The influencers may or may not end up using the product. Marketers need to identify key influencers in the buying centre and work to persuade them of their product's superiority.

● The *decider* is the member of the buying centre who makes the final decision. This person usually has the greatest power within the buying centre. He or she often has power within the organisation to authorise spending the company's money. For a routine purchase, the decider may be the purchasing officer. If the purchase is complex, a manager, director, or chief executive may be the decider. Quite obviously, the decider is key to a marketer's success and deserves a lot of attention in the selling process.

● The *buyer* is the person who has responsibility for executing the purchase. Although the buyer often has a role in identifying and evaluating alternative suppliers, this person's primary function is handling the details of the purchase. The buyer obtains competing bids, negotiates contracts, and arranges delivery dates and payment plans. Once a firm makes the purchase decision, marketers turn their attention to negotiating the details of the purchase with the buyer. Successful marketers are well aware that providing exemplary service in this stage of the purchase can be key to future sales.

The Business Buying Decision Process

Objective

6

Understand the stages in the business buying decision process

We've seen there are several players in the business buying process, beginning with an initiator and ending with a buyer. To make matters even more challenging to marketers, members of the buying team go through several stages in the decision-making process. The business buying decision process, as Figure 5.4 shows, is a series of steps similar to those in the consumer decision process. To help understand these steps, let's say you've just started working at the 'Big Skateboard Company' and you've been assigned to be in the buying centre for the purchase of new web page design computer software (a new-task buy) for your firm.

Step 1: Problem Recognition

As in consumer buying, the first step in the business buying decision process occurs when someone sees that a purchase can solve a problem. For straight re-buy purchases, this step may result because the firm has run out of paper, pens or bin bags. In these cases, the buyer places

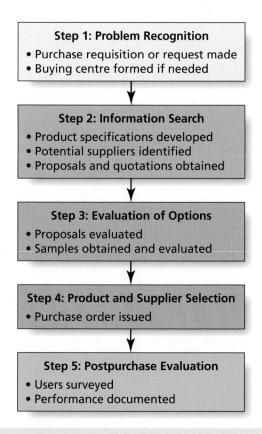

Step 1: Problem Recognition
- Purchase requisition or request made
- Buying centre formed if needed

Step 2: Information Search
- Product specifications developed
- Potential suppliers identified
- Proposals and quotations obtained

Step 3: Evaluation of Options
- Proposals evaluated
- Samples obtained and evaluated

Step 4: Product and Supplier Selection
- Purchase order issued

Step 5: Postpurchase Evaluation
- Users surveyed
- Performance documented

Figure 5.4	Steps in the Business Buying Process

The steps in the business buying decision process are the same as those in the consumer decision process. But for business purchases, each step may be far more complex and require more attention from marketers.

the order, and the decision-making process ends. Recognition of the need for modified re-buy purchases often comes from wanting to replace outdated equipment, from changes in technology, or from an ad, brochure or some other marketing communication that offers the customer a better product or one at a lower price. Two events may occur in the problem recognition step. First, a firm makes a request or requisition, usually in writing. Depending on the complexity of the purchase, the firm may form a buying centre.

The need for new-task purchases often occurs because the firm wants to enhance its operations in some way, or when a smart salesperson tells the business customer about a new product that will increase the efficiency of the firm's operations or improve the firm's end products. In the case of Big Skateboard's new software purchase, your marketing department has previously had its web page designed and maintained by an outside agency. The company has become dissatisfied with the outside supplier and has decided to move the design function in-house. Now the company needs new software to create a website.

Step 2: Information Search

In the second step of the decision process (for purchases other than straight re-buys) the buying centre searches for information about products and suppliers. Members of the buying centre may individually or collectively refer to reports in trade magazines and journals, seek advice from outside consultants, and pay close attention to marketing communications from different manufacturers and suppliers. As in consumer marketing, it's the job of marketers to make sure that information is available when and where business customers want it. This can be achieved by placing ads in trade magazines, through mailing out brochures and other printed material to prospects, and via having a well-trained, enthusiastic sales force regularly call on customers. For Big Skateboard's purchase, you may try to find out what software your outside supplier has been using (if the supplier will tell you), talk to the information technology experts in your firm, or review ads and articles in trade magazines.

There are thousands of specialised publications out there that cater for just about any industry you can think of, and each is bursting with information from competing companies that cater to a specific niche.

Developing Product Specifications   Business buyers often develop **product specifications**. That is a written description of the quality, size, weight, colour, features, quantity, training, warranty, service terms and delivery requirements for the purchase. When the product needs are complex or technical, engineers and other experts are the key players in identifying specific product characteristics and determining whether standard off-the-shelf or customised made-to-order goods and services are needed. Although there is excellent web design software available, for some computer applications custom-designed software is necessary.

Identifying Potential Suppliers and Obtaining Proposals   Once the product specifications are in hand, the next step may be to identify potential suppliers and obtain written or verbal proposals, or bids, from one or more of them. For standardised or branded products in which there are few if any differences in the products of different suppliers, this may be as simple as an informal request for pricing information, including discounts, shipping charges and confirmation of delivery dates. At other times, the potential suppliers will receive a formal written request for a proposal, or ask for a quotation that requires specific detail such as price and terms for supplying the product. For the Big Skateboard's software, which is likely to be a standardised package, you would probably just ask for general pricing information.

Step 3: Evaluation of Options

At this stage of the business decision process, the buying centre assesses the proposals. Total spending for goods and services can have a major impact on the firm's profitability, so all other things being equal, price is the primary consideration. Pricing evaluations must take into account discount policies for certain quantities, returned-goods policies, the cost of repair and maintenance services, terms of payment and the cost of financing large purchases. For capital equipment – such as large machinery, cost criteria can also include the life expectancy of the purchase, the expected re-sale value, as well as the disposal costs. In some cases, the buying centre may negotiate with the preferred supplier to match the lowest bidder.

Although a firm often selects a bidder because it offers the lowest price, there are times when the buying decision is based on other factors, and these may be related to a number of factors including reputation, quality, previous experience, history or even environmental concerns, as explained in Marketing Ethics. See how Marks & Spencer has been inspired to consider 'green' issues.

The more complex and costly the purchase, the more time buyers will spend searching for the best supplier (and the more marketers must try to win the order). In some cases, a company may even ask one or more of its current customers to participate in a *reference programme* where they recommend products to others. For example, Siebel Systems once asked over 350 corporate buyers of its computer systems to explain to new prospects how their system worked

| Photo 5.3 | You don't see too many everyday consumers driving Volvo trucks, but plenty of manufacturers and retailers buy them.
Source: Volvo Group UK Ltd |

Marketing Ethics

Many GreenPac Products Hangon the Selves of Top Retailers

It takes a lot of bottle to do what Simon Lee has achieved. Four years ago, he quit his job at a leading packaging supplier and bet everything he had to create a business to pioneer innovative recycling products. In 2007 year he convinced Marks & Spencer to manufacture some of its range of fleeces in Greenspun, a fabric made from 100 per cent recycled plastic bottles. One of the biggest problems has been finding products that can be commercialised. 'We have seen some fantastic environmental innovations. Some of it is not fit for purpose. Some is not right for the market.' Making sure that the product meets environmental standards and does not have any unethical skeletons in the closet is crucial.

Financial Times (London), 12 May 2007

Debate, Discuss, Disagree

1 What would you suggest for GreenPac to maximise its profits without having to change its company philosophy?

and why they chose Siebel's products. The payoff for customers was that they could network with other existing customers to gain insights about how to use the company's products. As a Siebel executive observes, customers become heroes – and by involving them in speaking engagements and articles in trade magazines, a real win–win scenario is evident for everyone.[2]

Marketers often make formal presentations and product demonstrations to the buying centre group. In the case of installations and large equipment, marketers sometimes arrange for buyers to speak to or even visit other customers to examine how the product performs. For less complex products, the buying firm may ask potential suppliers for samples of the products to evaluate alternatives. For the Big Skateboard Company website, your buying centre may ask salespeople from various companies to demonstrate their software for your group, so that you can compare the capabilities of different products.

Step 4: Product and Supplier Selection

Once buyers have assessed all proposals, the next step in the buying process is the purchase decision, that is the selection of the best product and supplier to meet the firm's needs. Reliability and durability rank especially high for equipment and systems that keep the firm's operations running smoothly without interruption. For some purchases, warranties, repair service and regular maintenance after the sale are important. For the Big Skateboard Company, the final decision may be based not only on the capabilities of the software itself, but also on the technical support provided by the software company. What kind of support is available and at what cost to the company?

One of the most important decisions of a buyer is how many suppliers can best serve the firm's needs. Sometimes a single supplier is more beneficial to the organisation than having several suppliers. **Single sourcing** occurs when a buyer and seller work quite closely together. It is particularly important when a firm needs frequent deliveries or specialised products. However, reliance on a single source means that the firm is at the mercy of the chosen supplier to deliver the needed goods or services without interruption.

In contrast, **multiple sourcing** means buying a product from several different suppliers. Under this system, suppliers are more likely to remain price competitive. If one supplier has problems with delivery, the firm has others to fall back on. However, using one or a few suppliers rather than many has its advantages. A firm that buys from a single supplier becomes a large customer with a lot of clout when it comes to negotiating prices and contract terms. Having one or a few suppliers also lowers the firm's administrative costs because it has fewer invoices to pay, fewer contracts to negotiate, and fewer salespeople to see than if it used many sources. Many hospitals are now moving towards single sourcing where possible. Historically, hospital buyers have had to negotiate with hundreds of suppliers for a vast range of products from disposable gloves to surgical implants. Some hospitals have more recently tried to reduce their supplier lists by only working with specific suppliers that can provide a diverse range of items.

Sometimes supplier selection is based on *reciprocity*, which means that a buyer and seller agree to be each other's customers by saying essentially, 'I'll buy from you, and you buy from me'. For example, a firm that supplies mechanical component parts to a company that manufactures vans would agree to buy their fleet vans only from that company.

Reciprocal agreements between firms often limit the effect of free market competition. New suppliers simply don't have a chance against the preferred suppliers. In certain less developed countries, reciprocity or counter trade is a practice that is common and even expected in business-to-business marketing.

Outsourcing occurs when firms obtain outside suppliers to provide goods or services that might otherwise be supplied in-house. Outsourcing is an increasingly popular strategy, but also a controversial one. Many critics object when companies contract with firms or individuals in remote places like China or India to perform work that used to be done at home. These tasks range from complicated jobs like writing computer code to fairly simple ones like manning reservation desks and call centres for telephone sales. Controversy aside, many companies are finding that it may be both cost-efficient and productive to call upon outsiders from around the world to provide such assistance. However, they must ensure that service is not compromised by moving their operations to less developed economies. The experience gained is now leading some companies to reconsider their initial strategies.

Yet another type of buyer–seller partnership is **reverse marketing**. Instead of sellers trying to identify potential customers and then 'pitching' for business. Buyers try to find suppliers capable of producing specific needed products and then attempt to 'sell' the idea to the suppliers. The seller aims to satisfy the buying firm's needs. Through advertising in well regarded international trade directories, like *Kompass*, European companies have been able to receive unsolicited business orders from buyers as far away as Saudi Arabia that are keen to acquire supply of a European standard.

Step 5: Post-purchase Evaluation

Just as consumers evaluate purchases, an organisational buyer assesses whether the performance of the product and the supplier is living up to expectations. The buyer surveys users to determine their satisfaction with the product as well as the installation, delivery and service provided by the supplier. For producers of goods, this may relate to the level of satisfaction of the final consumer of the buying firm's product. Has demand for the manufacturer's product increased, decreased or stayed the same? By documenting and reviewing supplier performance, a firm decides whether to keep or drop the supplier. Many suppliers recognise the importance of conducting their own performance reviews on a regular basis. Measuring up to a customer's expectations can mean winning or losing a big account. Many a supplier has lost business because of a past history of late deliveries or poor equipment repairs and maintenance.

Across the Hall

Shane Redding
is founder of Think Direct, experts in business-to-business marketing, and Chair of the Institute of Direct Marketing's B2B Council

I strongly recommend the board invest in further market research before proceeding with any of the options outlined. However, looking at each of the options in turn it is clear that none provides the ideal solution, but in combination would deliver results.

Option 1 – doing nothing in a highly competitive, saturated market will result in an eventual decline in the company's fortunes. The threat of new entrants, with a cheaper cost base cannot be ignored. The board needs a strategy for defending its strong domestic market. It is clear that Sash has a proven history of diversification, moving from the manufacture of wooden timber windows, to aluminium and eventually UPvC; as well as extending the product line to include doors and conservatories. It also extended its market from domestic new build, into refurbishment and eventually the industrial market. Based on this and Brian's engineering and B2B sales experience, together we have spotted a new opportunity for manufacturing highly energy efficient 'instant' offices, using existing materials and production line, that could be a high-end alternative to the Portakabin. Market research shows that demand is potentially high, with pressure on existing office space at a premium within the existing customer base of local government, education and large private sector businesses. This option is low risk, with high potential return and should be adopted.

Option 2 – outsourcing production and potentially reducing manufacturing costs is important for Sash to consider to remain competitive. One approach would be to identify suitable partners amongst the potential new low cost entrants (from Southern Europe – or Eastern Europe). In return for Sash's expertise in quality control, innovation and design; manufacturing capacity could be expanded quickly and at lower cost base. This gives a higher return for Sash to invest in the UK diversification outlined above. Risk of competition would be reduced and clear agreement could be reached over which markets each partner operated in, with Sash taking the UK, Eire and North America,

Option 3 – based on a few unsolicited enquiries from the US, the company has decided that the potential US demand is huge. Not only does the company admit that it has no exporting knowledge or skills, it also has not undertaken any robust market research into the true market size, local competitors, pricing, tax and legislation. This, coupled with exposure to exchange rates (at the current $1.95 = £1 exporting is difficult for any UK company!) and high shipping costs, will make pricing difficult. To base the expansion of plant investment requiring a loan on a new market with unproven sales is an extremely high-risk strategy. A much-lower-risk option would be to look for existing American sales channels with business customers that Sash could use to test the US market; before investing in any expansion in production. Extra capacity would be provided through the new European partner.

Objective 7
Understand the growing role of B2B e-commerce

Business-to-Business e-Commerce

The internet has brought about massive changes in marketing, from the creation of new products to providing more effective and efficient marketing communications, as well as assisting with the actual distribution of certain products. This is particularly true in business markets. **Business-to-business (B2B) e-commerce** refers to an online exchange between two or more businesses or organisations. B2B e-commerce includes the exchange of information, products, services and payment. It's not as flashy as consumer e-commerce, but it has changed the way businesses operate. Multinational enterprises are now saving significant amounts through obtaining supplies over the internet. For sellers, e-commerce also provides remarkable advantages. Boeing, for example, received orders worth over €100 million in spare parts in the first year that its website was established.[3]

Using e-commerce allows business marketers to link directly with suppliers, factories, distributors and their customers. It radically reduces the time necessary to order and deliver goods, track sales, and obtain customer feedback.

In the simplest form of B2B e-commerce, the internet provides an online catalogue of products and services that businesses need. Companies find that their website is important for delivering online technical support, product information, order status information, and customer service to corporate customers. Many companies, for example, save thousands of euros equivalent a year by replacing hard-copy manuals with electronic downloads.

Intranets, Extranets and Private Exchanges

Although the internet is the primary means of B2B e-commerce, many companies maintain intranets, which provide a more secure means for conducting business. The *intranet* is an internal corporate computer network that uses internet technology to link company departments, employees and databases. Intranets give access only to authorised employees. They allow companies to process internal transactions with greater control and consistency because of stricter security measures than those they can use on the entire web. Businesses also use intranets for videoconferencing, distributing internal documents, communicating with geographically dispersed branches and training employees.

In contrast to an intranet, an **extranet** allows certain suppliers, customers and others outside the organisation to access a company's internal system. A business customer that a company authorises to use its extranet can place orders online. Extranets can be especially useful for companies that need to have secure communications between the company and its channel members like dealers, distributors and/or franchisees.

Intranets and extranets can prove to be very cost efficient. Prudential Health Care's extranet allows its corporate customers to enrol new employees and check the eligibility and claim status themselves. This saves Prudential money because it can hire fewer customer service personnel. There are also no packages of insurance forms to mail back and forth, and Prudential doesn't even have to input policyholder data into the company database.[4]

In addition to saving companies money, extranets allow business partners to collaborate on projects (such as product design) and build relationships. Hewlett-Packard and Procter & Gamble swap marketing plans and review ad campaigns with their advertising agencies through extranets. They can exchange ideas quickly without having to spend money on travel and meetings.

Some of the most interesting online activity in the B2B world is taking place on **private exchanges**. These are systems that link a specially invited group of suppliers and partners over the web. A private exchange allows companies to collaborate with suppliers they trust – without sharing such sensitive information with others.

Security Threats

There are several security threats related to B2B e-commerce. You may be concerned about someone obtaining your credit card number and charging even more to your account. However, companies have even greater worries. When hackers break into company sites, they can destroy company records and steal trade secrets. Both B2C and B2B e-commerce companies worry about *authentication* and ensuring that transactions are secure. This means making sure that only authorised individuals are allowed to access a site and place an order. Maintaining security also requires firms to keep the information transferred as part of a transaction, such as a credit card number, from criminals' hard drives.

Well-meaning employees also can create security problems. They can give out unauthorised access to company computer systems and be careless about keeping their passwords secret. For example, hackers can guess at obvious passwords, such as nicknames, birth dates, hobbies or a spouse's name. To increase security of their websites and transactions, most companies now have safeguards in place, firewalls and encryption devices, to name the two most common methods.

Firewalls

A *firewall* is a combination of hardware and software that ensures that only authorised individuals gain entry into a computer system. The firewall monitors and controls all traffic between the internet and the intranet to restrict access. Companies may even place additional firewalls within their intranet when they wish only designated employees to have access to certain parts of the system. Although firewalls can be fairly effective (even though none is foolproof), they require costly and constant monitoring.

Encryption

Encryption means scrambling a message so that only another individual (or computer) that has the right 'key' for deciphering it can unscramble it. Otherwise, the message is unreadable. The message is inaccessible without the appropriate encryption software. Without encryption, it would be easy for unethical people to get your credit card number by creating a 'sniffer' program that intercepts and reads messages. A sniffer finds messages with four blocks of four numbers, copies the data, and voilà – someone else has your credit card number. Even with basic encryption software, hackers have been able to steal thousands of credit card numbers from various online retailers.

Now that you've learned the basics of B2B commerce, read 'Real People, Real Decisions: How it worked out at Sash' to see which strategy Brian and the board members at Sash decided on.

Real People, Real Decisions

How it worked out at Sash . . .

Brian and his colleagues chose option 3, and Sash began to embark on a strategy to invest and build a new production site and establish a US presence. Because of the physical size of the US market and the relatively greater complexities that this would bring compared with the UK, Sash decided to join forces with Veka (UK), the local subsidiary of a German firm that supplied Sash with high-quality PVCu profiles and ancillary items. Veka already had established a network of subsidiaries in the US and it was suggested to Brian that Sash should try and develop commercial links with Veka's US operations. The result was a four-way joint venture involving Sash, Veka (UK), Veka (Germany) and Veka (America).

> It was suggested to Brian that Sash should try and develop commercial links with Veka's US operations

A commercial decision was then made at Sash to jointly exhibit and share a large stand with Veka (America), at a trade convention in Las Vegas (Sash supplying the large portal structure to complement Veka's product lines). This convention paved the way and created huge interest for the Sash-designed portal structures, and subsequently enabled sales opportunities to flow in the US via Veka. On the back of this venture, further reciprocal business also emerged, and Sash was able to complement its own product line in the UK through acting as a distributor for Veka (America) and taking on the responsibility for marketing its fencing and decking materials.

Marketing Metrics

How Sash Measures Success

Sash uses three metrics that are applied to evaluate any capital investment: return on capital, internal rate of return and cash payback. In addition, the company uses a set of marketing metrics to test the success of the strategy. These include:

- Delivery to customer request: Is the delivery in full and on time? The firm's target is 95% delivery in full and on time.

- Market share of the window market.

- Market growth in the US in terms of revenue and units supplied.

Despite these and other measures, web security for B2B marketers remains a problem. The threat to intranet and extranet usage goes beyond competitive espionage. The increasing sophistication of hackers and internet criminals who create viruses, worms and other means for disrupting individual computers as well as entire company systems means that all organisations and consumers are vulnerable to attacks and need to remain vigilant.

Chapter Summary

Now that you have finished reading this chapter, you should be able to answer any of the following potential examination questions:

1. **Describe the general characteristics of business-to-business markets.** Business-to-business markets include business or organisational customers that buy goods and services for purposes other than for personal consumption. Business customers are usually few in number, may be geographically concentrated and often purchase higher-priced products in larger quantities.

2. **Explain the unique characteristics of business demand.** Business demand is derived from the demand for another good or service. It is generally not affected by price increases or decreases, is subject to great fluctuations, and may be tied to the demand and availability of some other good.

3. **Describe how business or organisational markets are classified.** Business customers include producers, re-sellers, governments and not-for-profit organisations. Producers purchase materials, parts and various goods and services needed to produce other goods and services to be sold at a profit. Resellers purchase finished goods to resell at a profit as well as other goods and services to maintain their operations. Governments and other not-for-profit organisations purchase the goods and services necessary to fulfil their objectives. The Standard Industrial Classification (SIC) system provides a numerical coding system that is widely used in business and organisational markets.

4. **Explain the business buying situation and describe business buyers.** The business buy class identifies the degree and effort required to make a business buying decision. Purchase situations can be straight re-buy, modified re-buy and new-task buying. Business buying is usually handled by trained professional buyers.

5. **Explain the roles in the business buying centre.** A buying centre is a group of people who work together to make a buying decision.

The roles in the buying centre are (1) the initiator who recognises the need for a purchase, (2) the user who will ultimately use the product, (3) the gatekeeper who controls the flow of information to others, (4) the influencer who shares advice and expertise, (5) the decider who makes the final decision and (6) the buyer who executes the purchase.

6. **Explain the stages in the business buying decision process.** The stages in the business buying decision process are similar to, but more complex than, the steps in consumer decision making. These steps include problem recognition, information search during which buyers develop product specifications and obtain proposals from prospective sellers, evaluating the proposals, selecting a supplier and formally evaluating the performance of the product and the supplier. A firm's purchasing options include single or multiple sourcing. In outsourcing, firms obtain outside vendors to provide goods or services that otherwise might be supplied in-house. Other business buying activities include reciprocity and reverse marketing.

7. **Explain the growing role of B2B e-commerce.** Business-to-business (B2B) e-commerce refers to the online exchange of information, products, services or payments between two or more businesses or organisations and allows business marketers to link directly to suppliers, factories, distributors and their customers. An intranet is a secure internal corporate network used to link company departments, employees and databases. Extranets link a company with authorised suppliers, customers or others outside the organisation. Companies can address security issues by using firewalls and encryption.

Key Terms

Business-to-business (B2B) e-commerce 203

Business-to-business (B2B) marketing 186

Business-to-business markets 186

Buy class 193

Buying centre 195

Derived demand 190

Extranet 204

Government markets 190

Inelastic demand 190

Joint demand 190

Modified re-buy 193

Multiple sourcing 201

New-task buy 193

Standard Industrial Classification System (SIC) 192

Not-for-profit institutions 192

Outsourcing 202

Private exchanges 204

Producers 191

Product specifications 199

Resellers 192

Reverse marketing 202

Single sourcing 201

Straight re-buy 193

Chapter Review

Marketing Concepts: Preparing for the examination and testing your knowledge

1. How do business-to-business markets differ from consumer markets? How do these differences affect marketing strategies?

2. Explain the unique characteristics of business demand.

3. How are business-to-business markets generally classified? What is the SIC system?

4. Describe new-task buys, modified re-buys and straight re-buys.

5. What are the characteristics of business buyers?

6. What is a buying centre? What are the roles of the various people in a buying centre?

7. What are the stages in the business buying decision process? What happens in each stage?

8. How are the stages in the business buying decision process similar to the steps in the consumer buying process? How are they different?

9. What is single sourcing? Multiple sourcing? Outsourcing?

10. Explain how reciprocity and reverse marketing operate in business-to-business markets.

11. Explain the role of B2B e-commerce in today's marketplace.

Marketing Concepts: Discussing Choices

1. E-commerce is dramatically changing the way business-to-business transactions take place. What are the advantages of B2B e-commerce to companies? To society? Are there any disadvantages of B2B e-commerce?

2. The practice of buying business products based on sealed competitive bids is popular among all types of business buyers. What are the advantages and disadvantages of this practice to buyers? What are the advantages and disadvantages to sellers? Should companies always give the business to the lowest bidder? Why or why not?

3. When firms implement a single sourcing policy in their buying, other possible suppliers do not have an opportunity. Is this ethical? What are the advantages to the company? What are the disadvantages?

4. Many critics of government say that strict engineering and other manufacturing requirements for products purchased by governments increase prices unreasonably and that taxpayers end up paying too much because of such policies. What are the advantages and disadvantages of such purchase restrictions? Should governments loosen restrictions on their purchases?

5. In the buying centre, the gatekeeper controls information flow to others in the centre. Thus, the gatekeeper determines which possible sellers are heard and which are not. Does the gatekeeper have too much power? What policies might be implemented to make sure that all possible sellers are treated fairly?

6. The chapter discussed how Siebel Systems operated a reference programme where previous purchasers of products were encouraged to discuss their experiences of a product with potential new customers. What are the advantages and disadvantages of such progress for companies like Siebel Systems? For previous customers? For prospective customers? For competitor firms?

7. Some critics complain that outsourcing sends much-needed jobs to competitors overseas while depriving our own national workers of these opportunities. Should a company consider this factor when deciding where to obtain raw materials or brainpower in order to compete efficiently?

Real People, Real Surfers

Exploring the Web

Sash isn't the only company that provides PVCu windows to business markets. Visit Sash's website (www.sashuk.com). Then explore the websites of one or more other similar manufacturers.

On the basis of your experience, answer the following questions:

1. Who are Sash's main competitors?

2. In general, how do the competitors' websites compare? Which are easier to navigate, and why? Which are more innovative and attractive, and why?

3. Evaluate each site from the perspective of a building construction manager. What feature in each site would be useful? What information is available that a manager might need? Overall, which site do you feel would be most useful to the manager? Why?

Now, take a look at the website at www.pearsoned.co.uk/solomon to see some videos from YouTube relating to aspects of this chapter.

Marketing in Action Case

Real decisions at Airbus

Does the world really need an airplane that will carry up to 555 passengers at once? The executives at Airbus Industries, the airplane manufacturer located in Toulouse, France, hope that the answer to this question is a resounding yes.

Airbus is a company that began in 1970 with funding provided by owners from Germany, Spain, Britain and France. It focuses on the business-to-business market as a producer of passenger airplanes. As such, the company is dependent on other companies, mostly airlines located throughout the world, to purchase its products.

To date, the company has been very effective at developing and building airplanes that compete successfully with its only world competitor, Boeing, which has

its headquarters in Chicago and has been in existence for almost 90 years. For example, Airbus's current product line features planes like the A320 and A330, which are configured to carry up to 150 and 200 passengers, respectively. These planes compete very effectively against planes of similar size produced by Boeing, such as the 737 and 777.

At first, Airbus had no plans to produce a plane that competed in the 'jumbo' category – the category dominated by Boeing's 747. That situation changed in 2005 when Airbus's A380 airplane was launched. The A380 is a complete double-decker plane, the first of its kind. It can carry 35 per cent more passengers than a Boeing 747. In addition, the plane was designed to cost approximately 2 cents per seat-kilometre to operate. Such a low cost makes the A380 the least expensive plane to fly in the world. However, despite the size increase and low operating cost, Airbus had to ask whether there was a market for this larger plane and whether introducing the 380 was the right decision to make.

As noted earlier, Airbus operates in a business-to-business environment. This means the company must gauge the potential demand for the new products such as this 'superjumbo' jet. Gauging an airline's demand for such a large plane is difficult because an airline's demand for new and larger planes is derived demand; that is, it depends on consumers' need for travel. As many airlines can confirm, determining travel trends and habits by consumers has been anything but an exact science lately. Such factors as terrorism, war, global economic uncertainty and the SARS outbreak have contributed to reduced travel. As a result, airlines around the world have lost approximately €30 billion since 2001, and many have cut back on plans to upgrade or expand their fleet of planes.

Another factor affecting the decision Airbus faces in the acceptance of this new plane is the selling effort that Airbus must put behind it. Purchasing a plane that costs around €280 million and lasts approximately 40 years will require a tremendous amount of study and research on the part of the potential customer airlines. Consequently, even though an airline may already be a customer of Airbus, the decision process to purchase the A380 will resemble more of a new-task purchase than a modified or straight re-buy.

In addition, the number of people involved in the purchase process for this plane will probably be rather

Airbus had to ask whether there was a market for this larger plane

large and could include people from the board level all the way down to flight attendants and maintenance personnel. As a result, identifying the right people with whom to discuss the merits of the A380 will be extremely important.

Finally, the size of the A380 requires Airbus executives to consider the potential that airports may not be large enough to handle the plane. Because of this factor, Airbus is working with 16 airports that will have to spend about €80 million each to get ready for the plane.

One advantage Airbus has when trying to sell the plane is that it knows who its customers are likely to be. Airlines flying large numbers of passengers on long routes, such as across the Pacific Ocean, are candidates. This means that Singapore Airlines, United, Northwest, British Airways and Japan Airlines were the most likely customers. Other potential customers are freight haulers such as FedEx and UPS. In fact, the first commercial flight was with Singapore Airlines in 2007.

However, the next few years saw the big jet programmes at both Airbus and Boeing run into technical and workforce problems and aircraft deliveries were delayed. Then the global economic downturn hit. However, at the start of 2009, Louis Gallois, chief of EADS, the European aerospace and defence group that owns Airbus, said most of the internal problems were behind the company. He told the *Financial Times*: 'The 2008 performance is globally satisfactory, EADS is back to business. But now we are facing the financial crisis and the economic downturn changes our perspective.'

Things to Think About

1. What are the issues facing Airbus?

2. What factors are important in understanding the situation?

3. What are the choices?

4. What decision(s) do you recommend?

5. What are some ways to implement your recommendation(s)?

Source: Adapted from Alex Taylor III, 'Lord of the Air: What's Left for Airbus after Overtaking Boeing in the Commercial Aircraft Market? Building a Really Big Plane', *Fortune*, 10 November 2003, 144–52. Sylvia Pfeifer, 'Global crisis slows EADS expansion plans', *Financial Times* (European edition), 13 January 2009, 16.

References

1. F. Robert Dwyer and John F. Tanner, *Business Marketing: Connecting Strategy, Relationships, and Learning* (Boston, MA: McGraw-Hill, 2005); Edward F. Fern and James R. Brown, 'The Industrial/Consumer Marketing Dichotomy: A Case of Insufficient Justification', *Journal of Marketing* (Spring 1984), 68–77.

2. Catherine Arnold, 'Reference Programs Keep B-to-B Customers Satisfied', *Marketing News*, 18 August 2003, 4.

3. Faye W. Gilbert, Joyce A. Young, and Charles R. O'Neal, 'Buyer–Seller Relationships in Just-in-Time Purchasing Environments', *Journal of Organizational Research* 29 February 1994, 111–20.

4. Andy Reinhardt, 'Log On, Link Up, Save Big', *Business Week*, 22 June 1998, 132–8.

Chapter 6
Segmentation, Targeting, Positioning and CRM

Meet Ken Moss,
former International Manager, Sheffield Chamber of Commerce and Industry

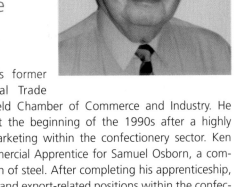

Q & A with Ken Moss

First job out of school:
Commercial Apprentice at Samuel Osbourne Steel Founders

Career high:
Instigating a TV campaign for Bassett's Liquorice Allsorts in Ireland, and being involved in replicating an International Trade Centre in Sheffield, that was originally developed in Johannesburg – South Africa

Business book I'm reading now:
Bottled for Business by Karan Bilimoria – the founder of Cobra Beer

My hero:
Geoffrey Boycott, an amazing batsman

My pet peeve:
Verbal aggression in a business context

Drink:
Jameson Irish Whisky

Food:
German pig's trotter

K enneth Lesley Moss is former Head of International Trade Services at the Sheffield Chamber of Commerce and Industry. He joined the Chamber at the beginning of the 1990s after a highly successful career in marketing within the confectionery sector. Ken started his career in 1956 as a Commercial Apprentice for Samuel Osborn, a company that specialised in the production of steel. After completing his apprenticeship, Ken took up various senior marketing and export-related positions within the confectionery industry. He was appointed to the post at the Chamber in 1992, where he held responsibility for the Chamber's international and members' services activities. Specifically, Ken's remit was to provide support services to the exporting community.

Ken served his commercial apprenticeship and went on to obtain various qualifications which led to his full membership of the Institute of Packaging, the Institute of Export and the Chartered Institute of Marketing. He is married with two daughters and has five grandchildren.

Real People, Real Decisions
Decision Time at the Chamber

Soon after the mid-nineteenth century the Sheffield Chamber of Commerce was established by a group of leading steel manufacturers with the aim of enhancing the city's reputation for manufacturing. Today, some 150 years later, the Chamber represents a thriving community with more than 2000 members. During the mid- to late-1990s the road to success was, however, a bumpy one.

Historically, UK Chambers of Commerce frequently differ in their legal and operational status to those in most other European towns and cities. The major fundamental difference is that often in Europe companies are obliged to officially register with their local Chamber, and pay for the privilege. In the UK becoming a member is completely optional. Just like deciding to be a member of a golf club or a gym, a company must weigh up the pros and cons – and can ultimately decide upon joining or not. The Sheffield Chamber, just like others in the UK, is a private entity (albeit operating in the non-profit sector) and needs to stay in surplus to justify its existence.

During the mid-1990s the Chamber ran into a significant deficit, but thankfully was able to continue to trade as it had some financial reserves to count upon. However, the Chamber's board – determined to overcome the financial problems – made some sweeping changes that meant increasing the pressures on its senior management team to operate more efficiently, effectively and move the business on.

For Ken Moss, this implied that his department (along with others) would be scrutinised to see how it contributed and would need to perform financially to remain in existence. Ken had to think long and hard and make decisions that could safeguard his own job as well as those around him.

Ken considers his options . . .

Option 1 Continue with the current strategy of targeting those companies that export, provide them with the same international trade services and lobby the chief executive for support

There are a couple of advantages to adopting this approach: (1) Ken and his colleagues do not have to get involved with the financial issues associated with the Chamber. He could argue that the core services supplied should be funded through membership subscriptions. As a result the department may get lucky, and some finance may be provided to keep it afloat. (2) By focusing on the existing segment, the team has the skills and ability to continue operating and providing a useful service, with a small deficit. In contrast, Ken may be given a lower budget to run his department, which may have detrimental implications.

Option 2 Strike a joint venture with the Chamber's cash rich commercial training department – target existing customers and provide different services

The advantage of this option is that Ken's department can be fully integrated within the Chamber's training arm and absorbed into its cost structure. Furthermore, the Chamber has the potential to increase revenues through using the facilities of this division to provide more training for exporters (or potential exporting companies) – including more tailored programmes and consultancy services, etc. The existing core services could continue to be provided and other opportunities explored accordingly. This may be a viable option, as management and staff in the two departments have good working relations.

Option 3 Go it alone: Provide more of the same services to the same segment and encourage staff to find more funding streams

This would allow the department to continue operating independently, and not have to share costs, profits (or losses) and management with another department. In the medium to long term the department could come out smelling of roses, but could fail in the short term if the finances did not improve. Choosing this option would also place more stress on Ken, particularly when he was aiming to retire in the medium term.

Now, put yourself in Ken's shoes: which option would you choose, and why?

Objectives

When you finish reading this chapter, you will be able to:

1 Understand the need for market segmentation in today's business environment

2 Know the different dimensions that marketers use to segment consumer and business-to-business markets

3 Show how marketers evaluate and select potential market segments

4 Explain how marketers develop a targeting strategy

5 Understand how a firm develops and implements a positioning strategy

6 Explain how marketers increase long-term success and profits by practising customer relationship management

Target Marketing Strategy: Selecting and Entering a Market

Objective

1

Understand the need for market segmentation in today's business environment

By now, we've heard over and over again that the goal of the marketer is to create value, build customer relationships and satisfy needs. In our modern, complex society, it is naive to assume that everyone's needs are the same. Understanding people's needs is an even more complex task today because technological and cultural advances in modern society have created a condition of **market fragmentation**. This condition occurs when people's diverse interests and backgrounds divide them into numerous different groups with distinct needs and wants. Due to this diversity, the same good or service will not appeal to everyone.

Consider, for example, the effects of fragmentation in the health and fitness industry. Back in the 1960s, dieting was simple. Pritikin was a best-selling weight loss system emphasising very low fat and high fibre, and health-conscious consumers thought that this combination would surely yield a lean body and good health. Today's consumers, however, have a wide range of diets from which to choose. There's Weight Watchers, Slim Fast and the Atkins diet to name a few, and dozens of herbal remedies for people with weight problems. Calories, fat, carbohydrates or all of the above – which to cut? The fact is, people have different requirements.

Marketers must balance the efficiency of mass marketing, serving the same items to everyone, with the effectiveness of offering each individual exactly what he or she wants. Mass marketing is certainly the most efficient plan. It costs much less to offer one product to everyone because that strategy eliminates the need for separate advertising campaigns and distinctive packages for each item. However, consumers see things differently; from their perspective, the best strategy would be to offer the perfect product for each individual. Unfortunately, that's often not realistic.

Instead of trying to sell something to everyone, marketers select a **target marketing strategy** in which they divide the total market into different segments based on customer characteristics, select one or more segments, and develop products to meet the needs of those specific segments. Figure 6.1 illustrates the three-step process of segmentation, targeting and positioning, and it's what we will build on in this chapter. Let's start with the first step – segmentation.

Step 1: Segmentation

Segmentation is the process of dividing a larger market into smaller pieces based on one or more meaningful, shared characteristics. Segmentation is a way of life for marketers. The truth is that you can't please everyone all the time, so you need to do your best. How do marketers segment a population? How do they divide the whole pie into smaller slices they can 'digest'? Segmenting the market is often necessary in both consumer and business-to-business markets.

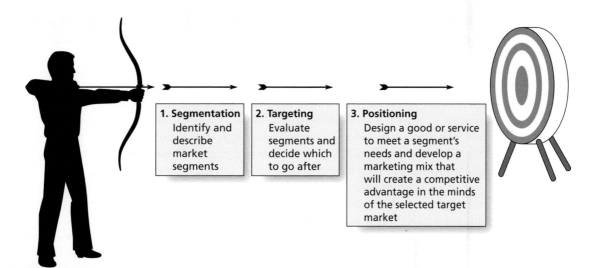

Figure 6.1	Steps in the Target-Marketing Process

Target marketing strategy consists of three separate steps. Marketers first divide the market into meaningful segments, then select segments, and finally design a unique marketing mix for each segment.

In each case, the marketer must decide on one or more useful **segmentation variables**. These represent dimensions that divide the total market into fairly homogeneous groups, each with different needs and preferences. In this section, we'll take a look at this process, beginning with the types of segmentation variables that marketers use to divide up end consumers.

Segmenting Consumer Markets

Objective

2

Know the different dimensions that marketers use to segment consumer and business-to-business markets

At one time, it was sufficient to divide the sports shoe market into athletes and non-athletes. However, a walk through any sports shop today reveals that the athlete market has fragmented in many directions – trainers designed for jogging, playing football, basketball, tennis, etc.

During the 1990s, obscure makers of such footwear focused their products on **Generation Y consumers** (those born between 1977 and 1994), and as a result managed to gain a significant share of the market.

Several segmentation variables can slice up the market for all the shoe variations available today. First, not everyone is willing to pay €150 for the latest sports shoes, so marketers need to consider income. Second, whilst men may be more interested in football boots, women look to buy the latest aerobics style, so marketers need to consider gender. Because not all age groups are going to be equally interested in buying specialised sport shoes, the large consumer 'pie' can be sliced into smaller pieces in a number of ways, including demographic, psychological and behavioural differences. Let's consider each variable in turn.

Objective

3

Show how marketers evaluate and select potential market segments

Segmenting by Demographics

Demographics are measurable characteristics such as gender and age. Demographics are vital to identify the best potential customers for a good or service. These objective characteristics are usually easy to identify, and then it's just a matter of tailoring messages and products to relevant groups. The demographic dimensions that marketers usually look at are age, gender, family structure, income and social class, race and ethnicity, and geography (where people live). Let's take a quick look at how marketers can use each of these dimensions to slice up the consumer pie.

Consumers of different age-groups have different needs and wants. Members of a generation tend to share the same outlook and priorities. A focus on such segments is often called **generational marketing**. Marketers need to know about the characteristics of such sub-segments in order to effectively market to them. During the famous 'cola wars' of the 1970s and 1980s, Pepsi managed to convince a generation (the 'Pepsi Generation') that its product reflected their core values of youth, idealism and casting off old ways. By default, Coca-Cola became identified as their parents' drink.[1]

Children have become an attractive age segment for marketers. Although kids obviously have a lot to say about purchases of toys and games, they influence other family purchases as well (just watch them at work in the supermarket!).

Teenagers/adolescents are also an attractive market segment. Much of the money spent by this segment goes towards 'feel-good' products, such as cosmetics, posters and fast food. Because they are so interested in many different products and have the resources to obtain them, many marketers focus on the teen market.[2] Of course, there are subgroups within the teen market with their own music idols and distinct styles, etc.

As we said, Generation Y consists of those consumers born between the years 1977 and 1994. Sometimes referred to as the baby 'boomlet', Generation Y is made up of the children of the baby boomer generation.[3] They are the first generation to grow up online and are more ethnically diverse than earlier generations. Generation Y is an attractive market for a host of consumer products, as it is significant in size, and is free-spending in nature. But Generation Y consumers may be hard to reach because they resist reading and increasingly turn the TV off. As a result, many marketers have had to develop other ways of reaching this generation, including online chat rooms, email promotions, and some of the more unusual 'guerrilla marketing' techniques we'll talk about later in this book.

The group of people born between 1965 and 1976 is sometimes known as **Generation X** consumers. Many of these people have a cynical attitude towards marketing. A chapter in a book called *Generation X* is 'I am not a target market!'[4] As one 20-year-old Japanese Xer commented, 'I don't like to be told what's trendy. I can make up my own mind.'[5]

Despite this tough reputation, members of Generation X, the oldest of whom are now entering their early 40s, have mellowed with age. In retrospect, they also have developed an identity for being entrepreneurial. An industry expert observed, 'Today's Gen Xer is both values-oriented and value-oriented. This generation is really about settling down.'[6] Many people in this segment seem to be determined to have stable families after being latchkey children themselves. Seven out of ten regularly save some portion of their income, a rate comparable to that of their parents. Xers tend to view the home as an expression of individuality rather than material success. More than half are involved in home improvement and repair projects.[7]

Baby boomers, consumers born between 1946 and 1964 and who are now in their 40s, 50s and 60s, are an important segment to many marketers – if for no other reason than because there are so many of them who are making a lot of money. Boomers were the result of their parents that wanted to start families after the Second World War interrupted their lives. Back in the 1950s and 1960s, couples started having children younger and had more of them than the previous generation. The resulting number of kids really changed the market infrastructure, resulting in the need for more single family houses, more schools, migration to suburban areas, and so on.

One aspect of boomers for marketers to always remember is that they never tend to age. At least, that's the way they look at it. Boomers are willing to invest significant money, time and energy to maintain their youthful image. Hence the growth of cosmetic surgery, nip and tucks for those in their 50s.

This helps to explain why women boomers in their 50s are becoming a hot new market for what the motor industry calls 'reward cars' – sexy and extravagant vehicles. These buyers say that for years they had let the roles of wife and mother restrict them. As their kids grow up and leave home, it's reward time. As one woman who bought a sporty Mercedes convertible for herself stated, 'I don't have the disease to please any more . . . I'm pleasing me.' She's not alone, the number of women over 45 who purchased such medium-sized sporty models has risen significantly since 2000. Among women of 45 and over earning at least €80,000, purchases of smaller luxury cars like the BMW 3 Series and the Audi A4 have also grown.[8]

Another important aspect of Boomers, a connection with the socio-cultural trends discussed in Chapter 2, is that because there are so many of them, they are clogging the upward mobility pipeline in employment. Generation Xers especially complain that the boomers hold all the power and position, and that the sheer number of boomers in managerial spots impedes promotion opportunities for Xers. This has fuelled the entrepreneurial spirit among the generations following boomers. Generation Xers and younger have no expectation of long-term employment with any one firm and are cynical about their prospects of ever receiving social security as a retirement benefit. These generations have had to very much make their own opportunities.

| Photo 6.1 | See how Honda attempts to capture the imagination of 'would-be' buyers. |
| | Source: The Advertising Archive |

A significant percentage of the population in Western Europe is now 65 years and older – and this segment is increasingly growing in size. Many older consumers are enjoying leisure time and continued good health. A key question nowadays is, what is a senior citizen/old age pensioner? As we will see later in the chapter, perhaps it isn't age but rather lifestyle factors, including mobility, that best define this group. More and more marketers are offering products that have strong appeal to those with able and active lifestyles. Disney challenges such consumers to re-live their youth by visiting their theme parks or joining one of their cruise liners – with or without their grandchildren.

Many products, from fragrances to footwear, appeal to men or women either because of the nature of the product or because the marketer chose to appeal to one sex or the other. Segmenting by gender starts at a very early age, even nappies come in pink for girls and blue for boys. In some cases, manufacturers develop parallel products to appeal to each gender. For example, male grooming products have traditionally been Gillette's priority since the company introduced the safety razor in 1903. Today the company offers the five-bladed Fusion for men and at the same time offers women a soothing shave from the Venus Vibrance system.

Whilst the ways in which products have been marketed to men and women have traditionally been very clear-cut, it may vary subject to trends and fashion, for example '**Metrosexual**' is a marketing buzzword you may have heard of. The term describes a man who is heterosexual, sensitive, educated and an urban dweller who is in touch with his feminine side.[9] This web posting from *The Urban Dictionary* sums up the metrosexual stereotype:[10]

You may be 'metrosexual' if:

1. You just can't walk past a Banana Republic shop without making a purchase.

2. You own 20 pairs of shoes, half a dozen pairs of sunglasses, just as many watches and you carry a man-purse.

3. You see a hair stylist instead of a barber, because barbers don't do highlights.

4. You can make her lamb shanks and risotto for dinner and Eggs Benedict for breakfast . . . all from scratch.

5. You only wear Calvin Klein boxer-briefs.

6. You shave more than just your face. You also exfoliate and moisturise.

7. You would never, ever own a pickup truck.

8. You can't imagine a day without hair styling products.

9. You'd rather drink wine than beer . . . but you'll find out what estate and vintage first.

10. Despite being flattered (even proud) that gay guys hit on you, you still find the thought of actually getting intimate with another man truly repulsive.

While many men are reluctant to identify with the metrosexual lifestyle, a renewed interest in personal care products, fashion accessories and other 'formerly feminine' product categories is creating many marketing opportunities. For example, men's jewellery, once considered a fringe market for rockers, rappers, gay men and gangsters, is moving towards the mainstream. US jeweller Tiffany quietly expanded its usual watch and cufflink collections to include a broad range of sporty men's jewellery including silver pendants, rings and bracelets. The famous retailer got a boost when supplying a silver pendant and cufflinks for actor Brad Pitt in the movie *Ocean's Twelve*. After photos of Brad wearing the jewellery appeared in the tabloid *Life and Style*, men started showing up at Tiffany's asking for the products.

SNAKESKIN FEEL. GOLDEN TOUCH.

Elegant 18k gold plating. Sensual snakeskin texture. Lavish laser-etched detailing. Sharper than ever, bellissimo.

RAZR 2

MOTOROLA

| Photo 6.2 | David Beckham epitomises the celebrity lifestyle that appeals to many metrosexual men.
Source: The Advertising Archives |

Because family needs and expenditures change over time, one way to segment consumers is to consider the stage of the family life cycle they occupy. Not surprisingly, consumers in different life cycle segments are unlikely to need the same products, or at least they may not need these things in the same quantities.[11] For example, Procter & Gamble introduced a brand of instant coffee for people who live alone and don't need to brew a full pot of coffee at a time.[12]

As families age and move into new life stages, different product categories ascend and descend in importance. Young bachelors and newlyweds are the most likely to exercise, go to bars and the cinema, and consume alcohol. Older couples and bachelors are more likely to use maintenance services. Old age pensioners are a prime market for exclusive second home apartments and golf products. Marketers need to discern the family life cycle segment of their target consumers by examining purchase data by family life cycle group.

The distribution of wealth is of great interest to marketers because it determines which groups have the greatest buying power. It should come as no surprise that many marketers yearn to capture the hearts and wallets of high-income consumers. Perhaps that explains a recent proliferation of ultra-high-end bottled waters such as Voss, which claims the water is extracted from a real Norwegian glacier (to taste this delicacy in gourmet restaurants and mini-bars, there is an expectation to pay for the privilege). At the same time, other marketers target lower-income consumers. Certainly, several European retailers such as Netto, Lidl and Aldi sell generic bottled water at a fraction of the price of Voss!

In the past, it was popular for marketers to consider social class segments, such as upper class, lower class, and the like. However, many consumers buy not according to where they may fall in that framework but rather according to the image they wish to portray. For example, readily available credit has facilitated many a sale of a BMW to a consumer who technically falls into the middle or lower class segment. Six years of making payments later, they finally own the car.

A consumer's national origin is often a strong indicator of preferences for specific magazines or TV shows, foods, clothing, and choice of leisure activities. Marketers need to be aware of these differences and sensitivities in order to try to appeal to consumers of diverse races and ethnic groups.

Recognising that people's preferences often vary depending on where they live, many marketers tailor their offerings to appeal to different regions. For example, whilst traditional beer drinkers in the south-east of England prefer to see their pint with little or no head of froth, this would not be quickly accepted in some parts of the north, where consumers expect to see a head of a centimetre or more.

When marketers want to segment regional markets even more precisely, they sometimes combine geography with demographics by using a technique called **geodemography**. A basic assumption of geodemography is that 'birds of a feather flock together', that is, people who live near one another share similar characteristics. Sophisticated statistical techniques identify geographic areas that share the same preferences for household items, magazines and other products. Through geodemography, marketers construct segments of households with a common pattern of preferences. This way the marketer can home in on those customers who are most likely to be interested in its specific offerings – in some cases so precisely that families living on one road will be included in a segment while those on the next may not. Companies can even customise web advertising by **geocoding** so that people who log on from different places will see ad banners for local businesses.

Segmenting by Psychographics

Demographic information is useful, but it does not always provide enough information to divide consumers into meaningful segments. Although we can use demographic variables to discover, for example, that the female student segment uses perfume, we won't be able to tell whether certain women prefer perfumes that express an image of, say, sexiness rather than athleticism. We can use psychographic data to understand differences among consumers who may be statistically similar to one another but whose needs and wants vary.

Psychographics segments consumers in terms of shared activities, interests and opinions (*AIOs*).[13] Psychographic segments usually include demographic information such as age or gender, but the richer descriptions that emerge go well beyond these characteristics. For example, most people are happy driving at the speed limit (or a little over) on the motorway, but others enjoy danger. For this psychographic segment, there is a variety of unique product offerings, including a tour of the sunken Titanic at 12,500 feet below the surface of the ocean, getting behind the wheel of a Formula One racing car or swimming with sharks.

Over the years, Harley-Davidson has done a great job of understanding buyers on the basis of psychographics. A Harley user's profile includes both thrill seeking and affinity for a countercultural image. In fact, your doctor, banker, lawyer or even marketing professor may be a member of HOG (the Harley Owners Group). However, demographics also come into play. Over the past decade, the age of the typical Harley buyer has risen to about 46, older than the motorcycle industry average of 38. But because the company knows the psychographics of its target buyers, it isn't lulled by age stereotypes of safety and conservatism. Harley-Davidson knows that in spite of the older age demographic, its buyers are still a thrill-seeking bunch.

Although some advertising agencies and manufacturers develop their own psychographic techniques to classify consumers, other agencies subscribe to services that divide the entire population into segments and then sell pieces of this information to clients for specific strategic applications.

An example of a psychographic segmentation system was developed by German research firm Sigma, and as a result the system paved the way for BMW's highly publicised reinvention and expansion of its car range. This system included 'upper liberals' (socially conscious, open-minded professionals who prefer roominess and flexibility), 'post-moderns' (high-earning innovators like architects, entrepreneurs and artists who like the individualistic statements made by driving convertibles and sports cars), 'upper conservatives' (made up of wealthy, traditional thinkers who like the upper crust) and 'modern mainstream' (family-oriented up-and-comers who want a luxury brand but probably can't afford more than the lowest priced model). Using this segmentation scheme as an anchor, BMW created vehicles for each category and also acquired Rolls Royce and the Mini to serve the extreme ends, with phenomenal success. As a result, its motor vehicle operations generated more profit than GM, Ford, Volkswagen and Renault combined. Psychographic segmentation is therefore very powerful in developing marketing strategy.[14]

Segmenting by Behaviour

In addition to demographics and psychographics, it is useful to study what consumers actually do with a product. **Behavioural segmentation** slices consumers on the basis of how they act

PHONE, CAMERA, EMAIL, GAMES, MUSIC...
MY BLACKBERRY HAS EVERYTHING.
A BIT LIKE MY HEALTH CLUBS, ACTUALLY.

Duncan Bannatyne. BlackBerry® User
and Shrewd Spotter of Opportunities.

See how BlackBerry can support, inspire and
surprise you. Go to blackberrypeople.co.uk

⠿ BlackBerry.

Photo 6.3	Increasingly popular for today's busy lifestyle segment is a Blackberry. Source: The Advertising Archives

towards, feel about or use a product. Fair Trade provides a range of products that appeal to consumers who want the benefits of consuming such produce, at the same time contributing to others in less developed regions.

One way to segment based on behaviour is to divide the market based on usage frequency. Marketers may therefore attempt to reward current users, and try to win over infrequent users. Typically marketers often distinguish between users and non-users by segmenting their current customers further into groups of heavy, moderate and light users.

Many marketers abide by a rule of thumb called the **80/20 or Pareto rule**: 20 per cent of purchasers account for 80 per cent of the sales revenue (the ratio is an approximation, not gospel). This rule means that it often makes more sense to focus on the smaller number of people who are really into a product rather than on the larger number who are just casual users.

While the 80/20 rule still holds in the majority of situations, the web's ability to offer an unlimited choice of goods to billions of people is starting to change how marketers think about segmentation. A new approach called the **long tail** is turning traditional thinking about the virtues of selling in high volume on its head. The basic idea is that we need no longer rely solely on big hit sales (like blockbuster movies or best-seller books) to generate profits. Companies can also make money by selling small amounts of items that only a few people want – if they sell enough different items. For example, Amazon.com maintains a stock of some 3.7 million books compared with the 100,000 or so you'll find in a Barnes & Noble bookshop. Most of these will sell only a few thousand copies (if that), but the 3.6 million books that Barnes & Noble does not carry make up a quarter of Amazon's revenue!

Another way to segment a market based on behaviour is to look at **usage occasions**, or when consumers use the product most. Many products are associated with specific occasions, whether time of day, holidays, business functions or casual get-togethers. Businesses often divide up their markets according to when and how their offerings are in demand. For many, Christmas and New Year are important times for sending greeting cards and providing gifts, so are theme days, such as Father's Day, or Mothering Sunday.

 ## Segmenting Business-to-Business Markets

We've reviewed the segmentation variables marketers use to divide up the consumer pie, but how about all those business-to-business marketers out there? Adding to what we learned about business markets in Chapter 5, it's important to know that segmentation also helps them slice up the pie of their customers. Though the specific variables may differ, the underlying logic of classifying the larger market into manageable pieces that share relevant characteristics is the same whether the product being sold is pasta or potatoes.

Organisational demographics also help a business-to-business marketer to understand the needs and characteristics of its potential customers. These classification dimensions include the size of the firms either in total sales or number of employees, the number of factories, whether they are a domestic or a multinational company, policies on how they purchase and the type of business they are in. Business-to-business markets may also be segmented on the basis of the production technology they use and whether the customer is a user or a non-user of the product. General Electric's Aviation division is one of the world's largest producers of jet engines. GE divides its customers by the types of jets they fly: commercial, corporate, military, and marine and industrial. The final category, in fact, doesn't include planes at all but rather large ships and other applications of jet engine technologies.[15]

Many industries use the Standard Industrial Classification (SIC) system discussed in Chapter 5 to obtain information about the number of companies operating in a particular industry. Business-to-business marketers often consult information sources. For example, the likes of Dun & Bradstreet and Kompass provide subscribers with up-to-date information on private and public companies worldwide.

Step 2: Targeting

www.pearsoned.co.uk/solomon

Objective

4

Explain how marketers develop a targeting strategy

We've seen that the first step in developing a target marketing strategy is segmentation, in which the firm divides the market into smaller groups that share certain characteristics. The next step is **targeting**, in which marketers evaluate the attractiveness of each potential segment and decide which of these groups they will invest resources against to try to turn them into customers. The customer group or groups selected are the firm's **target market**. In this section, we'll review how marketers assess these customer groups, and we'll discuss selection strategies for effective targeting.

Evaluating Market Segments

Just because a marketer identifies a segment does not necessarily mean that it's a useful target. A viable target segment should satisfy the following requirements:

Are members of the segment similar to each other in their product needs and wants and, at the same time, different from consumers in other segments?   Without real differences in consumer needs, firms might as well use a mass-marketing strategy. For example, it's a waste of time to develop two separate lines of skin care products for working women and non-working women if both segments have the same complaints about dry skin.

Can marketers measure the segment?   Marketers must know something about the size and purchasing power of a potential segment before deciding if it is worth their efforts.

Is the segment large enough to be profitable now and in the future?   For example, a graphic designer hoping to design web pages for Barbie doll collectors must decide whether there are enough hard-core interested parties to make this business worthwhile and whether the trend will continue.

Can marketing communications reach the segment?   It is easy to select television programmes or magazines that will efficiently reach older consumers, those with certain levels of education or residents of major cities because the media they prefer are easy to identify.

Can the marketer adequately serve the needs of the segment?   Does the firm have the expertise and resources to satisfy the segment better than the competition? Please read the Marketing Ethics box, as it is interesting to see how McDonald's appeals to the very young – a 'significant' market segment.

At the start of the chapter, you met Ken Moss of the SCCI. He needs to capture the attention of a specific segment of business customer. Read 'Real People, Other Voices' to learn how others advise Ken.

Real People, Other Voices

Professor Adrian Palmer, Swansea University

Each of the three options that we are presented with has some merits. From the brief description that we are given of Ken Moss, he sounds like a fairly conservative person, approaching retirement, and the first option might have some appeal to him. He could easily lose his financial accountability within the broader Chamber budget, on the fairly vague grounds that what he is doing is 'good for the Chamber' overall. However, this will most likely not be good in the long term for the Chamber. It will not give sufficient drive to individuals to really understand what its members (or should we talk about 'customers'?) really want from it. Companies only pay for the Chamber's services if they believe they are getting value, better than they could obtain elsewhere. If international trade services provided by the Chamber have a value, this should be reflected in the price that members are prepared to pay for them, rather than the Chamber simply assuming it.

Bits of the second and third alternatives are attractive. Certainly, Ken should work closely with the training department to try and extend the relationships with companies that have been successfully developed here. I hope there is no rivalry between Ken and the training department manager, so that they do not have jealously guarded lists of contacts. But I think that merging the two departments will not address the fundamental problem of how the Chamber delivers greater value in respect of its international trade services. In fact, having one manager responsible for both training and international trade services may lead to the latter being seen as the poor relation, and because it is not generating much cash, less management time could be spent on really understanding members' needs in this respect.

The third choice will in the long term be the best for the Chamber. It should preserve a focus on international trade services, and it will retain a manager who is dedicated to understanding how value can be created in this field. But this option will not be an easy one for Ken, who will have his work cut out in really understanding what customers want, and developing new alliances which will help to develop that value. Ken should investigate other funding streams which are available from the Department of Business and Regulatory Reform (previously the Department of Trade and Industry). But even further government funding will not solve the problem if the Chamber is not offering good value to its members, so Ken must build up a good knowledge of members' needs and interests. Part of this could be achieved through some kind of CRM system, but invariably, Ken will need to use a lot of personal knowledge and contacts to understand what will be attractive to members. He also needs to have a thorough understanding of forthcoming overseas trade events, and make sure that planned missions match the interests of members. A good database will ensure that members are given information about an event which is of particular relevance to them, rather than lots of information about events which they are not remotely interested in. Ken should also look at costs, so that members with tight budgets believe that they are obtaining value through their involvement with the Chamber, rather than going it alone or developing their own alliances with other organisations. In this respect, the Sheffield Chamber might look to collaborative ventures with nearby Chambers whose members have similar interests in attending international trade events.

Carol Kelleher, University College Cork

I would advise Kenneth Moss to adopt option 3. Pursuit of option 1 is not a viable option as it would mean that it would not be possible to secure an independent source of funding for the International Trade Services department and, with membership subscriptions under threat, it might not be long before the department would cease to exist. Pursuit of option 2 would result in the dissolution of the core offering of the International Trade Services department and might erroneously provide exporting members with training services which are not critical to expand their businesses internationally. Option 3, involving partnership with the DTI in relation to developing focused trade missions for companies in 'priority sectors' in key markets, secures funding and promotional support for the department, as well as enabling the department to segment its client base of existing exporters, to provide relevant services to them in order to develop their businesses as well as providing the department with an opportunity to segment and target the customer enquiry database for other potential companies that might be interested in participating in future trade missions. Based on treating the customer as an organisational asset, the department is successfully implementing a relationship marketing and CRM strategy to effectively engage new customers and to maximise retention of existing customers through superior levels of customer service and targeted cross-selling. Such a focused strategy based on effective segmentation, targeting and positioning should ensure the department's continued growth and expansion into the future.

▶

Eliska Janackova,
a student at the University of Surrey

If I was in Ken's position I would choose option 2. Integrating Ken's department with the commercial training division would bring many benefits to both departments. The benefits could be mostly identified in terms of increased efficiency, service effectiveness and levels of customer satisfaction, ultimately improving the organisational financial performance. Firstly, integrating the two departments would result in increased efficiency and service effectiveness as customer knowledge could be shared more easily within this new joint division. This would result in the ability to understand the customers and their needs better and would enable the organisation to reach its targeted audience more effectively. Secondly, having more resources and consolidated information about the customers would allow the company to manage this data more effectively and therefore deliver more tailored solutions to the needs of its customers. Hence, customer relationships could be created and managed which would result in improved customer satisfaction and company reputation leading to enhanced customer loyalty as well as the attraction of new customers.

To conclude, this option is in my opinion the most viable of the three options. It is important to consider implementing some major changes to the structure when a company faces difficult times and combining the two departments not only enables the organisation to become more cohesive but also links the processes between the two departments and creates a more organised and efficient working environment ultimately resulting in the delivery of better services to the customer.

Developing Segment Profiles

Once a marketer has identified a set of usable segments, it is helpful to generate a profile of each to really understand segment members' needs and to look for business opportunities. This segment profile is a description of the 'typical' customer in that segment. A **segment profile** might, for example, include customer demographics, location, lifestyle information and a description of how frequently the customer buys the product.

Marketing Ethics

'Half of all children aged four don't know their own name – but two thirds of three-year-olds can recognise the McDonald's golden arches'

There is an industry worth at least £70m every year: advertising aimed directly at children. The value of indirect marketing – ads that are not made expressly for kids but are seen by them anyway – runs into the hundreds of millions. The result is that today's average British child is familiar with up to 400 brand names by the time they reach the age of 10. One study found that 69 per cent of all three-year-olds could identify the McDonald's golden arches, while half of all four-year-olds did not know their own name. Schools are no longer a refuge from this commercial onslaught. There are poster sites promoting new films by the assembly hall. Until Education Secretary Ruth Kelly banned them in 2005, school vending machines were a prime outlet of crisps, chocolates and fizzy drinks. The marketing of food to young consumers is not only a matter of when, but how. The techniques are tried, tested and familiar. The appeal to young children is obvious: bright, primary colours; friendly, elastic faces. Except these lovable creations are not there to amuse or entertain but to sell.

The Guardian, 25 October 2005

Debate, Discuss, Disagree

1 What is your opinion about the fact that 'half of all children aged four don't know their own name – but two thirds of three-year-olds can recognise the McDonald's golden arches'?

Choosing a Targeting Strategy

A basic targeting decision is how finely tuned the target should be: should the company go after one large segment or focus on meeting the needs of one or more smaller segments? Let's look at four targeting strategies, which are summarised in Figure 6.2.

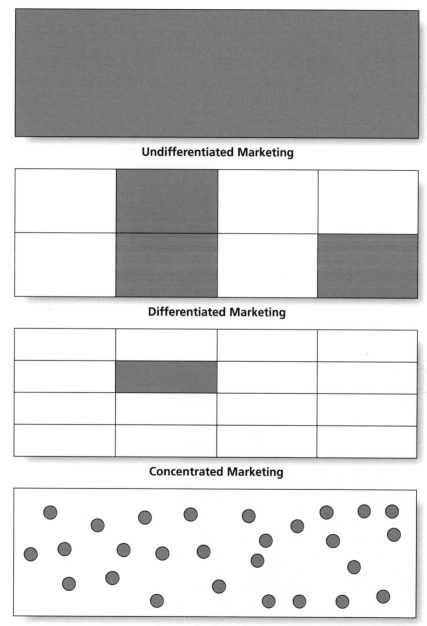

Undifferentiated Marketing

Differentiated Marketing

Concentrated Marketing

Customised Marketing

Figure 6.2	Choosing a Target Marketing Strategy
	After the market is divided into meaningful segments, marketers must decide on a target marketing strategy. Should the company go after one total market, one or several market segments, or even target customers individually?

A company such as Asda Wal-Mart that selects an **undifferentiated targeting strategy** is appealing to a broad spectrum of people. If successful, this type of operation can be very efficient, especially because production, research and promotion costs benefit from economies of scale. It's cheaper to develop one product or one advertising campaign than to choose several targets and create separate products or messages for each. The company must however be willing to gamble that people have similar needs, or that any differences among them will be so trivial that they will not matter so that the same product and message will appeal to many customers.

A company that chooses a **differentiated targeting strategy** develops one or more products for each of several customer groups with different product needs. A differentiated strategy is called for when consumers are choosing among well-known brands that have distinctive images and the company can identify one or more segments that have distinct needs for different types of products. The cosmetics giant L'Oréal follows this philosophy. The company has the resources to offer several product lines at a variety of prices. It targets the luxury market with such brands as Georgia Armani, Lancôme and Helena Rubinstein, while less expensive L'Oréal branded products are targeted to large department stores and discount stores, whilst Redken and Biotherm brands serve a more professional market.[16] Differentiated marketing can also involve connecting one product with different segments by communicating differently to appeal to those segments. VW has successfully achieved this in Europe through appealing to different segments via SEAT and Skoda.

When a firm focuses its efforts on offering one or more products to a single segment, it is using a **concentrated targeting strategy**. Smaller firms that do not have the resources or the desire to be all things to all people often use a concentrated strategy. UK tour operator Saga for example, purely markets its holidays at the growing segment of over 55s.

Ideally, marketers should be able to define segments so precisely that they can offer products and services that exactly meet the unique needs of each individual or firm. This level of concentration frequently does occur in the case of personal or professional services from doctors, lawyers and hairstylists. A **custom marketing strategy** is common in an industrial context whereby a supplier often works with one or a few large clients and develops products and services that only these clients will use, such as in the case of a design and build construction project.

Of course, in most cases this level of segmentation is neither practical nor possible when mass-produced products such as computers or cars enter the picture. However, advances in computer technology, coupled with new emphasis on building solid relationships with customers, have focused managers' attention on devising a new way to tailor specific products and the messages about them to individual customers. Thus, some forward-looking, consumer-oriented companies are moving toward **mass customisation** in which they modify a basic product or service to meet the needs of an individual.[17] Dell does this by offering customised computer products over the internet at Dell.com. Users can create their own computers – everything from personal computers to networking systems. We'll return to the issue of customisation later in this chapter when we introduce the idea of customer relationship management.

Photo 6.4   The diamond industry practises mass customisation; couples can create their own specific designs, diamond sizes and shapes, mounting styles and so forth.

Step 3: Positioning

www.pearsoned.co.uk/solomon

Objective

5

Understand how a firm develops and implements a positioning strategy

The final stage of developing a target marketing strategy process is to provide consumers who belong to a targeted market segment with a product or service that meets their unique needs and expectations. **Positioning** means developing a marketing strategy aimed at influencing how a particular market segment perceives a good or service in comparison to the competition. Developing a positioning strategy entails gaining a clear understanding of the criteria target consumers use to evaluate competing products and then convincing them that your product will meet those needs. Of course, ultimately the company must communicate this positioning to consumers.

Developing a Positioning Strategy

The success of a target marketing strategy hinges on marketers' abilities to identify and select an appropriate market segment. Then marketers must devise a marketing mix that will effectively target the segment's members by positioning their products to appeal to that segment. Here are the four steps marketers follow to develop a positioning strategy. We discuss each step in this section:

1. Analyse competitors' positions

2. Offer a good or service with competitive advantage

3. Match elements of the marketing mix to the selected segment

4. Evaluate the target market's responses and modify strategies if needed

The first step is to analyse competitors' positions in the marketplace. To develop an effective positioning strategy, marketers must understand the current state of the market. What competitors are out there, and how does the target market perceive them? Aside from direct competitors in the product category, are there other products or services that provide the same benefits people are seeking from indirect competitors?

Sometimes the indirect competition can be more important than the direct, especially if it represents an emerging consumer trend. For years, McDonald's developed positioning strategies based only on its direct competition, i.e. other fast-food chains (such as Burger King and KFC). McDonald's failed to realise that consumers' needs for a quick, tasty, convenient meal was being fulfilled by a plethora of indirect competitors, ranging from supermarket delicatessens and frozen microwavable single-serving meals to telephone order takeaways and full-service restaurants, such as T.G.I. Friday's, Pizza Hut and the like. Only recently has McDonald's begun to understand that it must react to this indirect competition by serving up a wider variety of adult-friendly and healthy food, as well as improving service.

The second step in developing a positioning strategy is to offer a good or service with a competitive advantage which provides a reason why consumers perceive the product as being better than the competition. If the company only offers a 'me-too product' it can induce people to buy for a lower price. Other forms of competitive advantage include offering a superior image like Giorgio Armani, a unique product feature at the time such as Levi's 501 button-fly jeans, better service like Singapore Airlines, or more experienced people, as B&Q.

Once a positioning strategy is set, the third step is for marketers to finalise the marketing mix by putting all the pieces into place. The elements of the marketing mix must match the selected segment. This means that the good or service must deliver benefits that

NIKE PRO VENT TIGHT IS FIRST LAYER APPAREL
ENGINEERED TO PERFORM.

UNIQUE DRI-FIT FABRIC RAPIDLY WICKS MOISTURE
AWAY FROM THE SKIN HELPING TO KEEP YOU COOL.

COLOUR CONTRAST STRETCH MESH VENTILATION
PANELS HELP CONTROL BODY TEMPERATURE.
AIDING OVERALL SPORTING PERFORMANCE.

LIGHTWEIGHT COMPRESSION TECHNOLOGY MEANS
NIKE PRO DOESN'T JUST GRIP THE BODY, IT ACTS
LIKE A SUPPORTIVE SECOND SKIN: MAKING YOU FEEL
INVINCIBLE AND READY TO PERFORM.

NIKE PRO
AN
ATHLETE'S
SECRET
WEAPON

NIKEPRO.COM

| Photo 6.5 | Nike uses football star Wayne Rooney to help position their brand alongside 'winners'. Source: The Advertising Archives |

the segment values, such as convenience or status. Put another way, it must add value and satisfy consumer needs. Furthermore, marketers must price this offering at a level these consumers will pay, make the offering available at places consumers are likely to go, and correctly communicate the offering's benefits in locations where consumers are likely to take notice.

In the fourth and final step, marketers must evaluate the target market's responses so they can modify strategies as needed. Over time, the firm may find that it needs to change which segments it targets, or even alter a product's position to respond to marketplace changes. Lucozade was originally positioned as a drink to be taken when ill to provide the body with increased energy levels. Nowadays, and through the use of high-profile celebrity endorsements from football stars such as Wayne Rooney, the drink is positioned as a sports drink that can improve endurance.

This type of change in strategy is called **re-positioning**, and it's fairly common to see a company try to modify its brand image to keep up with changing times. Re-positioning can also occur when brands once thought to be dead or near death get revived.

Bringing a Product to Life: The Brand Personality

Brands are almost like people in that we can often describe them in terms of personality traits. We may use adjectives such as cheap, elegant, sexy, or cool when talking about a shop, a perfume, a car, and so on. That's why a positioning strategy often tries to create a **brand personality** for a good or service – a distinctive image that captures its character and benefits. An advertisement for *Elle* magazine once said, 'She is not a reply card. She is not a category. She is not shrink-wrapped. Elle is not a magazine. She is a woman.'

Products as people? It seems funny to say, yet marketing researchers find that most consumers have no trouble describing what a product would be like 'if it came to life'. People often give clear, detailed descriptions, including what colour hair the product would have, the type of house it would live in, and even whether it would be thin, overweight or somewhere in between.[18] If you don't believe us, try doing this yourself.

Part of creating a brand personality is developing an identity for the product that the target market will prefer over competing brands. How do marketers determine where their products actually stand in the minds of consumers? One solution is to ask consumers what characteristics are important and how competing alternatives would rate on these attributes too. Marketers use this information to construct a **perceptual map** – a vivid way to construct a picture of where products or brands are 'located' in consumers' minds.

For example, suppose you wanted to construct a perceptual map of women's magazines as perceived by women in their 20s to give you some guidance while developing an idea for a new magazine. After interviewing a sample of female readers, you might determine questions women ask when selecting a magazine: (1) Is it 'traditional', that is, oriented towards family, home, or personal issues, or is it 'fashion forward', oriented towards personal appearance and fashion? (2) Is it for 'upmarket' women who are older and established in their careers or for

Across the Hall

Advice for Ken Moss

Professor Merlin Stone is a leading expert and author on direct and relationship marketing and Fellow of the Chartered Institute of Marketing and the Institute of Direct Marketing

I would go for option 3, but consider option 2 seriously. Option 1 is risky, both personally and professionally. It would demonstrate to the chief executive a serious failure to apply the marketing principles which the Chamber helps to promote. There is clearly a mismatch between the department's resources and its sales. It would make Ken look very weak. Therefore, the choice lies between options 2 and 3. Option 2 makes sense, but passes control to another department, whose objectives are not the same as Ken's. It would not be good to approach it from a position of weakness, but rather focus strongly on option 3, and if that works, turn to the commercial training department and cooperate with it on the basis of equality.

Option 3 is the brave option. It is also the only realistic one. However, if it does not work the viability of Ken's entire operation is questionable. If it does not work, it also shows that the rationale for the operation is disappearing. Of course, Ken's personal objectives of retiring in the medium term should not be a factor in the choice, although he does not seem to be the kind of person who would want to retire without having addressed the main challenge of the department he was leading. It seems that the rather reactive marketing stance of the Chamber meant that it did not understand the current and likely future needs of its customers (this knowledge is the basis of most good marketing), nor did it know to what extent its current customers were aware of the full range of its services. In most marketing, unless you know your customers' needs and ensure they are aware of what you do or can do for them, you have not passed first base in marketing. Given that Sheffield's industrial profile has changed so much in previous years, there was every chance that finding out more about customers' needs and increasing awareness of services would bring good results.

relatively downmarket women who are younger and just starting out in their careers? You might try to locate an unserved area, for example there may be room for a magazine aimed at 'cutting-edge' fashion for college-age women. An unserved segment is a gift for marketers: with luck, they can move quickly to capture a segment and define the standards of comparison for the category. This tactic paid off for European retailer Netto which identified a niche in the UK market to provide branded goods at lower prices.

Customer Relationship Management

www.pearsoned.co.uk/solomon

Objective 6

Explain how marketers increase long-term success and profits by practising customer relationship management

We've talked about identifying a unique group of consumers and developing products specifically to meet their needs. We also talked about how marketers can build products to meet the needs of individual consumers with mass customisation. Today many highly successful marketing firms embrace **customer relationship management (CRM)** programmes that allow companies to talk to individual customers and adjust elements of their marketing programmes in light of how each customer reacts to elements of the marketing mix.[19] In a nutshell, CRM aims to identify profitable customers and find effective ways to develop relationships with them, so that business is nurtured and expanded upon over the long term. The CRM trend facilitates one-to-one marketing, a term popularised in the writings of Don Peppers and Martha Rogers.[20]

Four Steps in One-to-One Marketing

Peppers and Rogers have identified four steps in one-to-one marketing:[21]

1. Identify customers and get to know them in as much detail as possible.

2. Differentiate among these customers in terms of both their needs and their value to the company.

Table 6.1
Four Steps to One-to-
One Marketing

Step	Suggested Activities
Identify	Collect and enter names and additional information about your customers. Verify and update, deleting outdated information.
Differentiate	Identify top customers. Determine which customers cost the company money. Find higher-value customers who have complained about your product more than once. Find customers who buy only one or two products from your company but a lot from other companies. Rank customers into A, B, and C categories based on their value to your company.
Interact	Call the top three people in the top 5 per cent of dealers, distributors and retailers that carry your product and make sure they're happy. Call your own company and ask questions; see how hard it is to get through and get answers. Call your competitors and compare their customer service with yours. Use incoming calls as selling opportunities. Initiate more dialogue with valuable customers. Improve complaint handling.
Customise	Find out what your customers want. Personalise your direct mail. Ask customers how and how often they want to hear from you. Ask your top 10 customers what you can do differently to improve your product. Involve top management in customer relations.

Source: Adapted from Don Peppers, Martha Rogers and Bob Dorf, "Is Your Company Ready for One-to-One Marketing?" *Harvard Business Review* (January–February 1999), 151–60.

3. Interact with customers and find ways to improve cost efficiency and the effectiveness of the interaction.

4. Customise some aspect of the products or services that you offer to each customer. This means treating each customer differently based on what has been learned through customer interactions.

Table 6.1 suggests some activities for implementing these four steps. Successful one-to-one marketing is dependent on CRM.

Peppers and Rogers define CRM as 'managing customer relationships. If I'm managing customer relationships, it means I'm treating different customers differently, across all enterprises. . . . The relationship develops a context over time, it drives a change in behaviour . . . [this] means that I have to change my behavior as an enterprise based on a customer'.[22] A CRM strategy allows a company to identify its best customers, stay on top of their needs and increase their satisfaction.

Is CRM for all companies? Should producers of consumer goods that target the entire market adopt CRM strategies? Of course, CRM seems to make more sense for firms such as business-to-business companies and consumer products companies that have a limited number of customers. But, as we'll see in the next section, even soft-drink and car companies have used CRM to build customer relationships and brand loyalty.

CRM: A New Perspective on an Old Problem

CRM is about communicating with customers and about customers being able to communicate with a company one to one. CRM systems are applications that use computers, CRM computer software, databases and often the internet to capture information at each touch-point (or interaction) between customers and companies to allow for overall better customer care. These systems include everything from websites that let you check on the status of a bill or package to call centres that solicit your business. When you log on to a website to track, for example, the expected delivery time for a product – that's part of a CRM system. When you get a phone message from the dentist reminding you about that filling appointment tomorrow, that's CRM. When you get a call from the car dealer asking how you would like your new vehicle, that's also CRM. In a nutshell, CRM helps firms communicate with and serve customers by understanding their needs. Remember how in Chapter 3 we said information is the fuel that runs the marketing engine? CRM is how much of that customer information is managed and acted on.

To fully appreciate the value of a CRM strategy, consider the following. In general, an investment banker needs to manage accounts as well as open new ones – often 30 to 50 per month. Just opening the account can take 45 minutes, not a satisfying process for the banker or for the customer. But with an automated CRM system, the banker can open an account, issue a welcome letter and produce an arbitration agreement in 10 minutes. He or she can create a unique marketing campaign for each client based on that person's life cycle – including such variables as when a person opened an account, their annual income, family situation, desired retirement age, and so on. The marketer can generate a happy anniversary letter to clients and include an invitation to update their investment objectives. These firms have found that this level of individualised attention results in a much higher rate of customer retention and satisfaction, so CRM creates a win–win situation for everyone.[23]

That success helps explain why CRM has become a driving philosophy in many successful firms. Industry sources estimated that in 2005 companies spent about €20 billion worldwide on CRM.[24]

The airline industry hit financial problems in the past decade, but is also concerned about customer relations and has invested heavily in CRM systems. These systems help flyers by automating crucial information and reducing phone call volume, and in the process those nasty 'holds' we're all accustomed to.[25] CRM also helps identify flying patterns, favoured destinations and loyal users so that extra perks (upgrades, tailored special offers and so on) can be sent their way. In addition to reducing angry customers, marketers can also use CRM systems to keep better track of enthusiastic ones.

Perhaps the most important aspect of CRM is that it presents a new way of looking at how to compete in the marketplace. This begins with looking at customers as partners. CRM proponents suggest that the traditional relationship between customers and marketers is an adversarial one where marketers try to sell their products to customers and customers seek to avoid buying.[26] The customer relationship perspective sees customers as partners, with each partner learning from the other every time they interact. Successful firms compete by establishing relationships with individual customers on a one-to-one basis through dialogue and feedback. What does this customer really want? That's one-to-one marketing.

 # Characteristics of CRM

In addition to having a different mind-set, companies that practise CRM have different goals, use different measures of success, and look at customers in some different ways. So, CRM marketers look at their share of the customer, at the lifetime value of a customer, at customer equity, and at focusing on high-value customers.

Share of Customer

Historically, marketers have measured success in a product category by their share of market. For example, if there are 100 million pairs of sports shoes sold each year, a firm that sells 10 million of them has a 10 per cent market share. If the manufacturer's marketing objective is to increase market share, it may lower the price of its shoes, increase its advertising, or offer customers a free football with every pair of shoes purchased. Such tactics may increase sales in the short run, but unfortunately may not do much for the long-term success of the firm. In fact, such tactics may actually decrease the value of the brand by weakening its image with giveaways.

Because it is always easier and less expensive to keep an existing customer than to get a new customer, CRM firms focus on increasing their **share of customer**, not share of market. Let's say that a consumer buys six pairs of shoes a year, two pairs from three different manufacturers. Let's assume one shoemaker has a CRM system that allows it to send letters to its current customers inviting them to receive a special price discount or a gift if they buy more of the firm's shoes during the year. If the firm can get the consumer to buy three, maybe four or perhaps all six pairs from them, the firm has increased its share of the customer. Incidentally, this may not be too difficult because the customer already buys and presumably likes the firm's shoes. Without the CRM system, the shoe company would probably use traditional advertising in an attempt to increase sales, which would be far more costly than the direct-mail campaign. So the company can increase sales and profits at a much lower cost than it would spend to get one, two or three new customers.

Lifetime Value of the Customer

As you'll recall from Chapter 1, the **lifetime value of a customer** is the potential profit generated by a single customer's purchase of a firm's products over the customer's lifetime. With CRM, a customer's lifetime value is identified and is the true goal, not an individual transaction. It just makes sense that a firm's profitability and long-term success are going to be far greater if it develops long-term relationships with its customers so that those customers buy from it again and again. Costs will be far higher and profits lower if each customer purchase is a first-time sale.

How do marketers calculate the lifetime value of a customer? They first estimate a customer's future purchases across all products from the firm over the next 20 or 30 years. The goal is to try to figure out what profit the company could make from the customer in the future. For example, a car dealer might calculate the lifetime value of a single customer by first calculating the total revenue that could be generated by the customer over his lifetime: the number of cars he would buy multiplied by their average price, plus the service the dealership would provide over the years, and even possibly the income from vehicle financing. The lifetime value of the customer would be the total profit generated by the revenue stream.

Customer Equity

Today an increasing number of companies are considering their relationships with customers as financial assets. Such firms measure success by calculating the value of their **customer equity** – the financial value of customer relationships throughout the lifetime of the relationships.[27] To do this, firms compare the investments they make in acquiring customers, retaining customers and relationship enhancement with the financial return on those investments. The goal is to reap a high return on the investments made in customer relationships and maximise the value of a firm's customer equity. Please analyse the Marketing Metrics case, to see how lifetime value and customer equity came into play at BCA.

Focusing on High-Value Customers

Using a CRM approach, customers must be prioritised and communication customised accordingly. For example, any banker will tell you that not all customers are equal – when it comes to

Marketing Metrics

Book Club Associates example

BCA is one of the world's biggest book clubs. Its business model, that of selling books by mail order to people who join its clubs, is one that has been around for a long time, but recent changes in its markets and channels have put it under severe financial pressures. The company decided to construct a customer equity optimisation model of the business, a spreadsheet which ran on data from their membership database and handled data for 30 book clubs (allowing a few extra for new clubs), 15 media channels and allowed for 450 different recruitment/spend decisions. The use of the optimisation model gave it guidance on:

- Targeting of marketing expenditure that maximises customer life-time value;

- Clubs that were candidates for closure;

- Profitability over five years that will result from customer equity strategy and the use of the model resulted in a substantial growth in the company's profitability.

profitability. So banks use CRM systems to generate a profile of each customer based on factors such as value, risk and interest in buying new financial products. This automated system helps the bank decide which current or potential customers it will target with certain communications, or how much effort to spend on retaining a person's account – whilst at the same time cutting its costs by as much as a third.[28] It just makes sense to use different types of communication contacts based on the value of each individual customer. For example, personal selling (the most expensive form of marketing communication per contact) may constitute 75 per cent of all contacts with high-volume customers, while direct mail or telemarketing is more often the best way to contact low-volume customers.

Now that you've learned more about segmentation, targeting and building relationships, read 'Real People, Real Decisions' to see which strategy Ken opted for.

Real People, Real Decisions

How it worked out at the Chamber

Ken decided to take the bull by the horns and go for option 3. It was not an easy decision, and it would have been much easier to look at option 1, or a safer gamble would have been option 2. It did, however, enable him to take control of his own department's destiny to some extent, and retain control. The selection was interesting as, building on the export promotion side, those issues relating to this chapter – segmentation, targeting and CRM – became fundamental issues of importance, and helped the department succeed with this option.

To start with, Ken and a close colleague decided to explore avenues for the Department of Trade and Industry (DTI) to support more of their work. As a result, a strategy was developed for the Chamber to bid to the DTI for more trade missions to take local companies to international destinations. Through carefully segmenting global markets on industrial sectors, and targeting those countries with high demand which the DTI labelled as 'priority sectors' for Sheffield's produce, such as power generation equipment, giftware, steel/engineering, hardware and healthcare, the Chamber was able to bid for business support to organise such events.

Obtaining support was no guarantee for making profitable business though, as many UK Chambers had experienced. Running international trade missions could actually lose money if the cost of generating company interest was not covered by management fees associated with the event. It was therefore important to recruit significant numbers that would actually cover the costs and hopefully generate a surplus.

In response, the Chamber targeted those firms that were already exporting in international markets where it planned to visit. In export there is always the need to visit international customers regularly, so it was decided to target existing exporters in general, and especially those that the Chamber knew were already exporting to such countries via export documentation evidence and through data stored on the Chamber database. Other potential recruits were targeted which were outside the locality, but which still had an interest in the market in question. These firms might have attended a governmental seminar on trading with the country in question, or had visited the market on a previous trade mission with another provider. Within a short amount of time, through successfully segmenting and targeting the market, revenue began to increase, and this twinned with developing further seminars and an Export Club initiative provided the ideal recipe for success.

Because of the segmentation and targeting strategy, the department was soon attracting lots of new business. Ken and colleagues were also happy to discover that many of the mission delegates were requesting further services. At this stage a decision was made to develop a relationship marketing approach and build on some of the CRM tactics to increase business. A marketing information system was developed to store data on exporting companies, and this data ranged from basic contact information relating to members of personnel in exporting departments, to more demographic detail relating to the countries where such companies did business.

> ## At this stage a decision was made to develop a relationship marketing approach and build on some of the CRM tactics to increase business

As a result, the Chamber was able to target individuals and cross-sell additional international services, as well as more of the same service. It was found for instance that an Export Manager who visited South Africa with the Chamber would later join the next delegation to say Hong Kong, would soon join the Export Club, later needed to use the Chamber's translation service, and, once obtained, a sales order in an international market would soon head to the Chamber to process export documents, etc. – so revenue spiralled in the right direction.

Chapter Summary

Now that you have finished reading this chapter, you should be able to answer any of the following potential examination questions:

1. **Is market segmentation needed in today's business environment.** Market segmentation is often necessary in today's marketplace because of market fragmentation. That is, the splintering of a mass society into diverse groups due to technological and cultural differences. Most marketers can't realistically do a good job of meeting the needs of everyone, so it is more efficient to divide the larger pie into slices in which members of a segment share some important characteristics and tend to exhibit the same needs and preferences.

2. **What are the different dimensions marketers use to segment consumer and business-to-business markets.** Marketers frequently find it useful to segment consumer markets on the basis of demographic characteristics, including age, gender, family life cycle, social class, race or ethnic identity and place of residence. A second dimension, psychographics, uses measures of psychological and social characteristics to identify people with shared preferences or traits. Consumer markets may also be segmented on the basis of how consumers behave towards the product. For example, their brand loyalty, usage rates (heavy, moderate or light) and usage occasions. Business-to-business markets are often segmented on the basis of industrial demographics, type of business based on the Standard Industrial Classification (SIC) codes, and geographic location.

3. **Describe how marketers evaluate and select potential market segments.** To choose one or more segments to target, marketers examine each segment and evaluate its potential for success as a target market. Meaningful segments have wants that are different from those in other segments, can be identified, can be reached with a unique marketing mix, will respond to unique marketing communications, are large enough to be profitable, have future growth potential, and possess needs that the organisation can satisfy better than the competition.

4. **Explain how marketers develop a targeting strategy.** After marketers identify the different segments, they estimate the market potential of each segment. The relative attractiveness of segments also influences the firm's selection of an overall marketing strategy. The firm may choose an undifferentiated, differentiated, concentrated or custom strategy based on the company's characteristics and the nature of the market.

5. **Describe how a firm develops and implements a positioning strategy.** After marketers select the target market(s) and the overall strategy, they must determine how they wish customers to perceive the brand relative to the competition. That is, should the brand be positioned like, against or away from the competition? Through positioning, a brand personality is developed. Marketers can compare brand positions by using such research techniques as perceptual mapping. In developing and implementing the positioning strategy, firms analyse the competitors' positions, determine the competitive advantage offered by their product, tailor the marketing mix in accordance with the positioning strategy, and evaluate responses to the marketing mix selected. Marketers must continually monitor changes in the market that might indicate a need to reposition the product.

6. **Explain how marketers increase long-term success and profits by practising customer relationship management.** Companies using customer relationship management (CRM) programmes establish relationships and differentiate their behaviour towards individual customers on a one-to-one basis through dialogue and feedback. Success is often measured one customer at a time using the concepts of share of customer, lifetime value of the customer and customer equity. In CRM strategies, customers are prioritised according to their value to the firm, and communication is customised accordingly.

Key Terms

Chapter Review

Marketing Concepts: Testing Your Knowledge

1. What is market segmentation, and why is it an important strategy in today's marketplace?

2. List and explain the major demographic characteristics frequently used in segmenting consumer markets.

3. Explain consumer psychographic segmentation.

4. What is behavioural segmentation?

5. What are some of the ways marketers segment industrial markets?

6. List the criteria used for determining whether a segment may be a good candidate for targeting.

7. Explain undifferentiated, differentiated, concentrated and customised marketing strategies. What is mass customisation?

8. What is product positioning? Describe the three approaches that marketers use to create product positions.

9. What is CRM? How do firms practise CRM?

10. Explain the concepts of share of customer, lifetime value of a customer and customer equity.

Marketing Concepts: Discussing Choices

1. One of the criteria for a usable market segment is its size. This chapter suggested that to be usable, a segment must be large enough to be profitable now and in the future and that some very small segments get ignored because they can never be profitable. So, how large should a segment be? How do you think a firm should go about determining if a segment is profitable? Have technologi-cal advances made it possible for smaller segments to be profitable?

2. Customer relationship management (CRM) focuses on share of customer, lifetime value of the customer, customer equity and high-value customers. What do you think are some problems with replacing earlier concepts such as share of market with these concepts?

Marketing Practice: Applying What You've Learned

1. Assume that a firm has hired you to develop a marketing plan for a small regional brewery. In the past, the brewery has simply produced and sold a single beer brand to the entire market – a mass-marketing strategy. As you begin work, you feel that the firm could be more successful if it developed a target marketing strategy. The owner of the firm, however, is not convinced. Write a memo to the owner outlining the following:

   a. The basic reasons for target marketing.

   b. The specific advantages of a target marketing strategy for the brewery.

2. As the marketing director for a company that is planning to enter the business-to-business market for photocopy machines, you are attempting to develop an overall marketing strategy. You have considered the possibility of using mass marketing, concentrated marketing, differentiated marketing and custom marketing strategies.

   a. Write a report explaining what each type of strategy would mean for your marketing plan in terms of product, price, promotion and distribution.

   b. Evaluate the desirability of each type of strategy.

   c. What are your final recommendations for the best type of strategy?

3. As an account executive for a marketing consulting firm, your newest client is a university – your university. You have been asked to develop a positioning strategy for the university. With a group of classmates, develop an outline of your ideas, including the following:

   a. Who are your competitors?

   b. What are the competitors' positions?

   c. What target markets are most attractive to the university?

   d. How will you position the university for those segments relative to the competition? Present the results to your class.

4. Assume that a firm hires you as marketing manager for a chain of bookshops. You feel that the firm should develop a CRM strategy. Outline the steps you would take in developing that strategy.

 # Marketing Miniproject: Learning by Doing

This miniproject will help you to improve your understanding of how firms make target marketing decisions. The project focuses on the market for women's beauty care products.

1. Gather ideas about different dimensions useful for segmenting the women's beauty products market. You may use your own ideas, but you probably will also want to examine advertising and other marketing communications developed by different beauty care brands.

2. Based on the dimensions for market segmentation that you have identified, develop a questionnaire and conduct a survey of consumers. You will have to decide which questions should be asked and which consumers should be surveyed.

3. Analyse the data from your research and identify the different potential segments.

4. Develop segment profiles that describe each potential segment.

5. Generate several ideas for how the marketing strategy might be different for each segment based on the profiles. Develop a presentation (or write a report) outlining your ideas, your research findings and your marketing strategy.

Real People, Real Surfers

In this chapter, we learned about the importance of segmentation and targeting at the Sheffield Chamber of Commerce. Please go on to their website, www.scci.org.uk/ and try to answer the following:

1. How does the Chamber segment its customer base?

2. Look closely at the services offered by the Chamber and identify which particular businesses they aim to target.

Now, take a look at the website at www.pearsoned.co.uk/solomon to see some videos from YouTube relating to aspects of this chapter.

Also on the website, try some analysis and calculations yourself by looking up the marketing metrics exercise called Customer Lifetime Value. This shows how to develop models of customer acquisition and retention for a mobile phone operator, to find the marketing strategies that deliver the maximum short-term and long-term value financially.

Marketing Plan Exercise

Check out a website for a company that manufacturers a product that you like and are familiar with. Pay special attention to the company's product lines and how it describes products and product uses. Select one particular product and answer the following questions:

1. What market segmentation approaches do you believe are most relevant for your chosen product given the type of product it is? Why do you recommend these over other possible approaches?

2. Describe the top three target markets for the product you selected. What makes these particular targets so attractive?

3. From your review of the website as well as your knowledge of the product, write out a positioning statement for the product. Keep it to a few sentences; start out with 'Product X is positioned as . . .'

4. In what ways could CRM help the company conduct successful target marketing and positioning of the product?

Marketing in Action Case

Real decisions at Les Gourmets Mondial

'Janet, could you present a review of your CRM programme at tomorrow's board meeting? Really sorry to ask at the last minute, but you could make it, couldn't you?' Janet knew that no matter how kind the request, Eric LeGrande, CEO of Les Gourmets Mondial, would not appreciate anything else but an affirmative response. In her six years as Marketing Director, Janet had never known Eric to ask for anything last-minute unless he had serious concerns.

It had been only 18 months ago that the board had signed off a €40m CRM programme that Janet had championed: the largest single investment the firm had made. Phase three of a four-stage CRM technology programme went live only last quarter: on time and on budget. A new global marketing group had been operating for over nine months and Les Gourmets Mondial had been transacting online for one year. Yet it was hard to assess what CRM was doing for revenue, customer loyalty and competitiveness. This, thought Janet, was what the board wanted to investigate before committing even more funds. She took out the document dated July 2007 entitled 'CRM Business Proposal' that the board accepted and blocked out the rest of the day to prepare for tomorrow's meeting.

Les Gourmets Mondial was a leading manufacturer of high-quality kitchenware (cooking utensils, pots,

knives, serving dishes) sold to consumers. Eric, a Cordon Bleu chef, founded the business in 1985 to sell specialist baking products and the firm built a worldwide reputation for style, innovation and superior quality. During the 1990s, the business listed on Le Bourse de Paris and used its expanded capital base to buy other, non-listed, high-quality kitchenware makers in Europe and Japan to become the world leader in its market. The firm's products were sold in department stores, specialist kitchenware shops, 30 company-owned shops, through a telephone ordering service and most recently online. The firm generated a turnover in excess of €400m and a net profit of €65m in 2002.

However, the firm now faced a much more competitive environment. Department stores, hypermarkets and grocery chains were increasingly offering high-quality products at lower prices. Sophisticated retailers employed savvy data analysts who used the retailers' databases to identify 'foodies', Les Gourmets' prime target group, from their readily identifiable purchasing profile. Retailers target foodies because this group is highly profitable. At the same time, exclusive (higher-priced) local competitors had finally ironed out their online business models and were extending their reach across the world: engaging with online 'foodie' communities to create awareness, purchase and loyalty. These communities provided competitors with useful data: for example, Royal and Sharp Knives of Sheffield

(UK) recently wrote to the husbands, wives or partners of their community members one month prior to their members' birthdays to encourage gift purchase.

As a result of increased competition, turnover in 2006 had grown to only €420m and profit margins eroded as the firm had to increase its promotional spending. Profits fell to only €50m. By February 2007, after a poor Christmas period, Janet concluded that Les Gourmet's brand name and reputation no longer commanded its traditional consumer loyalty and high prices. She commissioned various pieces of market research, engaged high-quality management consultants and consulted widely with peers in other companies. She concluded that the firm needed to move towards relationship marketing. Janet predicted that in future, retailers with whom consumers had relationships would dominate consumers' purchasing overall. Foodies would buy speciality items from their online communities: respected online experts would make a recommendation and the foodie would be 'one click' away from fulfilment. And they would concentrate more of their purchases through the major hypermarkets and grocers (e.g. Carrefour, Tesco) with whom they had a strong relationship and loyalty scheme incentives. Les Gourmets would be squeezed between low price mass marketers, full service retailers and the engaging customer experience afforded online. Already grocers were approaching it to make 'own-label' products at low margin: that could only spell trouble for Les Gourmets.

Janet faced a number of obstacles. Les Gourmets grew as a series of acquisitions and the business units did not have a common consumer strategy. Some sections already had online businesses and communities whereas others refused to compete with their existing retail distribution. The brand was represented differently in many markets. Prices were inconsistent. Customer data was scattered throughout innumerable and incompatible operational and local marketing databases. There was no best practice for direct marketing. Analytical tools used in the business were unsophisticated and none of the businesses had high-quality database analysts. Les Gourmets could not cross-sell to its best

After one year, Janet was not sure what relationship marketing was doing for Les Gourmets

customers because of this archipelago of practices and systems; indeed, it did not know what any one customer bought from it across all its product ranges. The firm had no metrics upon which to estimate the impact of relationship marketing.

With the help of a consultancy that had successfully addressed similar issues with comparable companies, Janet had built the business case for relationship marketing. The revenue side of the business case was built upon Janet's projections for share of market and models of best practice relationship marketing. She was particularly keen to exploit the breadth of Les Gourmets' product portfolio with foodies; this was a source of competitive advantage that the firm was not able to exploit at present.

New CRM business processes were designed in collaboration with IS (Information Systems) and national business unit marketers. The technology to manage these new processes was agreed and costed. With strong support from the CIO (Chief Information Officer), a far-reaching change programme was implemented. Business units were told to phase out their myriad of independent databases, analytical tools and campaign management tools in favour of a standard corporate solution which permitted a single view of the customer, best of breed tools, sophisticated cross-selling and an enhanced ability to understand individual customer profitability and respond to various campaigns. During the design phase, CRM solutions were evaluated by a team comprising IT, head office marketing and local marketers. A solution was specified and configured for Les Gourmets and the business processes associated with it tested before it was piloted in Germany in October 2007 and ultimately rolled out internationally. A similar process was undertaken for standardising and enhancing the various e-commerce platforms in use within the firm. The new solution incorporated the latest technology for managing online communities.

After one full year of operation, Janet was not sure what relationship marketing was doing for Les Gourmets. Market share was not rebounding, sales were getting better but the firm had reduced prices. Traffic on the websites was very high (500,000 unique visitors every month) but actual sales online were disappointing: averaging €400K per month versus an estimate of €1m. Telephone orders had increased and Monday morning was the busiest day of the week, suggesting people were surfing the site at the weekend but ordering on the phone. Perhaps customers were also going into the traditional outlets after seeing items online, but Janet had no evidence for this. Every business unit had launched a Les Gourmet online community but results were very patchy and the community members rarely bought online. Direct marketing campaigns were run in a more standardised and professional manner, but the promotions themselves were no more imaginative than they had been previously, or noticeably more effective.

There were some teething problems with the CRM system. Many marketers found it difficult to use, despite Marketing's involvement with its design. Data in the databases were not always accurate and customers were reluctant to provide all the data that Marketing had expected. The analytical tools that had looked so easy to use in the workshops of the previous year

(when the system was in design) proved difficult to work in the field and the business units could not find good-quality data analysts who knew both the tools and the Les Gourmets business. Head office had only managed to fill two of the five analyst positions for which it had budgeted and was lending its scarce resource to the business units to alleviate their problems. The breakthroughs in customer insight and cross-selling had not happened. But Janet was sure that this was normal for a change programme of this extent and that these problems would be reduced over time.

Yet there were criticisms. In the corridor two weeks ago, Joost van der Meer, Group Finance Director, said 'for all this money, €400K per month is not much. Your assumptions are optimistic. Price reduction would be a more cost effective way to return this business to growth. Had we invested all this money in lower prices, we would be ahead of the game. Price reduction funded by cost reduction seems sensible to me'.

Those words were still ringing in her ears as she sat down to prepare her presentation. She drew out a list of questions that she felt she would have to answer tomorrow.

Things to Think About

1. What had gone well? What could have been done better?

2. Will it work? Should Les Gourmet carry on and invest the remaining budget? Is Joost right about just cutting prices?

3. What are the specific actions Janet should recommend tomorrow? Merely suggesting more research and consultation would not be enough to satisfy the board?

4. How should Janet implement these actions?

Case study written by Dr Stan Maklan, Cranfield School of Management.

References

1. Stanley C. Hollander and Richard Germain, *Was There a Pepsi Generation before Pepsi Discovered It?: Youth-Based Segmentation in Marketing* (New York: NTC Business Books, 1992).

2. Amy Barrett, 'To Reach the Unreachable Teen', *Business Week*, 18 September 2000, 78–80.

3. Bruce Horovitz, 'Gen Y: A Tough Crowd to Sell', *USA Today*, 21 May 2002, www.usatoday.com/money/covers/2002-04-22-geny.htm.

4. Douglas Coupland, *Generation X: Tales for an Accelerated Culture* (New York: St. Martin's Press, 1991).

5. Quoted in Karen Lowry Miller, 'You Just Can't Talk to These Kids', *Business Week*, 19 April 1993, 104.

6. Robert Scally, 'The Customer Connection: Gen X Grows Up, They're in Their 30s Now', *Discount Store News*, 25 October 1999, 38 www.findarticles.com/p/articles/mi_m3092/ is_20_38/ai_57443548.

7. Ibid.

8. Alex Williams, 'What Women Want: More Horses', *New York Times Online*.

9. Michael Flocker, *The Metrosexual Guide to Style: A Handbook for the Modern Man* (Cambridge, MA: Da Capo Press, 2003).

10. www.urbandictionary.com/define.php?term=metrosexual.

11. Charles M. Schaninger and William D. Danko, 'A Conceptual and Empirical Comparison of Alternate Household Life Cycle Markets', *Journal of Consumer Research* 19 (March 1993), 580–94.

12. Christy Fisher, 'Census Data May Make Ads More Single-Minded', *Advertising Age*, 20 July 1992, 2.

13. See Lewis Alpert and Ronald Gatty, 'Product Positioning by Behavioral Life Styles', *Journal of Marketing* 33 (April 1969), 65–69; Emanuel H. Demby, 'Psychographics Revisited: The Birth of a Technique', *Marketing News*, 2 January 1989, 21; and William D. Wells, 'Backward Segmentation', in *Insights into Consumer Behavior*, ed. Johan Arndt (Boston: Allyn & Bacon, 1968), 85–100.

14. Neal E. Boudette, 'Navigating Curves: BMW's Push to Broaden Line Hits Some Bumps in the Road', *Wall Street Journal*, 10 January 2005, A1.

15. www.ge.com/en/product/business/aviation.htm.

16. L'Oréal, 'Our Brand Portfolio', www.loreal.com.

17. Chip Bayers, 'The Promise of One to One (a Love Story)', *Wired* (May 1998), 130.

18. For an example of how consumers associate food brands with a range of female body shapes, see Martin R. Lautman, 'End-Benefit Segmentation and Prototypical Bonding', *Journal of Advertising Research* (June/July 1991), 9–18.

19. 'A Crash Course in Customer Relationship Management', *Harvard Management Update*, March 2000 (Harvard Business School reprint U003B).

20. Don Peppers and Martha Rogers, *The One-to-One Future* (New York: Doubleday, 1996).

21. Don Peppers, Martha Rogers and Bob Dorf, 'Is Your Company Ready for One-to-One Marketing?', *Harvard Business Review* (January–February 1999), 151–60.

22. Quoted in Cara B. DiPasquale, 'Navigate the Maze', Special Report on 1:1 Marketing, *Advertising Age*, 29 October 2001, S1(2).

23. Jim Middlemiss, 'Users Say CRM Is Worth the Effort', at www.wallstreetandtech.com, third quarter 2001, 17–18.

24. Mary Jo Nott, 'CRM Spending Forecast and Analysis 2001–2005', *DM Review*, www.dmreview.com/specialreports/20020806/5607-1.html.

25. Marc L. Songini, 'Dimmed Utilities Plug into CRM', *Computer World* 35 (6 August 2001), 1(2).

26. Susan Fournier, Susan Dobscha and David Glen Mick, 'Preventing the Premature Death of Relationship Marketing', *Harvard Business Review* (January–February 1998), 42–44.

27. Robert C. Blattberg, Gary Getz and Mark Pelofsky, 'Want to Build Your Business: Grow Your Customer Equity', *Harvard Management Update* (August 2001, Harvard Business School reprint U0108B), 3.

28. Tonia Bruyns, 'Banking on Targeted Marketing', 7 November 2001, www.business2.co.za.

Chapter 7
Creating the Product

Meet Ben Tisdall,
Director of SpeedBreaks Ltd
(formerly SpeedDater)
www.speedbreaks.co.uk

Q & A with Ben Tisdall

What do you do when not working:
Road and mountain biking

First job out of university:
Making cheese and yoghurt at Neal's Yard Dairy, Covent Garden

Career high:
February 2003 when speed dating was at the height of its buzz

A job-related mistake you wish you hadn't made:
Franchising speed dating in Germany

Your hero:
Greg Lemond, Tour de France winner in 1986, 1989 and 1990

Motto to live by:
Do as you would be done by

My management style is:
Give people freedom and positive reinforcement

Don't do this when interviewing me:
Not knowing anything about me or my company

Ben Tisdall dropped out of an economics degree before going on to take a degree in Fine Art at Chelsea School of Art. After art school he moved into journalism and went on to edit a string of IT and business publications including *Personal Computer World* and oversee the launch in 1996 of *Internet World* in the UK. Between 1998 and 2002 Ben published magazines and newspapers for various publishers ranging from wedding magazine *Wedding Day* to the IT weekly *PC Week*.

Being made redundant in early 2002 after the first dot-com crash was the spur for founding SpeedDater with business partner Simon Prockter. SpeedDater was started on a shoestring and the logo was designed in exchange for fixing the designer's bike. However SpeedDater rapidly established itself as the UK market leader in speed dating and singles events. In March 2008, though, SpeedDater sold its dating interests to Easydate Ltd, to concentrate on building its singles holiday company SpeedBreaks. The company is now called SpeedBreaks Ltd and runs active holidays for single people in the UK and Europe.

Real People, Real Decisions

Decision time at SpeedBreaks

Whether looking for the love or your life, short-term fun or just new friends, the hottest product on the market in 2003 was speed dating. The concept was invented by Rabbi Yaccov Deyo and the first ever event took place in 1998 in the US and quickly spread across the Altantic on the back of an increasing need for people to find potential mates and dates, via bringing a group of strangers together to meet each other at high speed (3 minutes) in a sociable setting. Speed dating as it was called had its heyday in 2003 when nearly every newspaper journalist wanted a slice of the story and it was the newest social revolution around. From offices in Clerkenwell in London, the operation grew to organising speed dating events around the country and for niche markets such as marketing and media people, graduate professionals, Asian muslim and 'fit girls for fit guys' for the sporty types.

After that period, sales grew steadily but the company needed to develop new products around the speed dating concept. One idea stemmed from solving one of the problems with speed dating, which was its speed! Three minutes of conversation works brilliantly for instant chemistry; however, most meaningful relationships develop over a longer period of hours, days or even months. Thus anything which would increase the time together might work. One such solution to this was to think about mini breaks. Ben was a keen skier and had been on many very sociable skiing holidays before, so he thought mini speed dating holidays might be a way to develop the business and get into the singles travel market. But the question was: what type of mini break and speed dating format would work the best? The company decided to trial three new product/service options to see which might be most successful.

Ben considers his options . . .

Option 1 Organise speedbreaks in ski resorts

In this option, people would spend three nights in groups of 12–15 people which would usually be half male and half female. The cost would be around £300 per weekend. On the first night is a speed dating event for all the group and each person is given a name-badge to encourage interaction. There is a local host who makes introductions, arranges the best local restaurants, bars, etc. and gives local tourist information. The advantages of this option are that people on the break already share a common interest (skiing) and have to be reasonably active, outdoors-type people to want to go skiing in the first place. They are also put through an 'experience', i.e. skiing together, which helps to break down barriers and facilitate interaction. As the new product was promoted to speed daters on an existing database, it was an easy cross-selling opportunity and customers knew what to expect from the speed dating part of the holiday weekend. Also, three days is not much time to take off work and is less risky if you don't happen to like the people you are on holiday with. After the holiday, customers could go to the website and contact other people on the break just as you do with a normal speed date. The considerable disadvantages were that the ski season is only four months long and snow and weather conditions can be unpredictable, which can ruin the experience.

Option 2 Organise speedbreaks in cities

In this option, people go for 2–3 nights to places like Paris, Prague and Barcelona with 12–25 people in 3 or 4 star hotels. The package included usually a bike tour of the city and a local host who arranged nightclubs, bars and good restaurants. The host organised a speed dating event (like option 1) on the first evening. Advantages of this option were that it appealed to a much wider market encompassing both active people and general travellers. It could also be done all year round with locations varying by season so people might want to go on several holidays to different places whereas it was less likely that they would go on three mini skiing breaks. In addition, Ben did some research on speed dating participants and found that females' number one preferred activity was mini city breaks. The total cost of around £300 was not as much as option 3, but the daily rate was more expensive. The disadvantages of this option were that customers tended to be a random group of strangers and did not have the shared common interest and there was no real 'activity' to help break the ice and get people doing the same thing together. On a practical level, it was also sometimes difficult to find hotels with an appropriate room to host the first evening's speed dating event.

Option 3 Organise week-long activity speedbreaks

In this option, people went on a seven day activity holidays to do things like sailing, diving or multi-activities such as horse riding, mountain biking and hiking. To save embarrassment and increase enjoyment, people were put into ability groups for the activities.

Like the other breaks, they were often organised in Europe in order to get good hotels at a reasonable price. These activity holidays for singles started at £600–700 per week. They did not include the speed dating element on the first evening and had no name badges as people were together for longer and would naturally meet everyone in the group. Instead, they simply had a dinner on the first night which had a boy-girl-boy-girl seating plan and the local host arranged meeting points in bars and restaurants throughout the week. The advantages of this option were that there was a much

longer planning cycle in the consumer's mind so advance bookings were much greater for seven days than for 2–3 day breaks. Also, these activities could be run throughout the year.

The disadvantages of this option were the higher cost of the break, the fact that people had to take a week off work and were spending a full week with complete strangers. For the speedbreak business, a disadvantage was having to plan on much longer time horizons for booking hotels, flights and activities. It was also a more complicated product with higher customer expectations as a result of the time and money they were investing. Because of the greater things at stake, people needed more reassurance over potential concerns about spending a week with people you didn't know and might not like.

Now put yourself in Ben's shoes, which new product option do you think will be most successful and why?

Objectives

When you finish reading this chapter, you will be able to:

1 Explain the layers of a product

2 Describe the classifications of products

3 Understand the importance of new products

4 Show how firms develop new products

5 Explain the process of product adoption and the diffusion of innovations

Build a Better Mousetrap: The Value Proposition

'Build a better mousetrap and the world will beat a path to your door.' Although we've all heard that adage, the truth is that just because a product is better is no guarantee it will succeed. For decades, the Woodstream Company (under the brand name 'Victor') built wooden mousetraps. Then the company decided to build a better one. Woodstream's product development people researched eating, crawling and resting habits of mice (hey, it's a living . . .). They built prototypes of different mousetraps to come up with the best possible design and tested them in homes. Then the company unveiled the sleek-looking 'Little Champ', a black plastic miniature inverted bathtub with a hole. When the mouse went in and ate the bait, a spring snapped upward, and the mouse was history.

Sounds like a great new product (unless you're a mouse), but the Little Champ failed. Woodstream studied mouse habits, *not* consumer preferences. The company later discovered that husbands set the trap at night, but wives were left in the morning to dispose of the trap holding the dead mouse. Unfortunately, wives thought the Little Champ looked too expensive to throw away, so they felt they should empty the trap for reuse. This was a task most women weren't willing to do – they wanted a trap they could happily throw away.[1]

Woodstream's failure underscores the importance of creating products that provide benefits that people seek. It also tells us that any number of products, from low-tech cheese to high-tech traps, potentially deliver these benefits. Despite Victor's claim to be the 'World's Leader in Rodent Control Solutions', in this case cheese and a shoe box could trap a mouse as well as a high-tech trap.

We need to take a close look at how products successfully trap consumers' money. Chapter 1 showed us that the value proposition is consumers' perception of the benefits they will receive if they buy a product or service. So, the marketer's task is twofold: first, to create a better value than what's already out there and then to convince customers that this is true.

As we defined it in Chapter 1, a product is a tangible good, service, idea, place or person or some combination of these that satisfies consumer or business customer needs through the exchange process; a bundle of attributes including features, functions, benefits and uses. A good may be a pack of biscuits, a digital camera, a house, a fancy new computer or a pair of distressed jeans. A **good** is a tangible product, something that we can see, touch, smell, hear, taste or possess. In contrast, intangible products – services, ideas, people, places – are products that we can't always see, touch, taste, smell or possess. We'll talk more about intangible products in Chapter 9.

Marketers think of the product as more than just a thing that comes in a package. They view a product as a bundle of attributes that includes the packaging, brand name, benefits and supporting features in addition to a physical good. The key word here is *creating*, and a large part of the marketer's role in creating the value proposition is developing and *marketing* products appropriately. In this chapter, we'll first examine what a product is and see how marketers classify consumer and business-to-business products. Then we'll go on to look at new products, how marketers develop new products, and how markets accept them. In the chapters that follow, we'll look at issues such as managing and pricing products and services.

Layers of the Product Concept

Objective

1

Explain the layers of a product

No doubt you've heard someone say, 'It's the thought, not the gift that counts.' This means that the gift is a sign or symbol that the gift giver has remembered you. When we evaluate a gift, we may consider the following: Was the gift presented with a flourish? Was it wrapped in special paper? Was it obviously a 're-gift': something the gift giver got as a gift for himself but wanted to pass on to me? These dimensions are a part of the total gift you receive in addition to the actual goodie sitting in the box.

Like a gift, a product is everything that a customer receives in an exchange. As Figure 7.1 shows, we can distinguish among three distinct layers of the product – the core product, the actual product and the augmented product. In developing product strategies, marketers need to consider how to satisfy customers' wants and needs at each of these three layers. Let's consider each layer in turn.

The Core Product

The **core product** consists of all the benefits the product will provide for consumers or business customers. As we noted in Chapter 1, a benefit is an outcome that the customer receives from owning or using a product. Wise old marketers (and some young ones, too) will tell you, 'A marketer may make and sell a half-inch drill bit, but a customer buys a half-inch hole.' This timeworn saying tells us that people are buying the core product, in this case the ability to make a hole. If a new product such as a laser comes along that provides that outcome in a better way or more cheaply, the drill bit maker has a problem. The moral of this story? Marketing is about supplying benefits, not features. Table 7.1 shows how some marketers rigorously test their products 'in action' to be sure they deliver the benefits they promise.

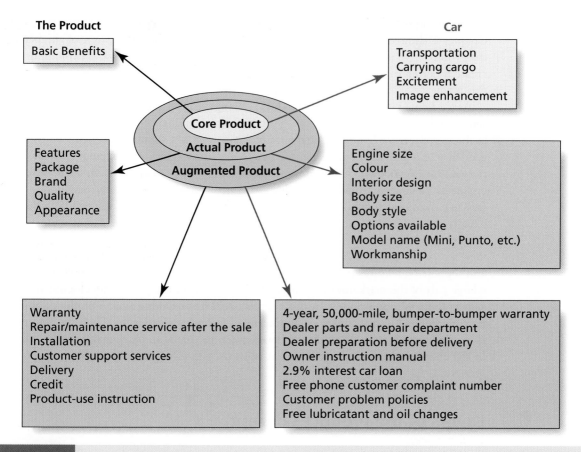

Figure 7.1	**Layers of the Product**
	A product is everything a customer receives – the basic benefits, the physical product and its packaging, and the 'extras' that come with the product.

Many products actually provide several benefits. For example, the primary benefit of a car is transportation – all cars (in good repair) provide the ability to travel from point A to point B. But products also provide customised benefits – benefits customers receive because manufacturers have added additional features to win over customers. Different drivers seek different customised benefits in a car. Some want economical transportation; others want a top-of-the-line, all-terrain vehicle; and still others look for a hot car that will be the envy of their friends.

The Actual Product

The second layer of the product, the actual product, is the physical good or the delivered service that supplies the desired benefit. For example, when you buy a washing machine, the core product is the ability to get clothes clean, but the actual product is a large, square, metal apparatus. When you have a medical examination, the core product is maintaining your health, but the actual product is a lot of annoying poking and prodding. The actual product also includes the unique features of the product, such as its appearance or styling, the package and the brand name. Canon makes a wide range of different cameras from inexpensive, disposable cameras to expensive digital models that do everything but take the photo for you – all offering the same core benefit of recording a person or event on film or in a digital format.

Table 7.1
Product Testing

Product	Testing Procedure	Benefit
Ikea furniture	Ikea puts its products through three years of 'everyday home use' in one week, such as opening and closing the doors of a closet. Only if the product passes this test does it go on the market.	Furniture which can survive in turbulent everyday family life and does not collapse after one week.
Motorola mobile phones	The phones are exposed to a large variety of tests, such as environmental stress tests, electromagnetic compatibility and reliability tests.	A high quality product which can meet the technological and safety requirements of the consumer.
Mercedes A-Class	The car had to pass the so-called 'Elk-test', which examined the stability of the car when it drives into a sharp curve at high speed. This simulated a situation in which an elk runs into the road and the car has to avoid it – a scenario which can be common in Scandinavia. For quite some time the car failed this test and kept falling over in the curve, to the amusement of the press and competitors.	Thanks to this product testing procedure, the company was able to correct mistakes made in the planning process and improve the product.

Source: www.motorola.com/testservices/; www.welt.de/motor/article1280688/Mercedes_und_der_Elch_Die_perfekte_Blamage.html

The Augmented Product

Finally, marketers offer customers an **augmented product** – the actual product plus other supporting features such as a warranty, credit, delivery, installation and repair service after the sale. Marketers know that adding these supporting features to a product is an effective way for a company to stand out from the crowd.

For example, Tesco DVD Rental provides rental of DVDs (the actual product) to customers who want access to films (the core product). Tesco successfully competes with video/DVD rental shops by letting customers rent an unlimited number of DVDs, with three titles out at a time, for a small monthly subscription. Unlike renting from a video shop, customers can keep the movies for as long as they want with no late fees, no contracts and you can cancel at anytime. Customers pay no delivery fees in either direction, and they can choose from 56,000 titles – a much more extensive collection than what the largest DVD rental shops can offer. Tesco DVD Rental also offers a movie recommendation service based on each customer's rating of previous discs. Tesco DVD Rental's augmented product (free shipping, no time limits, extensive selection and targeted recommendation) has paid off for the company.

A different example is that membership in a Virgin Active Health Club provides access to pieces of sports equipment and gym classes (the actual product) for customers who want to keep in good shape (the core product). However, as customers purchase the gym membership they also benefit from several additional and supporting features. Those include, for example, a free personal trainer session, the 'V-Club' where children are looked after while their parents exercise, free internet access and a large spa area. The company hopes that this augmented product offer will make customers feel especially well treated and more comfortable at the Health Club and that they will return the favour with loyalty and good word-of-mouth promotion.[2]

Classifying Products

Objective

2

Describe the classifications of products

So far, we've learned that a product may be a tangible good or an intangible service or idea and that there are different layers to the product. Now we'll build on that idea by looking at how products differ from one another. Marketers classify products into categories because the categories represent differences in how consumers and business customers feel about products and how they purchase them. Such an understanding helps marketers develop new products and a marketing mix that satisfies customer needs. Table 7.2 summarises these categories.

Generally, products are either consumer products or business-to-business products, although sometimes consumers and businesses buy the same products, such as toilet paper, vacuum cleaners

Table 7.2
Classification of Products

Marketers classify products to help understand how consumers make purchase decisions.
Consumer Products

Classified by how long they last
 Durable: products that provide a benefit over a long period
 • Example: Refrigerator
 	
 Nondurable: products that provide a benefit over a short time
 • Example: Toothpaste
 	
 Classified by how consumers buy them
 Convenience Products: products that are frequently purchased with little effort
 • Examples: Staples (milk)
            Impulse products (chocolate bars)
            Emergency products (drain cleaner)
 	
 Shopping Products: products that are selected with considerable time and effort
 • Examples: Attribute-based (shoes)
            Price-based (drain cleaner)
 	
 Speciality Products: products that have unique characteristics to the buyer
 • Examples: Favourite restaurant, Rolex watch
 	
 Unsought Products: products that consumers have little interest in until need arises
 • Example: Retirement plans

Business-to-Business Products

Classified by how organisational customers use them
 Equipment
 • Examples: Capital equipment (buildings)
            Accessory equipment (computer terminals)
 	
 Maintenance, Repair and Operating (MRO) Products
 • Examples: Maintenance products (lightbulbs, mops)
            Repair products (nuts, bolts)
            Operating supplies (paper, oil)
 	
 Raw Materials
 • Example: Iron ore
 	
 Processed Materials
 • Example: Sheets of steel
 	
 Specialised Services
 • Example: Legal services
 	
 Component Parts
 • Example: Car water pump

and light bulbs. In these cases, though, businesses tend to buy a lot more of them at once. Of course, as we saw in Chapters 4 and 5, customers differ in how they make the purchase decision depending on whether the decision maker is a consumer or a business purchaser. Let's first consider differences in consumer products based on how long the product will last and on how the consumer shops for the product. Then we will discuss the general types of business-to-business products.

Classifying Goods: How Long does the Product Last?

Marketers classify consumer goods as durable or non-durable depending on how long the product lasts. You expect a refrigerator to last many years, but a pint of milk will last only a week or so until it turns into a science project. **Durable goods** are consumer products that provide benefits over a period of months, years, or even decades, such as cars, furniture and appliances. In contrast, **non-durable goods**, such as newspapers and food, are consumed in the short term.

We are more likely to purchase durable goods under conditions of high involvement (as we saw in Chapter 4), while non-durable goods are more likely to be low-involvement decisions. When consumers buy a computer or a house, they will spend a lot of time and energy on the decision process. When they offer these products, marketers need to understand consumers' desires for different product benefits and the importance of warranties, service and customer support. So they must be sure that consumers can find the information they need. One way to do this is by providing a 'Frequently Asked Questions (FAQ)' section on a company website. Another way is to host a message board or blog to facilitate a sense of community around the product. When a company itself sponsors such forums, odds are the content will be much more favourable and the firm can police peripheral postings. For example, the section of the Microsoft website called 'Microsoft Technical Communities' allows users to solve problems by typing in any product (or even an error code that popped up on your computer) and then to track through a discussion board on that issue.[3]

In contrast, consumers usually don't consider the details so much when choosing among non-durable goods where there is little if any search for information or deliberation. Sometimes this means that consumers buy whatever brand is available and reasonably priced. In other instances, they base their decisions largely on past experience. Because a certain brand has performed satisfactorily in the past, customers see no reason to consider other brands and they choose the same one out of habit. For example, some consumers buy the box of Persil laundry detergent with that familiar red logotype again and again. In such cases, marketers can probably be less concerned with developing new product features to attract customers; they should focus more on pricing and distribution strategies.

Classifying Goods: How do Consumers Buy the Product?

Marketers also classify products based on where and how consumers buy the product. We can think of both goods and services as convenience products, shopping products, speciality products or unsought products. Recall that, in Chapter 4, we talked about how consumer decisions differ in terms of effort from habitual decision making to limited problem solving to extended problem solving. We can tie this classification of products in terms of how consumers buy them to these differences in consumer decision making. By understanding how consumers buy products, marketers have a clearer vision of the buying process that will help them to develop effective marketing strategies based upon the category into which their product falls.

A **convenience product** typically is a non-durable good or service that consumers purchase frequently with a minimum of comparison and effort, e.g. milk. As the name implies, consumers expect these products to be handy and they will buy whatever brands are easy to obtain. In general, convenience products are low priced and widely available. You can buy a litre of milk or a loaf of bread at grocery shops, at corner shops and even at many petrol stations. Consumers generally know all they need or want to know about a convenience product, devote little effort to purchases and willingly accept other brands if their preferred brand is not available in a convenient location. Most convenience product purchases are the results of habitual consumer decision making. What's the most important thing for marketers of convenience products? Unsurprisingly, it's to make sure the product is easily obtainable in all the places where consumers are likely to look for it.

But all convenience product purchases aren't alike. You may stop by a local shop on your way home from university or work to pick up that carton of milk because milk is something you always keep in the refrigerator. As long as you're there, why not grab a chocolate bar for the drive home? Later that night, you dash out to buy something to unblock your kitchen drain – also a convenience product. Marketers classify convenience products as staples, impulse products and emergency products.

Staples such as milk, bread and petrol are basic or necessary items that are available almost everywhere. Most consumers don't perceive big differences among brands. When selling staples, marketers must offer customers a product that consistently meets their expectations for quality and make sure it is available at a price comparable to the competition's prices.

Consider this situation: You are standing in the checkout queue at the supermarket and notice a copy of *Hello!* magazine featuring a photo of Victoria Beckham with a provocative headline. You've got to check out that article! This magazine is an **impulse product** – something people often buy on the spur of the moment. With an impulse product, marketers have two challenges: to create a product or package design that is enticing, that 'reaches out and grabs the customer', and to make sure their product is highly visible, for example by securing prime end-aisle or checkout-till space.

Emergency products are those products we purchase when we're in dire need. Bandages, umbrellas and something to unblock the bathroom sink are examples of emergency products. Because we need the product badly and immediately, price and sometimes product quality may be irrelevant to our decision to purchase. If you're caught out in a sudden downpour, any umbrella at almost any price may do.

What are the challenges to marketers of emergency products? As with any other product, emergency products are most successful when they meet customer needs – you won't sell a drain cleaner that doesn't unblock a drain more than once. And emergency products need to be offered in the sises customers want. If you cut your finger during a night out on the town you don't want to buy a box of 100 bandages – you want a box of 5 or 10. Of course, making emergency products available when and where an emergency is likely to occur is the real key to success.

In contrast to convenience products, **shopping products** are goods or services for which consumers will spend time and effort gathering information on price, product attributes and product quality. They are likely to compare alternatives before making a purchase. The purchase of shopping products is typically a limited problem-solving decision. Often consumers have little prior knowledge about these products. Because they gather new information for each purchase occasion, consumers are only moderately brand loyal and will switch whenever a different brand offers new or better benefits. They may visit several shops and devote considerable effort to comparing products.

Laptop computers are a good example of a shopping product because they offer an ever-expanding array of new features and functions. There are tradeoffs and decisions to make about the price, speed, screen size, weight and battery life. Consumers may ask, 'Does it have an internal DVD drive to play my movies?', 'How much does it weigh?', 'How long is the battery life?', 'Does it have built-in wireless networking?' or 'Does it have enough memory to drive my game?'[4] Designing successful shopping products means making sure they have the attributes that customers want. And it helps to design product packaging that points out those features consumers need to know about to make the right decisions.

Thinnovation.

The world's thinnest notebook. 13.3" widescreen display. Full-sized keyboard. ⍟ **MacBook** Air

Call 0800 048 0408 or visit www.apple.com/uk/macbookair for more information. © 2008 Apple Inc. All rights reserved. MacBook Air is a TM of Apple Inc.

| Photo 7.1 | Consumers will spend time and effort comparing shopping products. This MacBook Air advert focuses on its unique benefits – its size and weight – to inform the consumer's decision-making process. Source: The Advertising Archives |

Some shopping products have special characteristics. When people shop for *attribute-based shopping products*, such as a new party dress or a pair of designer jeans, they spend time and energy finding the best possible product selection. At other times, when choices available in the marketplace are just about the same, we consider these to be shopping products because of differences in price. For these *price-based shopping products*, such as a new lawnmower, determined shoppers will visit numerous shops in hopes of saving an additional €10 or €20.

In business-to-consumer e-commerce, shopping is easier when consumers use '**shopbots**' or 'intelligent agents': computer programs that find sites selling a particular product. Some of these programs also provide information on competitors' prices, and they may even ask customers to rate the various e-businesses that they have listed on their site so consumers can learn from other shoppers which sellers are good and which are less than desirable. It should be noted, however, that some sites do not wish to compete on price and don't give bots access to their listings.

Consumers can buy a mop in any supermarket for well under £10, right? Yet the demand for high-tech cleaning robots like the Kärcher RC3000 RoboCleaner is steadily increasing. The RoboCleaner promises 'cleaning at the touch of a button' as it sweeps and vacuums the floor all by itself. The only thing the consumer still needs to do is to switch it on. However, Kärcher charges a hefty price of around €1500 (about £1000) for this little knee and back saver.[5]

The RoboCleaner is a good example of a **speciality product**, as are Rolex watches. Speciality products have unique characteristics that are important to buyers at any price. We can even find speciality products competing in such mundane product categories as drinking water: Voss water has sleek packaging that makes it stand out from other bottled waters. Extracted from an aquifer that was buried under snow and ice for centuries in Norway, Voss markets its water as the purest in the world (for €10 or more a bottle in chic restaurants).

Consumers usually know a good deal about speciality products, and they tend to be loyal to specific brands. Generally, a speciality product is an extended problem-solving purchase that requires a lot of effort to choose. That means that firms selling these kinds of products need to create marketing strategies that make their product stand out from the rest. For example, advertising for a speciality product such as a flat-screen plasma TV may talk about plasma's unique and superior characteristics, attempting to convince prospective customers that savvy shoppers won't accept a substitute such as a mere LCD screen.

Unsought products are goods or services (other than convenience products) for which a consumer has little awareness or interest until a need arises. For university graduates with their first 'real' jobs, retirement plans and disability insurance are unsought products. It requires a good deal of advertising or personal selling to interest people in these kinds of products – just ask any life insurance salesperson. It's a real challenge to find convincing ways to interest consumers in unsought products. One solution may be to make pricing more attractive; for example, reluctant consumers may be more willing to buy an unsought product for 'only pennies a day' than if they have to think about their yearly or lifetime cash outlay.

Business-To-Business Products

Although consumers purchase products for their own use, as we saw in Chapter 5, organisational customers purchase items to use in the production of other goods and services or to facilitate the organisation's operation. Marketers classify business-to-business products based on how organisational customers use them. As with consumer products, when marketers know how their business customers use a product, they are better able to design products and craft the entire marketing mix. Let's briefly review the five different types of business-to-business products.

Equipment

Equipment refers to the products an organisation uses in its daily operations. Heavy equipment, sometimes called installations or capital equipment, includes items such as buildings and robotics used to assemble cars. Installations are expensive items and last for a number of years. Computers, photocopy machines and water fountains are examples of light or accessory equipment; they are portable, cost less, and have a shorter life span than capital equipment. Equipment marketing strategies usually emphasise personal selling and may mean custom-designing products to meet an industrial customer's specific needs.

MRO Products

Maintenance, repair and operating (MRO) products are goods that a business customer consumes in a relatively short time. Maintenance products include light bulbs, mops, cleaning supplies and the like. Repair products are such items as nuts, bolts, washers and small tools. Operating supplies include computer paper and oil to keep machinery running smoothly. Although some firms use a sales force to promote MRO products, others rely on catalogue sales, the internet and telemarketing to keep prices as low as possible.

Raw Materials

Raw materials are products of the fishing, lumber, agricultural and mining industries that organisational customers purchase to use in their finished products. For example, a food company may transform soya beans into tofu, and a steel manufacturer changes iron ore into large sheets of steel used by other firms to build cars, washing machines and lawnmowers.

Processed Materials and Special Services

Processed materials are produced when firms transform raw materials from their original state. Organisations purchase processed materials that become a part of the products they make. A builder uses treated timber to add a deck to a house, and a company that creates aluminium cans for Red Bull buys aluminium ingots for this purpose.

Some business customers purchase specialised services from outside suppliers. Specialised services may be technical, such as equipment repair, or non-technical, such as market research and legal services. These services are essential to the operation of an organisation but are not part of the production of a product.

Component Parts

Component parts are manufactured goods or subassemblies of finished items that organisations need to complete their own products. For example, a computer manufacturer needs silicon chips to make a computer, and a car manufacturer needs batteries, tyres and fuel injectors.

As with processed materials, marketing strategies for component parts usually involve nurturing relationships with customer firms and on-time delivery of a product that meets the buyer's specifications.

To review, we now understand what a product is. We also know how marketers classify consumer products based on how long they last and how they are purchased, and we've seen how they classify business-to-business products according to how they are used. In the next section we'll learn about the marketing of new products, or innovations.

Real People, Other Voices

Advice for Ben Tisdall

Matthew Wood,
University of Brighton

Option 2 is the weakest. The large size of the group and the suggested destinations and activities may create a downmarket image connected with stag parties and 'lager louts' abroad. The concept seems vague and would result in customer confusion: what exactly is on offer here – speed dating, city break or traditional British 'booze-up' abroad?

Option 3 has much more focus with a more clearly identified offer: an activity holiday for singles in good locations. The price is relatively high but would reinforce the more upmarket quality positioning. The market could be segmented according to interest and activity, opening up wider sales opportunities.

Option 1 has many strengths. There is a clear theme connected with a specific, attractive activity: skiing. Skiing is a very popular search term when consumers book holidays online and the resorts would offer suitable venues and social activities to meet other people.

Overall, options 1 and 3 both have potential. Option 1 has the clearest positioning and is an attractive proposition at that price. However, the skiing market is limited in terms of consumer demand and by seasonality. Option 3 is less clear but benefits from greater potential market and sales opportunities.

Zubin Sethna,
University of Westminster

I would choose Option 3.

The very essence of speed dating is relationships!

However, in order to develop strong relationships (that are going to last for more than one night!), the company and the participants require an understanding that the 'face-to-face' contact needs to be more substantial than the 'quick-and-dirty' contact that 'traditional' speed dating offers. There should also be a case for nurturing the relationship 'organically' rather than the 'genetic modification' that, again, one sees in traditional speed dating. People need time to understand each other and then decide on who they like and/or dislike. Therefore the idea of purposely dumbing down the speed dating elements should be appealing to a wider segment of the target market.

Although the prime disadvantage is one of cost (both for the company and the individual), one could make the assumption that if an individual invests more time and money in the planning and consumption of their holiday, they are far more likely to take it seriously, as opposed to the £300 price tag for what is, essentially, still a speed dating event, albeit abroad!

Toby Wade,
a student at the University of York

I would advise Ben to choose option 3. Option 3 opens up the singles experience to a much wider variety of clientèle than either of option 1 or 2 whilst not being dependent on weather conditions.

For the customer option 3 provides a much less intimidating scenario as there is no forced 'speed dating' aspect to the experience within the predetermined environment. Option 3 also provides the customer with a wider variety of activities and is still centred around the prospect of meeting other singles. Furthermore, although the customer would need to book further in advance this holiday would also be able to address different needs and any changes in circumstances that may arise during the booking period. This is an excellent marketing prospect.

For the company, option 3 is financially more viable as it will provide an increased cash flow based on a longer period of time. It it accepted that the bookings would need to be taken further in advance but this leaves more space for flexibility and the option to secure unique locations at better prices. Promotions and publicity will be able to be developed more thoroughly and through customer feedback Speed Breakes will be able to modify its current business model to increase overall sales and bookings year round.

'New and Improved!' The Process of Innovation

www.pearsoned.co.uk/solomon

Objective

3

Understand the importance of new products

'New and improved!' What exactly do we mean when we use the term *new product*? One interpretation is that a product must be entirely new or changed significantly to be called new and that a product may be called new for only six months.

That definition is fine from a legal perspective, but from a marketing standpoint, a new product or an **innovation** is anything that customers perceive as new and different. Innovations may be a cutting-edge style like the Motorola RAZR cellphone, a fad like Razor scooters, or a new personal care product like the Gillette Fusion razor (starting to see a pattern here?). It can also be a new communications technology such as Skype person-to-person telephony over the internet, or a new way to power a vehicle such as the Toyota Prius hybrid, which addresses consumer demand shifts driven by high petrol prices. An innovation may be a completely new product that provides benefits which were never available before, such as personal computers when they were first introduced, or it may simply be an existing product with a new style, in a different colour, or with some new feature like Kellogg's Special K Red Berries.

It's Important to Understand How Innovations Work

If an innovation is successful, it spreads throughout the population. First, it is bought and used by only a few people, and then more and more consumers adopt it. Or (more typically) an innovation can be a flop and it may not be around a year from now.

Understanding the process by which innovations succeed (or not) is critical to the success of firms for at least two reasons. First, technology is advancing at a dizzying pace. Products are introduced and become obsolete faster than ever before. In many industries, firms are busy developing another new-and-better product before the last new-and-better one even hits shop shelves. Nowhere is this more obvious than with personal computers, for which a steady change in technology makes consumers want a smaller, slimmer, faster machine before the dust even settles on the old one. Another reason why understanding new products is important is the high cost of developing new products and the even higher cost of new products that fail. In the pharmaceutical industry, the cost of bringing each new drug to market is over €4.5 billion.[6] Even the most successful firms can't afford many product failures with that kind of price tag.

Marketers must understand what it takes to develop a new product successfully. They must do their homework and learn what it is about existing products consumers find less than satisfactory and exactly what it will take to do a better job satisfying customer needs. Savvy marketers know they'll waste a lot of investment money if they don't.

Finally, new products contribute to society. We would never suggest that everything new is good, but many new products like those Table 7.3 lists allow us to live longer, happier lives of better quality than ever before. Although there are some who disagree, most of us feel that our lives are better because of mobile phones (if that person blabbing on his next to us would shut up . . .), televisions, PDAs, iPods, microwave ovens and laptop computers. And new medical products keep *us* from breaking down: in the near future, doctors will be able to replace or assist almost every part of the body with bionic products such as replacement spinal discs, insulin pumps that mimic a natural pancreas in diabetes patients by automatically testing blood-glucose levels, microdetectors

Table 7.3
Some innovations
since 1990

Products that have changed how we play	
1900	Kodak Brownie camera
1948	Polaroid camera
1970	Digital music
1976	JVC video recorder
1982	Philips/Sony CD player
1995	DVD player
1998	MP3 players

Products that have changed how we work	
1959	Xerox photocopier
1967	ATMs
1971	Intel microprocessor
1980	3M Post-it Notes
1984	Apple Macintosh
1996	Universal Serial Bus
1998	BlackBerry PDA

Products that have changed how we travel	
1908	Ford Model T
1936	DC-3
1949	de Havilland Comet
1950s	Skateboard
1993	Ryanair
2000	Global Positioning Systems (GPS)
2003	Toyota Prius hybrid car

Products that have changed our health and grooming	
1921	Johnson & Johnson Band-Aid
1928	Penicillin
1931	Tampax tampon
1960	Searle birth control pill
2003	Crest Whitestrips

Products that have changed our homes	
1907	Vacuum cleaner
1918	Frigidaire refrigerator
1955	TV remote
1967	Amana microwave oven
2003	TMIO internet-accessible refrigerated oven

Products that have changed the way we communicate	
1922	British Broadcasting Corporation formed
1936	BBC's first regular TV broadcasts
1991	World Wide web
2003	Treo cell phone/PDA/camera
2004	Web 2.0

Products that have changed our clothing	
1913	Zipper
1914	Bra
1939	Nylons
1954	Velcro
1961	Procter & Gamble Pampers

Sources: Adapted from Christine Chen and Tim Carvell, 'Products of the Century,' *Fortune*, 22 November 1999, 133–36; 'Best of What's Next,' *Popular Science*, 13 November 2003; http://inventors.about.com/library/inventors/bldvd.htm; www.time.com/time/2003/inventions/list.html; Thomas Hoffman, 'Segway's Tech Plans Look Down the Road to Growth,' *Computer World*, 26 January 2004, 4; Louis E. Frenzel, 'The BlackBerry Reaps the Fruits of Innovation,' *Electronic Design*, 29 March 2004, 41(5); David Stires, 'Rx for Investors,' *Fortune*, 3 May 2004, 158; and 'Procter & Gamble,' *Drug Store News*, 19 January 2004, 57; www.bbc.co.uk/heritage; www.tnenewsis.com/2006/11/02/10-inventions-that-changed-our-lives.

implanted into retinas allowing patients with retinal damage to see light, and bionic ears that allow the deaf to hear.[7]

 ## Types of Innovations

Innovations differ in their degree of newness, and this helps to determine how quickly the target market will adopt them. Because innovations that are more novel require us to exert greater effort to figure out how to use them, they are slower to spread throughout a population than new products that are similar to what is already available.

Marketers classify innovations into three categories based on their degree of novelty: continuous innovations, dynamically continuous innovations and discontinuous innovations. However, it is better to think of these three types as ranges along a continuum that goes from a very small change in an existing product to a totally new product. We can then describe the three types of innovations in terms of the amount of disruption or change they bring to people's lives. For example, the first cars caused tremendous changes in the lives of people who were used to getting to places under 'horse power'. While a more recent innovation like GPS systems that feed us driving directions by satellite are undoubtedly cool, in a relative sense we have to make fewer changes in our lives to adapt to them (other than not having to ask a stranger for directions when you're lost).

Continuous Innovations

A **continuous innovation** is a modification to an existing product, such as when Kellogg's introduced Special K Bliss Strawberry and Chocolate versions of its cereal. This type of modification can set one brand apart from its competitors. For example, Volvo cars are known for their safety, and Volvo comes out with a steady stream of safety-related innovations. Volvo was the first car to offer full front and side air bags, and its models come with an extensive menu of air bags, including Inflatable Curtain head-protection air bags for front and rear passengers, torso side air bags for front passengers, and the usual dual-stage front air bags. Additional crash protection for the Volvo V40 comes from whiplash-reducing front seats and seatbelt pretensioners.[8]

The consumer doesn't have to learn anything new to use a continuous innovation. From a marketing perspective, this means that it's usually pretty easy to convince consumers to adopt this kind of new product. For example, Samsung's high-definition plasma flat-screen monitors don't require computer users to change their behaviour. We all know what a computer monitor is and how it works. The system's continuous innovation simply gives users the added benefits of taking up less space and being easier on the eyes.

How different does a new product have to be from existing products before people think it's *too* different? We've all heard that 'imitation is the sincerest form of flattery', but decisions regarding how much (if at all) one's product should resemble those of competitors often are a centrepiece of marketing strategy. Sometimes marketers feel that the best strategy is to follow the competition. For example, the packaging of 'me-too' or lookalike products can create instant market success because consumers assume that similar packaging means similar products.

A **copycat** is a new product that copies, with slight modification, the design of an original product. Firms deliberately create copycats of clothing, jewellery or other items, often with the intent to sell to a larger or different market. For example, companies may copy the *haute couture* clothing styles of top designers and sell them at lower prices to the mass market. It is difficult to legally protect a design (as opposed to a technological invention) because an imitator can argue that even a very slight change – different buttons or a slightly wider collar on a dress or shirt – means the copycat product is not an exact copy.

Dynamically Continuous Innovations

A **dynamically continuous innovation** is a pronounced modification to an existing product that requires a modest amount of learning or change in behaviour to use it. The history of audio equipment is a series of dynamically continuous innovations. For many years, consumers enjoyed listening to their favourite Frank Sinatra songs on record players. Then in the 1960s, that same music became available on a continuous-play eight-track tape (requiring the purchase of an eight-track tape player, of course). Then came cassette tapes (oops, now a cassette

Photo 7.2	The Toyota Prius is an example of a dynamically continuous innovation. Source: Advertising Archives

player is needed). In the 1980s, consumers could hear Metallica songs digitally mastered on compact discs (that, of course, required the purchase of a new CD player).

In the 1990s, recording technology moved one more step forward with MP3 technology, allowing music fans to download music from the web or to exchange electronic copies of the music with other fans. Mobile MP3 players hit the scene in 1998, letting music fans download their favourite tunes into a portable player. In November 2001, Apple Computer introduced its first iPod. With the original iPod, music fans could take 1000 songs with them wherever they went. By 2006, iPods could hold 15,000 songs, 25,000 photos and 150 hours of video and now it's integrated into the iPhone.[9] Music fans go to the Apple iTunes music shop or elsewhere to download songs and to get suggestions for new music they might enjoy. Even though each of these changes required learning how to operate new equipment, consumers were willing to buy the new products because of the improvements in music reproduction, the core product benefit. Hopefully the music will continue to improve, too.

Convergence is one of the most talked-about forms of dynamically continuous innovations in the digital world. This term means the coming together of two or more technologies to create new systems that provide greater benefit than the original technologies alone. Think about the NeoReader Qode technology we discussed in Chapter 2 that combines mobile phones, cameras and web browsers in a unique way. Similarly, the phone, organiser and camera all come together in the Palm Treo. The Treo 700P Smartphone seamlessly combines a full-feature mobile phone with wireless email and text messaging, web browsing and digital camera into a pocket-sized, totally integrated device that includes a full QWERTY keyboard.[10]

Discontinuous Innovations

A **discontinuous innovation** creates major changes in the way we live. To use a discontinuous innovation, consumers must engage in a great amount of learning because no similar product has ever been on the market. Major inventions such as the airplane, the car and the television have radically changed modern lifestyles. Another discontinuous innovation, the personal computer, changed the way we shop and allowed more people to work from home or anywhere else. What's the next discontinuous innovation? Is there a product out there already that will gain that distinction? Usually, marketers only know for sure through 20-20 hindsight; in other words, it's tough to plan for the next big one (what the software industry calls 'the killer application').

Understanding the degree of newness of innovations helps marketers develop effective marketing strategies. For example, if marketers know that consumers may resist adopting a new and radically different product, they may offer a free product trial or place heavier emphasis on a personal selling strategy to convince consumers that the new product offers benefits worth the hassle. When Apple introduced its Macintosh computers (you've seen those in museums!), the company allowed bewildered customers to take them home and use them for a month for free to see their benefits first-hand. Business-to-business marketers often provide in-service training for employees of their customers who invest in new products.

Across the Hall

Advice for Ben Tisdall

Colin Mason

is Professor of Entrepreneurship in the Hunter Centre for Entrepreneurship, University of Strathclyde

All three options are interesting ways of stretching the brand. I am least convinced by option 3. With this option he is breaking the link with the speed dating concept and risks becoming just 'another holiday company'. In which case, has he any advantages over his competitors in running a travel company? Take away the speed dating concept and what is distinctive? Would there be any synergy between SpeedDater and the new travel company? My inclination would be to go for a combination of options 1 and 2 – retain the common activity theme of option 1 but go for a revised version of option 2 whereby the city breaks packages would be focused on specific themes or activities (e.g. opera, museums, theatre, sporting events) so that it attracts people who share the same interests.

Developing New Products

www.pearsoned.co.uk/Solomon

Objective

4

Show how firms develop new products

Building on our knowledge of different types of innovations, we'll now turn our attention to how firms go about developing new products. Product development doesn't simply mean creating totally new products never before on the market. Of course, a lot of companies do that, but for many other firms product development is a continuous process of looking for ways to make an existing product better or finding just the right width of leg for this year's new jean styles. No product category is immune to this process – even a 'boring' product like a toilet is constantly being improved by enterprising companies. Consider, for example, the Neorest toilet the Japanese firm Toto introduced in the EU. For a 'mere' €3000 you get a toilet that solves that age-old problem of toilet seat up versus toilet seat down. Motion sensors automatically open the lid as you approach and close it as you leave. It also has a heated seat, a temperature-controlled water spray and blow dryer, a catalytic air deodoriser, and even a 'white noise' control to mask sounds.[11]

The popular UK TV show *Dragons' Den* illustrates the lengths people and companies will go to come up with 'the next big thing' – whether screwy or sensible. Entrepreneurs with fresh and innovative ideas can pitch their business plans to five top British venture capitalists. After having been grilled by the 'five dragons', and after having shown that their idea has great potential, they hope to convince the venture capitalists to make an investment. Not only is this process quite entertaining for the TV viewers, it is also very important that young entrepreneurs have an opportunity to raise funding and turn their business concepts into reality. Without new business ideas and people who are willing to invest in them, new product development would be much more difficult and the whole business environment would slow down. For several reasons, new product development is increasingly important to firms. First, as we've already mentioned, technology is changing at an ever-increasing rate so that companies develop products, consumers adopt them, and then companies replace them with better products faster and faster. In addition, competition in our global marketplace makes it essential for firms to continuously offer new choices for consumers if they are to compete with companies all around the world rather than just down the street. Firms need to stay on top of current developments in popular culture, religion and politics to develop products that are consistent with consumers' mind-sets. Sometimes new hit products are based on careful research, but in many cases being in the right place at the right time doesn't hurt. For example Aston Martin experienced a big wave of customer recognition after the

Table 7.4
Phases in New-
Product
Development

Phases in Development	Outcome
1. Idea generation	Identify product ideas that will provide important customer benefits compatible with company mission.
2. Product concept development and screening	Expand product ideas into more complete product concepts and estimate the potential commercial success of product concepts.
3. Marketing strategy, development	Develop preliminary plan for target markets, pricing, distribution and promotion.
4. Business analysis	Estimate potential for profit. What is the potential demand, what expenditures will be required, and what is the cost of marketing the product?
5. Technical development	Design the product and the manufacturing-and-production process.
6. Test marketing	Develop evidence of potential success in the real market.
7. Commercialisation	Implement full-scale marketing plan.

James Bond films *Casino Royale* and *Quantum of Solace* hit the screens. The 'Bond factor' even helped Aston Martin to the top of the 'list of the UK's coolest brands'.[12]

Unfortunately, most new product introductions need a bit more than good timing to score big in the marketplace. If anything, it's becoming more and more difficult to successfully introduce new products. The costs of research and development are often so huge that firms must limit the number of new products in development. Because products are outdated faster than ever, firms have less time to recover their research-and-development costs. With so many products competing for limited shelf space, retailers often charge manufacturers exorbitant 'slotting' fees to stock a new product, increasing manufacturers' costs even more.[13] Firms must reduce the time it takes to get good products to market and increase the speed of adoption to recover these costs quickly. As Table 7.4 shows, new product development generally occurs in seven phases.

 ## Phase 1: Idea Generation

In the initial *idea generation* phase of product development, marketers use a variety of sources to come up with great new product ideas that provide customer benefits and that are compatible with the company mission. Sometimes ideas come from customers. Ideas also come from salespeople, service providers and others who have direct customer contact. And some companies encourage their designers to 'think outside the box' by exposing them to new ideas, people and places. When Lego decided to revitalise its Mindstorms programmable robotics kit, the Danish company recruited a panel of outside experts who were well known among Lego fans (and fanatics) for creating complex robots using the firm's 2001 version of the kit. These outsiders worked intensively with Lego's in-house design team for a year to create the next generation of Lego robotics and software (Mindstorms NXT) that includes drag-and-drop icons, sophisticated sound sensors and motors to allow the robots to roam free. It's worth noting that these self-proclaimed 'geeks' did all of this work without pay other than being given some Mindstorms prototypes. As one of the panellists observed, 'They're going to talk to us about Legos, and they're going to pay us with Legos? They actually want our opinion? It doesn't get much better than that.'[14] Now *that's* dedication! Often firms use marketing research activities such as the focus groups we discussed in Chapter 3 in their search for new product ideas. For example, a company such as MTV that is interested in developing new channels might hold focus group discussions across different groups of young people to get ideas for new types of programmes.

 ## Phase 2: Product Concept Development and Screening

The second phase in developing new products is product concept development and screening. Although ideas for products initially come from a variety of sources, it is up to marketers to expand these ideas into more complete product concepts. Product concepts describe what features the product should have and what benefits they will provide for consumers.

It has been said that McDonald's makes the world's best French fries – a claim that has annoyed arch-rival Burger King for decades. Unfortunately for BK, the chain achieved technical success but not commercial success when it invested heavily to out-fry McD's.[15] BK's food engineers came up with a potato stick coated with a layer of starch that makes the chip crunchier and keeps the heat in to stay fresh longer. Burger King created 19 pages of specifications for its new contender including a requirement that there must be an audible crunch present for seven or more chews. The €53 million rollout of the new product included a 'Free Fryday' when 15 million orders of fries were given away to customers free, and lavish advertising at major sporting events.

Unfortunately, the new chip was a 'whopper' of a product failure. Burger King blamed the product failure on inconsistent cooking by franchisees and a poor potato crop, but a more likely explanation is that consumers simply did not like the chips as well as those they might find at certain (golden) arch-rivals. Just because it's new doesn't always make it better.

BK's new product failure illustrates the importance of screening ideas for *both* their technical and commercial value. When screening, marketers and researchers examine the chances that a new product concept might be successful, while weeding out concepts that have little chance of making it. Estimating *technical success* means assessing whether the new product is technologically feasible – is it possible to build this product? Estimating *commercial success* means deciding whether anyone is likely to buy the product. The marketing graveyard is piled high with products that sounded interesting but that failed to catch on, including jalapeño pepper soda, aerosol mustard and edible deodorant.[16] Table 7.5 provides other examples of colossal new product failures and the ethics box describes a promotional campaign that hit the dust too.

Today, it's not just new functions that companies look for when they devise new product concepts. A product's *appearance* also plays a huge role – in a marketplace loaded with products that seem to do pretty much the same thing, people are attracted to the options that do what they need to do – but look good while doing it. Two young US entrepreneurs named Adam Lowry and Eric Ryan discovered that basic truth in the early days of 2000. They quit their day jobs to develop a line of house-cleaning products they called Method. Cleaning products – boring, right?

But, think again: For years companies like Procter & Gamble have plodded along, peddling boring boxes of soap powder to generations of housewives. Lowry and Ryan gambled that they could offer an alternative – cleaners in exotic scents like cucumber, lavender and ylang-ylang that come in aesthetically pleasing bottles. The bet paid off. Within two years the partners were cleaning up, taking in more than $2 million in revenue. Mass-market consumers are thirsting for great design, and they're rewarding those companies that give it to them with their enthusiastic patronage and loyalty, from razor blades like the Gillette Sensor to computers like Apple. To meet the demand for design, Maytag introduced lines of stylish home and kitchen equipment products such as refrigerators, (dish)washing machines and cookers. The

Table 7.5
New Products That
Bit The Dust

Product Introduced	Date	Company	Product Description	Why did the product fail?
Electrolux vacuum cleaner	1960s	Electrolux	Vacuum cleaner	Unfortunately the company translated their slogan a bit too literally and marketed their product with 'Nothing sucks like an Electrolux', which is a derogatory statement, especially in American English.
Thirsty Dog!, Thirsty Cat!	1995	Dr. George Hill Pet Drinks	Flavoured water for pets, such as with tangy beef.	Cats and dogs were highly unimpressed and preferred tap water after all.
Kellogg's Cereal Mates	1998	Kellogg's	All in one breakfast in a box, including a little packet of cereal, a small pint of milk and a plastic spoon.	In the supermarket, the product was stored in the cereal shelf. This made it easy to find the product but it also meant that consumers had to drink warm milk.
Clairol Mist Stick	2002	Clairol	Curling Iron	When introducing this product to the German market, the marketers did not know that 'Mist' in German is a slang word for manure. Not surprisingly, customers refused to have a 'manure stick' in their hair.

Source: www.bild.de/BTO/tipps-trends/geld-job/topthemen/allgemein/MARKEN/markenflops/markenflops.html;
http://findarticles.com/p/articles/mi_m3289/is_n5_v164/ai_16902133; www.sfgate.com/cgi-bin/article.cgi?file=/
chronicle/archive/2005/02/06/ING0VB42071.DTL; www.failuremag.com/arch_mcmath_kelloggs.html

product ranges not only offer convenience and smooth performance, they are also seen as *aesthetic* design pieces made out of *chic* materials such as stainless steel and glass.[17]

Even P&G is starting to get the idea. Although it's a bit like turning a battleship, Procter & Gamble now recognises the importance of integrating design into every product initiative. In the 'good old days', design was basically an afterthought. Marketing meant appealing to customers in terms of efficiency rather than aesthetics. Since 2002, Chairman-CEO A.G. Lafley has directed P&G to focus on what he calls 'the first moment of truth' – winning over consumers in the shop with packaging and displays. As a result, P&G now has a Vice President of design, strategy and innovation who sums up her philosophy as: 'Competitive advantage comes not just from patents, but also from incorporating design into products, much like Apple, Sony or Dell.'[18]

 ## Phase 3: Marketing Strategy Development

The third phase in new product development is to develop a marketing strategy to introduce the product to the marketplace. This means that marketers must identify the target market, estimate its size, and determine how the product can be positioned to address the target market's needs. And, of course, marketing strategy development includes planning for pricing, distribution and promotion expenditures both for the introduction of the new product and for the long run.

Marketing Ethics

Do kids get enough sleep for adults' liking?

It's the prize no company wants. But the victor in the Bad Products Awards 2007, organised by the US-based Consumers International (CI), certainly deserved to win. Takeda Pharmaceuticals was a worthy overall champion for its promotion of sleeping pills to children. This particular ad was released at the beginning of the school year and used images of children, black boards, school books and a school bus. The accompanying voiceover stated: 'Rozerem would like to remind you that it's back to school season. Ask your doctor today if Rozerem is right for you.' As CI said, announcing the award: 'It doesn't take PhD in marketing to see this is an effort to persuade parents to seek out the sleeping drug for their children – help them get through the stress of term starting.' It took six months before government agencies told Takeda to remove the ad. Despite the fact that Takeda is a $10 billion pharmaceutical company and had spent $118 million on advertising Rozerem, it was not fined and not penalised (Consumer International Press briefing, 2007).

New Statesman, 10 December 2007

Debate, Discuss, Disagree

1   What is your opinion about Takeda's sleeping pill promotion for children?

2   What do you think authorities should have done to handle this situation?

Phase 4: Business Analysis

Once a product concept passes the screening stage, the next phase is to conduct a *business analysis*. Even though marketers have evidence that there is a market for the product, they still must find out if the product can make a profitable contribution to the organisation's product mix. How much potential demand is there for the product? (see the Marketing Metrics box for an example). Does the firm have the resources that will be required for successful development and introduction of the product?

Larger firms typically develop new products in-house in their own laboratories, but in some cases even they prefer to scout out new ideas from entrepreneurs and just buy the technology. For example, Church and Dwight Company sell the Crest SpinBrush range of battery-powered toothbrushes. SpinBrush is a technology developed by four entrepreneurs whom Procter & Gamble then bought out (P&G then divested the product after the P&G/Gillette merger in 2005). Unlike electric toothbrushes that typically sell for upwards of €35 each, the SpinBrush sells for just slightly more than a decent old-fashioned toothbrush.[19] Another consideration in this phase may be the need to sell products more cheaply to some countries. See the Marketing Ethics box about pharmaceutical drugs.

Phase 5: Technical Development

If it survives the scrutiny of a business analysis, a new product concept then undergoes *technical development* in which a firm's engineers work with marketers in refining the design and production process. For example, when McDonald's recognised the need to bulk up its breakfast menu by adding something sweeter than its Egg McMuffin, the company's executive chef had to scramble to develop a pancake offering that could be eaten while driving. He first considered a pancake shaped like a muffin, but he decided this would be too confusing to customers – and

Marketing Ethics

Creating products to die for

It is not surprising that pharmaceutical companies' marketing plans call for heavy emphasis on new product development. These companies rely on a stream of new products to stay ahead of competitors. However, developing a new block-buster drug is expensive in R&D. To recoup the high cost of new product development these companies often charge high prices for their drugs. They do not lower the price even in countries where consumers cannot afford to pay high prices. Critics say that pharmaceutical companies have a moral obligation to subsidise drug prices in poor countries. The companies counter that they would have no incentive to develop life-saving drugs if they subsidised prices.

Debate, Discuss, Disagree

1 Should pharmaceutical companies be mandated by law to sell their products at lower prices in poor countries?

2 Discuss the pros and cons of this approach.

besides, how could he add in the all-important syrup? Fortunately, one of the company's suppliers had just developed a technology that crystallises syrup – just stir crystals into the batter and the syrup will seep through the entire pancake once it's heated. McDonald's did a lot of laboratory work to adapt this process so the syrup would melt uniformly and produce what the industry calls the correct 'mouth feel'. Enter the McGriddle, a breakfast sandwich that can be customised with combinations of sausage, bacon, egg and cheese. It's served between two 'high-tech syrup-infused' pancakes instead of bread and has become a very successful staple on the company's breakfast menu.[20]

The better a firm understands how customers will react to a new product, the better its chances of commercial success. For this reason, a company's research-and-development (R&D) department will typically develop one or more physical versions or **prototypes** of the product. Prospective customers may evaluate these mockups in focus group or in field trials at home.

Prototypes also are useful for people within the firm. Those involved in the technical development process must determine which parts of a finished good the company will make and which ones will be bought from other suppliers. If goods are to be manufactured, the company may have to buy new production equipment or modify existing machinery. Someone has to develop work instructions for employees and train them to produce the product. In developing service processes, technical development includes such decisions as which activities will occur within sight of customers and whether parts of the service can be automated to make delivery more efficient.

Technical development sometimes requires application for a patent. Because patents legally prevent competitors from producing or selling the invention, a patent may reduce or eliminate competition in a market for many years, allowing a firm 'breathing room' to recoup investments in technical development.

Phase 6: Test Marketing

The next phase of new product development includes **test marketing**. This means the firm tries out the complete marketing plan – the distribution, advertising and sales promotion – but in a small geographic area that is similar to the larger market it hopes to enter.

There are both pluses and minuses to test marketing. On the negative side, test marketing is extremely expensive. It can cost over €1 million to conduct a test market even in a single city. A test market also gives the competition a free look at the new product, its introductory price and the intended promotional strategy – and an opportunity to get to the market first with a competing product. On the positive side, by offering a new product in a limited area of the market, marketers can evaluate and improve the marketing programme. Sometimes test marketing uncovers a need to improve the product itself. At other times, test marketing indicates product failure, allowing the firm to save millions of euros by 'pulling the plug'. Remember Ben from SpeedBreaks you met at the beginning of the chapter? He's putting his three new single's holiday products out into the marketplace to test market them.

For years, Listerine manufacturer Warner-Lambert wanted to introduce a mint-flavoured version of the product to compete with Procter & Gamble's mouthwash Scope (it originally introduced this alternative under the brand Listermint). Unfortunately, every time Warner-Lambert tried to run a test market, P&G found out and poured substantial extra advertising and coupons for Scope into the cities in which the test market was conducted. This counter-attack reduced the usefulness of the test market results for Warner-Lambert when its market planners were trying to decide whether to introduce Listermint nationwide. As P&G's aggressive response to Listermint's test marketing actually *increased* Scope's market share in the test cities, there was no way to determine how well Listermint would actually do under normal competitive conditions. As a result, Warner-Lambert eventually introduced Listermint nationally, but achieved only marginal success, so the company eventually pulled it from the market.

Because of the potential problems and expense of test marketing, marketers instead may conduct simulated tests that imitate the introduction of a product into the marketplace, using special computer software as we saw in Chapter 3. These simulations allow the company to see the likely effect of price cuts and new packaging – or even to determine where in the shop the product should be placed to maximise sales. The process entails gathering basic research data on consumers' perceptions of the product concept, the physical product, the advertising and other promotional activity. The test market simulation model uses that information to predict the product's success much less expensively (and more discreetly) than a traditional test market. As this simulated test market technology improves, traditional test markets may become a thing of the past.

Phase 7: Commercialisation

The last phase in new product development is **commercialisation**. This means the launching of a new product, and it requires full-scale production, distribution, advertising and sales promotion. For this reason, commercialisation of a new product cannot happen overnight. A launch requires planning and careful preparation. Marketers must implement trade promotion plans that offer special incentives to encourage dealers, retailers or other members of the channel to stock the new product so that customers will find it on shop shelves the very first time they look. They must also develop consumer promotions such as coupons. Marketers may arrange to have point-of-purchase displays designed, built and delivered to retail outlets. If the new product is especially complex, customer service employees must receive extensive training and preparation.

As launch time nears, preparations gain a sense of urgency – like countdown to blastoff. Sales managers explain special incentive programmes to salespeople. Soon the media announce to prospective customers why they should buy and where they can find the new product. All elements of the marketing programme – ideally – come into play like a carefully planned liftoff of the space shuttle.

And there is always a huge element of risk in a new product launch – even for products that seem like a sure thing. For example, car manufacturer BMW introduced the C1 model, a small

Marketing Metrics

AC Nielsen Bases

BASES was founded in the mid-1970s as a method of forecasting sales of new products, and in the years since its inception has evaluated more than 75,000 new product ideas in more than 60 countries. Simulated Test Marketing (STM) is used to combine consumer reaction to new product ideas with marketing plan information to forecast likely sales volumes. STM has supplanted traditional in-market testing as the predominant method used by packaged goods manufacturers to evaluate new products, line extensions and other new business opportunities prior to large-scale in-market introduction. It is faster, less expensive, more secure and more accurate with regard to their forecasting capability and can answer the following questions.

- What is the volume potential for my new product?
- How will a line extension affect my overall brand franchise?
- What elements of my new initiative should be improved to increase the odds for consumer adoption?
- Who will be the core users of my new product and how can I reach them?
- How should I prioritise developing the ideas in my innovation pipeline?
- How should I price my new product?

---

motorcycle with a roof in 1992. In the eyes of the company, the motorcycle was bound to be a great success, with its emphasis on safety due to the cage roof top and a seatbelt which prevented the driver from hitting the road in case of an accident. Besides, the C1 was supposed to appeal to people who wanted to get around quickly in a crowded city. However, the consumers did not share this view and rather saw a vehicle in it which was less safe than a car, less fun to drive than a normal motorcycle and offered no real protection from rain anyway. As a result, the expected high demand failed to appear.[21]

What do you think about the C1's success or lack of it? Why do you think it didn't take of?

Objective

5

Explain the process of product adoption and the diffusion of innovations

Adoption and Diffusion

In the previous section, we talked about the steps marketers take to develop new products from generating ideas to launch. Moving on, we'll look at what happens *after* that new product hits the market – how an innovation spreads throughout a population.

A painting is not a work of art until someone views it. A song is not music until someone sings it. In the same way, new products do not satisfy customer wants and needs until the customer uses them. **Product adoption** is the process by which a consumer or business customer begins to buy and use a new good, service or idea.

The term **diffusion** describes how the use of a product spreads throughout a population. One way to understand how this process works is to think about a new product as if it was a computer virus that spreads from a few computers to infect many machines. A brand like Hush Puppies, for example, might just slog around – sometimes for years and years. It's initially bought by a small number of people, but change happens in a hurry when the process reaches the moment of critical mass. This moment of truth is called the **tipping point**. For example, Sharp created the low-price, home/small-office fax market in 1984 and sold about 80,000 in that year. There was a slow climb in the number of users for the next three years. Then, suddenly, in 1987 enough people had faxes that it made sense for everyone to have one – Sharp sold a million units that year. Along with such diffusion almost always come steep price declines – today you can buy a Sharp fax machine at Staples for less than £40.[22]

After months or even years spent developing a new product, the real challenge to firms is getting consumers to buy and use the product and to do so quickly to recover the costs of product development and launch. To accomplish this, marketers must understand the product-adoption process. In the next section, we'll discuss the stages in this process. We'll also see how consumers and businesses differ in their eagerness to adopt new products and how the characteristics of a product affect its adoption (or 'infection') rate.

Stages in Consumer Adoption of a New Product

Whether the innovation is better film technology or a better mousetrap, individuals and organisations pass through six stages in the adoption process. Figure 7.2 shows how a person goes from being unaware of an innovation through the stages of awareness, interest, evaluation, trial, adoption and confirmation. At every stage, people drop out of the process, so the proportion of consumers who wind up using the innovation on a consistent basis is a fraction of those who are exposed to it.

Awareness

Learning that the innovation exists is the first step in the adoption process. To make consumers aware of a new product, marketers may conduct a massive advertising campaign, called a **media blitz**. For example, to raise awareness of its entry into the electronic gaming product category, Microsoft launched a massive $500 million marketing campaign when it introduced the original Xbox, promoting the new product through in-store merchandising, retailer incentives, events and sponsorship in addition to traditional advertising.[23] At this point, some consumers will say, 'So there's a new gaming console out there. So what?' Many of these, of course, will fall by the wayside, out of the adoption process. But this strategy works for new products when consumers see a new product as something they want and need and just can't live without.

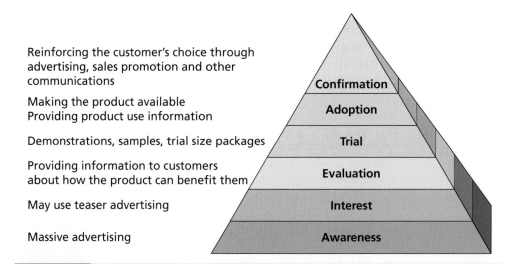

Reinforcing the customer's choice through advertising, sales promotion and other communications — **Confirmation**

Making the product available
Providing product use information — **Adoption**

Demonstrations, samples, trial size packages — **Trial**

Providing information to customers about how the product can benefit them — **Evaluation**

May use teaser advertising — **Interest**

Massive advertising — **Awareness**

Figure 7.2	Adoption Pyramid

Consumers pass through six stages in the adoption of a new product – from being unaware of an innovation to becoming loyal adopters. The right marketing strategies at each stage help ensure a successful adoption.

Interest

For some of the people who become aware of a new product, a second stage in the adoption process is *interest*. In this stage, a prospective adopter begins to see how a new product might satisfy an existing or newly realised need. Interest also means that consumers look for and are open to information about the innovation. Volkswagen's Jetta, for instance, developed a certain panache with the young 20s crowd around 2000 or so. But, as today's 20- and 30-something car buyers started having families and needing bigger cars with more carrying space, their interest in the Jetta declined. To get the lucrative young parent group interested in the product again, Volkswagen reintroduced the 2006 model with great advertising fanfare, touting seven more inches of room from front to back, 25 per cent more boot space and more safety features than the 2005 model. Ads hark back to those of another era, stressing 'German engineering' to make the car seem less frivolous and more appealing to families looking for quality and dependability.[24] Marketers often design teaser advertisements that give prospective customers just enough information about the new product to make them curious and to stimulate their interest. Despite marketers' best efforts, however, some consumers drop out of the process at this point.

Evaluation

In the *evaluation* stage, a prospect weighs the costs and benefits of the new product. On the one hand, for complex, risky, or expensive products, people think about the innovation a great deal before trying it. For example, a firm will carefully evaluate spending hundreds of thousands of euros on manufacturing robotics before purchase. Marketers for such products help prospective customers see how such products can benefit them.

But little evaluation may occur with an **impulse purchase**; a purchase made without any planning or search effort. As an example, consumers may do very little thinking before buying a virtual pet such as the Tamagotchi (Japanese for 'cute little egg'). For these products, marketers design the product to be eye-catching and appealing to get consumers to notice it quickly. Tamagotchis certainly grabbed the attention of consumers – 40 million of them bought the virtual pets. Toymaker Bandai Co. came out with a third generation of Tamagotchis in 2006, this time offering pets that not only communicate with other Tamagotchis via infrared ports, but that can recognise their owners' voices and respond to commands to speak, bark, walk, lie down, shake hands, perform tricks and follow clapping hands. Now the pets can make friends, 'marry' other Tamagotchis and even give birth.[25]

Some potential adopters will evaluate an innovation positively enough to move on to the next stage. Those who do not think the new product will provide adequate benefits drop out.

Trial

Trial is the stage in the adoption process when potential buyers will actually experience or use the product for the first time. Often marketers stimulate trial by providing opportunities for consumers to sample the product.

HMV, for example, opened up shops with a 'new generation' concept that was supposed to keep customers in the shop for longer and make them try out the products. Now it is easier to listen to CDs and watch extracts of DVDs in store by simply scanning the barcode of the product. Bright-coloured walls, a juice bar and free web access round up the home-like atmosphere for the shopper who, according to HMV's plan, will now easily spend hours and hours trying out the products and taking home a full shopping basket afterwards.[26]

Travel through some airports, for example, and you'll see Dell demonstration kiosks – a major departure from the company's usual focus on online direct marketing. That's because there is a drawback to online direct marketing: some consumers just can't stand to buy without first touching, holding, and using a product – in short, conducting a 'trial'. Interestingly, people are also buying right at the kiosks, which in retrospect is not too surprising given that the passenger demographics tend towards an age range of 24–49, most with annual household incomes above €50,000 – just the type of people who want the latest computer.[27]

Based on the trial experience, some potential buyers move on to adoption of the new product. Sometimes prospective customers will not adopt a new product because it costs too much. Initially, this was the case with onboard navigation systems in cars. Consumers could try out the system in rental cars from Hertz and Avis, but the price (over €1500) understandably put off most prospective customers. By 2006, with prices having dipped below €400 and continuing to fall, many more consumers were buying the units for their own cars and ordering them with new vehicles.[28]

Adoption

In the *adoption* stage, a prospect actually buys the product (Hallelujah!). If the product is a consumer or business-to-business good, this means buying the product and learning how to use and maintain it. If the product is an idea, this means that the individual agrees with the new idea.

Does this mean that all individuals or organisations that first choose an innovation are permanent customers? That's a mistake many firms make. Marketers need to provide follow-up contacts and communications with adopters to ensure they are satisfied and remain loyal to the new product over time.

Confirmation

After adopting an innovation, a customer weighs expected versus actual benefits and costs. Favourable experiences contribute to new customers becoming loyal adopters, as their initially positive opinions result in *confirmation*. Of course, nothing lasts forever – even loyal customers may decide that a new product is not meeting expectations and reject it. Some marketers feel that reselling to the customer in the confirmation stage is important. They provide advertisements, sales presentations and other communications to reinforce a customer's choice.

 ## The Diffusion of Innovations

Diffusion describes how the use of a product spreads throughout a population. Of course, marketers would prefer that their entire target market would immediately adopt a new product, but this is rarely the case. Consumers and business customers differ in how eager or willing they are to try something new, lengthening the diffusion process by months or even years. Based on adopters' roles in the diffusion process, experts have classified them into categories.

Adopter Categories

Some people like to try new products. Others are so reluctant you'd think they were afraid of anything new. As Figure 7.3 shows, there are five categories of adopters: innovators, early adopters, early majority, late majority and laggards.[29] To understand how the adopter categories differ, we'll focus on the adoption of one specific technology, Wi-Fi (wireless fidelity).

Innovators are roughly the first 2.5 per cent of adopters. This segment is extremely adventurous and willing to take risks with new products. Innovators are typically younger and better off financially than others in the population, as well as worldly and well educated. Innovators were the ones who knew all about Wi-Fi before other people, as they were fascinated and enthusiastic about trying this new technology. Because innovators pride themselves on trying new products, they purchased laptops with Wi-Fi cards way back in 1999, when Apple introduced them in its

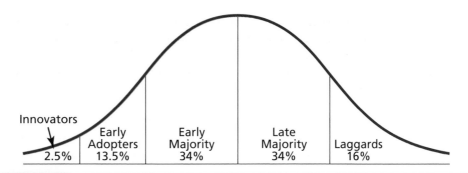

Innovators	Early Adopters	Early Majority	Late Majority	Laggards
2.5%	13.5%	34%	34%	16%

Figure 7.3	Categories of Adopters
	Because consumer differ in how willing they are to buy and try a new product, it often takes months or years for an innovation to be adopted by most of the population.

laptops. However, a company must take great care not to anger innovators such as through inconsistent pricing strategies. Apple lowered the prices for its iPhone quite drastically only three months after the launch. The consumers who first purchased the iPhone were very upset and protested heavily through online communities and forums. In the end Apple did indeed give in to the protests and each consumer received $100 back.[30]

Early adopters, approximately 13.5 per cent of adopters, buy product innovations early in the diffusion process but not as early as innovators. Unlike innovators, early adopters have greater concern for social acceptance. Typically, they are heavy media users and often are heavy users of the product category. Others in the population often look to early adopters for their opinions on various topics, making early adopters key to a new product's success. For this reason, marketers often target them in developing advertising and other communications efforts.

Columnists who write about personal technology for popular magazines like *Time* were testing Wi-Fi in mid-2000. They experienced some problems (like PCs crashing when setting up a wireless network at home) but touted the benefits of wireless connectivity. Road warriors adopted the technology as Wi-Fi access spread into airports and hotels. Intel, maker of the Centrino mobile platform, launched a major campaign with Condé Nast's *Traveller* magazine, offering a location guide to T-Mobile hotspots nationwide.

Photo 7.3	Apple's iPhone appealed to early adopters of new technologies and style gurus alike. Source: The Advertising Archives

The **early majority**, roughly 34 per cent of adopters, avoid being either first or last to try an innovation. They are typically middle-class consumers and are deliberate and cautious. Early majority consumers have slightly above average education and income levels. When the early majority adopts a product, it is no longer considered new or different – it is, in essence, already established. By 2002, Wi-Fi access was available in many Starbucks cafés, and monthly subscription prices were dropping rapidly.

Late majority adopters, about 34 per cent of the population, are older and more conservative and typically have lower than average levels of education and income. The late majority adopters avoid trying a new product until it is no longer risky. By that time, the product has become an economic necessity or there is pressure from peer groups to adopt. By 2004,

Wi-Fi capability was bundled into almost all laptops and you could connect in mainstream venues such as cafés and sports stadiums. Cities like London or Manchester were considering blanket Wi-Fi coverage throughout the entire town through WiMax technology.

Laggards, about 16 per cent of adopters, are the last in a population to adopt a new product. Laggards are typically lower in social class than other adopter categories and are bound by tradition. By the time laggards adopt a product, it may already be superseded by other innovations. By 2006, it would have seemed strange if Wi-Fi or a similar capability was not part of the standard package in even the lowest-priced laptop computer.[31]

By understanding these adopter categories, marketers are able to develop strategies that will speed the diffusion or widespread use of their products. For example, early in the diffusion process, marketers may put greater emphasis on advertising in special interest magazines to attract innovators and early adopters. Later they may lower the product's price or come out with lower priced models with fewer 'bells and whistles' to attract the late majority. We will talk more about strategies for new and existing products in the next chapter.

Product Factors Affecting The Rate Of Adoption

Not all products are successful, to say the least. As we saw in Table 7.5, all sorts of products litter the marketing graveyard. Other classic boobs include Crystal Pepsi, the Persil Power washing powder that turned out so powerful that it destroyed not only the stains but also the clothes; Thirsty Dog! (bottled water with crispy beef flavour for your pet); the Sony Betamax video player; and Snif-T-Panties (women's underwear that smelled like bananas, popcorn, whisky, or pizza).[32] The reason for such product failures is very simple – consumers did not perceive that they satisfied a need better than competitive products already on the market.

If you could predict which new products will succeed and which will fail, you'd quickly be in high demand as a marketing consultant by companies worldwide. That's because companies make large investments in new products, but failures are all too frequent. Experts suggest that between one-third and one-half of all new products fail. As you might expect, there is much research devoted to making us smarter about new product successes and failures.

Researchers have identified five characteristics of innovations that affect the rate of adoption: relative advantage, compatibility, complexity, trialability and observability.[33] Whether a new product has each of these characteristics affects the speed of diffusion. Think about Ben's options at SpeedBreaks in terms of these characteristics to help decide with option might be most successful. It may take years for a new product to become widely adopted. The five factors in Table 7.6 help to explain both why the new product was not adopted during its early years and why adoption sped up later. Let's take a closer look at the microwave oven to understand why these factors are important.

Table 7.6
Adoption-Rate
Factors – using a
Wi-Fi example

A variety of product factors cause adoption of the innovation by consumers to be faster or slower. Understanding these factors means marketers can develop strategies to encourage people to try a new product.			
Product Factors Affecting Rate of Adoption	**Product Rated High on Factor**	**Product Rated Low on Factor**	**Rating of Wi-Fi on the Factors**
Relative advantage	Faster	Slower	Low until consumer lifestyles changed
Compatibility	Faster	Slower	Low – required new PC card and base station
Complexity	Slower	Faster	Early setups were complex
Trialability	Faster	Slower	Low until infrastructure was established
Observability	Faster	Slower	Moderately low: wireless is invisible

Marketing Ethics

Bottled water or tap water? Which is better? – Dasani

Coca-Cola is undoubtedly one of the most recognised and successful brands on the planet, but even it pushed marketing into the realms of the ridiculous with its international bottled water – Dasani. In 2004, Coca-Cola was forced to take Dansani off the UK shelves after a public outcry because it contained nothing more than tap water. Coca-Cola itself says that Dansai isn't spring water and that it is sourced from local tap water supplies. But from its marketing and packaging, one could easily think otherwise. Dansai promotional material gushes with term like:

> 'Filtered for purity using state of the art processes' and
> 'enhanced with a special blend of minerals for a pure, crisp, fresh taste'

What it doesn't say quite as loudly is that Dansai comes from the same local municipal reservoirs as the water out of the tap. Coca-Cola is not doing anything illegal, but advertising which suggested its bottled water is significantly superior to local tap water is misleading. It is simply repackaging in plastic containers a common resource and charging consumers hundreds to thousands of times what it would cost out of the tap.

Consumers International – Press Briefing: International Bad Product Awards 2007, December 2007

Debate, Discuss, Disagree

1 What do you think about a big multinational company such as Coca-Cola repackaging tap water and selling it to the public at a high price?

2 Do you think it is just a clever strategy of Coca-Cola or it is actually deceiving its consumers?

Relative advantage is the degree to which a consumer perceives that a new product provides superior benefits. In the case of the microwave oven, consumers in the 1960s did not feel that the product provided significant benefits that would improve their lives. But by the late 1970s, that perception had changed because more women had entered the workforce. The 1960s woman had all day to prepare the evening meal, so she didn't need a microwave. In the 1970s, however, when many women left home for work at 8 a.m. and returned home at 6 p.m., an appliance that would 'magically' defrost a frozen chicken and cook it in 30 minutes provided a genuine advantage. However, what do you think the relative advantage was of Dasani? Read the Marketing Ethics box.

Compatibility is the extent to which a new product is consistent with existing cultural values, customs and practices. Did consumers see the microwave oven as being compatible with existing ways of doing things? Hardly. Cooking on paper plates? If you put a paper plate in a conventional oven, you're likely to get a visit from the fire brigade. By anticipating compatibility issues early in the new product development stage, marketing strategies can address such problems in planning communications programmes, or there may be opportunities for altering product designs to overcome some consumer objections.

Complexity is the degree to which consumers find a new product or its use difficult to understand. Many microwave users today haven't a clue about how a microwave oven cooks food. When appliance manufacturers introduced the first microwaves, they explained that microwaves cause molecules to move and rub together, creating friction, which produces heat. Voilà! Cooked roast beef. But that explanation was too complex and confusing for the homemaker of the early 1980s.

Trialability is the ease of sampling a new product and its benefits. Marketers took a very important step in the 1970s to speed up adoption of the microwave oven – product trial. Just

two **into one does go!**

◀ ◀ **smart** ▶ ▶

The new smart car is different - very different!

Designed by Swatch and built by Mercedes, it's an outrageous style and fashion statement. Smart cars fit into the tiniest of places - so parking is never a problem and with interchangeable body panels in seven wacky colours you're guaranteed never to get bored.

Go on treat yourself!!

Individuality to the extreme

the car to be seen about town in

for more information or a test drive call us on:

freephone 0500 123456

smart car uk ltd knightsbridge showroom 227 brompton road london sw3 2ep
just 150 metres from Harrods, heading out of town

Photo 7.4	This Smart car advert tries to convey the relative advantage of size over other cars to increase adoption. Source: The Advertising Archives

about every place that sold microwaves invited shoppers to pay a visit and sample an entire meal cooked in the microwave.

Observability refers to how visible a new product and its benefits are to others who might adopt it. The ideal innovation is easy to see. For example, for a generation of kids, scooters such as the Micro became the hippest way to get around as soon as one pre-teen saw his friends flying by. That same generation observed their friends trading Pokémon cards and wanted to join in. In the case of the microwave, it wasn't quite so readily observable for its potential adopters – only close friends and acquaintances who visited someone's home would see it in use by an early adopter. But the fruits of the microwave's labours – tasty food – created lots of buzz at the office and social events and its use spread quickly.

 ## How Organisational Differences Affect Adoption

Just as there are differences among consumers in their eagerness to adopt new products, businesses and other organisations are not alike in their willingness to buy and use new industrial products. New or smaller companies may be more nimble and able to jump onto emerging trends. Those that do often are rewarded with higher sales (though, of course, the risks are higher, too). Thus while Samsung recognised early on that colour screens on mobile phones were going to be in demand by consumers, some other companies (Nokia, for example) were slower to pick up on a trend that had originated in Samsung's home turf in Asia. While other firms continued to try to market monochrome screens for months longer than they should have, Samsung made strong gains with its more innovate product.

Firms that welcome product innovations are likely to be younger companies in highly technical industries with younger managers and entrepreneurial corporate cultures (think Apple). Early adopter firms are likely to be market-share leaders that adopt new innovations and try new ways of doing things to maintain their leadership. Firms that adopt new products only when they recognise that they must innovate to keep up are in the early majority. Late majority firms tend to be oriented toward the status quo and often have large financial investments in existing production technology. Laggard firms are probably already losing money.

Business-to-business products, like consumer products, also may possess characteristics that will increase their likelihood of adoption. Organisations are likely to adopt an innovation that helps them increase gross margins and profits. It is unlikely that firms would have adopted new products like voicemail unless they provided a way to increase profits by reducing labour costs. Organisational innovations are attractive when they are consistent with a firm's ways of doing business.

Cost is also a factor in the new products firms will adopt. Recall the concept of value as we introduced it in Chapter 1. For similar reasons, firms and institutions are more likely to accept a new product if they perceive the improvement to be large in relation to the investment they will have to make. This was the case when King's College London changed its IT system and adopted an open source network infrastructure. The advantages of using open source software include the ability to read, alter and improve the software and therefore tailor it to one's specific needs. King's College claims to have saved thousands of pounds through this investment and underlines that 'with open source software they spend their time focusing on education, not hardware or software'.[34] Many firms are starting turning their attention to the possible advantages of open source software. The European Commission funded a report which states that although open source software may lead to some increased short-term costs, it will reduce long-term costs significantly in almost all cases.[35]

Real People, Real Decisions

How it Worked Out at SpeedBreaks

After trials of each of the new products, option 3, the seven-day 'activity holidays for singles' was the most popular with a 200 per cent year-on-year growth in sales. The seven-day period allows much more time for people to get to know each other naturally and the activities provide a range of different situations and experiences to share. The range of activities means that people are very rarely excellent at all of them and provides a levelling experience which facilitates getting to know someone better. Because there is no 'speed dating' element, participants don't feel under any pressure to 'meet someone' on a holiday. It's less threatening to book

The format replicates the way people meet in normal situations

and they are less likely to cancel if they meet someone in the intervening time before the holiday. Without the speed dating element, the breaks have more the feel of a 'bunch of friends going away'. There is a less overt 'copping off' agenda. People, particularly women, feel more comfortable about booking a holiday and people are less concerned about exactly how old other participants are. The format replicates the way people meet in normal situations. For example, if you went away on a skiing holiday you are likely to meet other people staying in the same chalet.

Also, with no speed dating element there is no company responsibility to balance the genders, which sometimes

can be a problem. SpeedBreaks continues to run ski holidays, but the majority of them are the ski industry standard seven-night format.

speed breaks

great resorts
great crowd
great fun!

ski holidays for single travellers

Over 50 holidays in 11 great European resorts

| Photo 7.5 | Moving away from speed dating. Source: Ben Tisdall |

Marketing Metrics

Measuring the success of SpeedBreaks

The metrics used by SpeedBreaks to judge the success of the holidays were based on more advanced bookings to help with planning and cash flow. Because there is more money and commitment required, these breaks seem to attract a better calibre of person which reduces the number of 'desperate and dateless' people and has resulted in more repeat bookings. There is also more word of mouth from attendees, because an activity holiday which happens to be for singles is an easier thing to talk about to friends than a speed dating break. Recognising this, the company deliberately downplayed the speed dating element, marketing them as 'Active Holidays for Single Travellers' instead. In addition, while it continued to cross-sell the holidays to its speed dating customers, it does not promote speed dating to its holiday customers. There has been a huge increase in the numbers of visits to its site from the thousands of searches on 'singles holiday' and other similar terms such as 'singles skiing holiday' through Google and other search engines. Finally, the 'killer' feedback question, 'how likely are you to recommend this break to a friend' increased from 4–5 to 7–8 out of 10 compared with the other offerings.

Chapter Summary

Now that you have finished reading this chapter, you can:

1. **Explain the layers of a product.** A product may be anything tangible or intangible that satisfies consumer or business-to-business customer needs. Products include goods, services, ideas, people and places. The core product is the basic product category benefits and customised benefit(s) the product provides. The actual product is the physical good or delivered service including the packaging and brand name. The augmented product includes both the actual product and any supplementary services, such as warranty, credit, delivery, installation and so on.

2. **Describe the classifications of products.** Marketers generally classify goods and services as either consumer or business-to-business products. They further classify consumer products according to how long they last and how they are purchased. Durable goods provide benefits for months or years, whereas non-durable goods are used up quickly or are useful for only a short time. Consumers purchase convenience products frequently with little effort. Customers carefully gather information and compare different brands on their attributes and prices before buying shopping products. Speciality products have unique characteristics that are important to the buyer. Customers have little interest in unsought products until a need arises. Business products are for commercial use by organisations. Marketers classify business products according to how they are used, for example, equipment; maintenance, repair and operating (MRO) products; raw and processed materials; component parts; and business services.

3. **Explain the importance of new products.** Innovations are anything consumers perceive to be new. Understanding new products is important to companies because of the fast pace of technological advancement, the high cost to companies of developing new products, and the contributions to society that new products can

make. Marketers classify innovations by their degree of novelty. A continuous innovation is a modification of an existing product, a dynamically continuous innovation provides a greater change in a product, and a discontinuous innovation is a new product that creates major changes in people's lives.

4. **Show how firms develop new products.** In new product development, marketers first generate product ideas from which product concepts are developed and then screened. Next they develop a marketing strategy and conduct a business analysis to estimate the profitability of the new product. Technical development includes planning how the product will be manufactured and may mean obtaining a patent. Next, the effectiveness of the new product may be assessed in an actual or a simulated test market. Finally, the product is launched, and the entire marketing plan is implemented.

5. **Explain the process of product adoption and the diffusion of innovations.** Product adoption is the process by which an individual begins to buy and use a new product, whereas the diffusion of innovations is how a new product spreads throughout a population. The stages in the adoption process are awareness, interest, trial, adoption and confirmation. To understand the diffusion process better, marketers classify consumers according to their readiness to adopt new products as innovators, early adopters, early majority, late majority and laggards.

Five product characteristics that have an important effect on how quickly (or if) a new product will be adopted by consumers are relative advantage, compatibility, product complexity, trialability and observability. As with individual consumers, organisations differ in their readiness to adopt new products based on characteristics of the organisation, its management, and characteristics of the innovation.

Key Terms

Chapter Review

Marketing Concepts: Testing Your Knowledge

1. What is the difference between the core product, the actual product and the augmented product?

2. What is the difference between a durable good and a non-durable good? Provide examples of each.

3. What are the main differences among convenience, shopping and speciality products?

4. What is an unsought product? How do marketers make such products attractive to consumers?

5. What types of products are bought and sold in business-to-business markets?

6. What is a new product? Why is understanding new products so important to marketers?

7. What are the types of innovations?

8. List and explain the steps in developing new products.

9. What is a test market? What are some pros and cons of doing test markets?

10. List and explain the categories of adopters.

Marketing Concepts: Discussing Choices and Ethical Issues

1. Technology is moving at an ever-increasing speed, and this means that new products enter and leave the market faster than ever. What are some products you think technology might be able to develop in the future that you would like? Do you think these products could add to a company's profits?

2. In this chapter, we talked about the core product, the actual product and the augmented product. Does this mean that marketers are simply trying to make products that are really the same seem different? When marketers understand these three layers of the product and develop products with this concept in mind, what are the benefits to consumers? What are the hazards of this type of thinking?

3. Discontinuous innovations are totally new products – something seldom seen in the marketplace. What are some examples of discontinuous innovations introduced in the past 50 years? Why are there so few discontinuous

innovations? What products have companies recently introduced that you believe will end up being regarded as discontinuous innovations?

4. Consider the differences in marketing to consumer versus business markets. Which aspects of the processes of product adoption and diffusion apply to both markets? Which aspects are unique to one or the other? Provide evidence of your findings.

5. In this chapter, we explained that copycats are slightly modified copies of original product designs. Should copy-cat products be illegal? Who is hurt by them? Is the marketing of such products good or bad for consumers in the short run? In the long run?

6. It is not necessarily true that all new products benefit consumers or society. What are some new products that have made our lives better? What are some new products that have actually been harmful to consumers or to society? Should there be a way to monitor or 'police' new products that are introduced to the marketplace?

Marketing Practice: Applying What You've Learned

1. Assume that you are the director of marketing for a major mobile phone manufacturer. Your company has just developed a new product that does everything but tap dance. How would you go about convincing the late majority to go ahead and adopt this new technology?

2. Assume that you are employed in the marketing department of the firm that is producing a hybrid car. In developing this product, you realise that it is important to provide a core product, an actual product and an augmented product that meets the needs of customers. Develop an outline of how your firm might provide these three product layers in the hybrid car.

3. Firms go to great lengths to develop new product ideas. Sometimes new ideas come from brainstorming in which groups of individuals get together and try to think of as many different, novel, creative – and hopefully profitable – ideas for a new product as possible. With a group of other students, participate in brainstorming for new product ideas for one of the following (or some other product of your choice):

   ● An exercise machine with some desirable new features;

   ● A combination shampoo and body wash;

   ● A new type of university.

   Then, with your class, screen one or more of the ideas for possible product development.

4. As a member of a new product team with your company, you are working to develop an electric car jack that would make changing tyres for a car easier. You are considering conducting a test market for this new product. Outline the pros and cons for test marketing this product. What are your recommendations?

Marketing Miniproject: Learning by Doing

What product characteristics do consumers think are important in a new product? What types of service components do they demand? Most important, how do marketers know how to develop successful new products? This miniproject is designed to let you make some of these decisions.

Create (in your mind) a new product item that might be of interest to university students such as yourself. Develop a written description and possibly a drawing of this new product.

Show this new product description to a number of your fellow students who might be users of the product. Ask them to tell you what they think of the product. Some of the questions you might ask them are the following:

What is your overall opinion of the new product?

What basic benefits would you expect to receive from the product?

What about the physical characteristics of the product? What do you like? Dislike? What would you add? Delete? Change?

What do you like (or would you like) in the way of product packaging?

What sort of services would you expect to receive with the product?

Do you think you would try the product? How could marketers influence you to buy the product?

Develop a report based on what you found. Include your recommendations for changes in the product and your feelings about the potential success of the new product.

Real People, Real Surfers

Exploring the Web

Go to the Black & Decker website (www.blackanddecker.com). Check out the information on the ScumBuster as well as a few other Black & Decker products that interest you.

Pick any Black & Decker product and describe the core product, the actual product and the augmented product.

In your opinion, is Black & Decker engaged in product innovation? What clues from the website lead you to this conclusion?

What do you think of Black & Decker's 'How To' centre? Did you find the information there relevant and useful? Was it easy to navigate?

Why would a company such as Black & Decker include a 'How To' centre on its website instead of just focusing on the products themselves?

Now, take a look at the website at www.pearsoned.co.uk/solomon to see some videos from YouTube relating to aspects of this chapter.

Also on the website, try some analysis and calculations yourself by looking up the marketing metrics exercise called New Product Selection to learn how to model new product selection decisions for pre-prepared foods, including branding, pricing and product features.

Marketing Plan Exercise

Go to the Procter & Gamble website (www.pg.com) and click on 'Products' at the top of the page. Next, find and click on 'Oral Care' and then click on 'Crest'. Look over the information about Crest products, then answer these questions that Procter & Gamble must answer when doing marketing planning for the Crest product line:

Crest lists several product innovations, including Whitestrips, and Night Effects. How would you 'classify' each of these products based on the discussion in the chapter? What leads you to classify each as you do?

What type of innovation do you consider each of these products? Why?

Pick any one of the products and consider the process that Procter & Gamble probably went through when initially developing it. Give an example of how each of the steps in Table 7.4, 'Phases in New Product Development', might have been utilised for that product.

For the same product you selected, what stage in the adoption process do you believe that product currently occupies with most consumers? What leads you to this conclusion? Why is knowledge of the adoption process important in marketing planning? Go to the website (www.pcworld.com/printable/article/id125772/printable. html#)

Take a look at some of the flops of the IT industry. Pick several examples and using the five product characteristics that have an important effect on how quickly (or if) a new product will be adopted by consumers, explain why they might have failed.

Also, take a look at www.springwise.com, a website which features many innovative entrepreneurial ideas. Pick several examples and explain why you think they will or won't work in the future.

Marketing in Action Case

Real decisions at Voss Water

Creating a new product is challenging in any industry but even more so when that product is one consumers take for granted and can get for little or no cost. The people working at Voss Water, a producer of bottled water located in Norway, faced just this situation. Voss executives had an even bigger problem because they were trying to figure out how to convince people to pay up to €12 a bottle for the water when they dined in fine restaurants. The key question for the company was, what is the product? Is it just water – or something else? Voss bet it was something else.

In the product development process, Voss executives realised that ordinary water is a consumer, non-durable product that most consumers consider a commodity. Therefore, a high-quality, prestigious image had to be built around Voss to entice customers to pay a premium price. Developing such an image meant that the producers of Voss water had to plan carefully not only its core product offering but especially its actual and augmented product offerings.

For the actual product offering, the features that Voss water provides are a result of the source of the water: a 'virgin aquifer' that is protected from the air by both rock and layers of ice in the 'untouched wilderness' of central Norway (are you thirsty yet?). In addition, the water is said to be naturally pure, low in sodium and free of other minerals. As a result, Voss says no other water on the planet can match its quality level and clean taste. Another part of the actual product that sets Voss water apart is its packaging. Voss designed the bottle's shape to enhance the desired image of prestige, high quality and purity. A visit to the company's website (www.vosswater.com) should convince anyone that the bottle is 'stimulating' in terms of its sexiness and visual appeal.

From an augmented product standpoint, Voss will have to provide a high level of service to the companies that distribute the product. These include such services as (1) training on how to handle and sell the product, (2) market studies on the type of customers to target with the product and (3) providing credit to distributors so they can purchase an adequate amount of the product.

In addition to developing a superior product, Voss has begun to reach important adopters who can influence the tastes of the mainstream market. The company is developing a celebrity following, and it hopes these high-profile early adopters will influence a lot of other consumers to try the water.

However, although Voss has spent much time developing the product, the company still faces obstacles in terms of getting consumers to adopt the product. For one thing, what is the relative advantage offered by Voss water? Water is water, isn't it? Can one brand of water be so much better than others that it would command such a premium price?

Also, how can Voss encourage more people to try the product? There are many factors that influence a person to adopt a new product, and Voss seems sorely lacking in all of them. The level of awareness for Voss among the vast majority of consumers is extremely low or non-existent, and without awareness it is very difficult for people to become interested in the product and seek it out to conduct an evaluation. Despite the fact that some celebrities drink Voss, they will have to become more visible in their consumption of the product before usage will really begin to accelerate.

Finally, just how does someone try out a product like water? Very few, if any, companies provide taste tests for the water they sell. Consequently, the challenges for Voss to increase consumption of its water in the EU are great and not easy to overcome. However, if Voss succeeds in its quest, the company will be rewarded with a flood of orders.

> # A high-quality, prestigious image had to be built around Voss to entice customers to pay a premium price

Things to Think About

1. What are the decisions facing Voss?

2. What factors are important in understanding the decision situation?

3. What are the options?

4. What decision(s) do you recommend?

5. What are some ways to implement your recommendation(s)?

Sources: Bill Hensel Jr., 'A Crystalline Niche in Importing', *Houston Chronicle*, 7 April 2004, Business section, 1; Wesley Morris and Amy Graves, 'Food Hits Make Up for Ruby Room Misses', *Boston Globe*, 6 June 2004, Living, C2; 'Is Voss Sparkling Water Enhanced Water?' *The Water Connoisseur*, 10 April 2006, www.finewaters.com/Newsletter/September_2005/Is_Voss_Sparkling_Water_Enhanced_Water.aspand; VOSS Water, 'General', 3 June 2004, www.vosswater.com/general/html.

References

1. Woodstream Corp., *Victor* 27 March 2006, at www.victorpest.com.
2. Virgin Active Health Clubs website 2007
3. Microsoft Corp., 'Communities', 3 April 2006, www.microsoft.com/communities/default.mspx.
4. Walter S. Mossberg, 'Lots of Laptop Choices Mean Shoppers Have to Identify Their Needs', *Wall Street Journal*, 29 April 2004, B1.
5. Kärcher website 2004
6. Reuters News Service, 'Drugs Cost More, Return Less to Investors – Study', *Forbes.com*, 7 April 2006, www.forbes.com/business/newswire/2003/12/08/rtr1173648.html.
7. 'The Replacements', *Newsweek*, 25 June 2001, 50.
8. '2006 Volvo V40', *Top 100 Muscle Car Sites*, 30 March 2006, www.top100musclecarsites.com/Volvo-V40.html.
9. Steve Traiman, 'Goin' Digital', *Billboard*, 1 May 2004, 45(2); John Markoff, 'Oh, Yeah, He Also Sells Computers', *New York Times*, 25 April 2004, Section 3, 1; Devin Leonard, 'Songs in the Key of Steve', *Fortune*, 12 May 2003, 52+; Apple Computer, 'The New iPod' 29 March 2006, www.apple.com/ipod/ipod.html.
10. Palm Inc., *The Treo Store*, 30 March 2006, http://web.palm.com/products/communicators/treo600_overview.jhtml.
11. Becky Worley, 'Marriage-Saving Technology: Simple Devices Help Achieve Marital Bliss', *ABC News*, 1 April 2006, http://abcnews.go.com/GMA/Technology/story?id=1390155.
12. Sweney 2007 F. Keenan, 'G.I. Joe Heroics at Hasbro', *Business Week*, 26 November 2001, 16.
13. CBS Broadcasting Inc., 'Getting Products on Store Shelves', *CBS Evening News*, 28 March 2006, www.cbsnews.com/stories/2000/09/14/eveningnews/main233535.shtml.
14. Quoted in Brendan I. Koerner, 'Geeks in Toyland', *Wired* (February 2006), 105 (9).
15. Jennifer Ordonez, 'Burger King's Decision to Develop French Fry Has Been a Whopper', *Wall Street Journal.com*, 16 January 2001, http://interactive.wsj.com/articles/SB97960472517999878.
16. James Dao, 'From a Collector of Turkeys, a Tour of a Supermarket Zoo', *New York Times*, 24 September 1995, F12.
17. Maytag UK website 2007
18. Quoted in Jack Neff, 'P&G Boosts Design's Role in Marketing', *Advertising Age*, 9 February 2004, 1 (2), 52. This section adapted from Michael R. Solomon, *Consumer Behavior: Buying, Having, and Being*, 7th ed. (Upper Saddle River, NJ: Prentice Hall, 2006).
19. Robert Berner, 'Why P&G's Smile Is So Bright', *Business Week*, 12 August 2002, 58–60; Procter & Gamble Co., 'Crest Spin-Brush', 28 March 2006, www.spinbursh.com.
20. Dan Cray and Maggie Sieger, 'Inside the Food Labs', *Time*, 6 October 2003, 56–60; James Norton, 'The McGriddle', *flakmagazine*, 5 April 2006, http://flakmag.com/misc/mcgriddle.html.
21. Clarkson 2000 oglin 1998
22. Malcolm Gladwell, *The Tipping Point* (Newport Beach, CA: Back Bay Books, 2002).
23. Alice Z. Cuneo, 'Microsoft Taps "Puffy" for Xbox', *Advertising Age*, 20 October 2004, 4.
24. Neal E. Boudette and Lee Hawkins, 'Volkswagen Eyes Young Parents with Newest Version of Jetta', *Wall Street Journal*, 11 January 2005, D.9.
25. Polson Enterprises and Amazon.com, 'Virtual Pet Store', 6 April 2006), www.virtualpet.com/pe/books/vpbs/vpbs.htm.
26. Allen 2007
27. 'Dell Brings Kiosk-Based Marketing to DFW Airport', *Kiosk Marketplace*, 4 April 2006, www.kioskmarketplace.com/news_story.htm?i=16464.
28. Amy Gilroy, 'More Players Enter Portable Nav Market', *TWICE*, 5 April 2004, 28(2); Pioneer Electronics Co., 'XM NavTraffic', *Pioneer: Car Electronics*, 4 April 2006, www.pioneerelectronics.com/pna/article/0,,2076_3149_269505659,00.html.
29. Everett Rogers, *Diffusion of Innovations* (New York: Free Press, 1983), 247–51.

30. Steve Jobs, To all iPhone customers, Apple website www. apple.com/hotnews/openiphoneletter 2007

31. Sources used in this section: 'Wi-Fi's Big Brother', *Economist,* 13 March 2004, 65; 'Burgers, Fries and Wi-Fi', *Informationweek*, www.informationweek.com/showarticle.jhtml?articleID= 8700269; William J. Gurley, 'Why Wi-Fi Is the Next Big Thing', *Fortune*, 5 March 2001, 184; Joshua Quittner, 'Cordless Capers', *Time*, 1 May 2000, 85; Scott Van Camp, 'Intel Switches Centrino's Gears', *Brandweek*, 26 April 2004, 16; Benny Evangelista, 'SBC Park a Hot Spot for Fans Lugging Laptops', *San Francisco Chronicle*, 26 April 2004, A1; Todd Wallack, 'Santa Clara Ready for Wireless', *San Francisco Chronicle*, 19 April 2004, D1; http://wifinetnews.com.

32. Christine Chen and Tim Carvell, 'Hall of Shame', *Fortune*, 22 November 1999, 140.

33. Everett Rogers (2003) *Diffusion of Innovations*, 5th ed. (New York: Free Press).

34. Clement James, 'UK school saves thousands with open source software,' *VNUNet* (31 August 2006).

35. Richarcl Thurston, 'EU: Open source almost always cheaper option,' silicon.com (15 January 2007).

Chapter 8
Managing the Product

Meet Jamie Mitchell,
formerly of Innocent Drinks, Fruit Towers, London

Q & A with Jamie Mitchell

What do you do when not working?
I teach (I am a Teaching Fellow in Entre-preneurship at London Business School), sit on a couple of company boards, play a bit of hockey and pretend to be musical.

Career high?
Raising $50m for a venture capital fund and incubator in the dot-com boom.

A job-related mistake you wish you hadn't made?
Invested $50m in start-ups at the peak of the dot.com boom.

Your Hero?
My Dad. He had four completed different careers in his life, from being a jazz guitarist and band leader, to jingle writer, conference producer and public speaking coach.

Motto to live by?
Don't use mottos.

What drives me?
Happiness and fulfilment.

My management style is . . .
Challenging, but hands off.

Jamie was UK managing director at Innocent, a nice little place where people make smoothies and other healthy drinks. An entrepreneur and investor by background (he used to run a technology venture capital fund), he joined Innocent in September 2005 and lead the company's plans for rapid growth until January 2009.

Prior to Innocent, Jamie was managing partner and co-founder of Vesta Group. He is a Teaching Fellow in Entrepreneurship at London Business School, sits on the boards of E-Government Solutions, Frontiers Capital and Brunel University, and has been a government advisor on university governance. In 2008, he was named as a Young Global Leader by the World Economic Forum. He has an MBA from Harvard Business School and a BA from Oxford, and past jobs include number crunching at McKinsey and speech writing at the CBI (Confederation of British Industry).

Jamie is a regular speaker at marketing and FMCG industry events. He has published several business case studies, and written widely for the press on general business matters, including a monthly column on entrepreneurship for Germany's *Handlesblatt* newspaper. He has appeared on numerous television and radio programmes, from guest spots on *Newsnight* and the James Max show on LBC, to interviews for Sky News and the BBC.

Real People, Real Decisions
Decision time at Innocent

Innocent drinks makes 100 per cent natural, pure fruit smoothies and was established in 1999 by three entrepreneurs, Adam, John and Richard. At a music festival they set up a stall selling their smoothies and asked people to drop the bottles in a 'yes' or 'no' bin to vote on whether they should give up their day jobs and start making these smoothies full time. They are an unusual, quirky, fun and friendly company with delivery vans which are covered in grass, a consumer hotline called the banana phone and a managing director who has 'Chief Squeezer' on his business card. This natural, friendly approach epitomises the tone of voice their brand communication uses. Innocent are passionate about their product and encourage feedback from customers via blogs, email comments or visits to Fruit Towers – Innocent's HQ. (Go to www.innocent. co.uk.) At their first AGM (a grown-up meeting) the directors met 100 people selected from over 5000 who had applied, and discussed how the business was doing, and what they could do better.

As a result of this approach, Innocent is the number one smoothie brand in the UK with a turnover of £115 million in 2007 and a market share of 73 per cent.[1] The Innocent range has expanded to include: special smoothies for children, 1 litre cartons for families at home and thickies for a yoghurt and fruit blend. The drinks regularly win industry awards, including Best Soft Drink in the UK 2006 (for the fifth year running) and Growth Strategy and Business Innovation of the Year at the National Business Awards. The company wants to make it easy for people to do themselves some good. This is reflected in everything from the use of green electricity at Fruit Towers, to sourcing all bananas from Rainforest Alliance accredited farms. The company also recently launched the first 100 per cent compostable smoothie bottle, made from corn starch.

The problem Innocent faced was how to give something back to its loyal customers. Innocent's passion for smoothies had been infectious and there were now 70,000 people in the Innocent 'family' signed up to receive a weekly newsletter about the brand. Many of these people were as passionate about Innocent as Innocent itself. Innocent wanted to reward its brand advocates with some kind of event to say thanks. The company already ran a free music festival called Fruitstock, but didn't know whether to continue with this or not.

Jamie considers his options . . .

Option 1 Continue with Fruitstock

For four years Innocent organised a free music festival in Regent's Park to give something back to its customers. Originally this was a low key event with 20,000 people and mainly little known bands playing for small and affordable fees. It was organised by the Innocent team, who weren't experts at putting on events, but that was fine when it was small. There were drinks and food concessions, as well as free Innocent smoothie samples. Following good promoter's practice, there was always a headline act to attract people. Four years later, in 2006, 150,000 people attended the free event with Arrested Development headlining and it was a major success. The advantages of this option were: it was tried and tested, people loved the 'thank you' and it attracted major sponsors. Disadvantages were: the event was getting unmanageable, it had lost some of the original charm of a small event and risked nuisance to neighbours of the park and the park authorities themselves. It was no longer a family event, but one for festival goers.

Option 2 Devise a new event:
The Innocent Village Fete

This option would be modelled on a traditional British summer fete over two days with many activities. The theme was informal eclectic entertainment. There would be bandstands for country and folk music, as well as stages for new up-and-coming acts and a village green for such activities as duck herding, ferret racing, dog agility and Morris dancing. It would have a farmers' market, a tea tent and *al fresco* ballroom for old fashioned tea dances, a large children's play area, arts and crafts and lots of eating options. To keep numbers in check, the event would be ticketed, with some of the £5 ticket price going to charity. The advantages of this option were: it was an all-encompassing, anything goes format which was flexible and could change year on year; it was more family focused; it was natural and friendly like the Innocent brand. Disadvantages were: it had never been done before and was much more challenging to organise; there was no headliner, which breaks all promoting rules; the event was no longer free so reducing the 'thank you' element of the day.

Option 3 Do nothing for a year

Given how much time, effort and money went into planning, organising and executing such a large 'thank you' event, a realistic option was to do nothing for a year and plan something different, bigger and better the following year or give back via some other mechanism. There were problems with the other two options such as: it was very London focused and difficult to organise around the UK; it was a costly and time-consuming event to stage; doing an event every year can get boring and Innocent is not a boring brand. The advantages of doing nothing for a year were: saving money; avoiding the hassle and risks of either event; it would make it more special and more anticipated when the company did decide to do something. The disadvantages were: loyal customers would lose out on a 'thank you'; Innocent would lose out on the intensity of the experience and the connection with customers; brand experiences which engaged people emotionally were more of what Innocent is about than other types of 'give back' such as coupons.

Now put yourself in Jamie's shoes. Which option would you choose and why?

Objectives

When you finish reading this chapter, you will be able to:

1 Explain the different product objectives and strategies a firm may choose

2 Explain how firms manage products throughout the product life cycle

3 Discuss how branding creates product identity and describe different types of branding strategies

4 Explain the roles packaging and labelling play in developing effective product strategies

5 Describe how organisations are structured for new and existing product management

www.pearsoned.co.uk/solomon

Product Planning: Taking the Next Step

Objective

1

Explain the different product objectives and strategies a firm may choose

In 2006, Lexus introduced the GS450h – that's 'h' as in hybrid. It's the first hybrid ever brought to market on a rear-wheel drive car, with an acceleration claim of 0–60 mph in 5 1/2 seconds. The G450h is also the first 'luxury hybrid'; it's out to prove that phrase isn't an oxymoron. With an initial base price of about €41,450, Lexus is banking on re-educating high end car buyers that they can have their cake and eat it too with fuel economy, comfort and performance.[2]

Toyota's Prius has been a sales phenomenon at the lower end of the emerging hybrid market, although several other Prius rivals have posted more disappointing sales. Will the GS450h succeed? A lot depends on how this innovative product is marketed and managed. What makes one product fail and another succeed? It's worth repeating what we said in Chapter 2: firms that plan well succeed. Product planning plays a big role in the firm's *tactical marketing plans*. The strategies outlined in the product plan spell out how the firm expects to develop a product that will meet marketing objectives.

Today, successful product management is more important than ever. As more and more competitors enter the global marketplace and as technology moves forward at an ever-increasing pace, products are created, grow, reach maturity and decline at faster and faster speeds. Think about how quickly mobile phones are replaced. This means that good product decisions are more critical than ever.

In Chapter 7, we talked about what a product really is and about how companies develop and introduce new products. In this chapter, we'll finish the product focus of the book by seeing how companies manage products and examine the steps in product planning, as Figure 8.1 outlines. These steps include developing product objectives and the strategies required to successfully market products as they evolve from 'new kids on the block' to tried-and-tested favourites – and in some cases finding new markets for these favourites. Next, we'll discuss branding and packaging, two of the more important tactical decisions product planners make. Finally, we'll examine how firms organise for effective product management. Let's start by seeing how firms develop product-related objectives.

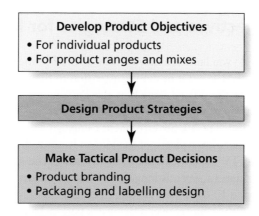

Figure 8.1	**Steps in Managing Products**
	Effective product strategies come from a series of orderly steps.

Using Product Objectives to Decide on a Product Strategy

When marketers develop product strategies, they make decisions about product benefits, features, styling, branding, labelling and packaging. But what do they want to accomplish? Clearly stated product objectives provide focus and direction. They should support the broader marketing objectives of the business unit in addition to being consistent with the firm's overall mission. For example, the objectives of the firm may focus on return on investment. Marketing objectives then may concentrate on building market share and/or the unit or sales volume necessary to attain that return on investment. Product objectives need to specify how product decisions will contribute to reaching a desired market share or level of sales.

To be effective, product-related objectives must be SMART, i.e. Specific, Measurable, Achievable, Relevant and Timebound, which means indicating a specific time frame. Consider, for example, how a frozen meal manufacturer might state its product objectives:

● 'In the next financial year, eliminate the product's trans fat content to satisfy consumers' health concerns.'

● 'Introduce three new items this quarter to the product line to take advantage of increased consumer interest in Brazilian foods.'

● 'During the next financial year, improve the chicken main course dishes to the extent that consumers will rate them as tasting better than the competition.'

Planners must keep in touch with their customers so that their objectives accurately respond to customer needs. An up-to-date knowledge of competitive product innovations also is important in developing product objectives. Above all, product objectives should consider the *long-term implications* of product decisions. Planners who sacrifice the long-term health of the firm to reach short-term sales or financial goals may be on a risky course. Product planners may focus on one or more individual products at a time, or they may look at a group of product offerings as a whole. In this section, we'll briefly examine both these approaches. We'll also look at one important product objective: product quality.

Objectives and Strategies for Individual Products

How do you launch a new car that's only 142 inches long and makes people laugh when they see it? BMW did it by calling attention to the small size and poking fun at the car itself.

After the official launch at the Paris motor show in 2000, the Mini Cooper hit the UK market in 2001 with an innovative marketing campaign which targeted young, well-to-do urbanites. The TV advertisement campaign called 'It's a Mini Adventure' wowed not only the car owners, but a plague of zombies and an invading army of Martians as well. One in the series of the TV advertisements was classified as the shortest film ever by the British Film Board, being just 12 seconds long. The Mini also went on a tour at the end of the summer which included 10 UK cities, visiting the biggest shopping centres and the most famous amusement park in the country over a five-week period. During the tour BMW organised games, convoys, drive-bys, stunts, plenty of give-aways and a Guinness World Record attempt. The Mini also picked up commuters from bus stops and hitchhikers held up 'Take me to a Mini Adventure' signs. A Sound System Mini – which has enough power to entertain a small nightclub – was featured at V music festival 2001 in Stafford, the Notting Hill Carnival and London's Mardi Gras. A remake of *The Italian Job* in 2003 also featured Minis which further helped to popularise BMW's little car in homage to their use in the original *The Italian Job* featuring Michael Caine.[3] If someone didn't know what a 'Mini Adventure' was by the end of the year, there probably wasn't much hope for them . . .[4]

Some product strategies, such as that for the new hybrid Lexus GS450h or the Mini Cooper, focus on a single new product. However, strategies for individual products may be quite different for new products, for regional products, and for mature products.

● For new products, not surprisingly, the objectives relate to successful introduction, such as retailer acceptance, 70 per cent awareness of the product, etc.

IS IT LOVE?

Photo 8.1   With a relatively tiny budget for a new car model, the marketers of the Mini Cooper had to be very creative.
Source: BMW Group (Germany)

Guess where 70% of her Immune System is?

Reinforce your family's Immune System

www.actimel.co.uk   Actimel - Feel the difference in 2 weeks.

| Photo 8.2 | Actimel's value proposition is to protect your immune system and keep you healthy.
Source: The Advertising Archives |

- After a firm has experienced success with a product in a local or regional market, it may decide to introduce it nationally. Scottish & Newcastle was a local brewer in 1985 focusing on Scotland and the North of England. By 2005 it became the UK's leading brewer. It has covered several markets in the world such as Europe, China and India with well-known beers like Foster's, Baltika and Kronenbourg 1664.[5]

- For mature products like Haribo sweets, originally founded in Germany in 1920,[6] product objectives may focus on breathing new life into a product while holding on to the traditional brand personality. Haribo, the sweets 'Kids and grown-ups love 'em so', has introduced a host of different tastes, such as MagicMix, Starmix, Strawbs, Liquorice and Jelly Beans. Haribo has been around for over 80 years but continues to try to stay fresh with more than 25 varieties offered in its pre-packed range and also selling other ranges.

Objectives and Strategies for Several Products

Although a small firm might make a go of focusing on one product, such as a small English winemaker, a larger firm often markets a set of related products. This means that strategic decisions affect two or more products simultaneously. The firm must think in terms of its entire portfolio of products. As Figure 8.2 shows, product planning means developing *product range* and *product mix* strategies encompassing several offerings. Figure 8.3 illustrates how this works for a selection of Procter & Gamble's products.

Product Range Strategies

A **product range** is a firm's total product offering designed to satisfy a single need or desire of a group of target customers. For example, Procter & Gamble's cleaning products include three laundry detergent brands: Ace focuses on reviving the brightness of coloured clothes; Ariel delivers outstanding whiteness; and Bounce is designed for tumble driers. To do an even better job of meeting varying consumer needs, each of the three brands comes in more than one formulation. In addition to regular Ariel, you can buy Ariel Sensitive which is gentler to your skin and Arial Handwash for your delicate fabrics.[7] The number of separate items within the same category determines the *length* of the product line.

A large number of variations in a product range is described as a *full line*, like Heinz soups, that targets many customer segments to boost sales potential. A *limited line strategy* with fewer product variations can improve the firm's image if it is perceived as a specialist with a clear, specific position in the market. A great example of such a strategy is Rolls-Royce Motor Cars, owned by BMW. Rolls-Royce makes expensive, handcrafted cars built to each customer's exact specifications and for decades has maintained a unique position in the automobile industry. Every Phantom and 101EX that rolls out of the factory door is truly a unique work of art.[8]

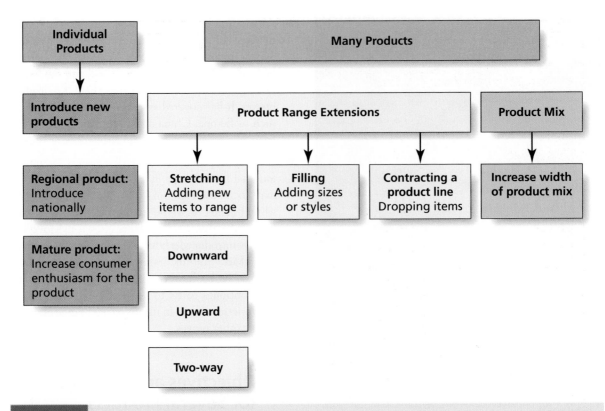

Figure 8.2	Objectives for Single and Many Products
	Product objectives provide focus and direction for product strategies. Objectives can focus on a single product or a group of products.

Organisations may also decide to extend their product range by adding more brands or models when they develop product strategies. For example, Gap extended its reach by adding children's clothing. When a firm stretches its product line, it must decide on the best direction to go. If a firm's current product line includes middle-range and cheaper items, an *upward line stretch* adds new items – higher priced and claiming more quality. For example, Hyundai decided it could tap the market for bigger, more luxurious cars and SUVs, and stretched its line upward in the form of models such as the Grandeur, Coupe SIII and Santa Fe SUVs.[9] Each of these is positioned against top end products by Toyota and Honda, but costs thousands of euros less.[10]

Conversely, a *downward line stretch* augments a range by adding cheaper items. Here the firm must take care not to blur the images of its higher-priced, upper-end offerings. Rolex, for example, may not want to run the risk of cheapening its image with a new watch line to compete with lower-priced watches such as Swatch.

In some cases, a firm may decide that it is targeting too small a market. In this case, the product strategy may call for a *two-way stretch* that adds products at both the upper and lower ends. Marriott Hotels, for example, added Fairfield Inns and Courtyard at the lower end and J.W. Marriott and Ritz Carlton at the upper end to round out its product line.

A *filling-out strategy* may mean adding sizes or styles not previously available in a product category. Kraft Foods did this by introducing a 4 × 35g multipack version of its Toblerone chocolate. In other cases, the best strategy may be to *contract* a product line, particularly when some of the items are not profitable. For example, Heinz scrapped its 'Bite Me' brand of frozen pizza snacks because of poor sales. The product, targeted to teenagers, failed to meet company expectations.[11]

We've seen that there are many ways a firm can modify its product line to meet the competition or take advantage of new opportunities. To further explore these strategic decisions, let's

← ——————————————— **Width of Product Mix** ——————————————— →

Fabric and Home Care	Beauty Care	Health Care/Baby and Family Care	Snacks and Beverages
Ace Laundry and Bleach	Aussie	Bounty	Millstone
Alomatik	Camay	Charmin	Pringles
Ariel	Clairol's Herbal Essences	Codi	Sunny Delight
Bold	Cover Girl	Crest	Torengos
Bonux	Evax	Didronel	
Bounce	Giorgio	Fixodent	
Dash	Head & Shoulders	Kandoo	
Daz	Hugo Boss	Luvs	
Dryel	Infasil	Macrobid	
Era	Infusion 23	Metamucil	
Fairy	Ivory Personal Care	Pampers	
Febreze	Lacoste	Pepto-Bismol	
Flash	Laura Biagiotti	Puffs	
Gain	Lines Feminine Care	PUR	
Hi Wash	Max Factor	Scope	
Ivory Dish	Mum Always Whisper	Tempo	
Joy	Muse	ThermaCare	
Lenor	Natural Instincts and Hydrience	Vicks	
Mr Clean/Proper	Naturella		
Rindex	Nice 'n Easy		
Salvo	Noxzema		
Tide	Olay		
Viakal	Old Spice		
Vizir	Pantene		
	Physique		
	Rejoice		
	Safeguard		
	Secret		
	SK-II		
	Sure		
	Tampax		
	Vidal Sassoon		
	Wash & Go		
	Zest		

Length of Product Range (vertical axis label on left)

Figure 8.3	Product Range Length and Product Mix Width

A product range is a firm's total offerings that satisfy one need, whereas the product mix includes all the products that a firm offers. Here we see an example of both for a selection of Procter & Gamble's extensive family of products. The figure illustrates the length of Procter & Gamble's product range as well as the width of its product mix.

Marketing Metrics

Branding in the Detergents Market

Liquid detergents provide a revealing example of evidence of consumer behaviour towards innovation. Technically, the new products were revolutionary, with seven years' of R&D to develop a fatty acid with water-softening capabilities equivalent to a phosphate, and new 'builders' to prevent redisposition of dirt in the wash. But the key question is how did consumers perceive the innovation? First to market was the new Unilever brand, named Wisk, in the final quarter of 1985. Procter & Gamble responded in the first quarter of 1987, but quite differently from Unilever and the product was launched as Ariel Liquid, a line extension. Unilever responded to the success of Ariel Liquid rather belatedly in the third quarter of 1988, and launched Persil Liquid (chemically identical to Wisk). Eventually, the more strongly differentiated product, Wisk, ended up in the weakest position and by mid 1989, Persil Liquid had 6 per cent share and Persil Powder 23 per cent, Wisk had decayed to 5 per cent, and Ariel Liquid and Powder had 9 and 11 per cent respectively. This suggests that strong differentiation can be less effective than hiding behind an existing identity. The key determinant is whether consumers see the differentiation. Despite all the technical innovation, most consumers saw the liquid as an example of the detergent category, not as a new category.

return to the world of detergents. What does Procter & Gamble do if the objective is to increase market share? One possibility would be to expand its range of laundry detergents. If the line extension meets a perceived consumer need currently not being addressed, such as bobbling on clothes, this would be a good strategic objective.

But whenever a product line or a product family is extended, there is risk of **cannibalisation**, which occurs when sales of an existing brand are eaten up by the new item as the firm's current customers switch to the new product. This is the risk Procter & Gamble took in meeting consumer demands for sensitive or handwash detergents by creating new versions of the existing brand Ariel, which could cannibalise sales of normal Ariel. But better that than consumers swapping to a competitor brand with sensitive properties.

Product Mix Strategies

Product planning can go beyond a single product item or a product line to entire groups of products. A firm's **product mix** is its entire range of products. For example, in addition to a deep line of shaving products, Procter & Gamble's 2005 acquisition of the Gillette line gave P&G new toiletries such as Old Spice and Secret deodorants, Oral B toothbrushes, Braun oral care products, Duracell batteries and Cricket cigarette lighters.

In developing a product mix strategy, planners usually consider the *width of the product mix*, that is, the number of different product lines produced by the firm. By developing several different product lines, firms can reduce the risk associated with putting all their eggs into one basket. Normally, firms develop a mix of product lines that have some things in common, be it distribution channels or manufacturing facilities.

Wine and spirits distributor Constellation Brands' entry into the mainstream supermarket wine space through its acquisition of Robert Mondavi is an example of a successful product mix expansion strategy. Europeans are drinking more wine of late, and the Mondavi brand gives Constellation the crown jewel in the €2.7 billion supermarket wine channel.[12]

 ## Quality as a Product Objective

Product objectives often focus on product quality; the overall ability of the product to satisfy customers' expectations. Quality is tied to how customers *think* a product will perform and not necessarily to some technological level of perfection so it can depend on how the company promotes the product.

In some cases, quality means fanatical attention to detail and also getting extensive input from actual users of a product as it's being developed or refined – this is known as integrating the *voice of the consumer* into product design. The Japanese take this idea a step further with a practice they call **Kansei engineering**, a philosophy that translates customers' feelings into design elements. In one application of this practice, the designers of the Mazda Miata focused on young drivers who saw the car as an extension of their body, a sensation they call 'horse and rider as one'. After extensive research, they discovered that making the gear stick exactly 9.5 centimetres long conveys the optimal feeling of sportiness and control.[13]

Total Quality Management

As noted in Chapter 1, many firms with a quality focus have adopted the principles and practices of **total quality management (TQM)**, a philosophy that calls for company-wide dedication to the development, maintenance and continuous improvement of all aspects of the company's operations. Indeed, many of the world's most admired, successful companies – top-of-industry firms such as 3M, Boeing and Coca-Cola – have adopted a total quality focus.

Product quality is one way that marketing can add value to customers. However, TQM as an approach to doing business is far more sophisticated and effective than simply paying attention to product quality. TQM firms promote the attitude among employees that *everybody* working there has customers – even employees who never interact with customers outside the firm. In such cases, employees' customers are *internal customers*; other employees with whom they interact. In this way, TQM seeks to ensure customer satisfaction by involving all employees, regardless of their function, in efforts to improve quality continually. For example, TQM firms encourage employees, even the lowest-paid factory workers, to suggest ways to improve products – and then reward employees for good ideas.

But how do you know when you've attained your goal of quality? Other than increased sales and profits, a few key award programmes recognise firms that are doing the job well. For example, in 1989 heads of prominent European businesses established the European Foundation for Quality Management (EFQM) to recognise excellence. The EFQM Excellence Award has been awarded to the best performing firms in Europe since 1992 (see Table 8.1). For example, the reason for Villa Massa's success is its focus on customer satisfaction and the creation of a top quality brand which is internationally recognised. The marketing strategy is to satisfy the consumer needs by offering a strong unique selling proposition based on 'quality, authenticity and premiumness'. Continuous improvement in activity performance is based on knowledge of customer satisfaction, competences of the people, suppliers, partnerships strengthening, technological innovations and evaluation of all process indicators and trends.

Around the world, many companies look to the uniform standards of the International Organisation for Standardization (ISO) for quality guidelines. This Geneva-based organisation developed a set of criteria in 1987 to improve and standardise product quality in Europe. The broad set of guidelines, known as **ISO 9000**, sets established voluntary standards for quality management. This means what the organisation does to achieve the customer's quality requirements, the applicable regulatory requirements, while aiming to enhance customer satisfaction, and achieve continual improvement of its performance in pursuit of these objectives.

Quality management ensures that an organisation's products conform to the customer's requirements. In 1996, the ISO developed **ISO 14000** standards, which concentrate on 'environmental management'. This means the organisation works to minimise any harmful effects it may have on the environment. Because members of the European Union and other European countries prefer suppliers with ISO 9000 and ISO 14000 certification, companies must comply with these standards, otherwise other companies won't buy from them.[14]

One way that companies can improve quality is by using the **Six Sigma** methodology. The term *Six Sigma* comes from the statistical term 'sigma', which is a standard deviation from the mean or average. Six Sigma, therefore, refers to six standard deviations from a normal distribution curve. In practical terms, that translates to no more than 3.4 defects per million – getting it right 99.9997 per cent of the time. As you can imagine, achieving that level of quality requires a very rigorous approach (try it on your coursework) – and that's what Six Sigma offers. The methodology involves a five-step process called DMAIC: define, measure, analyse, improve and control. Employees are trained in the methodology and, as in karate, progress towards 'black belt' status by successfully completing all the levels of training. Employees can use Six Sigma processes to remove defects from services, not just products. A 'defect' means failing to meet customer expectations. For example, hospitals can use Six Sigma processes to reduce medical errors, and airlines can use Six Sigma to improve flight scheduling.

Adding a Dose of Quality to the Marketing Mix

Marketing people research the level of quality consumers want and need in their products and what price they are willing to pay for them. The price-versus-quality decision is a major aspect

Table 8.1   The EFQM Excellence Award Winners

The EFQM Excellence Award is Europe's most prestigious recognition for organisational excellence given to Europe's best performing companies and not-for-profit organisations. In 2007, 18 organisations reached the final stage of the award.
The 2007 award and prize winners were:
Large Scope, Private Sector
• Trimo, Engineering and Production of Prefabricated Buildings, Slovenia Prize Winner in Leadership
Small and Medium Scope, Private Sector
• Villa Massa, Italy
Award Winner and Prize Winner in Partnership Development
• Tobermore Concrete Products, Northern Ireland
Award Winner and Prize Winner in Results Orientation
• TNT Express, Greece
Prize Winner in People Development and Involvement
• OBI Baumarkt Franken, Germany
Prize Winner in Customer Focus
• Siemens Standard Drives, Congleton, United Kingdom
Prize Winner in People Development and Involvement
Small and Medium Scope, Public Sector and Not-for-Profit
• The Cedar Foundation, Northern Ireland
Award Winner and Prize Winner in Customer Focus
• Lauaxeta Ikastola Sociedad Cooperativa, Spain
Award Winner and Prize Winner in Management of Processes
• Novia Salcedo Foundation, Spain
Prize Winner in Leadership

Source: www.efqm.org/uploads/Press/documents/PR2007EEA_Winners_Announced.pdf

of providing value to consumers. Marketing also has to *inform* consumers about product quality through its marketing communications.

But keeping on top of what customers want is just the beginning. Firms also have to deliver a (customer-perceived) quality product at the right place and at the right price. Instead of being satisfied with doing things the same way year after year, marketers must continuously seek ways to improve product, place, price and promotion. Let's see how quality concerns affect the marketing mix:

- **Product:** One way firms can offer quality for their customers is by improving their customer service support. For example, Whirlpool has been steadily improving the repair services it offers on its appliances. In the past, if your washing machine broke down, you'd call Whirlpool, they'd refer you to a service centre, and you'd call the service centre and try to arrange a repair time. Today, technology lets Whirlpool's customer service reps view the schedules of all its repair technicians in your area and then set a repair time that suits you – all during the first phone call. Whirlpool also offers an online service that lets customers schedule service themselves, without even talking with a rep. The easier it is for customers to interact with the company and get results, the more satisfied they will be. And Whirlpool's acquisition of Maytag in 2006 gave the company the opportunity to expand this service to include customers of its products.[15]

- **Place:** Dell has a general approach of manufacturing close to its customers thus improving delivery time to its clients which in turn improves the quality of its service. In the EU it manufactures in Ireland and Poland, in the US the company has three plants, it also owns three in Asia and one in South America.

- **Price:** Hewlett-Packard (HP) is lowering costs and improving service to customers at the same time. HP developed a 'sure supply' technology that is embedded into its printer cartridges. The technology has a sensor that detects when the ink supply is low, and the networked printer automatically orders a new cartridge. By building an automated cartridge supply service into the printer, HP also reduces its own costs related to processing a customer's phone order.[16]

- **Promotion:** Today's marketing firms realise that customers want information when they need it, not when it's convenient for the marketer. The Gap exemplifies this philosophy. At Gap's Old Navy stores, salespeople wear headsets so they can quickly get information to answer customers' questions. Another example is Marks & Spencer – the firm uses Radio Frequency Identification tags on several of its clothing lines which can be monitored to know exactly how many items are on the shop floor or in the store room to improve stock levels in store.[17]

Dimensions of Product Quality

But what exactly *is* quality? Figure 8.4 summarises some of the many meanings of quality. In some cases, product quality means durability. For example, trainers shouldn't develop holes after their owner plays football for a few weeks. Reliability also is an important aspect of product quality – just consider Toyota, its cars have been ranked among the top performers in reliability surveys for many years.[18]

For other products, quality means a high degree of precision. For example, high-tech audio equipment promises clearer music reproduction with less distortion. Quality, especially in business-to-business products, is also related to ease of use, maintenance and repair. Yet another crucial dimension of quality is product safety, e.g. a children's car seat. Finally, the quality of products such as a painting, a film or even a wedding dress relates to the degree of aesthetic pleasure they provide. Of course, evaluations of aesthetic quality differ dramatically among people: to one person, quality TV may mean a BBC period drama such as *Pride and Prejudice*, while to another it's MTV.

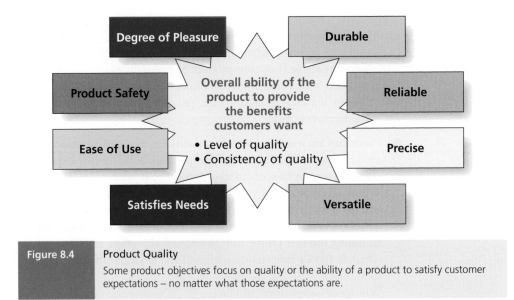

Figure 8.4	Product Quality
	Some product objectives focus on quality or the ability of a product to satisfy customer expectations – no matter what those expectations are.

Marketing planners often focus product objectives on one or both of two key aspects of quality: level and consistency. Customers often determine the *level of quality* of a product by comparison with other brands in the same product category. A handcrafted Rolls-Royce boasts higher quality than an assembly-line Fiat Punto, but this may be irrelevant to a Punto buyer inclined to compare his car with the quality of a Mini Cooper and not to an elite luxury car.

Consistency of quality means that customers experience the same level of quality in a product time after time, bringing repeat business and free word-of-mouth advertising or buzz. Consistent quality is also one of the major benefits of adopting TQM practices. Consumer perceptions can change overnight when quality is lacking. Ask anybody who's ever bought a new car only to find it back in the garage the following week with problems.

How E-Commerce Affects Product Quality

The web has made product quality even more important in product strategies. One of the most exciting aspects of the digital world is that consumers can interact directly with other people – around the corner or around the world. But this form of communication cuts both ways since it lets people praise what they like and criticise what they don't to an audience of thousands. Numerous websites like starbucked.com and microsoftsucks.org let consumers sound off about bad experiences they have had with products.

Marketing Throughout the Product Life Cycle

Objective

2

Explain how firms manage products throughout the product life cycle

Many products have very long lives, while others are 'here today, gone tomorrow'. The **product life cycle** is a useful way to explain how product features change over the life of a product. In Chapter 7, we talked about how marketers go about introducing new products, but the launch is only the beginning. Product marketing strategies must evolve and change as they continue through the product life cycle.

Alas, some brands don't have long to live. Who can remember the Nash car or Evening in Paris perfume? In contrast, other brands seem almost immortal. For example, Coca-Cola has been the number one cola brand for 120 years and Kleenex has been the number one tissue brand for 82 years.[19]

Real People, Other Voices

Nigel Bradley,
University of Westminster

There are three ways to make a decision: you can make a bad decision, you can make a good decision or you can make no decision by being indecisive. Indecision can be far more damaging than the wrong decision, so that would rule out option 3 for me. Option 1 is interesting but is starting to focus on a narrow segment of the market and is also running the risk of competing with major music events such as Glastonbury, Party in the Park and so on. This could work, but the name Innocent would be lost behind the big names of artists. It could benefit from strong associations but could also suffer by narrowing the marketplace. Moreover, the brand is a drink and that may be diluted in all the noise (excuse the pun).

I would choose option 2. Here is an original idea that can be memorable, offers scope for numerous side-shows and incorporates product sampling. We are faced with a credit crunch and we are being encouraged to live in a sustainable way. The village-style fete would have a farmers' market and 'sustainable entertainment'. The entry fee would be an issue for some people but clever communications can overcome that one. A summer fete must be the right choice because Innocent has a family image that is peppered with fun. These toddlers, tweenagers and teenagers are the marketplace of tomorrow, so make them laugh and remember Innocent today. Word of mouth is extremely powerful and this is a breeding ground for positive messages, in fact it is a word of mouth farm. As to the future, the formula can easily be exported to other places in Britain and youngsters can always be offered a free music concert when they grow up.

Peter Ruddock,
University of Central Lancashire

Option 3 to do nothing is not an option, and rarely is, unless there are exceptional circumstances, either internally and externally to make it so, for instance a disaster. All that you do is lose time. Continuing with option 1 could work, but has been done before and so will lose its freshness, not a concept that Innocent would want to be associated with. It has limitations too in that it aligns with a narrow target group of young, or want to be young, hippy-rockers – does one detect some association here with the directors of the company? This brand has a much wider target group than this that it appeals to. Option 2 is brilliant in concept as it is both 'fresh', like the fruit in the smoothies that Innocent makes, and it appeals to a wider target audience. This embraces all ages, and that all-important stalwart of all that is British – the family group. In choosing the country fete they are making an association with a strong British tradition, as they did with the Fruitstock, but one with a much longer history and one which is both acceptable and endearing to all. You might get complaints about a pop festival but whoever complains about a country fete? The formula is set for the next 1–3 years, but then they may have a difficult decision to make – how to make it fresh again? The Regent's Park event is more for Londoners and even in these days of easy travel it is geographically exclusive. Given the national market that they have they could consider rolling this concept around the country, possibly on a smaller scale as a fete in its own right, or as part of the traditional regional country shows which run from May to August (but with some dilution of their brand identity as the main sponsor). Then again they may want to do something completely fresh.

Dr Laurent Muzellec,
Dublin City University

I would go for option 2. Option 3 is lazy. Brand communities need to be nurtured and rewarded. Brand communities and brand advocates need to be managed delicately yet very proactively. In business, doing nothing is an invitation for the competitors to fill in the void. Option 1 is rather complacent and may be hazardous in the long run. At first sight, option 1 makes some sense. The event has been successful in the past: 'never change a winning team!' But there are signs that the event is rapidly growing out of line with the brand image and the Fruitstock festival may be becoming a brand with its own differentiated community. As a family drink, Innocent should appeal to (young) parents, i.e. adults between the ages of 28 to 45 and their children, i.e. under 13. Festival-goers do not primarily belong to those two age categories. Another issue is that 'the event is becoming unmanageable'. What could be the implications for the brand? What damages could the festival inflict on the brand image if it were to become associated with littering, damage to the environment, or even drugs and binge drinking? It seems that now is the right time for a new event.

Option 2 seems to be the best option if done properly. The idea should be to create a real family event, which would attract young parents with their young kids. The idea of a 'boutique' festival where green, health-conscious parents could enjoy themselves while entertaining their children could be the winning formula. After all, it is the essence of the Innocent product. Health is a constituent of the brand's DNA, but unlike the bio cauliflower, Innocent is also fun and quirky! Of course, from a management point of view this option is also the most challenging. However, the short history of the company demonstrates a culture of entrepreneurship and innovation which should help Innocent to reinvent its brand fests and stay on top of its success.

The Introduction Stage

Like people, products are born, they 'grow up', and eventually they die. We can divide the life of a product into four separate stages; introduction, growth, maturity and decline. The first stage Figure 8.5 shows is the **introduction stage**. Here customers get the first chance to purchase the good or service. During this early stage, a single company usually produces the product. If it works and is profitable, competitors will follow with their own versions.

During the introduction stage, the goal is to get first-time buyers to try the product. Sales (hopefully) increase at a steady but slow pace. As is also evident in Figure 8.5, the company usually does not make a profit during this stage. Why? Research-and-development (R&D) costs and heavy spending for advertising and promotional efforts cut into revenue.

During the introduction stage, pricing may be high to recover the R&D costs (demand permitting) or low to attract large numbers of consumers (see Figure 8.6). For example, the introductory base price of the Lexus GS450h described at the beginning of this chapter was €41,450, nearly the same as the BMW 550i's base of €43,050. The price is designed to appeal to consumers who are willing to pay for the GS450h's unique combination of comfort, great mileage and superb performance. The high cost helps Lexus recover its R&D costs for this revolutionary engineering design.

How long does the introduction stage last? As we saw in Chapter 7's Wi-Fi example, it can be quite long. A number of factors come into play, including marketplace acceptance and the producer's willingness to support its product during start-up.

Not all products make it past the introduction stage. For a new product to be successful, consumers must first know about it. Then they must believe that it is something they want or need. Marketing during this stage often focuses on informing consumers about the product,

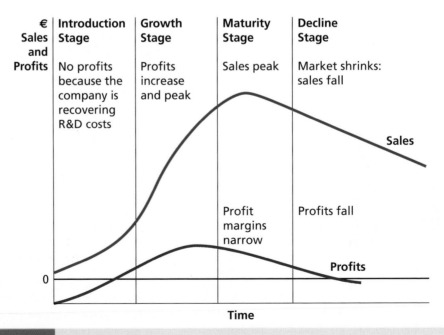

Figure 8.5	The Product Life Cycle
	The product life cycle helps marketers understand how a product changes over its lifetime and suggests how marketing strategies should be modified accordingly.

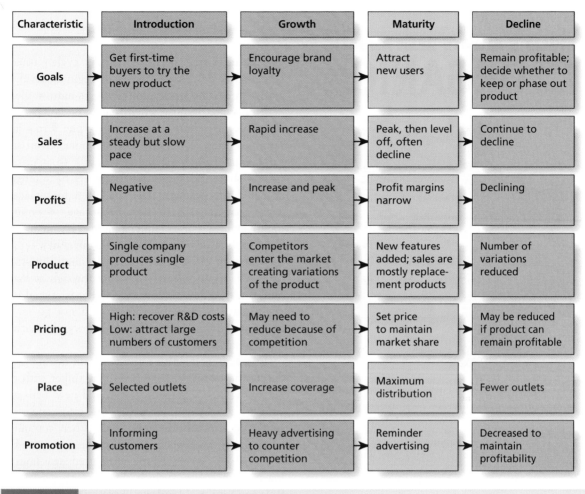

Characteristic	Introduction	Growth	Maturity	Decline
Goals	Get first-time buyers to try the new product	Encourage brand loyalty	Attract new users	Remain profitable; decide whether to keep or phase out product
Sales	Increase at a steady but slow pace	Rapid increase	Peak, then level off, often decline	Continue to decline
Profits	Negative	Increase and peak	Profit margins narrow	Declining
Product	Single company produces single product	Competitors enter the market creating variations of the product	New features added; sales are mostly replacement products	Number of variations reduced
Pricing	High: recover R&D costs Low: attract large numbers of customers	May need to reduce because of competition	Set price to maintain market share	May be reduced if product can remain profitable
Place	Selected outlets	Increase coverage	Maximum distribution	Fewer outlets
Promotion	Informing customers	Heavy advertising to counter competition	Reminder advertising	Decreased to maintain profitability

Figure 8.6   Marketing Mix strategies through the product life cycle
Marketing mix strategies—the Four Ps—change as a product moves through the life cycle.

how to use it, and its promised benefits. Think about Apple's iPhone. However, this isn't nearly as easy as it sounds: nearly 40 per cent of all new products fail.[20]

 ## The Growth Stage

In the **growth stage**, sales increase rapidly while profits increase and peak. Marketing's goal here is to encourage brand loyalty by convincing the market that this brand is superior to others. In this stage, marketing strategies may include the introduction of product variations to attract market segments and increase market share. The mobile phone is an example of a product that is still in its growth stage as worldwide sales continue to increase (though they might have peaked in some countries). A large part of its continued growth is due to relentless product innovation and the building in of converging communication features.

When competitors appear, marketers must use heavy advertising and other types of promotion. Price competition may develop, driving profits down. Some firms may seek to capture a particular segment of the market by positioning their product to appeal to a certain group. And, if pricing has initially been set high, it may be reduced to meet the increasing competition.

PHILLY'S ALWAYS BEEN ANGELIC
NOW IT
CAN BE ORGANIC TOO

IF YOU LOVE PHILLY BUT LIKE TO EAT ORGANIC, THERE'S NOW NEW PHILADELPHIA ORGANIC.
ALL THE COOL, CREAMY TASTE OF YOUR FAVOURITE PHILLY BUT MADE USING
THE FINEST ORGANICALLY SOURCED INGREDIENTS. A LITTLE TASTE OF HEAVEN.

Photo 8.3   Companies continue to modify their products to breathe life into them when in the maturity phase.
Source: The Advertising Archives

The Maturity Stage

The **maturity stage** of the product life cycle is usually the longest. Sales peak and then begin to level off and even decline while profit margins narrow. Competition grows intense when remaining competitors fight for their share of a shrinking pie. Firms may resort to price reductions and reminder advertising ('did you brush your teeth today?') to maintain market share. Because most customers have already accepted the product, sales are often to replace a 'worn-out' item or to take advantage of product improvements. For example, almost everyone owns a TV, which means most people who buy a new set are replacing an older one. During the maturity stage, firms will try to sell their product through as many outlets as possible because availability is crucial in a competitive market. Consumers will not go far to find one particular brand if satisfactory alternatives are close at hand.

To remain competitive and maintain market share during the maturity stage, firms may tinker with the marketing mix. Competitors may add new 'bells and whistles', as when producers of potato crisps and other snack foods modify their products. When consumers became concerned about carbohydrates and turned to diets such as Atkins, Nestlé introduced new lines of low-carb chocolate, such as the low-carb versions of Rolo and Kit Kat.[21] Unilever likewise rolled out 18 new low-carb products, rejuvenating venerable brands like Ragu spaghetti sauce and Wishbone salad dressing.[22]

Attracting new users of the product can be another strategy that marketers use in the maturity stage. Market development means introducing an existing product to a market that doesn't currently use it. Many UK and Scandinavian firms are finding new markets in developing countries such as China for products whose domestic sales are stagnant. For example, Nokia, the world's largest mobile phone manufacturer, is offsetting stagnated domestic sales with aggressive investment in growth in the Chinese market, where it holds a 35 per cent share of the market.[23]

 ## The Decline Stage

The **decline stage** of the product life cycle is characterised by a decrease in product category sales. The reason may be obsolescence forced by new technology – where do you see a new typewriter in this computer age or VHS video or a cassette tape? Although a single firm may still be profitable, the market as a whole begins to shrink, profits decline, there are fewer variations of the product and suppliers pull out. In this stage, there are usually many competitors, with none having a distinct advantage.

A firm's major product decision in the decline stage is whether to keep the product at all. An unprofitable product drains resources that could be better used to develop newer products. If the decision is to keep the product, advertising and other marketing communications may be decreased to cut costs, and prices may be reduced if the product can remain profitable. If the decision is to drop the product, it can be eliminated in two ways: phase it out by cutting production in stages and letting existing stocks run out, or simply drop the product immediately. If the established market leader anticipates that there will be some residual demand for the product for a long time, it may make sense to keep the product on the market. The idea is to sell a limited quantity of the product with little or no support from sales, merchandising, advertising and distribution and just let it 'wither on the vine'.

In the web era, some products that otherwise would have died a natural death in the shops continue to sell online to a cadre of fans, backed by zero marketing support. Banana Mojos, Blackcurrant Chewits and Cola Frosties are sold direct to consumers by online purveyors such as handycandy.co.uk. Before the web, those sweets would have been doomed by aggressive marketing budgets for all the new product introductions in the category by competitors such as Haribo or M&M's.

Oil of Olay has been a great example of a product that, like a cat, has had many lives through the product life cycle. The pink moisturiser was developed during the Second World War for Britain's Royal Air Force as a lotion to treat burns. In 1962, another company bought it and started to market it as a 'beauty fluid'. Procter & Gamble acquired that company in 1985 and reinvigorated it by pumping in a lot of advertising spend. In the early 1990s, P&G started to launch line extensions built around the Oil of Olay name. The company also began revamping the product's image to make it more appealing to women. P&G found through research that some consumers were put off by the word 'oil' because they equate it with greasy. Now the €260 million range of skin-care products and cosmetics is known simply as Olay, aimed at women who want to 'love the skin you're in'. The Olay line now includes over a dozen brand extensions such as Total Effects (to diminish middle-aged consumers' fine lines and wrinkles), Complete (an all-day moisturiser with ultraviolet protection), and Ribbons body wash (with your choice of aloe extract, almond oil or jojoba butter). Olay's an example of a product with life cycle staying power![24]

Creating Product Identity: Branding Decisions

Objective

3

Discuss how branding creates product identity and describe different types of branding strategies

Marketers keep close tabs on their products' life cycle status, and plan accordingly. Equally important, though, is giving that product an identity, as Ferrero did with Kinder Bueno; which is made of layers of crispy waffle with hazelnut filling and a milk chocolate wrapping. That's where branding comes in. The brand personality connotes pure, unadulterated fun, and the launch featured TV adverts with the animated Nutshells, a band of musical elephants. How important is branding? In 2007 the total amount spent on advertising in the UK was £19.4 billion. One of the heaviest advertisers was the government, which spent over £158 million on advertisements. The global total for 2009 is expected to be $21 billion.[25]

We said earlier that nearly 40 per cent of all new products fail, but for new brands the failure rate is even higher – up to 80 to 90 per cent.[26] Branding is an extremely important (and expensive) element of product strategies. In this section, we'll examine what a brand is and how certain laws protect brands. Then we'll discuss the importance of branding and how firms make branding decisions.

What's in a Name (or a Symbol)?

How do you identify your favourite brand? By its name? By the logo (how the name appears)? By the packaging? By some graphic image or symbol, such as the Guinness harp? A **brand** is a name, a term, a symbol, or any other unique element of a product that identifies one firm's product(s) and sets it apart from the competition. Consumers easily recognise the Coca-Cola logo, and the illuminated golden arches of McDonald's when driving at night. Branding provides the recognition factor products need to succeed in regional, national and international markets.

There are several important considerations in selecting a brand name, brand mark or trade character. First, it must have a positive connotation and be memorable. Kentucky Fried Chicken changed its name to KFC in 1991. The reasons for the name change included the move to de-emphasise 'chicken' as the company started to offer more varied menus that included other types of food, to eliminate the word 'fried' because it had a negative connotation as consumers became more health-conscious, and to use an abbreviation to make the brand name more memorable.[27]

A brand name is probably the most used and most recognised form of branding. Coca-Cola and Disney are sometimes two of the first words children learn. Smart marketers use brand names to maintain relationships with consumers 'from the cradle to the grave'. For example, McDonald's now markets Salads Plus to appeal to adults who live a healthy lifestyle or are on a diet.

A good brand name may position a product by conveying a certain image or personality (Nature Valley, crunchy granola bar) or by describing how it works (Kleenoff, Vanish). Brand names such as Palmolive and Shield help position these different brands of bath soap by saying different things about the benefits they promise. Carex handwash provides an unerring image of gentle hand cleaning. The Nissan Xterra combines the word *terrain* with the letter *X*, which many young people associate with extreme sports, to give the brand name a cutting-edge, off-road feel.

How does a firm select a good brand name? Good brand designers say there are four 'easy' tests: easy to say, easy to spell, easy to read and easy to remember – like Daz, Bold, Lenor and Head & Shoulders. And the name should also 'fit' four ways: fit the target market, fit the product's benefits, fit the customer's culture and fit legal requirements.

When it comes to graphics for a brand symbol, name or logo, the rule is that it must be recognisable and memorable. No matter how small or how large, the triangular Nabisco logo in the corner of the box is a familiar sight. In addition, it should have visual impact. That means that from across a shop or when you are quickly flicking through the pages in a magazine, the brand will catch your attention. Some marketers enhance brand recognition by creating a trade character such as the Pillsbury Dough Boy or the Playboy Bunny.

Trademarks

A **trademark** is the legal term for a brand name, brand mark or trade character. The symbol for legal registration in the UK is a capital 'R' in a circle:® Marketers register trademarks to make their use by competitors illegal. Because trademark protection applies only in individual countries where the brand has been registered, unauthorised use of marks on counterfeit products made in foreign countries is a huge headache for many companies.

A firm can have protection for a brand even if it has not legally registered it. In the UK, *common-law protection* exists if the firm has used the name and established it over a period of time. Although a registered trademark prevents others from using it on a similar product, it may not bar its use for a product in a completely different type of business. Consider the range of 'Quaker' brands: Quaker Oats (cereals), Quaker Funds (mutual funds), Quaker State (motor oil), Quaker Bonnet (gift food baskets) and Quaker Safety Products Corporation (firemen's clothing). This principle was recently applied when Apple Corp., the Beatles' music company, sued Apple Computers in 2006 over its use of the Apple logo. The plaintiff wanted to win an injunction to prevent Apple Computer from using the Apple logo in connection with its iPod and iTunes products; it argued that the application to music-related products came too close to the Beatles' musical products. The judge didn't agree; he ruled that the logo was clearly used in relation to the download service, not to the music itself.[28]

Marketing Metrics

Millward Brown Brand Dynamics

Millward Brown tracks the importance of over 50,000 brands in 60 countries. It offers summary measurements under the name Brand Dynamics, which it describes as measures of past performance (called Brand Presence) and future potential (called Brand Voltage); these two figures are distilled from research data using proprietary formulae. The company has also used its Brand Dynamics scores to estimate the brand valuations of the world's top brands, which it publishes every year in its BrandZ survey (www.brandz.com). For 2008 the top three brands were Google (valued at $86,057m), General Electric ($71,379m) and Microsoft ($70,887m).

 ## The Importance of Branding

A brand is a lot more than just the product it represents – the best brands build an emotional connection with the consumer. Strong brands don't just meet rational needs, they create an emotional reaction. Think about the most popular nappy brands – they're named Pampers and Huggies, not some functionally descriptive name like AbsorbancyMaster. The point is that Pampers and Huggies evoke the joys of parenting, not the utility of the nappy.

Marketers spend huge amounts of money on new product development, advertising and promotion to develop strong brands. When they succeed, this investment creates **brand equity**, which is a brand's value to its organisation over and above the value of the generic version of the product (that is, how much extra will you pay for a golf shirt with a Ralph Lauren logo on it than for the same shirt with no logo?). (See the Marketing Metrics boxes on the subject for what they get back for their money.) We can identify different levels of loyalty or lack thereof by assessing how customers feel about the product. At the lowest level, customers really have no loyalty to a brand and will change brands for any reason, often jumping ship if they find something else at a lower price. At the other extreme, some brands command fierce devotion, and loyal users will go without rather than buy a competing brand.

Figure 8.7 shows one way to think about these escalating levels of attachment to a brand. At the lowest level of the 'brand equity pyramid', consumers are aware of a brand's existence. Moving up the pyramid, they might look at the brand in terms of what it literally does for them or how it performs relative to competitors. Going up still further, they may think more deeply about the product and form beliefs and emotional reactions to it. The truly successful brands, however, are those that make the long climb to the top of the pyramid – they 'bond' with their customers so that people feel they have a real relationship with the product. Here are some of the types of relationships a person might have with a product:

- **Self-concept attachment:** The product helps establish the user's identity. (For example, do you feel more like yourself in Ralph Lauren or Diesel clothing?)

- **Nostalgic attachment:** The product serves as a link with a past self. (Does eating the inside of a Cadbury Creme Egg remind you of childhood?)

- **Interdependence:** The product is a part of the user's daily routine. (Could you get through the day without a Starbucks or Caffe Nero coffee?)

- **Love:** The product elicits emotional bonds of warmth, passion or other strong emotion. (Ever been to a match between Arsenal and Manchester United?)[29]

As the pyramid in Figure 8.7 shows us, the way to build strong brands is to build strong bonds with customers – bonds based on *brand meaning*. Try and apply this to Innocent drinks.

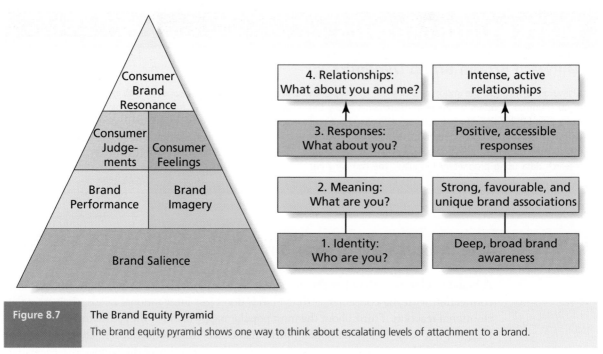

Figure 8.7	**The Brand Equity Pyramid** The brand equity pyramid shows one way to think about escalating levels of attachment to a brand.

Source: Kevin Lane Keller, Building Customer-Based Brand Equity: A Blueprint for Creating Strong Brands, Working Paper Series, Report 01–107 (Cambridge, MA: Marketing Science Institute, 2001), 7.

What attachments spring to mind? This concept encompasses the beliefs and associations that a consumer has about the brand. In many ways, the practice of brand management revolves around the management of meanings. Brand managers, advertising agencies, package designers, name consultants, logo developers and public relations firms are just some of the collaborators in a global industry devoted to the task of meaning management. This complex and synergistic system is based on one simple but critical truth: strong brands are built on strong meanings. The corollary: brands die when their meanings lose value in consumers' worlds. Table 8.2 shows some of the dimensions of brand meaning.

Brand equity means that a brand enjoys customer loyalty because the customers are not only aware of it but they also perceive it to be superior to the competition. For a firm, brand equity provides a competitive advantage because it gives the brand the power to capture and hold on to a larger share of the market and to sell at prices with higher profit margins. For example, among pianos, the Steinway name has such brand equity that 95 per cent of concert pianists use a Steinway.[30]

What makes a brand successful? Here are ten characteristics of the world's top brands:[31]

1. The brand excels at delivering the benefits customers truly desire.

2. The brand stays relevant.

3. The pricing strategy is based on consumers' perceptions of value.

4. The brand is properly positioned.

5. The brand is consistent.

6. The brand portfolio and hierarchy make sense.

7. The brand makes use of and coordinates a full repertoire of marketing activities to build brand equity.

8. The brand's managers understand what the brand means to consumers.

Dimension	Example
Brand identification markers	Coca-Cola's red and white colours, the Nike logo, Harley-Davidson's characteristic sound
Product attribute and benefit associations	Starbucks as good coffee; BMW as the ultimate driving machine
Gender	World Wrestling Forum, Harley-Davidson, Marlboro and masculinity; Laura Ashley and femininity
Social class	Mercedes and the old-guard elite; Primark and the lower classes
Age	Nokia and the iPod
Reference group	Marks & Spencer and the smart-casual workforce; B&Q and the serious home improver
Life stage	Dewar's and the coming of age; Fisher Price and babies
Lifestyles and taste subcultures	BMW and the 'yuppie'; Red Bull and the club culture
Place	Coke and America; Chelsea FC and London
Time and decade	Marylin Monroe and the 1950s; VW and the 1960s' countercultural revolution
Trends	John Lewis and cocooning; Pret A Manger and small indulgences
Traditions and rituals	Häagen-Dazs ice cream and the pampering of self

Table 8.2 Dimensions of Brand Meaning

Source: Adapted from Susan Fournier, Michael R. Solomon, Basil G. Englis and Jeff Green, 'How Brands Mean: Resonance as a Mediator of the Brand Meaning – Brand Strength Connection', unpublished manuscript, March 2004.

9. The brand is given proper support, and that support is sustained over the long run.

10. The company monitors sources of brand equity.

Products with strong brand equity provide enticing opportunities. A firm may leverage a brand's equity with **brand extensions**: new products sold with the same brand name. For example, in 2004 premium ice cream maker Häagen-Dazs decided to get into the growing 'low fat' ice cream market. Its choices were to create a new brand or modify the existing one. They chose to introduce the line as Häagen-Dazs Light, sold as having 'all the taste and texture of original Häagen-Dazs with only half the fat'. The brand extension was an immediate success, and soon 14 flavours carried the Light banner, many of which were available only as Light. More generally, this success highlights the potential value of a strong brand name: although many people assume the European sounding name assures high quality, in reality the name is made up. The company started in the Bronx, New York, and today Pillsbury owns it![32]

Playboy also expanded its brand to increase recognition of the magazine and to support its sales. It sells a wide range of merchandise. You can find Playboy branded cushions, cosmetics, lingerie, mobile phone and party accessories in high street Playboy Stores in Oxford Street, London, or in other retailers like Argos.

Because of the existing brand equity, a firm is able to sell its brand extension at a higher price than if it had given it a new brand, and the brand extension will attract new customers immediately. Of course, if the brand extension does not live up to the quality or attractiveness of the original brand, brand equity will suffer, as will brand loyalty and sales. Having read this section, how does it help to you to decide which of the options for saying 'thank you' given at the start of the chapter fits in with Innocent's brand image?

Branding Strategies

Because brands are important to a marketing programme's success, branding strategies are a major part of product decision making. Marketers have to determine whether to create individual or family brands, national or shop brands, or co-brands – it's not that easy.

Individual Brands Versus Family Brands

Part of developing a branding strategy is deciding whether to use a separate, unique brand for each product item – an *individual brand strategy* – or market several items under the same brand name – a **family brand** or *umbrella brand* strategy. Individual brands may do a better job of communicating clearly and concisely what attributes, values and benefits the consumer can expect from the specific product while a well-known company like Apple may find that its high brand equity in other categories (like computers) can sometimes 'rub off' on a new brand (like the iPod). The decision of whether to use an individual or family branding strategy often depends on characteristics of the product and whether the company's overall product strategy calls for introduction of a single, unique product or for the

Marketing Metrics

Brand Equity

Brand equity is the comparative value of a product with a particular brand name compared with the value of a product without the brand name. Many corporations, marketing research firms and ad agencies have devised various measures of brand equity because this is an effective way to assess if a branding strategy has been successful. For example, Interbrand conducts a study every year to measure the equity of global brands and rank the best 100. The company analyses the brands according to three aspects: financial contribution of the brand, the role of the brand within the company strategy and the brand strength, i.e. awareness of what the brand stands for. In its 2008 rankings the top five brands were: (1) Coca-Cola, (2) IBM, (3) Microsoft, (4) General Electric and (5) Nokia.[33] Check out www.interbrand.com for full details.

If consumers have strong, positive feelings about a brand and are willing to pay extra to choose it over others, you are in marketing heaven. Each of the following approaches to measuring brand equity has some good points and some bad points:

1. *Customer mind-set metrics* focus on consumer awareness attitudes and loyalty towards a brand. However, these metrics are based on consumer surveys and don't usually provide a single objective measure that can be used to assign a financial value to the brand.

2. *Product-market outcomes metrics* focus on the ability of a brand to charge a higher price than the one charged by an unbranded equivalent. This usually involves asking consumers how much more they would be willing to pay for a certain brand compared with others. These measures often rely on hypothetical judgements and can be complicated to use.

3. *Financial market metrics* consider the purchase price of a brand if it is sold or acquired. They may also include subjective judgements about the future stock price of the brand.

A team of marketing academics has proposed a simpler measure that they claim reliably tracks the value of a brand over time. Their *revenue premium* metric compares the revenue a brand generates with the revenue generated by a similar private-label product (that doesn't have any brand identification). In this case, brand equity is just the difference in revenue (net price times volume) between a branded good and a corresponding private label.[34]

development of a group of similar products. For example, Microsoft serves as a strong umbrella brand for a host of diverse individually branded products such as Office, internet Explorer, Xbox and MSN web Search, while Procter & Gamble prefers to brand each of its household products separately.

National and Own-Label Brands

Retailers today often are in the driver's seat when it comes to deciding what brands to stock and push. In addition to choosing from producers' brands, called **national or manufacturer brands**, retailers decide whether to offer their own versions. **Own-label brands**, also called **private-label** or *own brands*, are the retail shop's or chain's exclusive trade name. Tesco, for example, sells own brand Tesco Healthy Living ready meals and Tesco Diet Cola along with national brands such as Weight Watchers and Coca-Cola. Own brands are gaining in popularity for many value-conscious shoppers. Retailers continue to develop new ones, and some are adding services to the mix: Asda now has opticians and pharmacies in its shops and Sainsbury's is planning to offer an out-of-hours GP walk-in service.

Retailers choose an own-label branding strategy because they generally make more profit on these than on national brands. Even mid-range retailers such as John Lewis now offer private-label clothing to lure millions of customers away from more upmarket department stores as well as lower end discounters. John Lewis' own-label shirts, trousers and coats for men have become a significant competitive force against national brands like French Connection fcuk, Timberland and Levi's.

In addition, if you stock a unique brand that consumers can't find in other shops it makes it much harder for shoppers to compare 'apples with apples' across shops and simply buy the brand where they find it sold for the lowest price. Tesco, the UK's largest supermarket chain, developed its own Tesco Finest 'premium quality' own-label brand. Tesco sells over 1100 food items under the Tesco Finest label, from biscuits to beef, olive oil, copying paper and kitchen utensils. Under the own-label, Tesco can introduce new products at high quality but lower prices than brand names. It can also keep entire categories profitable by its mix of pricing options. Competitors that sell only national brands can cut prices on those brands, but that hurts their overall profitability. Tesco can bring prices down on national brands but still make money on its own-label products.[35]

Generic Brands

An alternative to either national or store branding is **generic branding**, which is basically no branding. Generic branded products are typically packaged in white with black lettering that name only the product itself (for example, 'green beans'). Generic branding is one strategy to meet customers' demand for the lowest prices on standard products such as dog food or kitchen towels. Generic brands were first popularised during the inflationary period of the 1980s, when consumers became especially price conscious because of rising prices. However, today generic brands account for very little consumer spending.

Licensing

Some firms choose to use a **licensing** strategy to brand their products. A licensing agreement means that one firm sells another firm the right to use a legally protected brand name for a specific purpose and for a specific period of time. Firms do this for a variety of reasons. Licensing can provide instant recognition and consumer interest in a new product, and this strategy can quickly position a product for a certain target market by trading on the high recognition of the licensed brand among consumers in that segment. For example, distiller Brown-Forman licensed

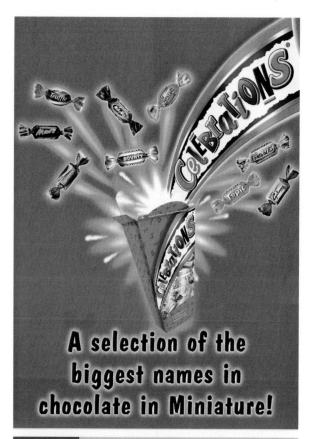

A selection of the biggest names in chocolate in Miniature!

Photo 8.4   Adverts for Celebrations are a good example of ingredient branding as they focus on the strength of the component brands within the product.
Source: The Advertising Archives

its Jack Daniels bourbon name to T.G.I. Friday's for use on all sorts of menu items from shrimp to steak to chicken. The menu partnership has been highly successful, contributing to a turnaround in sales at Friday's in the highly competitive mid-range family restaurant space.[36]

Much better known, however, is the licensing of entertainment names, such as when film producers license their properties to manufacturers of a seemingly infinite number of products. Each time the blockbuster Harry Potter films hit the screens, a plethora of Potter products packed the shops. In addition to toys and games, you can buy Harry Potter sweets, clothing, all manner of back-to-school items, home items, and even wands and cauldrons.

Co-Branding

Co-branding examples include Nat West and Mastercard credit card, Ford and *Elle* magazine to form Ford Focus Elle, Brita on Electrolux fridge freezers. Strange marriages? No, these are examples of **co-branding**, as is the Jack Daniels/T.G.I. Friday's combination. This branding strategy benefits both partners when combining the two brands provides more recognition power than either enjoys alone. For example, Panasonic markets digital cameras that use Leica lenses. Leica lenses are legendary for their superb image quality. Panasonic is known for its consumer electronics. Combining the best in traditional camera optics with a household name in consumer electronics helps both brands.

A new and fast-growing variation on co-branding is **ingredient branding**, in which branded materials become 'component parts' of other branded products.[37] This was the strategy behind the classic 'Intel inside' campaign that encouraged millions of consumers to ask by name for a highly technical computer part (a processor) that they wouldn't otherwise recognise if they fell over it.[38] Today, consumers can buy Häagen-Daz Bailey's Ice Cream, Carl Zeiss lenses in Sony cameras or Scotchguard in fabrics. The ultimate co-branding deal for chocolate lovers may be a box of Celebrations sweets, which includes up to six brands in a single package. Mars, Bounty, Snickers, Galaxy, Malteaser and Milkyway are all part of the package. Brand heaven!

The practice of ingredient branding has two main benefits. First, it attracts customers to the host brand because the ingredient brand is familiar and has a strong brand reputation for quality. Second, the ingredient brand's firm can sell more of its product, not to mention the additional revenues it gets from the licensing arrangement.[39]

Creating Product Identity: Packaging and Labelling Decisions

How do you know if the cola you are drinking is 'normal' or 'caffeine free'? How do you keep your low-fat grated cheese fresh after you have used some of it? Why do you always leave your bottle of Kylie's new perfume out on your dresser so everyone can see it? The answer to all

Marketing Ethics

Tesco and Disney: attempting to enforce a snow white food policy

Disney is increasing its focus on healthy snacks with the introduction of a new co-branded line with UK supermarket Tesco. While helping present the company as a responsible business, the move could also be highly lucrative for Disney as it further exploits consumer interest in healthier foods. The deal will allow Disney cartoon characters to appear on selected fresh fruit lines at Tesco and it will expand to include yogurt and breakfast cereals. Disney is not merely forming these deals for altruistic reasons, but because it believes the healthy snack area will be highly lucrative in the long term. As long as the company remembers to keep its products fun-looking, it should succeed in appealing to children as well as parents. The advantages for Tesco are that Disney is well known in the children's market and could stimulate children to buy more fruit while at the same time it fits with Tesco's ethical policy of promoting good food to children.

Food MarketWatch, December 2007

Debate, Discuss, Disagree

Disney had a partnership with McDonald's Happy Meals for 10 years and when it ended the deal cost the company approximately $100 million a year in royalties.

1 What would be the main purpose of Disney licensing its cartoon characters to Tesco?

2 Where do you draw the line at this kind of promotion directly aimed at children?

these questions is effective packaging and labelling. So far, we've talked about how marketers create product identity with branding. In this section, we'll learn that packaging and labelling decisions also are important in creating product identity.

Packaging Functions

A **package** is the covering or container for a product, but it's also a way to create a competitive advantage. The important functional value of a package is that it protects the product. For example, packaging for computers, TV sets and stereos protects the units from damage during shipping, storage and shelf life. Cereal, crisps or packs of grated cheese wouldn't be edible for long if packaging didn't provide protection from moisture, dust, odours and insects. The chicken broth in Figure 8.8 is protected (before opening) from spoilage by a multilayered soft box. In addition to protecting the product, effective packaging makes it easy for consumers to handle and store the product. Figure 8.8 shows how packaging serves a number of different functions.

Over and above these utilitarian functions, however, the packaging plays an important role in communicating brand personality. Effective product packaging uses colours, words, shapes, designs and pictures to provide brand and name identification for the product. Packaging is the silent salesperson sitting next to the competition on retail shelves. The product's packaging not only needs to get busy consumers' attention but also has to 'scream' BUY ME as they pass by. In addition, packaging provides specific information consumers want and need, such as information about the specific variety, flavour or fragrance, directions for use, suggestions for other uses (for example, recipes), product warnings and product ingredients. Packaging may also include warranty information and a free phone number for customer service.

Figure 8.8	Functions of Packaging
	Great packaging provides a covering for a product, and it also creates a competitive advantage for the brand.

Marketing Ethics

To eat or not to eat? That is the question

In February 2007, Cadbury had a problem with thousands of Easter eggs which were distributed without nut allergy warnings. It was criticised for sending retailers stickers to place on the packaging rather than recalling all the eggs. This followed an incident in June 2006 where Cadbury recalled 1 million bars of chocolate after salmonella contamination.

The company has been accused of a cover-up after failing to notify the authorities months after it knew about the problem. It still faces prosecution.

'An Unexpected Bitter Taste',
Marketing Week, 5 April 2007

Debate, Discuss, Disagree

1   Did Cadbury act in an ethical way?

2   How should it have acted?

We've already talked about Häagen-Dazs; now let's see how rival Ben & Jerry's redesigned its ice-cream packaging in the late 1990s to make its more user friendly.[40] Because the top of the carton is the first thing customers see in a chest freezer, the company replaced the photo of Ben and Jerry that used to appear on the top lid with text identifying the flavour. Other changes included a more upmarket look with a black-on-gold colour scheme and enticing realistic watercolours of the product's ingredients. The result was increased ease of shopping for consumers.

A final communication element is the **Universal Product Code (UPC)**, which is the set of black bars or lines printed on the side or bottom of most items sold in grocery shops and other mass-merchandising outlets. The UPC is a national system of product identification. Each product has a unique 10-digit number assigned to it. These numbers supply specific information about the type of item (grocery item, meat, produce, medicines, or a discount voucher), the manufacturer (a 5-digit code), and the specific product (another 5-digit code). At checkout counters, electronic scanners read the UPC bars and automatically transmit data to a computer controlling the cash register, allowing retailers to track sales and control inventory.

 ## Designing Effective Packaging

Should the package have a zip closing, feature an easy-to-pour spout, be compact for easy storage, be short and fat so it won't fall over, or be tall and skinny so it won't take up much shelf space? Designing effective packaging involves a multitude of decisions.

Planners must consider the packaging of other brands in the same product category. For example, milk usually comes in plastic bottles. Waitrose, the UK supermarket, offers milk in a bag, which uses 75 per cent less packaging. Not all customers are willing to accept a radical change in packaging, however, and other retailers may be reluctant to sell milk bags because they would need to adjust their shelf space to accommodate such packages. In addition to functional benefits, the choice of packaging material can make an aesthetic statement. Enclosing a fine liqueur in a velvet or silk bag may enhance its image. A fine perfume packaged in a beautifully designed glass bottle means consumers are buying not only the fragrance but an attractive dressing table accessory as well.

Firms seeking to act in a socially responsible manner must also consider the environmental damage caused by packaging. Shiny gold or silver packaging transmits an image of quality and opulence, but certain metallic inks are not biodegradable and are harmful to the environment. Some firms are developing innovative *green packaging* that is less harmful to the environment than other materials. Of course, there is no guarantee that consumers will accept such packaging. They didn't take to plastic pouch refills for certain spray bottle products even though the pouches may take up less space in landfills than the bottles do. They didn't like pouring the refill into their old spray bottles. Still, customers have accepted small packages of concentrated products such as laundry detergent, dishwashing liquid and fabric softener.

What about the shape: Square? Round? Triangular? Hourglass? How about an old-fashioned bottle that consumers can reuse as an attractive storage container? What colour should it be? White to communicate purity? Yellow because it reminds people of lemon freshness? Brown because the flavour is chocolate? Sometimes these decisions trace back to irrelevant personal factors. The familiar Campbell's Soup label is red and white because a company executive many years ago liked the sports kit at a university!

Finally, what graphic information should the package show? Should there be a picture of the product on the package? Should cans of green beans always show a picture of green beans? Should there be a picture of the results of using the product, such as beautiful hair? Should there be a picture of the product in use, perhaps a box of crackers showing crackers with delicious looking toppings arranged on a silver tray? Should there be a recipe or coupon on the back? Of course, all these decisions rest on a marketer's understanding of consumers, ingenuity and perhaps a little creative luck.

 ## Labelling Regulations

The Trade Descriptions Act of 1968 prevents manufacturers, retailers or service industry providers in the UK from supplying misleading information to customers about their products. The law empowers courts to punish those companies that make false statements about their products or services. The EU introduced the Unfair Commercial Practices Directive, it gives consumers a high level of protection and it also aims to harmonise the fair trading laws of the member states.

In the UK the Customer Protection Act 1987 relates to liabilities a firm has to face if its defective pharmaceutical products, bio-mechanical devices and general medical equipment

---

Across the Hall

Advice for Jamie Mitchell

Marcel Knobil is a leading expert, author and consultant on branding, founder of Superbrands and chair of Creative & Commercial

This is easier than the first question on *Who Wants to be a Millionaire*? Success isn't just about numbers: in this case it must be about an event that reflects and promotes the Innocent brand. They could have had a lapdancing show in the park (very fruity) and attracted even more attendees, but what does it say about the brand?

I visited a number of Fruitstocks and enjoyed them. However, besides being free, there was little distinction from some other music festivals I have attended.

Innocent is meant to be different. In so much of what it does it stands apart from its competitors. Whether it be its product, packaging, vehicles or customer service, Innocent has delivered in exceptional fashion. Yet Fruitstock was not exceptional.

What was required was an event that echoed the values and personality of the brand. Yes, 'friendly' and 'quirky' but also (I would guess) pure, natural and honest. Innocent village fete certainly walks (dances, skips and waddles) the talk far better than any of the other options. The village fete idea reeks of innocence and purity. Whilst I can think of far more appropriate attractions than mechanical diggers, the theme makes eminent sense.

Not only would I anticipate that this event would far better reflect and promote the Innocent brand, but it reinforces its freshness. And a pragmatic anticipated bonus is less noise and a better-behaved crowd. The donation to charity only reinforces the good nature of the brand.

Although I feel that Fruitstock was misguided, it is a rare mistake from a brand that I have great admiration for. Having accomplished so much within a short time, I fear that a huge multinational vulture or two are hovering over the Innocent. Crunch decision time will not be its village fete, but its corporate fate.

cause an injury. The General Product Safety Regulation 1994 amends the Customer Protection Act 1987 and extends it to all suppliers of all consumer goods and requires them to supply products that are safe in normal or reasonably foreseeable use.

The Sale of Goods Act states that what your company sells in the UK must fit its description, be of satisfactory quality and be fit for its purpose. If not, then the supplier is obliged to sort out the problem.[41]

The Food Labelling Regulations 1998 and 1999 describe requirements that pre-packed food sold in the UK needs to contain on the label. The name of the food, date mark, weight and alcohol strength (if applicable) must be in the same field of vision. The producer also needs to list the place of origin, storage conditions and instructions for use if it would be difficult to use the product without it, for example how to make a cake from cake mix. The list of ingredients must be indicated as well, in a descending order by weight, certain categories such as additives must be indentified by category name and by chemical name or serial number.[42]

Organising for Effective Product Management

Of course, firms don't create great packaging, brands or products – people do. Like all elements of the marketing mix, the effectiveness of product strategies depends on marketing managers. In this section, we'll talk about how firms organise themselves to manage existing products and develop new products.

Management of Existing Products

Objective

5

Describe how organisations are structured for new and existing product management

In small firms, a single marketing manager usually handles the marketing function, being responsible for new product planning, advertising, working with the company's few sales representatives, marketing research and just about everything else. But in larger firms there are managers responsible for different brands, product categories or markets. Depending on the organisation, product management may include brand managers, product category managers and market managers. Let's take a look at how each operates.

Brand Managers

Sometimes a firm sells different brands within a single product category. For example, Nestlé produces quite a few different brands of its Nescafé, including Gold Blend, Collection, Half Caff, Black Gold and Dolce Gusto. In such cases, each brand may have its own **brand manager** who is responsible for coordinating all marketing activities for a brand: positioning, identifying target markets, research, distribution, sales promotion, packaging and evaluating the success of these decisions.

While this assignment is still common, some big firms are changing the way they allocate responsibilities. For example, today Procter & Gamble's brand managers function more like internal consultants to cross-functional P&G teams located in the field that have responsibility for managing the complete business of key retail clients across all product lines. Brand managers still are responsible for positioning of brands and developing brand equity, but they also work closely with people from sales, finance, logistics and others to serve the needs of the major retailers that comprise the majority of P&G's business.

By its very nature, the brand management system is not without potential problems. Acting independently, and sometimes competitively against each other, brand managers may fight for increases in short-term sales for their own brand. They may push too hard with vouchers, 50 eurocents-off packages, or other price incentives to a point at which customers will refuse to buy the product without them. Such behaviour can hurt long-term profitability and damage brand equity.

Product Category Managers

Some larger firms have such diverse product offerings that they need more extensive co-ordination. Take IBM, for example. Originally known as a computer manufacturer, IBM now generates much of its revenue from a wide range of consulting and related client services across the spectrum of IT applications (and the company doesn't even sell personal computers any more!). In cases such as IBM, organising for product management may include **product category managers**, who coordinate the mix of product lines within the more general product category, such as all products related to telephony solutions, and who consider the addition of new product lines based on client needs.

Market Managers

Some firms have developed a **market manager** structure in which different managers focus on specific customer groups rather than on the products the company makes. This type of organisation can be useful when firms offer a variety of products that serve the needs of a wide range of customers. For example, Raytheon, a company that specialises in consumer electronics products, special mission aircraft and business aviation, sells some products directly to consumer markets, others to manufacturers and still others to the government. Their customers are best served by a differing focus on these very different markets.

Organising for New Product Development (NPD)

Because launching new products is so important, the management of this process is a serious matter. In some instances, one person handles new product development, but within larger organisations, new product development almost always needs many people. One person, however, may be assigned the role of *new product manager*. Often individuals who are assigned to manage new product development are especially creative people with entrepreneurial skills.

The challenge in large companies is to get specialists in different areas to work together in **NPD teams** or **venture teams**. These teams focus exclusively on the new product development effort. Sometimes the venture team is located away from traditional company offices, usually in a remote location called a 'skunk works'.

Now that you've learned about product management and branding, read 'Real People, Real Decisions' to see which strategy Jamie Mitchell at Innocent drinks selected to say thanks to Innocent customers.

Real People, Real Decisions

How It Worked Out at Innocent

Innocent decided on option 2, the village fete idea. The company hired Sledge, an experienced events management agency, to manage the production of the event. The two-day event in Regent's Park brought a little bit of the country into the city and was attended by 60,000 people including 6000 children.

It brought a little British nostalgia and evoked the innocence of a bygone era. It was friendly, natural and easy to talk about; a bit like Innocent. Customers and business partners alike enjoyed the experience and compared it favourably with other events they attended. The small stages and closeness meant that even the performers said how much they enjoyed getting some intimacy back with the audience. The event wasn't slick and overmanufactured, having a low-tech, old-world charm about it. A key success factor was that because there was so much going on, there was something for everyone; a real family event, which is what Innocent wanted as its smoothies were becoming as popular with children as with their parents. It succeeded in creating a community feeling for a day and a sense of belonging, which is in keeping with

It was friendly, natural and easy to talk about; a bit like Innocent

the Innocent family approach. There was also a VNP (Very Nice People) area for trade partners who sold or supplied Innocent. Not only were Innocent's trade partners treated right royally in the royal park, but also they saw first hand the passion of the participants for the Innocent brand. Finally, as no one else was doing a fete as a brand experience, it was novel and, being the first to do this, Innocent now 'owns' the fete concept.

| Photo 8.6 | Simple, quirky packaging.
Source: Jamie Mitchell |

| Photo 8.7 | Duck herding at the village fete.
Source: Jamie Mitchell |

Marketing Metrics

Measuring success of Innocent's village fete

Interviews with consumers on the day revealed that many thought the event was very 'Innocent'. A follow-up email questionnaire attached to the weekly newsletter to the Innocent 'family' resulted in nearly 1800 replies from which 37 per cent said it was an amazing day; 87 per cent described it as 'an event for all the family' which pleased both Sledge and Innocent as this was the intended target audience. In addition, 51 per cent said they preferred it to Fruitstock. Innocent also tracked all the feedback on its website and email traffic as well as doing a staff survey, since all Innocent staff worked over the two days. In addition, a university student did a video ethnographic study for the company which he could use for his degree. One key advantage was that the fete generated a much better, more cohesive and more aligned set of brand partners than Fruitstock had done, who also contributed financially to the two-day event; the result was that the fete raised £150,000 for three charities. As the event was designed to charm loyal drinkers, Innocent didn't expect to see an increase in sales, but metrics from brand advocacy to PR coverage help understand the value it brings the brand.

Chapter Summary

Now that you have finished reading this chapter, you should be able to

1. **Explain the different product objectives and strategies a firm may choose.** Objectives for individual products may be related to introducing a new product, expanding the market of a regional product, or rejuvenating a mature product. For multiple products, firms may decide on a full or a limited line strategy. Often companies decide to extend their product range with an upward, downward, or two-way stretch or with a filling out strategy, or they may decide to contract a product line. Firms that have several product lines may choose a wide product mix with many different lines or a narrow one with few. Product quality objectives refer to the durability, reliability, degree of precision, ease of use and repair, or degree of aesthetic pleasure.

2. **Explain how firms manage products throughout the product life cycle.** The product life cycle explains how products go through four stages from birth to death. During the introduction stage, marketers seek to get buyers to try the product and may use high prices to recover research and development costs or low prices to get it into the market. During the growth stage, characterised by rapidly increasing sales, marketers may introduce new product variations. In the maturity stage, sales peak and level off. Marketers respond by adding desirable new product features or with market development strategies. During the decline stage, firms must decide whether to phase a product out slowly, to drop it immediately, or, if there is residual demand, to keep the product without costly sales support but maybe some minimal advertising.

3. **Discuss how branding creates product identity and describe different types of branding strategies.** A brand is a name, term, symbol, or other unique element of a product used to identify a firm's product. A brand should be selected that has a positive connotation and is recognisable and memorable. Brand names need to be easy to say, spell, read and remember and should fit the target market, the product's benefits, the customer's culture, and legal requirements. To protect a brand legally, marketers obtain trademark protection. Brands are important because they help maintain customer loyalty and because brand equity or value means a firm is able to attract new customers. Firms may develop individual brand strategies or market many items with a family or umbrella brand strategy. National or manufacturer brands are owned and sold by producers, whereas private-label or shop brands carry the retail or chain store's trade name. Licensing means a firm sells another firm the right to use its brand name. In co-branding strategies, two brands form a partnership in marketing a new product.

4. **Explain the roles packaging and labelling play in developing effective product strategies.** Packaging is the covering or container for a product and serves to protect a product and to allow for easy use and storage of the product. The colours, words, shapes, designs, pictures and materials used in package design communicate a product's identity, benefits, and other important product information. Package designers must consider cost, product protection and communication in creating a package that is functional, aesthetically pleasing and not harmful to the environment. Product labelling in the UK and EU are controlled by laws aimed at making package labels more helpful to consumers.

5. **Describe how organisations are structured for new and existing product management.** To successfully manage existing products, the marketing organisation may include brand managers, product category managers and market managers. Large firms, however, often give new product responsibilities to new product managers or to venture teams, groups of specialists from different areas who work together for a single new product.

Key Terms

Brand 299
Brand equity 301
Brand extensions 303
Brand manager 311
Cannibalisation 290
Co-branding 306
Decline stage 298
Family brand 304
Generic branding 305
Growth stage 297
Ingredient branding 306

Introduction stage 296
ISO 14000 291
ISO 9000 291
Kansei engineering 291
Licensing 305
Market manager 312
Maturity stage 298
National or manufacturer brands 305
Own-label 305
Package 307
Private-label brands 305

Product category managers 312
Product life cycle 294
Product line 287
Product mix 290
Six Sigma 292
Total quality management (TQM) 291
Trademark 300
Universal Product Code (UPC) 309
Venture teams 312

Chapter Review

Marketing Concepts: Testing Your Knowledge

1. Why might a company decide to expand a product range? What are some reasons for contracting a product range? Why do many firms have a product mix strategy?

2. Why is quality such an important product strategy objective? What are the dimensions of product quality? How has e-commerce affected the need for quality product objectives?

3. Explain the product life cycle concept. What are the stages of the product life cycle?

4. How are products managed during the different stages of the product life cycle?

5. What is a brand? What are the characteristics of a good brand name? How do firms protect their brands?

6. What is a national brand? A shop brand? Individual and family brands?

7. What does it mean to license a brand? What is co-branding?

8. What are the functions of packaging? What are some important elements of effective package design?

9. What should marketers know about package labelling?

10. Describe some of the different ways firms organise the marketing function to manage existing products. What are the ways firms organise for the development of new products?

Marketing Concepts: Discussing Choices and Ethical Issues

1. Brand equity means that a brand enjoys customer loyalty, perceived quality and brand name awareness. What brands are you personally loyal to? What is it about the product that creates brand loyalty and thus brand equity?

2. Quality is an important product objective, but quality can mean different things for different products, such as durability, precision, aesthetic appeal and so on. What does quality mean for the following products?
   a. Car;
   b. Pizza;
   c. Trainers;
   d. Hair dryer;
   e. Deodorant;
   f. University education.

3. Firms often take advantage of their popular, well-known brands by developing brand extensions because they know that the brand equity of the original or parent brand will be transferred to the new product. If a new product is of poor quality, it can damage the reputation of the parent brand while a new product that is of superior quality can enhance the parent brand's reputation. What are some examples of brand extensions that have damaged and that have enhanced the parent brand equity?

4. Sometimes marketers seem to stick with the same packaging ideas year after year regardless of whether they are the best possible design. Following is a list of products. For each one, discuss what, if any, problems you have with the package of the brand you use. Then think of ways the package could be improved. Why do you think marketers don't change the old packaging? What would be the results if they adopted your package ideas?

   a. Breakfast cereal;

   b. Washing-up liquid;

   c. Orange juice;

   d. Carton of milk;

   e. Crisps;

   f. Loaf of bread.

5. You learned in the chapter that it's hard to *legally* protect brand names across product categories – Quaker and Apple, for example, and also Delta, which is an airline and a tap. But what about the *ethics* of borrowing a name and applying it to some unrelated products? Think of some new business you might like to start up. Now consider some possible names for the business that are already in use as brands in other unrelated categories. Do you think it would be ethical to borrow one of those names? Why or why not?

Marketing Practice: Applying What You've Learned

1. The web allows consumers to interact directly through blogs and other means with other people so they can praise products they like and criticise those they don't. With several of your fellow students, conduct a brief survey of students and of older consumers. Find out if consumers complain to each other about poor product quality. Have they ever used a website to express their displeasure over product quality? Make a report to your class.

2. You may think of your college or university as an organisation that offers a range of different educational products. Assume that you have been hired as a marketing consultant by your university to examine and make recommendations for extending its product line. Develop alternatives that the university might consider:

   a. Upward line stretch;

   b. Downward line stretch;

   c. Two-way stretch;

   d. Filling-out strategy.

   Describe how each might be accomplished. Evaluate each option.

3. Assume that you are the head of marketing for a firm that markets a large number of speciality food items (gourmet sauces, marinades, relishes and so on). Your firm is interested in improving its marketing management structure. You are considering several alternatives: a brand manager structure, having product category managers or focusing on market managers. Outline the advantages and disadvantages of each type of organisation. What is your recommendation?

4. Assume that you are working in the marketing department of a major manufacturer of athletic shoes. Your firm is introducing a new product, a line of disposable sports clothing. You wonder if it would be better to market the line of clothing with a new brand name or use the family brand name that has already gained popularity with your existing products. Make a list of the advantages and disadvantages of each strategy. Develop your recommendation.

5. Assume that you have been recently hired by Kellogg, the cereal manufacturer. You have been asked to work on a plan for redesigning the packaging for Kellogg's cereals. In a role-playing situation, present the following report to your marketing superior:

   a. Discussion of the problems or complaints customers have with current packaging;

   b. Several package options;

   c. Your recommendations for changing packaging or for keeping the packaging the same.

Marketing Miniproject: Learning by Doing

In any supermarket in any town, you will surely find examples of all the different types of brands discussed in this chapter: individual brands, family brands, national brands, shop brands, and co-branded and licensed products. This miniproject is designed to give you a better understanding of branding as it exists in the marketplace.

1. Go to a typical supermarket in your community.

2. Select two product categories of interest to you: ice cream, cereal, laundry detergent, soup, paper products and so on.

3. Make a list of the brands available in each product category. Identify what type of brand each is. Count the number of shelf facings (the number of product items at the front of each shelf) for each brand.

4. Arrange to talk to the shop manager at a convenient time. Ask the manager to discuss the following:

   a. How the shop decides which brands to carry;

   b. Whether the shop is more likely to carry a new brand that is an individual brand versus a family brand;

   c. What causes a shop to drop a brand;

   d. The profitability of shop brands versus national brands;

   e. Other aspects of branding that the shop manager sees as important from a retail perspective.

5. Present a report to your class on what you learned about the brands in your two product categories.

Real People, Real Surfers

Exploring the Web

As we discussed in this chapter and in Chapter 7, companies protect their products by obtaining patents and legal protection for their brands with trademarks. The UK Intellectual Property Office issues both of these forms of protection. Visit the Intellectual Property Office website at www.ipo.gov.uk. Use the website to answer the following questions.

1. What is a patent? What can be patented?

2. Who may apply for a patent? Can foreign individuals or companies obtain a UK patent? Explain.

3. What happens if someone infringes on a patent?

4. What does the term *patent pending* mean?

5. What is a trademark? What is a service mark?

6. Who may file a trademark application? Do firms have to register a trademark? Explain.

7. What do the symbols TM, SM and ® mean?

8. What are the benefits of trademark registration?

9. What are common-law rights regarding trademarks?

10. How long does a trademark registration last? How long does a patent last?

11. How would you evaluate the Patent and Trademark Office website? Was it easy to navigate? Was it useful? What recommendations do you have for improving the website?

Now, take a look at the website at www.pearsoned.co.uk/solomon to see some videos from YouTube relating to aspects of this chapter.

Also on the website, try some analysis and calculations yourself by looking up the marketing metrics exercise called Product Mix about how brewers model the effects of changing product mix on volume, revenue and profit objectives.

Marketing Plan Exercise

Irn-Bru is an interesting brand with a long history (the history is worth reading – go to www.irn-bru.co.uk, then click on 'History Timeline'). Suffice to say, it is one of the oldest soft drinks brands in the United Kingdom. Assume for a moment that A.G. Barr plc, the owner of Irn-Bru, is doing some marketing planning involving this brand.

1. What are some product line strategies you might suggest that Irn-Bru consider?

2. How important is TQM and product quality in general to a brand like Irn-Bru? How do these issues play into the company's marketing plan?

3. Take a look at the different Irn-Bru products portrayed on its website. Where does each fall on the product life cycle? What leads you to conclude this?

4. What realistic opportunities do you believe exist for brand extensions for Irn-Bru? Explain how the company might go about introducing each to the market.

5. Does Irn-Bru have high brand equity? What evidence do you have for your answer? What can Irn-Bru do to enhance its brand equity, given the 800-pound gorillas it competes against (Coke and Pepsi)?

Marketing in Action Case

Real decisions at Procter & Gamble

You probably use several Procter & Gamble products. The company's well-known brands include Crest toothpaste, Ivory soap, Old Spice Deodorant, Tide and Cheer laundry detergent, Folgers coffee and Pringles potato crisps. How did Procter & Gamble (P&G) become one of the most respected consumer goods companies in the world? The company has stuck to a consistent formula: develop great products, give them a distinctive brand name and bold packaging, promote them heavily to both supply chain members and consumers, and distribute them efficiently to as many retail locations as possible. P&G's ability to execute its formula for success is well documented (sales exceeding $60 billion with profits over $8 billion) and is one that should lead to even greater success in the future.

Given its already amazing history of success, why would P&G spend $57 billion to acquire Gillette – a company that had total sales and profits of only $10.48 billion and $1.69 billion, respectively, in the two years before the 2005 acquisition? One reason is because of Gillette's stable of well-known brands, including its lucrative razor and blade line (Sensor, Venus, Mach 3 and Fusion brands, for example), which account for an over 70 per cent market share in the razor product category. Even with this added brand strength, there's an even bigger reason P&G wanted Gillette – the opportunity for economies of scope P&G can realise from pushing Gillette's line of products through P&G's already established (and legendarily efficient) channels of distribution. To understand just how extensive and efficient the P&G channels are, let's

compare the market coverage achieved by two razor products: one introduced by pre-P&G Gillette (Mach 3) and one introduced post-acquisition (Fusion, five-blade razor).

When Gillette introduced the Mach 3 razor in 1998, the company took an entire year to set up 180,000 shop displays that featured the new razor. After the P&G purchase of Gillette, P&G was able to set up 180,000 store displays of the Fusion razor and blades in just *one week*! Furthermore, P&G plans to take the Fusion razor into China and Eastern Europe – locations where Gillette by itself traditionally had weak distribution systems. P&G also plans to blanket the marketplace with related grooming products like HydraGel shaving gel, sold under the same Fusion brand name. The distribution plan for Fusion can be summed up by the phrase 'you'll see Fusion absolutely everywhere you go'. Distributing these new shaving products through the extensive P&G channels of distribution will help the company gain a much bigger market presence in the growing men's grooming line of products. In fact, according to one investment firm, these actions should allow the Fusion brand alone to grab 15 per cent of the US market, adding $120 million to P&G's bottom line.

> After the P&G purchase of Gillette, P&G was able to set up 180,000 shop displays of the Fusion razor and blades in just *one week*!

Despite all that P&G has done so far to make its investment in Gillette pay off, the long-term outcome of the acquisition is still uncertain. One problem is that P&G has so many brands – maybe too many. The task of managing and distributing its brands is formidable. In addition, given continuously increasing costs for new product development, should the company continue to drive the lightning fast pace of advancements in razor technology? After all, isn't a five-bladed razor enough to provide customers with a good shave? How much more of a premium will customers pay for the next technological leap in shaving? And where will P&G look next for growth opportunities once its distribution channel has been saturated with Gillette products? Distributing Gillette products through the existing P&G channels represents the 'low-hanging fruit' resulting from the acquisition, and growth by acquisition breeds expectations of the next big takeover. After P&G achieves full market coverage, the company will have to look elsewhere for increases in sales and profits. How can P&G improve on Gillette's 70+ per cent overall market share in the razor and blade category? Product management strategies will play a key role in addressing these challenges.

Things to Think About

1. What is the decision facing Procter & Gamble?

2. What factors are important in understanding this decision situation?

3. What are the alternatives?

4. What decision(s) do you recommend?

5. What are some ways to implement your recommendation?

Sources: Dan Sewell, 'Procter & Gamble Profit Rises 37 Percent on Stronger Sales', *Associated Press Financial Wire*, 2006; Mark Jewell, 'Gillette Earnings Rise 13 Percent Heading Into Acquisition by P&G', *Associated Press*, 3 February 2005; Paul Lukas, 'How Many Blades is Enough?' *Fortune*, 31 October 2005; William C. Symonds and Robert Berner, 'Gillette's New Edge: P&G Is Helping Pump Up the Fusion Razor', *BusinessWeek online*, 6 February 2006.

References

1. IRI Infoscan EPOS sales for weekending 3 November 2007.
2. Joseph B. White, 'Lexus Tries to Redefine Hybrids', online.wsj.com/article_email/SB114242707250600173-1MyQjAxMDE2NDIyMDUyMjA3Wj.html.
3. www.imdb.com/title/tt0317740/.
4. www.austin-rover.co.uk/index.htm?r50storyf.htm; www.mini2.com/2001/09/10/its-a-mini-adventure-across-the-uk/.
5. www.scottish-newcastle.com/.
6. www.haribo.com/planet/uk/info/frameset_verbraucherinfo.php?verbraucher=1.
7. www.uk.pg.com/products/products/ariel.html.
8. www.rolls-roycemotorcars.com.
9. www.hyundai.co.uk/.
10. Joann Muller and Robyn Meredity, 'Last Laugh', *Forbes*, 18 April 2005 98.
11. Daniel Thomas, 'Relaunches: new Life or Last Gasps?', *Marketing Week*, 29 January 2004, 20(2).
12. Lea Goldman, 'Big Gulp', *Forbes*, 10 January 2005, 68.
13. Material adapted from a presentation by Glenn H. Mazur, QFD Institute, 2002.
14. 'The Magical Demystifying Tour of ISO 9000 and ISO 14000' www.iso.ch/iso/en/iso9000-14000/understand/basics/general/basics_1.html.
15. 'The Sabre System of the Appliance Service Industry', *Appliance*, 69(2) (March 2004).
16. Mohanbir Sawhney *et al.*, 'Creating Growth with Services', *MIT Sloan Management Review* 34(10) (Winter 2004).
17. www.computerweekly.com/Articles/2007/02/20/221914/marks-spencer-extends-rfid-technology-to-120-stores.htm.
18. http://blogs.consumerreports.org/cars/toyota/.
19. Al Ries and Laura Ries, *The Origin of Brands* (New York: Collins, 2005).
20. Philip H. Francis, 'New product development, the soul of the enterprise', memagazine.org/contents/current/webonly/webex.html.
21. www.low-carb.org.uk/main.htm.
22. 'Today's Buzzword: Low-Carb', *Chain Drug Review*, 2 February 2004, 40.
23. http://search.ft.com/ftArticle?queryText=nokia+asia&aje=true&id=071212000271&ct=0.

24. 'P&G Joins Forces with MTV Asia to Attract Young Chinese', *European Cosmetic Markets* (March 2004), 84; 'Will P&G's Moisturinse Boost Personal Cleanser Sales?', *Household & Personal Products Industry* (April 2004), 125; www.pg.com/product_card/product_card_main_olay.shtml.

25. www.marketingmagazine.co.uk/news/868873/Marketings-Top-100-advertisers-2008; www.guardian.co.uk/media/2008/jun/09/advertising1; www.telegraph.co.uk/finance/newsbysector/mediatechnologyandtelecoms/3659492/global-advertising-spend-to-tumble-21bn.html; www.brandrepublic.com/ digital/news/851330/online-adspend-21-total-ad-market-falls-07/?dcmp=emc-digital-bulletin).

26. Julian Hunt, 'Making Great Ideas Pay Off', *Grocer*, 27 March 2004, 2; Glen L. Urban, *Digital Marketing Strategies* (Englewood Cliffs, NJ: Prentice Hall, 2004).

27. http://snopes.com/horrors/food/kfc.asp.

28. Apple wins logo lawsuit against Beatles, www.macnn.com/articles/06/05/08/apple.wins.logo.lawsuit/.

29. Susan Fournier, 'Consumers and Their Brands: Developing Relationship Theory in Consumer Research', *Journal of Consumer Research* 24 (March 1998), 343–73.

30. 'The Most Famous Name in Music', *Music Trades*, September 2003, 118(12).

31. Kevin Lane Keller, 'The Brand Report Card', *Harvard Business Review* (January–February 2000) (Harvard Business School reprint R00104).

32. www.haagen-dazs.com/.

33. www.interbrand.com.

34. Kusum L. Ailawadi, Donald R. Lehmann and Scott A. Neslin, 'Revenue Premium as an Outcome Measure of Brand Equity', *Journal of Marketing* 67 (October 2003), 1–17.

35. www.competition-commission.org.uk/Inquiries/completed/2003/safeway/pdf/tescosummary.pdf.

36. Ron Ruggless, 'T.G.I. Friday's Beefs Up Menu with New Atkins Partnership', *Nation's Restaurant News*, 15 December 2003, 1(2).

37. D.C. Denison, 'The Boston Globe Business Intelligence Column', *Boston Globe*, 26 May 2002.

38. 'Putting Zoom into Your Life', *Time International*, 8 March 2004, 54.

39. Stephanie Thompson, 'Brand Buddies', *Brandweek*, 23 February 1998, 26–30; Jean Halliday, 'L.L. Bean, Subaru Pair for Co-Branding', *Advertising Age*, 21 February 2000, 21.

40. Ed Brown, 'I Scream You Scream – Saaay, Nice Carton!', *Fortune*, 26 October 1998, 60.

41. www.businesslink.gov.uk/bdotg/action/layer?topicId=1074016261; www.accident999.eu/jurisdiction.html.

42. www.rbkc.gov.uk/EnvironmentalServices/foodhygieneand-standards/labelling.asp.

Chapter 9
Services Marketing

Q & A with Patricia Vaz

Career high:
Reaching Managing Director at BT

My hero:
I have many – all great leaders – such as Martin Luther King

Don't do this when interviewing with me:
Shorten my name to Pat

Holiday resort:
Anywhere in Jamaica

Hobby/Sport:
Shooting

Drink:
Champagne

Food:
Fish and chips

Meet Patricia Vaz,
a decision maker at BT

Patricia Vaz is former Managing Director of UK customer service for British Telecom. She began her career with BT in 1975, joining the company as a clerical officer and progressively working her way up the corporate ladder, gaining extensive experience in a number of disciplines across the company. In October 2002, Patricia was awarded the 'Customer Service Strategy of the year Award' at the National Business Awards. She was also the winner of the Veuve Clicquot (UK) Business Woman of the Year and was awarded an OBE for 'services to telecommunications' in 2002. She was later recognised by HM The Queen as a Pioneer of the Nation at a reception at Buckingham Palace. In 1990, Patricia was appointed Director of BT Payphones. She set up and managed BT's entire payphones business with a staff of 3000, transforming the business from a poor-quality loss maker into a profitable business. She doubled the turnover and dramatically improved the quality of service by a) working with local communities to protect pay phones from vandalism, b) replacing the old-fashioned red telephone boxes with more modern and clean-looking kiosks and c) relocating the pay phone kiosks in more prominent locations. The changes helped restore the image of the company on the streets. In the late 1990s Patricia then took on the responsibility for the company's call centres and technical services help. She initiated and drove through to implementation a transformation programme.

Real People, Real Decisions
Decision Time at BT

In the early 1980s the telecommunications sector became one of the first targets for the former Conservative government in its quest to deregulate state-owned assets, end monopoly control and create a free-market 'laissez-faire' economy. The 1990s saw the erosion of trade barriers within the European Union and represented challenging times for the company, as other providers began to establish an interest in the UK telecoms market and obtain market share. During this time and well into the new millennium, growing competition meant that BT had to deliver both efficient and effective service in order to retain customers and prevent them from switching to new entrants (which were advertising some excellent packages aimed at enticing customers away from BT).

Whilst Patricia had the benefit of working with the former monopoly supplier and a huge customer base, many customers began to switch to alternative providers as the market became more open. This represented a key challenge for Patricia, as she grappled to woo customers and retain their business. She and the company realised that there was a positive association between high customer service levels and customer retention. Accordingly the company invested heavily in customer research and regularly measured service performance. Those measures were telling a very favourable story – customer service as measured by internal statistics was at a 98 per cent high. However, despite this, Patricia was receiving a growing number of complaints from disgruntled customers – something was not right. Why was service supposedly running at a record high, yet complaints were increasing and customers were leaving?

The need to improve customer satisfaction became a key issue for the company – all divisions of the company were required to share the challenge and Patricia appointed a director to work full time on analysing the 'voice of the customer' to help understand what was driving the customers' satisfaction and so help focus the improvement programmes.

As Patricia probed further into the problems, it became clear that customer service had not been adequately measured at BT. The internal statistics were measuring processes rather than the things that were causing customers to be dissatisfied. There was a fairly large gap between the process measures of success and what the voice of the customer was telling her. Although the research indicated that there were many things that affected customer satisfaction it was clear that one of the key areas was the experience they had when calling into the company's call centres. The call centres were very much the shop window of the company and if the experience the customers had when accessing the call centres was bad then they were left with a poor impression of the company as a whole.

It was decided to undertake a full investigation of the call centre process as Patricia was determined to turn the situation around and achieve the double win by at the same time transforming the network of call centres to improve efficiency and reduce costs.

Examination of the processes indicated there were many flaws – the systems were not designed to provide the most efficient way of routing calls; there was no effective knowledge management system to support the agents; there were over 130 call centres of various sizes, not all of which were of a size or quality to be fit for purpose and not all of which were networked together effectively so that often some centres were overloaded whilst others were waiting for calls. All these things were having a negative effect on call centre morale as well as creating inefficiencies – both of which were damaging the service being provided to customers and this was showing up in the levels of customer dissatisfaction being identified and measured.

After several months of consumer research, Patricia had identified that one of the root causes of the problem stemmed from the attitudes and service of a significant number of call centre staff. It was clear that up to 35 per cent of the customers' satisfaction was determined by the experience they had when they spoke to one of the call centre agents. But because of the inefficiencies identified above there was a significant number of these employees who were uneasy about their environment, anxious about their future and unhappy at having to face customers. As a result, they were dissatisfied with the nature of their job and were expressing their anxiety to customers in an unfriendly way.

Patricia realised that this was not a healthy sign for the company, i.e. employees, managers, customers and most importantly company shareholders. Patricia had to think long and hard and make a decision for the future that would satisfy a number of stakeholders including investors, the group's board of directors and the Chairman.

Patricia considers her options . . .

Option 1 Discard the call centres altogether and look to outsource

There were huge financial savings that could be made by going down this route, particularly if the option of off-shoring was adopted. The company had been doing some research in this area, and outsourcing the service to India had already been tabled.

Option 2 Consolidate call centres to improve efficiency

Offer redundancies to existing staff and employ new agents with the required skills and attitudes. The advantage of this option is that staff could reapply for a limited number of jobs. Those that were dissatisfied might be happy to take voluntary redundancy, particularly if they were to be offered an incentive.

Option 3 Consolidate call centres and invest more money in training the staff

A risky strategy, Patricia could argue to try and obtain a larger budget for training. The idea being that if more money was available, employees could be trained more on understanding the needs of customers, and/or be moved to other non-customer facing roles where permitted.

Now, put yourself in Patricia's position: Which option would you choose, and why?

Objectives

When you have finished reading this chapter, you will be able to:

1 Describe the four characteristics of services

2 Understand how services differ from goods

3 Explain marketing strategies for services

4 Explain how marketers create and measure service quality

5 Explain the marketing of people, places, and ideas

Marketing What Isn't There

Instead of something tangible like toothpaste or a new car, the product that BT offers is a service experience. Patricia Vaz understands the challenges of marketing what people can't touch. As a former director of the company, she realises that a customer's decision to remain loyal to BT is not likely if the service experience isn't a pleasant one. It's a challenge that Patricia needed to manage daily, and not in just one location with just one employee, but at a national level.

These same challenges apply to other types of services. For example, studying at university represents the consumption of a service, and so does going to watch your favourite football team. Each represents a product (a service) that combines experiences with physical goods to create an event that the buyer consumes. You can't have a university without a library of textbooks, or sit and watch football without a seat. But these tangibles are secondary to the primary product, which is some act that in these cases can produce enjoyment, knowledge or excitement.

This chapter will consider some of the challenges and opportunities facing marketers such as Patricia Vaz, whose primary offerings are **intangibles**: services and other experience-based products that cannot be touched. The marketer whose job it is to build and sell a better football, car, or iPod (all tangibles) must deal with different issues from someone who wants to sell tickets for a football match, arrange a taxi to the airport, or sell seats at a music concert. In the first part of this chapter, we'll discuss services, a type of intangible that tends to be the fastest-growing sector in developed economies. As we'll see, all services are intangible, but not all intangibles are services. Then we'll move into other types of intangibles.

Does Marketing Work for Intangibles?

Does marketing work only for companies that sell washing detergent and cars, or does it apply to many types of 'products', including politicians, the arts, and the places we live and visit? Yes, marketing does work for intangibles.

Even intangibles such as electricity or gas which we normally think of as commodities are now branded and marketed directly to consumers. Throughout the UK customers can select from a range of competing utility suppliers. Sound marketing concepts don't apply only to companies solely looking to make profit. Indeed, not-for-profit organisations, including charities, social welfare organisations, zoos, museums and religious congregations increasingly are thinking about branding and image building. The not-for-profit sector plays a significant role in many leading economies, and with millions of volunteers the competition for both customers and donors is fierce. These organisations have to come up with innovative marketing strategies all the time.[1] Even the Salvation Army operates a state-of-the-art website complete with a chat room and online press kit (www.salvationist.org).[2]

Still, some producers of intangibles have been slow to accept the idea that what they do *should* be marketed. Sometimes, people who work in healthcare, the legal profession or the arts resist the notion that the quality of what they produce and the demand for their services are affected by the same market forces driving the fortunes of paper producers, food suppliers or even power utilities. It is sometimes hard, for example, for nursing and administrative staff in hospitals to realise that they need to treat you as a customer and not just any old patient.

Let's take a quick look at how some basic marketing concepts would apply to an artistic product. Suppose a local theatre company wanted to increase attendance at its performances. Remembering the basics of developing a marketing plan, here are some marketing actions the organisation may consider to reach its goals:

- The organisation could develop a *mission statement*, such as 'We seek to be the best provider of quality theatre in the region.'

- A *SWOT analysis* could include an assessment of the organisation's strengths and weaknesses and the environmental threats and opportunities. The arts marketer is, after all, competing for the consumer's disposable income against other theatre groups. The marketer is also up against other forms of entertainment. The consumer may choose instead to attend a pop concert at Wembley Stadium, go to the cinema to see a film or watch a football game.

- The theatre company should use information obtained in the SWOT analysis to develop measurable *objectives*, such as to 'increase the number of season ticket holders by 20 per cent over the next two years'.

- Next, the organisation must develop marketing strategies. For example, it must consider which *target markets* it wishes to attract. If audience levels for its plays have been stable for several years, it should consider new markets for its performances. This might

Photo 9.1	Many not-for-profit organisations, including charities, know that marketing is key to their success. This advert for Greenpeace uses the iconic visual style from the iPod advertising campaign to get attention. Source: Greenpeace UK

Marketing Metrics

M&S Mini Cash ISA

Marks & Spencer started selling financial services in the 1990s and by the year 2000 it was looking at ways of broadening its offer. It considered the highly competitive ISA tax-free savings market as a candidate, but wanted evidence that it could succeed. The company commissioned a conjoint research study with MORI to determine the product specification that would maximise returns. This used consumer research to determine the effects of interest rates, bonus, tiering, rate guarantees and withdrawal conditions on sales volumes, and used these to construct a 'what-if' financial model. Findings of this model were used by management to select the optimum product, which was launched successfully.

lead to product modifications such as some opera companies have done by projecting English translations above the stage to draw new patrons who are unfamiliar with opera's international languages.

As you can see, by using the principles of effective marketing planning, just like with any tangible product, an organisation such as a theatre can reach its goals. More important, service organisations can be sure they are meeting the needs of their 'customers'. One way to develop an appropriate service offering is to undertake research to identify which attributes of service appeal to customers and can contribute effectively to bottom-line profits. This is exactly what Marks & Spencer did when diversifying from predominantly retail clothing into financial service retailing (see Marketing Metrics box).

What is a Service?

Objective

1

Describe the four characteristics of services

As we've said, marketing can help sell all kinds of intangibles, from theatre performances to ideas about birth control. But first, let's take a look at services, an important type of intangible.

Services are acts, efforts or performances exchanged from producer to user without ownership rights. Like other intangibles, a service satisfies needs by providing pleasure, information or convenience. Nowadays in most developed economies the vast majority of employment is in services. If you pursue a marketing career, it's highly likely that you will work somewhere in the services sector of the economy.

Of course, the service industry includes many consumer-oriented services, ranging from dry cleaning to retail travel. But it also includes a vast number of services provided for organisations. Some of the more commonly used business services include vehicle leasing, computer technology services, insurance, security, legal advice, food services, consulting, cleaning and maintenance. In addition, businesses also purchase some of the same services as consumers, such as utilities, telecommunications and travel.

The market for business services has grown rapidly because it is often more cost effective for organisations to hire outside firms that specialise in these services than to try to hire a workforce and handle the service themselves. In other instances, firms buy business services because they do not have the expertise necessary to provide the service. Even the marketing function itself is not immune to being outsourced by organisations. It's not unusual for companies to hand over their advertising, public relations and other related functions to outside agencies.

Characteristics of Services

Services come in many forms, from those performed for you, such as a massage or teeth cleaning, to those done to something you own, such as having your DVD player repaired or getting a respray on your classic 1965 Aston Martin. Regardless of whether they affect our bodies or

Table 9.1
Marketing Strategies
for Different Service
Characteristics

Characteristic	Marketing Response
Intangibility	Provide tangibility through physical appearance of the facility Furnishings Employee uniforms Logo Websites Advertising
Perishability	Adjust pricing to influence demand Adjust services to match demand (capacity management)
Variability	Institute total quality management programmes Offer service guarantees Conduct gap analysis to identify gaps in quality
Inseparability	Train employees on successful service encounters Explore means for disintermediation

our possessions, all services share four characteristics: intangibility, perishability, inseparability and variability. Table 9.1 shows how marketers can address the unique issues related to these characteristics of services that don't pop up when they deal with tangible goods.

Intangibility

Intangibility is the characteristic of a service that means customers can't see, touch or smell a service. Unlike the purchase of a tangible good, we can't inspect or handle services before we buy them. This makes many services much more difficult for consumers to evaluate. Although it may be easy to evaluate your new haircut, it is far less easy to determine whether the dental hygienist has done a great job cleaning your teeth.

Because they're buying something that isn't there, customers look for reassuring signs before purchasing, and marketers must ensure that these signs are readily available. That's why marketers try to overcome the problem of intangibility by providing physical cues to reassure the buyer. These cues might be the 'look' of the facility, its furnishings, logo, stationery, business cards, the appearance of its employees, and well-designed advertising and websites, just to name a few. Universities and business schools in Europe and beyond are now frequently trying to promote that their MBAs are accredited by AMBA (the Association of MBAs) or EQUIS (European Quality Improvement System) in an attempt to reassure MBA students that what they are buying is a high quality programme.

Perishability

Perishability refers to the characteristic of a service that makes it impossible to store for later sale or consumption. It's a case of use it or lose it. When rooms go unoccupied at a ski resort, there is no way to make up for the lost opportunity to rent them for the weekend. Marketers try to avoid these problems by using the marketing mix to

IT'S BEING ABLE TO TELL
THE WORLD TO GET LOST.

WEALTH. WHAT'S IT TO YOU?

Barclays Wealth is a new division of Barclays devoted to the management of wealth.
With high levels of personal service, we can help you achieve your ambitions.
Whatever wealth means to you, call +44 (0) 141 352 3952 or visit barclayswealth.com today.

International and Private Banking · Financial Planning · Investment Services · Brokerage

BARCLAYS WEALTH

Photo 9.2 Financial services are highly intangible, so companies need to use vivid imagery to communicate their benefits.
Source: The Advertising Archives

encourage demand for the service during slack times. One option is to reduce prices to increase demand for otherwise unsold services. Some chartered airlines do this by offering more lower-priced seats in the final weeks before a flight. TV channels also offer advertisers low-priced airtime at the last minute.

This relates to effective **capacity management** – representing the process by which organisations adjust their services in an attempt to match supply with demand. Capacity management may mean adjusting the product, or it may mean modifying the price. In the summer, for example, a winter ski resort could combat its perishability problem by opening its lifts to mountain bikers who tear down the sunny slopes. Rental car companies, for example, offer discounts on days of the week when business travel is light, and many hotels offer special weekend packages to increase their occupancy rates. Even cinemas are starting to catch on to the idea of encouraging greater usage of their facilities by offering incentives to pensioners and students during less busy periods.

Variability

Perhaps Steven Gerrard was on fire on Saturday when he netted his hat trick for Liverpool Football Club, however he may have a quiet game the next time out – there is no guarantee. **Variability** is the characteristic of a service that means that even the same service performed by the same individual for the same customer can vary. This means that there may be inevitable differences in a service provider's performances over time. It's rare when you get *exactly* the same cut from a hairstylist.

It is difficult to standardise services because service providers and customers vary. Think about your experiences in your university classes. A business school can standardise its offerings to some extent – course catalogues, content and classrooms. Lecturers, however, vary in their training, life experiences and personalities, so there is little hope of being able to make teaching uniform (not that this would necessarily be desirable anyway). Also, because students with different backgrounds and interests vary in their needs, the lecture that you find fascinating may put your friend to sleep. The same is true for customers of organisational services. Differences in the quality of individual security guards or cleaners mean variability in how these services get delivered.

In fact, we don't necessarily *want* standardisation when we purchase a service. Most of us want a hairstyle that fits our face and personality and a personal trainer who will address our unique physical training needs. Because of the nature of the tasks performed in services, customers often appreciate the firm that customises its service for each individual.

One solution to the problem of variability is to implement total quality management (TQM) programmes for continuous improvement of service quality. As we learned earlier, TQM is a management effort to involve all employees from the assembly line onward in continuously working towards product quality improvement. This, briefly, is achieved through empowering staff at each level and providing them with the opportunity to have an input and make decisions. In addition to instituting TQM programmes, offering service guarantees assures consumers that if service quality fails, they will be compensated. We'll talk later in this chapter about how service marketers can provide greater quality and consistency in service delivery through gap analysis and employee empowerment.

Inseparability

Inseparability is the characteristic of a service, meaning that it is impossible to separate the production of a service from the consumption of that service. Although a firm can manufacture goods prior to sale, a service can take place only at the time the service provider performs an act on either the customer or the customer's possession. It's hard to take notes on a lecture when the professor doesn't show up. In some cases, of course, the service can be sold before delivery, such as buying a ticket to see Celtic play Ajax in Amsterdam months before attending the event.

Still, the expertise, skill and personality of a provider or the quality of a firm's employees, facilities and equipment cannot be detached from the offering itself. The central role employees play in making or breaking a service underscores the importance of the **service encounter**, or the interaction between the customer and the service provider.[3] The most expertly cooked meal is not appreciated if an unpleasant or incompetent waiter brings it to the table. We'll talk more about the importance of service providers later in this chapter.

To minimise the potentially negative effects of bad service encounters and to save on labour costs, some service businesses are experimenting with **disintermediation**, which means removing the 'middleman' and thus eliminating the need for customers to interact with people at all. Good examples include self-service petrol stations and hotels, which are becoming increasingly popular in places like France, and self-service checkouts at Tesco retail stores in the UK. Even salad and dessert bars reduce reliance on a waiter or waitress. Although some consumers resist dealing with machines, or composing their own salad, most prefer the speed and efficiency that disintermediation provides.

The internet provides many opportunities for disintermediation, especially in the financial services area. Banking customers can access their accounts, transfer funds from one account to another, and pay their bills with the click of a mouse. Many busy consumers can check on mortgage interest rates and even apply for a loan at their convenience – a much better option than taking an afternoon off work to sit in a branch and discuss your mortgage options. Online brokerage services are increasingly popular as many consumers seek to handle their investments themselves, thus eliminating the commission a full-service brokerage firm would charge.

Classifying Services

Objective

2

Understand how services differ from goods

By understanding the characteristics of different types of services and just which type of service they offer, marketers can develop strategies to improve customer satisfaction. As Figure 9.1 shows, we can classify services in terms of whether the service is performed directly on the customer or on something the customer owns and whether the service consists of tangible or intangible actions. Customers themselves receive tangible services to their bodies – a haircut

	Tangible Services	*Intangible Services*
Customer	Haircut	University education
	Plastic surgery	A religious service
	Manicure	A TV programme
	Personal trainer	A flower-arranging course
		Marriage counselling
Possessions	Dry cleaning	Banking
	Car repair	Accounting services
	Housecleaning	Insurance
	Package delivery	Home security service

Figure 9.1   Classification of Services by Inputs and Tangibility

Services can be classified according to whether the customer or his or her possessions are the recipient of the service and whether the service itself consists of tangible or intangible elements.

or a heart transplant. The education you are receiving from your course is an intangible service directed at the consumer. A customer's possessions are the recipient of such tangible services as the repair of a favourite watch. Intangible services directed at a consumer's possessions include insurance, and even security – which is particularly valued for residents who live in blocks of flats, or own second homes in exclusive resorts.

Services can be classified according to whether the customer or his or her possessions are the recipient of the service and as to whether the service itself consists of tangible or intangible elements.

The Goods/Services Continuum

In reality, most products are a *combination* of goods and services. The purchase of a 'pure good' like a Mercedes-Benz still has service components, such as bringing it to the dealer for maintenance work. The purchase of a 'pure service' such as a makeover at a department store has product components, for example, make-up, eye shadow, lipsticks, etc. that the beautician uses.

The service continuum in Figure 9.2 shows that some products are dominated by either tangible or intangible elements. Where salt and teaching represent two extremes on the continuum, others tend to include a mixture of goods and services, such as a commercial airline flight. A product's placement on this continuum gives some guidance as to which marketing issues are most likely to be relevant. As the product approaches the tangible pole of this continuum, there is fairly little emphasis on service. The physical product itself is the focal point, and people will choose one option over others because of the product's function or image.

However, as the product gets near the intangible pole, the issues we've discussed such as intangibility and inseparability play a key role in shaping the service experience. In the middle of the continuum, both goods and services contribute substantially to the quality of the product because these products rely on people to satisfactorily operate equipment that will in turn deliver quality service. Let's consider each of these three positions as we move from products dominated by tangibles to those dominated by intangibles.

1. **Goods-dominated products.** Even if this only means that a company provides a free phone number for questions, or provides a 30-day warranty, companies that sell tangible products still must provide supporting services. Car manufacturers, home appliances and electronics firms can realise a major competitive advantage when they provide customers with this support better than their competitors. Services may be even more important for marketers of business-to-business tangibles. Business customers often will not even consider buying from manufacturers who don't provide services such as employee training and equipment maintenance. For example, hospitals that buy lifesaving patient care and monitoring equipment that costs hundreds of thousands of euros demand not only in-service training for their nursing and technical staff, but also require regular maintenance of the equipment (if needed) and a quick response to breakdowns.

2. **Equipment- or facility-based services.** As we see in Figure 9.2, some products include a mixture of tangible and intangible elements. While a restaurant is a balanced product because it includes the preparation and delivery of the food to your table plus the food itself, the tangible elements of the service are less evident for other products. Many hospitals and hotels fall in the middle of the continuum not because customers take a tangible good away from the service encounter, but because these organisations rely on expensive equipment or facilities to deliver a product. The Park Lane Hilton in London is just one example that relies on using expensive equipment and facilities to help portray a 'world class' image for its visitors. Facility-driven services, such as theme

Scale of (In)Tangibility

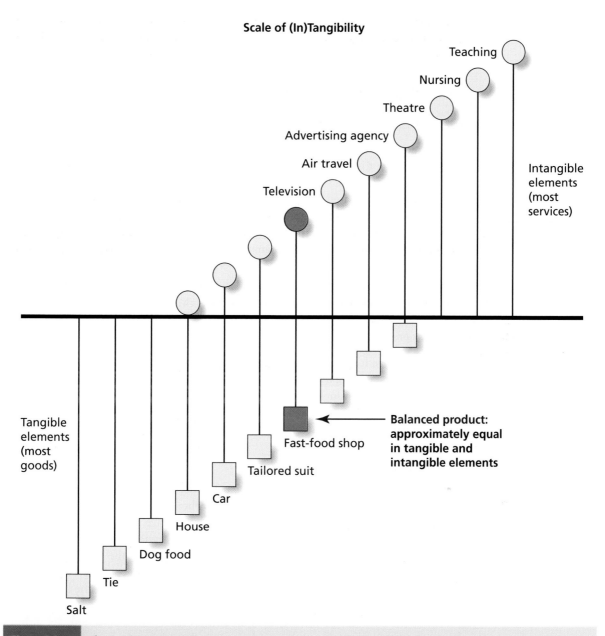

Figure 9.2   The Service Continuum

Products vary in their level of tangibility. Salt is a tangible product, teaching is an intangible product, and the products offered by fast-food restaurants include both tangible and intangible elements.

Source: Adapted from G. Lynn Shostack, 'How to Design a Service,' *European Journal of Marketing* 16, no. 1 (1982): 52.

parks and others like amusement arcades, museums, health clubs, etc. must be concerned with these factors:[4]

● **Operational factors:** Clear signs and other guidelines must show customers how to use the service. In particular, firms need to minimise waiting times. Marketers have developed a number of tricks to give impatient customers the illusion that they aren't waiting too long. One hotel chain, responding to complaints about the long wait for lifts, installed mirrors in the lobby. People tended to look at their appearance until the lift arrived and, lo and behold, the number of complaints reduced.[5]

● **Locational factors:** These are especially important for frequently purchased services, such as dry cleaning or retail banking, that we obtain from a fixed place. When you select a bank, a restaurant, an estate agent or a health club, its location often influences your decision. Marketers make sure their service sites are convenient and in places that are attractive to prospective customers.

● **Environmental factors:** Service managers who manage a retail presence and require people to come to their location realise they must create an attractive environment to lure customers. That's one of the reasons why Arsenal upgraded its seating, eating and toilet facilities when moving to its Emirates Stadium. One trend is for services to adopt a more retail-like philosophy, borrowing techniques from clothing shops or restaurants to create a pleasant environment as part of their marketing strategy. Banks, for example, are creating signature looks for their branches through the use of lighting, colour, art and music, and even local shops are now baking bread on their premises.

3. **People-based services.** At the intangible end of the continuum are pure people-based services. A roaming masseur, a mobile hair dresser, or car valeter are examples of people in professions that provide services for others.

Because people have less and less time to get things done, the importance of people-based services is increasing. Self-improvement services such as wardrobe consultants and personal trainers are becoming increasingly popular, and in some places even professional dog walkers and mobile pet washing services do good business. Many of us hire someone to do our legal work, repair our cars and file our tax returns.

Core and Augmented Services

When we buy a service, we may in fact be buying a *set* of services. The **core service** is a benefit that a customer gets from the service. For example, when your car breaks down, repairing the problem is a core service you seek from your car dealer or garage. In most cases, though, the core service alone just isn't enough. To attract customers, a service firm often tries to offer **augmented services**, i.e. additional service offerings that differentiate the firm from the competition. When the car dealership provides the pick-up and delivery of your car, a free carwash, or a lounge with nice chairs, satellite TV and delicious coffee, these represent the kind of items that can help the provider to gain your loyalty as a customer.

Think about the core service you buy with an airline ticket – transportation. Yet airlines rarely stress the basic benefit of arriving safely at your destination. Instead, they emphasise augmented services such as frequent-flyer miles, speedy check-in and in-flight entertainment. In addition, augmented services may be necessary to deliver the core service. In the case of air travel, airports have added attractions to encourage travellers to fly to one site rather than another.[6] Here are some augmented services now available at airports around the world:

● London Gatwick: internet café, Planet Hollywood restaurant, personal shopper services.

● Amsterdam Schiphol: casino, airport television station, sauna, dry cleaner, grocery shop.

● Frankfurt International: supermarket, disco, sex shop.

● Singapore Changi: fitness centre, karaoke lounge, putting green.

And what about your university education? With increased competition for students, universities are finding that their augmented products must provide a variety of amenities that provide added value, such as cafés and bars, sports and recreation facilities, etc.

Services on the Web

From DVD rentals to fine restaurant cuisine, anything that can be delivered can be sold on the web. In some cities, website companies will arrange to have your dry cleaning picked up, your family photos developed, or your shoes repaired. Here are some of the newest and most popular web services:

● **Banking:** Customers can check their statements, pay bills, transfer money and balance their accounts 24 hours a day, seven days a week whether they're at home or travelling around the world. Some banks offer online customers better incentives, including higher interest rates on deposits and lower rates on loans.

● **Software:** Siebel Systems – market leaders in customer relationship management software, is spearheading an industry shift toward internet-accessed software sold or rented to user companies and paid for monthly.[7]

● **Travel:** Airline travel, and tourism websites now command a large portion of the travel business for both business customers and individual consumers. Traditional travel agencies now tend to focus on specialised markets such as outsourcing a firm's business travel function or booking unique packaged travel deals for consumers.

● **Career-related sites:** Employment agencies and recruiting firms such as Monster.com provide important job services and a less expensive way for applicants and employers to advertise their availability.

To stay in the game, marketers of such services need to think seriously about developing an online presence as well. Effective websites not only allow customers to access the services online but also provide information on how to contact them for those customers who still want personal contact. Because customers seek access to internet-based services for convenience, marketers must make sure internet sites are fast, simple, continuously updated and easy to navigate around.

The Service Encounter

Objective 3

Explain marketing strategies for services

Earlier we said that the service encounter occurs when the customer comes into contact with the organisation. This usually means interacting with one or more employees who represent that organisation. The service encounter has several dimensions of importance to marketers.[8] First, there is the social contact dimension, of one person interacting with another person. The physical dimension is also important, and customers often pay close attention to the environment where the service is delivered – where the consumer and the service provider interact. The interactive contact is also referred to as 'the moment of truth', and specifically the employee can often determine whether the customer will come away with a good or bad impression of the service. Our interactions with service providers can range from the most superficial, such as buying a cinema ticket, to telling a doctor our most intimate secrets. In each case, the quality of the service encounter can play a big role in determining how we feel about the service we receive.

Social Elements of the Service Encounter: Employees and Customers

Because services are intimately tied to company employees who deliver the service, the quality of a service is only as good as its poorest employees. The employee represents the organisation. Actions, words, physical appearance, courtesy, and professionalism, or a lack of it reflect the values of the organisation. Customers entrust themselves and/or their possessions to the care of the employee, so it is important that employees look at the encounter from the customer's perspective.

Real People, Other Voices

Philip Warwick,
University of York

I would choose option 3 because the customer experience is so important in a service encounter and it seems that staff attitudes are the main problem Patricia faces. Conversations with company representatives are even more important in the context of a call centre than in other service settings such as hotels, restaurants and leisure clubs because there is often physical evidence to counter any poor face-to-face experiences. Service employees simply must be enthusiastic advocates of the organisation; we all know how frustrating it is when service employees are going through the motions of providing a service without any interest in the customer or the service they are providing.

Having said that, it appears from the other option choices listed that Patricia is under some pressure to reduce costs. There would be no point training her team now, if cost saving measures need to be implemented in the near future, so if she does have to reduce costs then she must do that straight away by redeploying staff and possibly offering voluntary redundancies. Handled well, this type of downsizing could help the morale of the team, especially if this is then followed up with training and development initiatives. Patricia will be aware that she cannot provide a standard customer service training package, as this could be interpreted as a criticism of the staff by their manager. So I am sure she will want to develop a tailor-made programme which builds on existing staff abilities as well

as one that offers new skills and motivates the call centre staff to provide an improved service experience for BT customers.

Tony Bqain,
a student at University of Worcester

I would choose option 2. Investing more money in training the staff is an expensive strategy and may not generate the required level of employee satisfaction. An increase in incurred costs may also cause discontent among stakeholders and other interest groups, especially if the measures are not cost-effective. Similarly – despite significant financial savings that might gratify interest groups – outsourcing will engender a problem similar to the initial one, in which low employee loyalty, motivation and attitudes might lead to further customer dissatisfaction. By offering voluntary redundancies to disgruntled or unmotivated employees, the company can retain motivated workers and allow more flexibility to those who have unfavourable attitudes towards customer service and possibly augment their motivation. The impact of this method would not directly generate considerable financial savings, but would establish a valuable foundation for eventually improving the level of customer service and customer retention, and for further growth – together satisfying the needs of employees, interest groups and customers. Ultimately, the method should reinforce customer loyalty and generate word-of-mouth communication as a basis for attracting more customers.

The customer also plays a part in ensuring that a quality experience will result from a service encounter. When you visit a medical centre, the quality of the healthcare you receive depends not only on the doctor's competence but also on your ability to communicate accurately and clearly the problems you are experiencing and how well you comply with advice. The business customer must provide accurate information to his accounting firm. Even the best personal trainer is not going to make the desired improvements to a client's body if the client refuses to do the designated workout.

Physical Elements of the Service Encounter: Servicescapes and Other Tangibles

As we noted earlier in the chapter, because services are intangible, marketers focus attention on providing *physical evidence* of the service they deliver. An important part of this physical evidence is the **servicescape**; the environment in which the service is delivered and where the firm and the customer interact. Servicescapes include facility exteriors, elements such as the exterior design of the facility, the signs, parking and even the landscaping. They also include interior elements, such as the design of the office or shop, equipment, colours, air quality, temperature and smells. For hotels, restaurants, banks, airlines and business schools the servicescape is quite elaborate. For other services, such as a dry cleaning service, the servicescape can be very simple.

Marketers know that carefully designed servicescapes can have a positive influence on customers' purchase decisions, their evaluations of service quality, and their ultimate satisfaction with the service. Thus, when Arsenal considered moving to the Emirates Stadium, much planning needed to go into the design, not only the actual playing field, but also the exterior design of the stadium for its turnstyle entrances, landscaping, seating areas, toilets, etc. Similarly, marketers pay close attention to the design of other tangibles that facilitate the performance of the service or provide communications. For the visiting supporters, these include signs that direct fans to the ground, the game tickets themselves, the match day programmes, the kit design and colours, and hundreds of staff that help in the delivery of the service on match days.

Nowadays, for many consumers the first tangible evidence of a business (service or otherwise) is its website. Websites that are unattractive or frustratingly dysfunctional provide a horrible first impression of the company and its service. Investments by service firms in user-friendly websites pay back through increased business and higher customer satisfaction and loyalty. Consider Lastminute.com as an example. Users can price their flight using various airlines, and consider a range of hotels. Users are therefore easily able to design a tailor-made package that suits their needs. This functionality not only makes customers happy, it also saves the company money by reducing the number of telephone enquiries.

Providing Quality Service

Objective

4

Explain how marketers create and measure service quality

If a service experience isn't positive, it can turn into a *disservice* with nasty consequences. Quality service ensures that customers are satisfied with what they have paid for. However, satisfaction is relative because the service recipient compares the current experience to some prior set of expectations. That's what makes delivering quality service tricky. What may seem like excellent service to one customer may be mediocre to another person who has been 'spoiled' by earlier encounters with an exceptional service provider. So, marketers must identify customer expectations and then work hard to exceed them.

Of course, meeting or exceeding customer expectations is not always so easy. These expectations can be influenced by stories people hear from friends and acquaintances, and they are not always realistic in the first place.[9] Exaggerated customer expectations, such as level of personal service, may be impossible for a large company to accomplish, and account for about 75 per cent of the complaints reported by service businesses. However, providing customers with logical explanations for service failures and compensating them in some way can substantially reduce dissatisfaction.[10]

Service Quality Attributes

Because services are inseparable in that they are not produced until the time they are consumed, it is difficult to estimate how good a service will be until you buy it. Most service businesses cannot offer a free trial. Because services are variable, it is hard to predict the consistency of quality and there is little or no opportunity for comparison shopping. The selection process for services is somewhat different than for goods, especially for services that are highly intangible, such as those on the right end of the continuum in Figure 9.2. Service

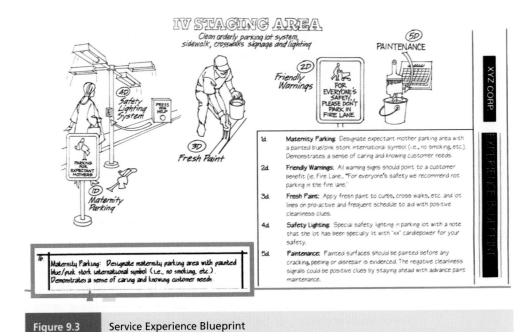

Figure 9.3	Service Experience Blueprint
	Firms often build in cues their customers can easily see because services quality is often difficult to determine. Grocery shops such as this one often use a variety of cues to convince consumers of superior quality.

Source: Lewis P. Carbone and Stephan H. Haeckel, 'Engineering Customer Experiences,' *Marketing Management* 3 (winter 1994), reprint, exhibit 4.

marketers have to come up with creative ways, such as developing 'search qualities', building on 'experience qualities' and utilising 'credence qualities' to illustrate the benefits their service will provide.

Search qualities are product attributes that the consumer can examine prior to purchase. These include colour, style, price, fit, smell and texture. Tangible goods, of course, are more likely to have these characteristics, so services need to build them in by paying attention to such details as the style of flight attendants' uniforms or the decor of a hotel room. The 'Service Experience Blueprint' in Figure 9.3 illustrates how one design firm tried to build in such cues for a retailer. The company planned an upgraded, freshly painted parking lot that included a special preferred parking space for expectant mothers (complete with a stork logo) to signal that the company cared.[11] Attention to detail makes a difference.

Experience qualities are product attributes that customers can determine during or after consumption. For example, we can't really predict how good a holiday we'll have until we experience it, so marketers need to reassure customers *before* the fact that they are in for a good time. A travel agency may invest in developing a presentation complete with alluring images of a tropical resort and perhaps even supply enthusiastic recommendations from other clients who had a positive experience at the same location.

Credence qualities are product attributes we find difficult to evaluate even *after* we've experienced them. For example, most of us don't have the expertise to know if our doctor's diagnosis is correct.[12] Evaluations here are difficult, and to a great extent the client must trust the service provider. That is why tangible clues of professionalism, such as diplomas or an organised office, count toward purchase satisfaction, and is the reason as mentioned earlier why so many European business schools wish to acquire AMBA and EQUIS accreditation to support their MBAs.

Measuring Service Quality

Because the customer's experience of a service is crucial to determining future patronage, service marketers feel that measuring positive and negative service experiences is the 'Holy Grail' for the services industry. Marketers gather consumer responses in a variety of ways. For example, some companies hire 'mystery shoppers' to check on businesses and provide feedback. These shoppers usually work for a research firm, although some airlines reportedly recruit 'spies' from the ranks of their most frequent flyers.

The **SERVQUAL** scale is a popular instrument to measure consumers' expectations and perceptions of service quality. SERVQUAL identifies five dimensions or components of service quality:

- *Tangibles* – the physical facilities and equipment and the professional appearance of personnel.

- *Reliability* – the ability to provide dependably and accurately what was promised.

- *Responsiveness* – the willingness to help customers and provide prompt service.

- *Assurance* – the knowledge and courtesy of employees, and the ability to convey trust and confidence.

- *Empathy* – the degree of caring and individual attention provided to customers.[13]

The SERVQUAL scale developed by Parasuraman and his colleagues has been applied in thousands of service settings across the service continuum. It is most often administered in a survey format through a written, online or telephone questionnaire. Firms often track SERVQUAL scores over time to see how their service quality is (hopefully) improving. SERVQUAL can be used in the gap analysis approach we describe next.

Gap analysis is a measurement approach that gauges the difference between a customer's expectation of service quality and what actually occurred. By identifying specific places in the service system where there is a wide gap between what is expected and what is received, service marketers can get a handle on what needs improvement. Some major gaps include the following:[14]

- **Gap between consumer expectations and management perceptions:** A major quality gap can occur when the firm's managers don't understand what its customers' expectations are in the first place. Many service organisations have an operations orientation rather than a customer orientation. For example, banks often used to close branches early in order to balance transactions because that was more efficient for them, even though it was not convenient for customers who wanted to do their banking during their lunch hour or on their way home. Today more and more banks are open late, those located in shopping streets open at weekends and cash machines are widely available.

- **Gap between management's perception and quality standards that the firm sets:** Successful service firms develop written quality goals. If for example a company found that customers complained most about its responsiveness, accuracy and timeliness, it would be possible to develop action goals to correct such problems, and monitor for example how quickly employees answer phones in an effort to be more responsive. Management therefore ideally need to focus on appropriate quality standards that will ultimately be valued among consumers.

- **Gap between established quality standards and service delivery:** One of the biggest threats to service quality is poor employee performance. When employees do not deliver the service at the level specified by the company, quality suffers. Teamwork is crucial to service success. Unfortunately, many companies don't clearly specify what they expect of employees.

- **Gap between service quality standards and consumer expectations:** Sometimes a firm makes exaggerated promises or does not accurately describe its service to customers. When the Holiday Inn hotel chain developed an advertising campaign based on the promise that guests would receive 'No Surprises', many operations personnel opposed the idea, saying that *no* service organisation, no matter how good, can anticipate every single thing that can go wrong. Sure enough, the campaign was unsuccessful. A service firm is better off communicating *exactly what the customer can expect* and what will happen if the company does not deliver on its promises.

- **Gap between expected service and perceived service:** Sometimes consumers misperceive the quality of the service. Thus, even when communications accurately describe what service quality is provided and what customers can expect, buyers are less than satisfied. It's therefore important that companies verify that all forms of communication do not mislead customers.

The **critical incident technique** is another way to measure service quality.[15] Using this approach, the company collects and closely analyses very specific customer complaints. It can then identify *critical incidents*, i.e. specific contacts between consumers and service providers that are most likely to result in dissatisfaction. An airline for example may analyse its customer complaints and discover that business customers are more likely to switch carriers if their planes fail to arrive on time. This then becomes 'critical' for the airline to rectify, and the company would be wise to develop mechanisms to reduce the number of delayed take-offs that occur, and compensate business passengers accordingly.

Some critical incidents happen when the service organisation simply can't meet a customer's expectations. For example, it is impossible to satisfy a passenger who says to a flight attendant, 'Come sit with me, I don't like to fly alone'. In other cases, though, the firm is capable of meeting these expectations but fails to do so. For example, the customer might complain to a flight attendant, 'My seat won't recline'.[16] A potentially dissatisfied customer can be turned into a happy one if the problem is addressed or perhaps even if the customer is told why the problem can't be solved at this time. Customers tend to be fairly forgiving if they are given a reasonable explanation for the problem.

Strategies for Developing and Managing Services

We've seen that delivering quality should be the aim of every successful service organisation. What can the firm do to maximise the likelihood that a customer will choose its service and become a loyal customer? With services differing from goods in so many ways, decision makers struggle to market something that isn't there. An interesting example of marketing something that doesn't exist appears in the Marketing Ethics box. Here we see that the Co-operative Bank turns away significant business in return for promoting environmentally friendly issues. Attracting and retaining appropriate and like-minded ethical customers is more appealing to the bank. However, many of the same strategic issues apply. For example, Table 9.2 illustrates how three different types of service organisations can devise marketing strategies.

Of course, sometimes service quality does fail. Some failures, such as when your dry cleaner places glaring red spots on your new white sweater, are easy to see at the time the service is performed. Other service failures, such as when the dry cleaner shrinks your sweater, may be less obvious for you to recognise immediately. But no matter when or how the failure is discovered, the important thing is that the firm takes fast action to resolve the problem. Quick action means that the problem won't occur again (hopefully) and that the customer's complaint will be resolved. The key is speed: research shows that customers whose complaints are resolved quickly are far more likely to buy from the same company again than when complaints take longer to be resolved.[17]

	Dry Cleaner	City Theatre Company	University
Marketing objective	Increase total revenues by 20 per cent within one year by increasing business of existing customers and obtaining new customers.	Increase to 1000 the number of season memberships to theatre productions within two years.	Increase applications to undergraduate and postgraduate programmes by 10 per cent for the coming academic year.
Target markets	Young and middle-aged professionals living within an 8 km radius of the business.	Clients who attend single performances but do not purchase season tickets.	Primary market: prospective undergraduate and postgraduate students who live within the region.
		Other local residents who enjoy theatre but do not normally attend local performances.	Secondary market: prospective undergraduate and graduate students living in other regions and in foreign countries.
Benefits offered	Excellent and safe cleaning of clothes in 24 hours or less.	Experiencing professional quality theatre performances while helping ensure the future of the local theatre company.	High-quality education in a student-centred campus environment.
Strategy	Provide an incentive offer to existing customers such as one suit cleaned for free after 10 suits cleaned at regular price.	Write letters to former membership holders and patrons of single performances encouraging them to purchase new season tickets.	Increase number of recruiting visits to local secondary schools. Arrange a special day of events for secondary school teachers and career advisers to visit campus.
	Use newspaper advertising to communicate a limited time discount offer to all customers.	Arrange for theatre company personnel and performers to be guests of local television and radio talk shows.	Send letters to alumni encouraging them to recommend the university to prospective students they know.

Table 9.2 Marketing Strategies for Service Organisations

Marketing Ethics

Co-op Bank develops ethical financial products, but at a cost of £9m

The Co-operative Bank turned away nearly £9m of business in 2004–5 from companies it deemed to be unethical or environmentally unfriendly. Turning away business because of concerns over the prospective customer's approach to animal welfare lost the bank £1.2m, declining business from companies with a poor record on human rights and labour practices lost it close to £4m. However, the Co-op's tough stand on ethical screening is also attracting customers in record numbers. More than a third of its profits come from people who decided to sign up to the bank because of its ethical values.

The Independent (London), 25 July 2005

Debate, Discuss, Disagree

1   What are the main reasons why companies try to be involved in ethical/socially responsible activities?

To make sure that service failures are kept to a minimum and that recovery is fast, managers should first understand the service and the potential places where failures are most likely to occur and then make plans ahead of time to recover.[18] That's why the process of identifying critical incidents can be so important. In addition, employees should be trained to listen for complaints and be empowered to take appropriate actions immediately.

As we look into the future, we recognise that the importance of service industries as part of the global economy will continue to grow. In fact, in recent years the accelerating importance of services as an integral part of any firm's value proposition has led to discussions of a new **dominant logic for marketing** that in part redefines service as the core deliverable and the actual physical products purveyed as somewhat incidental to the business proposition.[19]

Let's consider several important trends that will provide both opportunities and challenges for the marketers of services. In the future, we can expect services we can't even imagine yet. Of course, they will also provide many new and exciting job opportunities for future marketers.

- **Changing demographics:** As populations age, service industries that meet the needs of older consumers will see dramatic growth. Companies offering recreational opportunities, health care and living assistance for senior citizens will be in demand.

- **Globalisation:** The globalisation of business will increase the need for logistics and distribution services to move products around the world, and for accounting and legal services that facilitate these global exchanges. In addition, global deregulation will affect the delivery of services by banks, insurance and other financial service industries because globalisation means greater competition. For example, many patients now are going to countries like Thailand and India, where common surgical procedures may cost significantly less than half what they would in Europe. In the hotel industry, demand for luxury properties is growing around the world. Hyatt International has expanded its five-star hotels in Tokyo, Hong Kong and Paris, and the company has an aggressive building campaign for luxury hotels in mainland China, where it expects to have as many as 24 properties by 2013.[20]

- **Technological advances:** Changing technology will provide opportunities for growth and innovation in global service industries such as telecommunications, healthcare, banking and online services. We can also expect technological advances to provide opportunities for services that we haven't even thought of yet but that will change and improve the lives of consumers.

- **Shift to flow of information:** In many ways, we have become an information society. Both organisations and individuals have experienced a dramatic increase in the importance of obtaining, manipulating, reporting and using information. The availability, flow and access of information are becoming increasingly critical to the success of organisations. These changes will provide greater opportunities for database services, artificial intelligence systems, communications systems and other services that facilitate the storage and transfer of knowledge.

Objective

5

Explain the marketing of people, places and ideas.

Marketing People, Places and Ideas

By now, you understand that services are intangibles that marketers work hard to sell. But as we said earlier, services are not the only intangibles that organisations need to market. Intangibles such as people, places and ideas often need to be 'sold' by someone and 'bought' by someone else. Let's consider how marketing is relevant to each of these.

Across the Hall

Advice for Patricia Vaz

Derek Williams,
Managing Director of
The WOW! Awards
www. TheWowAwards.co.uk

With the benefit of more recent research and experiences, here's what I would do:

1. I would want to understand why there were so many people with an inappropriate attitude in the business. If we accept that most people come into work each day intending to do a good job, then the attitudes that they develop are simply a reflection of the leadership, the communication and the support that they receive.

2. Specifically I would want to look at:

  a. Mission and values of the business. Are these being lived and breathed by senior management?

  b. How seriously is customer service/retention being taken at board level? Is there a customer service director?

  c. How are these guiding principles being communicated to the employees? Is the communication adequate and consistent? Is there an opportunity for feedback and ongoing improvement?

  d. Are we measuring and managing the right things? So often, the focus might be on a short-term result, i.e. a sale, and forgetting the long-term goal of keeping the customer.

  e. What systems do we have to catch people doing things right from the customer's point of view? Most management has historically been about catching people doing things wrong. If the only time that people see their manager is when 'You're off target!' or 'I've had a complaint about you!' then we cannot expect our people to have a great attitude. And remember that public recognition is much more important to an individual than money.

Do more research. Get to the root cause and you may find a solution that doesn't require huge investment that avoids damaging redundancies and is a much better long-term solution than more training.

Don Hales,
World of Customer Service Founder and Chairman of Judges National Customer Service Awards

BT is a unique company within the UK – it is extremely large and has a long history, including many decades of being a complete monopoly.

It has been subject to much change since the 1980s and its reputation for customer service was very poor. Not all of the problems can be solved quickly.

Option 3 would be a very brave decision one but is undoubtedly correct. By applying the rule of 'root cause' analysis to identify the cause of the problem she would take the first and most important step in finding a solution that will really fix the problem. Training will undoubtedly be a major part of the solution but unlikely to provide the complete solution. Appropriate training can help people deliver service better and the training needs to be made 'real' and seen to be able to work for people in their specific roles. Identifying and establishing a service style for the whole organisation is paramount. All activity should then be based around this – it is a style that should be lived and breathed and role modelled from the top down. People who do not work to this 'style' would then need to be performance managed as they would not be working in line with the company' expectations. This way people who do deliver service in the company style can then be measured and rewarded accordingly through the appraisal and review system.

Working to ensure the right people are in the right jobs is a good step as we know that there are many people in customer-facing jobs who perhaps do not naturally 'enjoy' this. Recruiting the right people with the appropriate mindset is key – if they are good – but perhaps if the mindset is not quite there, this can be trained. Training can provide people with tools and techniques. Training people to manage their mindset is also important. Even someone trained with all the tools can come across in a poor way if they are not managing their mindset appropriately.

People who are trained appropriately and given the right techniques will start to have successes in their dealings with clients and will then start to see the rationale behind giving great service and will also start to feel more confident in their ability to deal with queries/issues. This will subsequently start to turn their mindsets to being more positive and optimistic – a reinforcing cycle.

The ultimate aim is to ensure that people are equipped with the right techniques to handle any situation in a professional and positive manner and to train them in 'how' to use these techniques in their own roles. Customers should feel confident that when they phone anyone from the company, they will receive a professional, caring and solution-focused service – consistency of service delivery is key! Monitoring workers' performance in service delivery is essential to ensure that this consistency is maintained.

Marketing People

As we saw in Chapter 1, people are products, too. If you don't believe that, you've never been for a job interview. Many of us find it distasteful to equate people with products. In reality though, a sizeable number of people hire personal image consultants to devise a marketing strategy for them, and others undergo plastic surgery, physical conditioning or cosmetic makeovers to improve their 'market position' or 'sell' themselves to potential employers, friends, or lovers.[21] Let's briefly touch on a few prominent categories of people marketing.

Politicians are created and marketed by sophisticated consultants who 'package' candidates and compete for 'market share' of votes. Actors, musicians, athletes, supermodels, the famous and near-famous are all competing for market position in popular culture. Agents carefully package celebrities by working to get their clients exposure on TV, star roles in films, recording contracts or product endorsements.[22] Like other products, celebrities even rename themselves to craft a 'brand identity' using the same strategies marketers use to ensure that their products make an impression on consumers (did you know that Harry Webb's stage name is Cliff Richard).

In addition to these branding efforts, there are other strategies marketers use to 'sell' a celebrity, as Figure 9.4 shows.[23] These include (1) the *pure selling approach*, in which an agent presents a client's qualifications to potential 'buyers' until he finds one who is willing to act as an intermediary; (2) the *product improvement approach*, in which the agent works with the

Marketing Approach	Implementation
Pure Selling Approach	*Agent presents a client to* – record companies – film studios – TV production companies – talk show hosts – advertising agencies – talent scouts
Product Improvement Approach	*Client is modified* – New name – New image – Voice lessons – Dancing lessons – Plastic surgery – New back-up band – New music genre
Market Fulfilment Approach	*Agent looks for market opening* – Identify unmet need – Develop a new product (band, singer) to the specifications of consumer wants

Figure 9.4   Strategies to Sell a Celebrity
There is more than one approach to selling an intangible – even for selling a celebrity, Successful marketing has to determine the best approach to take for each product.

| Photo 9.3 | Superstar Beyonce Knowles is one of the latest celebrities to extend her 'brand identity' by branching out to other areas. In addition to her singing career, she has starred in films and is a spokeswoman for various products, including Pepsi and the Tommy Hilfiger perfume, True. Source: The Advertising Archives |

| Photo 9.4 | Many cities, counties, and countries recognise that by using effective marketing strategies, they can increase vital tourism revenues and attract business investment needed for growth. Source: The Advertising Archives |

client to modify certain characteristics that will increase market value; and (3) the *market fulfilment approach*, in which the agent scans the market to identify unmet needs. After identifying a need, the agent then finds a person or a group that meets a set of minimum qualifications and develops a new 'product'.

There is more than one approach to selling an intangible – even for selling a celebrity. Successful marketing has to determine the best approach to take for each product.

 ## Marketing Places

Place marketing strategies regard a city, country or other location as a brand, and attempt to position it so that consumers select this over competing destinations when they plan their travel. Because of the huge amount of money associated with tourism, the competition to attract visitors is fierce. This probably explains the rivalry between Hong Kong, Singapore and Dubai as stopover destinations for passengers going to Australasia.

The marketing of ideas can be even more difficult than marketing goods and services. Consumers often do not perceive that the *value* they receive from recycling their household waste or reducing global warming is worth the *cost* – the extra effort necessary to realise these goals. Governments and other organisations use marketing strategies, often with only limited success, to sell ideas that will save the lives of millions of unwilling consumers or will help save our planet.

Now that you've learned about marketing intangibles, read 'Real People, Real Decisions' to see which strategy Patricia Vaz selected.

Real People, Real Decisions

How it worked out at BT

After long and careful deliberation, and several discussions at board level, Patricia decided to put her head on the line and go for option 3. The decision was not an easy one. In light of the competitive intensity within the industry, perhaps option 1 would have been the shareholders' choice as by outsourcing the call centres to India, BT could make massive cost savings which would have helped both profitability and share price. Establishing a presence in India however would be disruptive in the short term as the company attempted to grapple with the transition phase. This option might not have been a winner with the public, particularly since the company previously belonged to the state. There was always a fear that by going down this route, more customers would switch to other suppliers, based on the ethical arguments of taking work overseas at the expense of the UK. For these reasons, option 1 was discarded.

Option 2 did provide some additional benefits for the company. Firstly, BT had the opportunity here to retain the management of the service within the UK. Quality standards would therefore be easier to control, and the management of the call centres by Patricia and her team would be simpler due to the geographic proximity. This option also provided the opportunity for Patricia to inform staff of the consolidation plans, and offer opportunities for a number of staff to consider a redundancy offer. The main concern here was ensuring her highly motivated and influential employees did not leave. This represented a sensitive area, as allowing some people to take redundancy because you want them to go, whilst at the same time refusing to allow others the same option is not good PR and it also affects the morale of the existing staff, who are left wondering when the next round of redundancies will take place. It would need much support from middle management. At an organisational level, to this date BT had never before made one single employee compulsorily redundant – which was the only way of making sure the ones you wanted to leave took the redundancy option. However, the company was proud of its record on redundancy being totally voluntary and for these reasons it was felt that option 2 should not be considered.

> **Patricia took the challenge of option 3 and decided to invest in improving the environment for the call centre agents**

Patricia took the challenge of option 3 and decided to invest in improving the environment for the call centre agents, focusing heavily on employee training whilst at the same time adopting a comprehensive reorganisation and consolidation programme. The main themes of the programme were as follows:

● The network of call centres across the UK was consolidated from 130 to 30.

- Each of the 30 residual centres was located in 'place of best fit' for existing call centre agents to minimise the number of agents who would find it impossible to work in the new centres.

- Each of the 30 centres was upgraded with state-of-the-art environment and equipment to ensure the best quality environment for the agents.

- New systems were designed and implemented to overcome all networking problems and ensure the call traffic was directed to the right place first time.

- A new and comprehensive knowledge management system was introduced to assist agents whilst they dealt with customers' needs.

- A process of talent casting was adopted, backed up by a comprehensive training programme, to ensure the agents were aware of the needs of the job and had the aptitude and talent to do well in it.

This last point was critically important. The company took the opportunity of restructuring the workforce of agents based on their talent, aptitude and enthusiasm for the job – one of the problems with the previous strategy had been that some agents were really not happy with their role as they dreaded speaking with customers. It was soon realised that what was right for one may not be right for another and a concerted effort was made to address the issue. Whilst the vast majority of employees in the call centres enjoyed their work and were delivering excellent service, these staff were 'empowered' to continue serving the public in very much the same way. With the others, however, there were basically two sorts of problems. The first group lacked the confidence to manage and deal with the public. They disliked their jobs because of this. These employees were therefore offered other jobs, or the opportunity to continue in their current posts, but with further mentoring support and training (MST). This strategy was

| Photo 9.5 | BT Customer Service Advisors. Source: BT Image Library |

successful, and over 90 per cent of the staff progressed down the MST route. However, for those that did not wish to continue dealing with customers, other jobs were found in the organisation that better suited their capabilities and talents.

Overall this complex programme took three years to complete; it succeeded in reducing costs for the company by £150m per annum and delivered a significant improvement in customer satisfaction with the service experience. Today no one gets a long-term contract for a job in the call centres until they have gone through a comprehensive selection process based on the specific requirements of the job and in particular the need to like the idea of talking to customers. In addition all agents have to complete a period of time working as an agency staff member in order to validate the selection procedures under real-time working supervision – only when they have proved their capabilities and their enthusiasm for the job are they then offered full-time contracts to deal with that most precious of responsibilities, the service interaction with customers.

Chapter Summary

Now that you have finished reading this chapter, you should be able to answer any of the following potential examination questions:

1. **Describe the principal characteristics of services.** Services are products that are intangible and that are exchanged directly from producer to customer without ownership rights. Generally, services are acts that accomplish some goal and may be directed either towards people or towards an object. Both consumer services and business-to-business services are significant parts of the economy. Important service characteristics include (1) intangibility (they can not be seen, touched, or smelled), (2) perishability (they can not be stored), (3) variability (they are never exactly the same from time to time) and (4) inseparability from the producer (most services are produced, sold and consumed at the same time).

2. **Explain how services differ from goods.** In reality, most products are a combination of goods and services. Some services are goods dominant (i.e. tangible products are marketed with supporting services). Some are equipment- or facility-based (i.e. elaborate equipment or facilities are required for creation of the service). Other services are people-based (i.e. people are actually a part of the service marketed). Like goods, services include both a core service or the basic benefit received and augmented services, including innovative features and convenience of service delivery.

3. **Explain how marketers create and measure service quality.** The customer's perception of service quality is related to expectations. Because services are intangible, evaluation of service quality is more difficult, and customers often look for cues to help them decide whether they received satisfactory service. Gap analysis measures the difference between customer expectations of service quality and what actually occurred. Using the critical incident technique, service firms can identify the specific contacts between customers and service providers that create dissatisfaction. The SERVQUAL instrument can be used to identify service quality gaps and look at remedies for improvement.

4. **Explain the marketing of people, places and ideas.** Managers follow the steps for marketing planning when marketing other intangibles as well. People, especially politicians and celebrities, are often packaged and promoted. Place marketing aims to create or change the market position of a particular location, whether a city, country, resort or institution. Idea marketing (gaining market share for a concept, philosophy, belief or issue) seeks to create or change a target market's attitude or behaviour. Marketing is used by religious organisations and to promote important causes. Marketing of ideas may be especially difficult, as consumers may not see the value to be worth the cost.

Key Terms

Augmented services 332

Capacity management 328

Core service 332

Credence qualities 336

Critical incident technique 338

Disintermediation 329

Dominant logic for marketing 340

Experience qualities 336

Gap analysis 337

Inseparability 328

Intangibility 327

Intangibles 324

Perishability 327

Place marketing 343

Search qualities 336

Service encounter 329

Services 326

Servicescape 334

SERVQUAL 337

Variability 328

Chapter Review

Marketing Concepts: Testing Your Knowledge

1. What are intangibles? How do basic marketing concepts apply to the marketing of intangibles?

2. What is a service? What are the important characteristics of services that make them different from goods?

3. What is the goods/services continuum? What are goods-dominated services, equipment- or facility-based services and people-based services?

4. What are core and augmented services? How do marketers increase market share with augmented services?

5. What are the physical and social elements of the service encounter?

6. Describe some popular means of marketing for services on the internet.

7. What dimensions do consumers and business customers use to evaluate service quality? How do marketers work to create service quality?

8. How do marketers measure service quality?

9. What are some ideas about the future of services?

10. What do we mean by marketing people? Marketing places? Marketing ideas?

Marketing Concepts: Discussing Choices

1. Why are first impressions formed on the internet about a service so important? What can a service firm do to ensure a favourable first impression online?

2. Sometimes service quality may not meet customers' expectations. What problems have you experienced with quality in the delivery of the following services?

   a. A restaurant meal

   b. An airline flight

   c. Motor vehicle repairs

   d. Your university education

   What do you think is the reason for the poor quality?

3. Many not-for-profit and religious organisations have found that they can be more successful by marketing their ideas. What are some ways that these organisations market themselves that are similar to and different from the marketing of for-profit businesses?

Marketing Practice: Applying What You've Learned

1. Because of increased competition in its community, you have been hired as a marketing consultant by a local bank. You know that the characteristics of services (intangibility, perishability, variability and inseparability) create unique marketing challenges. You also know that these challenges can be met with creative marketing strategies. Outline the challenges for marketing the bank created by each of the four characteristics of services. List your ideas for what might be done to meet each of these challenges.

2. Assume that you are a doctor. You are opening a new family practice clinic in your community. You feel that you have the best chance of being successful if you can create a product that is superior to that offered by competing businesses. Put together a list of ways in which you can augment the basic service offering to develop a better product. List the advantages and disadvantages of each.

3. You are currently a customer for a university, a very expensive service product. You know that a service organisation can create a competitive advantage by focusing on how the service is delivered after it has been purchased, i.e. making sure the service is efficiently and comfortably delivered to the customer. Develop a list of recommendations for your university for improving the delivery of its service. Consider both classroom and non-classroom aspects of the educational product.

4. Assume that you work for a marketing firm that has been asked to develop a marketing plan for a new up-and-coming pop band called Stalagmite, and their new CD 'Slow Drip'. Prepare an outline for your marketing plan. First, list the special problems and challenges associated with marketing people rather than a physical product. Then outline your ideas for product, price and promotion strategies.

5. Address the same issues in question 4 for a marketing plan for your own home town or city.

6. Assume that you have been recently hired by your city government to head up a programme to create 100 per cent compliance with recycling regulations. Develop a presentation for the local government in which you will outline the problems in 'selling' recycling. Develop an outline for the presentation. Be sure to focus on each of the four Ps.

 ## Marketing Miniproject: Learning by Doing

1. Select a service that you as a consumer will purchase in the next week or so.

2. As you experience the service, record the details of every aspect, including the following:
   a. People
   b. Physical facilities
   c. Location
   d. Waiting time
   e. Hours
   f. Transaction
   g. Other customers
   h. Tangible aspects
   i. Search qualities
   j. Credence qualities

3. Recommend improvements to the service encounter.

Real People, Real Surfers

Exploring the Web

Theme and entertainment parks fall in the middle of the goods/services continuum – half goods and half services. To be successful in this highly competitive market, these parks must carefully develop targeting and positioning strategies. Through looking at the websites of two or three theme parks of your choice, investigate the following:

1. How is each website designed to appeal to each theme park organisation's target market?

2. How does each park position its product? How is this positioning communicated through the website?

3. What changes or improvements would you recommend for each website?

Now, take a look at the website at www.pearsoned.co.uk/solomon to see some videos from YouTube relating to aspects of this chapter.

Marketing Plan Exercise

Organisations that market services face special challenges because services are intangible. One way they address the challenges created by intangibility is by designing an effective servicescape. This represents the environment where the service is delivered and where the firm and the customer interact.

1. Select a service that you are familiar with, such as a bank, an airline, or even your university.

2. Describe the weaknesses there might be in a SWOT analysis for the business that occur because of the intangibility of the service.

3. Develop strategies for creating a servicescape that will be a positive influence on customers' purchase decisions, their evaluations of the service quality, and their ultimate satisfaction with the service.

Marketing in Action Case

Real decisions at Betfair.com

On a May evening in 1998, Alan Black had one of those insightful neuron surges. He imagined building an online gambling exchange operating on similar principles to a stock exchange. As he commented in an interview published by *Scotland on Sunday*,

> 'The big jump was realising the numbers in the model didn't have to be a price. If you substituted these numbers for odds, it still worked.'

By 2004, Betfair was the world's largest betting exchange, with around 50,000 people placing bets each week on the many events the website features. Elections, major horse races, golf tournaments and football matches invariably trade more than €4.5 million at a time. Yet Black, co-founder Ed Wray and the senior management of the firm face a number of dilemmas. Topics that dominate management meetings include:

Who is our competition, how should we react and where might new competition come from?

How should we develop Betfair into a truly global firm, what challenges can we expect and how do we deal with vested interests and governments in countries where betting exchanges are seen as a significant challenge to the status quo?

How can we develop the Betfair business model? Are we a gambling and wagering company, or are we a technology company whose competences and processes allow us to expand into other markets and businesses as well?

How do we continue to deliver great service, fun and, hopefully, profits, to our customers?

Bookmakers and Totalisator Systems

Traditionally, those wanting to bet on the outcome of an event, such as the Epsom Derby, the European Cup Final or Wimbledon, have had to resort to a pari-mutuel totalisator system, or bookmaker. Pari-mutuel or totalisator systems deduct a percentage of all bets (normally around 15 per cent), and winners are then paid as a ratio of the remaining pool to their stake. The disadvantage for gamblers is that as the weight of money for their selection increases after they have placed their bet, so their odds, or payoffs, decrease. This means that it is difficult for players to use any kind of betting system to maximise profits or minimise losses. A player at a racetrack might for example be £100 down by the last race, and places a bet of a £100 on the favourite in an attempt to recoup his losses. At the time of placing the bet, the horse is showing a £2 payout for a £1 bet on the totalisator board. At these odds, our player will indeed recoup losses if the horse wins. However, the subsequent sheer weight of money then reduces the payout on the horse to £1.50 by the start of the race. If the horse wins, our player will still be £50 down for the day, and there are no rewards for skilfully placing the bet early. The totalisator can never lose – much like a lottery; it simply takes as its income a fixed percentage of all funds wagered.

Bookmakers offer fixed odds on the outcome – odds of 6/1 (£6 to £1), for example, means that the punter will be paid £6 plus the £1 stake should the bet win the event. The advantage to the gambler is that the odds are fixed, and will not be reduced by the subsequent weight of money placed on this choice, as in the totalisator case. On the other hand, however, if the bookmaker later increases the odds, the early gambler does not benefit from this change. The disadvantage to the gambler, in this case, is that bookmakers, like casinos, have a significant edge because they offer odds shorter than the true probabilities in order to profit in the long run – typically around 14 per cent of turnover.

In many countries, bookmaking is illegal. In those in which it is not illegal, bookmaking is strictly controlled and licensed, because there have been instances of unethical bookmakers influencing the outcome of sporting events for personal gain. For example, bookmakers have been accused of fixing races, bribing jockeys and other corrupt actions, and this is not in the ordinary player's interest. It is difficult enough to find a winner without having the odds unfairly stacked against one through cheating. Where bookmaking is legal, jurisdictions have often taxed winning bets as a form of governmental revenue, thereby increasing the odds against players, and in some cases authorities tax the stake, which means a further disadvantage. Unlike totalisator systems, bookmakers can and do lose on some events. For example, when they have misjudged the probabilities and the odds that they have offered have been too generous, or when some of the potential outcomes do not attract the anticipated volume of bets.

While the models for the totalisator and bookmaker differ in many ways, their basic premise is the same: use the money taken from losing bets to pay winning ones, and allow for a percentage 'rake-off' before doing so.

Betfair

When Betfair launched in 2000 with £1 million raised from Black's and co-founder Ed Wray's (a former vice-president of JP Morgan) network of contacts, it was taking less than £50,000 a week in bets. This number began to climb gradually and within nine months Betfair exceeded £1 million a week in turnover. Betfair won a Queen's Award for Innovation in 2003. To give a better indication of the volumes of cash being turned over by mid-June 2004, Betfair made more turnover on the Kentucky Derby than the totalisator on the track. More than £14 million was wagered on the 2007 US Open golf tournament, simply on the final outcome (and not taking novelty bets into consideration, such as would Tiger Woods make the cut, and who would be the top European player). A week before the Men's Final at Wimbledon in 2007, more than £12 million had been wagered on the overall outcome, and betting on each individual match exceeded £400,000.

Betfair provides an opportunity for speculators to bet on events that range from the more conventional sports such as horse and greyhound racing at tracks around the world, football, golf and tennis to more exotic activities such as hurling, darts and snooker. There is also the opportunity for bets to be laid or taken on non-sporting events such as the outcome of political elections, Big Brother competitions, and the Oscars. The company also offers a range of financial bets on most of the world's major markets (turning over more than £100,000 daily simply on whether the FTSE will rise or fall).

The Betfair System

Unlike conventional bookmakers, and like totalisator systems, Betfair is not really interested in the outcome of an event. It simply provides a market for opinions and for trade to take place. Unlike totalisator systems, and like bookmakers, the odds offered on Betfair are fixed, and Betfair also doesn't take a percentage of the money wagered. Rather, its income is derived from a small percentage commission (ranging between 2 and 5 per cent, depending on a player's turnover) on a player's net winnings on an event. So, for example, if a player backed two horses in a race, lost £5 on one and won £20 on another, then a commission would be taken on the net winnings of £15. Similarly if a player had accepted a bet of £5 against Tiger Woods winning the 2008 US Masters, and laid him at odds of 3/1, the player would have won £5 (because Tiger Woods lost) and paid a small percentage commission to Betfair accordingly.

> # Betfair is not really interested in the outcome of an event. It simply provides a market for opinions and for trade to take place

For events, Betfair shows the possible outcomes (for example, horses or dogs in a race, the players in a golf tournament, or the two teams in a game, which may also include a draw), and columns entitled 'Bet' and 'Lay'. The 'Bet' column shows the odds available to a player who wants to back an outcome and how much money a player can place on those odds. So, for example, if the 'Bet' column showed a price of 4.00 and £100 available, then a player will get odds of 3/1 (the price represents the payout plus the stake), and so by wagering £100, would get £300 plus the stake of £100 back if the selection won. Likewise, the 'Lay' column shows what players want as odds, and how much they wish to bet. So a 'Lay' price of 3.00 and amount of £200 means that someone who thought the outcome might lose could take up to £200 on the outcome at that price. So, for example, if one took £10 of the £200 (leaving £190) at these odds, one would keep the £10 if the outcome lost, and lose £20 as well as forfeiting the stake of £10 if the outcome won (for a net loss of £30).

Even for those not inclined to gambling, but nevertheless interested in the mechanics of markets, it is worth visiting Betfair just to see how narrow are the differences between the 'Bet' and 'Lay' columns on the larger markets (such as horse races and golf competitions). Prices are inevitably made and taken, and the margins are minuscule, much smaller than those of even the most generous bookmaker.

Rather than profit by taking a percentage of losing bets, Betfair profits by taking a small percentage of net winnings. Therefore, the greater the turnover on events, the more revenue Betfair will generate. It is successful if it can assemble large numbers of customers – and provide a market for them to interact with each other. Customers place funds with Betfair by making an online deposit through a credit card (or by cheque or bank draft through special arrangement), and Betfair then maintains a record of the account's balance and transactions. The balance is reduced every time a customer takes a bet (e.g. backs a horse), and is also reduced on reserve every time a customer lays a bet (i.e. incurs a potential liability by laying an outcome at odds). When a player wins, the net winnings are credited to that player's account. Customers with a positive balance can withdraw at any time and request to have all or part of their positive balance re-credited to their credit cards or bank accounts. The company also allows customers to make payments in advance by cheque, or to have cheques mailed to them or deposited into their bank accounts by prior arrangement.

A feature of Betfair is that it permits players to bet 'in the running' – that is, after a race has started until a winner eventually crosses the finishing line. In the event of a very close photo-finish, or an objection, Betfair will also reopen in-play betting so that bets can be taken on the outcome of the photo-finish or the objection. Players can also bet on games and matches while these are 'in play,' a particularly popular feature in sports such as football, golf and tennis.

Growth in Revenues and Business

Betfair continued to grow rapidly, and its turnover in 2003 was substantially higher than in 2002. From April 2002 to April 2003, Betfair's pretax profits rose from £1 million to £11.9 million. Growth since then has matched these rates.

By the end of 2004, Betfair had more than 300,000 registered customers, of whom some 50,000 were regular punters betting every week. Major events could attract up to 12,000 wagers per minute.

The Incumbents Retaliate and Competitors Enter the Market

As would be expected, a number of competing online betting exchanges have been established in countries such as the United Kingdom, the US and South Africa, with variations on the Betfair business model. Some of the major operators are listed in Table 9.3. So far none of these offers the selection and range of wagering possibilities that Betfair does. Tradesports[1] tends to concentrate on sport and racing in the US, and also runs markets in political events, and prominent issues such as the Michael Jackson trial, and whether Osama Bin Laden will be captured.

The Way Forward

There are many issues that confront the group, including potential corruption, aggressive conflict with incumbents, technology, international growth and the possible expansion of the business into other areas. These all demand the attention of top management, whose problems are compounded by the diversity of legislation surrounding internet gambling.[2]

---

[1] www.tradesports.com.

[2] For a current summary of the climate in the various jurisdictions, see http://online.casinocity.com/jurisdictions/.

BETDAQ www.betdaq.co.uk	Revamped its site to offer many new features including, when laying a selection, you can now enter the backers' stake you hope to win as opposed to your own liability. Maximum commission rate of 3 per cent.
GGBet www.gg.com	Horse racing betting exchange from GG.com. Standard commission is 5 per cent, but this can reduce to 1 per cent based on bets placed.
iBetX www.ibetx.com	International person-to-person betting exchange. Provides coverage for UK and US horse racing. In addition to normal betting exchange features, it allows you to upload a text file to place multiple bets simultaneously. Commission charges range from 1 per cent to 3 per cent. Free £20 bonus for new customers.
Sporting Options www.sportingoptions.co.uk	Functionally similar to Betfair. Went into receivership in November 2004, and Betfair bailed out the 5000 customers.
Tradesports www.tradesports.com	Person-to-person betting (mostly on American sports). Deposit and trade $50 and receive a $50 free bet. Frequently quoted in respected magazines such as *The Economist* as a source of indication of probability.
Trading Sports www.tradingsports.net	Not a betting exchange, rather it provides the technology to enable websites to offer branded person-to-person betting exchange. Used to power sites such as Tradbets, Betfanatic and Matchedbets.
SABookmaker www.sabookmaker.co.za	Allows licensed South African bookmakers to both take and lay bets, and players to ask for bets (but not to lay bets)

Table 9.3   Betfair's competition

Things to Think About

1. What do you think are the key questions confronting Betfair executives?

2. What business is Betfair in?

3. How might Betfair provide even better service to its customers?

4. How would you go about implementing your recommendations if you worked for Betfair?

Case study written by Professor Leyland Pitt at the Segal Graduate School of Business, Simon Fraser University.

References

1. *Giving and Volunteering in the United States: Key Findings* www.independentsector.org/PDFs/GV01keyfind.pdf.

2. www.salvationist.org/intnews.nsf/vw_web_images_only?openview&start=1&count=10.

3. John A. Czepiel, Michael R. Solomon and Carol F. Surprenant, eds., *The Service Encounter: Managing Employee/Customer Interaction in Service Businesses* (Lexington, MA: D.C. Heath and Company, 1985).

4. Lou W. Turley and Douglas L. Fugate, 'The Multidimensional Nature of Service Facilities: Viewpoints and Recommendations', *Journal of Services Marketing* 6 (Summer 1992), 37–45.

5. David H. Maister, 'The Psychology of Waiting Lines', in Czepiel *et al.*, *The Service Encounter*, 113–24.

6. Jennifer Chao, 'Airports Open Their Gates to Profits', *Montgomery Advertiser*, 26 January 1997, 16A.

7. Jim Kerstetter and Jay Greene, 'Pay-As-You-Go Is Up and Running', *Business Week*, 12 January 2004, 69–70.

8. Cengiz Haksever, Barry Render, Roberta S. Russell and Robert G. Murdick, *Service Management and Operations* (Englewood Cliffs, NJ: Prentice Hall, 2000), 25–26.

9. Cynthia Webster, 'Influences upon Consumer Expectations of Services', *Journal of Services Marketing* 5 (Winter 1991), 5–17.

10. Mary Jo Bitner, 'Evaluating Service Encounters: The Effects of Physical Surroundings and Employee Responses', *Journal of Marketing* 54 (April 1990), 69–82.

11. Lewis P. Carbone and Stephan H. Haeckel, 'Engineering Customer Experiences', *Marketing Management* 3 (Winter 1994), reprint, exhibit 4.

12. Valarie A. Zeithaml, Mary Jo Bitner and Dwayne Gremler, *Services Marketing*, 4th ed. (Englewood Cliffs, NJ: Prentice Hall, 2005).

13. A. Parasuraman, Leonard L. Barry and Valarie A. Zeithaml, 'SERVQUAL: A Multiple-Item Scale for Measuring Consumer Perceptions of Service Quality', *Journal of Retailing* 64 (1) (1988), 12–40; A. Parasuraman, Leonard L. Barry and Valarie A. Zeithaml, 'Refinement and Reassessment of the SERVQUAL Scale', *Journal of Retailing* 67 (4) (1991), 420–50.

14. Valarie A. Zeithaml, Leonard L. Berry and A. Parasuraman, 'Communication and Control Processes in the Delivery of Service Quality', *Journal of Marketing* 52 (April 1988), 35–48.

15. Jody D. Nyquist, Mary F. Bitner and Bernard H. Booms, 'Identifying Communication Difficulties in the Service Encounter: A Critical Incident Approach', in Czepiel *et al.*, *The Service Encounter*, 195–212.

16. Nyquist *et al.*, 'Identifying Communication Difficulties in the Service Encounter', 195–212.

17. Kristin Anderson and Ron Zemke, *Delivering Knock Your Socks Off Service* (New York: American Management Association, 1998).

18. Haksever *et al.*, *Service Management and Operations*, 342–43.

19. Stephen L. Vargo and Robert F. Lusch, 'Evolving to a New Dominant Logic for Marketing', *Journal of Marketing* 68 (January 2004): 1–17.

20. Joe Sharkey, 'Hotels to Flaunt Brands and Add Amenities', 1 December 2003, www.nyt.com.

21. Michael R. Solomon, 'The Wardrobe Consultant: Exploring the Role of a New Retailing Partner', *Journal of Retailing* 63 (Summer 1987), 110–28.

22. Michael R. Solomon, 'Celebritisation and Commodification in the Interpersonal Marketplace', unpublished manuscript, Rutgers University, 1991.

23. Adapted from a discussion in Rein *et al.*, *High Visibility*, p. 573.

Chapter 10
Pricing the Product

Meet Phil Byrne,
Chief Executive at BR
Pharmaceuticals

Q & A with Phil Byrne

First job out of school:
Shop floor operative at Leeds Alloys Ltd.

Business book I'm reading now:
The History of the Middle East
by Peter Mansfield.

My hero:
Sam Goldman, a highly successful and
influential local businessman – he's my
mentor and business guru.

**Don't do this when interviewing
with me:**
Lack self-confidence.

My pet peeve:
People that are 'unaware' – the world is
full of them (including myself at times).

Hobby/sport:
Travelling, especially on business or with
my wife and family.

Phil Byrne is Chief Executive, the major shareholder and co-founder of BR Pharmaceuticals. Previously he had spent over 20 years working with a number of healthcare companies in various management and marketing roles. Having left school at the age of 17 with no formal qualifications, Phil began work at a local firm on the shop floor manufacturing vehicle number plates. He always had the drive and desire to become a commercial airline pilot and achieved his personal goal before his 20th birthday. Due to unforeseen circumstances that were beyond his control, he was unable to pursue his dream to have a career in commercial aviation and in 1985 decided to start his own business in the healthcare sector.

Through learning on the job, Phil was able to develop the skills and experience necessary that would later serve him well at BR. He is married with three children and lives in a village just ten minutes from his business.

Real People, Real Decisions
Decision Time at BR Pharmaceuticals

Formed in the mid 1990s, BR Pharmaceuticals is the shared vision of Phil Byrne and Patrick Roche. These two entrepreneurs came together combining over 25 years' experience in over-the-counter sales with 10 years' involvement in pharmacy retail, to establish the company. In 1996, Phil and Patrick identified a marketing opportunity in the UK to supply the first value-for-money home pregnancy test kit and this became their first commercial product which they labelled 'Reveal'. Based on the marketing ethos of entering the market at a low price to attract customers and achieve market share, the kit quickly penetrated the market.

However, Phil and Patrick realised that being dependent on just one product would not generate sufficient business for the company to survive. As a result the two partners decided to focus their attention on the vitamin, mineral and supplements (VMS) market. Phil had previous experience of marketing in this sector and Patrick was a qualified pharmacist.

Historically the VMS market consisted of three different market segments:

1. At the top end of the market, a number of specialist and health food shops would typically display and market high specification produce, at high prices. Sales tended to be low volume with good margins for the suppliers and retailers alike. A number of domestic players operate in this segment, and imported goods from US suppliers such as Solgar and GNC had also found their way into the market.

2. At the low-price end of the market, supermarket 'own label' tended to lead the way, as powerful retailers used their strength to squeeze the supply chain and obtain relatively good quality products at low prices.

3. Finally, and somewhere in the middle of the road, retailers, pharmacists and speciality shops were also looking for branded produce to increase their range. This segment is fragmented, with all the key players aiming for a slice of the action.

Phil had to consider which segment of the VMS market the company should aim at. It was essential that the right choice was made, as it would probably make the difference between business success or failure. Three options came to mind.

Phil considers his options . . .

Option 1 Aim to enter at the low end of the market and compete on price

This would be a risky strategy for BR to follow as the company would be up against the major supermarket chains that offer their 'own label' produce. Whilst this option may not be impossible, particularly if other retailers would buy into the idea, the margins would be so low that big volume sales needed to be generated.

Option 2 Focus on supplying high spec VMS products for big income earners at high prices

This represented a viable option for BR. Supplying low volume with high profit would particularly appeal to the company's needs at this stage of its development, as well as retail stores, which could benefit from substantial margins on the merchandise. The only downside of this strategy is that the 'Reveal' brand was targeted at the opposite end of the market. However, a differentiated strategy may not be a bad approach.

Option 3 Price match and aim to compete in the middle-of-the-road market

The main advantage associated with this option is the huge market size and potential. Both Phil and Patrick could use their existing contacts within the sector to break into this segment. Through nurturing such contacts and developing new relationships, achieving success would probably take some time to evolve, as in order to grow significantly BR must fight to achieve market share in a competitive arena.

Now, put yourself in Phil's position: Which option would you choose, and why?

Objectives

When you finish reading this chapter, you will be able to:

1 Explain the importance of pricing and how prices can take both monetary and non-monetary forms

2 Understand the pricing objectives that marketers typically have in planning pricing strategies

3 Describe how marketers use costs, demands and revenue to make pricing decisions

4 Understand some of the environmental factors that affect pricing strategies

5 Understand pricing strategies

6 Explain pricing tactics for single and multiple products and for pricing on the internet

7 Understand the opportunities for online pricing strategies

8 Describe the psychological, legal and ethical aspects of pricing

Objective

1

Explain the importance of pricing and how prices can take both monetary and non-monetary forms

'Yes, but What Does it Cost?'

As Phil Byrne discovered, the question of what to charge for a product is a central part of marketing decision making. In this chapter, we'll tackle the basic question, what is price? We'll also see how marketers begin to determine pricing strategies by developing pricing objectives and by looking at the role of demand, costs, revenues and the environment in the pricing decision process. Then we'll explore how the pricing decision process leads to specific pricing strategies and tactics.

We've all heard that 'if you have to ask how much it is, you can't afford it', but how often do you buy something without asking the price? If price was not an issue, we'd all drive great cars, take trips to exotic places, and live like royalty. In the real world, though, most of us need to consider a product's price before we buy it.

Price is the value that customers give up or exchange to obtain a desired product. Payment may be in the form of money, goods, services, favours, votes or anything else that has *value* to the other party. As explained in Chapter 1, marketing is the process that creates exchanges of things of value. We usually think of this exchange as people trading money for a good or a service. However, in some marketplace practices, price can mean the exchange of non-monetary value as well. Long before societies produced currency, people exchanged goods and services. This practice still occurs today. For example, someone who owns a home at a mountain ski resort may exchange a weekend stay for car repair or dental work. No money changes hands, but there is an exchange of value.

Other non-monetary costs are often important to marketers. What is the cost of wearing seat belts? What is it worth to people to camp out in a clean national park? It is also important to consider an *opportunity cost*, or the value of something that is given up to obtain something else. For example, the cost of going to university includes more than tuition – it also includes the income that the student could have earned by working instead.

How important are good pricing decisions? Even during the best of economic times, most consumers rank 'reasonable price' – a price that makes the product affordable and that appears to be fair – as the most important consideration in a purchase and one that counts the most when they decide where to shop.[1]

Developing Pricing Objectives

As Figure 10.1 shows, there are six steps in price planning. The first crucial step is developing pricing objectives. Pricing objectives must support the broader objectives of the firm, such as maximising shareholder value, as well as its overall marketing objectives, such as increasing market share. Table 10.1 provides examples of different types of pricing objectives, which we'll discuss next.

| 1. Develop Pricing Objectives |
| 2. Estimate Demand |
| 3. Determine Costs |
| 4. Evaluate the Pricing Environment |
| 5. Choose a Pricing Strategy |
| 6. Develop Pricing Tactics |

Figure 10.1   Steps in Price Planning
Successful price planning includes a series of orderly steps beginning with setting pricing objectives.

Step 1: Develop Sales or Market Share Objectives

Objective

2

Understand the pricing objectives that marketers typically have in planning pricing strategies

Often the objective of a pricing strategy is to maximise monetary sales or to increase market share. Does setting a price that is intended to increase unit sales, market share or focus on sales objectives simply mean pricing the product lower than the competition? Sometimes this is the case. Providers of mobile phone services such as O$_2$, Orange or Vodafone relentlessly offer consumers better deals that include more minutes for a standard fee, free airtime minutes, rollover minutes, and low-cost phones to keep them ahead in the mobile market. Service providers pay for numerous television and radio commercials to promote these changes, but lowering prices is not always necessary to increase market share. Table 10.1 illustrates that if a company's product has a competitive advantage, keeping the price at the same level as other firms may satisfy sales objectives.

Profit Objectives

As discussed earlier in the book, often a firm's overall objectives relate to a certain level of profit it hopes to realise. When pricing strategies are determined by profit objectives, the focus is on a target level of profit growth or a desired net profit margin. A profit objective is important to firms that believe profit is what motivates shareholders and bankers to invest in a company.

Although profits are an important consideration in the pricing of all goods and services, they are critical when the product has a short market life. Fashion garments for example have a relatively short market life, making a profit is therefore essential to allow the firm to recover its investment in a short period of time. In such cases, the firm must achieve profits before customers lose interest and move on to the next fashion or fad.

Table 10.1
Pricing Objectives

Type of Objective	Example
Sales or market share	Institute pricing strategy changes to support a 5 per cent increase in sales.
Profit	During the first six months, set a price to yield a target profit of €200,000 or set prices to allow for an 8 per cent profit margin on all goods sold.
Competitive effect	Alter pricing strategy during first quarter of the year to increase sales during the competitor's introduction of a new product or maintain low end pricing policies to discourage new competitors from entering the market.
Customer satisfaction	Simplify pricing structure to simplify decision process for customers or alter price levels to match customer expectations.

 ## Competitive Effect Objectives

Competitive effect objectives mean that the pricing plan is intended to have a certain effect on the competition's marketing efforts. Sometimes a firm may deliberately seek to pre-empt or reduce the effectiveness of one or more competitors. That's what happened when the likes of easyJet entered the European market with low-fare flights. In response, national and former national carriers began to reduce their fares in order to become more competitive on such routes.

 ## Customer Satisfaction Objectives

Many quality-focused firms believe that profits result from making customer satisfaction the primary objective. These firms believe that by focusing solely on short-term profits a company loses sight of keeping customers for the long term. During the summer period in Dubai (July – August), traditionally a poor season for hotel occupancy due to the excessively hot climate, several of the leading hotel chains have managed to attract European visitors and retain business through providing greater value, and upgrading guests to full board and even club facilities.

 ## Image Enhancement Objectives

Consumers often use price to make inferences about the quality of a product. In fact, marketers know that price is often an important means of communicating not only quality but also image to prospective customers. The image enhancement function of pricing is particularly important with **prestige products** (or luxury products) that have a high price and appeal to status-conscious consumers. Most of us would agree that the high price tag on a Rolex watch, a Louis Vitton handbag, or a Rolls-Royce car, although representing the higher costs of producing the product, is vital to shaping an image of an extraordinary product with ownership limited to wealthy consumers.

LOUIS VUITTON

In vendita unicamente nei negozi esclusivi Louis Vuitton. Tel. 800 30 89 80 www.louisvuitton.com

Photo 10.1	People are often willing to pay a premium price for a luxury product because they believe (rightly or wrongly) that it makes a statement about their own worth. Source: The Advertising Archives

Step 2: Estimate Demand

Objective

3

Describe how marketers use costs, demands and revenue to make pricing decisions

The second step in price planning is to estimate demand. *Demand* refers to customers' desires for a product: how much of a product are customers willing to buy as the price goes up or down? Obviously, marketers should know the answer to this question before setting prices. Therefore, one of the earliest steps that marketers take in price planning is to estimate demand for their products.

Demand Curves

A graph using a *demand curve* nicely illustrates the effect of price on the quantity demanded of a product. The demand curve, which can be a curved or straight line, shows the quantity of a product that customers will buy in a market during a period of time at various prices if all other factors remain the same.

Figure 10.2 shows demand curves for normal and prestige products. The vertical axis for the demand curve represents the different prices that a firm might charge for a product (P). The horizontal axis shows the number of units or quantity (Q) of the product demanded. The demand curve for most goods (shown on the left side of Figure 10.2) slopes downward and to the right. As the price of the product goes up (P_1 to P_2), the number of units that customers are willing to buy goes down (Q_1 to Q_2). If prices decrease, customers will buy more. This is known as the *law of demand*. For example, if the price of bananas goes up, customers will probably buy fewer of them. If the price really goes so high, customers will simply switch to alternatives.

There are, however, exceptions to this typical price – quantity relationship. In fact, there are situations in which people desire a product more as it *increases* in price. For prestige products such as luxury cars or jewellery, an increase in price may actually result in an *increase* in the quantity demanded because consumers see these products as more valuable. In such cases, the demand curve slopes upward. If the price decreases, consumers perceive the product to be less desirable and demand may decrease. The right-hand side of Figure 10.2 shows the 'backward-bending' demand curve associated with prestige products.

Still, the higher price/higher demand relationship has its limits. If the firm increases the price too much, making the product unaffordable for all but a few buyers, demand will begin to decrease, as shown by the backward direction taken by the top portion of the backward-bending curve.

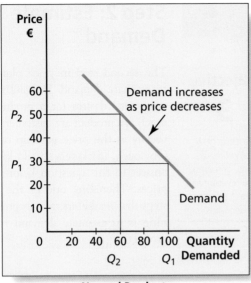

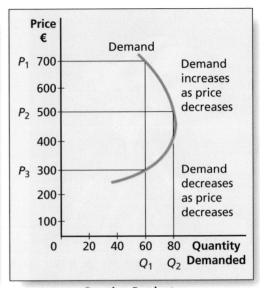

Normal Products	**Prestige Products**

Demand Curves for Normal and Prestige Products

For normal products, there is an inverse relationship between price and demand. For prestige products, demand will increase – to a point – as price increases or will decrease as price decreases.

 ## Shifts in Demand

The demand curves shown assume that all factors other than price stay the same. But what if they don't? What if the product is improved? What happens when there is a trendy new advertising campaign that turns a product into a 'must-have' for a lot of people? What if a paparazzi photographer catches Hugh Grant using the product at home? Any of these things could cause an *upward shift* of the demand curve. An upward shift in the demand curve means that at any given price, demand is greater than before the shift occurs.

Figure 10.3 shows the upward shift of the demand curve as it moves from D_1 to D_2. At D_1, before the shift occurs, customers will be willing to purchase the quantity Q_1 (or 80 units in Figure 10.3) at the given price, P (or €60 in Figure 10.3). For example, customers at a particular shop may buy 80 barbecue grills at €60 a grill. Then the shop decides to run a huge advertising campaign, featuring celebrity chef Gordon Ramsay on his patio using the barbecue grill. The demand curve shifts from D_1 to D_2 (the shop keeps the price at €60). Take a look at how the quantity demanded has changed to Q_2. In our example, the shop is now selling 200 barbecue grills at €60 per grill. From a marketing standpoint, this shift is the best of both worlds. Without lowering prices, the company can sell more of its product. As a result, total revenues go up, and unless the new promotion costs as much as the increase in revenues it triggers, so do profits.

Changes in the environment or in company efforts can cause a shift in the demand curve. A great advertising campaign for example, can shift the demand curve upward.

Of course, demand curves may also shift downward. That's what has happened with the demand for first-class airline seats. As companies and families become more concerned about costs, fewer customers buy first-class seats. In response, airlines are offering some first-class tickets at 50 to 70 per cent off the standard rate.[2] In the real world, factors other than the price and marketing activities influence demand. If it rains heavily, the demand for umbrellas increases and the demand for playing golf or tennis declines. The development of new products may also influence demand for old ones. Even though some firms may still produce

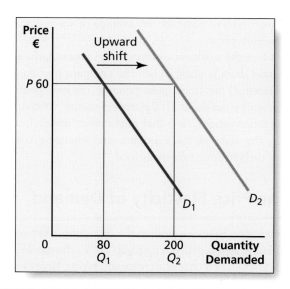

Figure 10.3	**Shift in Demand Curve**
	Changes in the environment or in company efforts can cause a shift in the demand curve. A great advertising campaign, for example, can shift the demand curve upwards.

cassette tapes, the introduction of CDs and MP3s has greatly reduced the demand for vinyl records and turntables to play them on.

Estimating Demand

Understanding and estimating demand is extremely important for marketers. First, a firm's production scheduling is based on anticipated demand that must be estimated well in advance of when products are brought to market. In addition, all marketing planning and budgeting must be based on reasonably accurate estimates of potential sales.

So how do marketers reasonably estimate potential sales? Marketers predict total demand first by identifying the number of buyers or potential buyers for their product and then multiply that estimate by the average amount each member of the target market is likely to purchase. Table 10.2 shows how a small business, such as a start-up pizza restaurant, estimates demand in markets. For example, a pizza entrepreneur may estimate that there are 180,000 consumer households in his market that would be willing to buy his pizza, and that each

Table 10.2
Estimating Demand
for Pizza

Number of families in market	180,000
Average number of pizzas per family per year	6
Total annual market demand	1,080,000
Company's predicted share of the total market	3 per cent
Estimated annual company demand	32,400 pizzas
Estimated monthly company demand	2,700
Estimated weekly company demand	675

household will purchase an average of six pizzas a year. The total annual demand is over 1 million pizzas.

Once the marketer estimates total demand, the next step is to predict what the company's market share is likely to be. The company's estimated demand is then its share of the whole (estimated) pie. In our pizza example, the entrepreneur may feel that he can gain 3 per cent of this market, or about 2700 pizzas per month. Of course, such projections need to take into consideration other factors that might affect demand, such as new competitors entering the market, the state of the economy, and changing consumer tastes like a sudden demand for low-carbohydrate take-away food.

The Price Elasticity of Demand

In addition to understanding the relationship between price and demand, marketers also need to know how sensitive customers are to *changes* in price. In particular, it is critical to understand whether a change in price will have a large or a small impact on demand. How much can a firm increase or decrease its price before seeing a marked change in sales? If the price of a pizza goes up €1, will people switch to Chinese or Indian take-aways? What would happen if the pizza went up €2? Or even €5?

Price elasticity of demand is a measure of the sensitivity of customers to changes in price: if the price changes by 10 per cent, what will be the percentage change in demand for the product? The word *elasticity* indicates that changes in price usually cause demand to stretch or retract like a rubber band. Price elasticity of demand is calculated as follows:

$$\text{Price elasticity of demand} = \frac{\text{percentage change in quantity demanded}}{\text{percentage change in price}}$$

Sometimes customers are very sensitive to changes in prices, such a change may result in a substantial change in the quantity demanded. In these instances, we have a case of **elastic demand**. In other situations such as **inelastic demand**, a change in price tends to have little or no effect on the quantity that consumers are willing to buy.

For example, using the formula, suppose the pizza maker finds (from experience or from marketing research) that lowering the price of his pizza 10 per cent (from €10 per pizza to €9) will cause a 15 per cent increase in demand. He would calculate the price elasticity of demand as 15 divided by 10. The price elasticity of demand would be 1.5. If the price elasticity of demand is greater than one, demand is elastic; that is, consumers respond to the price decrease by demanding more. Or, if the price increases, consumers will demand less. Figure 10.4 shows these calculations.

As Figure 10.5 illustrates, when demand is elastic, changes in price and in total revenues (total sales) work in opposite directions. If the price is increased, revenues decrease. If the price is decreased, total revenues increase. With elastic demand, the demand curve shown in Figure 10.5 is more horizontal. With an elasticity of demand of 1.5, a decrease in price will increase the pizza maker's total sales.

Price elasticity of demand represents how demand responds to changes in prices. If there is little change in demand, then demand is said to be price inelastic. If there is a large change in demand, demand is price elastic.

As we noted earlier, in some instances demand is *inelastic* so that a change in price results in little or no change in demand. For example, if the 10 per cent decrease in the price of pizza resulted in only a 5 per cent increase in pizza sales, then the price elasticity of demand calculated would be 5 divided by 10, which is 0.5 (less than 1), and our pizza maker faces inelastic demand. When demand is inelastic, price and revenue changes are in the same direction; that is, increases in price result in increases in total revenue, while decreases in

---

Elastic demand

Price changes from €10 to €9.

€10 − 9 = €1

1/10 = 10% change in price

Demand changes from 2,700 per month to 3,100 per month

$$3,100$$
$$-\,2,700$$

Increase · 400 pizzas

Percentage increase · · · · · · · · · · · · · 400/2,700 = 0.148 ~ 15% change in demand

$$\text{Price elasticity of demand} = \frac{\text{percentage change in quantity demanded}}{\text{percentage change in price}}$$

$$\text{Price elasticity of demand} = \frac{15\%}{10\%} = 1.5$$

Inelastic demand

Price changes from €10 to €9.

€10 − 9 = €1

1/10 = 10% change in price

Demand changes from 2,700 per month to 2,835 per month

$$2,835$$
$$-\,2,700$$

Increase · 135 pizzas

Percentage increase · · · · · · · · · · · · · 135/2,700 = 0.05 ~ 5% change in demand

$$\text{Price elasticity of demand} = \frac{\text{percentage change in quantity demanded}}{\text{percentage change in price}}$$

$$\text{Price elasticity of demand} = \frac{5\%}{10\%} = 0.5$$

Figure 10.4	Price Elasticity of Demand

price result in decreases in total revenue. With inelastic demand, the demand curve in Figure 10.5 becomes more vertical. Generally, the demand for necessities such as food and electricity is inelastic. Even large price increases do not cause us to buy less food or to give up our lights and hot water.

If demand is price inelastic, can marketers keep raising prices so that revenues and profits will grow larger and larger? What if demand is elastic? Does it mean that marketers can never raise prices? The answer to these questions is no. Elasticity of demand for a product often differs for different price levels and with different percentages of change.

As a general rule, pizza makers and other companies can determine the *actual* price elasticity only after they have tested a pricing decision and calculated the resulting demand. Only then will they know whether a specific price change will increase or decrease revenues.

To estimate what demand is likely to be at different prices for new or existing products, marketers often do research. One approach is to conduct a study in which consumers tell marketers how much of a product they would be willing to buy at different prices. For example, researchers might ask participants if they would rent more DVD films if the price was reduced from €4 to €3, or how many bags of their favourite chocolates they would buy at €3, €4, or €5. At other times, researchers conduct *field studies* in which they vary the

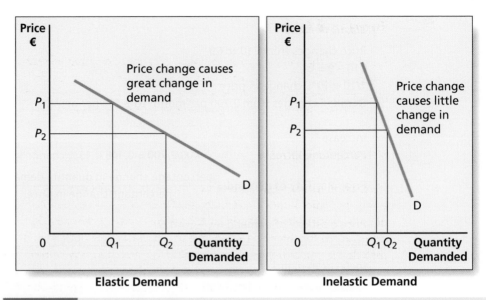

Elastic Demand   **Inelastic Demand**

Figure 10.5	Price Elastic and Inelastic Demand Curves
	Price elasticity of demand represents how demand responds to changes in prices. If there is little change in demand, then demand is said to be price inelastic. If there is a large change in demand, demand is price elastic.

price of a product in different shops and measure how much is actually purchased at the different price levels.

Other factors can affect price elasticity and sales. Consider the availability of *substitute* goods or services. If a product has a close substitute, its demand will be elastic; that is, a change in price will result in a change in demand, as consumers move to buy the substitute product. For example, Coke and Pepsi may be considered close substitutes. If the price of Pepsi goes up, many people may buy Coke instead. Marketers of products with close substitutes are less likely to compete on price, recognising that doing so could result in less profit as consumers switch from one brand to another. Many consumers are finding that the cost of a mobile phone service is so reasonable that they are now giving up their land lines.

Changes in prices of other products also affect the demand for an item, a phenomenon called **cross-elasticity of demand**. When products are substitutes for each other, an increase in the price of one will increase the demand for the other. For example, if the price of bananas goes up, consumers may instead buy more strawberries, kiwis, or apples. However, when products are complements, that is, when one product is essential to the use of a second, an increase in the price of one decreases the demand for the second. For example, if the price of petrol goes up, consumers may drive less or take public transport. As a result, the demand for tyres will decrease.

Step 3: Determine Costs

Estimating demand helps marketers develop possible prices to charge for a product. It tells them how much of the product they think they'll be able to sell at different prices. Knowing this brings them to the third step in determining a product's price: making sure the price will cover costs. Before marketers can determine price, they must understand the relationship of cost, demand and revenue for their product. In this next section, we'll talk about different types of costs that marketers must consider in pricing. Then we'll show two types of analyses that marketers use in making pricing decisions.

Types of Costs

It's obvious that the cost of producing a product plays a big role when firms decide what to charge for it. If an item's selling price is lower than the cost to produce, it doesn't take a rocket scientist to figure out that the firm will lose money. Before looking at how costs influence pricing decisions, it is necessary to understand the different types of costs that firms incur.

Variable Costs

First, a firm incurs **variable costs**; per-unit costs of production that will fluctuate depending on how many units or individual products a firm produces. For example, if it takes 25 cents' worth of nails (a variable cost) to build a single bookcase, it will take 50 cents' worth for two, 75 cents' worth for three and so on. For the production of bookcases, variable costs would also include the cost of timber, paint as well as the salaries factory workers would be paid.

Figure 10.6 shows some examples of the variable cost per unit or average variable cost and the total variable costs at different levels of production (for producing 100, 200 and 500 bookcases). If the firm produces 100 bookcases, the average variable cost per unit is €50, and the total variable cost is €5000 (€50 × 100). If production is doubled to 200 units, the total variable cost now is €10,000 (€50 × 200).

In reality, calculating variable costs is usually more complex than shown here. As the number of bookcases the factory produces increases or decreases, average variable costs may change. For example, if the company buys just enough wood for one bookcase, the timber yard will charge top price. If it buys enough for 100 bookcases, the company gets a better deal. If the company buys enough for thousands of bookcases, it may cut variable costs even more. Even the cost of labour goes down with increased production as manufacturers are likely to invest in labour-saving equipment that allows workers to produce bookcases faster. Figure 10.6 shows this to be the case. By purchasing wood, nails and paint at a lower price (because of volume discount) and by providing a means for workers to build bookcases more quickly, the cost per unit of producing 500 bookcases is reduced to €40 each.

Of course, variable costs don't always go down with higher levels of production. Using the bookcase example, at some point the demand for the labour, timber or nails required to produce

Variable Costs for Producing 100 Bookcases		Variable Costs for Producing 200 Bookcases		Variable Costs for Producing 500 Bookcases	
Wood	€13.25	Wood	€13.25	Wood	€9.40
Nails	0.25	Nails	0.25	Nails	0.20
Paint	0.50	Paint	0.50	Paint	0.40
Labour (3 hours × €12.00 per hr)	€36.00	Labour (3 hours × €12.00 per hr)	€36.00	Labour (2½ hours × €12.00 per hr)	€30.00
Cost per unit	€50.00	Cost per unit	€50.00	Cost per unit	€40.00
Multiply by number of units	100	Multiply by number of units	200	Multiply by number of units	500
Cost for 100 units:	€5,000	Cost for 200 units:	€10,000	Cost for 500 units:	€20,000

One bookcase = one unit.

Figure 10.6   Variable Costs at Different Levels of Production

the bookcases may exceed the supply. The bookcase manufacturer may have to pay employees overtime to keep up with production. The manufacturer may have to buy additional wood from a distant supplier that will charge more to cover the costs of shipping. The cost per bookcase rises.

Fixed Costs

Fixed costs are costs that do *not* vary with the number of units produced – the costs that remain the same whether the firm produces 1000 bookcases this month or only 10. Fixed costs include rent or the cost of owning and maintaining the factory, utilities to heat or cool the factory, and the cost of equipment such as hammers, saws and paint sprayers used in the production of the product. While the cost of factory workers to build the bookcases is part of a firm's variable costs, the salaries of a firm's executives and marketing managers are fixed costs. All these costs are constant no matter how many items are manufactured.

Average fixed cost is the fixed cost per unit; the total fixed costs divided by the number of units (bookcases) produced. Although total fixed costs remain the same no matter how many units are produced, the average fixed cost will decrease as the number of units produced increases. Say, for example, that a firm's total fixed costs of production are €300,000. If the firm produces one unit, the total of €300,000 is applied to the one unit. If it produces two units, €150,000, or one-half of the fixed costs, is applied to each unit and so on. As we produce more and more units, average fixed costs go down, and so does the price we must charge to cover fixed costs. Of course, like variable costs, in the long term total fixed costs may change. The firm may find that it can sell more of a product than it has manufacturing capacity to produce, so it builds a new factory, its executives' salaries go up, and more money goes into manufacturing equipment.

Combining variable costs and fixed costs yields **total costs** for a given level of production. As a company produces more and more of a product, both average fixed costs and average variable costs may decrease. Average total costs may decrease, too, up to a point. As explained, as output continues to increase, average variable costs may start to increase. These variable costs ultimately rise faster than average fixed costs decline, resulting in an increase to average total costs. As total costs fluctuate with differing levels of production, the price that producers have to charge to cover those costs changes accordingly. Therefore, marketers need to calculate the minimum price necessary to cover all costs – the *break-even price*.

Break-Even Analysis

Break-even analysis is a technique marketers use to examine the relationship between cost and price, and to determine what sales volume must be reached at a given price before the company will completely cover its total costs, so will begin making a profit. Simply put, the **break-even point** is the point at which the company doesn't lose any money and doesn't make any profit. All costs are covered, but there isn't a penny extra. A break-even analysis allows marketers to identify how many units of a product they will have to sell at a given price to exceed the break-even point and be profitable.

Using break-even analysis, marketers can determine what sales volume to reach before the company makes a profit.

Figure 10.7 uses our bookcase manufacturing example to demonstrate break-even analysis. The vertical axis represents the amount of costs and revenue in euros, and the horizontal axis shows the quantity of goods produced and sold. In this break-even model, we assume that there is a given total fixed cost and that variable costs do not change with the quantity produced.

In this example, let's say that the total fixed costs (the costs for the factory, the equipment, and electricity) are €200,000 and that the average variable costs (for materials and labour) are

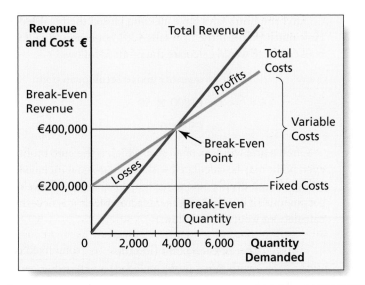

Figure 10.7	**Break-Even Analysis**
	Using break-even analysis, marketers can determine what sales volume to reach before the company makes a profit. This company needs to sell 4,000 bookcases at €100 each to break even.

constant. The figure shows the total costs (variable costs plus fixed costs) and total revenues if varying quantities are produced and sold. The point at which the total revenue and total costs lines intersect is the break-even point. If sales are above the break-even point, the company makes a profit. Below that point, the firm will suffer a loss.

To determine the break-even point, the firm first needs to calculate the **contribution per unit**, or the difference between the price the firm charges for a product (the revenue per unit) and the variable costs. This figure is the amount the firm has after paying for the wood, nails, paint and labour to contribute to meeting the fixed costs of production. For our example, we will assume that the firm sells its bookcases for €100 each. Using the variable costs of €50 per unit that we had before, contribution per unit is €100 − €50 = €50 . Using the fixed cost for the bookcase manufacturing of €200,000, we can now calculate the firm's break-even point in units of the product:

$$\text{Break-even point (in units)} = \frac{\text{total fixed costs}}{\text{contribution per unit to fixed costs}}$$

$$\text{Break-even point (in units)} = \frac{€200{,}000}{€50} = 4000 \text{ units}$$

We see that the firm must sell 4000 bookcases at €100 each to meet its fixed costs and to break even. We can also calculate the break-even point in euros. This shows us that to break even the company must sell €400,000 worth of bookcases:

$$\text{Break-even point (in euros)} = \frac{\text{total fixed costs}}{1 - \dfrac{\text{variable cost per unit}}{\text{price}}}$$

$$\text{Break-even point (in euros)} = \frac{€200{,}000}{1 - \dfrac{€50}{€100}} = \frac{€200{,}000}{1 - 0.5} = \frac{€200{,}000}{0.5} = €400{,}000$$

After the firm's sales have met and passed the break-even point, it begins to make a profit. How much profit? If the firm sells 4001 bookcases, it will make a profit of €50. If it sells 5000 bookcases, we would calculate the profit as follows:

$$\text{Profit} = \text{quantity above break-even point} \times \text{contribution margin}$$

$$= €1000 \times 50$$

$$= €50,000$$

Often a firm will set a *profit goal*, which is the euro profit figure it desires to earn. The break-even point may be calculated with that euro goal included in the figures. In this case, it is not really a 'break-even' point we are calculating because we're seeking profits. It's more of a 'target amount'. If our bookcase manufacturer feels it is necessary to realise a profit of €50,000, the calculations would be as follows:

$$\text{Break-even point (in units with target profit included)} = \frac{\text{total fixed costs} + \text{target profit}}{\text{contribution per unit to fixed costs}}$$

$$\text{Break-even point (in units)} = \frac{€200,000 + 50,000}{€50} = 5000 \text{ units}$$

Sometimes the target return or profit goal is expressed as a *percentage of sales*. For example, a firm may say that it wants to make a profit of at least 10 per cent on sales. In such cases, this profit is added to the variable cost in calculating the break-even point. In our example, the company would want to earn 10 per cent of the selling price of the bookcase, or 10 per cent × €100 = €10 per unit. We would simply add this €10 to the variable costs of €50 and calculate the new target amount as we calculated the break-even point before.

$$\text{Contribution per unit} = \text{selling price} - (\text{variable costs} + \text{target profit})$$

$$= €100 - (€50 + €10) = €40$$

$$\text{Break-even point (in units)} = \frac{\text{total fixed costs}}{\text{contribution per unit to fixed costs}}$$

$$\text{Break-even point (in units)} = \frac{€200,000}{€40} = 5000 \text{ units}$$

Break-even analysis does not provide an easy answer for pricing decisions. It provides answers about how many units the firm must sell to break even and to make a profit, but without knowing whether demand will equal that quantity at that price, companies can make big mistakes. It is therefore useful for marketers to estimate the demand for their product and then perform a marginal analysis.

Marginal Analysis

Marginal analysis provides a way for marketers to look at cost and demand at the same time and to identify the output and the price that will generate the maximum profit. Figure 10.8 shows the various cost and revenue elements considered in marginal analysis. Like Figure 10.7, the vertical axis in Figure 10.8 represents the cost and revenues in euros, and the horizontal axis shows the quantity produced and sold. Figure 10.8 shows the average revenue, average cost, marginal revenue and marginal cost curves. When doing a marginal analysis, marketers examine the relationship of **marginal cost** – the increase in total costs from producing one

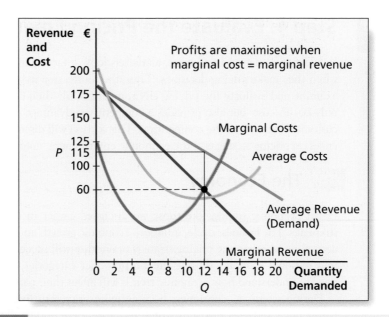

Revenue € and Cost

Profits are maximised when marginal cost = marginal revenue

200
175
150
125
P 115
100
60

Marginal Costs

Average Costs

Average Revenue (Demand)

Marginal Revenue

0 2 4 6 8 10 12 14 16 18 20   **Quantity Demanded**
Q

Figure 10.8	**Marginal Analysis**
	Marginal analysis allows marketers to consider both costs and demand in calculating a price that maximises profits.

additional unit of a product – to **marginal revenue** – the increase in total income or revenue that results from selling one additional unit of a product. Average revenue is also the demand curve and thus represents that amount customers will buy at different prices – people buy more only if price and thus revenue decrease. Thus, both average revenue and marginal revenue decrease with each additional unit sold.

Marginal analysis allows marketers to consider both costs and demand in calculating a price that maximises profits.

If the manufacturer produces only one bookcase, the average total cost per unit is the same as the marginal cost per unit. After the first unit, the cost of *producing each additional unit* (marginal cost) and the average cost at first decrease. Eventually, however, both marginal costs and average costs begin to increase since, as we discussed earlier, both average fixed costs and average variable costs may increase in the long term.

Profit is maximised at the point at which marginal cost is *exactly* equal to marginal revenue. At that point, the cost of producing one unit is exactly equal to the revenue to be realised from selling that one unit. If, however, one additional unit is produced, the cost of producing that unit is *greater than* the revenue from the sale of the unit, and total profit actually begins to decrease. So it makes sense for firms to keep production and sales at the point of maximum profit.

One word of caution when using marginal analysis: although in theory the procedure is straightforward, in the real world things seldom are. Production costs may vary unexpectedly because of shortages, inclement weather, unexpected equipment repairs, and so on. Revenues may also unexpectedly move up and down because of the economy, what the competition is doing or a number of other reasons. Predicting demand, an important factor in marginal analysis, is never an exact science. This makes marginal analysis a less than perfect way to determine the best price for a product. Indeed, it is theoretically sounder than break-even analysis, but most firms find the break-even approach more useful.

Step 4: Evaluate the Pricing Environment

In addition to demand and costs, marketers look at factors in the firm's external environment when they make pricing decisions. Thus, the fourth step in developing pricing strategies is to examine and evaluate the pricing environment. Only then can marketers set a price that not only covers costs but also provides a competitive advantage – a price that meets the needs of customers better than the competition. This section will discuss some important external influences on pricing strategies – the economic environment, competition and consumer trends.

The Economy

Broad economic trends, like those we discussed earlier in the book, tend to direct pricing strategies. The business cycle, inflation, economic growth and consumer confidence all help to determine whether one pricing strategy or another will succeed. The upswings and downturns in a national economy do not affect all product categories or all regions equally. Marketers need to understand how economic trends will affect their particular business.

During *recessions*, consumers become more price-sensitive. They switch brands to get a better price and seek discount stores and warehouse outlets. Even wealthy households, relatively unaffected by the recession, tend to cut back on conspicuous consumption. As a result, during periods of recession, many firms find it necessary to cut prices to levels at which costs are covered but the company doesn't make a profit to keep factories in operation.

massive delivery
of top brand surf and
swimwear is in stores now
always up to 60% less

BIG LABELS SMALL PRICES

TK·maxx

Photo 10.2 When the economy is weak, consumers are more interested in paying lower prices – and they're more sceptical about high-priced status symbols.
Source: The Advertising Archives

There are also some economic trends that allow firms to increase prices, altering what consumers see as an acceptable or unacceptable price range for a product. Inflation may give marketers cause to either increase or decrease prices. First, inflation gets customers used to price increases. Customers may remain insensitive to price increases even when inflation goes away, allowing marketers to make real price increases, not just those that adjust for the inflation. Of course, during periods of inflation consumers may grow fearful of the future and worry about whether they will have enough money to meet basic needs. In such a case, they may cut back on purchases. Then, as in periods of recession, inflation may cause marketers to lower prices and temporarily sacrifice profits to maintain sales levels.

The Competition

Marketers try to anticipate how the competition will respond to their pricing actions. They know that consumers' expectations of what constitutes a fair price largely depend on what the competition is charging. However, it's not always a good idea to fight the competition with lower and lower prices. Pricing wars such as those in the fast-food industry can change consumers' perceptions of what is a 'fair' price, leaving them unwilling to buy at previous price levels.

Most industries, such as airlines, restaurants and hotels, consist of a number of firms. These firms can belong to one of three industry structures – an oligopoly, monopolistic competition or pure competition. Which industry structure a firm belongs to will influence price decisions. Generally, firms like the airline KLM that do business in an oligopoly, in which the market has few sellers and many buyers, are more likely to adopt status quo pricing objectives in which the pricing of all competitors is similar. Such objectives are attractive to oligopolistic firms because avoiding price competition allows all players in the industry to remain profitable. In a business like the restaurant industry that is characterised by monopolistic competition in which there are a lot of sellers each offering a slightly different product, it is possible for firms to differentiate products and to focus on non-price competition. Each firm can therefore price its product on the basis of its cost without much concern for matching the exact price of competitors' products. Consumers don't necessarily have the time to shop and study the price of a burger at McDonald's versus Burger King before deciding which outlet to use.

Providers of commodity goods like wheat farmers in a purely competitive market have little opportunity to raise or lower prices. Rather, the price of wheat, corn or fresh peaches is directly influenced by supply and demand. When bad weather decreases the supply of crops, prices go up and the price for almost any kind of fish has increased dramatically since health-conscious consumers began turning away from beef and other red meat.

Consumer Trends

Another environmental influence on price is consumer trends. Culture and demographics determine how consumers think and behave and so have a great impact on all marketing decisions. Take for example, the purchasing habits of women who opted for a career in their 20s, but now are hearing the ticking of their biological clocks as they enter their late 30s and 40s. Couples having babies later in their lives are often better off financially than younger parents, and on average they will have fewer children to spoil, so they are more willing to spend whatever it costs to give their babies the best.

Another important trend is that even well-off people no longer consider it shameful to hunt for bargains – particularly in today's economic climate. As a marketing executive for a chain of shopping centres observed, 'Everybody loves to save money. It's a badge of honour today.' Luxury consumers are looking for prestigious brands at low prices, though they're still willing to splash out on some high-priced items. Industry analysts have called this new interest in hunting for sales 'strategic shopping'.[3]

Objective

5

Understand
pricing strategies

Step 5: Choose a Price Strategy

An old Russian proverb says, 'There are two kinds of fools in any market. One doesn't charge enough. The other charges too much.'[4] In modern business, there seldom is any one-and-only, now-and-forever, best pricing strategy. Like playing a chess game, making pricing moves and countermoves require thinking two and three moves ahead.

The next step in price planning is to choose a price strategy. Some strategies work for certain products, with certain customer groups, in certain competitive markets. When is it best for the firm to undercut the competition and when is best to just match the competition's prices? When is the best pricing strategy one that covers costs only and when is it best to use one based on demand?

Pricing Strategies Based on Cost

Marketing planners often choose cost-based strategies because they are simple to calculate and relatively risk free. They promise that the price will at least cover the costs the company incurs in producing and marketing the product.

Cost-based pricing methods have drawbacks, however. They do not consider such factors as the nature of the target market, demand, competition, the product life cycle and the product's image. Moreover, although the calculations for setting the price may be simple and straightforward, accurate cost estimating may prove difficult. Think about firms such as 3M, Nestlé and Heinz, all of which produce many products. How do financial analysts or accountants allocate the costs for the plant, research and development, equipment, design engineers, maintenance, and marketing personnel so that the pricing plan accurately reflects the cost of producing any one product? For example, how do you allocate the salary of a marketing executive who oversees many different products? Should the cost be divided equally among all products? Should costs be based on the actual number of hours spent working on each product? Or should costs be assigned based on the revenues generated by each product? There is no one right answer. Even within these limitations, cost-based pricing strategies may often be a marketer's best choice.

The most common cost-based approach to pricing a product is **cost-plus pricing**, in which the marketer totals all the costs for the product and then adds an amount (or marks up the cost of the item) to arrive at the selling price. Many marketers, especially retailers and wholesalers, use cost-plus pricing because of its simplicity (users need only estimate the unit cost and add the mark-up). To calculate cost-plus pricing, marketers usually calculate either a mark-up on cost or a mark-up on selling price. With both methods, you calculate the price by adding a predetermined percentage to the cost, but as the names of the methods imply, for one the calculation uses a percentage of the costs and for the other a percentage of the selling price. Which of the two methods is used seems often to be little more than a matter of 'the way our company has always done it'.

Pricing Strategies Based on Demand

Demand-based pricing means that the selling price is based on an estimate of volume or quantity that a firm can sell in different markets at different prices. To use any of the pricing strategies based on demand, firms must determine how much product they can sell in each market and at what price. As we noted earlier, marketers often use customer surveys where consumers indicate whether they would buy a certain product and how much of it they would buy at various prices. More accurate estimates may be obtained by some type of field experiment. For example, a firm might actually offer the product at different price levels in different test markets and gauge the reaction. Two specific demand-based pricing strategies are target costing and yield management pricing. Let's take a quick look at each approach:

Today, firms are finding that they can be more successful if they match price with demand using a process called **target costing**.[5] A firm first determines the price at which customers would be willing to buy the product and then works backward to design the product in such a way that it can produce and sell the product at a profit.

Step 1: Determine the price customers are willing to pay for the jeans
  €39.99

Step 2: Determine the markup required by the retailer
  40% (0.40)

Step 3: Calculate the maximum price the retailer will pay, the price customers are
  willing to pay minus the markup amount

  Formula: Price to the retailer = Selling price × (1.00 − markup percentage)
      Price to the retailer =   €39.99   × (1.00 − 0.40)
                =   €39.99   × 0.60 =   **€23.99**

Step 4: Determine the profit required by the firm
  15% (0.15)

Step 5: Calculate the target cost, the maximum cost of producing the jeans
  Formula: Target cost = Price to the retailer × (1.00 − profit percentage)
        Target cost = €23.99 × 0.85 =   **€20.39**

Figure 10.9	Target Costing Using a Jeans Example
	With target costing, a firm first determines the price at which customers would be willing to buy the product and then works backward to design the product in such a way that it can produce and sell the product at a profit.

With target costing, firms first use marketing research to identify the quality and functionality needed to satisfy attractive market segments and what price they are willing to pay *before the product is designed*. As Figure 10.9 shows, the next step is to determine what margins retailers and dealers require as well as the profit margin the company requires. On the basis of this information, managers can calculate the target cost, i.e. the maximum it will cost the firm to manufacture the product. If the firm can meet customer quality and functionality requirements and control costs to meet the required price, it will manufacture the product. If not, it abandons the product.

Yield management pricing is another type of demand-based pricing strategy that hospitality companies like airlines, hotels and cruise lines use. These businesses charge different prices to different customers in order to manage capacity while maximising revenues. Many service firms practice yield management pricing because they recognise that different customers have different sensitivities to price. Some customers don't mind paying a standard price for an airline ticket, while others will travel only if there is a discount available. The goal of yield management pricing is to accurately predict the proportion of customers who fall into each category and allocate the percentages of the airline's or hotel's capacity accordingly – so that no product goes unsold.

For example, an airline may charge two prices for the same seat: the full fare (€899) and the discount fare (€299). The airline must predict how many seats it can fill at full fare and how many can be sold only at the discounted fare. The airline begins months ahead of the date of the flight with a basic allocation of seats – perhaps it will place 25 per cent in the full-fare 'bucket' and 75 per cent in the discount-fare 'bucket'. While it can't sell the seats in the full-fare bucket at the discounted price, the airline may be able to sell the seats it allocated at the discounted price for the full fare if it's lucky.

As flight time gets closer, the airline might make a series of adjustments to the allocation of seats in the hope of selling every seat on the plane at the highest price possible. If the Real Madrid football team needs to book the flight, the chances are some of the discount seats will be sold at full fare (the journalists will be happy to pay) – decreasing the number available at the discounted price. If, as the flight date nears, the number of full-fare ticket sales falls below the forecast, some of those seats may be moved to the discount bucket. This process continues until the day of the flight as the airline attempts to have every seat filled when the plane takes off. This is why you may be able to get a fantastic price on a late charter flight from say London Gatwick to Alicante or Malaga.

Pricing Strategies Based on the Competition

Sometimes a firm's pricing strategy may be near to, at, above or below the competition. For many years, Esso for example operated a 'price watch' campaign on its petrol pump prices. It simply announced its prices and other players more or less fell into line. A **price leadership** strategy, which usually is the rule in an oligopolistic industry dominated by a few firms, may be in the best interest of all players because it minimises price competition. Price leadership strategies are popular because they provide an acceptable and legal way for firms to agree on prices without ever talking with each other.

Pricing Strategies Based on Customers' Needs

When firms develop pricing strategies that cater to customers, they are less concerned with short-term results than with keeping customers for the long term. New Era firms constantly assess customers' responses in developing pricing strategies. O_2 for example negotiates with its business customers in an attempt to determine the best package of air time and features available.

Firms that practise **value pricing**, or **everyday low pricing (EDLP)**, develop a pricing strategy that promises ultimate value to consumers. What this really means is that, in the customers' eyes, the price is justified by what they receive.[6] Northern European retailer Netto views everyday low pricing as being a fundamental part of the company's success. The company aims to buy branded goods at low prices, with the aim of passing on such savings to its customers.

When firms base price strategies solely or mainly on cost, they are operating under the old production orientation that we discussed in Chapter 1, rather than with a marketing orientation. Value-based pricing begins with customers, then considers the competition, and then determines the best pricing strategy. Changing pricing strategies at Procter & Gamble (P&G) in recent years illustrate value pricing in action. Until about a decade ago, P&G watched as sales volume dropped for its Charmin toilet tissue, Dawn dishwashing liquid, Pringles potato crisps, and many other well-established brands. More and more shoppers were buying whatever brand was on sale or had a special promotion offer. To rebuild loyalty, P&G switched to an EDLP strategy. The company reduced everyday prices 12 to 24 per cent by cutting the amount it spent on trade promotions. P&G said, in effect, 'This really *is* our best price, and it's good value for the money. Buy now. There will be no sale next week. We won't do business that way.'

New Product Pricing

As discussed earlier, new products are vital to the growth and profits of a firm, but they also present unique pricing challenges. When a product is new to the market or when there is no established industry price norm, marketers may use a skimming price strategy, a penetration pricing strategy or trial pricing when they first introduce the item to the market.

Setting a **skimming price** means that the firm charges a high, premium price for its new product with the intention of reducing it in the future in response to market pressures. For example, when Top-Flite introduced its Strata golf balls with a dimple design and more solid core for better flight with metal clubs, the price was three times that of regular balls. Pro shops still couldn't keep them in stock.[7]

If a product is highly desirable and it offers unique benefits, demand is price inelastic during the introductory stage of the product life cycle, allowing a company to recover R&D and promotional costs. When rival products enter the market, the price is lowered in order for the firm to remain competitive. Firms focusing on profit objectives in developing their pricing strategies often set skimming prices for new products.

A skimming price is more likely to succeed if the product provides some important benefits to the target market that make customers feel they must have it no matter what the cost. Handheld calculators were such a product when they were introduced in the late 1960s. To the total astonishment of consumers at that time, these magic little devices could add, subtract, multiply and divide with just the push of a button. It's equally hard for consumers today to believe that back then they sold for as much as €200 equivalent.

Second, for skimming pricing to be successful, there should be little chance that competitors can get into the market quickly. With highly complex, technical products, it may be quite a while before competitors can put a rival product into production. Finally, a skimming pricing strategy is most successful when the market consists of several customer segments with different levels of price sensitivity. There must be a substantial number of initial product customers who have very low price sensitivity. After a period of time, the price can go down, and a second segment of the market with a slightly higher level of price sensitivity will purchase and so on.

Penetration pricing is just the opposite of skimming. This strategy means that a new product is priced very low in order to sell more in a short period of time, thus gaining market share early on. One reason marketers use penetration pricing is to discourage competitors from entering the market. The firm first out with a new product has an important advantage. Experience shows that a pioneering brand often is able to maintain dominant market share for long periods of time. Penetration pricing may act as a *barrier to entry* for competitors if the prices the

Real People, Other Voices

Advice for Phil Byrne

Dr Fiona Cheetham,
University of Salford

I would choose option 2, supply high spec VMS products at high prices. Phil needs to consider the needs and wants of two groups of customers if BR Pharmaceuticals is to succeed in the VMS market in the UK: retailers and consumers. Targeting the high end segment with high priced products would allow the company to provide retailers with high margins; an attractive proposition to interest and encourage these retailers to 'push' a new brand into an already reasonably competitive marketplace. On the issue of branding, I feel that it would not be feasible to attempt to 'stretch' the 'Reveal' brand into both a new product category *and* a new price point and would therefore recommend that BR Pharmaceuticals develop a new brand to target the high end consumer. If Phil is to succeed in getting the big income earners to 'pull' his high spec, high priced brand into the market he must ensure that the brand offers a clear differential advantage relative to the competition.

Bill Barlow,
University of Abertay, Dundee

Philosophically, I prefer being associated with high price, high specification speciality brands but, in this case, I will go against my natural instinct (i.e. option 2) and select instead option 1, for several inter-related reasons.

It is not clear that the firm has either the expertise or the financial resources to launch a speciality brand into the already crowded premium-priced segment of the vitamins, minerals and supplements market. In addition, a high price brand would not fit well alongside the firm's existing value-for-money brand, 'Reveal'. On the other hand, one of the firm's strengths is its knowledge of and contacts with retail pharmacies and health food shops – a sector which would welcome something to counteract supermarkets' own-label products. Furthermore, this is a sector which already has confidence (as a result of 'Reveal') in the firm's ability to launch and sustain a successful value brand. If the retailers believe in the new brand and if it addresses their needs, it is more likely to succeed.

market will bear are so low that the company will not be able to recover development and manufacturing costs. Hoover (vacuum cleaners) is an example of a brand that was first to the market decades ago and still competes strongly today.

Trial pricing means that a new product carries a low price for a limited period of time to generate a high level of customer interest. Unlike penetration pricing, in which the low price is maintained, the trial price is increased after the introductory period. The idea is to win customer acceptance first and make profits later, as when a new health club offers an introductory membership to start pulling people in. Marketers aim to lure customers to try the product at the lower price and then if they're impressed will consume at normal prices as well as persuade others to buy at the full price.

Step 6: Develop Pricing Tactics

Objective

6

Explain pricing tactics for single and multiple products and for pricing on the internet

Once marketers have developed pricing strategies, the last step in price planning is to implement them. The methods companies use to set their strategies in motion are their *pricing tactics*.

Pricing for Individual Products

Once marketers have settled on a product's price, the way they present it to the market can make a big difference. Here are two tactics with examples of each:

- *Two-part pricing* requires two separate types of payments to purchase the product. For example, golf and tennis clubs may charge yearly or monthly fees plus fees for each round of golf or game of tennis. Likewise, mobile phone service providers offer customers a set number of minutes for a monthly fee plus a per-minute rate for extra usage.

- *Payment pricing* makes the consumer think the price is 'do-able'[8] by breaking up the total price into smaller amounts payable over time. For example, many customers now opt to lease rather than buy a car. The monthly lease amount is an example of payment pricing, which tends to make people less sensitive to the total price of the car.[9]

Pricing for Multiple Products

A firm may sell several products that consumers typically buy at one time. A fast-food restaurant selling food for lunch usually invites the purchase of a soft drink and maybe a dessert as well. The sale of a paper-cup dispenser usually means a package of cups is not far behind. The two most common tactics for pricing multiple products are price bundling and captive pricing.

Price bundling means selling two or more goods or services as a single package for one price. A music follower can buy tickets to an entire concert series for a single price. A PC typically comes bundled with a monitor, a keyboard and software. Even an all-you-can-eat special at the local Chinese restaurant is an example of price bundling. Phone service companies such as TalkTalk Telecom offer customers unlimited national and European phone calls plus broadband for a flat monthly fee.

From a marketing standpoint, price bundling makes sense. If products are priced separately, then it is likely that customers will buy some but not all the items. They might choose to put off some purchases until later, or they might buy from a competitor. Whatever revenue a seller loses from the reduced prices it makes up in increased total purchases.

Captive pricing is a pricing tactic a firm uses when it has two products that work only when used together. The firm sells one item at a very low price and then makes its profit on the second high-margin item. This tactic is commonly used to sell shaving products where the razor is relatively cheap but the blades are not. Similarly, some film manufacturers practically give away the camera in order to keep selling you the film.

Distribution-Based Pricing

Distribution-based pricing is a pricing tactic that establishes how firms handle the cost of shipping products to customers near, far and wide. Characteristics of the product, the customers and the competition figure in the decision to charge all customers the same price or to vary according to shipping cost.

Often a price is given as FOB factory or FOB delivered. FOB stands for 'free on board', which means the supplier will pay to have the product loaded onto a truck or some other carrier. Also, and this is important – *title passes to the buyer* at the FOB location. FOB factory or **FOB origin pricing** means that the cost of transporting the product from the factory to the customer's location is the responsibility of the customer. **FOB delivered pricing** means that the seller pays both the cost of loading and the cost of transporting to the customer, which is included in the selling price.

Delivery terms for pricing of products sold in international markets are especially important. Some of the more common terms are the following – get ready for a bunch of initials:[10]

- *CIF* (cost, insurance, freight) is the term used for ocean shipments and means the seller quotes a price for the goods (including insurance), all transportation, and miscellaneous charges to the point of debarkation from the vessel.

- *CFR* (cost and freight) means the quoted price covers the goods and the cost of transportation to the named point of debarkation but the buyer must pay the cost of insurance. The CFR term is typically used only for ocean shipments.

- *CIP* (carriage and insurance paid to) and *CPT* (carriage paid to) include the same provisions as CIF and CFR but are used for shipment by modes other than water.

Another distribution pricing tactic, **base-point pricing**, means marketers choose one or more locations to serve as base points. Customers pay shipping charges from these base points to their delivery destinations whether the goods are actually shipped from these points or not. For example, a customer in Lille may order a product from a company in Geneva. The product is shipped to Lille from the Brussels warehouse. However, if the designated base point is Paris, the customer pays transport charges from Paris to Lille, charges that were never incurred by the seller.

When a firm uses **uniform delivered pricing**, it adds an average shipping cost to the price, no matter what the distance from the manufacturer's plant – within reason. For example, when you order a CD from a music supplier, you may pay the cost of the CD plus €2.99 shipping and handling, no matter what the actual cost of the shipping to your particular location. Internet sales, catalogue sales, home television shopping and other types of non-store retail sales usually use uniform delivered pricing.

Freight absorption pricing means the seller takes on part or all of the cost of shipping. This policy works well for high-ticket items when the cost of shipping is a negligible part of the sales price and the profit margin. Marketers are most likely to use freight absorption pricing in highly competitive markets or when such pricing allows them to enter new markets.

Discounting for Channel Members

So far we've talked about pricing tactics used to sell to end customers. Now we'll talk about tactics used for pricing to members of the channel of distribution.

Whether a firm sells to businesses or directly to consumers, most pricing structures are built around list prices. A **list price**, also referred to as a *recommended retail price (RRP)*, is the price that the manufacturer sets as the appropriate price for the end consumer to pay. In pricing for members of the channel, marketers recognise that retailers and wholesalers have costs to cover and profit targets to reach as well. Thus, they often begin with the list price and then use a number of discounting tactics to implement pricing to members of the channel of distribution – wholesalers, distributors and retailers. Such tactics include the following:

- **Trade or functional discounts:** Because the channel members perform selling, credit, storage and transportation services that the manufacturer would otherwise have to provide, manufacturers often offer **trade or functional discounts**, usually set percentage discounts off list price for each channel level.

- **Quantity discounts:** To encourage larger purchases from distribution channel partners or from large organisational customers, marketers may use **quantity discounts**, or reduced prices for purchases of larger quantities. *Cumulative quantity discounts* are based on a total quantity bought within a specified time period, often a year, and encourage a buyer to stick with a single seller instead of moving from one supplier to another. Cumulative quantity discounts may be in the form of *rebates*, in which case the firm sends the buyer a rebate cheque at the end of the discount period or a credit against future orders. *Non-cumulative quantity discounts* are based only on the quantity purchased with each individual order and encourage larger single orders but do little to tie the buyer and the seller together.

- **Cash discounts:** Many firms try to entice their customers to pay their bills quickly by offering cash discounts. For example, a firm selling to a retailer may state that the terms of the sale are '2 percent 10 days, net 30 days', meaning that if the retailer pays the producer for the goods within 10 days, the amount due is cut by 2 per cent. The total amount is due within 30 days, and after 30 days the payment is late.

- **Seasonal discounts:** *Seasonal discounts* are price reductions offered only during certain times of the year. For seasonal products such as garden furniture or lawn mowers, marketers use seasonal discounts to entice retailers and wholesalers to buy off-season and either store the product at their locations until the right time of the year or pass the discount along to consumers with off-season sales programmes. Alternatively, discounts may be offered when products are in-season to create a competitive advantage during periods of high demand.

Pricing and Electronic Commerce

As we have seen, pricing for 'bricks-and-mortar' firms is a complex decision process. But our e-commerce world creates even more options. Because sellers are connected to buyers around the globe as never before through the internet, company networks and wireless setups, marketers can offer deals tailored to a single person at a single moment.[11] On the other hand, they're also a lot more vulnerable to smart consumers who can easily check out competing prices at the flick of a mouse.

For firms that want to sell to other businesses (B2B firms), the web means that they can change prices rapidly to adapt to changing costs. For consumers who have lots of stuff in the attic they need to put in someone else's attic (C2C e-commerce), the internet means an opportunity for consumers to find ready buyers. Finally, for B2C firms, firms that sell to consumers, the internet offers other opportunities. In this section, we will discuss some of the more popular web online pricing strategies.

 ## Dynamic Pricing Strategies

One of the most important opportunities the internet offers is **dynamic pricing**, where the seller can easily adjust the price to meet changes in the marketplace. If a retailer wants to change prices, employees/workers must place new price tags on items, create and display new display signage and media advertising, and input new prices input into the retailer's computer system. For business-to-business marketers, employees/workers must print catalogues and price lists and distribute them to sales people and customers. These activities can be very costly to a firm, so they simply don't want to change their prices too often.

Because the cost of changing prices on the web is so low, firms are able to respond quickly, and if necessary frequently due to changes in costs, in supply, and/or in demand. For example, Lastminute.com periodically adjusts the price of flights and hotels on the basis of supply and demand so that a five-star hotel in London might cost more or less depending on which day you log on to buy it.

Auctions

Hundreds of **online auctions** allow shoppers to bid on everything from golf clubs to health-and-fitness equipment to children's toys. Auctions provide a second internet pricing strategy. Perhaps the most popular auctions are the C2C auctions such as those on eBay. The eBay auction is an *open auction*, meaning that all the buyers know the highest price bid at any point in time. In many auction websites, the seller can set a *reserve price*, a price below which the item will not be sold.

Pricing Advantages for Online Shoppers

The web also creates unique pricing challenges for marketers because consumers and business customers are gaining more control over the buying process. With the availability of search engines, they are no longer at the mercy of firms that dictate a price they must accept. The result is that customers have become more price sensitive. For example, online pharmacies have been stealing customers from traditional chemists by offering much lower prices.

Detailed information about what products actually cost manufacturers, available from sites such as Consumerreports.org, can give consumers more negotiating power when shopping for new cars and other high price items. Finally, e-commerce potentially can lower consumers' costs because of the time and hassle associated with a trip to the shops or supermarket.

Objective

8

Describe the psychological, legal and ethical aspects of pricing

Psychological Issues in Pricing

Much of what we've said about pricing depends on economists' notions of a customer who evaluates price in a logical, rational manner. For example, the concept of demand is expressed by a smooth demand curve, which assumes that if a firm lowers a product's price from €10 to €9.50 and then from €9.50 to €9 and so on, then customers will simply buy more and more. In the real world, though, it doesn't always work that way. Let's look at some psychological factors that keep those economists up at night.

Buyers' Pricing Expectation

Often consumers base their perceptions of price on what they perceive to be the customary or *fair price*. For example, in the mid 1970s for many years a chocolate bar or a pack of chewing gum in the UK was priced at 5p. Consumers would have perceived any other price as too high or low. So when costs went up and inflation kicked in, some confectionary suppliers tried to reduce the size of the bar instead of changing the price. Eventually, inflation prevailed, consumers' salaries rose, and so did the price.

When the price of a product is above or even sometimes when it's below what consumers expect, they are less willing to purchase the product. If the price is above their expectations, they may think of it as a rip-off. If it is below expectations, consumers may think quality is below par. By understanding the pricing expectations of their customers, marketers are able to develop better viable pricing strategies.

Internal Reference Prices

Sometimes consumers' perceptions of the customary price of a product depend on their **internal reference price**. That is, based on past experience, consumers have a set price or a price range in mind that they refer to in evaluating a product's cost. The reference price may be the last price paid, or it may be the average of all the prices they know of similar products. In the early 1990s no matter in which Parisian bakery you visited, the cost of a baguette would be 4 francs. In some hypermarkets it might have been 3.75FF, and in plush bakeries 4.25FF, but the average was 4FF. If consumers found a baguette priced much higher than this – say at 5FF – they would feel it was overpriced and not buy. If they found it significantly lower – say at 2.50FF or 3FF – they might shy away from the purchase, wondering 'what is wrong' with the baguette.

In some cases, marketers try to influence consumers' expectations of what a product should cost by employing reference pricing strategies. For example, manufacturers may show their price compared with competitors' prices in advertising. Similarly, a retailer will display a product next to a higher priced version of the same or a different brand. The consumer must choose between the two products with different prices.

Two results are likely. On the one hand, if the prices (and other characteristics) of the two products are fairly close, the consumer will probably feel the product quality is similar. This is called an *assimilation effect*. The customer might think, 'The price is about the same, they must be alike. I'll be smart and save a few euros' – so the customer chooses the item that is priced lower because the low price made it look attractive next to the higher priced alternative. This is why shop brands of deodorant, vitamins, pain relief tablets and shampoo sit beside national brands, often accompanied by a shelf display pointing out how much shoppers can save by purchasing the retailer's own label brand. On the other hand, if the prices of the two products are too far apart, a *contrast effect* may result in which the customer equates it with a big difference in quality. 'This lower-priced one is probably not as good as the higher-priced one. I'll buy the more expensive one.' Using this strategy, an appliance store may place an advertised €300 refrigerator next to a €699 model to convince a customer the bottom-of-the-line model just won't do.

Price/Quality Inferences

Imagine that you are in a shoe shop looking for a pair of running shoes. You notice one pair that is priced at €89.99. On another aisle you see a second pair looking almost identical to the first pair but priced at only €24.95. Which pair do you want? Which pair do you think is the better quality? Many of us will pay the higher price because we believe the bargain-basement shoes aren't worth the risk at any price.

Consumers make *price–quality inferences* about a product when they use price as a cue or an indicator of quality (an inference means we believe something to be true without any direct evidence). If consumers are unable to judge the quality of a product through examination or experience, they usually will assume that the higher priced product is the higher quality product.

 ## Psychological Pricing Strategies

Setting a price is part science, part art. Psychological aspects of price are important for marketers to understand in making pricing decisions.

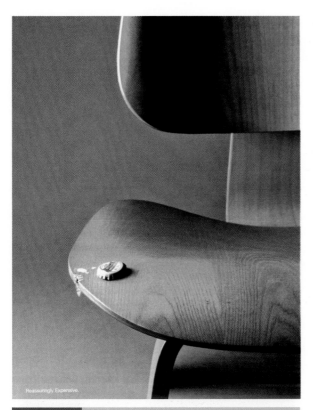

Reassuringly Expensive.

Photo 10.4	Consumers often associate higher prices with higher quality. This ad for Stella Artois uses the line 'reassuringly expensive'. Source: The Advertising Archives

Odd–Even Pricing

In Europe, we usually see prices in euros and cents – €1.99, €5.98, €23.67, or even €599.95. We see prices in even euro amounts – €2, €10, or €600 – far less often. The reason? Marketers assume that there is a psychological response to odd prices that differs from the responses to even prices. Habit might also play a role here. Research on the difference in perceptions of odd versus even prices supports the argument that prices ending in 99 rather than 00 lead to increased sales.[12]

At the same time, there are some instances in which even prices are the norm or perhaps necessary. Theatre and concert tickets, admission to sporting events, and lottery tickets tend to be priced in even amounts. Professional fees are normally expressed in even amounts too. If a dentist charged €39.99 for treatment, the patient might think the quality of medical care was less than satisfactory. Many luxury items such as jewellery, golf course green fees, and resort accommodation use even figure prices to set them apart.

Price Lining

Marketers often apply their understanding of the psychological aspects of pricing in a practice called **price lining**, where items in a product line sell at different prices, called *price points*. If you want to buy a new refrigerator, you will find that most manufacturers have one 'stripped-down' model for about €400. A better quality but still moderately priced model will be around €600. A better one will be about €800, and a large refrigerator with lots of special features will be around €1000. Recently, some appliance manufacturers have come out with new models, branded and marketed as special premium lines, with price tags of €3000 or more. Price lining provides the different ranges necessary to satisfy each segment of the market.

Why is price lining a good practice? From the marketer's standpoint, price lining is a way to maximise profits. In theory, a firm would charge each individual customer the highest price that they were willing to pay. If the maximum one particular person would be willing to pay for a refrigerator is €550, then that would be the price. If another person would be willing to pay €900, that would be his price. Charging each consumer a different price is really not possible. Having a limited number of prices that generally fall at the top of the range customers find acceptable is a more workable alternative.

Legal and Ethical Considerations in Pricing

The free enterprise system is founded on the idea that the marketplace will regulate itself. Prices will rise or fall according to demand. Firms and individuals will supply goods and services at fair prices if there is an adequate profit incentive.

Unfortunately, the business world includes the greedy and the unscrupulous. National and local governments have found it necessary to enact legislation to protect consumers and to protect businesses from predatory rivals. For example, under current laws in Europe, car companies

Across the Hall
Advice for Phil Byrne

Alan Griffiths
is Reader in Economics at the Ashcroft International Business School of Anglia Ruskin University and co-author of *Economics for Business and Management* (Financial Times/Prentice Hall)

I would advise BR Pharmaceuticals to choose option 1 because it appears to builds on the inherent skills and experience which the company has developed since 1996. The reasons for my choice are threefold. First, the early success of its 'Reveal' home pregnancy test has shown that the company can produce and distribute successful products which combine high quality with low price. The company's focus on high quality but with low costs through economies of scale and from efficient logistics systems has already given the company a successful brand image in this 'value for money' end of the market. In this way, the decision to enter the vitamin and mineral supplements (VMS) market means that the company should play to its inherent strengths (or comparative advantage) in the lower price market. Second, the choice of option 1 is also the best if one recognises the fact that demand for VMS products is worldwide. For example, in the developed countries the growth of the number of elderly population with their relatively high income means that the company has a market for good quality products which enhance lifestyle e.g. fish oils for better health, etc. In the less developed countries where poor diet is the problem, then the

VMS are an ideal way to compensate for poor nutrition. In this low income market, the fact that the company concentrates on volume and cost minimisation is an important way to extend the demand for its VMS products.

Thirdly, the barriers to entry into the VMS market are relatively low so that a company such as BR Pharmaceuticals should be able to exist quite well in such a market since the capital and 'set-up' costs are not as high as other parts of the pharmaceutical industry. However, the problem for the company is the competition from the supermarkets' 'own brand' products. However, with the accumulated experience of Phil Byrne and Patrick Roche in the pharmaceutical market they should be able to lead the supermarkets by being focused, flexible and fast changing. For example moving from single to multi-vitamins; producing a variety of vitamin strengths; producing different combinations of vitamins for different countries/markets; developing children's VMS products which combine basic ingredients with pleasant taste, etc. As a result, option 1 can be a viable and profitable option if costs can be kept low and quality above the norm.

I feel that the main problem with adopting option 2 is that high priced pharmaceutical products are often those where the research and development costs have been high and companies such as BR Pharmaceuticals may not have the resources needed to move into these markets. It is also not the area which the company has been known to be successful in the past. The difficulties with option 3 is that it is a more complex market with the requirement of possibly having to employ more company representatives and the cost/complexity of the time involved in dealing with different types of pharmaceutical outlets i.e. high transaction costs.

---

are allowed to charge wildly different prices for the same vehicle in different countries – prices can vary by as much as 30 per cent. New regulations are now being proposed to create a more level playing field among countries belonging to the European Union – despite fierce opposition by some car manufacturers that want to retain control over their pricing decisions.[13] In this section, we'll talk about deceptive prices, unfair prices, discriminatory prices, price fixing, and some regulations to combat them. Please peruse the Marketing Ethics box to see how British Gas has attempted to use a form of 'predatory' pricing tactics to try and retain business.

Deceptive Pricing Practices

Unscrupulous businesses may advertise or promote prices in a deceptive way. One deceptive pricing practice that has been prevalent in North America and has been adapted in Europe is the **bait-and-switch** tactic, where a retailer will advertise an item at a very low price – the *bait* – to lure customers into the shop. However, it is almost impossible to buy the advertised item. Salespeople like to say (privately) that the item is 'nailed to the floor'. The salespeople do everything possible to get the unsuspecting customers to buy a different, more expensive, item – the *switch*. They might tell the customer 'confidentially' that 'the advertised item is really poor quality, lacking important features and full of problems'. Enforcing laws against

Marketing Ethics

Pricing gas causes sparks

The energy regulator Ofgem has been urged by the UK's consumer watchdog Energywatch to investigate claims that British Gas has been undercutting rivals with predatory pricing when customers give notice to leave British Gas. There is an industry agreed code on customer switching. According to Energywatch Business Manager Paul Savage, British Gas's interpretation of it was 'unanimously opposed' by the rest of the industry. 'If this is consolidated into business practice, it will damage the vibrant competitive market Ofgem says it wants.'

Utility Week, 27(16), 5

Debate, Discuss, Disagree

1 This seems to be a great deal for consumers, so why shouldn't British Gas be allowed to offer great deals to consumers in order to keep them?

bait-and-switch tactics is complicated because such practices are similar to the legal practice of 'trading up'. Simply encouraging consumers to purchase a higher priced item is an acceptable sales technique, but it is illegal to advertise a lower priced item when it's not a legitimate, *bona fide* offer that is available on demand.

Loss Leaders

Not every advertised bargain is a bait-and-switch. Some retailers advertise items at very low prices or even below cost and are glad to sell them at that price because they know that once in the shop, customers may buy other items at regular prices. This is called **loss leader pricing** and is aimed at building traffic and sales volume.

Price Fixing

Price fixing occurs when two or more companies conspire to keep prices at a certain level. Oil companies have been accused of working a cartel in order to control supply and fix high prices. Such pricing can take two forms: horizontal and vertical.

Horizontal Price Fixing

In 2003, a number of top US fashion-modelling agencies were charged with conspiring to fix commissions they charge models. Because such practices mean higher prices for customers, in this case the models who were buying the services of the agencies.[14] *Horizontal price fixing* occurs when competitors making the same product jointly determine what price they each will charge. In industries in which there are few sellers, there may be no specific price-fixing agreement, but sellers will still charge the same price to 'meet the competition'. Such parallel pricing is not of itself considered price fixing. There must be an exchange of pricing information between sellers to indicate illegal price-fixing actions.

Vertical Price Fixing

Sometimes manufacturers or wholesalers attempt to force retailers to charge a certain price for their product. This is called *vertical price fixing*. If the retailer wants to carry the product, for example, it should charge the 'recommended' retail price.

Predatory Pricing

Predatory pricing means that a company sets a very low price for the purpose of driving competitors out of business. Later, when they take over the supply and have a monopoly, they will increase prices.

Now that you've learned about product pricing read 'Real People, Real Decisions' to see which strategy Phil Byrne of BR Pharmaceuticals selected.

Real People, Real Decisions

How it worked out at BR Pharmaceuticals

Phil decided to go for option 1, and BR began to establish an operational site that would soon focus on highly efficient production and distribution – in order to achieve cost advantages. As a result, the company rapidly went on to offer an attractive range of products to retailers and pharmacists that would compete on price with supermarket 'own label' produce. However, and importantly, Phil did not wish the company to compromise in any way on quality.

BR Pharmaceuticals was able to revolutionise the VMS market and pass on value to retailers and consumers alike

Through adopting a low-cost strategy, BR Pharmaceuticals was able to revolutionise the VMS market and pass on value to retailers and consumers alike. Vitamins were launched through retailers at consumer prices of £0.99. Herbals and supplements followed at £1.49. Larger container packs were also available for £2.49 and £3.99 respectively. The products soon began to penetrate the market, and the real price to consumers has reduced as the company still maintains the same prices and pricing structure.

Based on the above strategy, since a humble beginning in 1996, BR has now become a key player in the UK VMS market. Phil's pioneering approach to pricing has enabled the company to obtain a significant command of the market, and based on the early success, BR is now marketing a 'joint care' and 'life style' range of products that are all geared around the company's same core values of supplying quality products at very competitive prices.

| Photo 10.5 | Operations site for BR Pharmaceuticals. Source: Phil Byrne |

Chapter Summary

Now that you have finished reading this chapter, you should be able to answer any of the following potential examination questions:

1. **Explain the importance of pricing and how prices can take both monetary and non-monetary forms.** Pricing is important to firms because it creates profits and influences customers to purchase or not. Prices may be monetary or non-monetary, when consumers or businesses exchange one product for another.

2. **Explain some of the pricing objectives that marketers typically have when planning pricing strategies.** Effective pricing objectives are designed to support corporate and marketing objectives and are flexible. Pricing objectives often focus on sales (to maximise sales or to increase market share), on a desired level of profit growth or profit margin, on competing effectively to increase customer satisfaction or on communicating a certain image.

3. **Describe how marketers use costs, demands and revenue to make pricing decisions.** In developing prices, marketers must estimate demand and determine costs. Marketers often use break-even analysis and marginal analysis to help in deciding on the price for a product. Break-even analysis uses fixed and variable costs to identify how many units must be sold at a certain price in order to begin making a profit. Marginal analysis uses both costs and estimates of product demand to identify the price that will maximise profits. In marginal analysis, profits are maximised at the point at which the revenue from selling one additional unit of a product equals the costs of producing the additional unit.

4. **Explain some of the environmental factors that affect pricing strategies.** Like other elements of the marketing mix, pricing is influenced by a variety of external environmental factors. These include economic trends such as inflation, recession, the firm's competitive environment – including the industry in which it operates, i.e. oligopoly, monopoly or a more competitive environment. Pricing may also be influenced by changing consumer trends.

5. **Illustrate some of the key pricing strategies used by firms.** Though easy to calculate and safe, frequently used cost-based strategies do not consider demand, competition, stage in the product life cycle, plant capacity or product image. The most common cost-based strategy is cost-plus pricing.

   Pricing strategies based on demand such as target costing and yield management pricing can require marketers to estimate demand at different prices in order to be certain the firm can sell what they produce. Strategies based on the competition may represent industry wisdom but can be tricky to apply. A price leadership strategy is often used in an oligopoly. Firms that focus on customer needs may consider everyday low price or value pricing strategies. New products may be priced using a high skimming price to recover research, development and promotional costs, or a penetration price to encourage more customers and discourage competitors from entering the market. Trial pricing means setting a low price for a limited time.

6. **Explain pricing tactics for single and multiple products.** To implement pricing strategies with individual products, marketers may use two-part pricing or payment pricing tactics. For multiple products, marketers may use price bundling, whereby two or more products are sold and priced as a single package. Captive pricing is often chosen when two items must be used together; one item is sold at a low price and the other at a high, profitable price. Distribution-based pricing tactics, including FOB, base-point and uniform delivered pricing address differences in how far products must be shipped. Similar pricing tactics are used for products sold internationally. Pricing for members of the channel may include trade or functional discounts, cumulative or non-cumulative quantity discounts to encourage larger purchases, cash discounts to encourage fast payment and seasonal discounts to spread purchases throughout the year or to increase off-season or in-season sales.

7. **To what extent is the internet having an impact on pricing strategies.** E-commerce may offer firms an opportunity to initiate dynamic pricing – meaning prices can be changed frequently with little or no cost. Auctions offer opportunities for customers to bid on items in C2C, B2C, and B2B e-commerce. The web allows buyers to compare products and prices, gives consumers more control over the price they pay for items and has made customers more price sensitive.

8. **Describe the psychological, legal and ethical aspects of pricing.** Consumers may express emotional or psychological responses to prices.

Customers may use an idea of a customary or fair price as an internal reference price in evaluating products. Sometimes marketers use reference pricing strategies by displaying products with different prices next to each other. A price-quality inference means that consumers use price as a cue for quality. Customers respond to odd prices differently than to even prices. Marketers can manipulate pricing with price lining strategies, a practice of setting a limited number of different price ranges for a product line. Most marketers try to avoid unethical or illegal pricing practices. One deceptive pricing practice is the bait-and-switch tactic.

Key Terms

Average fixed cost 366
Bait-and-switch 382
Base-point pricing 377
Break-even analysis 366
Break-even point 366
Captive pricing 376
Contribution per unit 367
Cost-plus pricing 372
Cross-elasticity of demand 364
Demand-based pricing 372
Dynamic pricing 378
Elastic demand 362
Everyday low pricing (EDLP) 374
FOB delivered pricing 377
FOB origin pricing 377

Fixed costs 366
Freight absorption pricing 377
Inelastic demand 362
Internal reference price 380
List price 377
Loss leader pricing 383
Marginal analysis 368
Marginal cost 368
Marginal revenue 369
Online auctions 379
Penetration pricing 375
Prestige products 358
Price 356
Price bundling 376
Price elasticity of demand 362

Price fixing 383
Price leadership 374
Price lining 381
Quantity discounts 378
Skimming price 374
Target costing 372
Total costs 366
Trade or functional discounts 378
Trial pricing 376
Uniform delivered pricing 377
Value pricing 374
Variable costs 365
Yield management pricing 373

Chapter Review

 ## Marketing Concepts: Testing Your Knowledge

1. What is price, and why is it important to a firm? What are some examples of monetary and non-monetary prices?

2. Describe and give examples of some of the following types of pricing objectives: market share, competitive effect, customer satisfaction and image enhancement.

3. Explain how the demand curves for normal products and for prestige products differ. What are demand shifts and why are they important to marketers? How do firms go about estimating demand? How can marketers estimate the elasticity of demand?

4. Explain variable costs, fixed costs, average variable costs, average fixed costs and average total costs.

5. What is break-even analysis? What is marginal analysis? What are the comparative advantages of break-even analysis and marginal analysis for marketers?

6. How does recession affect consumers' perceptions of prices? How does inflation influence perceptions of prices?

7. Explain cost-plus pricing, target costing, and yield management pricing. Explain how a price leadership strategy works.

8. For new products, when is skimming more appropriate, and when is penetration pricing the best strategy? When would trial pricing be an effective pricing strategy?

9. Explain two-part payment pricing, price bundling, captive pricing and distribution-based pricing tactics. Give an example of when each would be a good pricing tactic for marketers to use.

10. Why do marketers use trade or functional discounts, quantity discounts cash discounts and seasonal discounts in pricing to members of the channel? What is dynamic pricing? Why does the internet encourage the use of dynamic pricing?

11. Explain these psychological aspects of pricing: price–quality inferences, odd–even pricing, internal reference price and price lining

12. Explain how unethical marketers might use bait-and-switch tactics, price fixing and predatory pricing.

 ## Marketing Concepts: Discussing Choices

1. Consumers often make price–quality inferences about products. What does this mean? What are some products for which you are likely to make price–quality inferences? Do such inferences make sense?

2. In pricing new products, marketers may choose a skimming or a penetration pricing strategy. While it's easy to see the benefits of these practices for the firm, what is the advantage or disadvantage of the practice for consumers? For the industry as a whole?

 ## Marketing Practice: Applying What You've Learned

1. Assume that you are the director of marketing for a firm that manufactures confectionary goods. You feel the time is right for your company to increase the price of its products, but you are concerned that increasing the price may not be profitable. You feel you should examine the elasticity of demand. How would you go about doing this? What findings would lead you to increase the price? What findings would cause you to rethink the decision to increase prices?

2. Assume that you and your friend have decided to go into business together manufacturing your personally designed women's handbags. You know that your fixed costs (rent on a building, equipment, and so on) will be €120,000 a year. You expect your variable costs to be €28 per handbag.

   a. If you plan on selling the handbags to shops for €35, how many must you sell to break even; that is, what is your break-even quantity?

   b. Assume that you and your partner feel that you must set a goal of achieving a €50,000 profit with your business this year. How many units would you have to sell to make that amount of profit?

   c. What if you feel that you will be able to sell no more than 10,000 handbags? What price will you have to charge to break even? To make €50,000 in profit?

3. You are a marketing consultant, and your new client is the owner of a small chain of ice cream shops. The client has sold his ice cream at the same price since opening the shops seven years ago. Over time the costs of operating the shops has increased, cutting profits. The client feels he needs to increase his prices but is concerned that increasing prices may not be a good decision. Design a plan to measure price elasticity and thus determine if increasing prices will be good or bad for your client's profit. In a role-playing situation, explain to the client what you recommend.

4. Assume that you have been hired as the assistant manager of a local greengrocer. As you look over the shop, you notice that there are two different displays of tomatoes. In one display the tomatoes are priced at €1.39 per kilo, and in the other the tomatoes are priced at €0.89 per kilo. The tomatoes look very much alike. You notice that many people are buying the €1.39 tomatoes. Write a report explaining what is happening and give your recommendations for the shop's pricing strategy.

5. As the director of marketing for a firm that markets computer software, you must regularly develop pricing strategies for new software products. Your latest product is a software package that automatically translates any foreign language e-mail messages to the user's preferred

language. You are trying to decide on the pricing for this new product. Should you use a skimming price, a penetration price, or something in between? With a classmate taking the role of another marketing professional with your firm, argue in front of your class the pros and cons for each option.

 ## Marketing Miniproject: Learning by Doing

The purpose of this miniproject is to help you become familiar with how consumers respond to different prices by conducting a series of pricing experiments.

For this project, you should first select a product category that students such as yourself normally purchase. It should be a moderately expensive purchase such as trainers, a bookcase or a piece of luggage. You should next obtain two photographs of items in this product category or, if possible, two actual items. The two items should not appear to be substantially different in quality or in price.

Note: You will need to recruit separate research participants for each of the activities listed in the next section.

● **Experiment 1: Reference Pricing**

a. Place the two products together. Place a sign on one with a low price. Place a sign on the other with a high price (about 50 per cent higher will do). Ask your research participants to evaluate the quality of each of the items and to say which one they would probably purchase.

b. Reverse the signs and ask other research participants to evaluate the quality of each of the items and to tell which one they would probably purchase.

c. Place the two products together again. This time place a sign on one with a moderate price. Place a sign on the other that is only a little higher (less than 10 per cent higher). Again, ask research participants to evaluate the quality of each of the items and to tell which one they would probably purchase.

d. Reverse the signs and ask other research participants to evaluate the quality of each of the items and to say which one they would probably purchase.

● **Experiment 2: Odd–Even Pricing**   For this experiment, you will only need one of the items from experiment 1.

a. Place a sign on the item that ends in €.99 (for example, €59.99). Ask research participants to tell you if they think the price for the item is very low, slightly low, moderate, slightly high or very high. Also ask them to evaluate the quality of the item and to tell you how likely they would be to purchase the item.

b. This time place a sign on the item that ends in €.00 (for example, €60.00). Ask different research participants to tell you if they think the price for the item is very low, slightly low, moderate, slightly high or very high. Also ask them to evaluate the quality of the item and to tell you how likely they would be to purchase the item.

Develop a presentation for your class in which you discuss the results of your experiments and what they tell you about how consumers view prices.

Real People, Real Surfers

Exploring the Web

Barter exchange is undertaken by organisations that facilitate barter or counter trade between each other. In the US, many such exchanges are members of the National Association of Trade Exchanges (NATE).

First, visit the NATE web page at www.nate.org. Using links on that page to NATE member exchanges or an internet search engine, locate and explore several barter exchange web pages. Based on your internet experience, answer the following questions:

1. What is NATE?

2. What are the benefits to a business of joining a barter exchange?

3. What types of products are bartered?

4. How does trade actually work with a barter exchange?

5. How does the exchange make its money? Who pays the exchange and how much is charged?

6. Assuming that the goal of barter exchange websites is to attract new members, evaluate the different websites you have recently visited. Which website do you think was best? What features of the site would make you want to join if you were the owner of a small business? What features of the other sites made them less appealing than this one?

Now, take a look at the website at www.pearsoned.co.uk/solomon to see some videos from YouTube relating to aspects of this chapter.

Also on the website, try some analysis and calculations yourself by looking up the marketing metrics exercise called Pricing to learn how to model the effect of pricing decisions on volumes, revenues and profits; and how to incorporate price elasticity and cross-elasticity into financial models.

Marketing Plan Exercise

For many service organisations such as restaurants, hotels, airlines and resorts, pricing strategies are particularly important because of the perishability of services (i.e. services can't be stored). Pricing is a vital part of effective marketing strategies because it ensures that a maximum number of seats on the plane or rooms in the hotel are purchased – every day.

Think about a new seaside resort complex that offers holiday makers luxury villas, available for rent for a few days, a week, or longer. Consider possible pricing strategies such as cost-plus, yield management, everyday low pricing, skimming, penetration and trial pricing.

1. What pricing strategy do you recommend for the resort complex that would maximise their occupancy?
2. What recommendations for pricing tactics or for how to implement the strategy do you have?

Marketing in Action Case

Real decisions in Pricing in UK Supermarkets: Does Winning the Battle Mean Winning the War?

What factors influence your decision to shop at a particular supermarket? Prices? Proximity to the shop? Where the food is sourced from? The shop's values and ethical practices? Whatever factors influence your decision, price is a key attribute in most people's decision-making process.

Often supermarkets compete for market share in the UK grocery market through aggressively promoting low prices and special offers. For instance, the proliferation of price comparison websites such as www.CompareSupermarketPrices.co.uk and the likes of retailers such as Asda advertising on TV and challenging customers to compare its prices with those of other supermarkets are having a major impact on UK consumers. Asda's website[1] reinforces this claim by stating 'Winner of Britain's lowest priced supermarket award – 11 years running'. Many supermarkets do however claim low price 'high ground' in their battle for customers and market share, including Tesco ('Every little helps'), Aldi ('Spend a little. Live a lot'), Lidl ('Where quality is cheaper') and others. But how should others compete?

The Co-operative seems to target a smaller, but perhaps more profitable segment of consumers who wish to purchase ethically. The company seems to position itself as a supermarket that cares about you and your environment, rather than profits *per se*. For instance, its website[2] alludes to government health campaigns by promoting its commitment to health and offering half price offers on different colours of fruit and vegetables all year round. It also promotes the number of fair-trade products it sells relative to other supermarkets.

Similarly, supermarkets such as Sainsbury's and Waitrose try to position themselves away from the low price segment, focusing on other attributes that might be important to customers. For instance, Sainsbury's ('Try something new today') seems to promote less aggressively on price but emphasises other ways to help customers by promoting its 'feed your family for a fiver' (£5) campaign with celebrity chef Jamie Oliver. It also promotes the quality of the food it sells and associates with customers' ethnocentric tendencies through a campaign devoted to 'great British food' such as Welsh Lamb. Likewise, Waitrose's advertising campaign claims that, whilst other supermarkets claim to sell 'local' food, it is the only supermarket which

[1] www.asda.com/asda_shop/sys/web_sys01_b_initialise.jsp.

[2] www.co-operative.coop/food/.

defines 'local' as food produced within 30 miles of the shop. In an effort to take the moral high ground, rather than compete on price, it is promoting a commitment to low food miles and high ethical standards.

Of course supermarkets like the Co-operative, Sainsbury's and Waitrose also try to keep prices low but their business model is based around a different group of customers who find value in aspects of the product other than low price. By targeting customers who are less likely to buy on price, such companies are differentiating themselves and positioning away from price competition. As such, these markets, whilst smaller are likely to be more profitable.

Recent changes in the external environment may affect these dynamics and the way that supermarkets compete. Between 1974 and 2005 food prices fell in *real* terms[3]. Since 2005 food prices have climbed rapidly and by mid-2008 were as high as they had ever been as governments subsidised the production of ethanol and as consumers in emerging economies switched to eating meat products, which take more resources to produce. As the economy grapples with issues arising from the credit crunch and from inflation, the importance of price has increased to consumers. In June 2008 British supermarkets responded in what was touted as the beginning of a price war.

In June 2008 British supermarkets responded in what was touted as the beginning of a price war

Tesco and Asda threw down the gauntlet and initiated price cuts on thousands of products. For instance, Asda promised to sell staples such as bread and eggs for only 50p. Tesco promised to reduce the price of several thousand products by up to 50 per cent to win back customers from newly emerging discount chains such as Lidl and Aldi.

Price wars have often been blamed for damaging whole industries and fundamentally changing how consumers think about value to the detriment of firms in those industries. They tend to increase the 'share of the pie', rather than increase the 'size of the pie', and are often viewed as short term, damaging tactics, rather than a concerted, well defined strategy. So what is *in store* for supermarkets?

[3]The Economist, 8-14 December, page 11.

Things to Think About

1. How are these competitors positioned? Draw some perceptual maps to show the main competitors in the supermarket industry and how they are positioned against each other, using price and other attributes of importance to the customer.

2. What is the decision facing low price competitors such as Asda? What is the decision facing other competitors, which tend to compete less on price, such as Waitrose?

3. What factors are important in understanding the decision situation for these competitors?

4. What are the options for the different supermarkets?

5. How would you implement your recommendations?

Case written by Dr Ben Lowe, Kent Business School.

References

1. Leslie Vreeland, 'How to Be a Smart Shopper', *Black Enterprise* (August 1993), 88.

2. Melanie Trottman, 'First Class at Coach Prices', 17 February 2004, http://online.wsj.com/article_email?article?pring/O,,SB107698413620331110-H0je4Nhl.

3. Quoted in Mercedes M. Cardonna, 'Affluent Shoppers Like Their Luxe Goods Cheap', *Advertising Age*, 1 December, 2003, 6.

4. Steward Washburn, 'Pricing Basics: Establishing Strategy and Determining Costs in the Pricing Decision', *Business Marketing*, July 1985, reprinted in Valerie Kijewski, Bob Donath and David T. Wilson, eds., *The Best Readings from Business Marketing Magazine* (Boston: PWS-Kent Publishing, 1993), 257–69.

5. Robin Cooper and W. Bruce Chew, 'Control Tomorrow's Costs Through Today's Design', *Harvard Business Review* (January–February 1996), 88–97.

6. Nikki Swartz, 'Rate-Plan Wisdom', *Wireless Review*, 15 June 2001, http://industry click.com.

7. Jennifer Merritt, 'The Belle of the Golf Balls', *Business Week*, 29 July 1996, 6.

8. 'Numerical Nirvana', *Business Week*, 10 November 2003, 13.

9. Douglas Lavin, 'Goodbye to Haggling: Savvy Consumers Are Buying Their Cars Like Refrigerators', *Wall Street Journal*, 20 August, 1993, B1, B3.

10. 'Pricing, Quotations, and Terms', *Advertising and Marketing Review*, www.ad-mkt-review.com/public_html/govdocs/bge/bgec10.html.

11. Amy E. Cortese and Marcia Stepanek, 'Good-Bye to Fixed Pricing?', *Business Week*, 4 May 1998, 71–84.

12. Robert M. Schindler and Thomas M. Kibarian, 'Increased Consumer Sales Response through Use of 99-Ending Prices', *Journal of Retailing* 72 (1996), 187–99.

13. Edmund L. Andrews, 'Europe to Seek Uniformity in Car Pricing', 5 February 2002, www.nyt.com.

14. John R. Wilke, 'Top Modeling Agencies Face Federal Price-Fixing Inquiry', 4 August 2003, www.wsj.com.

Chapter 11
Integrated Marketing Communications

Meet Ian Bruce,
Director of the Centre for Charity Effectiveness, and Former chief of the RNIB, a UK non-profit organisation for blind and partially sighted people

Q & A with Ian Bruce

What do you do when not working?
Go to contemporary dance, plays and concerts with my wife Tina

Career high?
Leading a campaign that led to the Disability Living Allowance, which put over £40 million per year into the pockets of blind people

Motto to live by?
'Do as you would be done by'

My management style is
Build on people's strengths

My pet peeve
People who think quantitative targets are sufficient to produce the right outcomes rather than motivating and trusting colleagues

Don't do this when interviewing me . . .
Put words in my mouth

rofessor Ian Bruce CBE, is the founder Director of the Centre for Charity Effectiveness at London City University's Cass Business School (Cass CCE) and Vice President of the Royal National Institute of Blind People (RNIB). Cass CCE runs five part-time postgraduate degrees in charity/non-profit work; undertakes research, consultancy, professional development and mentoring, and is launching an online learning resource for non-profit workers. Previously he was Director General of RNIB, Assistant Chief Executive of the London Borough of Hammersmith and Fulham, Chief Executive of Volunteering England, Assistant Chief Executive of Age Concern England and a marketing manager with Unilever. He is the founder or co-founder of seven voluntary organisations. He was 29 when he achieved his first charity chief executive role. He has written extensively on charity marketing, strategic planning and other aspects of charity management and leadership. His book *Charity Marketing – Meeting Need through Customer Focus* is in its third edition. He was awarded a CBE in 2004, was the first charity chief executive to be made a Companion of the Chartered Institute of Management (1991), and is the first person to have been elected to the Outstanding Achievement Awards of both the National Charity Awards (2001) and the UK Charity Awards (2003)

Real People, Real Decisions
Decision time at RNIB

Can you imagine what is must be like not to be able to see what you are buying or the people you love? Over 2 million people with uncorrectable sight problems and their families in the UK are helped by the Royal National Institute of Blind People (RNIB), which is the UK's largest charity. Its mission is 'to challenge blindness by empowering people who are blind or partially sighted, removing the barriers they face, and helping to prevent blindness'. While it is not a business, it is a large and extraordinarily diverse enterprise employing 2500 staff on 40 sites across the UK and involving several hundred thousand volunteers. To keep it in touch with its purpose, the majority of the elected trustee board are, and are required to be, blind or partially sighted.

To assist blind and partially sighted people, it provides services such as schools, colleges, libraries, rehabilitation centres, residential homes, help lines, social security advice services, Braille and large print publishing. Campaigning to improve the situation of people with sight problems is a major priority and there can be as many as 30 campaigns going on at any one time. For example, the RNIB is a leading member of the European Blind Union and led the campaign in the 1900s to persuade the European institutions to design the euro notes with high contrasts and different sizes for different denominations – rather than have 'same size' notes for different denominations which would have made it impossible for blind people to differentiate the values.

A major problem facing the RNIB, like most charities, is how to raise more money for its cause. As a result, its main promotional strategies are linked to fundraising. Historically, the RNIB had been very good at what's known as 'regional fundraising', i.e., employing local people who know the area and the people to organise street collections, door to door collections, dance events, raffles, fetes, etc. Local fundraising presence is important to RNIB because of awareness raising of the brand and the cause with its beneficial impact on securing legacies, i.e., money people leave to RNIB in their wills. However, this local source of money was diminishing and the cost of doing these activities were rising. Ian, who was chief executive of the RNIB at the time, was looking for ways to reverse this downturn. He was, and is, convinced that marketing has so much to offer non-profit organisations and nowhere more so than in fundraising. He and his fundraising team considered three options.

Ian considers his options . . .

Option 1 Use telemarketing for raffles

This could be used to cold-call one person in a street and ask them to sell raffle tickets on behalf of the RNIB to their friends and neighbours. If they said yes, then books of tickets would be posted to them and they simply returned the money equivalent or the unsold books. The advantages were that it is relatively cheap and has a good return on expenditure with a minimum of 50 per cent of the money raised going to help blind people. It could be coordinated nationally from RNIB HQ and this allowed some economies of scale as opposed to having each area of the country try to establish its own telemarketing operation. Disadvantages were that many charities had tried telesales for fundraising without real success, the public did not like cold-calling telemarketing that asked people directly for money, and RNIB was concerned that its good image and the goodwill it had with the public might be eroded.

Option 2 Begin 'Chugging'

Chugging was a drive to get people to sign up to monthly direct debit donations using special subcontracted paid agents intercepting people on the street. The advantages of this option were that it gives regular income to RNIB, called 'planned giving', which aids planning within the organisation because they can be guaranteed a steady income rather than a fluctuating one which means that people's jobs were more secure and they could plan other campaigns well in advance knowing they would have the money. Once recruited, the donors are relatively low cost to maintain, e.g. requiring only occasional thank you letters. In addition, the street recruiters have high visual impact and this is a very interactive and personal form of promotion which helped to establish trust and rapport with the RNIB. Another advantage was that direct debits were also favoured by younger donors and so it would enable the RNIB to move into a new donor market. However, younger donors also tend to favour younger causes such as climate change, overseas aid and HIV, rather than more traditional causes like the RNIB. Also, it is quite costly to get donors this way and can take up to 18 months before the charity sees a profit from the person's donations because of the costs in acquiring a donor. Finally, there is a high rejection rate on the street and many people approached object to the invasion of privacy and RNIB was worried that its image might be damaged.

Option 3 Revamp and reinvigorate their box collecting

This method, also known as 'static media', would involve identifying better and more placements for collection boxes in places such as pubs which had the best returns. The advantages of this option were the clever recruiting of retired ex-pub suppliers to become part of the RNIB volunteer base meant that these volunteers were used to visiting pubs and selling things to them; also the RNIB had a lot of experience in this type of fundraising and this method was the most profitable for them, giving a 70 per cent return on marketing expenditure. However, competition was rising between charities for box placements, retailers were becoming more resistant to accepting boxes and the method was seen as tired and associated with old-fashioned charities by the public.

Put yourself in Ian's shoes. Which option would you choose and why?

Objectives

When you finish reading this chapter, you will be able to:

1 Understand the role of marketing communications

2 Understand the communications model

3 List and describe the traditional elements of the promotion mix

4 Explain how word-of-mouth marketing, buzz marketing, viral marketing and guerrilla marketing provide effective marketing communications

5 Describe integrated marketing communications and its characteristics

6 Explain the important role of database marketing in integrated marketing communications (IMC)

7 Explain the stages in developing an IMC plan

Tailoring Marketing Communications to Customers

Objective
1
Understand the role of marketing communications

See how many of the following questions you can answer:

1. 'Have a break, have a _____'

2. Name one or more products for which Lewis Hamilton is a spokesperson.

3. Which bank is the world's local bank?

4. At Burger King, you can have it '_____,' whereas at Hesburger from Finland the burgers are '_____' flame grilled.

5. Which brand makes you say 'Because I'm worth it'?

Did you get them all right? You owe your knowledge about these and 1000 other trivia questions to the efforts of people who specialise in marketing communications. As we said in Chapter 1, promotion is the coordination of marketing communications efforts to influence attitudes or behaviour. This function is one of the famous Seven Ps of the marketing mix and it plays a vital role – whether the goal is to sell hamburgers, insurance, ringtones or healthy diets. Of course, keep in mind that marketers use *all* the elements of the marketing mix to communicate with customers. The package in which the product comes, the price of the product, and the type of retail outlet where the product is available are all part of effective marketing communications because they make statements about the nature of the product and the image it intends to convey.

Marketing communications can take many forms: quirky television commercials, sophisticated magazine ads, web banner ads boasting the latest Java-language applications, funky T-shirts, and even do-it-yourself, customer-made advertising.

Some Companies publicise their brands by buying space on hot air balloons. This promotional programme might be done independently of an ad campaign.
Source: BP plc

Marketing communications have different purposes; some can be to push specific products, whereas others try to create or reinforce a corporate image:

- Marketing communications *inform* consumers about new goods and services and where they can purchase them.[1]

- Marketing communications *remind* consumers to continue using certain products.

- Marketing communications *persuade* consumers to choose one product over others.

- Marketing communications *build* relationships with customers.

In today's competitive marketplace, the role of the successful marketer in communicating the value proposition means adopting an IMC perspective as this is the best way to get reinforcing messages. In this chapter, we'll first review the communication process of marketing. Next, we'll discuss both the traditional elements of the promotion mix and some of those new tricks marketers are using to communicate with us. Finally, we'll describe the characteristics of IMC and the communications planning process.

The Communications Model

Objective

2

Understand the communications model

A good way to understand what marketing communications is all about is to examine the **communications model** in Figure 11.1. In this model, a message is transmitted through some medium from a sender to a receiver who (we hope!) is listening and understands the message. *Any* way that marketers reach out to consumers, from a roadside hoarding to a customised message sent via e-mail, is part of the basic communications process. The communications model specifies the elements necessary for communication to occur: a source, a message, a medium, and a receiver. Regardless of how messages are sent – whether by a Jaguar mascot on luxury cars, a distinctive yellow and blue logo from IKEA, or a televised fashion advert with supermodel Kate Moss promoting her clothing line for Topshop – they are designed to capture receivers' attention and relate to their needs. Now let's look at defining and explaining the terms in the communication model.

 ## Encoding By the Source (the Marketer)

Encoding is the process of translating an idea into a form of communication that will convey the desired meaning. This involves deciding on what words and visuals will be used. The **source** is the organisation or individual sending the message. It's one thing for marketers to form an idea about a product in their own minds, but it's not quite as simple to express the idea so that other people get the same picture. To encode a message in the language of the intended audience, the National Health Service in the UK developed

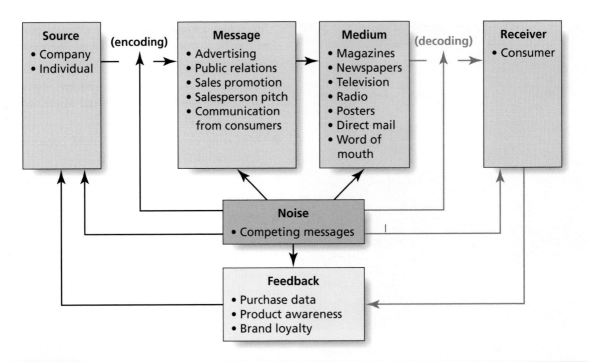

Figure 11.1	**The Communications Model**	
	The communications model explains how ideas are translated into messages and transmitted from the marketer (the source) to the consumer (the receiver) who (we hope) understands what the marketer intended to say.	

an anti-smoking campaign that featured patients talking about their smoking-related cancer. These testimonials can be a very convincing way of raising awareness and preventing people from smoking.[2] Danone presented ordinary people when it advertised its new healthy yoghurt drink 'Danone Bio Activia' on TV. The product users shown were all middle-aged women who talked about their positive experience after using Danone's drink. To make their messages more believable or more attractive to consumers, marketers sometimes choose a celebrity or expert to do the encoding (football player David Beckham for Motorola), hire an actor or a model (Keira Knightley for Chanel), or create a character (Tony the Tiger for Kellogg's Frosties) to represent the source. The toothpaste manufacturer Sensodyne uses similar techniques in promoting its products. Often, qualified dentists talk about Sensodyne toothpaste and try to convince the viewer of the good results the products brings with it.[3]

The Message

The **message** is the actual communication going from sender to receiver. It must include all the information necessary to persuade, inform, remind, or build a relationship. Messages may include both verbal and non-verbal elements, such as beautiful background scenery or unusual music. These elements must be carefully constructed so that they can connect with a wide variety of consumers or business customers. Think about a typical well crafted Guinness commercial. In contrast, the message a salesperson delivers can be carefully tailored for each individual customer, and the salesperson can respond to questions or objections.

GEORGE CLOONEY'S CHOICE.

AVAILABLE AT
OMEGA BOUTIQUES:

12 OLD BOND STREET
LONDON

ROYAL EXCHANGE
LONDON

TERMINAL 1
HEATHROW AIRPORT

AND AT FINE JEWELLERS AND
WATCH SPECIALISTS NATIONWIDE.

Ω
OMEGA

Photo 11.2 Marketers often hire celebrities as spokespersons for their products, thus adding excitement to the 'source' of the message.
Source: The Advertising Archives

The Medium

No matter how the message is encoded, it must then be transmitted via a **medium**, a communications vehicle used to reach members of a target audience. This vehicle can be television, radio, a magazine, a company website, a blog, a personal contact, a poster, or even a product logo printed on a coffee mug. Ideally, the attributes of the product should match those of the medium. For example, magazines such as *Vogue*, with high prestige are more effective at communicating messages about overall product image and quality for Chanel or D&G, whereas specialised magazines, such as *What Car?*, do a better job of conveying factual information.[4]

Decoding by the Receiver

Communication cannot occur unless a **receiver** is there to get the message. The receiver can be any individual or organisation that intercepts and interprets the message. Assuming that the customer is even paying attention (a big assumption in our overloaded, media-saturated society), he or she interprets the message in light of his or her unique experiences. **Decoding** is the process whereby a receiver assigns meaning to a message, that is, translates the message back into an idea. A good example of decoding is comedy. Sometimes you hear a joke and you don't understand it, but others around you are laughing. That's because they've decoded the message. Check out some funny international ads from YouTube on our website (www.pearsoned.co.uk/solomon) and type in 'Berlitz language ad' (www.youtube.com/watch?v=_1Vn9OwDjgQ) to see if you get the humour. It happens in the marketing communication process too. Marketers hope that the target consumer will decode the message the way they intended; that the idea in the mind of the receiver is identical to the idea the source sought to communicate.

Effective communication occurs only when the source and the receiver have a mutual frame of reference. They must share the same understanding about the world. For example, when in 2004 the Italian fashion producer Colours of Benetton published some advertisements with black children showing the word 'HIV' on their skin, not everyone who saw the commercial interpreted it quite the same way. Some saw it as a positive political statement showing the plight of millions of children who are born with HIV, others were furious that Benetton would use the suffering of young people to gain publicity for their brand. United Colours of Benetton's advertisements are famous for being provocative, showing for example a nun kissing a priest or a white infant being breast-fed by a black woman.[5] Indeed they do not want everyone to interpret it in the same way otherwise there would be no debate. The British HM Revenue and Customs advertisement from 2007 is another example of misunderstood commercials. It showed a self-employed plumber evading tax by hiding under the kitchen sink. The advertisement attracted complaints from a number of institutions who said that the ad implied self-employed people – plumbers in particular – were tax-evaders and was thus both misleading and offensive.[6]

High   **Low**

| Advertising | Sales promotion | Personal selling | Direct marketing | Public relations | Word of mouth |

| Figure 11.2 | **Control Continuum**
The messages that consumers receive about companies and products differ in the amount of control the marketer has over the message delivered to the consumer. |

 ## Noise

The communications model also acknowledges that **noise** – anything that interferes with effective communication – can block messages. As the many arrows between noise and the other elements of the communication model in Figure 11.2 indicate, noise can occur at any stage of communication. It can pop up at the encoding stage if the source uses words or symbols that the receiver will not understand. Or the receiver may be distracted from receiving the message by a nearby conversation. There may be a problem with transmission of the message through the medium – especially if it's drowned out by the chorus of other marketers clamouring for us to look at *their* messages instead. Gaining attention is one of the key challenges in today's crowded communication marketplace, which is why techniques like word-of-mouth (WOM) and guerrilla marketing techniques are being used which almost guarantee the consumers' attention. Marketers try to minimise noise by placing their messages where there is less likely to be distractions or competition for consumers' attention. Calvin Klein, for example, will often buy a block of advertising pages in a magazine so that the reader sees only pictures of its clothing.

 ## Feedback

To complete the communications loop, the source gets **feedback** from receivers (see section on copy testing and pre- and post-ad testing). Feedback is a reaction to the message that helps marketers gauge the effectiveness of the message so they can fine-tune it. Obtaining feedback reminds us of the importance of conducting marketing research (as we discussed in Chapter 3) to verify that a firm's strategies are working.

 # Marketing Communications Strategy and the Promotion Mix

Objective

3

List and describe the traditional elements of the promotion mix

Although **promotion** is one of the seven Ps, virtually *everything* an organisation says and does is a form of marketing communications. The ads it creates, the packages it designs, the uniforms its employees wear and even what other consumers say, contribute to the impression people have of the company and its products. We can argue that *every element of the marketing mix is actually a form of communication*. After all, the price of a product, where it is sold, and even the nature of the product itself contribute to the impression we form of it.

Within the marketing mix, we call the communication elements that the marketer controls the **promotion mix**. These elements include the following:

- Personal selling (e.g. Clinique make-up assistants);
- Advertising (Nicole Kidman and Daniel Craig wearing Omega watches);
- Sales promotions (a voucher in a student magazine for 2 for 1 meals at a local pub);
- Public relations (an Amnesty International press conference to highlight human rights issue in Burmah).

Just as a DJ combines songs or phrases to create an entertainment experience, the term mix implies that a company's promotion strategy is focused on more than one element, so the challenge is to integrate these different communication tools in an effective way.

Another challenge is to be sure that the promotion mix works in harmony with the overall marketing mix, which combines elements of promotion with place, price and product information to position the firm's offering in people's minds. For example, ads for luxury products such as Mont Blanc pens or Jaguar cars must be designed to communicate that same luxury character of the product and they should appear in places that reinforce that upmarket image such as *Monocle* magazine or in business class lounges in airports.

Marketers have a lot more control over some kinds of messages than they do others. As Figure 11.3 (page 412) shows, mass-media advertising and sales promotion are at one end of the continuum, where the marketer has total control over what message is delivered. At the other end is WOM communication, where everyday people rather than the company run the show. Marketers know what consumers hear from one another is a vitally important component of the brand attitudes consumers form – and of their decisions about what to buy. Between the ends we find personal selling, where marketers have a lot but not total control over the message delivered, and public relations, where marketers have even less control because journalists and editors value their independence and will write what they think, not what the company wants them to write. Table 11.1 presents some of the pros and cons of each element of the promotion mix, which we discuss next.

Promotional Element	Pros	Cons
Advertising	• The marketer has control over what the message will say, when it will appear, and who is likely to see it.	• Often expensive to produce and distribute. • May have low credibility and/or be ignored by audience.
Sales promotion	• Provides incentives to retailers to support one's products. • Builds excitement for retailers and consumers. • Encourages immediate purchase and trial of new products. • Price-oriented promotions cater to price-sensitive consumers.	• Short-term emphasis on immediate sales rather than a focus on building brand loyalty. • The number of competing promotions may make it hard to break through the promotional clutter.
Public relations	• Relatively low cost. • High credibility.	• Lack of control over the message that is eventually transmitted and no guarantee that the message will ever reach the target. • Hard to track the results of publicity efforts.
Personal selling	• Direct contact with the customer gives the salesperson the opportunity to be flexible and modify the sales message to coincide with the customer's needs. • The salesperson can get immediate feedback from the customer.	• High cost per contact with customer. • Difficult to ensure consistency of message when it is delivered by many different company representatives. • The credibility of salespeople often depends on the quality of their company's image, which has been created by other promotional strategies.
Direct marketing	• Can target specific groups of potential customers with different offers. • Marketers can easily measure the results. • Can provide extensive product information and multiple offers within a single appeal. • Provides a means for collecting information for company marketing databases.	• Consumers may have a negative opinion of some types of direct marketing. • Costs more per contact than mass appeals.

Table 11.1 A Comparison of Elements of the Promotion Mix

If electromagnetic waves can penetrate walls, imagine what they can do to your skin. Today, electromagnetic waves generated by a host of modern day electronic devices join a list of well-known pollutants which can damage skin. For the first time, Clarins Research reveals the link between exposure to artificial electromagnetic waves and accelerated skin ageing'. Clarins introduces Expertise 3P™ (Poly Pollution Protection).

WORLDWIDE FIRST. Clarins Expertise 3P™

Exceptional plant extracts with super-adapting powers against all types of pollution: Thermus Thermophilus from the ocean and Rhodiola Rosea from Siberia. Together with free radical fighters, White Tea and Succory Dock-Cress, they form an advanced anti-pollution complex to help maintain skin's health and beauty. Innovative skin protection for today's world.

*Clarins discovery. The subject of a scientific research paper.

Photo 11.3	For many products, factual information is essential. Magazine advertising provides an opportunity to deliver the desired information. Source: The Advertising Archives

Personal Appeals

The most immediate way for a marketer to make contact with customers is simply to tell them how wonderful the product is. This is part of the *personal selling* element of the promotion mix we mentioned previously. It is the direct interaction between a company representative and a customer that can occur in person, by phone, or even over an interactive computer link. We'll learn more about this important process in Chapter 12. Salespeople are a valuable source of communications, because customers can ask questions and the salesperson can immediately address objections and describe product benefits.

Personal selling can be tremendously effective, especially for expensive and complicated consumer items such as computers or cars and for industrial products where the 'human touch' is essential. It can be so effective that some marketers, if given a choice, might neglect other forms of promotion. Unfortunately, for many products, especially consumer goods – a bottle of shampoo or a pair of running shoes – it's often too expensive to connect personally with each and every customer, so marketers need to use other forms of promotion as well.

Mass Appeals

The other pieces of the promotion mix are those messages intended to reach many prospective customers at the same time which are impersonal and lack the 'human touch'. Whether a company posts an announcement to a few hundred local residents about a new restaurant opening or broadcasts a television commercial to millions, it is promoting itself to a mass audience. The following are the elements of the promotion mix that provide mass appeal opportunities:

- **Advertising:** Advertising is for many the most familiar and visible element of the promotion mix. It is non-personal communication from an identified sponsor using the mass media. Because it can convey rich and dynamic images, advertising can establish and reinforce a distinctive brand identity. Think about the ads for mobile phone companies which convey much more than just the talk plan. Advertising also is useful in communicating factual information about the product or reminding consumers to buy their favourite brand. Think about the ads that remind you of why you shop at Tesco. However, advertising sometimes suffers from a credibility problem because cynical consumers ignore messages they think are biased or are intended to sell them something they don't need. Advertising can also be very expensive, so firms must ensure their messages are effective. Reaching the university student market in the UK, Denmark, Holland, Sweden and Norway with their large discretionary spending power is a unique challenge for marketers since students are less likely to be influenced by advertising in traditional media. Instead, the university newspapers have proven effective for many companies.[7] For example, marketers like Google, Amazon and major film studios spend millions on university newspaper advertising.[8] In some countries an estimated 95 per cent of university students read the campus paper and newspaper ads can cost more than €1500 each.

- **Sales promotion:** Sales promotions are programmes such as contests, coupons or other incentives that marketers design to build interest in or encourage purchase of a product during a specified time period. Unlike other forms of promotion, sales promotions are intended to stimulate immediate action (often in the form of a purchase) rather than building long-term loyalty. More on this in Chapter 12.

- **Public relations:** Public relations relates to communications activities that seek to create and maintain a positive image of an organisation and its products among various audiences, including customers, government officials and shareholders. As we'll see in Chapter 12, public relations activities include writing press releases about product and company-related issues, dealing with the news media and organising special events. Public relations also includes efforts to present bad company news in the best way, thus minimising harmful consequences. In contrast to sales promotions, public relations components of the promotion mix usually do not seek a short-term increase in sales. Instead, they try to influence feelings, opinions, or beliefs for the long term. For example, car manufacturers might take motor journalists to Monaco to wine and dine them and let them test drive a new model.

Buzz Appeals

In addition to these tried-and-tested methods, many marketers are starting to figure out that they must find alternatives to traditional advertising – partly because there is so much

| Photo 11.4 | Marketers have a wide range of communications tools from which to choose, ranging from glitzy TV commercials to neon signs. |

advertising it's hard to get noticed and partly because some consumers, especially young consumers, are very cynical about the efforts of big corporations to buy their allegiance. For these and other 'hard-to-get' consumers, marketers must find new 'out-of-the-box' tactics. These new tactics come under a variety of names including word-of-mouth marketing, viral marketing and buzz and guerrilla marketing.

Buzz, Word-of-Mouth and Viral Marketing

Everywhere you turn in marketing today, it seems someone is talking about '**buzz**'. In fact, we hear so much about buzz and its counterparts viral marketing and word-of-mouth marketing that it's hard to know exactly what all the terms mean. The Word of Mouth Marketing Association (WOMMA), founded in 2004, has written the following definitions:[9]

Word-of-mouth: The act of consumers providing information to other consumers.

Word-of-mouth marketing: Giving people a reason to talk about your products and services, and making it easier for that conversation to take place.

Buzz marketing: Using high-profile entertainment or news to get people to talk about your brand.

Viral marketing: Creating entertaining or informative messages that are designed to be passed along in an exponential fashion, often electronically or by email.

In more general terms, marketers think of 'buzz' as people helping their marketing efforts by talking about a product or a company to their friends and neighbours.[10] As the examples in Table 11.2 illustrate, companies spend millions to create consumer buzz. Companies such as Dell even have word-of-mouth teleconferences where their named WOM marketing managers will share tactics and techniques covering this topic.[11] According to JWT Worldwide, the fourth-largest advertising agency in the world, over 85 percent of top 1000 marketing firms now use some form of word-of-mouth tactics.[12]

Of course buzz isn't *really* new. Many refer to the Mona Lisa as one of the first examples of buzz marketing. In 1911 the famous painting was stolen from the Louvre and became the topic of consumer talk around the globe, giving the previously little recognised painting fame that exists until today. When you think of the effect of consumers talking one-on-one nearly a century ago, imagine the exponential increase in influence of the individual consumer 'connectors' or 'e-fluentials' who use blogs and other computer-generated media to increase their reach.[13] Compared with traditional advertising and public relations activities, these endorsements are far more credible because they are generated by other consumers and thus more valuable to the brand.

Buzz works best when companies put unpaid consumers in charge of creating their own messages because the message is more credible and trusted. In the UK, Kellogg's is currently trying to make its first foray into buzz marketing with a campaign to promote FruitaBu, its range of bagged fruit snacks. Consumers can sign up to be sent product samples which in turn they will promote and recommend to friends. Kellogg's believes that this type of marketing offers an ideal way to introduce UK consumers to FruitaBu. The company gets help from buzz specialist agency BzzAgent, which established itself in the UK in 2007 and also assists clients such as Kraft, Procter & Gamble and Philips.[14] As Table 11.3 shows, WOMMA considers hiring actors to create buzz deceptive and unethical (more on this at the end of the chapter!). This is just what Sony Ericsson Mobile Communications did when it hired 60 actors to go to tourist attractions to act like tourists and get unsuspecting passers-by to take their photos using the new Sony Ericsson camera phone and then rave about the phone. WOMMA now has rules that state that anyone promoting products should identify for whom they work.[15] Some critics say buzz marketing should never be directed at children and teens as these consumers are more impressionable and

Company	Buzz Marketing Tactic
IKEA	To create attention for its mattresses, IKEA created a buzz having people sleeping on IKEA mattresses all over downtown Toronto in a one-day event.[1]
Burger King	At www.Subservientchicken.com, consumers could have fun giving a man in a chicken suit orders to follow. The site attracted 418 million visitors who stayed on an average of 6 minutes.[2] Result: Burger King was seen as a more empathetic and relevant company for young people.
Nike	Nike was supposedly the 'brains' behind a cool, illegal warehouse club in Berlin.[3]
Hasbro	Consumers were encouraged to play Monopoly on the streets of London.[4] The fines and clean-up fees Hasbro was forced to pay to the city were far less than advertising costs.
Puma	Encouraged consumers to stencil its cat logo all over Paris.
Diesel (the retailer)	Lets dogs come in and gives them biscuits.[5]
Audi	To introduce its A3 model, Audi staged a fake car theft at a New York Auto Show. Posters placed near the theft appealed to consumers for help and sent then to a website where they could participate in an alternate reality game (ARG) and find hidden clues to solve the mystery.[6]
Kellogg's	Gave a video of never-before-seen ads for Pop-Tarts to 12,000 'tween' girl influencers.[7]
Hard Rock Hotel	A blonde model in the Hard Rock Hotel dressing gown created buzz for the café by wandering around a park in Chicago, asking commuting businessmen if they knew the way back to the Hard Rock Hotel.[8]
Procter & Gamble	P&G sent product and information to 250,000 teens who were not paid but were free to form their own opinions and talk about them.[9]
Microsoft	When introducing its Halo 2 videogame, gave players identified as influencers bits of information about the game before its release so they could talk about the product with other avid gamers who, conveniently, were also heavy users of chat rooms and videogame message boards.[10]
Nestlé	Nestlé created a buzz in London by hiring an agency which deliberately jackknifed a lorry in Covent Garden, spilling boxes and boxes of Nestle chocolate bars on the pavement. Roughly 70,000 passer-by were only too pleased to fill their pockets.[11]
Scottish and Newcastle	The brewer Scottish and Newcastle achieved a buzz with its 250-strong team which visited 6,000 pubs, chatted to customers about their boozing habits and then bought them a drink. Thousands of pints of Foster's, Kronenbourg 1664 and Strongow were handed out.[12]

Notes:

[1] Bruce Philp, 'IKEA's buzz might wake consumers', *The Hamilton Spectator*, 22 September 2007 (Final Edition).
[2] 'Word-of-Mouth: Brands of the Unexpected', *Brand Strategy*, 5 December 2005, 24.
[3] Ibid.
[4] Ibid.
[5] Ibid.
[6] Ibid.
[7] Todd Wasserman, 'Blogs Cause Word of Mouth Business to Spread Quickly', *Brandweek*, 3 October 2005, 9.
[8] Jonny David, 'The Stealth Sell', *The Sunday Times (London)*, 5 August 2007; Todd Wasserman, 'Word Games', *Brandweek*, 24 April 2006, 24.
[9] Suzanne Vranica, 'Getting Buzz Marketers to Fess Up', *The Wall Street Journal*, 9 February 2005, B9.
[10] Ibid.
[11] David, 'The Stealth Sell'.
[12] Ibid.

Table 11.2 How Some Marketers Have Created Buzz

Positive Word of Mouth Marketing Strategies	Unethical Word of Mouth Marketing Strategies
1. Encouraging communication Developing tools to make telling a friend easier Creating forums and feedback tools Working with social networks **2. Giving people something to talk about** Information that can be shared or forwarded Advertising, stunts and other publicity that encourages conversation Working with product development to build WOM elements into products **3. Creating communities and connecting people** Creating user groups and fan clubs Supporting independent groups that form around your product Hosting discussions and message boards about your products Enabling grassroots organisations such as local meetings and other real-world participation **4. Working with influential communities** Finding people who are likely to respond to your message Identifying people who are able to influence your target customers Informing these individuals about what you do and encouraging them to spread the word Good-faith efforts to support issues and causes that are important to these individuals **5. Creating evangelist or advocate programmes** Providing recognition and tools to active advocates Recruiting new advocates, teaching them about the benefits of your products, and encouraging them to talk about them **6. Researching and listening to customer feedback** Tracking online and offline conversations by supporters, detractors and neutrals Listening and responding to both positive and negative conversations **7. Engaging in transparent conversation** Encouraging two-way conversations with interested parties Creating blogs and other tools to share information Participating openly in blogs and discussions **8. Co-creation and information sharing** Involving consumers in marketing and creative (feedback on creative campaigns, allowing them to create commercials, etc.) Letting customers 'behind the curtain' have first access to information and content	**1. Stealth marketing** Any practice designed to deceive people about the involvement of marketers in a communication. **2. Shilling** Paying people to talk about (or promote) a product without disclosing that they are working for the company; impersonating a customer. **3. Infiltration** Using fake identities in an online discussion to promote a product; taking over a website, conversation, or live event against the wishes or rules set by the proprietor. **4. Comment spam** Using automated software 'bots' to post unrelated or inappropriate comments to blogs or other online communities. **5. Defacement** Vandalising or damaging property to promote a product. **6. Spam** Sending bulk or unsolicited e-mail or other messages without clear, voluntary permission. **7. Falsification** Knowingly disseminating false or misleading information.

Table 11.3   Positive and Unethical Word of Mouth Marketing Strategies

Source: "Word of Mouth 101: An Introduction to Word of Mouth Marketing" (accessed July 17, 2006, at www.woman.org/wom101.htm).

easier to deceive than adults.[16] Companies must therefore be careful using buzz marketing because campaigns can backfire when the press get hold of them and publicise the way people are potentially being duped into believing the word of mouth is genuine.

Of course marketers don't have a hand in creating all the buzz around a product or service. WOMMA refers to buzz resulting from buzz marketing campaigns as 'amplified WOM' while it calls buzz that occurs naturally 'organic WOM'. Organic buzz allowed Procter & Gamble to discover that its Home Café coffee maker had a tendency to start fires after 3000 buzz agents complained.[17] Naturally occurring buzz also can create negative publicity as when ex-journalist Jeff Jarvis detailed on a blog his problem getting a $1600 PC fixed due to poor service from Dell computers.[18] To create positive buzz, companies need to have a total customer focus, to empathise and care about their customers. To what extent do you think Ian Bruce at RNIB might be able to generate Buzz with his option 1, telemarketing and raffles?

Guerrilla Marketing

When you see anyone dressed up as a light bulb, a cigarette or a sweet, the chances are it's an attempt at guerrilla marketing. A few years back, some companies with smaller advertising budgets developed innovative ways of getting consumers' attention. These activities – from putting advertising stickers on apples and heads of lettuce to placing product-related messages on the backs of theatre tickets and flags on a golf course – became known as **guerrilla marketing**. The term is not to be confused with Gorilla marketing which was used in a recent commercial for Cadbury's (go to www.youtube.com and type in 'Cadbury's Gorilla Advert Aug 31st 2007' (http://www.youtube.com/watch?v=TnzFRV1LwIo). This strategy involves 'ambushing' consumers with promotional content in places where they are not expecting to encounter this kind of activity.[19]

Marketing Ethics

Blogging or Flogging: Can you tell the difference?

As a marketing communications tool, 'Blogs' have not caused much concern in the digital marketing environment to date. Technocrati.com, a leading technology website and commentator estimates there are 35.5 million blogs in existence, as well as 75,000 created daily. As the prominence of blogs and their authors rise, blogs attract growing corporate attention as a digital word of mouth technique.

A number of businesses have fallen foul of the blogosphere community due to ethically questionable blogging practices. In 2007, reports emerged alleging that Microsoft delivered brand new high spec laptops with new Vista software to influential tech bloggers before the Vista launch. However, perhaps the most infamous blogging misdemeanour was allegedly committed by Wal-Mart. In 2006, it was reported by the press that its communications agency, Edelman Public Relations Worldwide, 'masterminded the authorship of several pro-Wal-Mart blogs'.

It appears that the popularity and influence of blogs has led to a growing number of companies rewarding bloggers financially or in kind to report favourably on a company's product or service, otherwise known as 'flogging'.

Debate, Discuss, Disagree

1   Is the practice of flogging, corporate deception or a legitimate form of advertising?

Today, big companies are using guerrilla marketing strategies extensively. During the World Cup year, the British company MindShare created 'Sure Fans United', a reality TV show sponsored entirely by Unilever for its Sure deodorant brand. The show portrayed extreme fans who even sold their mortgages to support local football teams. The reality TV show was shown on ITV1 and 'garnered an average of 490,000 viewers per episode, gaining a 9.9 per cent share'.[20] Burger King began a guerrilla marketing campaign to increase sales in its Asia-Pacific outlets by 25 per cent.[21] The company sent CDs with quirky marketing suggestions to local restaurant managers. These included putting 'I♥BK' on T-shirts and placing the shirts on Ronald McDonald, placing large footprints from McDonald's outlets to Burger King outlets, placing signs on empty benches saying 'gone to BK – Ronald' and placing large signs at BK locations that are near KFC locations that read 'It's why the chicken crossed the road.'

Companies can use guerrilla marketing to promote new drinks, cars or clothing styles. Nike, for example, mentions its website or celebrity tie-ins in chat rooms. This method has been hugely successful in attracting hundreds of thousands of visitors to its website. The website suits the young market offering sport-focused video clips, email games or MP3 downloads.[22] Given the success of these campaigns, many of which operate on a shoestring budget, expect to see even more of this kind of tactic as other companies climb on the guerrilla bandwagon. Type in 'guerrilla marketing' to look for example videos on www.youtube.com.

Integrated Marketing Communications

The traditional forms of marketing communications are *advertising*, including mass media, direct mail, outdoor advertising and online advertising; *sales promotions* such as coupons, samples, rebates or contests; press releases and special events that *public relations* professionals organise; and *sales presentations*. Today's marketers have added newer types of communications tactics such as buzz, viral marketing and guerrilla marketing to their bag of tricks.

Many marketing experts now believe that integrating all forms of marketing communications is essential for successful marketing. **Integrated marketing communications (IMC)** is the process that marketers use to plan, develop, execute and evaluate coordinated, measurable, persuasive brand communication programmes over time to targeted audiences. The IMC approach argues that consumers see the variety of messages they receive from a firm – a TV commercial, a coupon, an opportunity to win a sweepstake and a display in a shop – as a whole, as a single company speaking to them but in different places and different ways. Take, for example, the Harry Potter books. The communications there are managed from the pre-release publicity events and online marketing to create buzz, through to event marketing and opening nights, to poster and newspaper advertising to remind people and finally the merchandising for all of the characters all communicate the same ideas.

That's a lot different from how traditional marketing communication programmes are created, where little effort is made to coordinate the varying messages consumers receive. An advertising campaign typically is run independently of a sweepstake, which in turn has no relation to a Formula One car racing sponsorship. These disjointed efforts can send conflicting messages that leave the consumer confused and unsure of the brand's identity. The customer is the focus for companies that adopt an IMC perspective. With IMC, marketers seek to understand what information consumers want as well as how, when and where they want it – and then to deliver the information about the product or service using the best combination of communications methods available to them. This should mean that communication becomes part of people's lives and not a distraction.

Marketers have been developing promotion strategies and using the elements of the promotion mix for many years, but the concept of integrated marketing communications is relatively new. While IMC has not been adopted by all firms, many marketing experts believe that IMC provides a competitive advantage to firms in the twenty-first century.

With IMC, marketers plan and then execute marketing communication programmes that create and maintain long-term relationships with customers by satisfying customer needs. This means that promotion tools are used in such a way as to build loyal relationships with customers or other stakeholders, rather than simply causing a one-time product purchase or short-term change in behaviour.[23] With IMC, marketers like Ian Bruce at RNIB look at communication the way customers see it – as a flow of information from a single source. Thus, marketers who understand the power of IMC seek to 'unify all marketing communication tools – from advertising to packaging – to send target audiences a consistent, persuasive message that promotes company goals'.[24]

So why is IMC so important today? A few years ago, marketers could communicate with consumers by placing a few ads on major television networks and perhaps in a few popular magazines. Today, with increased global competition, customers are bombarded with more and more marketing messages. And the sheer number of media outlets also is mushrooming. Marketers can choose from literally hundreds of cable and satellite stations, each of which can deliver its messages to a selected portion of the television viewing audience. All this means that consumers are less likely to be influenced by any single marketer-generated message. At the same time, widely available technology now enables even small firms to develop and effectively use customer databases, giving firms greater opportunities for understanding customers and for developing one-to-one communication programmes. And technology gives customers the ability to communicate among themselves about products and companies and even to view ads on the web at their leisure.[25]

 # Characteristics of IMC

To fully understand what IMC is all about and before a firm can begin to implement an IMC programme, it is essential to understand some important characteristics of IMC.

IMC Creates a Single Unified Voice

Perhaps the most important characteristic of IMC is that it creates a single unified voice for a firm. If we examine the traditional communication programme of a typical consumer goods firm, say, a manufacturer of frozen foods, we see that they often develop communication tactics in isolation. If marketers decide they need advertising, what do they do? They hire an ad agency to produce great advertising. Or they may even hire several different ad agencies to develop advertising aimed at different target markets. They may also realise they need public relations activities, so they hire a public relations firm. Then some other genius decides to sponsor a sweepstakes and hires a sales promotion firm to do this. The sales department hires a different firm to develop trade show materials, and someone in the corporate communication department hires a sports-marketing firm to work on sponsoring a car race.

Each of these firms may well do a good job, but each may also be sending out a different message. The customer can't help but be confused. What is the product? What is the brand image? Whose needs will this product satisfy? IMC strategies present a unified selling proposition in the marketplace by eliminating duplication and conflicting communication. Because a company develops an IMC programme as a whole, there is a focus on *all* communications elements – advertising, public relations, sales promotion, and so forth – speaking with one voice, creating a single and powerful brand personality.

Having a single brand message, however, doesn't mean that marketers don't communicate to different segments of the market or different stakeholder groups with different tactics. The same brand message can be communicated to employees with a story in the company newsletter about how local workers have helped flood victims, to loyal customers via direct mail that explains how to make their home safe for toddlers, and to prospective customers through mass media and internet advertising.

The one-voice/one-message focus of IMC also considers other less obvious forms of communication. For example, a firm's communication with customers includes the letters sent to customers, the way company personnel talk on the phone with clients or customers, the uniforms delivery people or other employees wear, signage and other policies and procedures that may have an unintended effect on consumers' perceptions of the firm (even the stationery the company uses to correspond with vendors and customers).

Real People, Other Voices

Advice for Ian Bruce

Sally McKechnie,
University of Nottingham

I would choose option 1. If the RNIB is to become successful again at fundraising on a local level, it needs to turn to new initiatives that enable the charity to use database marketing technology to increase the number of volunteers who work on its behalf as well as the number of donors. Databases of past donors can be profiled using geodemographic segmentation systems, so that cold prospects can be identified for targeted direct marketing campaigns. Using telemarketing to recruit potential volunteers in selected locations will be more expensive than using direct mail but should result in a much higher acceptance rate. The two-stage approach of getting these volunteers to then sell raffle tickets on the charity's behalf to their friends and neighbours provides the RNIB with a cost-effective opportunity to raise awareness of its campaigns through word-of-mouth marketing. Since information received through informal and personal communication channels is generally considered to be more reliable and trustworthy than information received through more formal and impersonal ones, individuals are not only more likely to buy raffle tickets if they already know who is selling them, but also more likely to conform through reference group influence to the expectations of the volunteers and actually buy them. Another reason why I would choose this option is because it would help the charity to get a better understanding of its target markets. Given that it is more costly to attract new volunteers and donors than retain existing ones, by monitoring the effectiveness of raffle ticket campaigns and capturing names and addresses of donors from ticket stubs, it should be in a better position to identify volunteers and donors with whom it would be worth building a longer term relationship in order to increase the level of local fundraising.

Marilyn Hunt,
University of Worcester

I would choose option 1 because it offers RNIB the opportunity to combine the power of word-of-mouth marketing with the cost-effective benefits of telemarketing. The key factor here is that RNIB is not selling a product/service, but using telemarketing to recruit donation collectors. As the UK's largest charity, RNIB clearly has a well-known and acceptable brand, so rejection by respondents is less likely. Collectors will sell tickets to individuals with whom they have a personal connection, so the likelihood of successful conversion is further increased. The regional fundraising model is not new to RNIB and appears to be an area of strength, so past experience could possibly inform street targeting. It is not clear whether RNIB has any experience of outbound telemarketing. If not, it will need to devote time and money to the recruitment and training of appropriate staff/volunteers. It will also be important to plan telemarketing campaigns carefully so that they provide extensive market coverage (and funds) over time and support and complement the wide range of other campaigns that RNIB is likely to be undertaking at any one point in time.

IMC Begins with the Customer

The customer is the primary focus of the communication, *not* the goals of the company or the creative genius of the communication specialists whose creative ideals can become too abstract for the consumer to follow. First and foremost, the goal of IMC is to provide the information customers want when they want it, where they want it, and in the amount needed. Remember it's about becoming part of people's lives not a distraction from it! Sometimes that's as simple as letting consumers 'vote' on the shows or products they want to see, as when fans of the hit TV comedy *Friends* were allowed to choose their six favourite episodes at a website when the producers decided to end the series.[26]

IMC Seeks to Develop Relationships with Customers

As mass-marketing activities have become less effective, many marketers are finding that the road to success is through one-to-one or relationship marketing, where the focus is on building and maintaining a long-term relationship with each individual customer. To achieve this, marketers must continuously communicate with each customer or else risk losing them to the competition.

What we said earlier bears repeating – *it simply is easier and less expensive to keep an existing customer than to attract a new one*. Thus, IMC firms also measure their success by share of customer, not share of market, and on the lifetime value of a customer. This means prioritising customers so that greater resources go to communicating with high-value buyers or clients.

Because IMC also is much about building and maintaining relationships with customers, IMC strategies often incorporate databases and the CRM programmes and practices we talked about in Chapter 6. With these tools, marketers have the information they need to understand customers and to deliver unique messages to each consumer – messages that meet the needs of each consumer and that build relationships.

IMC Involves Two-Way Communication

Traditional communication programmes were built on one-way communication activities. Television, magazine, newspaper and outdoor advertising spouted clever messages at the consumer, but there was little if any way for the consumer to talk back. Today, we know that one-way, impersonal communication is highly ineffective at building long-term relationships with customers. Instead, marketers seek first to learn what information customers have and what additional information they want and then develop communication tactics that let them give information to their customers.

IMC Focuses on Stakeholders, Not Just Customers

Stakeholders (not to be confused with shareholders) are any individuals or organisations that are important to the long-term health of an organisation. Some of these stakeholders include employees, suppliers, stockholders, the media, trade associations, regulators and even neighbours. One reason these other stakeholders are so important is that customers and prospective customers don't just learn about a company and its products from the firm. Their attitudes, positive or negative, are also heavily influenced by the mass media, government regulatory bodies, or even their neighbour who happens to work for the company. Thus, while the primary stakeholder is usually the customer, a myriad of other groups or individuals can significantly influence customers' attitudes and behaviours.

IMC Generates a Continuous Stream of Communication

A major characteristic of an IMC strategy is that tactics using many different elements of the communication programme – advertising, publicity, personal selling, sales promotion, customer testimonials, and so on – are included in a single IMC plan. As a result, IMC strategies provide a continuous stream of communication. Instead of consumers being bombarded with messages from various sources for a week or two and then hearing nothing from the brand for months, IMC planning ensures that consumers receive information on a regular basis and in the right amount.

IMC Measures Results Based Upon Actual Feedback

Many IMC supporters suggest that the only adequate measure of effectiveness is to evaluate the return on investment. This means that if a firm spends €1 million on advertising, it should be able to determine what euro amount of revenue the firm receives as a result of that expenditure. While this type of relationship between promotion euros and revenues may be difficult to measure exactly because of such things as the long-term effects of advertising and other communication, most firms are seeking measures of accountability for their communication budgets and demand results. That's why we've made such a big deal out of *marketing metrics* in this book. (See Chapter 12 on how to measure advertising effectiveness.)

IMC and Database Marketing

Objective

6

Explain the important role of database marketing in integrated marketing communications (IMC)

The effective use of databases is crucial for building relationships with consumers, a key characteristic of IMC. The development of a customer database allows an organisation to learn about the preferences of its customers, fine-tune its offerings, and build a relationship with its market. Tesco is a great example of database marketing: when you use your loyalty card, you tell Tesco what products you like buy buying from its shops. Your loyalty card also provides you with coupons and vouchers, and Tesco knows how effective it has been by how many you redeem.

Database marketing is the creation of a relationship with a set of customers with an identifiable interest in a product or service and whose responses to promotion efforts become part of the communications process.

Let's look at an example of how an IMC firm may make effective use of database marketing. What if you ordered a dozen roses to be delivered to a friend for his or her birthday last year? You (and your friend) have become a part of the florist's database. What are the possibilities for the florist? First, the database is a goldmine of information. By examining (or *mining* as it is often called) the records of thousands of customers, including you, the florist can find out which customers order flowers frequently (heavy users) and which order only occasionally (light users). They can identify customers who order flowers for themselves. They know which customers order flowers only for funerals, and which send flowers to their partners. And they can determine what type of customer accounts for their greatest sales and their greatest profits. This helps them to develop a better understanding of their target markets.

Of course, using the information in the database for understanding a firm's market is only the beginning. Even more important is how firms such as our florist *use* the database to create that one-to-one communication with their target markets. So you, our florist's customer, may get a call or an e-mail next year reminding you of your friend's birthday and asking if you want the same dozen roses sent again this year. The customer who hosts dinner parties frequently may receive a brochure before the Christmas holiday season that shows various table arrangements. Heavy users might receive a special thank you for their business and an offer to receive a free arrangement after purchasing 12 arrangements. And by the way, what about your friend who received flowers but who has never purchased from our florist? Since we may assume that a consumer who likes to receive flowers will sooner or later want to purchase them as well, they become part of the florist's prospective customer database. As such, they may receive a catalogue of the most popular arrangements or perhaps a coupon for a discount on the first order.

The following list explains what database marketing can do:[27]

- **Database marketing is interactive:** Recall that interactive marketing requires a response from consumers, be it filling out an order form or calling an 0800 number for product information. For example, Jaguar.com wanted to rebuilt its website to get the online brand in sync with the look of its ongoing traditional campaign. It hired a marketing agency which asked 200 Jaguar owners to rank their website preferences. As a result, the website was redesigned to show more information about security and the company's history.[28] This type of interactivity gives marketers more than one opportunity to develop a dialogue with the customer and possibly to create add-on sales by engaging the customer in a discussion about the product and related items or services in which they might be interested.

- **Database marketing builds relationships:** It's easier for the marketer to build promotion programmes that continue over time with database marketing because the marketer can best adapt them in light of consumers' responses. *The best predictor of who will buy a product is knowing who bought it in the past.* That's why *Reader's Digest*'s 12 full-time statisticians sort its customers by likelihood of purchase and predict the probability that each will respond to a given offer.[29] Once sophisticated database marketers know who has already purchased, they can keep in touch with these consumers. They can reward loyal customers with money-saving coupons and keep them informed of upcoming prizes and promotions. As one executive whose company tracks high value customers explained, 'They are members of a club, but they don't know they are members.'[30]

- **Database marketing locates new customers:** In some cases, a marketer can create new customers by focusing communications on likely prospects with characteristics similar to current users. For example, after Tesco launched its Clubcard the company did not rest on its laurels. It soon introduced a Clubcard Plus which offered holders interest paid on their balances and therefore could be used like any other debit card. Within 12 months of being lauched, the Clubcard Plus became the most popular UK loyalty scheme.[31]

- **Database marketing stimulates cross-selling:** Database marketers can find it easy to offer related products to their customers. Interest in one product category boosts the odds that the customer is a good candidate for similar items. This explains why companies bombard consumers with mail offers for computer software, magazines, or clothing after they purchase a similar product over the phone or through a catalogue. At British Gas, answering customer calls and solving their queries are not only important to achieve high customer satisfaction but are also crucial for a successful cross-selling strategy. Customer information is stored in a database and helps to sell appropriate products which are in line with customer's needs in the long term.[32] The European low-cost airline Germanwings uses its customer database to send out e-mails informing customer of cheap ticket deals for given periods. Some mailings have included questionnaires regarding specific interests of customers to help them decide on future product offerings.

- **Database marketing is measurable:** A common complaint of many marketers is the difficulty in pinpointing the impact a promotion had on the target market – what is a specific promotion's return on investment (ROI)? Who can say for sure that a single TV commercial motivated people to switch mobile phone? But the database marketers know exactly who received a specific message, so they are able to measure the effectiveness of each communication because they track each promotion and enter it into the database against your name.

- **Responses are trackable:** The marketer can assess the proportion of message recipients that responded, compare the effectiveness of different messages, and compile a history of which consumers are most likely to respond over time.[33]

Developing the IMC Plan

www.pearsoned.co.uk/solomon

Objective

7

Explain the stages in developing an IMC plan.

Now that we've talked about the characteristics of an IMC strategy, we need to see how to make it happen. How do we develop an IMC plan that delivers just the right message to a number of different target audiences when and where they want it in the most effective and cost-efficient way? Just as with any other strategic decision-making process, the development of this plan includes several steps, as Figure 11.3 shows. Let's review each step.

Step 1: Identify the Target Audiences

An important part of overall marketing planning is to determine who the target market is. This is where a good customer database is most important. With a well-designed database, marketers can know who their target market is as well as the buying behaviour of different segments within the total market. This means they can develop targeted messages for each customer.

Step 2: Establish the Communications Objectives

The next step in communications planning is to establish communications objectives. The whole point of communicating with customers and prospective customers is to let them know that the organisation has a product to meet their needs in a timely and affordable way. It's bad enough when a product comes along that people don't want or need. But the bigger marketing sin is to have a product that they *do* want – but you fail to let them know about it. Of course, seldom can we deliver a single message to consumers that magically transforms them into loyal customers. In most cases, it takes a series of messages that move consumers through several stages.

We can view this process as an uphill climb, such as the one Figure 11.4 depicts. The consumer is 'led' through a series of steps, often referred to as a **hierarchy of effects**, from initial awareness of a product to brand loyalty. The task of moving the consumer up the hierarchy becomes more difficult at each step. Many potential buyers may drop out along the way,

Figure 11.3   Steps in Developing the IMC Plan.

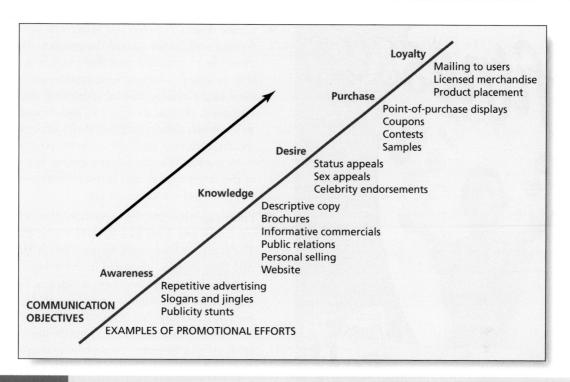

Figure 11.4	**The Hierarchy of Effects**
	Communication objectives seek to move consumers through the hierarchy of effects.

leaving less of the target group inclined to go the distance and become loyal customers. Each part of this path entails different communication objectives to 'push' people to the next level.

To understand how this process works, consider how a firm would have to adjust its communication objectives as it tries to establish a presence in the market for a new men's cologne called Homme. Let's say that the primary target market for the cologne is single men aged 18 to 24 who care about their appearance and who are into health, fitness, working out and looking very fit. The company would want to focus more on some promotion methods (such as advertising) and less on others (such as personal selling). Here are some steps the company might take to promote Homme:

● **Create awareness:** The first step is to make members of the target market aware that there's a new brand of cologne on the market. Marketers would accomplish this through simple, repetitive advertising in magazines, on television and on the radio that push the brand name. The company might even consider creating a 'teaser' campaign where ads heighten interest because they don't reveal the exact nature of the product (for example, newspaper ads that simply proclaim, 'Homme is coming!'). The promotion objective might be to create an 80 per cent awareness of Homme cologne among 18- to 24-year-old men in the first two months.

● **Inform the market:** The next step would be to provide prospective users with knowledge about the benefits the new product has to offer, that is, how it is positioned relative to other fragrances (see Chapter 6). Perhaps the cologne has a light, slightly mentholated scent with a hint of a liniment smell to remind the wearer of how he feels after a good workout. Promotion would focus on communications that emphasise this position. The objective at this point might be to communicate the connection between Homme and muscle building so that 70 per cent of the target market develops some interest in the product.

Photo 11.5	The second step in the hierarchy of effects is knowledge. Fitnesse informs consumers about its new product. Source: The Advertising Archives

- **Create desire:** The next task is to create favourable feelings and desires toward the product. The aim should be to convince men that Homme is preferable to other colognes. Communications at this stage might employ splashy advertising spreads in magazines, perhaps including an endorsement by a well-known celebrity such as a Pierce Brosnan. The specific objective might be to create positive attitudes towards Homme cologne among 50 per cent of the target market and brand preference among 30 per cent of the target market.

- **Encourage trial:** As the expression goes, 'How do you know you don't like it, until you've tried it?' The company now needs to get some of the men who have become interested in the cologne to try it. A promotion plan might encourage trial by mailing samples of Homme to members of the target market, inserting 'scratch-and-sniff' samples in bodybuilding magazines, placing elaborate displays in shops that dispense money-saving coupons, or even sponsoring a contest in which the winner gets to have a personal trainer for a day. The specific objective now might be to encourage trial of Homme among 25 per cent of 18- to 24-year-old men in the first two months.

- **Build loyalty:** Of course, the real test is loyalty: convincing customers to stay with Homme after they've gone through the first bottle. Promotion efforts must maintain communications with current users to reinforce the bond they feel with the product. As before, they will accomplish this with some mix of strategies, perhaps including direct mail advertising to current users, product placements in popular television programmes or films, and maybe even the development of a workout clothing line bearing a Homme logo. The objective might be to develop and maintain regular usage of Homme cologne among 10 per cent of men from 18 to 24 years old.

Step 3: Determine and Allocate the Marketing Communications Budget

While setting a budget for marketing communications might seem easy – you just calculate how much you need to accomplish your objectives – in reality it's not that simple. Determining and allocating communications budgets includes three distinct decisions:

- determining the total communications budget;
- deciding whether to use a push strategy or a pull strategy; and
- allocating how much to spend on specific promotion activities.

In the real world, firms often view communications costs as an expense rather than as an investment leading to greater profits. When sales are declining or the company is operating in a difficult economic environment, it is often tempting to cut costs by reducing spending on advertising, promotions and other 'soft' activities whose contributions to the bottom line are hard to quantify. When this is the case, marketers must work harder to justify these expenses.

Economic approaches to budgeting rely on marginal analysis (discussed in Chapter 10), in which the organisation spends money on promotion as long as the revenues realised by these efforts continue to exceed the costs of the promotions themselves, e.g, BOGOF offers, buy one get one free, often fall into this category. This perspective assumes that promotions are always intended solely to increase sales when in fact these activities may have other objectives, such as enhancing a firm's image.

Also, the effects of promotions often lag over time. For example, a firm may have to spend a lot on promotion when it first launches a product without seeing any immediate return. Because of these limitations, most firms rely on two budgeting techniques: top down and bottom up.

Top-down budgeting techniques require top management to establish the overall amount that the organisation allocates for promotion activities, and this amount is then divided among advertising, public relations and other promotion departments.

The most common top-down technique is the **percentage-of-sales method**, in which the promotion budget is based on last year's sales or on estimates for the present year's sales. The percentage may be an industry average provided by trade associations that collect objective information on behalf of member companies. The advantage of this method is that it ties spending on promotion to sales and profits.

Unfortunately, this method can imply that sales cause promotional outlays rather than viewing sales as the *outcome* of promotional efforts. As sales drop, firms might be reluctant to spend more on promotion even though the drop might be due to environmental changes, such as a change in economic conditions or a rival's recent introduction of a new product. If so, cutting promotion spending might not help the firm in the long run.

The **competitive-parity method** is another way of saying 'keep up with the Joneses'. In other words, match whatever competitors are spending. Some marketers think this approach simply mirrors the best thinking of others in the business. However, this method often sees each player maintaining the same market share year after year. This method also assumes that the same euros spent on promotion by two different firms will yield the same results, but spending a lot of money doesn't guarantee a successful promotion. Firms certainly need to monitor their competitors' promotion activities, but they must combine this information with their own objectives and capacities.

The problem with top-down techniques is that budget decisions are based more on established practices than on promotion objectives. Another approach is to begin at the beginning: identify promotion goals and allocate enough money to accomplish them. That is what **bottom-up budgeting techniques** attempt. For example, some marketers devise a budget that attempts to project the revenues and costs associated with a product over several years and then match promotion expenditures to a pattern – such as spending more on promotion in the first year to build awareness of the brand market share and then spending less once the product catches on.

This bottom-up logic is at the heart of the **objective-task method**, which is gaining in popularity. Using this approach, the firm first defines the specific communications goals it hopes to achieve, such as increasing by 20 per cent the number of consumers who are aware of the brand. It then tries to figure out what kind of promotional efforts it will take to meet that goal. Although this is the most rational approach, it is hard to implement because it obliges managers to specify their objectives and attach euro amounts to them. This method requires careful analysis – and a bit of lucky 'guesstimating'.

One crucial issue in determining the promotion mix is whether the company is relying on a push strategy or a pull strategy. A **push strategy** means that the company wants to move its products by convincing members of the distribution channel such as wholesalers, agents or retailers to offer them and entice their customers to select these items. In this case, promotion efforts will 'push' the products from producers to consumer by focusing on personal selling, trade advertising and sales promotions, such as exhibits at trade shows.

In contrast, a company relying on a **pull strategy** is counting on consumers wanting its products and so convincing retailers to respond to this demand by stocking them. In this case, efforts will focus on media advertising and consumer sales promotion to stimulate interest among end consumers who will 'pull' the product onto shop shelves and then into their

Marketing Metrics

Ford Advertising Models

Ford of Europe spends hundreds of millions of euros on advertising. Management wanted to optimise the allocation of spend across the main car brands and the countries in Europe. They used econometric modelling to assess the incremental sales value of advertising for different brand/country combinations, and also the saturation curves as advertising spend is increased. These 'elasticities' were then incorporated into an optimisation model that determined the allocation of advertising money that would produce the maximum financial returns. When management first ran the model it triggered vigorous debate, followed by refinement of the assumptions, and after an iterative process management agreed on a new allocation that significantly enhanced the financial results.

shopping baskets. So no supermarket would dare not to stock Heinz tomato ketchup because Heinz makes sure through lots of promotions that customers put it in their basket when they go shopping.

Once the organisation decides how much to spend on promotion and whether to use a push or a pull strategy, it must divide its budget among the elements in the promotion mix. Although advertising used to get most of the promotion budget, today sales promotions are playing a big role in marketing strategies. UK-based Dynamo Marketing Communications, for example, spurred its Christmas sales for three consecutive years by offering consumers personal and interactive promotions. In 2007, the company gave its customers a pot of earth, a miniature watering can and an amaryllis bulb. The customer had to nurture the plant and send a photo of the plant to the company. If successful, the customer won an Easter Egg. If the customer produced a red flower, he or she could win a weekend away.[34] Procter & Gamble reduced consumer sales promotion spending in the early 1990s when adopting its 'value pricing' strategy. Since then, P&G has revamped its $2 billion-plus annual trade promotion budget to focus more on activities such as in-store merchandising, temporary price reductions and end-of-aisle displays.[35]

Whether we use a push or a pull strategy and how the promotion mix for a product is designed must vary over time because some elements work better at different points in the product life cycle than others. As an example, we might think about the state of electronic audio and video equipment in today's market and the relative positions in the product life cycle.

An Example of an IMC Strategy In the *introduction phase*, the objective is to build awareness of and encourage trial of the product among consumers, often by relying on a push strategy. That's the situation today with WiFi. Advertising is the primary promotion tool for creating awareness, and a publicity campaign to generate news reports about the new product may help as well. Business-to-business marketing that emphasises personal selling – that is, the marketing that a manufacturer does to retailers and other business customers – is important in this phase in order to get channel members to carry the product. For consumer goods sold through retailers, trade sales promotion may be necessary to encourage retailers to stock the product.

In the *growth phase*, promotions must now start stressing product benefits. For products such as MP3 players, advertising increases now, while sales promotions that encourage trial usually decline because people are more willing to try the product without being offered an incentive. Sales promotions (free samples and such, as when retailers like Starbucks or McDonald's set up free WiFi zones for customers) may be used to encourage trial.

The opposite pattern often occurs with products such as DVD players, now in their *maturity phase*, when many people have already tried the product. As sales stabilise, strategy now shifts to encouraging people to switch from competitors' brands. This can be tough if consumers don't see enough differences to bother. Usually, sales promotions, particularly coupons and special price deals, have greater chances of success than advertising because advertising is great at generating awareness but not great a creating action, i.e. buying. In some cases an industry revamps a widely used technology by introducing one or more new versions or formats that force consumers to convert (sometimes kicking and screaming), thus transforming a mature category back to a new one. That's what's happened in the 'DVD format wars', a high-stakes showdown between the Blu-ray disc that offered 50 gigabytes of storage and was backed by a large group of consumer electronics and computer companies and the HD DVD format, backed by Toshiba and favoured by a majority of film studios, which was more similar to the standard DVD.[36] In 2008, Toshiba blinked first and so became the decade's equivalent of the losing Betamax (versus the winning VHS format) in the earlier 'VCR format wars'.[37]

All bets are off for products such as VCR players, now in their *decline phase*. As sales plummet, the company dramatically reduces spending on all elements of the promotion mix. Sales will be driven by the continued loyalty of a small group of users who keep the product alive until it is sold to another company or discontinued.

Factors affecting the size of the IMC budget are:

- **Organisational factors:** Characteristics of the specific firm influence how it allocates its money. These characteristics include the complexity and formality of the company's decision-making process, preferences for advertising versus sales promotions or other elements in the promotion mix, past experiences with specific promotion vehicles, and the 'comfort level' of the firm's advertising and promotion agencies with different approaches in marketing communications.

- **Market potential:** Some consumer groups are more likely to buy the product than others. For example, the marketers of Homme might find that men in blue-collar occupations would be more interested in the product than men in white-collar occupations. It makes sense for marketers to allocate more resources to areas with more sales potential.

- **Market size:** As a rule, larger markets are more expensive places in which to promote. The costs of buying media (such as local TV spots) are higher in major metropolitan areas, but high population density means it will be easier to reach more consumers at the same time. Advertising is good for mass-market products, while personal selling is good for expensive, specialised or highly technical products.

Step 4: Design the Promotion Mix

Designing the promotion mix is the most complicated step in marketing communication planning. It includes determining the specific communication tools that will be used, what message is to be communicated, and the communication channel(s) to be employed. Planners must ask how advertising, sales promotion, personal selling and public relations can be used most effectively to communicate with different target audiences. Each element of the promotion mix has benefits and shortcomings, all of which must be considered in making promotion decisions.

The message should focus on one of four objectives: it should get attention, hold interest, create desire, and produce action. These communications goals are known as the **AIDA model**. Here we'll review some different forms the message can take as well as how the information in the message might be structured. You could also use AIDA to help decide on the options Ian Bruce at the RNIB has to consider. For example, which option might be best in pulling potential donors through from awareness of the RNIB to action in giving?

There are many ways to say the same thing, and marketers must take care in choosing what type of appeal, or message strategy, they will use when encoding the message. To illustrate, consider two strategies employed by rival car companies to promote similar cars. A few years ago, both Toyota and Nissan introduced a large luxury car that sold for more than €30,000. Toyota's

Across the Hall

Janet Hull

is Consultant Head of Marketing at the Institute of Practitioners in Advertising and has been a judge of the IPA Effectiveness Awards and the CIM Effectiveness Awards

I would choose option 1. The RNIB example represents grassroots campaigning in action. It's a really worthy cause, offering huge benefit to those partially sighted people it reaches out to, but it's not 'sexy' or 'high profile'. And it can't command the high marketing budgets of some of the major charities. The majority of its beneficiaries are elderly, and many of its regular donors, I imagine, have direct experience of a parent or relative in need. It's a genuine case of 'charity begins at home'. The fact that its front-line ambassadors are themselves partially sighted, in most cases, only serves to emphasise the point. Applying this thinking to the three fundraising options presented leads me to believe that the first is potentially the most effective. In image terms, it fits best with my perception of this charity's ethos. The approach is neighbourly and unthreatening. After the initial cold-call, people self-select to get involved. Each recruit is simply asked to knock on doors in their own street. The mechanic of the raffle ticket provides both an easy talking point and a potential reward. Provided there are enough people on the ground, substantial funds could be raised at minimum marketing cost. And there is also a good opportunity to build a marketing database of participants. Personally, I am not a huge fan of 'chugging'. Typically aggressive and confrontational, it seems out of kilter with my 'soft and cuddly' image of the RNIB. As for collection boxes, in my experience they attract small change rather than substantial sums, and are a nightmare to manage. And, as our society moves ever closer to becoming 'cashless' and cheques go out of usage, I have to believe their days are numbered.

advertising for its Lexus model used a rational appeal that focused on the technical advancements in the car's design. This approach is often effective for promoting products that are technically complex and require a substantial investment. Nissan, in contrast, focused on the spiritual fulfilment a driver might feel driving down the road in a fine machine. Much like Nissan, Volkswagen launched an international advertising campaign based on love poems linked to vehicles in an attempt to reach the strong emotions that underlie consumers' preferences for cars. In Germany, double-page newspaper and magazine ads featured a love poem with a paragraph explaining the feelings one of Volkswagen's cars represented.[38]

Many marketing messages are similar to debates or trials in which someone presents arguments and tries to convince the receivers to shift their opinions. The way the argument is presented can be important. Most messages merely tout one or more positive attributes of the product or reasons to buy it. These are known as *supportive arguments* or *one-sided messages*. An alternative is to use a *two-sided message*, with both positive and negative information. Two-sided ads can be quite effective, but marketers seldom use them.[39]

A related issue is whether the argument should draw conclusions. Should the ad say only 'our brand is superior', or should it explicitly tell the consumer to buy it? The answer depends on the degree of a consumer's motivation to think about the ad and the complexity of the arguments. If the message is personally relevant, people will pay attention to it and draw their own conclusions. But if the arguments are hard to follow or the person's motivation to follow them is lacking, it is best to make these conclusions explicit.

Even the best message is wasted if it is not placed in communication channels that will reach the target audience effectively. See the marketing metrics insert for the latest way of measuring what media people are consuming. Communication channels include the mass media: newspapers, television, radio, magazines and direct mail. Other media include outdoor display signs and boards and electronic media, the most important of which is the internet. Sponsorships provide another channel for communications. Volvo heavily invests in tennis sponsorship. Its banners are displayed at tournaments, as are examples of its model range. As well as transporting celebrity tennis players in a Volvo car, the company also increases its TV advertisements

Marketing Metrics

IPA Touchpoints survey

The UK's Institute of Practitioners and Advertisers' TouchPoints Survey questioned 5010 people through a substantial self-completion questionnaire and a PDA (personal digital assistant) time-based diary that collected data every half hour for a week on how they were spending their time, their opinions and the role of media in their lives. It has been designed as a stand-alone survey and to be integrated with other media research. A snapshot of the research shows:

- The media hierarchy in hours for all adults between Monday and Friday is: 3.9 television, 1.3 radio and 0.8 internet. On Saturday and Sunday this changes to: 4.5 television, 1.5 radio and 1.0 internet

- On a typical weekday a 15–24-year-old home internet user spends 2 hours surfing the web – this rises to 2.4 hours at the weekend and averages 14.8 hours for the week.

- The average individual receives 8.5 pieces of advertising mail each week, 4.9 (57 per cent) are personally addressed and 3.6 (43 per cent) are 'random' pieces of mail.

- Only 13 per cent of all written communication is now using pen and paper; 49 per cent is via email, 29 per cent via SMS text, 10 per cent via internet instant messaging.

Details from: www.ipa.co.uk/content/touchpoints-site-home.

---

during tournaments.[40] In Munich, golf players can play from tees sponsored by BMW for the International Open and the English football club Arsenal has a stadium which is called 'Emirates Stadium', which is related to the Saudi Arabian airline, reinforcing the message that these organisations are at the top of their game and compete at the highest levels.[41]

The internet provides a unique environment for promotional messages because it can include text, audio, video, hyperlinking and personalisation, not to mention opportunities for interaction with customers and other stakeholders. Websites can come alive with the right mix of technical wizardry and good design. One advantage of the web is that companies can give customers a 'feel' for their products or services before they buy. Even nightclubs are going to the web to draw virtual crowds.[42] Sites like Thewomb.com feature real-time footage of what's happening in the clubs.

Step 5: Evaluate the Effectiveness of the Communications Programme

The final step in managing marketing communications is to decide whether the plan is working. The marketer needs to determine whether the communication objectives are adequately translated into marketing communications that are reaching the right target market.

It would be nice if a marketing manager could simply report, 'The €3 million campaign for our revolutionary glow-in-the-dark surfboards brought in €15 million in new sales!' It's not so easy. There are many random factors in the marketing environment: a rival's manufacturing problem, a coincidental photograph of a movie star carrying one of the boards, or perhaps a surge of renewed interest in surfing sparked by a cult film hit like *Blue Crush*.

Still, there are ways to monitor and evaluate the company's communication efforts. The catch is that the effectiveness of some forms of communication is easier to determine than others. As a rule, sales promotions are the easiest to evaluate because they occur over a fixed, usually short period, making it easier to link to sales volume. Advertising researchers measure brand awareness, recall of product benefits communicated through advertising and even the image of the brand before and after an advertising campaign. The firm can analyse and compare the performance of salespeople in different territories, although again it is difficult to rule out other factors that make one salesperson more effective than another. For example, in 2007, the average Media Impact Unit for the Rugby World Cup 2007 was 14,983 UBM in comparison to 32,900 during the Football World Cup in 2006. UBM represents a composite which

Marketing Metrics

Thomson Intermedia

Thomson Intermedia's advertising monitoring service captures pretty much every advertisement run in the UK in every medium – TV, press, direct mail, door drop, internet, outdoor, radio and cinema. It uses advanced technology to capture the images and these are matched with advertising expenditure data which are obtained from the fastest, most authoritative sources. The resulting data – creative and expenditure – is stored on its database and made available over the web 24 hours a day, 7 days a week, 365 days a year. Data goes back several years, and covers every advertiser in every industry. Clients can download individual ads, whole campaigns, or information about the expenditure across entire industry sectors – for any period of time.

integrates audiences from TV, press and radio who are likely to have received the information (age 15+). The score impact on the Rugby World Cup was much lower than the World Cup's in relation to the length of the total games, which lasted for one month and three weeks and one month respectively.[43]

Public relations activities are more difficult to assess because their objectives relate more often to image building than sales volume.

Now that you've read about IMC, and heard the advice for Ian Bruce at the RNIB, read how it worked our for his promotional efforts.

Real People, Real Decisions

How it Worked out at the RNIB

After testing, option 1 was chosen because raffles combined with telemarketing was a fresh fundraising method and the sums of money raised were substantial. Cold-calling turned out to have a high, one in three, acceptance rate and did not create the antagonism or seemingly any brand image damage which cold-calling for donations can sometimes do. This was due to the fact that the RNIB was not directly asking for money, just a little time. In particular the scheme created value for the volunteers selling the tickets, who not only felt good about themselves and were seen to do good by their friends who bought some tickets, but also were able to give time as well as money which increased the value of the exercise for those who participated. At a time when charity telemarketing efforts had a bad reputation, this was a welcome development. In reality, once people had committed to help they often felt obliged to buy any unsold books themselves.

The raffles allowed RNIB to experiment with different prizes to see which was most effective and cash proved better than cars or holidays. Conventional lottery wisdom of having few very large prizes did not seem to be necessary because the lotteries were viewed by purchasers as local (hence expected smaller prizes) and people were buying as much to support a good cause as to win the raffle. RNIB found using blind people to make some of the calls was also an effective and credible strategy. Initially blind volunteers were used to make the calls, but as soon as the operation became successful and

> **Once people had committed to help they often felt obliged to buy any unsold books themselves**

bigger, the sheer volume required telesales agencies to be used which employed mainly fully sighted people. This was a potential problem as the telesales people needed heavy briefings to handle the wide variety of questions asked by people being recruited, which increased costs and slightly decreased the authenticity. The big advantage was that once someone became a volunteer raffle ticket salesperson for their street, their name was on the database for next year's campaign, which meant the following year's call was 'warm' and they were much more likely to participate again. Positive response rates rose to two out of three even though the scheme was being aggressively expanded across the UK. This meant that for the same amount of money spent on recruiting people to sell raffle tickets, each year the number of raffle ticket salespeople grew. Remember it costs up to eight times more to recruit a customer than to keep one!

| Photo 11.6 | Ian Bruce (left) meets Stevie Wonder, a supporter of the RNIB. Source: Ian Bruce |

Marketing Metrics

RNIB

The money raised in the first year of going national was around £400,000 and this reached £7 million after six years. In addition to the total amount, the profitability of the marketing effort was 50 per cent, which was a good return on the marketing investment. Quite apart from the money being raised, the benefit to brand awareness was huge. Each year there are over 400,000 volunteers recruited via telemarketing, many of whom are now very loyal to RNIB. In turn they sell tickets on to their friends and neighbours so the fundraising product and the RNIB brand is reaching many millions of people each year. So RNIB has a double win – more money and more awareness. As Ian Bruce says 'there is a thrill seeing any product's sales go through the roof, but when it is a product raising money for blind people and raising awareness for the charity, then it is really special!'

Chapter Summary

Now that you have finished reading this chapter, you should be able to:

1. **Understand the role of communications for successful marketing.** Firms use promotion and other forms of marketing communication to influence attitudes and behaviour. Through marketing communications, marketers inform consumers about new products, remind them of familiar products, persuade them to choose one alternative over another and build strong customer relationships. Today, firms believe that the integration of marketing communications, where firms look at the communication needs of customers, is essential for successful marketing communication programmes.

2. **Understand the communications model.** The traditional communications model includes a message source that creates an idea, encodes the idea into a message, and transmits the message through some medium. The message is delivered to the receiver, who decodes the message and may provide feedback to the source. Anything that interferes with the communication is called 'noise'.

3. **List and describe the traditional elements of the promotion mix.** The four major elements of marketing communications are known as the promotion mix. Personal selling provides direct contact between a company representative and a customer. Advertising is non-personal communication from an identified sponsor using mass media. Sales promotions stimulate immediate sales by providing incentives to the trade or to consumers. Public relations activities seek to influence the attitudes of various audiences.

4. **Explain how word of mouth marketing, buzz marketing, viral marketing and guerrilla marketing provide effective marketing communications.** Marketers have developed several new options to traditional marketing communications in order to reach 'hard-to-get' consumers. Viral marketing means firms create messages designed to be passed on in an exponential fashion, often electronically. With buzz marketing, marketers use entertainment or news to stimulate consumers to talk about a product or a company to friends and neigh-

bours. These word-of-mouth (WOM) marketing messages are more credible and thus more valuable, especially when unpaid consumers create their own messages. Guerrilla marketing includes promotional strategies that 'ambush' consumers in places they are not expecting it.

5. **Describe integrated marketing communications and its characteristics.** Integrated marketing communications (IMC) includes the planning, development, execution and evaluation of coordinated, measurable persuasive brand communications. IMC programmes mean a firm's marketing communication programmes include a single unified voice, begin with the customer, seek to develop relationships with customers, use targeted communications, use two-way communications, focus on all stakeholders rather than customers only, rely on the effective use of databases, generate a continuous stream of communications, and measure results based on actual feedback.

6. **Explain the important role of database marketing in integrated marketing communications (IMC).** The effective use of databases, key to an IMC strategy, allows organisations to learn about its customers, fine-tune its offerings and build a relationship with its market. Database marketing is interactive, i.e. it requires a response from consumers and it builds relationships allowing the marketer to adapt to consumers' needs. Database marketing provides a means to locate new customers and to stimulate cross-selling of related products. With database marketing, a company can measure the impact of its communication efforts and track which consumers responded.

7. **Explain the stages in developing an IMC plan.** An IMC plan begins with communication objectives, usually stated in terms of communications tasks such as creating awareness, knowledge, desire, product trial and brand loyalty. Which promotion mix elements will be used depends on the overall strategy (that is, a push versus a pull

strategy, the type of product and the stage of the product life cycle).

Promotion budgets are often developed from such rules of thumb as the percentage-of-sales method, the competitive-parity method and the objective-task method. Monies from the total budget are then allocated to various elements of the promotion mix. Designing the promotion mix includes determining what communication tools will be used and the message that will be delivered.

Marketing messages use a variety of different appeals, including those that are rational and others that are emotional in nature. The message may provide one- or two-sided arguments and may or may not draw conclusions. Communication channels must be selected. The internet provides both challenges and opportunities for communication. Finally, marketers monitor and evaluate the promotion efforts to determine if the objectives are being reached.

Key Terms

Chapter Review

 ## Marketing Concepts: Testing Your Knowledge

1. How is IMC different from traditional promotion strategies?

2. Describe the traditional communications model.

3. List the elements of the promotion mix and describe how they are used to deliver personal and mass appeals.

4. What are word-of-mouth marketing, buzz marketing and viral marketing? Why are such activities gaining in popularity?

5. Explain what guerrilla marketing means.

6. What is IMC? Explain the characteristics of IMC.

7. What is database marketing? How do marketers use databases to meet the needs of their customers?

8. List the stages in developing an IMC strategy.

9. Explain the hierarchy of effects and how it is used in communication objectives.

10. Describe the major ways in which firms develop marketing communications budgets.

11. How does the promotion mix vary with push versus pull strategies?

12. What are some different types of appeals marketers may use in their communications strategies?

13. How do marketing evaluate the effectiveness of their communications programmes?

Marketing Concepts: Discussing Choices and Ethical Issues

1. Some people would argue that there is really nothing new about IMC. What do you think?

2. More and more companies are developing word-of-mouth or buzz marketing campaigns. Is buzz marketing just a craze that will fade in a year or two or is it here to stay? Do you think buzz is effective? Why do you feel that way?

3. With an IMC programme, firms need to coordinate all of the marketing communications activities. What do you see as the problems inherent in implementing this?

4. Consumers are becoming concerned that the proliferation of databases is an invasion of an individual's privacy. Do you feel this is a valid concern? How can marketers use databases effectively and, at the same time, protect the rights of individuals?

 ## Marketing Practice: Applying what you've Learned

1. As a marketing consultant, you are frequently asked by clients to develop recommendations for marketing communication strategies. The traditional elements used include advertising, sales promotion, public relations and personal selling. Which of these do you feel would be most effective for each of the following clients?

   a. A company that provides mobile phone services;

   b. A hotel;

   c. A university;

   d. A new soft drink.

2. Again, assume that you are a marketing consultant for one of the clients in question 1. You believe that the client would benefit from guerrilla marketing. Develop several ideas for guerrilla marketing tactics that you feel would be successful for the client.

3. As the director of marketing for a small firm that markets environmentally friendly household cleaning supplies, you are developing a marketing communication plan. With one or more of your classmates, provide suggestions for each of the following items. Then, in a role-playing situation, present your recommendations to the client:

   a. Marketing communication objectives;

   b. A method for determining the communication budget;

   c. The use of a push strategy or a pull strategy;

   d. Elements of the promotion mix you will use.

4. Assume that you are the word-of-mouth marketing manager for a sports shoe company such as Footlocker. Develop ideas on how to create buzz for your company's products.

5. As the marketing manager for a chain of bookshops, you are interested in developing a database marketing plan. Give your recommendations for the following:

   a. How to generate a customer database;

   b. How to use the database to better understand your customers;

   c. How to increase sales from your existing customers using your database;

   d. How to get new customers using your database.

6. As a member of the marketing department for a manufacturer of handheld power tools for home improvement, you have been directed to select a new agency to do the promotion for your firm. Of two agencies solicited, one recommends an IMC plan and the other has developed recommendations for a traditional advertising plan. Write a memo to your boss explaining each of the following:

   a. What is different about an IMC plan?

   b. Why is the IMC plan superior to conventional advertising?

 ## Marketing Miniproject: Learning by Doing

This miniproject is designed to help you understand how organisations use database marketing.

1. Visit your university alumni office and ask to discuss how it uses database marketing to enhance participation of alumni in the programmes of the university and in fundraising. Some of the questions you might ask include the following:

   a. How the office obtains names for an initial or expanded database;

   b. What information is included in the initial database;

   c. What information is added to the database;

   d. How the office uses the database for communicating with alumni.

2. Based on what you learn, consider other ways the school might use database marketing for enhancing its alumni programmes and its fundraising.

3. Make a presentation of your findings and recommendations to your class.

Real People, Real Surfers

Exploring the Web

A vast majority of traditional media (television stations, newspapers, magazines and radio stations) are now using the web to build relationships with readers and viewers. For the media, the internet provides an excellent way to build a database and to communicate one on one with customers.

Although individual sites change frequently, some media sites that have provided opportunities for interactive communications with customers and for building a database are the following:

Business Week (www.businessweek.com)

Financial Times (www.ft.com)

Advertising Age (www.adage.com)

Brand Republic (www.brandrepublic.com)

Explore these or other sites that provide opportunities for consumers to register, answer questionnaires, or in some other way use the internet to build a database. After completing your exploration of each site, answer the following questions:

1. In what ways does each website facilitate interactive communications between the firm and customers?

2. How does each firm use the internet to gather information on customers? What information is gathered? Which site does a superior job of gathering information, and why?

3. How do you think the firm might use the information it gathers through the internet in database marketing activities? How can the information be used to build relationships with customers and prospective customers?

4. What recommendations do you have for each company to improve the interactive opportunities on its website?

Now, take a look at the website at www.pearsoned.co.uk/solomon to see some videos from YouTube relating to aspects of this chapter.

Marketing in Action Case

Real decisions – Psst! Have you heard?

The next time someone in a pub insists on telling you about an exciting new band or drink, be very suspicious. They may have been paid to talk it up as companies adopt 'stealth' and 'buzz' marketing.

Several years ago, a Premiership football club was trying to sign up fans to its text bulletin service. For 25p a message (working out at around £100 a year), fans would get a text whenever something interesting happened at the club – team selections, injury updates, half-time scores, that sort of thing.

Despite promoting the service in club literature, on its website, and with armies of attractive girls handing out leaflets on match days, the club could not get the rate of new subscriptions to rise above a disappointing 20 a week. So it hired a small marketing agency called Sneeze.

'We got a group of 14 or 16 actors, who were not all football fans, but pretended to be fans', explains Graham Goodkind, Sneeze's founder and chairman. And they went round bars and clubs around the ground, in groups of two, saying that one of their mates had been sacked from work because he kept on getting these text messages and talking to everyone about it, and his boss had had enough and given him the boot. So they were going round with this petition trying to get his job back – kind of a vaguely plausible story.

'And then the actors would pull out of their pocket some crumpled-up leaflet, which was for the text subscription service. They'd have a mobile phone in their pocket, and they'd show them how it worked. "What's the harm in that?" they'd say. And they could have these conversations with lots of people – that was the beauty of it. Two people could spend maybe 20 minutes or half an hour in each pub, working the whole pub. We did it at two home games and reckon we got about 4000 people on the petition in total.'

The petition went in the bin, of course, but subscriptions to the club's texting service soared. 'The week after we had done the activity it went up to 120 sign-ups,' says Goodkind, who is also boss of the Frank PR agency. 'Then you saw that after that it was 125, and the next week was 75, and the next week was 60. That was the talkability, because obviously if you get that service you tell your mates about it. We saw a massive effectiveness.'

> # That was the talkability, because obviously if you get that service you tell your mates about it. We saw a massive effectiveness

Many people might not consider it ethical to promote things to people in this way (although I have checked and it does not seem to constitute fraud). Does Goodkind? '"Ethical" is a funny word', he says. 'That one, I would say, is quite clever and quite sneaky, but no more sneaky than lots of other forms of marketing that go on every day.' Certainly there were no complaints. But when you consider that none of the fans ever discovered that there had been anything to complain about, this is not surprising. Welcome to stealth marketing, one of the new frontiers in twenty-first century selling.

Things to Think About

1. What is your opinion of this marketing campaign?

2. What are the ethical issues involved in stealth marketing?

3. Who should monitor these marketing activities; the club or the agency, the ASA, Ofcom?

Source: Leo Benedictus *The Guardian*, Tuesday 30 January 2007

References

1. Leiss *et al.*, *Social Communication*; George Stigler, 'The Economics of Information', *Journal of Political Economy* (1961), 69.

2. 'Anti-smoking ads to shock parents', *BBC News/Health,* 2004, http://news.bbc.co.uk/1/hi/health/4118857.stm.

3. Shane Coleman, 'PD dentist touches raw nerve with broadcaster', *Sunday Tribune (Ireland),* 28 January 2007.

4. Gert Assmus, 'An Empirical Investigation into the Perception of Vehicle Source Effects', *Journal of Advertising* 7 (Winter 1978), 4–10; for a more thorough discussion of the pros and

cons of different media, see Stephen Baker, *Systematic Approach to Advertising Creativity* (New York: McGraw-Hill, 1979).

5. Sandra O'Loughlin and Steve Miller, 'Marketers Struggle With the "Dark" Side', *Brandweek.com*, 20 February 2007.

6. ASA Annual report, 2007, www.asa.org.uk/ASA_2004_Rebuild/ASAAppBase/AnnualReport2006/ASA_Top10.htm.

7. Sandra Yin, 'Degree of Challenge', *American Demographics* (May 2003), 20–22.

8. Nick Summers, 'College Papers Grow Up; They Have the Ads, the Readers – and Budgets to Match', *Newsweek*, 5 December 2005, 48.

9. Catharine P. Taylor, 'What's In a Word?', *Brandweek*, 24 October 2005, 30.

10. Lois Geller, 'Wow – What a Buzz', *Target Marketing,* June 2005, 21.

11. 'Word of Mouth Marketing Experts Launch New Training Series', *Market Wire*, 9 March 2006.

12. Todd Wasserman, 'Word Games', *Brandweek*, 24 April 2006, 24.

13. Todd Wasserman, 'Blogs Cause Word of Mouth Business to Spread Quickly', *Brandweek*, 3 October 2005, 9.

14. Gemma Charles, 'Buzz finds favour in the UK', *Marketing*, 27 February 2008, 2.

15. Suzanne Vranica, 'Getting Buzz Marketers to Fess Up', *The Wall Street Journal*, 9 February 2005, B9.

16. Wasserman, 'Word Games'.

17. Wasserman, 'Blogs Cause Word of Mouth Business to Spread Quickly'.

18. Ibid.

19. T.L. Stanley, 'Guerrilla Marketers of the Year', *Brandweek*, 27 March 2000, 28; Jeff Green, 'Down with the Dirt Devils', *Brandweek*, 27 March 2000, 41–44; Stephanie Thompson, 'Pepsi Favors Sampling Over Ads for Fruit Drink', *Advertising Age*, 24 January 2000, 8.

20. 'ENGAGEMENT: Trying to score with elusive male demo?', *Advertising Age*, 26 February 2007, S–10

21. Jaimie Seaton, 'Burger King Guns for Rivals in Guerilla Push', *Media*, 9 September 2005, 6.

22. S. Dibb, L. Simkin, M. William and O.C. Ferrel, *Marketing, Concepts and Strategies*, 5th European ed. (Houghton Mifflin, 2006).

23. Tom Eppes, 'From Theory to Practice', Price/McNabb corporate presentation, 2002.

24. John Burnett and Sandra Moriarty, *Marketing Communications: An Integrated Approach* (Upper Saddle River, NJ: Prentice Hall, 1998).

25. Danny Kucharsky, 'Ads on Demand', *Marketing*, 15 May 2006, 9.

26. 'NBC to Hold Online Vote for Top "Friends" Episodes', 7 January 2004, www.wsj.com.

27. Curt Barry, 'Building a Database', *Catalog Age* (August 1992), 65–68.

28. Adrienne Mand, 'IQ News: Jaguar.com Redesign on the Prowl for Luxury Car Buyers', *Adweek.com*, 06 July 1998.

29. Ian P. Murphy, 'Reader's Digest Links Profits Directly to Research', *Marketing News*, 31 March 1997, 7.

30. Elaine Santoro, 'NBO Markets with Style', *Direct Marketing* (February 1992), 28–31, quoted on p. 30.

31. David Benardy, 'Tesco plays its Clubcard right', *Marketing Week*, 3 November 1995, pp. 30–1.

32. Claire Foss, 'Service with a Sale', *Marketing Direct,* 26 July 2007, Special Report, 5.

33. Martin Everett, 'This one's just for you,' *Sales and Marketing Management*, June 1992, 119–126.

34. Paul Gander, 'Make it a season to remember', *Marketing Week* 30(42), 18 October 2007, 35–38.

35. Jack Neff, 'P&G Trims Fat Off its $2B Trade-Promotion System', *Advertising Age*, 5 June 2006, 8.

36. John Borland, 'All Eyes on New DVD Format War', *CnetNews.com*, 11 July 2005.

37. Mariko Sanchanta and Paul Taylor, 'Toshiba ready to abandon DVD war', *Financial Times* (Asia edition), 18 February 2008, 1.

38. Bill Britt, 'Volkswagen Waxes Poetic to Stir Up Emotions and Sales', *Advertising Age*, 29 September 2003, 8.

39. Linda L. Golden and Mark I. Alpert, 'Comparative Analysis of the Relative Effectiveness of One- and Two-Sided Communication for Contrasting Products', *Journal of Advertising* 16 (1987): 18–25; Robert B. Settle and Linda L. Golden, 'Attribution Theory and Advertiser Credibility', *Journal of Marketing Research* 11 (May 1974), 181–85.

40. Dibb *et al.*, *Marketing Concepts and Strategies*, p. 569.

41. 'Emirates back as official airline of S'pore Masters', *The Straits Times (Singapore),* 7 March 2007.

42. Khanh T.L. Tran, 'Lifting the Velvet Rope: Nightclubs Draw Virtual Throngs with Webcasts', 30 August 1999, www.wsj.com.

43. 'Worldwide Event', *The Media Intelligence Journal,* 20 (Fall 2007) www.tnsmi.co.uk/assets/issue20.pdf.

Chapter 12

Advertising, PR, Sales and Sales Promotion

Meet Rick Goings,
a Decision Maker at Tupperware Brands Corporation

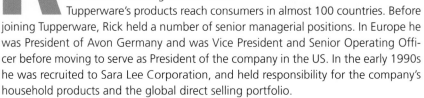

Rick Goings is Chairman and Chief Executive of Tupperware Brands Corporation. Tupperware is one of the world's leading direct sellers. Tupperware's products reach consumers in almost 100 countries. Before joining Tupperware, Rick held a number of senior managerial positions. In Europe he was President of Avon Germany and was Vice President and Senior Operating Officer before moving to serve as President of the company in the US. In the early 1990s he was recruited to Sara Lee Corporation, and held responsibility for the company's household products and the global direct selling portfolio.

In March 2000, the People's Republic of China recognised him with the Marco Polo Award for his visionary leadership, and his role in China's economic development and concern for Chinese society.

Q & A with Rick Goings

Business book I'm reading now:
The One Thing You Need to Know: About Great Managing, Great Leading, and Sustained Individual Success by Marcus Buckingham

My motto to live by:
Character is what you do when no one is watching

What drives me:
To make a difference

My management style:
Hire great people and get out of their way

Don't do this when interviewing with me:
Be boring

My pet peeve:
People who stand on the moving pavements in airports – they are meant to move things faster, not to replace walking

Real People, Real Decisions
Decision Time at Tupperware

Tupperware Brands is a US company that has the privilege of being one of the most recognised brands worldwide. Unfortunately, the company often is remembered for what the product line was and not for what it is today. Additionally, many consumers don't yet understand that selling Tupperware provides an opportunity for women to achieve a better standard of living. Faced with stagnant sales, Tupperware Brands embarked on a series of significant steps to revitalise the company and its products. First, it updated its product line. While protecting its core category of food storage, it expanded into fashion and functionality across housewares to include cookware, cutlery, kitchen tools and gadgets.

The second task was to update Tupperware's brand image and expand aggressively into more countries to promote steady growth for the company. Additionally, Tupperware needed to inform women in these new export markets that they had a chance to achieve their financial and personal goals by selling its products. Tupperware has successfully expanded into the primary emerging markets of Russia, Turkey and Poland as well as China, India and Indonesia. Women in all of these countries have embraced the opportunity to earn money through their own self-motivation instead of being limited by education and background.

However, if the consumer doesn't know about the opportunity or the products, then existing sales force members cannot book parties to sell products and recruit new sales force members, and Tupperware cannot increase its revenue. Rick and his management team had to find a way to refresh the Tupperware brand perception from a seller of plastic food storage to a lifestyle brand full of opportunity that would succeed around the world.

Rick considers his options . . .

Option 1 Increase advertising in new markets

This strategy quickly exposes the brand to millions of consumers. However, mass advertising is very expensive and it's hard to quantify the return on this investment. Additionally, it is now easy for viewers to skip over TV advertisements. Also, Tupperware products are primarily available through parties. This means that rather than seeking out a Tupperware agent to buy a product she likes in an ad, a consumer can instead go to the nearest retailer to purchase a similar product. In addition to being expensive, paid advertising messages placed in women's magazines and other media do not always reach women in foreign markets who still need to be educated about the new Tupperware image. Also, Tupperware will be 'at the mercy' of editors who may decide either not to run a story or to spin a story whichever way they decide. Tupperware currently doesn't advertise, so the company has to convince consumers through its agents that they will get a better value by purchasing a genuine Tupperware product rather than a competing option.

Option 2 Use public relations

PR could be used to spread the word about the fashionability and innovative functionality of the product line as well as the updated party format that makes it easier for salespeople to achieve their goals. A public relations campaign – working with and alongside the press to obtain favourable publicity – in the form of news stories is not as expensive as advertising, yet it can still have a broad reach if it's successful at generating publicity about the new Tupperware product line in television shows and print media.

Option 3 Motivate the salesforce

Build demand for Tupperware products using word of mouth encouraged by the sales force. This strategy allows the sales force to generate business by educating consumers about the brand. But there are probably not enough existing sales force members to reach the millions of new consumers that Tupperware needs to expand, particularly in areas of large population like the emerging markets of China, India and Indonesia. To make matters worse, the current brand perception in these markets isn't strong enough to let Tupperware recruit the number of consultants it needs to increase the sales force to allow it to reach the numbers it needs.

Now, put yourself in Rick's shoes: which option would you choose, and why?

Objectives

When you finish reading this chapter, you will be able to:

1 Explain what advertising is and describe the main types of advertising

2 Explain what sales promotion is and describe the different types of trade and consumer sales promotion activities

3 Explain the role of public relations

4 Understand the important role of personal selling

5 Understand direct marketing

Advertising: The Image of Marketing

Objective

1

Explain what advertising is and describe the main types of advertising

Advertising is so much a part of marketing that many people think of the two as the same thing. As we saw in Chapter 11, that's not the case – there are many ways to get a message out to a target audience. Advertising is still very important – in 2006 the 25 Top Global Marketers spent over €71.25 billion to do it.[1] The top spender in Finland was Elisa with €25.63 million, whereas the Dansk Supermarket was the leading spender in Denmark with €49.25 million. Telenor and Royal Ahold were the biggest advertising spender in Norway and Sweden with €61.88 and €149.38 million respectively.[2] Still, in today's competitive environment, even the biggest companies such as Procter & Gamble and Unilever are rethinking how much they want to invest in pricey ad campaigns as they search for other ways to get their messages out there.

This is especially true as the number of media outlets mushrooms along with the number of TV viewers who use their trusty remote control or perhaps TiVo or Sky+ to skip over ads. 'Personal video recorders' that let viewers skip through commercials are forecast to reach 30 per cent of UK households by 2010 and increasingly these gadgets are available as part of cable-TV boxes.[3] That's why product plugs in films, known as **product placement**, are turning up much more often (no, it's no accident that the logos are so visible!):[4]

● Audi cars are heavily featured in *I, Robot* with Will Smith

● The famous movie *Fight Club* with Brad Pitt includes scenes where an Apple shop is broken into and the headlights of a Volkswagen Beetle are smashed.

● In *Desperate Housewives*, three characters drive Nissans.

● Nokia phones had played a very visible role in the first *Matrix* movie in 1999. They were visible as the entrance and exit points for the characters beaming themselves into the virtual reality mindset.

● Aston Martins are prominently featured in the James Bond film A *Quantum of Solace*.

Check out www.brandchannel.com for more recent examples in their 'brand cameo' section.

Meanwhile, other marketers are taking their messages to the streets as they rely on public relations events in addition to traditional advertising. For example, Coca-Cola opened lounges for teenagers at shopping centres, while BMW scored big points with its series of short films from famous directors that appeared on its website and included people like Madonna (www.bmw.com).[5] There are many ways to communicate with a mass audience. In this chapter, we'll learn about some of the major approaches, beginning with advertising.

Wherever we turn, advertising bombards us. Television commercials, radio spots, banner ads and huge hoardings scream, 'Buy me!' **Advertising** is nonpersonal communication paid for by an identified sponsor using mass media to persuade or inform an audience.[6] Advertising can be fun, glamorous, annoying, informative – and hopefully an effective way to let consumers know what they're selling and why people should run out and buy it *today*.

Advertising has been with us a long time. In ancient Greece and Rome, advertisements appeared on walls and were etched on stone tablets. Would the ancients have believed that today we get messages about products almost wherever we are, whether driving down the road or surfing the web? Some of us even get advertising messages on our mobile phones. It's hard to find a place where ads don't try to reach us.

Advertising is also a potent force that creates desire for products by transporting us to imaginary worlds where the people are happy, beautiful, rich or, annoyingly, all three! In this way, advertising allows the organisation to communicate its message in a favourable way and to repeat the message as often as it deems necessary to have an impact on receivers.

Types of Advertising

Although almost every business advertises, the types of media they choose to use for advertising can vary. In 2004, newspapers were the biggest advertisement medium in Europe, where companies and governments spent a total of €29 billion to advertise various products and services. €27 billion was spent on television and only €5 billion and €2.2 billion were spent on outdoor and internet respectively.[7] Because they spend so much on advertising, marketers must decide which type of ad will work best given their organisational and marketing goals. The advertisements an organisation runs can take many forms, so let's review the most common kinds.

| Photo 12.1 | This advert is designed to stimulate primary demand for milk, a generic product category rather than a brand or organisation. Source: The Advertising Archives |

Product Advertising

When people give examples of advertising, they may recall the provocative poses in Agent Provocateur ads or a catch phrase such as 'Beanz Meanz Heinz' or the artwork from a Guinness poster. These are examples of **product advertising**, where the message focuses on a specific good or service. While not all advertising focuses on a product or a brand, most of the advertising we see and hear is indeed product advertising.

Institutional Advertising

Rather than focusing on a specific brand, **institutional advertising** promotes the activities, personality or point of view of an organisation or company or can be used for recruitment purposes to attract potential employees to jobs. Some institutional messages state a firm's position on an issue to sway public opinion, a strategy called **advocacy advertising**.[8] For example, the Metropolitan Police launched its advocacy campaign against gun crime in London in November 2006. The police force worked closely with creative agencies and media planners and placed the gun-crime video on sites like Myspace.com and Youtube.com to raise awareness.[9] Other messages called **public service advertisements (PSAs)** are advertisements the media run free of charge. These messages promote not-for-profit organisations that serve society in some way, or they champion an issue such as increasing literacy or discouraging drunk driving. Advertising agencies often take on one or more public service campaigns

Photo 12.2	This advert conveys an institutions viewpoint on carbon footprints. Source: The Advertising Archives

on a *pro bono* (for free) basis. Public service advertising has included a campaign featuring the actress Emma Thompson aimed at promoting legislation to fight human trafficking. The campaign, in collaboration with The Body Shop and the Helen Bamber Foundation, shows Thomson from the view of her assailant as she is subjected to forcible, rough sex. Throughout the spot, she relates to two memories, those of Elena, a good girl full of hope and optimism and those of Maria, a prostitute, forced into many sex acts daily. As the spot finishes, Thompson shows that Elena and Maria are the same – a before and after picture of a life destroyed.[10]

Retail and Local Advertising

Both major retailers and small, local businesses advertise to encourage customers to shop at a specific shop or use a local service. Much local advertising informs us about shop hours, location and products that are available or on sale.

Consumer-generated Advertising

Today, in what has been referred to as the 'Generation C' phenomenon, consumer-generated content such as that included in blogs is building on the web. To take advantage of this blog craze, some marketers are encouraging consumers to contribute to their next advertising campaign. In its Dove Cream Oil Body Wash contest, Unilever's Dove brand asked consumers to create their own 30-second commercial to support the launch of its Body Wash collection. The company worked closely with AOL to host the website which carried the contest rules, sample Dove ads, step-by-step tutorials and editing tools. The consumer-made ads were reviewed by an anonymous panel of judges and the winners received an all expenses paid trip to Los Angeles.[11] Other companies that have experimented with DIY advertising are L'oréal ('You Make the Commercial'), JetBlue ('Travel Stories') and McDonald's ('Global Casting').[12] As we saw in Chapter 1, though, putting content in the hands of consumers is risky. During a commercial on the TV show 'The Apprentice' in the US, Chevrolet directed viewers to a website (www.chevyapprentice.com) to create their own ads for the Chevy Tahoe, a popular SUV. As Chevy expected, not all the submissions were complimentary (or suitable for airing on network TV!). In one video, a shiny SUV motors down a country road lined with sunflower fields, jaunty music playing in the background. But then, white lettering appears on the screen: '$70 to fill up the tank, which will last less than 400 miles. Chevy Tahoe'. Another submission asked: 'Like this snowy wilderness? Better get your fill of it now. Then say hello to global warming.' A spokeswoman for Chevrolet observed, 'We anticipated that there would be critical submissions. You do turn over your brand to the public, and we knew that we were going to get some bad with the good. But it's part of playing in this space.'[13]

Who Creates Advertising?

Although the trend towards DIY advertising illustrates how high-tech picture modifying software like Photoshop and Final Cut Pro can help almost anyone to become a director, most advertising is far more complicated. An **advertising campaign** is a coordinated, comprehensive plan that carries out promotion objectives and results in a series of advertisements placed in media over a period of time. Although a campaign may be based around a single ad, most employ multiple messages with all ads in the campaign having the same look and feel.

Creating and executing an advertising campaign often means many companies work together, and it requires a broad range of skilled people to do the job right. Some firms may do their own advertising. In many cases, though, the firm will retain outside *advertising agencies* to develop advertising messages on its behalf. A **limited-service agency** provides one or more specialised services, such as media buying or creative development. A **full-service agency** provides most or all of the services needed to mount a campaign, including research, creation of ad copy and art, media selection and production of the final messages. The five largest global agencies are the J. Walter Thompson Co., McCann-Erickson Worldwide, Leo Burnett Worldwide BBDO Worldwide, and Ogilvy and Mather Worldwide.[14]

A campaign requires many different people to produce. Big or small, an advertising agency hires a range of specialists to craft a message and make the communications concept a reality:

- **Account management:** The *account executive*, or account manager, is the 'soul' of the operation. This person develops the campaign's strategy for the client, supervises the day-to-day activities on the account, and is the primary liaison between the agency and the client. The account executive has to ensure that the client is happy while verifying that people within the agency are executing the desired strategy.

- **Creative services:** *Creatives* are the 'heart' of the communications effort. These are the people who actually dream up and produce the ads. They include the agency's creative director, copywriters and art director. Creatives are the artists who breathe life into marketing objectives and craft messages that (hopefully) will interest consumers.

- **Research and marketing services:** *Researchers* are the 'brains' of the campaign. They collect and analyse information that will help account executives develop a sensible strategy. They assist creatives in getting consumer reactions to different versions of ads or by providing copywriters with details on the target group.

- **Media planning:** The *media planner* is the 'legs' of the campaign. He or she helps to determine which communication vehicles are the most effective, and recommends the most efficient means for delivering the ad by deciding where, when and how often it will appear.

As we saw in Chapter 11, more and more agencies practise integrated marketing communications (IMC) in which advertising is only one element of a total communications plan. Because IMC includes more than just advertising, client teams composed of people from account services, creative services, media planning, research, public relations, sales promotion and direct marketing may work together to develop a plan that best meets the communications needs of each client.

| Photo 12.3 | Advertisers often include imagery to capture the attention of their audiences. Source: The Advertising Archives |

Developing the Advertising Campaign

The advertising campaign is about much more than creating a cool ad and hoping people notice it. The campaign should be intimately related to the organisation's overall communications goals. That means the firm (and its outside agency if it uses one) must have a good idea of whom it wants to reach, what it will take to appeal to this market, and where and when the messages should be placed. Let's examine the steps required to do this (see Figure 12.1).

Step 1: Identify the Target Audiences

The best way to communicate with an audience is to understand as much as possible about them and what turns them on and off. An ad that uses the latest slang may relate to teenagers but not to their parents – and this strategy may backfire if the ad copy reads like a 40-year-old trying to sound like a 20-year-old.

Most advertising is directed towards customers, whether the target audience includes college students or industry executives. As we discussed in Chapter 6, marketers/researchers often identify the target audience for an advertising campaign from research related to a segmentation strategy. Researchers try to get inside the customer's head to understand just how to create a message to which he or she will understand and respond. For example Toyota and Honda sent staff to live with families in order to test how they use their vehicles. This tactic led to the Honda's decision to add backseat room to the 1998 Accord.

Step 2: Establish Message and Budget Objectives

Advertising objectives should be consistent with the overall communications plan. That means that both the underlying message and its costs need to be related to what the marketer is trying to say about the product and what the marketer is willing or able to spend. Thus, advertising objectives generally will include objectives for both the message and the budget.

| Step 1: Identify the Target Audience |
| Step 2: Establish Message and Budget Objectives |
| Step 3: Design the Ads |
| Step 4: Test What the Ads Will Say |
| Step 5: Choose the Media Type(s) and Media Schedule |
| Step 6: Evaluate the Advertising |

Figure 12.1   Steps in Developing an Advertising Campaign
Developing an advertising campaign includes a series of steps that will ensure that the advertising meets communication objectives.

Marketing Metrics

Measuring Value

More and more television viewers are bypassing commercials – whether by switching the channel, fast forwarding, or just getting up to get a snack. Advertisers are demanding a more precise system that will let them know just which of their ads people are actually watching and how captivating their ads are. The firm PreTesting developed a system that 'records saccadic eye motion, the involuntary flicks and darts of the eye as consumers watch TV commercials and read billboards or print advertising'. This passive eye monitoring is a better and more accurate way of gauging a subject's response than focus groups or diaries. With the help of this new technology, the major pharmaceutical company Pfizer figured out that its latest TV ad for its Lipitor cholesterol medicine did not do very well among customers. The commercial featured Robert Jarvik, a well known American scientist and physician known for his role in developing the Jarvik-7 artificial heart medicine. During the ad, he was talking about the benefits of this new Lipitor cholesterol medicine. The saccadic tests revealed however that consumers had a 'blank stare' on Robert Jarvik's face instead on focusing on what he was saying. People were obviously trying to figure out who he was rather than listening to the commercial message.[15]

Setting Message Objectives

As we noted earlier, because advertising is the most visible part of marketing, many people assume that marketing *is* advertising. In truth, advertising alone is quite limited in what it can achieve. What advertising *can* do is to inform, persuade and remind. Accordingly, some advertisements are *informational*; they aim to make the customer knowledgeable about features of the product or how to use it. At other times, advertising seeks to *persuade* consumers to like a brand or to prefer one brand over the competition. But many ads are simply aimed at keeping the name of the brand in front of the consumer – *reminding* consumers that this brand is the one to choose when they go looking for a soft drink or a beefburger or a chocolate bar.

Setting Budget Objectives

Advertising is expensive. In 2006, Unilever, which led all European companies in advertising expenditures, spent €5.75 billion while second and third place ad spenders, l'Oréal and Nestlé spent €3.875 billion and €2.63 billion respectively.[16]

An objective of many firms is to allocate a percentage of its overall communications budget to advertising, depending on how much and what type of advertising the company can afford. Major corporations like Renault advertise heavily, using expensive media such as television to promote multiple products throughout the year. Other companies may be more selective, and smaller firms may want to put their advertising euros into cheaper media outlets, such as direct mail or trade publications.

The major approaches and techniques to setting overall promotional budgets, such as the percentage-of-sales and objective-task methods we discussed in Chapter 11, also set advertising budgets.

 ## Step 3: Design the Ads

Creative strategy is the process that turns a concept into an advertisement. It's one thing to know *what* a company wants to say about itself and its products, and another to figure out *how* to say it. Some marketers like to think of the creative process for an advertising campaign as the 'spark between objective and execution'.

The goal of an advertising campaign is to present a series of messages and repeat it to a sufficient degree to meet the desired objectives. To do this, advertising creatives – art directors, copywriters, photographers and others – must develop a 'big idea', a concept that expresses aspects of the product, service or organisation in a tangible, attention-getting, memorable manner.

An **advertising appeal** is the central idea of the ad. Some advertisers use an emotional appeal complete with dramatic colour or powerful images, while others bombard the audience with facts. Some feature sexy people or stern-looking experts – even professors from time to time. Different appeals can work for the same product, from a bland 'talking head' to a montage of animated special effects. An attention-getting way to say something profound about cat food or laundry detergent is more art than science, but we can describe some common appeals:

- **Reasons why: A unique selling proposition (USP)** gives consumers a single, clear reason why one product is better at solving a problem. The format focuses on a need and points out how the product can satisfy it. For example, 'M&Ms melt in your mouth, not in your hands' is a USP. In general, a USP strategy is effective if there is some clear product advantage that consumers can readily identify and that is important to them.

- **Comparative advertising:** A comparative advertisement explicitly names one or more competitors. Comparative ads can be very effective, but there is a risk of turning off consumers who don't like the negative tone. While in many countries comparative advertising is illegal, it's a widely used tactic in the UK. Think about supermarkets such as Tesco and Sainsbury's who compare each other's prices in ads. Comparative advertising is best for brands that have a smaller share of the market, and for those firms that can focus on a specific feature that makes them superior to a major brand. When market leaders use comparative advertising, there is the risk consumers will feel that 'Goliath is picking on David!'

- **Demonstration:** The ad shows a product 'in action' to prove that it performs as claimed: 'It slices, it dices!' Demonstration advertising is most useful when consumers are unable to identify important benefits except by seeing the product in use. Who has not seen the numerous TV product advertisement shows where entire products like juice mixer, rasps or vacuum cleaners are seen in action under various conditions. The British firm Acdoco ran an ad for its laundry colour protector Glo Care Colour Catcher. The advertisements were set inside a washing machine and showed the product in action.[17]

- **Testimonial:** A celebrity, an expert, or a 'man in the street' states the product's effectiveness. Think about toothpaste ads that use dental practice managers, or make-up ads that use 'Hollywood make-up artists' to endorse products. The use of *celebrity endorsers* is a common, but expensive strategy, e.g. David Beckham and Motorola or Kate Moss and Rimmel. It is particularly effective for mature products that need to differentiate themselves from competitors, such as Coke and Pepsi that enlist celebrities to tout one cola over another.[18]

- **Slice of life:** A *slice-of-life* format presents a (dramatised) scene from everyday life. Slice-of-life advertising can be effective for everyday products such as washing powders and headache remedies that consumers may feel good about if they see 'real' people buying and using them. Washing powder commercials often feature typical dirty washing family scenarios or the 'Bisto family' sitting down to dinner each night.

- **Lifestyle:** A lifestyle format shows a person or persons attractive to the target market in an appealing setting. The advertised product is 'part of the scene', implying that the person who buys it will attain the lifestyle.

- **Fear appeals:** This tactic highlights the negative consequences of *not* using a product. Some fear appeal ads focus on physical harm, while others try to create concern for social harm or disapproval. Mouthwash, deodorant, dandruff shampoo makers and life insurance companies have successfully used fear appeals, as have ads aimed at changing behaviour, such as messages discouraging drug use or encouraging safe sex. Over-50s life insurance ads often start with 'what would happen to your loved ones if you were taken seriously ill or died?'

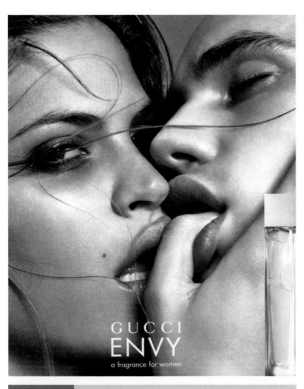

| Photo 12.4 | Companies often create eye-catching campaigns by using sex appeal to draw attention.
Source: The Advertising Archives |

- **Sex appeals:** Some ads appear to be selling sex rather than products. In a Dolce & Gabbana advertisement for watches, various topless men and women lie next to each other while showing their watches. Ads such as these rely on sexuality to get consumers' attention. Sex appeal ads are more likely to be effective when there is a connection between the product and sex (or at least romance). For example, sex appeals will work well with a perfume but are less likely to be effective when selling a lawn mower.

- **Humorous appeals:** Humorous ads can be a way to break through advertising clutter. But humour can be tricky, because what is funny to one person may be offensive or stupid to another. Different cultures also have different senses of humour. A Reebok commercial in the US showed women at a basketball game checking out the all-male cheerleading squad – people from countries who don't have cheerleaders (you don't find too many pom-poms at football matches) might not 'get it'. Perhaps the benefit of humorous advertising is that it attracts consumers' attention and leaves them with a pleasant feeling. Of course, humour can backfire. In the UK, a Renault Megane 225 ad featuring people in everyday situations shaking uncontrollably as the car passed by was banned by the government's Office of Communications after viewers complained that the ad mocked people with illnesses such as Parkinson's disease.[19] Check out www.pearsoned.co.uk/solomon to see some of the funniest ads.

- **Slogans and jingles:** Slogans link the brand to a simple linguistic device that is memorable. Jingles do the same but set the slogan to music. We usually have no trouble reciting successful slogans (sometimes years after the campaign has ended) think of such die-hards as McDonald's 'I'm lovin' it', Sainsbury's 'Try Something New', Merrill Lynch's 'Be bullish', Thomas Cook's 'Don't just book it, Thomas Cook it', Nokia's 'Nokia has everyone talking', Orange's 'The future's bright, the future's Orange', IKEA's 'Make yourself at home' or P&G's 'Please don't squeeze the Charmin'.

 ## Step 4: Pre-test What the Ads will Say

Now that the creatives have worked their magic, how does the agency know if the campaign ideas will work? Advertisers try to minimise mistakes by getting reactions to ad messages before they actually place them. Much of this **pre-testing**, the research that goes on in the early stages of a campaign centres on gathering basic information that will help planners be sure they've accurately defined the product's market, consumers and competitors. As we saw in Chapter 3, this information comes from quantitative sources, such as syndicated surveys, and qualitative sources, such as focus groups.

As the campaign takes shape, the players need to determine how well the advertising concepts will perform. **Copy testing** measures the effectiveness of ads. This process determines whether consumers are receiving, comprehending, and responding to the ad according to plan.

Marketing Ethics

Puffery

Often ads, although not illegal, create a biased impression of products with the use of **puffery** – claims of superiority that neither sponsors nor critics of the ads can prove are true or untrue. For example, Nivea bills itself as 'the world's number 1 name in skin care', Neutrogena claims that its cream cleanser produces 'the deepest feeling clean', and DuPont says that its Stainmaster Carpet is 'a creation so remarkable, it's practically a miracle'.

Debate, Discuss, Disagree

1   How harmful is a little exaggeration?

2   Don't consumers expect and adjust for it?

3   What are the dangers to the marketing discipline of puffery in advertising?

Step 5: Choose the Media Type(s) and Media Schedule

Media planning is a problem-solving process for getting a message to a target audience in the most effective way. When reading this section, think about which media type might suit option 1 for Rick at Tupperware. Planning decisions include audience selection and where, when, and how frequent the exposure should be. Thus, the first task for a media planner is to find out when and where people in the target market are most likely to be exposed to the communication. This is called an **aperture**, the best 'window' to reach the target market. Many university students read the campus newspaper in the morning, so their aperture would include this medium at this time.

There is no such thing as one perfect medium for advertising. The choice depends on the specific target audience, the objective of the message, and, of course, the budget. For the advertising campaign to be effective, the media planner must match up the profile of the target market with specific media vehicles. For example, many young consumers are avid web users, so marketers wishing to reach this segment might allocate a relatively large share of their advertising budget to buying online advertising.

Choosing the right mix of media is no laughing matter, especially as new options including videos and DVDs, video games, personal computers, the internet, MP3 players, hundreds of new TV channels, and even satellite radio now vie for our attention. Consider that by 2008, approximately 13 million British households had satellite and cable TV in their households, a 35 per cent increase since 2002. In the UK, the battle for dominance in the world of satellite and cable TV had boiled down to a fight between two main players: BSkyB and Virgin Media. In recent years, people are spending a lot more time watching cable and satellite channels, which explains the fierce fight for further market share by the two companies.[20] Figure 12.2 highlights some of these dramatic changes.

Where to Say It: Traditional Media

What does a 52-inch plasma TV with Dolby Surround Sound have in common with a bus ticket? Each is a media vehicle that permits an advertiser to communicate with a potential customer. Depending on the intended message, each medium has its advantages and

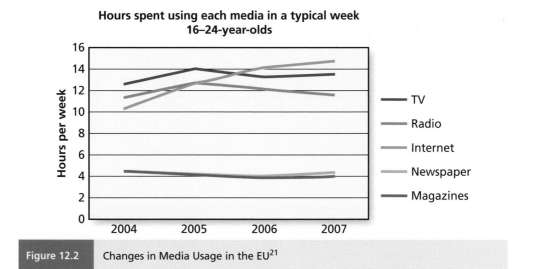

Figure 12.2 | Changes in Media Usage in the EU[21]

disadvantages. Let's take a look at the major categories of media (Table 12.1 summarises some of the pros and cons of each type).

● **Television:** Because of television's ability to reach so many people at once, it's the medium of choice for regional or national companies. Today there are literally hundreds of television choices available to advertisers. However, advertising on a television network can be very expensive. The cost to place a single 30-second ad on a popular prime-time TV show normally ranges between €300,000 and €750,000, depending on the size of the show's audience. Advertisers may prefer to buy cable, satellite or local television time rather than national network time because it's cheaper or because they want to reach a more targeted market, such as 'foodies' who are into cooking. Nevertheless, 78 per cent of advertisers say TV advertising has become less effective as DVRs and video-on-demand grow in popularity.[22]

Marketing Ethics

Secrets and Lies of Beauty Industry Laid Bare by Advertising

The cosmetics market is thought to be worth more than £15 billion worldwide, but expensive beauty products are not doing what they say on the pack. They are promoted as products that will rejuvenate and bring bounce to your hair and a little brilliance to your demeanour. In a ruthlessly competitive market, pseudoscientific claims have become common. In a warning shot to an industry reliant on increasingly extreme claims, the Advertising Standards Authority upheld complaints about 'amino-acid replenishing' shampoo. Some claims attached to the product – Procter & Gamble UK's Pantene Pro-V shampoo – were found to be misleading and unsubstantiated, the watchdog ruled. A television advertisement for Pantene Pro-V, which promised to make hair 'up to ten times stronger' and would 'put back what life takes out', also misled viewers.

The Times, 11 May 2005

Debate, Discuss, Disagree

1 What is the main cause of misleading advertising?

2 Should companies be forced to run ads explaining how it was misleading and correcting the perception?

Vehicle	Pros	Cons
Television	• Extremely creative and flexible. • National TV is the most cost-effective way to reach a mass audience. • Cable and satellite TV allow the advertiser to reach a selected group at relatively low cost. • A prestigious way to advertise. • Can demonstrate product in use. • Can provide entertainment and generate excitement. • Messages have high impact because of the use of sight and sound.	• The message is quickly forgotten unless it is repeated often. • The audience is increasingly fragmented. • Although the relative cost of reaching the audience is low, prices are still high on an absolute basis – often too high for smaller companies. • Fewer people are viewing national television. • People switch from station to station zapping commercials. • Rising costs have led to more and shorter ads, causing more clutter.
Radio	• Good for selectively targeting an audience. • Is heard out of the home. • Can reach customers on a personal and intimate level. • Can use local personalities. • Relatively low cost, both for producing a spot and for running it repeatedly. • Because of short lead time, radio ads can be modified quickly to reflect changes in the marketplace. • Use of sound effects and music allows listeners to use their imagination to create a vivid scene.	• Listeners often don't pay full attention to what they hear. • Difficulty in buying radio time, especially for national advertisers. • Not appropriate for products that must be seen or demonstrated to be appreciated. • The small audience of individual stations means ads must be placed with many different stations and must be repeated frequently.
Newspapers	• Wide exposure provides extensive market coverage. • Flexible format permits the use of colour, different size ads, and targeted editions. • Ability to use detailed copy. • Allows local retailers to tie in with national advertisers. • People are in the right mental frame to process advertisements about new products, sales, etc. • Timeliness, i.e., short lead time between placing ad and having it run.	• Most people don't spend much time reading the newspaper. • Readership is especially low among teens and young adults. • Short life span – people rarely look at a newspaper more than once. • Very cluttered ad environment. • The reproduction quality of images is relatively poor. • Not effective in reaching specific audiences.
Magazines	• Audiences can be narrowly targeted by specialised magazines. • High credibility and interest level provide a good environment for ads. • Magazines have a long life and are often passed along to other readers. • Visual quality is excellent. • Can provide detailed product information with a sense of authority.	• Expensive: with the exception of direct mail, the highest cost per exposure. • Long deadlines reduce flexibility. • The advertiser must generally use several magazines to reach the majority of a target market. • Clutter.
Outdoor	• Most of the population can be reached at low cost. • Good for supplementing other media. • High frequency when signs are located in heavy traffic areas. • Effective for reaching virtually all segments of the population. • Geographic flexibility.	• Hard to communicate complex messages because of short exposure time. • Difficult to measure advertisement's audience. • Controversial and disliked in many communities. • Cannot pinpoint specific market segments.
Direct response	• Ads can target extremely narrow audiences. • Messages can be timed by the advertiser at his or her convenience. • Easy to measure the effectiveness of ads.	• High cost per exposure. • Target lists must be constantly updated. • Ads lack credibility among many consumers.

Table 12.1 Pros and Cons of Media Vehicles

Sources: Adapted from Thomas J. Russell and Ron Lane, *Kleppner's Advertising Procedure*, 15th ed. (Upper Saddle River, NJ: Prentice Hall, 2002); Terence A. Shimp, *Advertising, Promtion and Supplemental Aspects of Integrated Marketing Communications*, 6th ed. (Australia: Thomson Southwestern, 2003); and William Wells, John Burnett, and Sandra Moriarty, *Advertising: Principles and Practice*, 6th ed. (Upper Saddle River, NJ: Prentice Hall, 2003).

Marketing Metrics

Measuring Magazine Value

Marketing managers and media planners have a difficult time measuring a magazine's reach in time spans shorter than several months. Lately, magazines have been getting pressure to devise a system that provides readership measures more quickly and that also do a better job of tracking the total audience and the effectiveness of specific ads that run in an issue. More and more advertisement pricing in magazines is being linked to its effectiveness and return on investment – and on a short-term timescale. McPheters & Co. runs a website called Readership.com that is designed to do just this task: provide real-time information about a magazine's audience and distribution as well as audience engagement on an individual-issue basis.[23]

- **Radio:** Radio as an advertising medium goes back to 1922 in the US, when a New York City apartment manager went on the air to advertise properties for rent. One advantage of radio advertising is flexibility. Marketers can change commercials quickly, often on the spot by an announcer and a recording engineer.[24] Radio is attractive to advertisers seeking low cost and the ability to reach specific consumer segments.

- **Newspapers:** The newspaper is among the oldest types of media. Retailers in particular have relied on newspaper ads since the Victorian era to inform readers about sales and deliveries of new merchandise. Newspapers are an excellent medium for local advertising and for events (such as shop sales) that require a quick response. Today, most newspapers also offer online versions of their papers to expand their exposure.

- **Magazines:** Approximately 92 per cent of adults look through at least one magazine per month. New technologies such as *selective binding* allow publishers to personalise their editions, so that advertisements for local businesses can be included in issues distributed at specific locations only.

| Photo 12.5 | Out-of-home media provide an excellent way to reach consumers on the go. Posters such as this one certainly grab our attention. Source: The Advertising Archives |

- **Directories:** Directory advertising is the most 'down-to-earth', information-focused advertising medium. In 1883, a printer in the US ran out of white paper while printing part of a telephone book, so he substituted yellow paper instead. Today, the Yellow Pages are still well-known throughout the world. The Yell Group is a leading international directories business covering markets such as the United Kingdom, United States, Spain and Latin America with products such as Yellow Pages, Business Pages, Yell.com and Yellow Book USA. Its Yellow Pages have been connecting buyers and sellers in the UK for over 40 years; 28.3 million copies were distributed in 2007 in the UK, having approximately 480,000 unique advertisers included. In 2007, the group had revenues of £2.075 billion.

- **Out-of-home media: Out-of-home media**, such as airships, transit ads and hoardings, reach people in public places. This medium works best when it tells a simple, straightforward story.[25] For example, to make sure it was not upstaged by Nike or other rivals, Adidas constructed a massive 3D advertisement at

Munich airport for the 2006 World Cup. The billboard was stretched over the whole highway and received a lot of attention.[26] In the Netherlands, Hotels.nl, an online reservation company fitted 144 sheep with logo-emblazoned blankets. The advertising agency that created the 'sheep boards' plans to offer blankets for horses and cows in the future.[27]

● **Place-based media:** Marketers are constantly searching for new ways to get their messages out to busy people. The European low-cost airline Germanwings even transformed the entire interior of its aeroplanes into advertising spaces. The inside of the airplane is painted in the firm's colours – lilac and yellow. Further ads can be seen on areas like the front wall or the luggage flap. **Place-based media** like 'The Airport Channel' transmit messages to 'captive audiences' in public places, such as doctors' offices and airports. At Luton Airport (London) easyJet shows videos on various screens before the check-in to educate people about the procedures that will take place (check-in, security check, boarding process). In one scene of the film, a woman goes through the security check and takes out her Apple laptop in order to let it be X-rayed. Throughout the whole video, you also see various easyJet ads of their products. Another example of place-based media is *in-store TV*. For example, the British supermarket chain ASDA sells advertising space on its in-store TV channel 'ASDA live'.[28] Tesco uses the outdoor media company JCDecaux, the bus stop poster people, to sell space for its Tesco TV network.

And now, some retailers can even follow you around the shop to deliver more intimate and personal messages: a new technology called *RFID* (radio frequency identification) tracks customers as they make their way through the aisles. So a shopper might receive a beep to remind her she just passed her family's favourite peanut butter.[29] You're not paranoid; they really *are* watching you!

Internet Advertising

The web gives marketers the ability to reach customers in new and exciting ways. Online advertising has grown in the European Union to €6.8 billion in 2007, having substantially increased in the latter years. In the EU in 2005, the UK was the biggest spender on the internet with €2 billion, closely followed by France and Germany with €382 and €369 million respectively.[30] Online advertising offers several advantages. First, the internet provides new ways to finely target customers. Web user registrations and *cookies* allow sites to track user preferences and deliver ads based on previous internet behaviour. In addition, because the website can track how many times an ad is 'clicked', advertisers can measure how people are responding to online messages. Finally, online advertising can be interactive – it lets consumers participate in the advertising campaign. Guinness ran an interactive ad on Sky TV in the UK which aimed to educate viewers on how to pour the perfect pint of Guinness. The campaign consisted of video footage, a game to win a pint glass, a poll for the best Guinness ad and references to Guinness' association with the Premiership.[31] Vodafone Netherlands recently launched its KijkMij TV (Look at me) initiative, which involves not only customers uploading their (cameraphone) videos in different categories (funniest, sexiest, most informative) but also pays these 'minipreneurs' 10 per cent of revenues generated when other customers download their video. Vodafone works with PayPal's MassPay in order to pay out accrued earnings when accounts surpass €10 (which equals approximately 400 downloads).[32]

Specific forms of internet advertising include banners, buttons, pop-up ads, search engines and directories, and e-mail:

- **Banners:** These rectangular graphics at the top or bottom of web pages were the first form of web advertising. Although the effectiveness of banners remains in question (banners now receive less than a one per cent click-through rate), they still remain the most popular form of web advertising.

- **Buttons:** These are small banner-type advertisements that a company can place anywhere on a page. Early in the life of the internet, buttons encouraging surfers to 'Download Netscape Now' became a standard on many websites and were responsible for much of Netscape's early success.

- **Search engine and directory listings:** Just as the Yellow Pages and other directories are advertising media, so too are search engines and online directory listings. Increasingly, firms are paying search engines for more visible or higher placement on results lists. Who have you Googled today?

Marketing Metrics

The more clicks, the more sticks

As more and more companies start to allocate some of their advertising budgets to the online space, they need to know whether this is an effective strategy and to learn more about which kinds of ads are more likely to have an impact on web surfers. A metric called 'stickiness' is the Holy Grail for many web advertisers. A 'sticky' website is one that holds people's attention so that they are motivated to stay at the site for a long time – which in turn means they are more likely to absorb the advertising information they see there and/or make a purchase. Stickiness can be computed by combining some of the same metrics (like reach and frequency) that marketers use to calculate the effectiveness of other forms of advertising:[33]

Frequency = the number of visits to a website divided by the number of unique visitors (since the same person can click on a website as frequently as they want).

Duration = the total number of minutes visitors spend viewing web pages divided by the number of visits during the month.

Reach = the number of unique visitors during the month divided by the total number of visitors to the site.

Stickiness = frequency × duration × reach.

Consider the following example of visits to a company's website in two successive months. Although more people visited the website in February, this basic measure of website attractiveness can be misleading. In reality, the content on the website in January was 'stickier', because those people came back more times.

	January	February
Number of visits	10,000	11,000
Number of unique visitors during month	4,000	5,000
Total unique visitors acquired by site	8,000	9,000
Frequency	2.5	2.2
Total number of viewing minutes	1,920,000	2,112,000
Duration	192.00	192.00
Reach	50%	55.6%
Monthly stickiness	240.00	234.67

- **Pop-up ads:** A pop-up ad is an advertisement that appears on the screen while a web page is being loaded or after it is loaded. Because pop-up ads take the centre of the screen while surfers are waiting for the desired page to load, they are difficult to ignore. Because many surfers find pop-ups a nuisance, most internet access software provides an option that blocks all pop-ups. A pop-up ad opens a separate browser window. Web advertisers are typically charged only if people actually click through to the ad.

- **E-mail:** For advertising, e-mail is becoming as pervasive as radio and television. It is one of the easiest ways of communicating with consumers because marketers can send unsolicited e-mail advertising messages to thousands of users by *spamming* – sending unsolicited e-mail to five or more people not personally known to the sender. Many websites that offer e-mail give surfers the opportunity to refuse unsolicited email via junk email blockers. This **permission marketing** gives the consumer the power to opt in or out. Spamming, however, is not always legal and can result in lawsuits if it is proven that practices have violated laws. In 2003, Microsoft claimed a victory in the fight against spamming when a man who called himself the 'Spam King' agreed to pay the company €8.05 million. The man's US-based company was alleged to have been one of the world's biggest spammers, sending out 38 billion emails a year.[34]

Media Scheduling: When to Say It

After choosing the advertising medium, the planner then creates a **media schedule** that specifies the exact media to use for the campaign as well as when and how often the message should appear. Figure 12.3 shows a hypothetical media schedule for the promotion of a new video game. Note that much of the advertising reaches its target audience in the months just before Christmas and that much of the expensive television budget is focused on advertising during specials at a time when people are buying presents. An extension of this logic is the purchase frequency. For weekly purchases such as bread, a weekly ad schedule would be more appropriate than for cold remedies, which are highly seasonal.

The media schedule outlines the planner's best estimate of which media will be most effective in attaining the advertising objective(s) and which specific media vehicles will do the most effective job. The media planner considers such factors as the match between the demographic and psychographic profile of a target audience and the people reached by a

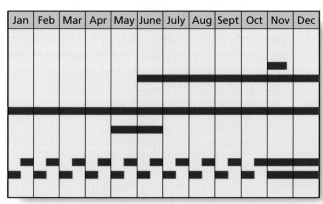

	Figure 12.3	Media Schedule for a Video Game
		Media planning includes decisions on where, when and how much advertising will be done. A media schedule such as this one for a video game shows the plan visually.

media vehicle, the advertising patterns of competitors, and the capability of a medium to convey the desired information adequately. The planner must also consider such factors as the compatibility of the product with editorial content. For example, viewers might not respond well to a lighthearted ad for a new snack food during a sombre documentary on world hunger.

When analysing media, the planner is interested in assessing **advertising exposure**; the degree to which the target market will see an advertising message in a specific medium. Media planners speak in terms of **impressions**; the number of people who will be exposed to a message placed in one or more media vehicles. For example, if 5 million people watch *MTV Total Request Live* on television, then each time an advertiser runs an ad during that programme it gets 5 million impressions. If the advertiser's spot runs four times during the programme, the impression count would be 20 million (even though some of these impressions would represent repeated exposure to the same viewers).

To calculate the exposure a message will have if placed in a certain medium, planners consider two factors: reach and frequency. **Reach** is the percentage of the target market that will be exposed to the media vehicle at least one time. This measure is particularly important for widely used products when the message needs to get to as many consumers as possible. **Frequency** is the average number of times that these members of the target market will be exposed to the message. This measure is important for products that are complex or those that are targeted to relatively small markets for which many exposures to the message are necessary to make an impact.

Say that a media planner wants to be sure her advertising for 18–30s holidays reaches university students. She learns that 25 per cent of the target market reads at least a few issues of *NME* music magazine each year (that's *reach*). She may also determine that these students on average are likely to see three of the 12 monthly ads that 18–30s holidays will run in *NME* during the year (that's *frequency*). Now, she calculates the magazine's **gross rating points (GRPs)** by multiplying reach by frequency, which in this case allows the media planner to compare the effectiveness of *NME* with other media. By using this same formula, the planner could then compare this GRP number to another magazine or to the GRP of placing an ad on television or on a bus or any other advertising medium.

Although some media vehicles deliver superior exposure, they may not be cost efficient. More people will see a commercial aired during the European Football Championship than during a 3.00 a.m. re-run of a Tarzan film. But the advertiser could run late-night commercials every night for a year for the cost of one 30-second European Football Championship Final spot. To compare the relative cost effectiveness of different media and of spots run on different vehicles in the same medium, media planners use a measure called **cost per thousand (CPT)**. This figure reflects the cost to deliver a message to 1000 people. CPT allows advertisers to compare the relative cost effectiveness of different media vehicles that have different exposure rates. CPM, the cost of a thousand impressions, is used for websites.

A medium's popularity with consumers determines how much advertisers must pay to put their message there. Television networks are concerned about the size of their audiences because their advertising rates are determined by how many viewers their programming attracts. Similarly, magazines and newspapers try to boost circulation (that explains all the freebies you get) so they can charge higher rates to their advertising clients.

Media Scheduling: How Often to Say It

After deciding where and when to advertise, the planner must decide how often. What time of day? And what overall pattern will the advertising follow?

A *continuous schedule* maintains a steady stream of advertising throughout the year. This is most appropriate for products that we buy on a regular basis, such as shampoo or bread as well as unwanted goods such as household services like plumbers and electricians who often advertise continually in classified ads or directories. Some advertising industry trade groups maintain that continuous advertising sustains market leadership even if total industry sales fall.[35] On the downside, some messages can suffer from *advertising wear-out* because people ignore the same old ad messages.

A *pulsing schedule* varies the amount of advertising throughout the year based on when the product is likely to be in demand. A suntan lotion might advertise year-round but more heavily during the summer months. *Flighting* is an extreme form of pulsing in which advertising appears in short, intense bursts alternating with periods of little to no activity. It can produce as much brand awareness as a steady dose of advertising at a much lower cost if the messages from the previous flight were noticed.

Step 6: Evaluate the Advertising

A famous comment usually attributed to Lord Leverhulme goes: 'I am certain that half the money I spend on advertising is completely wasted. The trouble is, I don't know which half.'[36] Now that we've seen how advertising is created and executed, let's step back and see how we decide if it's working.

There's no doubt that a lot of advertising is ineffective. Ironically, as marketers try harder and harder to reach their customers, these efforts can backfire. Many consumers have a love–hate relationship with advertising. Over half the respondents in one survey said they 'avoid buying products that overwhelm them with advertising and marketing', and 60 per cent said their opinion of advertising 'is much more negative than just a few years ago'.[37] With so many messages competing for the attention of frazzled customers, it's especially important for firms to evaluate their efforts to increase the effect of their messages. How can they do that? Often advertisers do this by post-testing their advertising campaigns.

Post-testing means conducting research on consumers' responses to advertising messages they have seen or heard (as opposed to *pre-testing*, which as we've seen collects reactions to messages *before* they're actually placed in 'the real world'). Ironically, many creative ads that are quirky or even bizarre make an advertising agency look good within the industry (and on the CV of the art director), but are ultimately unsuccessful because they don't communicate what needs to be said about the product itself. On the other hand, nowadays to say less is to say more to consumers. The audience is bombarded with so much information that advertisers are left with little option but to try a different approach to reach people. If you think of brands such as Apple, O_2, easyJet, Tesco or Nike you will have an instant impression. These advertisers understand this concept. By saying less, they seem to tell the viewer more. Just think of the ad for the iPods from Apple. In the spot you see the black profile of dancing people and the only shiny object in the spot is the white iPod.[38]

Three ways to measure the impact of an advertisement are *unaided recall*, *aided recall* and *attitudinal measures*. **Unaided recall** tests by telephone survey or personal interview whether a person remembers seeing an ad during a specified period of time without giving the person the name of the brand. An **aided recall** test uses the name of the brand and sometimes other clues to prompt answers. For example, a researcher might show a group of consumers a list of brands and ask them to choose which items they have seen advertised within the past week. **Attitudinal measures** probe a bit more deeply by testing consumer beliefs or feelings about a product before and after being exposed to messages about it. If, for example, Colgate's messages about '24 hour protection' make enough consumers believe that Colgate can protect their teeth for a whole day, marketers can consider the advertising campaign successful.

Marketing Metrics

Measuring Value

Traditional television advertising is being challenged by direct-response advertising; one reason is that it's easier to evaluate the immediate impact of spots that call upon viewers to call an 0800 number or log on to a website NOW to order the advertised product. Direct response TV (DRTV) was once utilised only for gimmicks during daytime hours on rarely watched cable channels. Today, it's a different story: Even Procter & Gamble, the largest conventional advertiser in many EU markets, has bought into the idea. P&G initially explored DRTV with Dryel, a low-priority brand, but the company has now broadened its direct response advertising to include spots for Cover Girl, Iams, Old Spice and Olay. The Olay commercials, for example, direct consumers to a website with special offers on a facial skincare kit. This provides P&G

not only the number of viewers who see the commercial, but those actively engaged with it. Researchers have predicted that by 2012 all television advertising will have some form of direct response, whether a freephone number, website, mobile phone response, or video on demand. Ultimately, the readily available measure of ROI for advertising euros will be the key influence in the shift in television advertising expenditures.[39]

Utilising technology to track and analyse responses to advertising, a database has been set up in Britain through Avongate and data specialist Maestro. The list is called 'Pooling Power' and contains over a million names of people who have purchased health or beauty products due to direct response advertisement or direct mail inserts.[40]

Marketing Ethics

Has America got it right?

Some deceptive ads make statements that can be proven false. For example, the US Federal Trade Commission (FTC) fined Volvo and its ad agency $150,000 each for an ad containing a 'rigged' demonstration. The Volvo 'Bear Food' ad campaign showed a monster truck running over a row of cars and crushing all but the Volvo station wagon. The Volvos, however, had been structurally reinforced, while the structural supports in some of the other cars had been cut.[41] In addition

to fining firms for deceptive advertising, The FTC also has the power to require firms to run corrective advertising, messages that clarify or qualify previous claims. For example, an FTC ruling required Novartis AG to spend $8 million to change packaging and advertising information about its Doan's Pills back medication saying 'Although Doan's is an effective pain reliever, there is no evidence that Doan's is more effective than other pain relievers for back pain'.[42]

Debate, Discuss, Disagree

1   What are the pros and cons of every country having an agency that can force companies to do corrective advertising?

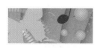

Objective

2

Explain what sales promotion is and describe the different types of trade and consumer sales promotion activities.

Sales Promotion

Sometimes taking a simple walk through your student union on campus puts you in contact with a parade of people eager for you to enter a contest, taste a new chocolate bar, or take home a free T-shirt with a local bank's name on it. These are examples of **sales promotion**; programmes that marketers design to build interest in or encourage purchase of a product or service during a specified time period.[43] Marketers have been placing an increasing amount of their total marketing communication budget into sales promotion for one simple reason – these strategies deliver short-term sales results.

Sales promotion sometimes can be elaborate and high profile. For example, Burger King launched a worldwide sales promotion for its Whopper hamburger to celebrate its 50th anniversary. The promotion centred around the website www.whopperat50.com, which feature facts about the Whopper.[44] Another example was McDonald's Tigger Happy Meal promotion that ran throughout Europe to coincide with the launch of Disney's *The Tigger Movie*. Countries such as the UK, Finland, Sweden, Germany, Norway and Belgium participated in this programme, which lasted about four weeks.[45]

How does sales promotion differ from advertising? Both are paid messages from identifiable sponsors intended to change consumer behaviour or attitudes. In some cases, the sales promotion itself is publicised using a traditional advertising medium. But while marketers craft many advertising campaigns to create long-term positive feelings about a brand, company or shop, sales promotion tends to focus on more short-term objectives, such as an immediate boost in sales or the introduction of a new product.

Sales promotion is very useful if the firm has an *immediate* objective, such as quickly bolstering sales for a brand or encouraging consumers to try a new product. The objective of sales promotion may be to generate enthusiasm among retailers to take a chance on a new product or provide more shelf space for an item they already carry. Thus, like advertising, sales promotion can target channel partners (the 'trade') or the selling firm's own employees, as well as end consumers.

As you learned in Chapter 11, sales promotion is but one part of a firm's integrated marketing communication programme and thus must be coordinated with other promotion activities. For example, if a brand's marketing communication tries to position the product as an expensive, luxury item (think Porsche), a sales promotion activity that reduces the price or involves giving away free beefburgers and lemonade at the Porsche dealer served by a man dressed in a clown suit will undoubtedly send conflicting messages to the customer about the Porsche brand. And, importantly, sales promotion rarely if ever is used by itself as the sole form of marketing communication. By its nature, sales promotion is most often used to support a more extensive advertising, direct marketing, public relations and/or personal selling initiative.

Table 12.2 summarises key sales promotion techniques. Sales promotion is directed at two key groups: trade and consumers. Let's start with trade promotions and then learn about consumer promotions.

 ## Sales Promotion Directed at the Trade

Trade promotions focus on members of the trade, which includes distribution channel members, such as retail salespeople or wholesale distributors, that a firm must work with to sell its products. (We'll discuss these and other distribution channel members in more detail in Chapter 13)

Trade promotions take one of two forms: (1) discounts and deals and (2) increasing industry visibility. Discount promotions (deals) reduce the cost of the product to the retailer or help defray its advertising expenses. The promotions are designed to encourage shops to stock the item and be sure it's given a lot of attention. Trade promotions that focus on increasing awareness and sales (increasing industry visibility) do so by creating enthusiasm among salespeople and customers. Let's take a look at both types of trade promotions in more detail.

Discounts and Deals

One form of trade promotion is a *price break*. A manufacturer can reduce a channel partner's costs through sales promotions that discount its products. For example, a manufacturer can offer a **merchandising allowance** that reimburses the retailer for in-store support of a product, such as when a shop features an off-shelf display for a brand. Another way in which a

Technique	Primary Target	Description	Example
Trade shows	Trade	Many manufacturers show their products to convention attendees.	The Cebit in Hannover (Germany) is the worlds biggest trade show for computer hardware and software.
Incentive programmes	Trade	A prize is offered to employees who meet a pre-specified sales goal or who are top performers during a given period.	The British Carphone Warehouse flew 30 top retail staff out to the Primavera festival in Barcelona with a VIP access to the festival.[1]
Point-of-purchase displays	Trade and consumers	In-store exhibits make retail environments more interesting and attract consumers' attention.	As sombre music plays in the background, a huge plastic rat draped in a black shroud lies next to a tombstone to promote the Farnam Company's Just One Bite rat poison.
Push money	Trade	Salespeople are given a bonus for selling a specific manufacturer's product.	A retail salesperson at a cosmetics counter at a Nordstrom shop in the US gets $5 every time she sells a bottle of Glow by JLo.
Promotional products	Trade and consumers	A company builds awareness and reinforces its image by giving out items with its name on them.	Coors distributors provide bar owners with Coors Light neon signs promoting the beer.
Cross promotion/ cooperative promotions	Trade and consumers	Companies team up to promote their products jointly.	Burger King promotes its Spidey Sense game in conjunction with Columbia Pictures' *Spider-Man* 2.
Coupons	Consumers	Certificates for money off on selected products, often with an expiry date, are used to encourage product trial.	Tesco's wine club provides a magazine with coupons and exclusive offers.[2]
Samples	Consumers	Retailers might get a demonstration product to help in sales presentations; consumers get a free trial size of the product.	A free small bottle of Clairol Herbal Essences shampoo arrives in the post.
Contests/ sweepstakes	Trade and consumers	A sales contest rewards wholesalers or retailers for performance; consumers participate in games to win prizes; builds awareness and reinforces image.	Publisher's Clearing House announces its latest sweepstake.
Special/bonus packs	Consumers	Additional product is given away with purchase; rewards users. Note that bonus packs usually mean the package must be altered in some way to accommodate the extra merchandise.	Maxell provides 10 free blank CDs with purchase of a pack of 50.
Gifts with purchase	Consumers	A consumer gets a free gift when a product is bought; reinforces product image and rewards users.	The drink-maker Ribena offers a fridge jug as a giveaway; Andrex gave bathroom door hangars away with toilet tissue with messages encouraging good toilet behaviour from children.[3]

[1] Yasmin Razak, 'Carphone Warehouse assigns incentives to fledging agency', *Conference and Incentive Travel*, 21 May 2007, 4.
[2] Carol Angrisani, 'The Grapevine', *Supermarket News*, 26 May 2008, 43.
[3] 'Nothing comes for free', *Marketing*, 15 March 2006, 37.

Table 12.2   Sales Promotion Techniques: A Sampler

Marketing Metrics

Measuring Value

Duracell invested heavily in promotion of its batteries but soon found out that proliferation of trade promotions, deals and product giveaways actually had a negative effect. Consumers felt bewildered and the retail partners were complaining about the complexity of pricing and promotional activity. As a result of this and being faced with tough competition, heavy promotional spending and product confusion in the market-place, Duracell decided to lower its list prices for the top-selling AA and AAA batteries. The company further decided to eliminate inefficient promotions, lessen the overall depth and frequency of trade promotions and instead increase support for its new campaign called 'Trusted Everywhere'.[46]

manufacturer can reduce a channel partner's cost is through a **case allowance** that provides a discount to the retailer or wholesaler during a set period of time based on the sales volume of a product it orders from the manufacturer.

However, allowances and deals have a downside. As with all sales promotion activities, the manufacturer's expectation is that they will be of limited duration after which the distribution channel partner will again pay full price for the items. Unfortunately, some channel members engage in a practice called *forward buying*, in which they purchase large quantities of the product during a discount period, store them, and don't buy them again until the manufacturer offers another discount. Some large retailers and wholesalers take this to an extreme by engaging in *diverting*, an ethically questionable practice. Here the retailer buys the product at the discounted promotional price, stores it, and, after the promotion has expired, sells the inventory to other retailers at a price that is lower than the manufacturer's non-discounted price but high enough to turn a profit for the retailer. Both forward buying and diverting go against the manufacturer's intent in offering the sales promotion.

Increasing Industry Visibility

Other types of trade sales promotions increase the visibility of a manufacturer's products to channel partners within the industry. Whether an elaborate exhibit at a convention or a coffee mug with the firm's logo it gives away to channel partners, these efforts seek to keep the company's name topmost when distributors and retailers make decisions about which products to stock and push. These forms of sales promotions include the following:

● **Trade shows:** The thousands of industry **trade shows** held in Europe and around the world each year are major vehicles for manufacturers to show off their product lines to wholesalers and retailers. Usually, large trade shows are held in big convention centres, such as Earl's Court in London or NEC Birmingham, where many companies set up elaborate exhibits to show their products, give away samples, distribute product literature, and trawl for new business contacts. One example of how technology is changing traditional marketing is the advent of online trade shows where potential customers can preview a manufacturer's wares remotely. This idea is growing in popularity, though many industry people are finding it a challenge to 'schmooze' in cyberspace (it's also a little harder to collect all the great freebies they give out at real life shows!). An important benefit of traditional trade shows is the opportunity to develop customer leads that the company then forwards to its sales force for follow-up. We'll talk more about the role of a sales force later in this chapter.

Marketing Ethics

Drug firms a danger to health – International research exposes flaws in £33bn marketing budget

Drug companies are promoting their products through patients' groups, students and internet chat rooms to bypass the ban on advertising except to doctors. They offer information to the public on 'modern' lifestyle diseases, such as stress and poor eating habits, to encourage people to ask their doctors for medicines. Doctors are offered incentives to prescribe and promote drugs including kickbacks, gifts, free samples and consulting agreements. 'This kind of "nice-and-friendly" marketing is often disguised as corporate social responsibility and has been shown to create a subtle need among consumers to demand drugs for the conditions, while giving consumers a sense of trust in the pharmaceutical companies,' says Consumer International.

Guardian, 26 June 2006

Debate, Discuss, Disagree

1   Do you think this is just good sales promotion or stealth marketing?

- **Promotional products:** We have all seen them: coffee mugs, visors, T-shirts, hats, key chains, refrigerator magnets, and countless other items emblazoned with a company logo. They are examples of **promotional products**. Unlike licensed merchandise sold in shops, sponsors give away these goodies to build awareness of their organisation or specific brands. In many industries, companies vie for the most impressive promotional products and offer business customers and channel partners such upmarket items as watches, fleece jackets and expensive leather desk accessories – all emblazoned with the firm's logo so recipients never forget who gave them such cool stuff.

- **Incentive programmes:** The British supermarket chain Asda has an incentive programme that rewards employee teams for boosting product sales at their shop. The programme requires teams to choose a product that they think will be popular within their community. Regional winning teams receive a cash prize of £150 to spend in store, on gifts or on travel. From the winning teams, two are awarded the use of an Asda branded Mini S convertible over a three-week period.[47] These incentives, known as **push money**, may come in the form of cash bonuses, trips or other prizes.

Sales Promotion Directed at Consumers

Some sales promotions directed at consumers create a buzz in the form of a contest or a special event. For example, Red Bull, the high-octane energy drink (and popular mixer), has became famous for this approach by making its auspicious Red Bull vans available at rave and hip-hop clubs to raise the party atmosphere profile for the venue. Red Bull's consistent efforts at consumer sales promotion became the signature aspect of its marketing communication to consumers, and for the early stages of Red Bull's product life cycle the company did very little traditional consumer advertising. The buzz created by these special events added to the mystique of the brand, fuelling popularity among its young target market much more effectively than would traditional advertising. Let's take a closer look at several popular forms of consumer-targeted sales promotion.

Marketing Metrics

Typhoo tea sales promotions

Typhoo, a leading tea brand, wanted to understand whether it had allowed sales promotions to dilute its brand advertising too much. Under pressure from major retailers, its sales promotion expenditure had grown, but at the cost of advertising. It commissioned an econometric modelling study to find the answer. Analysts studied retail audit data from the main supermarket chains, identifying 19 types of sales promotions and the size of the promotional spike. For example, BOGOF (buy one get one free) promotions caused an uplift many tens of times above baseline sales. It also calculated the sales effect of advertising. These figures were incorporated into a simulation model that Typhoo management used to compare the effects of different combinations of advertising and promotions. As a consequence, the mix between promotions and advertising was changed, and financial performance improved.

Price-Based Consumer Sales Promotion

Many sales promotions target consumers' wallets. They emphasise short-term price reductions or rebates that encourage people to choose a brand – at least during the deal period. Price-based consumer promotion, however, has a downside similar to trade promotions that involve a price break. If used too frequently, consumers become conditioned to purchase the product at only the lower promotional price. Price-based consumer sales promotions include the following:

● **Coupons:** Try to pick up any Sunday newspaper without spilling some coupons. These certificates, redeemable for money off a purchase, are the most common price promotion. Indeed, they are the most popular form of sales promotion overall, with billions distributed annually. The company Tarantula Responsive Communications worked with Kimberly-Clarke and launched a European campaign in order to promote its product Brevia. The promotion ran in countries such as the UK, Netherlands, France and Germany. The campaign itself was identical, just the mechanics varied from country to country. In France, for example, the company offered money-off coupons.[48] Even industries like pharmaceuticals that have never tried this approach before are turning to it in a big way. This industry sends out coupons that customers can redeem for free initial supplies of drugs. Coupons are also available through sites such as Viagra.com and Purplepill.com. Companies use the coupons to prompt patients to ask their doctor for the specific brand instead of a competing brand or a more economical generic version.[49]

  Today, many firms simply send consumers to their website for coupons. For example, Google uses a coupon service. This service lets advertisers embed their coupons in Google maps, offering savings from local businesses including pizza restaurants, local cleaners, supermarkets or pet shops. Google teamed up with the American direct marketing firm Valpak to offer the coupons to its clients, with new offers added on a daily basis. Currently, this service only exists in the US but Google is very keen to launch it in Europe as soon as possible.[50] In September 2006, the smoothie maker Innocent Drinks started its first e-couponing campaign. The company wanted to reward customers for their continued loyalty to the brand. Every individual who received the e-mail was a recipient of the regular e-newsletter that Innocent sent out every week.[51]

● **Price deals, refunds, and rebates:** In addition to coupons, manufacturers often offer a temporary price reduction to stimulate sales. This *price deal* may be printed on the package itself, or it may be a price-off flag or banner on the shop shelf or it may even be included in credit cards. Shell and Citigroup have launched a co-branded Mastercard in the UK, which gives customers a fuel rebate.[52]

Marketing Ethics

Cadbury's buried treasure hunt

In February 2007, a sales promotion for soft drink Dr Pepper went disastrously wrong. A series of clues led treasure hunters seeking a £760,000 prize to a graveyard in Boston containing the remains of historic American figures such as Samuel Adams. The managers of the graveyard – where Cadbury buried the winning gold coin – complained and a national outcry ensued. Cadbury admitted to 'poor judgement' but said none of the graves was damaged.

Debate, Discuss, Disagree

1 Who is responsible for the event and how can you prevent this happening again?

- **Frequency (loyalty/continuity) programmes: Frequency programmes**, also referred to as *loyalty* or *continuity programmes*, offer a consumer a discount or a free product for multiple purchases over time. The famous Miles & More frequent flyer programme of 12 European airlines was introduced by the German airline Lufthansa in 1993. The programme enables its 13 million members to earn and redeem frequent flyer miles on all of the fully integrated airlines as well as the Star Alliance members. All members are also able to build status, which gives them access to certain privileges, like upgrading seating options for example. Virgin Atlantic has gone one step further with its frequent flyer programme that allows Virgin Atlantic Flying Club members the chance to redeem miles for a trip to outer space – only 2 million miles required.[53] More 'down to earth' is Six Flags theme park's Carrothead Club that offers kids 6–10 who attend 'Brunch with Bugs' a club hat, a monthly newsletter and insider information about the park.[54]

- **Special/bonus packs:** Another form of price promotion involves giving the shopper more product instead of lowering the price.[55] How nice to go to Boots and find a 500ml bottle of Nivea lotion with 50ml free! A *special pack* also can be a separate product given away along with another product, such as a GoodNews! razor wrapped with a can of Gillette Foamy shaving cream.

Attention-Getting Consumer Promotions

Attention-getting consumer promotions stimulate interest in and publicity for a company's products. Some typical types of attention getting promotions include the following:

- **Contests and sweepstakes:** According to their legal definitions, a contest is a test of skill, and a sweepstake is based on chance. Some examples of such programmes are:

  - Lynx ran a 'get-in-there' UK campaign, which aimed to help men to 'break the ice' with women and help them to take the first step. On its website, www.lynxeffect.com, people could send in their best videos on how to approach a woman. The winner received an iPod and other Lynx goodies. This campaign also got promoted on YouTube and the social networking site Bebo.[56]

  - As part of the kickoff for Disney's global marketing campaign themed 'Where Dreams Come True', Disney offered consumers an online sweepstake called Keys to the Magic Kingdom. The winning family received a trip to Walt Disney World Resort and a day at the Magic Kingdom.[57]

- Several wireless network operators in Europe offer contests among players in a mobile phone-based game called 'Mobile Millionaire', which resembles the famous TV show 'Who Wants to be a Millionaire'. The game is played with short message service (SMS) or wireless application protocol (WAP). Contestants are declared winners if they have the highest scores using the shortest time during a given period (e.g. a month). Prizes vary among countries, but the winner in the UK, for example, wins a weekend for two in Monte Carlo worth £10,000 whereas in Belgium the winner gets a weekend away including a helicopter flight, use of a sports car and luxury hotel.[58]

- **Premiums:** **Premiums** are items offered free for buying a product. The prize in the bottom of the box of cereal – the reason many university students open the box from the bottom – is a premium. In the 1990s, prepaid phone cards were highly popular premiums. Companies jumping on the phone card bandwagon offered cards emblazoned with pictures of sports heroes, products and rock bands. Phone cards made ideal premiums because they are compact, they can display brand logos or attractive graphics and they provide opportunities for repeat exposure. And an important benefit for the marketer is the ability to build databases by tracking card usage.[59]

- **Sampling:** How many starving university students at one time or another have managed to scrape together an entire meal by scooping up free food samples at their local grocery shop? Some shops, such as wine merchants, actually promote Saturdays as sampling day in their advertising. **Sampling** encourages people to try a product by distributing trial-size versions in shops, in public places such as student unions, or through the post. Many marketers now distribute free samples through sites on the internet.[60] Companies like Procter & Gamble, Unilever, S.C. Johnson & Son and SmithKline Beecham are readily taking advantage of websites such as www.freesamples.com and www.startsampling.com that not only distribute the firms' samples but also follow up with consumer satisfaction surveys. Other free sample sites covering European countries such as the UK, Germany or Netherlands are www.free-stuff.co.uk, www.gratisproben.com or www.freetemplates.nl respectively.

- **Point-of-sale promotion (POS):** This attempts to influence consumers while they are in the shop by catching their attention with creative displays or signs.[61] Marketers are challenged to come up with new and innovative POS displays that will grab attention, such as the promotion Bausch & Lomb ran in Spain. The company wanted to encourage consumers with good vision to buy contact lenses that changed their eye colour. By letting shoppers upload their pictures to a computer in the shop and then digitally altering the photos, the promotion allowed people to see how they would look with five different eye colours without actually inserting the contacts.[62]

  POS activities also include the use of *in-store media*, such as placards on shopping trolleys or TVs inside the shop to promote specific products. As the chief executive officer of one company that produces these in-store messages put it, 'Does it make any sense to spend millions of euros talking to people in their living rooms and cars and then let them wander around a supermarket with 30,000 product choices without something to remind them to buy your product?'[63] One very noticeable technique of this genre of POS promotion uses a motion detector box that flashes lights in the voucher dispenser as a shopper approaches a section of the shelf.

- **Product/brand placements:** As we've seen, *product placement* refers to getting your brand featured in film or television shows. When consumers see a popular celebrity using a brand when they watch a favourite film or TV programme, they might develop a more positive attitude towards the brand. Successful brand placements have included the Aston Martins driven by James Bond since the 1960s, the Nike shoes worn by Forrest Gump, and the Dodge Grand Caravan and the Dodge Sprinter Cargo van in *Mr. & Mrs. Smith* driven by Brad Pitt and Angelina Jolie.[64] MasterCard recently combined its placement in the Jennifer Aniston and Vince Vaughn film *The Break Up* with special offers for free cinema tickets in its Priceless.com website, as well as a sweepstake in which consumers could win tickets to the film premier and free DVDs for consumers who use their MasterCard debit cards a certain number of times.[65]

Beyond movies and television shows, what better way to promote to the video generation than through brand placements in video games, an approach called **advergaming**. If you are a video game fanatic, watch for placements of real life brands such as Adidas, Burger King, Intel, Toyota and Sony embedded in the action of your game. Adidas approached the advergame by adapting an existing online title, Double Fusion's Powerchallenge – a virtual football game. It promoted their Predator and f50 boots and let gamers choose virtual 3D football team players wearing either pairs of the shoes. Each type had different qualities and in a survey 98 per cent of the game players thought that it was a good or excellent experience.[66]

- **Cross-promotion:** When marketers do a **cross-promotion (or cooperative promotion)**, this means that two or more products or services join forces to create interest using a single promotional tool. In a way, this is similar to product/brand placement in that each promoted product appears on each other's turf. Cross-promoted products should share some logical connection, be compatible in image, and put forth a message that helps both brands. The Burger King/*Spider-Man 2* sales promotion is an example of a cross-promotion that worked. In the cinema, moviegoers got a dose of the Burger King 'Spidey Sense' contest in the trailers that play before the feature. Then, when consumers went to their nearby Burger King they saw *Spider-Man 2* cups and all sorts of Spidey decor throughout the restaurant.

| Photo 12.7 | A cross-promotion lets companies join forces to push their products using a single promotional tool. That's the plan behind DHL's partnerships, shown in this advert with Mercedes Benz. Source: DHL (Germany) |

| Photo 12.8 | Another DHL cross-promotion, this time with London Fashion Week. Source: DHL (Germany) |

Marketing Metrics

Measuring Product Placements

Marketers' opportunities for product placement, where they embed their products into entertainment vehicles, are rapidly expanding. No longer are they limited to television and movies; iPods, mobile phones, TiVo or Skyplus, concerts, events and downloadable web-based films are providing numerous new platforms for marketers to showcase their brands. Unfortunately, as the opportunities become more and more complex it is more difficult to determine the relevance of a placement and measure its reach and effectiveness. There are now some companies who can measure this for you. Marketing Evolution offers a system to measure directly the impact, counting how many people recognise the product placement. Other programmes such as BuzzMetrics and Intelliseek look for more indirect measures such as word of mouth

and perceptions of the product placement. TNS Media Intelligence provides the newest service with a technology measuring products and brand appearances (such as symbols or logos) on selected basic cable shows, all six broadcast networks' prime-time programming, and the three major late-night talk shows. TNS tracks such detailed information as any connection the plot or storyline in the programme has with the product placement as well as measures that relate to the impact of the product. iTVX is yet another company exploring the value of product placements, creating a measure called Q-Ratio that calculates and assigns a relative value of the traditional 30-second advertising spot to a product placement opportunity and will provide a starting rate for the cost of product placements.[67]

Public Relations

www.pearsoned.co.uk/Solomon

Objective 3

Explain the role of public relations.

Public relations (PR) is the communications function that seeks to build good relationships with an organisation's *publics*; these include consumers, stockholders, legislators and other stakeholders in the organisation. Today marketers use PR activities to influence the attitudes and perceptions of various groups not only towards companies and brands but also towards politicians, celebrities and not-for-profit organisations.

The basic rule of good PR is: *Do something good, and then talk about it.* A company's efforts to get in the limelight – and stay there – can range from humanitarian acts to more lighthearted 'exposure'. Consider for example the British Flora Family Marathon that takes place every year in London. The marathon is used to raise awareness to control your weight and to help keep your heart and lungs healthy.[68]

The big advantage of this kind of communication is that when PR messages are placed successfully they are more credible than if the same information appeared in a paid advertisement. As one marketing executive observed, 'There's a big difference between hearing about a product from a salesman and from your trusted local newsreader.'[69] The value of publicity was clearly demonstrated by the huge success of Mel Gibson's controversial film *The Passion of the Christ*. Frequent news stories, TV appearances by Mr. Gibson, radio debates and even a *Newsweek* cover that asked 'Who Really Killed Jesus?' built momentum. Even before the film opened, 81 per cent of cinema goers were aware of it. This high level of interest didn't just 'happen' – a year before the film's release, Gibson toured churches with a rough cut of his movie, giving speeches and charming pastors. His film production company, Icon, signed up consultants to advise pastors on how best to use the film to promote the church and recruit new members.[70]

Public relations is crucial to an organisation's ability to establish and maintain a favourable image. Some types of PR activities, referred to as *proactive PR*, stem from the company's marketing objectives. For example, marketers create and manage **publicity**; unpaid communication about an organisation that gets media exposure. This strategy helps to create awareness about a product or an event, as when a local newspaper reporting on an forthcoming concert features an interview with the band's lead guitarist around the time that tickets go on sale. Although some publicity happens naturally, more typically a 'buzz' needs to be created by a firm's publicists. For example, take the drug Botox. Everyone has heard of it. But how? As Botox has 13 different clinical uses and can only be prescribed by doctors, it cannot be promoted directly to the public because the law prevents companies promoting prescription medicines to consumers. The answer is PR. The company uses the press to get Botox written about to create awareness and consumer interest.

The internet has expanded the capabilities of the traditional PR function.[71] Corporate websites post testimonials from customers, make new product announcements and respond quickly to important events. The internet can also be very effective in handling crises. Companies can respond to a crisis online in far less time than other forms of communication, such as press releases or conferences.[72] For example, as news regarding danger from Dell's batteries surfaced, Dell's digital media manager Lionel Menchaca used a corporate blog entry to announce that battery replacements would take 20 days to reach customers. Further, Dell reported that changes in lead times would be reported on the blog (www.direct2dell.com).[73]

 ## Objectives of Public Relations

Companies that practise IMC know that PR strategies are best used in concert with advertising, sales promotions and personal selling to send a consistent message to customers and other stakeholders. As part of the total IMC plan, PR is often used to accomplish the following objectives:

- **Introducing new products to manufacturers:** When Weyerhaeuser Co. introduced Cellulon, a new biotechnology product, it distributed information kits that clearly explained the technical product and its applications in each of 12 markets to ensure that the trade press properly covered the introduction.[74]

- **Introducing new products to consumers:** When First Drinks Brands sponsored the launch of the premium vodka brand Russian Standard in the UK through TV, it hoped to gain a foothold in the growing expensively priced vodka market. The TV ad was boosted by sales promotion and public relations to get the vodka into magazine editorials in order to gain a good share in the almost £1.9 billion strong market.[75]

- **Influencing government legislation:** Airplane maker Boeing spent over a decade in public relations activities to persuade regulators that jetliners with two engines were as safe as those with three or four engines even for non-stop international flights, some as long as 16 hours. Boeing's rival Airbus argued that four-engine planes were necessary for the desired level of safety for such flights.[76]

- **Enhancing the image of an organisation:** Budget Rent-A-Car International, a car company operating in Europe, the Middle East and Africa and lying third in the European league table behind Hertz and Avis, used a variety of public relations and other promotions activities to generate business. The company wanted to secure a stronger presence in the international business traveller market and introduced the VIP Traveller card, which entitled the holder to unlimited mileage throughout Budget offices worldwide. Inflight magazines, such as *High Life* (British Airways), *Atlas* (Air France) or *Bordbuch* (Lufthansa) were used as a vehicle to promote this card offering coupons and information.[77]

- **Enhancing the image of a city, region or country:** Faced with international criticism about possible human rights abuses and restriction of trade, the Chinese government established an office in charge of 'overseas propaganda' to present a more favourable image of China to the rest of the world.[78]

- **Crisis management:** Whether it's product tampering or an accident at a company's facilities or some other company-related problem, such as British Airways' Terminal Five fiasco, a crisis can cause permanent damage to a company, the success of its products, and its stockholder equity. Public relations professionals know that when a firm handles crises well, it can minimise damage. Thus, a vitally important role of PR is to prepare a *crisis management plan*; a document that details what an organisation will do *if* a crisis occurs – who will be the spokesperson for the organisation, how the organisation will deal with the press, and what sort of messages it will deliver to the press and the public. Public relations may be even more important when the company's image is at risk due to bad publicity, for example, product tampering.[79] The goal here is to manage the flow of information to address concerns so that consumers don't panic and distributors don't abandon the product. For example, in 2006 Dell and Sony suffered after bloggers posted images of 'exploding' laptops. This news resulted in Dell's largest recall in its 22-year history. The lithium laptop batteries made by Sony and used by Dell could overheat and catch fire. Dell responded quickly by providing essential information on its website, which registered 23 million visitors during that time.[80] The British firm Cadbury faced a salmonella scandal in 2006, when a rare Montevideo strain of salmonella was found in seven of its products. A major recall began and millions of products had to be destroyed. The product withdrawal cost Cadbury approximately £20m. The negative PR was even worse because Cadbury faced huge criticism for its handling of the crisis and for the delay in coming clean and admitting its fault.[81]

- **Calling attention to a firm's involvement with the community:** In 2005, companies globally spent approximately £17.4bn on sponsorship according to the European Sponsoring Association (ESA). For example, the US insurance company AIG signed a £56m four-year deal to be the shirt sponsor for Manchester United. Norwich Union as another example announced a £50m injection into UK Athletics as the dominant Olympic sport.[82] PR specialists work behind the scenes to ensure that sponsored events receive ample press coverage and exposure.

 ## Planning a Public Relations Campaign

A public relations campaign is a coordinated effort to communicate with one or more of the firm's audiences. This is a three-step process of developing objectives, executing and evaluating. Let's review each step.

Like an advertising campaign, the organisation must first develop clear objectives for the PR programme that define the message it wants people to hear. Next, the PR specialists must develop a campaign strategy that includes the following:

- A statement of objectives;

- A situation analysis;

- Specification of target audiences (publics), messages to be communicated and specific programme elements to be used;

- A timetable and budget;

- Discussion of how the programme will be evaluated.

For example, the International Apple Institute, a trade group devoted to increasing the consumption of apples, had to decide if a campaign should focus on getting consumers to cook more with apples, drink more apple juice, or simply to buy more fresh fruit. Because fresh apples brought a substantially higher price per pound to growers than apples used for apple sauce or apple juice, the group decided to push the fresh fruit angle. It used the theme 'An

Table 12.3
Measuring the
Effectiveness of
Public Relations
(PR) Efforts.

Method	Description	Pros	Cons
In-house assessments conducted by a PR manager	Analyse media coverage in publications, looking for number and prominence of mentions	Relatively inexpensive because the major cost is the manager's time	Cannot guarantee objectivity in the analysis; crucial to specify up-front what the relevant indicators are
Awareness and preference studies	Assess company's standing in the minds of customers relative to competition	Good for broad-based strategy setting or to demonstrate the progress of a large programme	Difficult to connect results to specific PR events and to identify which actions had what level of impact on awareness; very expensive
Measurement of print and broadcast coverage generated by PR activities	The basic measurement tool in PR	Provides a quantifiable measure of press coverage; relatively inexpensive	Quantitative only; does not consider the content of the press coverage
Impression counts	Measure the size of the potential audience for a given article	Because a similar measure is used to assess advertising effectiveness, this method provides a common measure for comparison	Usually limited to the circulation of selected publications, so this method does not include pass-along readership; can be expensive

Source: Adapted from Deborah Holloway, 'How to Select a Measurement System That's Right for You,' *Public Relations Quarterly*, Fall 1992, pp. 15–17.

apple a day . . .' (sound familiar?) and mounted a focused campaign to encourage people to eat more apples by placing articles in consumer media extolling the fruit's health benefits.

Execution of the campaign means deciding precisely how the message should be communicated to the targeted public(s). An organisation can get out its positive messages in many ways: news conferences, sponsorship of charity events and other attention-getting promotions.

A barrier to greater reliance on PR campaigns is the difficulty of devising metrics to gauge their effectiveness. Who can say precisely what impact appearances by company executives on talk shows or sponsoring charity events has on sales? It is possible to tell if a PR campaign is getting media exposure, though compared with advertising it's much more difficult to assess bottom-line impact. Table 12.3 describes some common measurement techniques. Check out our PR case 'Eat in colour' at www.pearson.co.uk/solomon.

 ## Public Relations Activities

Public relations professionals engage in a wide variety of activities. While some of these may seem more related to marketing and to marketing communications than others, they all lead to the same goal – creating and maintaining that positive image the organisation needs. Some of these efforts are as follows:

● **Press releases:** The most common way for PR specialists to communicate is a **press release**, which is a report of some event that an organisation writes itself and sends to the media in the hope that it will be published for free. A newer version of this idea is a *video news release*

(VNR) that tells the story in a film format instead. Some of the most common types of press releases include the following:

- *Timely topics* deal with topics in the news. For example, the British company WebitPR developed a way of sending press releases to news websites globally and then monitoring their impact. When the company started in 2001, it created a video news release to inform clients about its service. Nowadays you can look at the video on its website www.webitpr.com or on www.youtube.com.[83]

- *Research project stories* are published by universities highlighting breakthroughs by faculty researchers.

- *Consumer information releases* provide information to help consumers make product decisions, such as helpful tips from a gravy manufacturer about preparing dishes for Sunday lunch.

- **Internal PR:** These activities aimed at employees often include company newsletters and closed-circuit television. Internal releases help keep employees informed about company objectives, successes or even plans to 'downsize' the workforce. Often company newsletters also are distributed outside the firm to suppliers or other important publics.

- **Investor relations:** For publicly held companies, investors are a vitally important public as their financial support is critical to the future of the company. It is the responsibility of the PR department to develop and distribute annual and quarterly reports and to provide other essential communications with individual and corporate stockholders, with investment firms and with capital market organisations.

- **Lobbying:** Lobbying means talking to and providing information to government officials to persuade them to vote a certain way on pending legislation or even to initiate legislation that would benefit the organisation.

- **Speech writing:** An important job of a firm's PR department is to write speeches on a topic for a company executive to deliver. While some executives do actually write their own speeches, it is more common for a speechwriter on the PR staff to develop an initial draft of a speech after which the executive might add his or her own input.

- **Corporate identity:** PR specialists may provide input on corporate identity materials, such as logos, brochures, building design and even stationery that communicate a positive image for the firm.

- **Media relations:** One of the tasks of the PR professional is to work to develop and maintain positive relationships with the media. Of course, this is important if the company is going to receive the best media exposure possible for positive news, such as publicising the achievements of an employee who has done some notable charity work or for a product it developed that saved someone's life. For example, Tesco and Asda attracted favourable publicity following positive coverage of a trial involving radio frequencies to replace bar-codes and a 'tough' stance on underage drinking and the cheapest supermarket petrol prices respectively.[84] And, as we've seen, good media relations can be even more important when things go wrong. News editors are simply less inclined to present a story of a crisis in its most negative way if they have a good relationship with PR people in the organisation.

- **Sponsorships:** These are PR activities through which companies provide financial support to help fund an event in return for publicised recognition of the company's contribution. Many companies today find that their promotion euros are well spent to sponsor a golf tournament, a Formula One driver, a symphony concert, or global events such as the London Olympics 2012 or World Cup football competition. These sponsorships are partic- ularly effective because consumers often connect their enjoyment of the event with the

Photo 12.9	Marketers often sponsor events or teams to gain publicity and exposure in their target markets. Source: The Advertising Archives

sponsor, thus creating brand loyalty. McDonald's, a sponsor of the FIFA World Cup since 1994, has built on its sponsorship to create promotions in its restaurants around the world. McDonald's global Player Escort Programme sent 1408 children aged 6–10 to the World Cup in Germany where they escorted players onto the field for all 64 FIFA matches. In Brazil, McDonald's restaurants offered customers sandwiches with flavours from countries competing in the World Cup. World Cup beverage cups were available for customers in some countries including China and the US and some locations in Europe offered consumers a World Cup burger which was 40 per cent larger than a Big Mac.[85]

- **Special events:** Another job of a PR department is the planning and implementation of special events. Whether it is the visit of a group of foreign investors to a firm's manufacturing facilities, a Bank Holiday picnic for company employees, or a hospitality booth set up during a motorcycle race where the company is a sponsor, the PR staff's job is to make sure the event happens without a glitch and people go home happy. For example, Skoda created a reception for the launch of the Fabia vRS model at the Tram Studios in North London. This event was exclusively for 100 motoring and lifestyle journalists. Afterwards, the company invited 60 regional press delegates to participate in a ride and drive event to test the new model.[86]

- **Buzz-building:** Because people have increasingly criticised such traditional PR techniques as video news releases, many PR agencies are turning to word of mouth to build a positive buzz about an organisation. One PR firm even hires noted bloggers to help clients develop an expertise in blogging.[87]

- **Advice and consultancy:** When a firm fully understands and appreciates the importance of the PR function, top management recognises that PR professionals have much more to offer than just planning parties and writing news releases. Because of their expertise and understanding of the effects of communication on public opinion, PR professionals also play the role of consultants to top management. So when a firm needs to shut down a plant or to build a new one, to discontinue a product or add to the product line, to fire a director, or to give an award to an employee who spends hundreds of hours a year doing volunteer work in his community, it needs the advice of its PR staff. What is the best way to handle the situation? How should the announcement be made? Who should be told first? What is to be said and how?

Having read the PR section, do you think Rick's option 2 to use PR is a good thing for Tupperware? Now you've covered some of the key impersonal media such as advertising and PR, which are designed to create awareness, interest and even desire (remember AIDA?) in a product, the role of sales promotion, personal selling and direct marketing is to create action, the final stage of the AIDA communications model. In the next part we take a closer look at personal selling and direct marketing.

Real People, Other Voices

Advice for Rick Goings

Dr Fiona Ellis-Chadwick,
Loughborough University

I would choose option 2. By updating and extending the product range, Tupperware has taken steps towards repositioning the brand. However in doing so the company is adopting a high-risk strategy as it is changing the product and entering new international markets simultaneously. In this situation, Tupperware is pursuing tangible repositioning and in order to do this effectively it needs to encourage target customers to really 'buy-into' the brand.

A PR campaign is a great way to achieve this through the use of media reporting in lifestyle magazines, other suitable print media and online. However, selection of the *right* PR agency would be critical to the success of any such campaign as the agency will need to have a good publication success rate and understanding of particular international markets. To maximise the potential of the campaign it should be supported by a series of highly visible promotional events. Depending on the age of the target market, this could take the form of a contest or series of challenges. One of the advantages of PR is that it can help to enhance the reputation and prestige of a brand as well as promoting sales.

By following this option Tupperware has the opportunity to build the profile of the brand, which should drive retail sales as well as encourage more sale agents to join the company.

Hannah Geddes,
Student at University of Surrey

As with every decision a company must make there are a number of positive and negative aspects associated with each viable option. While, by their own merit, each option offers to some degree an element of advantage, the negative aspects evident in option 1 and option 3 seem to outweigh the positives to a more considerable degree than option 2.

While advertising serves to promote the product in a definitive and prominent manner, the costs which the company would incur implementing this option are significant; this option does not carry a strong enough guarantee of success to warrant the high investment levels required. Reliance on word of mouth, as put forth in option 3, is a strong candidate for altering public perception of the Tupperware brand; however while it continues to be an inadequately recognised brand the limitations are too great to enable mass success. This option would be more efficient and effective used as a secondary marketing strategy once the initial push has been made. While there *is* a degree of risk associated with developing the brand through PR this option has potential to be the most valuable option presented. There is a degree of malleability intrinsic within the PR approach, which facilitates the manipulation of the final outcome. This approach allows the final 'story' to be shaped and influenced to construct a strong degree of positive association with the brand. Overall option 2 would seem to be the pre-eminent viable option presented, not only due to the lower costs (in comparison with option 1) but also the widespread awareness it can generate, which would initially be unachievable through option 3.

Personal Selling

www.pearsoned.co.uk/solomon

Objective 4

Understand the important role of personal selling.

Personal selling occurs when a company representative interacts directly with a customer or prospective customer to communicate about a good or service. This form of promotion is a far more intimate way to talk to the market. Many organisations rely heavily on personal selling because at times the 'personal touch' can carry more weight than mass-media material. In a business-to-business market situation, such as at Sash UK, as earlier discussed as our Chapter 5 case, participating in international trade shows provides an example for salespeople at Sash to demonstrate their goods, provide a personal touch, and begin to develop crucial relationships with clients. Also, many industrial products and services are too complex or expensive to market effectively in impersonal ways (such as through mass advertising).

Another advantage of personal selling is that salespeople are the firm's eyes and ears in the marketplace. They learn which competitors are talking to customers, what is being offered, what new rival products are on the way and all sorts of competitive intelligence. As such, salespeople perform a vital role in the success of a firm's customer relationship management system that we discussed earlier in the book – providing a source of timely and accurate informational input about customers and the market.

Personal selling has special importance for students because many graduates with a marketing background will enter professional sales jobs. Jobs in selling and sales management often provide high upward mobility if you are successful, because firms value employees who understand customers and who can communicate well with them. The old business adage 'nothing happens until something is sold' translates into many firms placing quite a bit of emphasis on personal selling in their promotion mixes.

Now let's take a close look at how personal selling works and how professional sales people develop long-term relationships with customers.

 ## The Role of Personal Selling

When a man calls Dell Computer to place an order for a new PC configured with a DVD drive and gaming memory, he is dealing with a salesperson. When he sits in on a presentation by a computer technician presenting a new spreadsheet software package, he is dealing with a salesperson. And when that same man agrees over a business dinner at an expensive restaurant to buy a new computer network for his company, he also is dealing with a salesperson. For many firms, some element of personal selling is essential to land a commitment to purchase or a contract, making this type of marketing communication an important part of any marketing plan. To put the use of personal selling into perspective, Table 12.4 summarises some of the factors that make it a more or less important element in an organisation's promotion mix.

Generally, a personal selling emphasis is more important when a firm engages in a *push strategy*, in which the goal is to 'push' the product through the channel of distribution so that it is available to consumers. As a vice-president at Hallmark Cards observed, 'We're not selling to the retailer, we're selling *through* the retailer. We look at the retailer as a pipeline to the hands of consumers.'[88]

Personal selling is also likely to be crucial in a business-to-business context when direct interaction with a client's management is required to clinch a big deal, and often when intense negotiations about price and other factors will occur before the deal is signed. In a consumer context, inexperienced customers may need the hands-on assistance that a professional salesperson can provide. Firms selling products which consumers buy infrequently – houses, cars, computers, lawnmowers, even university education – often rely heavily on personal selling.

Table 12.4
Factors Influencing a Firm's Emphasis on Personal Selling

Factors Increasing Emphasis on Personal Selling	Factors Limiting Emphasis on Personal Selling
• If a push strategy is used • If the decision maker has higher status within the organisation • If the purchase is a 'new task' for the customer • If the product is highly technical or complex • If the customer is very large • If the product is expensive • If the product is a custom good or personalised service • If there are trade-in products • If negotiation is required	• If the amount of individual orders will be small • If there are many small customers • If the image of the salesperson is poor

Likewise, firms whose products or services are complex or very expensive often need a salesperson to explain, justify, and sell – in both business and consumer markets.

If personal selling is so useful, why don't firms do away with their advertising and sales promotion budgets and hire more salespeople? Because there are some drawbacks that limit the role personal selling plays in the marketing communications mix. First, when the amount of individual purchases is low, it doesn't make sense to use personal selling. The cost per contact with each customer is very high compared with other forms of promotion. Analysts estimated that in 2007 the average total cost for a sales call with a consultative (or problem-solving) approach to selling was about €300, and this cost was increasing at a rate of 5 per cent per year. Of course this figure is an average, and depending on the industry some sales calls are much more expensive to make. In contrast, the per-contact cost of a national television commercial is miniscule by comparison. A 30-second, prime-time commercial may be €300,000 to €500,000 (or much much more during big events like the FIFA World Cup final), but with millions and millions of viewers, the cost per contact may be only €10 or €15 per 1000 viewers. For low-priced consumer goods like Coca-Cola, personal selling to end users doesn't make sense either.

Salespeople – even the *really* energetic types – can make only so many calls a day. Thus, reliance on personal selling is effective only when the success ratio is at its highest. **Telemarketing**, sometimes called *teleselling*, involves person-to-person communication taking place via the phone. Because the cost of field salespeople is so high, telemarketing continues to grow in popularity – much to the dismay of many prospect customers who are interrupted during their evening meal to answer sales calls for double glazing, new kitchens or insurance.

Ironically, consumer resistance to telemarketing has provided a powerful boost for a form of selling that has been around for a long time: *direct selling*. *Direct selling is not the same thing as direct marketing*. Direct sellers bypass channel intermediaries and sell directly from manufacturer to consumer through personal, one-to-one contact. Typically, independent sales representatives, or even members of the public do the selling in person in a customer's home, a place of business, or even in their own home. Well-known examples include Avon, Ann Summers and Tupperware. Many of these firms utilise a *party plan* approach to selling in which salespeople demonstrate products in front of groups of neighbours or friends. Direct selling is on the up with domestic sales volume increasing significantly.[89]

Technology and Personal Selling

Personal selling is supposed to be 'personal'. By definition, a company uses personal selling for marketing communication in which one person (the salesperson) interacts directly with another person (the customer or prospective customer) to communicate about a good or service. All sorts of technologies are available to enhance the personal selling process. However, as anyone making sales calls knows, technology cannot and should not *replace* personal selling. As we'll discuss later in this chapter, nowadays a key role of personal selling is to manage customer *relationships* – and remember, relationships occur between people, not between computers.

However, without doubt, a number of technological advancements have made it easier for salespeople to do their jobs more effectively. One such technological advance is *customer relationship management (CRM) software*. For years now, salespeople have used and benefited from account management software such as ACT and GoldMine. Account management software is inexpensive, easy to use, and allows salespeople to track all aspects of customer interaction. Currently, many firms are turning to 'on demand' online CRM applications, accessible online, which are more customisable and integrative than ACT or GoldMine yet are less expensive than major company-wide CRM installations. Examples of widely used online CRM products include SalesForce.com and SalesNet, both of which are user-friendly for salespeople. A key benefit of online CRM systems is that the firm 'rents' them for a flat fee per month and avoids major capital outlay.[90] Recently, sales organisations have begun using a new generation system called *partner relationship management (PRM)* that links information between selling and buying firms. PRM differs from CRM in that at least some of the databases and systems of both supplier and buyer firms are shared in order to maximise the utility of the data for decision-making purposes. When firms' information is shared, they are more likely to strive for win–win solutions.

Beyond CRM and PRM, numerous other technology applications are enhancing personal selling, including teleconferencing, videoconferencing, and improved corporate websites that include FAQ pages that answer many customer queries. Many firms also use intranets and blogs to link internal and external communication.

Voice-over Internet Protocol (VoIP) – using a data network to carry voice calls – is beginning to get a lot of use in day-to-day correspondence between salespeople and customers. With VoIP, the salesperson on the road can just plug into a fast internet connection and then start making and receiving calls just as if he or she is in the office. Unlike using mobile phones, there are no bad reception areas, and unlike using hotel phones, there are no hidden charges. One popular VoIP product is Skype, whose tagline is 'The whole world can talk for free.' According to its website, Skype 'is a little piece of software that allows you to make free calls to other Skype users and really cheap calls to ordinary phones'.

Of course, salespeople are using wireless technology in general more and more to provide seamless communication process with clients. BlackBerry has been around a while, but predictions are that as wireless becomes more and more predominant, the various devices salespeople use to communicate (mobile phone, fax, laptop and so on) will become more and more integrated.

Across the Hall

Advice for Rick Goings

Tom Beaumont-Griffin is Strategy Director at Sledge Integrated, a leading brand experience agency in the UK

I would choose option 2. Firstly I believe that the heritage and authenticity of the Tupperware brand is one of its greatest strengths in a society that is moving rapidly from 'throw away' to 'save and re-use'.

As other brands move to position themselves in that space, Tupperware must overtly celebrate the fact that it has always been there. I do however agree with the 'innovation' strategy, but I see it as the other side of the same coin.

Tupperware continues to be valued by successive generations because it continues to innovate for the evolving needs of women who care about doing the right thing for their family and the right thing for the environment.

This combination of heritage and innovation equally appeals to those who sell Tupperware. They are domestic activists for practical and ecological house keeping. In selling Tupperware they are not only doing their bit for themselves, they are doing their bit for the environment. A fabulous feel-good motivator!

It is the authenticity of these messages and the relevance of the brand to the daily lives of women that leads me towards the second option provided by a PR-led approach. However, I would view PR as a fire-starter.

Subsequent campaigns should become an *integral part* of people's lives in a way that reaches beyond the magazines they read and connects to the real world of their homes, their friends and the 'parties' they go to.

The most persuasive form of marketing is a conversation and recommendation from a friend. Tupperware should add up how many hours of this potent highly targeted 'conversational media space' they 'own' and ask themselves how much it would cost if they had to buy it!

Surely the long-term solution will see Tupperware recognising itself as the major media mogul it is and then rising to the creative challenge of how to exploit this potent business asset. What fun!

Types of Sales Jobs

As you might imagine, sales jobs vary considerably. The person who processes an IBM computer purchase over the phone is primarily an **order taker** – a salesperson who deals with transactions that the customer initiates. Many retail salespeople are order takers, but often wholesalers, dealers, and distributors also employ salespeople to look after their business customers. Because little creative selling is involved in order taking, this type of sales job typically is the lowest paying sales position.

In contrast, a **technical specialist** contributes expertise in the form of product demonstrations, recommendations for complex equipment, and the setup of machinery. The technical specialist's job is to provide *sales support* rather than to actually close the sale. He or she promotes the firm and tries to stimulate demand for a product to make it easier for colleagues to actually achieve the sale.

Sometimes a person whose job is to stimulate clients to buy is called a **missionary salesperson**. Like technical specialists, missionary salespeople promote the firm and work to stimulate demand for its products but don't actually take orders for products.[91] Pfizer's salespeople do missionary sales work when they call on doctors to influence them to prescribe the latest and greatest Pfizer medication over competing products. However, no 'sale' is made until doctors' prescriptions are passed to pharmacies, that in turn place orders for the drug through their wholesalers or distributors.

The **new-business salesperson** is responsible for finding new customers and calling on them to present the company's products or services. As you might imagine, gaining the business of a new customer usually means that the customer stops doing business with one of the firm's competitors. New-business selling requires a high degree of creativity and professionalism, so this type of salesperson is usually very well paid. Once a new-business salesperson establishes a relationship with a client, he or she often continues to service that client as the primary contact as long as the client continues to buy from the company. In that long-term relationship building role, this type of salesperson is an **order getter**. Order getters are usually the people most directly responsible for a particular client's business and may also have titles such as 'account manager'.[92]

More and more, firms are finding that the selling function is best handled by **team selling**. A selling team may consist of a salesperson, a technical specialist, someone from engineering and design, and other players who work together to develop products and programmes that satisfy the customer's needs. Inclusion of people from these various functional areas gives rise to the term *cross-functional team*.

Approaches to Personal Selling

Personal selling is one of the oldest forms of marketing communication. Unfortunately, its image was tarnished by smooth-talking sales representatives who would say anything to make a sale. The profession was not helped by Pulitzer Prize-winning playwright Arthur Miller's famous character Willie Loman in *Death of a Salesman*. Willie Loman is a pathetic, burned-out pedlar who leaves home for the road on Monday morning and returns late Friday evening, selling 'on a smile and a shoeshine'. His personal life is in shambles, with two dysfunctional sons and a disaffected wife who hardly know him.

Fortunately, personal selling today is not as harsh as Arthur Miller's portrayal. Selling has moved from a transactional, hard-sell approach to an approach based on relationships with customers. Let's see how.

Transactional Selling: Putting On The Hard Sell

The *hard sell* practised by Willy Loman is a high-pressure process. We've all been exposed to the pushy electronics salesperson that puts down the competition by telling shoppers that if they buy elsewhere they will be stuck with an inferior product that will fall apart in six months. Or how about the crafty used-car salesman who plays good cop/bad cop games using the sales manager or finance manager at the dealership as a tactic? These type of hard-sell approaches reflect **transactional selling** – which focuses on making an immediate sale with no concern for developing a long-term relationship with the customer.

As customers, the hard sell makes us feel manipulated and resentful and thwarts customer satisfaction and loyalty. It is a very short-sighted approach to selling. As we said earlier in the book, constantly finding new customers is much more expensive than getting repeat business from the customers you already have. The behaviour promoted by transactional selling (that is, doing anything to get the order) also contributes to the poor image many of us have of sales people, i.e. obnoxious and untrustworthy. Such sales people engage in such behaviour because they don't care if they ever have the chance to sell to you again.

Relationship Selling: Building Long-Term Customers

Today's professional salesperson is more likely to practise relationship selling than transactional selling. This means that the salesperson seeks to develop a mutually satisfying, win–win relationship with the customer. **Relationship selling** involves securing, developing, and maintaining long-term relationships with profitable customers.[93] *Securing* a customer relationship means converting an interested prospect into someone who is convinced that the product or service holds value for him. *Developing* a customer relationship means ensuring that you and the customer find more ways to add value. *Maintaining* a customer relationship means building customer satisfaction and loyalty – thus, the customer can be counted on to provide future business and won't switch to another source to purchase the products or services you sell. If doing business with the customer isn't *profitable* for you (unless you're a charitable organisation), you would probably like to see that customer go somewhere else. This is part of Rick's option 3 at Tupperware to get his salesforce to generate more word of mouth to stimulate new customers.

The Creative Selling Process

Many people find selling to be a great profession, partly because something different is always going on. Every customer, every sales call, and every salesperson is unique. Some salespeople are successful primarily because they know so much about what they sell. Others are successful because they've built strong relationships with customers so that they're able to add value to both the customer and their own firm – a win–win approach to selling. Successful salespeople understand and engage in a series of activities to make the sales encounter mutually beneficial.

Successful personal selling is probably more likely if the salesperson undergoes a systematic series of steps called the **creative selling process**. These steps require the salesperson to seek out potential customers, analyse their needs, determine how product attributes provide benefits, and then decide how best to communicate this to the prospects. As Figure 12.4 shows, there are seven steps in the process. Let's take a look at each step.

Step 1: Prospecting and Qualifying

Prospecting is the process of identifying and developing a list of potential customers, called *prospects* or *sales leads*. Leads can come from existing customer lists, telephone directories and

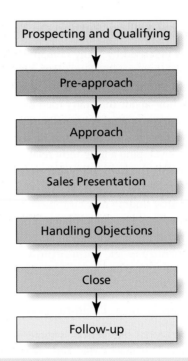

Figure 12.4	**Steps in the Creative Selling Process**
	In the creative selling process, sales people follow a series of steps to ensure successful long-term relationships with customers.

commercially available databases. The local library usually contains directories of businesses (including those published by government agencies) and directories of association memberships. Sometimes companies generate sales leads through their advertising or sales promotion by letting customers request more information. As you learned earlier, trade shows are often an important source of sales leads, as are website visits by potential customers.

An emerging technology available to salespeople for prospecting is the development of online *social networks*. These are not 'friendship' social networks, but rather business networks. These sites enable salespeople to create profiles, upload their personal address books to the site, and invite business colleagues to join the network. The site protocol then provides for contact, request for formal introductions and information exchange.

Another way to generate leads is through *cold calling*, when the salesperson simply contacts prospects 'cold' without introduction or arrangement. It always helps to know the prospect, so salespeople might rely instead on *referrals*. Current clients who are satisfied with their purchase often give referrals – yet another reason to maintain good customer relationships.

However, the mere fact that someone is willing to talk to a salesperson doesn't guarantee a sale. Along with identifying potential customers, salespeople need to *qualify* prospects to determine how likely they are to become customers by asking questions such as the following: Are the prospects likely to be interested in what I'm selling? Are they likely to switch their allegiance from another supplier or product? Is the potential sales volume large enough to make a relationship profitable? Can they afford the purchase? If they must borrow money to buy the product, what is their credit history?

Step 2: Pre-Approach

The **pre-approach** consists of compiling background information about prospective customers and planning the sales interview. Important purchases are not made lightly, and it's often difficult even to get an appointment to see a prospect. It's foolish for a salesperson to blindly call on a qualified prospect and risk losing the sale because of a lack of preparation. Salespeople try to learn as much as possible about qualified prospects early on. They may probe purchase history, look at current needs or, in some cases, find information about their interests.

Salespeople can draw information about a prospect from a variety of sources. In the case of larger companies, salespeople can find financial data, names of top executives, and other information about a business in publications like Dun & Bradstreet. They can also find a great deal of information for the pre-approach on customers' websites.

If the salesperson's firm has a CRM system, he or she can use it to see whether information on the prospect exists in the system's database. Say, for example, a salesperson at Michael's Bikes is planning a call on a buyer at Greg's Rentals. If Michael's Bikes has had a CRM system in place for some time, any contacts with customers and potential customers (prospects) will have been recorded in the CRM database. The salesperson can simply run an inquiry about Greg's Rentals and, with luck, the CRM database will have information on the company, purchases from Michael's Bikes, when and why they stopped buying from Michael's Bikes, and even the preferences of the particular buyer (if he was with Greg's Rentals at the time the data were recorded).

As useful as external databases and internal CRM systems are, the inside scoop on a prospect often comes from informal sources, such as non-competing salespeople who have dealt with the prospect before. This background information helps salespeople set their goals and plan their strategy for the sales call.

Step 3: Approach

After laying the groundwork with the pre-approach, it is time to **approach**, or contact, the prospect. During these important first minutes when the salesperson initiates contact with the prospective customer, several key events occur. The salesperson tries to learn even more about the prospect's needs, create a good impression, and build rapport. If the salesperson made contact with the prospect through a referral, he or she will probably say so up front: 'Katie Stevens from Pearson suggested I call you.'

During the approach, the customer is deciding whether the salesperson has something to offer that is of potential value to him. Also, the old saying, 'You never get a second chance to make a good first impression', rings true here. A professional appearance tells the prospect that the salesperson means business and is competent to handle the sale. A good salesperson is well-groomed and wears appropriate business dress, doesn't chew gum, use poor grammar or inappropriate language, mispronounce the customer's name, or seem uninterested in the call.

Step 4: Sales Presentation

Many sales calls involve a formal **sales presentation** that lays out the benefits of the product and its advantages over the competition. When possible and appropriate, salespeople should incorporate technology such as laptops and DVDs into their sales presentations to facilitate demonstrations.

The focus of the sales presentation should always be on ways the salesperson, the products, and the company can add value to the customer (and, in a business-to-business setting, to the customer's company). It is important for the salesperson to present this value proposition clearly, inviting involvement by the customer in the conversation. Let the customer ask questions, give feedback, and discuss their needs. Pre-formulated approaches to sales presentations are a poor choice for salespeople attempting to build long-term relationships. In fact, sales managers rate *listening* skills, not talking skills, as the most important attribute they look for when hiring relationship salespeople.[94]

Step 5: Handling Objection

It is rare when a prospect accepts everything the salesperson has to say without question. The effective salesperson anticipates *objections*, or reasons why the prospect is reluctant to make a commitment, and is prepared to respond with additional information or persuasive arguments. Actually, the salesperson should *welcome* objections because they show the prospect is at least interested enough to have considered the offer and seriously weigh its pros and cons. Handling the objection successfully can move a prospect to the decision stage. For example, the sales person might say, 'Ms. Buonanno, you've said before that you don't have room to carry our new line of mountain bikes, although you mentioned that you might be losing some sales by carrying only one brand with very few different models. If we could come up with an estimate of how much business you're losing, I'd be willing to bet you'd consider making room for our line, wouldn't you?'

Step 6: Close the Sales

The win–win nature of relationship selling should take some of the pressure off salespeople to make 'the dreaded close'. But there still comes a point in the sales call where one or the other party has to move towards gaining commitment to the objectives of the call – presumably a purchase. This is the decision stage, or **close**. Directly asking the customer for business doesn't need to be painful or awkward. If the salesperson has done a great job in the previous five steps in the creative selling process, closing the sale should be a natural progression of the dialogue between the buyer and seller.

There are a variety of approaches salespeople can use to close the sale. For example, a *last objection close* asks customers if they are ready to purchase, providing the salesperson can address any concerns they have about the product: 'Are you ready to order if we can prove our delivery time frames meet your expectations?' Using an *assumptive close*, the salesperson acts as if the purchase is inevitable with only a small detail or two to be settled: 'What quantity would you like to order?' In some cases, the salesperson interjects urgency by using a *standing-room-only* or *buy-now close* that suggests the opportunity might be missed if the customer hesitates. 'This price is good until Saturday, so to save 20 per cent you should place the order now.' When making such closes, salespeople must be sure the basis they state for buying now is truthful. Relationship selling-minded sales people don't stretch the truth for short-term gain, they know the customer's long-term loyalty to them, their company, and its products is worth much more than booking one order today.

Step 7: Follow-up

The **follow-up** after the sale includes arranging for delivery, payment and purchase terms. It also means the salesperson makes sure the customer received delivery and is satisfied. Follow-up also allows the salesperson to *bridge* to the next purchase. Once a relationship develops, the selling process is only beginning. Even as one cycle of purchasing draws to a close, a good salesperson is already laying the foundation for the next one.

 ## Sales Management

Few, if any, firms can succeed with just one star salesperson. Personal selling is a team effort that requires careful planning and salespeople available when and where customers need them. **Sales management** is the process of planning, implementing and controlling the personal selling function. Let's review some of the major decisions sales managers who oversee this function must make, as outlined in Figure 12.5.

Figure 12.5 | The Sales Force Management Process
Personal selling is a team effort that requires careful planning to place sales people in the best locations at the best times.

Setting Sales Force Objectives

Sales force objectives state what the sales force is expected to accomplish and when. Sales managers develop such sales force performance objectives as 'acquire 100 new customers,' 'generate 100 million in sales', or even 'reduce travel expenses by 5 per cent'. Firms engaged in relationship selling also state objectives related to customer satisfaction, loyalty and retention. Other common objectives are new customer development, new product suggestions, training, reporting on competitive activity and community involvement.

Sales managers also work with their salespeople to develop *individual* objectives. We can identify two types of individual objectives. *Performance objectives* are readily measurable outcomes, such as total sales and total profits per salesperson. *Behavioural objectives* specify the actions salespeople must accomplish, such as the number of prospects to identify, the number of sales calls, and the number of follow-up contacts they should make.

Creating a Sales Force Strategy

A sales force strategy establishes important specifics such as the structure and size of a firm's sales force. Each salesperson has the responsibility for a set group of customers – their **sales territory**. The territory structure allows salespeople to have an in-depth understanding of customers and their needs through frequent contact, both business and personal. The most common way to allocate territories is geographically, minimising travel and other field expenses. A *geographic sales force structure* usually is sized according to how many customers are in a given area. If the product line is diverse or technically complex, however, a better approach may be to structure sales territories based on different classes of products to enable the sales force to provide more focused product expertise to customers. Kraft Foods, for example, has separate sales teams for its major product areas, such as beverages, cheese and dairy, and grocery items.

Another structure is *industry specialisation*, in which salespeople focus on a single industry or a small number of industries. Firms can often refer to large clients as *key accounts* or *major accounts*. Procter & Gamble uses cross-functional key account teams to focus on each of its major customers. The idea behind this is the old Pareto rule – 20 per cent of your customers account for 80 per cent of your sales (and profits). Those 20 per cent therefore deserve the bulk of your personal selling attention.

Putting salespeople out into the field is a very expensive proposition that greatly affects a company's profitability. Remember, cost per customer contact is far higher for personal selling than for any other form of promotion. Thus, determining the optimum number of salespeople is an important decision. A larger sales force may increase sales, but at what cost? A smaller sales force will keep costs down, but this could backfire if competitors move in with larger sales forces and are able to develop strong customer relationships because each of their salespeople doesn't have to call on as many customers.

A key contributor to the success of a sales force is keeping salespeople in front of customers as much of the time as possible, as opposed to spending their time travelling, in meetings, doing paperwork, or otherwise engaging in non-selling activities. Fortunately, the advent of *virtual meetings* (or *videoconferencing*) has cut down substantially on non-selling time for salespeople. Also, the ability to videoconference and have members of a geographically diverse sales team hold meetings from their home offices can cut non-customer-related travel costs substantially. Along the same lines, more and more companies are allowing salespeople to work from virtual offices through *telecommuting*. This trend keeps salespeople from having to make trips back and forth from home to some office location, allowing them instead to use precious travel time visiting customers.[95]

 ## Recruiting, Training and Rewarding the Sales Force

Because the quality of a sales force can make or break a firm, a top priority for sales managers is to recruit and hire the right set of people to do the job. These are people who have good listening skills, effective follow-up skills, the ability to adapt their sales style from situation to situation, tenacity (sticking with a task), and a high level of personal organisation, among a variety of other well-documented key factors for salesperson success.[96] Companies screen potential salespeople to reveal these skills, along with useful information about interests and capabilities. Pencil-and-paper tests can determine quantitative skills and competencies in areas not easily assessed through interviews.

Closely related to training, *development* (often called professional development) strives to prepare salespeople personally and professionally for new challenges, such as promotions and management responsibilities. It focuses on developing the salesperson more broadly than knowledge or skills training. Training and development should take place not just after the initial hire but throughout the salesperson's career. Many sales organisations turn to outside consultants to help them develop sales force training and development programmes. Sometimes a boost in creative thinking from the outside can do wonders for developing more productive salespeople. Today, with budgets tighter than ever, sales organisations are expecting identifiable returns on investments in training, and outside firms can often deliver these quantifiable results.[97]

Of course, a way to motivate salespeople is to pay them well. This can mean tying compensation to performance. A *straight commission plan* is based solely on a percentage of sales the person closes. Under a *commission-with-draw plan*, earnings are based on commission plus a regular payment, or 'draw', that may be charged against future commissions if current sales are inadequate to cover the draw. With a *straight salary plan*, the salesperson is paid a set amount regardless of sales performance. Sometimes straight salary plans are augmented with a *quota-bonus plan*, in which salespeople are paid a salary *plus* a bonus for sales above an assigned quota or for selling certain products that may be new or more profitable. *Sales contests* provide prizes (cash or otherwise) for selling specific products during a specific time period and can provide a needed short-term boost to sales. However, sales contests can be easily over-used, motivating salespeople to simply wait to sell some products until the contest period, resulting in no real long-term sales increase. Popular prizes for contest winners include cruises, other types of travel, and product selections from prize catalogues.

Although many salespeople like to work independently, supervision is essential for an effective sales force. Sales managers often require sales people to develop monthly, weekly or daily *call reports*, a plan of action detailing which customers were called on and how the call went. These call reports are likely to be generated electronically, often on laptop computers or even as a part of the firm's overall CRM initiative. They allow the sales manager to track what the salespeople are doing in the field, and they provide marketing managers with timely information about customers' responses, competitive activity and any changes in the firm's customer base.

 ## Evaluating the Sales Force

The job of sales management isn't complete until the total effort of the sales force is evaluated. First, it is important to determine if the sales force is meeting its objectives. If not, the sales manager must figure out the causes. Is it due to flaws in the design and/or implementation of the sales force strategy, or are there uncontrollable factors that have contributed? An overall downturn in the economy, such as the recessions of 2000–2002 and more recently, can make it impossible for the best of sales force plans to meet its original sales objectives.

Managers normally measure individual sales person performance against sales quotas for individual sales territories, even when compensation plans do not include bonuses or commissions based on the quotas. They may also use quantitative measures, such as number of sales calls and sales reports, in the evaluation. In addition to quantitative measures, many firms also evaluate their salespeople on qualitative indicators of performance, such as salesperson attitude, product knowledge and communication skills. Increasingly, as firms focus on relationship selling, the level of several important customer metrics such as customer satisfaction, loyalty and retention/turnover have become key measures of superior salesperson performance. Please read the Marketing Metrics box to see how Northlight Sanitation worked on salesperson performance to improve the overall business performance of the company.

Finally, the company can consider the salesperson's expense account for travel and entertainment since the best sales record can mean little to a company's bottom line if the salesperson is bleeding the company dry with outrageous expenses. You think you're creative when spending money? Here are some expenses a few salespeople actually submitted according to *Sales and Marketing Management* magazine:[98]

● Chartering a private plane to make an appointment after missing a regularly scheduled flight.

● A round of golf for four people that cost about €2300.

Marketing Metrics

Northlight Sanitation

Northlight Sanitation manufactures and sells bathroom and kitchen fixtures and accessories. Its sales force had considerable autonomy negotiating prices, terms and conditions. However, after collecting and analysing data on salesperson performance and contributions, it discovered major differences between contributions, and in particular 'star performers' did not contribute much profit. After in-depth interviews it emerged that some salespeople were good at communicating the value proposition and held their ground in price negotiations, whereas others were bad at communicating value and conceded on price. As a consequence of this analysis the company retrained, reassigned or dismissed salespeople; it also adjusted the incentive system to focus on contribution more than volume. These steps boosted profits from 11.6 per cent to almost 14 per cent.

- A set of china for a salesperson's wife to use for a client dinner party.
- A three-day houseboat rental with a crew and chef for equivalent to €30,000.

We'll now turn our attention to direct marketing, which can often represent a useful mechanism for supporting and complementing personal selling.

Direct Marketing

Objective

5

Understand
direct marketing.

Are you one of those people who love to get lots of catalogues in the post, spend hours reading them, and then order just exactly what you want without leaving home? Do you order DVDs, computer software, and books on the web? Have you ever responded to a direct advertising commercial (an infomercial) on TV? All these are examples of direct marketing, the fastest growing type of marketing communications. **Direct marketing** refers to 'any direct communication to a consumer or business recipient that is designed to generate a response in the form of an order, a request for further information, and/or a visit to a shop or other place of business for purchase of a product'.[99] The Direct Marketing Association reported in 2005 that direct marketing-driven sales were on the increase and would grow by over 6 per cent through to 2009.[100]

Clearly, direct marketing has potential for high impact. Let's look at the most popular types of direct marketing, starting with the oldest – buying through the postal system.

Mail Order

In 1872, retailers Aaron Montgomery Ward and two partners decided to mail a one-page flyer that listed their merchandise and prices, hoping to inspire a few more sales.[101] Thus the mail-order industry was born and today consumers can buy just about anything through the mail. Mail order comes in two forms: catalogues and direct mail.

Catalogues

A **catalogue** is a collection of products offered for sale in book form, usually consisting of product descriptions that are accompanied by photos of the items. Catalogues came on the scene within a few decades of the invention of movable type over 500 years ago, but they've come a long way since then.[102]

The early catalogues of Montgomery Ward were designed for people in remote areas who lacked access to shops. Today, the catalogue customer is likely to be an affluent career woman with access to more than enough shops but without the time or desire to go to them. Many shops use catalogues to complement their in-store efforts, for example European fashion retailer Next provides high-quality catalogues as a way to maintain its company image as a leading player.

A catalogue strategy allows the shop to reach people who live in areas too small to support a shop or are too distant. US companies Lands' End and Eddie Bauer are doing good business in Europe and Asia, where consumers tend to buy a lot of products through mail order. Lands' End opened up a central warehouse in Berlin to supply the German market with catalogues. The company trained phone operators in customer service and friendliness and launched an aggressive marketing campaign to let consumers know of the Lands' End lifetime warranty (German catalogue companies require customers to return defective merchandise within two weeks). Although local competitors protested, and even took the company to court, the case was settled in Lands' End's favour.[103]

Direct Mail

Unlike a catalogue retailer that offers a variety of merchandise through the mail, **direct mail** is a brochure or pamphlet offering a specific product or service at one point in time. A direct mail offer has an advantage over a catalogue because it can be personalised to the receiver. Direct mail also is widely used by charities, political groups and other not-for-profit organisations.

Just as with e-mail spam, many of us are becoming overwhelmed with direct-mail offers – 'junk mail' that mostly ends up in the recycle paper bin. This problem was amplified following the anthrax scare of 2001 in the US, when a lot of people became more reluctant to open mail from a source they couldn't identify. Procter & Gamble held back on shipment samples of Always Maxi Pads because consumers received lumpy packages without a clearly identified sender. Nissan also cancelled a direct-mail campaign for one of its new models for similar reasons.[104] The direct-mail industry is always working on ways to monitor what is sent through the mail and provides some help by allowing consumers to 'opt out' of at least some mailing lists. The Direct Marketing Association works to maintain a proactive stance with its members to promote professional practice.

Telemarketing

Telemarketing is direct marketing conducted over the telephone. It might surprise you to learn that telemarketing actually is more profitable for business markets than for consumer markets. When business-to-business marketers use the telephone to keep in contact with smaller customers, it costs far less than a face-to-face sales call, yet still lets small customers know they are important to the company.

 ## Direct-Response Advertising

Direct-response advertising allows the consumer to respond to a message by immediately contacting the provider to ask questions or order the product. This form of direct marketing can be very successful. For example, Richard Thalheimer, founder of high-tech retailer Sharper Image, began his business with a full-page ad in *Runner's World* for a chronograph watch that you could buy by calling a freephone number.[105] While the internet has for many companies become the media of choice for direct marketing, direct advertising in magazines, newspapers and television still represents an active way of doing business.

As early as the 1950s, department stores brought the retailing environment into the television viewer's living room by offering a limited number of products the viewer could buy by calling the advertised company. Television sales picked up in the 1970s when two companies, Ronco Incorporated and K-Tel International, began to present such products as the Kitchen Magician, the Mince-O-Matic and the Miracle Broom on television sets around the world.[106] This form of advertising called **direct-response TV (DRTV)** includes short commercials of less than two minutes, 30 minutes or longer, and home shopping networks such as QVC. Top-selling DRTV product categories include exercise equipment, self-improvement products, diet and health products, kitchen appliances and music.

 ## M-Commerce

One final type of direct marketing is M-commerce. The 'M' stands for mobile, and **M-commerce** refers to the promotional and other e-commerce activities transmitted over mobile phones and other mobile devices, such as personal digital assistants (PDAs).[107] With about a billion mobile phones in use worldwide, many of them internet-enabled, it makes sense that marketers would want to reach out and touch this large target audience. Young people in particular are big users of mobile phones, which of course explains why all the mobile phone companies advertise aggressively to attract university students and often have a retail presence on campus.

M-commerce through text messages (such as an ad for a concert or a new restaurant) is known as *short-messaging system marketing* (SMS marketing). Perhaps you're in the market for a new computer. You visit a local retailer and decide what you want. While you're there, you use your NeoReader/Qode software on mobile phone or PDA to check prices and access a promotion, and then you go online to compare prices of the same computer elsewhere on the web. If you decide you have the best price, you'll be able to handle the transaction on your phone as well, paying for the computer through a secure internet connection.

Now that you've learned about the promotional mix, read 'Real People, Real Decisions' to see which strategy Rick selected.

Real People, Real Decisions

How it worked out at Tupperware

Rick chose option 2 to utilise PR, and Tupperware Brands instigated a comprehensive public relations campaign to inform consumers and update the brand perception of the product and the opportunity for achievement. The company is working hard to redefine itself in pop culture. For example, Tupperware Brands worked with designer Cynthia Rowley to design shoes and headbands of the same plastic resin utilised to mould Tupperware products. Tupperware will not sell these items, but had them designed to associate Tupperware with high fashion and change its historical image. These are some of the specific actions Tupperware took as part of this PR effort:

> ## The company is working hard to redefine itself in pop culture

- It launched a global design contest encouraging individuals to design something from Tupperware whereby a unique design is crafted utilising Tupperware products. Once again, these items would not be sold as Tupperware products but would be displayed in museums around the world to associate Tupperware with design, in order to get people to perceive the products in a new light. The company has now run this contest in all of its major markets, including Germany, France, Mexico, Indonesia and the United States, to name a few.

- It is launching an international cookbook featuring recipes from celebrities and well-known chefs that it will distribute globally.

- It created a video to be used with the press that talks through the history of the company and features women throughout the world who have achieved their dreams through the earnings opportunity at Tupperware.

Since the campaign launched in April 2005, Tupperware has seen a significant increase in terms of media exposure. Instead of trying to convince the media to feature the company, print and TV editors have requested coverage. Other foreign exposure comes from placing the winners of the design contest in famous museums in markets like Germany, France and Mexico. Indonesia planned to put all of the design submissions in a shopping centre to be viewed and voted on by consumers, with the winner being submitted to the global contest. Allowing public viewing of these designs globally helps remind consumers about Tupperware and allows them to know and understand Tupperware with a new and different viewpoint.

design a
tupperware
masterpiece

click here for details
cliquez ici pour les détails en français
haga clic aquí para obtener detalles en español

Translations in
Tupperware
Global Design Contest

Photo 12.11	Cynthia Rowley's wedge shoes and head-bands updated the brand perception of Tupperware. Source: www.translationsintupperware.com

Marketing Metrics

How Tupperware Measures Success

Tupperware conducted a baseline market study in 2004 to ascertain brand perception in its top 10 markets, and it updated this study in the middle of 2006 to determine changes in brand perceptions. The brand perception studies were done globally in many of Tupperware's major markets, like Germany, France, Mexico and Russia. They included questions to determine brand penetration, including product awareness, product perception such as leading-edge and high design, ability to locate a consultant, product and company image, price points and value for money. It takes 2–3 years to change a perception, but the company already has seen strong evidence of improvement in its Australian market, which today is one of its strongest growth markets.

Chapter Summary

Now that you have finished reading this chapter, you should be able to answer any of the following potential examination questions:

1. **Explain what advertising is and describe the major types of advertising.** Advertising is non-personal communication from an identified sponsor using mass media to persuade or influence an audience. Advertising informs, reminds and creates consumer desire. Product advertising is used to persuade consumers to choose a specific product or brand. Institutional advertising is used to develop an image for an organisation or company, to express opinions (advocacy advertising), or to support a cause (public service advertising) and retail advertising informs customers about where to shop. Some advertisers are now encouraging consumers to participate in do-it-yourself advertising. Most companies rely on the services of advertising agencies to create successful advertising campaigns. Full-service agencies include account management, creative services, research and marketing services, and media planning, while limited service agencies provide only one or a few services.

2. **Describe the process of developing an advertising campaign.** Development of an advertising campaign begins with identifying the target audience and developing advertising message and budget objectives. Next, advertisers design the advertising, and select an effective type of advertising appeal. Pre-testing advertising before placing it in the media prevents costly mistakes. A media plan determines where and when advertising will appear. Media options include broadcast media (network and spot television and radio), print media (newspapers, magazines and directories), out-of-home media (outdoor advertising and place-based media), and internet advertising. A media schedule specifies when and how often the advertising will be seen or heard.

3. **Explain how marketers evaluate advertising.** Marketers evaluate advertising through post-testing. Post-testing research may include aided or unaided recall tests that examine whether the message had an influence on the target market.

4. **Explain what sales promotion is and describe some of the different types of trade and consumer sales promotion activities.** A sales promotion is a short-term programme designed to build interest in or encourage purchase of a product. Trade sales promotions include merchandising and case allowances, trade shows, incentive programmes, push money and promotional products, among others. Consumer sales promotions include coupons, price deals, refunds, rebates, frequency or loyalty programmes, bonus packs contests/ sweepstakes, premiums, sampling, point-of-purchase promotions, product placements and cross-promotions among others.

5. **Explain the role of public relations.** The purpose of PR is to build good relationships between an organisation and its various publics and to establish and maintain a favourable image. Public relations is useful in introducing new products, influencing legislation, enhancing the image of a city, region, or country, enhancing the image of an organisation and calling attention to a firm's community involvement.

6. **Describe the steps in developing a public relations campaign.** The steps in a PR campaign begin with setting objectives, creating and executing a campaign strategy, and planning how the PR programme will be evaluated. PR specialists often use print or video news releases to communicate timely topics, research stories, and consumer information. Internal communications with employees include company newsletters and internal TV programmes. Other PR activities include lobbying, speechwriting, developing corporate identity materials, media relations, arranging sponsorships and special events, and providing advice for management.

7. **Explain the important role of personal selling in marketing.** Personal selling occurs when a company representative interacts directly with a prospect or customer to communicate about a good or service. Many organisations rely heavily on this approach because at times the 'personal touch' can carry more weight than mass-media material. Generally, a personal selling effort is more important when a firm engages in a 'push' strategy, in which the goal is to push the product through the channel of distribution so that it is available to consumers. Today's salespeople are less likely to employ transactional selling (hard-sell tactics) in favour of relationship selling in which they pursue win–win relationships with customers.

8. **List the steps in the personal selling process.** The steps in the personal selling process include prospecting and qualifying, pre-approach, approach, sales presentation, handling objections, close and follow-up. These steps combine to form the basis for communicating the company's message to the customer. Learning the intricacies of each step can aid the salesperson in developing successful relationships with clients and in bringing in business for their companies.

9. **Explain the role of the sales manager.** Sales management includes planning, implementing and controlling the selling function. The responsibilities of a sales manager include the following: creating a sales force strategy, including the structure and size of the sales force; recruiting, training, and compensating the sales force; and evaluating the sales force.

Key Terms

Advergaming 455

Advertising 430

Advertising appeal 436

Advertising campaign 432

Advertising exposure 445

Advocacy advertising 431

Aided recall 446

Aperture 438

Approach 469

Attitudinal measures 446

Banners 443

Buttons 443

Case allowance 450

Catalogue 474

Close 470

Copy testing 437

Cost per thousand (CPT) 445

Creative selling process 467

Creative strategy 435

Cross-promotion (or cooperative promotion) 455

Direct mail 475

Direct marketing 474

Direct-response advertising 475

Direct-response TV (DRTV) 475

Follow-up 470

Frequency 445

Frequency programmes 453

Full-service agency 433

Gross rating points (GRPs) 445

Impressions 445

Institutional advertising 431

limited-service agency 433

M-commerce 475

Media planning 438

Media schedule 444

Merchandising allowance 448

Missionary salesperson 466

New-business salesperson 466

Order getter 466

Order taker 466

Out-of-home media 441

Permission marketing 444

Personal selling 462

Place-based media 442

Point-of-sale (POS) 454

Post-testing 446

Premiums 454

Press release 459

Pre-approach 468

Pre-testing 437

Product advertising 431

Product placement 430

Promotional products 451

Prospecting 467

Public relations (PR) 456

Public service advertisements (PSAs) 431

Puffery 438

Publicity 456

Push money 451

Reach 445

Relationship selling 467

Sales management 470

Sales presentation 469

Sales promotion 447

Sales territory 471

Sampling 454

Sponsorships 460

Team selling 466

Technical specialist 466

Telemarketing 475

Trade promotions 448

Trade shows 450

Transactional selling 467

Unaided recall 446

Unique selling proposition (USP) 436

Chapter Review

Marketing Concepts: Testing Your Knowledge

1. What is advertising, and what is its role in marketing?

2. What are the types of advertising that are most often used?

3. How do advertising agencies create campaigns for their clients? Describe the steps in developing an advertising campaign.

4. Describe some of the different advertising appeals used in campaigns.

5. What are the strengths and weaknesses of television, radio, newspapers, magazines, directories, out-of-home media, place-based media and the internet for advertising? What are the ways marketers advertise on the web?

6. Describe the media planning process. How do marketers pre-test their ads? How do they post-test ads?

7. What is sales promotion? Explain some of the different types of trade and consumer sales promotions frequently used by marketers.

8. What is the purpose of public relations? What is proactive PR? What is a crisis management plan?

9. What are the steps in planning a PR campaign?

10. Describe some of the activities that are a part of PR.

11. What role does personal selling play within the marketing function?

12. What is relationship selling? How is it different from transactional selling?

13. What is prospecting? What does it mean to qualify the prospect? What is the pre-approach? Why are these steps in the creative selling process that occur before you ever even contact the buyer so important to the sale?

14. What are some different ways you might approach a customer? Would some work better in one situation or another?

15. What is the objective of the sales presentation? How might you overcome buyer objections?

16. Why is follow-up after the sale so important in relationship selling?

17. Describe the role of sales managers. What key functions do they perform?

18. What is direct marketing? Describe the more popular types of direct marketing.

Marketing Concepts: Discussing Choices

1. Some people are turned off by advertising because they say it is obnoxious, that it insults their intelligence, and that advertising claims are untrue. Others argue that advertising is beneficial and actually provides value for consumers. What are some arguments on each side? How do you feel?

2. Technology through television remotes, VCRs, computers and cable television is giving today's consumers more and more control over the advertising images they see. How has this affected the advertising industry so far, and do you think this will affect it in the future? What are some ways that advertising can respond to this?

3. Companies sometimes teach consumers a 'bad lesson' with the overuse of sales promotion. As a result, consumers expect the product always to be 'on offer' or have a rebate available. What are some examples of products where this has occurred? How do you think companies can prevent this?

4. Some people criticise PR specialists, calling them 'spin doctors' whose job is to hide the truth about a company's problems. What is the proper role of PR within an organisation? Should PR specialists try to put a good face on bad news?

5. In general, professional selling has evolved from hard-sell to relationship selling. Is the hard-sell style still used? If so, in what types of organisations? What do you think the future holds for these organisations? Will the hard-sell continue to succeed – that is, are there instances where transactional selling is still appropriate? If so, when?

6. One reason cited by experts for the increase in consumer catalogue shopping is the poor quality of service available at retail stores. What do you think about the quality of most retail salespeople you come in contact with? What are some ways retailers can improve the quality of their sales associates?

7. Would training and development needs of salespeople vary depending on how long they have been in the business? Why or why not? Would it be possible (and feasible) to have different training programmes for salespeople who are at different career stages?

8. What would be the best approach for a sales manager to take in determining the appropriate rewards programme to implement for his or her salespeople? What issues are important when determining the rewards to make available?

9. M-commerce allows marketers to engage in location commerce where they can identify where consumers are and send them messages about a local shop. Do you think consumers will respond positively to this? What do you think the benefits for consumers of M-commerce are?

Marketing Practice: Applying what you've Learned

1. As an account executive for an advertising agency, you have been assigned to a new client, a new line of high quality, high price make-up. As you begin development of the creative strategy, you are considering different types of appeals:

   a. USP

   b. Comparative advertising

   c. A fear appeal

   d. A celebrity endorsement

   e. A slice-of-life ad

   f. Sex appeal

   g. Humour

   Outline the strengths and weaknesses of using each of these appeals for advertising the makeup.

2. Spend some time looking through magazines. Find an ad that fits each of the following categories:

   a. USP strategy

   b. Testimonial

   c. Lifestyle format

   d. Humour appeal

   Assess each ad. Explain who the target market appears to be. Describe how the appeal is executed. Discuss what is good and bad about the ad. Do you think the ad will be effective? Why or why not?

3. Assume that you are the head of PR for a regional fast-food chain that specialises in fried chicken and fish. A customer has claimed that he became sick when he ate a fried cockroach that was in his meal along with the chicken. As the director of PR, what recommendations do you have for how the firm might handle this crisis?

4. As a PR professional employed by your university, you have been asked to develop strategies for improving your school's PR programme. Write a memo to your university vice chancellor with your recommendations.

5. Assume that you have just been hired as a field salesperson by a firm that markets university textbooks. As part of your training, your sales manager has asked you to develop an outline of what you will say in a typical sales presentation. Write that outline.

6. This chapter introduced you to several key success factors sales managers look for when hiring relationship salespeople. Are there other key success factors you can identify for relationship salespeople? Explain why each is important.

Marketing Miniproject: Learning by Doing

(A) The purpose of this miniproject is to give you an opportunity to experience the advertising creative process.

   1. With one or more classmates, create (imagine) a new brand of an existing product (such as toothpaste, perfume, soft drink, or the like).

   2. Decide on an advertising appeal for your new product.

   3. Create a series of at least three different magazine ads for your product, using the appeal you selected. Your ads should have a headline, a visual, and copy to explain your product and to persuade customers to purchase your brand.

   4. Present your ads to your class. Discuss the advertising appeal you selected and explain your ad executions.

(B) The purpose of this miniproject is to help you understand the advantages of following the creative selling process.

   1. With several of your classmates, create a new product in a category that most students buy regularly (for example, toothpaste, shampoo, pens, pencils, soft drinks . . . anything that interests you that might be sold through a supermarket). Make up a new brand name and some creative features and benefits of the new product you come up with.

   2. Develop a plan for executing each of the steps in the creative selling process. Ensure that you cover all the bases of how you would go about selling your product to an organisational buyer at the supermarket for distribution to all their shops.

   3. Report on your plan to your class and ask the other students for feedback on whether or not your approach will convince the buyer to purchase.

Real People, Real Surfers

Exploring the Web (A)

Much of the advertising you see every day on television and in magazines is created by a small number of large advertising agencies. To make their agency stand out from the others, the different agencies develop unique personalities or corporate philosophies. Visit the websites of several advertising agencies:

Leo Burnett Worldwide (www.leoburnett.com)

BBDO Worldwide (www.bbdo.com)

WPP (www.wpp.com)

Fallon (www.fallon.co.uk)

J. Walter Thompson (www.jwt.com)

Explore the websites to see how they differ. Then answer the following questions:

1. What is the mission of each agency? How does each agency attempt to position itself compared to other agencies?

2. Who are some of the major clients of the agency?

3. How does the site demonstrate the creative ability of the agency? Does the site do a good job of communicating the mission of the agency? Explain.

4. If available, tell a little about the history of the agency.

5. Of the agencies you visited, which would you most like to work for, and why?

6. As a client, based on your exploration of the websites, which agency would you choose for your business, and why?

Exploring the Web (B)

A critical part of successful selling today is the effective use of technology and information by salespeople. Sometimes salespeople feel like they have information and technology 'overload' – just too much to cope with. A well-run CRM system can go a long way towards organising the important elements of selling.

Visit the websites www.crmguru.com and www.salesforce.com. Peruse some of the content and then answer the following questions:

1. What do you gather are some of the most important issues surrounding successful use of CRM?

2. Pick any two experts featured on the sites and briefly summarise their key messages.

3. How do you suppose CRM can help link the marketing and sales functions in a firm? Hint: Consider the information needed by both groups, and how that information is collected, analysed and distributed for use.

4. Assume that you have been hired as a sales manager for a small firm with 20 outside salespeople. Would CRM be useful in such a setting? Why or why not?

Now, take a look at the website at www.pearsoned.co.uk/solomon to see some videos from YouTube relating to aspects of this chapter.

In addition, read our PR case study called 'Eat in colour' and work out which option received the most PR coverage. Finally, do our special online sales promotion exercise and you could throughout the year save enough to pay for this book.

Also on the website, try some analysis and calculations yourself by looking up the marketing metrics exercise called Advertising to learn how to develop advertising models.

Marketing Plan Exercise

(A) An advertising campaign consists of a series of advertisements placed in media over time. While ads may be placed in different media, all will have the same look, feel, and message. Think about one of the following products:

1. A new brand of toothpaste
2. Your home town or city
3. Your university

Assume that you are developing an advertising campaign. Outline how you would develop the campaign. Be sure to discuss the following:

1. The type of appeal you would use
2. The main message you will seek to communicate
3. The media you would use (be sure to include at least one print and one broadcast medium)
4. How you will develop the ads so that they have the same look and feel

(B) Assume for a moment that you are Rick Goings at Tupperware. Consider the nature of the business, its products and services and the markets in which the company competes for business. In developing a marketing plan, one must be very careful to use the elements of the marketing communication mix (1) in an integrated way so that one communicates a consistent message and (2) in a way that represents the best investment of promotional spend that will give the greatest returns.

1. Should personal selling be a high priority in the future? Why or why not?

2. What approach to personal selling would you recommend to be built into the plan? Why do you recommend this approach?

3. Is there any place for direct marketing? Justify your answer. If you believe direct marketing should be planned for, what type(s) do you recommend, and why?

Marketing in Action Case

Real decisions at Hamilton Wishaw (HW), City of London

William Duncan looked at his watch. Half an hour before meeting his brother at the wine bar on the ground floor, he thought he ought, perhaps, to prepare for his appraisal next week. It was a year since he took his job as Business Development Manager at Hamilton Wishaw and he reflected that there were lots of things that he now knew about which he had not picked up on his MBA studies. In particular he was responsible for sales in a sales-led firm which let him do very little direct selling.

Hamilton Wishaw (HW) was a significant firm in the London legal market. It was not quite in the league of the famed Magic Circle top four legal firms but had aspirations to get itself to that level. 'Sooner rather than later,' growled HW's Managing Partner as he noted June 2008's reporting season numbers from Magic Circle member firms. These indicated that

Magic Circle partners (owners of the firm and practising lawyers) had typically received somewhat more than £1.2 million each in profits for the previous year. William well remembered the comment 'Nice work! But you are going to have to help us drive towards these numbers, William. That's what you're here for'.

HW currently had 65 equity partners and 130 lawyers, some 200 solicitors in all. These were complemented by a similar number of support staff, some like William highly qualified, many not. Rewards, as in any successful City of London firm, were high. Standards of expertise were high too, as were expectations of effort. Weekend and through-the-night working were common enough. HW had, like many firms, its particular areas of expertise within a general framework of legal services. These ranged from the comparatively general (such as banking law) to the somewhat unusual (e.g. derivatives). The firm had been around in London for generations and was reasonably well thought of by its peers. The current Managing Partner had been in post for some time. As part of his strategy to modernise the firm, he had been the mover behind the establishment of the Business Development function which William now managed.

Business Development Issues

In terms of winning new business, the key figure in most clients' decision-making unit would likely be the General Counsel. This would be the most senior legally qualified lawyer employed by the client and would usually be supported by a team of other lawyers, some of whom would be senior people in their own right, such as a Deputy General Counsel. The GC would normally have a very significant say in which law firms were on the company panel. Unsurprisingly, since almost all GCs have been in private practice earlier in their career, such panels often had representation from these previous firms. In terms of gaining business, the process seemed to work as follows. Firstly, when a new GC was appointed or when there was a change in senior management of the firm, it was common for a review of panel membership to be instituted. This provided an opportunity for

firms previously excluded from the panel to pitch for panel membership. However, success at this stage did not necessarily guarantee work coming their way for the new panel member. For substantial pieces of business, the norm was to invite two or more panel members to put up their response to an RFP (request for proposal) and if the law firm wished to become involved, they might then participate in a competitive 'beauty parade' with other panel members. As William wryly used to say 'Getting on the panel is a bit like buying a ticket to a disco. It gets you entrance but you've still got to dance and chat before you may get the chance to take someone home!' Work gained from clients in this manner could have very significant value, with fees into many millions of pounds per year per client.

Implications of the Panel

The two-step panel process had provided William with food for thought. The client side invariably fielded a team of solicitors (perhaps flanked by a procurement professional) who liked to deal with matters in their own 'language' and whose agenda was often driven by cost reduction. This virtually obliged HW to respond in like vein, with himself as a possible attendee. The well-tried formula of 'Find out what the client wants and then give them it' was never far from William's mind in such situations. The RFP process certainly gave some clues but not everything would necessarily be disclosed therein, and now and then the prospect of 'personality incompatibility' loomed. As William noted, even bookish colleagues can have large egos. Questions of price were inevitable although not necessarily mission critical. Technical expertise was an expected norm unless the area was considered very specialist/exotic; more often, the determining factors were perceived to be experience and the ability to match the commercial objectives of the firm. To be able to convincingly answer 'What have you done that can help my company deliver its commercial objectives and manage its legal and regulatory risk more effectively?' was to hear the entry door opening in front of one.

Because of the extent of the stakes and the nature of the process, William had found it useful not only to advise on the make-up of the teams for each beauty contest, but also to gather these teams together for rehearsal before meeting the potential client. In the beginning, partners thought this was time-consuming and costly as they were potentially giving up client servicing time (at upwards of several hundreds of pounds per hour income generated); and 'they were lawyers not actors'. However, after a few early good results from this approach, the resistance had subsided somewhat.

One of the unexpected plus points from the rehearsal had been a more thorough exploration and quantification of what he had learned at business school as the 'augmented product'. Language which he would never dare use at work, he thought. In the context here, the augmented product would probably involve analysing environmental/legal changes relevant to the client for free and providing these via electronic or face-to-face means on a regular basis. It was a regular occurrence for legal firms to second their own staff (at the legal firm's own expense) to work as in-house solicitors for the client for periods of six months or more, he mused. Whilst times were good, touch wood, at the moment, there had been occasions in the past when HW had reduced its contract fees well below market level in order to keep fee-earners occupied as a contribution to fixed cost overhead so the price issue could rarely be totally discounted.

> # The well-tried formula of 'Find out what the client wants and then give them it' was never far from William's mind

Personal Networks

William was proud of his alumni list. This was a database of every qualified solicitor who had worked for the firm in the last ten years. These alumni were cultivated generously as they provided a source of early intelligence as to potential items of business. In a quiet way they were also company advocates. William and his team were assiduous in keeping list members up to date with HW's 'successes' by e-mail and hard copy newsletter. Personal interaction was also facilitated by invitation to social events and sporting occasions such as music concerts and tennis at Wimbledon. He was confident that the alumni programme was a most useful aid to business development. It did cost, though – lots! Perhaps a time would come when the expense would be challenged. He needed to institutionalise this as best he could in order to defend the list for the future.

Ethical Concerns

It should not be thought, however, that HW was prepared to accept just any old piece of business which came its way. That was the *raison d'être* for a central team quite separate from Business Development which had the function, basically, of being guardian of HW's values and ethics. After all, if a major law firm could not be trusted to act with integrity, then it had little future. So this was an area which was taken very seriously. Examples here went beyond the obvious of refusing to act illegally and encompassed items such as the choice of which party (if any) to act for in a contested takeover when both firms were already existing clients. Or similarly, in a situation where two clients, say a sovereign state and a foreign investor, disagreed about the scale of compensation appropriate in a nationalisation of the investor's assets, with which side should HW run? The existence of this central team and similar groups in other major legal practices was, in the main, a blessing for William. Admittedly, it could be a delaying factor when he sometimes wanted to move on quickly, but on the other hand it removed a lot of difficulties in taking decisions from his remit. And anyway, his firm sometimes picked up referrals from other firms which felt that they could not afford to be seen to be choosing between existing clients, thus ushering HW into a 'hot prospect'. Personal networks in evidence once more!

Back to the Forthcoming Appraisal

Faced with the need to answer his boss's likely questions at the appraisal, William had formulated in anticipation a difficult one to deal with, viz 'What do we need to do better to win more business?' His response, he concluded, was likely to be in three parts. Firstly, he believed that communication still needed to be stronger. The concept of internal marketing had much resonance in the HW context; in essence virtually everyone was a business developer for the firm, whether it was a partner presenting at a beauty contest or a member of the support team putting together an analysis for a client. Everyone needed to be kept in the picture and to want to be kept in the picture. Cue for a cross-disciplinary chat with the folks in human resources perhaps? Secondly, he was aware of client pressure for increased transparency, particularly in respect of fee structure and expenses charged. This clearly needed some coordination and the nod of approval from the Managing Partner to get going. Finally, there was little doubt in his mind that the personal network concept needed nourishing. Those alumni, those co-suppliers, and, crucially, those existing and past clients all had their different needs and preferences for contact with HW but there was little other than anecdotal commentary to help him do this more effectively.

Things to Think About

1. In what way does William's job as a Business Development Manager seem different from traditional views of being a sales manager?

2. Would you agree with William's assessment of what needs doing?

3. Are there areas to which you would additionally turn your attention in the longer term?

4. What will William need to do in order to make his ideas work in practice?

Source: Written by Frederick Thomson, Kent Business School.

Note: the organisation mentioned in this case is entirely fictitious although based on typical issues. All the material was modified from sources in the public domain.

References

1. 'Marketers', *Advertising Age*, 31 December 2007, 78(52).
2. '21st Annual Global Marketers', *Advertising Age*, http://adage.com/images/random/datacenter/2007/global-marketing2007.pdf.
3. www.wpp.com/nr/rdonlyres/25779704-cab8-4fa7-9240-3febb388f1d8/0/mediaedge_what_next_for_pvrs_apr05.pdf (accessed 28 January 2009).
4. Stuart Elliott, 'On ABC, Sears Pays to Be Star of New Series', 3 December 2003, www.nytimes.com; Brian Steinberg and Suzanne Vranica, 'Prime-Time TV's New Guest Stars: Products', 12 January 2004, www.wsj.com.
5. Brian Steinberg and Suzanne Vranica, 'Five Key Issues Could Alter the Ad Industry', 4 January 2004, www.wsj.com.
6. William Wells, John Burnett and Sandra Moriarty, *Advertising: Principles and Practice,* 5th ed. (Englewood Cliffs, NJ: Prentice Hall, 2000).
7. 'European Advertising and Media Forecast', 19(1) (October 2004), 10–11.
8. Bob D. Cutler and Darrel D. Muehling, 'Another Look at Advocacy Advertising and the Boundaries of Commercial Speech', *Journal of Advertising* 20 (December 1991), 49–52.

9. W. Cooper, 'The Met reaches out to young people with gun-crime video', *New Media Age*, 16 November 2006, 5.

10. 'The Body Shop takes on human trafficking', *Creativity*, 15(11) (November 2007), 50.

11. 'Dove joins DIY Ad creative marketplace', *Brandweek.com*, 15 December 2006.

12. 'Customer-Made', www.trendwatching.com/briefing/; 'Generation C', www.trendwatching.com/trends/GENERATION_C.htm.

13. Quoted in Stuart Elliott, 'Chevy Tries a Write-Your-Own-Ad Approach, and the Potshots Fly', *The New York Times Online*, 6 April 2006.

14. 'Top U.S. Agency Brands by Advertising Revenue', *Advertising Age*, 28 April 2006, www.adage.com/datacenter/article?article_id=108857.

15. G.E. Jordan, 'To gauge ads' effectiveness, watch those eyes', *Newhouse News Service*, August 2007.

16. 'Marketers', *Advertising Age* 78(52), 31 December 2007.

17. 'Insider Information', *The Grocer*, 31 January 2004, 56.

18. Douglas C. McGill, 'Star Wars in Cola Advertising', *New York Times*, 22 March 1989, D1.

19. Jeremy Lee, 'Ofcom Bans Follow-Up Renault Megane Spot', *Campaign*, 6 August 2004, 10.

20. 'Satellite and Cable TV', *Mintel Reports,* October 2007.

21. www.eiaa.net/ftp/casestudiesppt/eiaa_mediascope_europe_2007_pan_european_executive_summary.pdf (accessed 28 January 2009).

22. 'TV Advertising is Less Effective: Survey', *PROMO Magazine*, www.promomagazine.com/news/tvadvertising_survey_032406/index/html.

23. N. Ives, 'Print buyers search for real-time ad metrics', *Advertising Age* (February 2006), S–2.

24. Phil Hall, 'Make Listeners Your Customers', *Nation's Business*, June 1994, 53R.

25. Lisa Marie Petersen, 'Outside Chance', *Mediaweek*, 15 June 1992, 20–23.

26. 'New Campaigns the World', *Asia's Media and Marketing Newspaper*, 16 June 2006.

27. Doreen Carvajal, 'Advertiser Counts on Sheep to Pull Eyes Over the Wool', *The New York Times*, 24 April 2006, www.nytimes.com.

28. J. Quilter, 'Asda hunts agency to handle in-store TV ad sales', *Marketing*, 29 March 2006, 3.

29. Jeremy Wagstaff, 'Loose Wire', 31 July 2003, www.wsj.com (accessed 21 January 2004).

30. 'European Advertising and Marketing Forecast', 21 (April 2007), supplement, 9–127.

31. R. Britton, 'iTV data', *New Media Age*, 5 October 2007, 26.

32. www.springwise.com/telecom_mobile/user_generated_content_meets_p/.

33. Embellix Software, *eMarketing Planning: Accountability and eMetrics*, www.templatezone.com/pdfs/ems_whitepaper. pdf.

34. J. Wilson and B. Johnson, 'He sent 38 billion emails and called himself the Spam King. Then Bill Gates went after him: World's biggest spammer faces $7m bill after legal battle', *The Guardian*, 11 August 2005, 3.

35. Bristol Voss, 'Measuring the Effectiveness of Advertising and PR', *Sales and Marketing Management*, October 1992, 123–24.

36. This remark has also been credited to British businessman Lord Leverhulme; see Charles Goodrum and Helen Dalrymple, *Advertising in America: The First 200 Years* (New York: Harry N. Abrams, 1990).

37. Stuart Elliott, 'New Survey on Ad Effectiveness', 14 April 2004, www.nytimes.com.

38. S. Far, 'Only visual thought can beat today's information overload', *Marketing Week* 29(13), 30 March 2006, 35.

39. J. Neff, 'What P&G learned from Veg-O-Matic', *Advertising Age*, 77(15) (April 2006), 1–3.

40. 'Pooling Power List up for sale', *Precision Marketing* 18(34), 23 June 2006, 26.

41. Federal Trade Commission, *FTC Policy Statement on Deception*, 14 October 1983, www.ftc.gov/bcp/policystmt/addecept.htm; Dorothy Cohen, *Legal Issues in Marketing Decision Making* (Cincinnati: South-Western College Publishing, 1995).

42. 'Appeals Court Backs FTC Call for Changes to Doan's Pills Ads', *The Wall Street Journal*, 21 August 2000, 1, http://0-proquest.umi.com.lib.aucegypt.edu/pqdweb?index=4&did=58381387&SrchMode=1&sid=5&Fmt=3&VInst=PROD&VType=PQD&RQT=309&VName=PQD&TS=1148116805&clientId=.

43. Howard Stumpf and John M. Kawula, 'Point of Purchase Advertising', in *Handbook of Sales Promotion*, ed. S. Ulanoff (New York: McGraw-Hill, 1985); Karen A. Berger, *The Rising Importance of Point-of-Purchase Advertising in the Marketing Mix* (Englewood Cliffs, NJ: Point-of-Purchase Advertising Institute).

44. 'The Whopper Waxes Nostalgic at 50', *Brandweek* 48(45), 12 October 2007.

45. R. Miller, 'Promotions aim to cross borders', *Marketing*, 24 May 2001, 31.

46. J. Malester, 'Duracell to cut prices', *TWICE: This week in Consumer Electronics* 18(2), 20 January 2003, 39.

47. 'Asda reviews incentive plans', *Employee Benefits* (September 2007), 9.

48. Miller, 'Promotions aim to cross borders'.

49. Gardiner Harris, 'Drug Makers Offer Consumers Coupons for Free Prescriptions', 13 March 2002, www.wsj.com.

50. J. Whitehead, 'Redeeming features', *New Media Age*, 14 September 2006, 25.

51. O. Raeburn, 'Online couponing', *Direct Response*, 5 September 2007, 12.

52. 'In Brief', *Marketing Week*, 20 September 2007, 30(38), 5.

53. 'Virgin Atlantic Rolls Out Space Miles', *PROMO Magazine*, www.promomagazine.com/incentives.virgin_atlantic_miles_011106/index.html.

54. 'Six Flags Launches Kids Loyalty Club', *PROMO Magazine*, www.promomagazine.com/entertainmentmarketing/news/sixflagskids/iondex.html.

55. This section based on material presented in Don E. Schultz, William A. Robinson and Lisa A. Petrison, *Sales Promotion*

Essentials, 2nd ed. (Lincolnwood, IL: NTC Business Books, 1993).

56. www.lynxeffect.com/.

57. 'Lengthy Research Leads Disney to Global "Dreams" Theme', *Promo Magazine*, www.Promomagazine.com/research/ Disney_research_061206/index.html.

58. D. Liu, X. Geng and A. Whinston, 'Optimal Design for Consumer Contests', *Journal of Marketing*, 71(4) (October 2007), 140–156.

59. Kerry J. Smith, 'It's for You', *PROMO: The International Magazine for Promotion Marketing*, 41(4) (August 1994); Sharon Moshavi, 'Please Deposit No Cents', *Forbes*, 16 August 1993, 102.

60. Amanda Beeler, 'Package-Goods Marketers Tune in Free-Sampling Sites', *Advertising Age*, 12 June 2000, 58.

61. *The Point-of-Purchase Advertising Industry Fact Book* (Englewood Cliffs, NJ: Point-of-Purchase Advertising Institute, 1992).

62. 'Bausch & Lomb Makes Eyes with Consumers in Spain', *Promo: The International Magazine for Promotion Marketing* (October 1994), 93.

63. Patricia Sellers, 'Winning Over the New Consumer', *Fortune*, 29 July 1991, 113.

64. J. Stein, 'Automakers go Hollywood', *Automotive News* 78(6085), 22 March 2004, 42–43.

65. 'Mastercard and Bud Tie Unique Concepts to *Break Up*', *Promo Magazine*, www.promomagazine,com/entertain mentmarketing/news/mastercard-breakup_060806/ index.html.

66. R. Gray, 'Play the brand', *Marketing,* 25 July 2007, 33.

67. K.J. Bannan, 'No end to placement data services', *Advertising Age* (February 2006), S–3.

68. www.florafamilymarathon.com/florahealthheartinitiatives/ family-marathon.aspx.

69. Fitzgerald, "Homemade Bikini Contest Hits Bars, Beach for 10th Year," 18.

70. Melissa Marr, 'Publicity, PR and "Passion"', 20 February 2004, www.wsj.com.

71. Steve Jarvis, 'How the Internet Is Changing Fundamentals of Publicity', *Marketing News*, 17 July 2000, 6–7.

72. Dana James, 'When Your Company Goes Code Blue', *Marketing News*, 6 November 2000, 1, 15.

73. 'Dell battery replacement to take 20 days', *Electronic News* 52(34), 21 August 2006, 49.

74. Judy A. Gordon, 'Print Campaign Generates Sales Leads for Biotechnology Product', *Public Relations Journal* (July 1991), 21.

75. 'Russian Vodka in UK launch drive', *Marketing,* 20 June 2007, 9.

76. Andy Pasztor, 'FAA Ruling on Long-Haul Routes Would Boost Boeing's Designs', *Wall Street Journal*, 5 June 2006, A.3.

77. F. McEwan, 'Case history: Budget rent a car', *Financial Times (London)*, 24 April 1984, 10.

78. Ni Chen and Hugh M. Culbertson, 'Two Contrasting Approaches of Government Public Relations in Mainland China', *Public Relations Quarterly* (Fall 1992), 36–41.

79. Willie Vogt, 'Shaping Public Perception', *Agri Marketing* (June 1992), 72–75.

80. 'Dell's Exploding battery debacle', *Bulldog Reporter's Daily Dog*, 18 August 2006, Vol. 1, 2.

81. M. Carmichael, 'Cadbury', *The Grocer*, 23 September 2006, 43.

82. C. Turner, '*AIG* banks on the red army for expansion in UK . . . and China?', *Marketing Week* 29(16), 20 April 2006, 9.

83. 'Expansion enables teenager to become MD', *BBC*, 13 April 2002, www.bbc.co.uk/lincolnshire/asop/people/jonathan_ dolby.shtml.

84. J. Lepper, 'M&S slumps as retailer rivals retain reign at top', *PR Week*, 1 October 2004, 4.

85. 'McDonald's Celebrates World Cup Fever with Global Campaign', *Promo Magazine*, www.promomagazine,com/ eventmarketing/news/mcds_worldcup_camapign_060906/ index.html.

86. 'Mmm secures Skoda deal for PR event work', *Event*, September 2003, 5.

87. Brian Steinberg, 'PR Executive Turns to Bloggers to Spread Messages for Clients', *Wall Street Journal*, 17 May 2006, B3A.

88. Quoted in Jaclyn Fierman, 'The Death and Rebirth of the Salesman', *Fortune*, 25 July 1994, 38(7), 88.

89. Direct Selling Association, www.dsa.org; Scott Reeves, '"Do Not Call" Revives Door-to-Door Sales', *Marketing News*, 8 December 2003, 13; Maria Puente, 'Direct Selling Brings It All Home', *USA Today*, 28 October 2003, 5D.

90. www.salesforce.com; Daniel Tynan, 'CRM Software: Who Needs It?', *Sales and Marketing Management* (July 2003), 30; Daniel Tynan, 'CRM: Buy or Rent?', *Sales and Marketing Management* (March 2004), 41–45.

91. Dan C. Weilbaker, 'The Identification of Selling Abilities Needed for Missionary Type Sales', *Journal of Personal Selling and Sales Management* 10 (Summer 1990), 45–58.

92. Derek A. Newton, *Sales Force Performance and Turnover* (Cambridge, MA: Marketing Science Institute, 1973), 3.

93. Mark W. Johnston and Greg W. Marshall, *Relationship Selling and Sales Management*, 2nd ed. (Boston, MA: McGraw-Hill, 2008).

94. Greg W. Marshall, Daniel J. Goebel and William C. Moncrief, 'Hiring for Success at the Buyer – Seller Interface', *Journal of Business Research*, 56 (April 2003), 247–55.

95. Andy Cohen, 'Selling from Home Base', *Sales and Marketing Management* (November 2003), 12.

96. Marshall *et al.*, 'Hiring for Success at the Buyer-Seller Interface'.

97. Julia Chang, 'Making the Grade', *Sales and Marketing Management* (March 2004), 24–29.

98. Adapted from Erin Strout, 'The Top 10 Most Outrageous T&E Expenses', *Sales and Marketing Management* (February 2001), 60.

99. Direct Marketing Association, www.the-dma.org.

100. Direct Marketing Association, www.the-dma.org/research/ economicimpact2005ExecSummary.pdf.

101. Frances Huffman, 'Special Delivery', *Entrepreneur*, 81(3) (February 1993).

102 Paul Hughes, 'Profits Due', *Entrepreneur*, 74(4) (February 1994).

103. Cacilie Rohwedder, 'U.S. Catalog Firms Target Avid Consumers Overseas', www.wsj.com.

104. C. B. DiPasquale, 'Direct Hit after Anthrax Threat', *Advertising Age*, 22 October 2001, 1, 60.

105. 'How We Got Started, Richard Thalheimer', *Fortune*, www.fortune.com/fortune/fsb/specials/innovators/thalheimer.html.

106. Alison J. Clarke, '"As Seen on TV": Socialization of the Tele-Visual Consumer' (paper presented at the Fifth Interdisciplinary Conference on Research in Consumption, University of Lund, Sweden, August 1995).

107. William Safire, 'M-Commerce', www.nytimes.com/library/magazine/home/20000319mag-onlanguage.html.

Chapter 13
Retail and Distribution

Meet Jill Stanley and Kate Crapper-Reardon,
Decision Makers at the Holiday Shop

Q & A with Jill Stanley and Kate Crapper-Reardon

Career high:
Both are still climbing.

Our heroes:
Jill – Stelios Haji-Ioannou;
Kate – Richard Branson.

Don't do this when interviewing with me:
Jill – answer your mobile phone;
Kate – chew gum.

Our pet peeve:
We dislike smoking in all forms.

Holiday resort:
Jill – Thailand; Kate – Madeira.

Drink:
Jill – white wine, or vodka;
Kate – red wine or gin and tonic.

Food:
Italian.

J ill and Kate are partners of the Holiday Shop Ltd, an independent retail travel agent that sells flights and holidays to the general public. The business was established in 1979. Prior to joining the company Kate had spent 10 years in retail travel management, Jill meanwhile had been the personal assistant to four company directors before deciding to run her own business. Both partners had significant management experience, and had participated in thorough management training programmes whilst employed in the steel and engineering sectors.

Soon after establishing the business, Jill and Kate worked hard towards Association of British Travel Agents (ABTA) accreditation for the travel agency, and after a period of time were accepted as members of the association. Both Jill and Kate are married. Jill has one daughter, and Kate has a son and daughter – all three are grown up and have professional careers.

Real People, Real Decisions

A New Wheel of Retailing and its Effect on the Holiday Shop

Up until the late 1970s the Association of British Travel Agents (ABTA) controlled the level of commission that travel agents were able to charge clients for booking flights or taking holidays – and this was fixed at 10 per cent. It was illegal for agents to discount or take larger rates of commission. Regulations changed towards the end of the 1970s and it was Pickfords (a chain of retail agents) that first started to differentiate their offering – and provided a beach towel as an incentive for anyone purchasing a holiday from them. They later offered a free five-minute international phone call for customers who reserved a long-haul flight. This incentive was designed to appeal to the British public who wanted to visit friends and family that had emigrated to Australia and New Zealand. Providing incentives and reducing the commission rate soon became the trend for travel agents as they competed with one another to obtain business.

In the 1980s, when the Holiday Shop was first established, direct forms of advertising became the norm for a number of suppliers. Having a visible or tangible retail presence was no longer a necessity – as companies used teletext (television) to promote their flights and holidays which saved on the overheads associated with having retail premises and allowing further discounts to be passed on to customers.

In the mid 1990s, however, a different form of competition emerged which posed a greater threat to independents like Jill and Kate's business. This stemmed from vertical integration in the supply chain, where holiday companies themselves (the tour operators) decided to acquire their own planes, and more significantly establish control of a number of household names in retail travel. Thomson Holidays, for example, purchased Lunn Poly, and its main competitor Air Tours established a retail arm through acquiring Going Places. These became known as the 'multiples' within the sector, as such companies grappled to take control of the supply chain. Shortly after – towards the mid to late 1990s, telecommunication company Sky decided it wanted a slice of the action too and was quick to establish a TV channel to promote holidays – 'Sky Travel'. The company was able to physically film at destinations, and offered holidays to such places at direct prices – in a bid to obtain market share in a highly competitively intense industry.

Having successfully weathered the storm in the 1980s and 1990s, the Holiday Shop made modest profits and was able to consolidate its position as an independent retailer. However, Jill and Kate were not prepared for what was about to hit them at the next stage of the retail cycle going into the new millennium. From having steady profits for the previous 20 years, the turn of the century did not bring good times for the Holiday Shop. Sales were significantly down in a sector that was still growing year on year. The owners came to the conclusion that their previous loyal customers were surfing the web to find better holiday deals online. It was true, and a number of companies such as Expedia and Lastminute.com had established themselves as key suppliers to holidaymakers. As customers were moving from retail 'bricks' to computer 'clicks', the shape of retail travel was changing quickly. Jill and Kate had to think long and hard concerning a possible future.

Jill and Kate consider their options . . .

Option 1 Look to establish a presence in the corporate business sector by providing bespoke travel services to companies sending their employees on overseas business trips, whilst continue to serve the declining consumer segment of the market

This option was feasible, particularly as both Jill and Kate had experience of working with company directors and operating themselves at director level. Both appreciate the importance of good customer service and felt confident that they could tap into a growing market here, as companies were becoming more and more dependent on export and international travel. The segment was also lucrative, as business and first class passengers pay significantly more for their flights and the commission per flight reservation would therefore be much greater than for the consumer market.

Option 2 Remain independent and try to compete in the direct sell market

This would be a risky option, particularly with state of play regarding consumers and the internet. However, the wide publicity surrounding internet fraud offered a slim hope that consumers might return in fear of undertaking transactions online. However, greater emphasis could be placed on service and security which could win the hearts and minds of some consumers. Whether or not this segment would be large enough would be something that only time would tell.

Option 3 Sell the business to a key retail player, and continue to operate in the market

This was a safe option and companies like Apollo and Co-op Travel had been acquiring such independent players. The approach provides a 'win–win' situation, as larger market share can be obtained, and at the same

time the new agency obtains greater bargaining power with suppliers. Specifically it would provide leverage to negotiate better commission rates with tour operators, airlines, hoteliers and the like, so that further discounts could be passed on to consumers in order to compete with e-tailers. Selling the business would provide a lump sum for Jill and Kate as the ownership of the company would transfer hands, and at the same time they would be able to command reasonable salaries and benefits as joint managers of the newly branded retail business. However, they would lose overall control and be answerable to others.

Now, put yourself in Jill and Kate's position. Which option looks most feasible? Which one would you go for, and why?

Objectives

When you finish reading this chapter, you will be able to:

1 Understand what a distribution channel is and what functions distribution channels perform

2 Describe the types of distribution channels and the steps in planning distribution channel strategies

3 Define retailing and understand how retailing evolves

4 Describe B2C e-commerce and its benefits, limitations and future promise

5 Understand the importance of shop image to a retail positioning strategy and explain how a retailer can create a desirable image in the marketplace

Objective

1

Understand what a distribution channel is and what functions distribution channels perform

Place: The Final Frontier

Distribution may be the 'final frontier' for marketing success. After years of hype, many consumers no longer believe that 'new and improved' products really *are* new and improved. Nearly everyone, even upmarket manufacturers and retailers, tries to gain market share through aggressive pricing strategies. Advertising and other forms of promotion are so commonplace they have lost some of their impact. Marketers know that *place* may be the only one of the Four Ps to offer an opportunity for competitive

advantage – especially since many consumers have come to expect 'instant gratification' by getting just what they want when the urge strikes.

This chapter is about the science and art of getting goods and services to customers. A large part of the marketer's role in delivering the value proposition deals with understanding and developing effective distribution strategies. In this chapter, we will begin with a broad view of the company through the lens of the value chain concept. You'll recall from earlier on that the *value chain* is a broad concept that spans all the activities involved in designing, producing, marketing, delivering and supporting any product. Then we focus on the supply chain, which spans activities across many firms. The *supply chain* includes all the activities necessary to turn raw materials into a good or service and put it into the hands of the consumer or business customer. Often, of course firms outside your own company accomplish these activities – firms with whom your company has probably developed some form of partnership or cooperative business arrangement.

Next, we talk about distribution channels, which are a subset of the supply chain. Distribution channels are important because a large part of the marketer's role in delivering the value proposition deals with understanding and developing effective distribution strategies. Finally, we look at logistics management, which is the process of actually moving goods through the supply chain. We will define each of these terms in greater detail in subsequent sections of this chapter, but for now let's look at the broader activities of the value chain.

The Value Chain

Delivering value to the customer is of primary importance. As we saw way back in the book, the value chain concept is a way of looking at how firms deliver benefits to consumers. They do this by coordinating a range of activities that result in providing a product or service to the customer. As we can see in Figure 13.1, the value chain consists of five primary activities (inbound logistics, operations, outbound logistics, marketing and sales, and service) and four support activities (procurement, technology development, human resource management and firm infrastructure).

Specifically, during the stage of *inbound logistics* activity the company receives materials it needs to manufacture its products. This activity includes receiving the input materials, warehousing and stock control. In *operations*, activities transform the materials into a final product form by machining, packaging and assembly. *Outbound logistics* involve shipping the product out to customers, while *marketing and sales* handle advertising, promotion, channel selection and pricing. *Service* activities enhance or maintain the value of the product, via offering installation or repair. The process is called a value chain because each of these activities adds value to the product or service the customer eventually buys.

Links in the Supply Chain

Whereas the value chain is an overarching concept of how firms create value, the **supply chain** also encompasses components external to the firm itself, including all activities that are

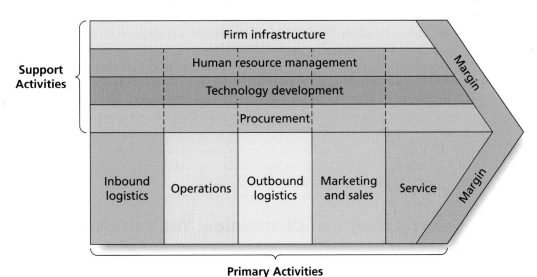

Primary Activities

Figure 13.1	The Generic Value Chain
	The value chain (a concept first proposed by Professor Michael Porter) encompasses all the activities a firm does to create goods and services that in turn create value for the consumer and make a profit for the company.

necessary to convert raw materials into a good or service and put it in the hands of the consumer or business customer. Thus, **supply chain management** is the coordination of flows among the firms in a supply chain to maximise total profitability. These 'flows' include not only the physical movement of goods but also the sharing of information about the goods. That is, supply chain partners must synchronise their activities with one another. For example, they need to communicate information about which goods they want to purchase (the procurement function), about which marketing campaigns they plan to execute (so that the supply chain partners can ensure there will be enough product to supply the increased demand from the promotion), and about logistics (such as sending advance shipping notices informing their partners that products are on their way). Through these information flows, a company can effectively manage all the links in its supply chain, from sourcing to retailing.

One interesting development in supply chain management is that some companies traditionally known for other things are remaking themselves as specialists who take over the coordination of clients' supply chains for them. UPS is perhaps the best example of a former messenger delivery service that today is much, much more because it specialises in **insourcing**; a term used when companies contract with a specialist who services their supply chains. Unlike outsourcing, where a company delegates non-essential tasks to subcontractors, insourcing implies that an external company is brought in to the client company to run its essential operations. While we tend to associate UPS with transportation and the delivery of boxes, etc., the company also provides several other functions for its customers. For example, if your Toshiba laptop needs to be repaired, you can drop it off at a UPS shop and it's shipped to a UPS unit where UPS employees (not Toshiba) actually get your machine back on track. If you order a pair of trainers at Nike.com, it could be a UPS employee who fills the order, bags it, labels it and delivers.[1]

The difference between a supply chain and a *channel of distribution* is the number of members and their function. A supply chain is broader; it consists of those firms that supply the raw materials, component parts and supplies necessary for a firm to produce a good or service, plus the firms that facilitate the movement of that product to the ultimate users of the product. This last part, the firms that get the product to the ultimate users – is the **channel of distribution**.

HP Pavilion uses hundreds of suppliers in manufacturing its notebooks and it sells those items through hundreds of online and offline retailers worldwide. It is noteworthy that the role of individual firms within the supply chain will depend on your perspective. If we are looking at Hewlett-Packard's supply chain, Intel is a supplier, and PC World is a member of its channel of distribution. From Intel's perspective, Hewlett-Packard is a customer. From the perspective of PC World, Hewlett-Packard is a supplier. Intel takes raw materials such as silicon and adds value by turning them into Pentium chips. Intel ships these chips to Hewlett-Packard, which combines them with the other components of a computer, again adding value. PC World takes the finished product and adds value by providing display, sales support, financing and so forth for the customer. Now that you understand the basics of the value chain and the supply chain, let's go deeper into the importance of distribution.

The Importance of Distribution: You Can't Sell What Isn't There!

So you've created your product, priced it and you've done the research to understand your target market and created a marketing message. It does not finish there! You now need to deliver what you make to the marketplace. As we noted earlier, a channel of distribution is a series of firms or individuals that facilitates the movement of a product from the producer to the final customer. In many cases, these channels include an organised network of producers (also called manufacturers), wholesalers, and retailers that develop relationships and work together to make products conveniently available to keen buyers.

Distribution channels come in different shapes and sizes. The bakery around the corner where you buy nice cakes is a member of a channel, as is the baked goods section at the local supermarket, and the café bistro on the high street that sells biscotti to go with your cappuccino.

A channel of distribution consists of, at a minimum, a producer – the individual or firm that manufactures or produces a good or service – and the customer. This is a *direct channel*. For example, when you buy a kilo of strawberries at a farm where they're grown, that's a direct channel relationship. Firms that sell their own products through catalogues, use freephone numbers and factory outlet shops use direct channels.

But life and marketing usually isn't that simple: channels often are *indirect* because they include one or more **channel intermediaries**; firms or individuals such as wholesalers, agents, brokers and retailers who in some way help move the product to the consumer or business user. For example, a baker may choose to sell his buns to a wholesaler that will in turn sell boxes of buns to supermarkets and restaurants that in turn sell them to consumers.

Functions of Distribution Channels

Distribution channels perform a number of functions that make possible the flow of goods from the producer to the customer. These functions must be handled by someone, be it the producer or a channel intermediary. Sometimes the activities are delegated to the customer, like the person who picks up a new chair from the warehouse instead of having it delivered to his home.

Channels that include one or more organisations or intermediaries often can accomplish certain distribution functions more effectively and efficiently than can a single organisation. This is especially true in international distribution channels where differences in countries' customs, beliefs and infrastructures can make global marketing a nightmare. Even small companies can be successful in global markets by relying on distributors that know local customs and laws.

Overall, channels provide the time, place and ownership utility we described earlier in the book. They make desired products available when, where and in the sizes and quantities that customers desire. Suppose for example, you want to buy that perfect bouquet of flowers for someone special. You *could* grow them yourself? Fortunately, however, you can probably just accomplish this task with a simple phone call or a few mouse clicks, and 'like magic' the flowers are delivered to your fiancé's door.

Just think about what happened behind the scenes to make this possible. These days large growers harvest and electronically sort acres of flowers, then auction them to buyers at a huge wholesale flower market in Amsterdam. From there they are shipped by air to importers in other European locations who inspect them for insects and disease, and who in turn transport them to various wholesalers within the EU, who finally distribute the cut flowers to local florists who combine them into bouquets for their customers. The channel members consist of the growers, the auction house, the importers, the wholesalers and the local florists, who all work together to create just the gifts for admirers – and save you lots of time and hassle.

| Photo 13.1 | Supermarkets like this one are channel intermediaries. They buy fresh fruits and vegetables from farmers and make them available to consumers on a daily basis. |

Distribution channels provide a number of logistics or physical distribution functions that increase the efficiency of the flow of goods from producer to customer. How would we buy groceries without our modern system of supermarkets and hypermarkets? We'd have to get our milk from a dairy, our bread from a bakery, our tomatoes from a local farmer, and so on. The companies that make these items would then have to handle literally hundreds of transactions to sell to every individual who wanted to buy.

Distribution channels create *efficiencies* by reducing the number of transactions necessary for goods to flow from many different manufacturers to large numbers of customers. This occurs in two ways. The first is called **breaking bulk**. Wholesalers and retailers purchase large quantities (usually cases) of goods from manufacturers but sell only one or a few at a time to many different customers. Second, channel intermediaries reduce the number of transactions by creating **assortments**, i.e. providing a variety of products in one location so that customers can conveniently buy many different items from one seller at one time.

Figure 13.2 provides a simple example of how distribution channels work. This simplified illustration includes five producers and five customers. If each producer sold its product to each individual customer, 25 different transactions would have to occur, which is not an efficient way to distribute products. But with a single intermediary who buys from all five manufacturers and sells to all five customers, the number of transactions is cut to 10. If there were 10 manufacturers and 10 customers, an intermediary would reduce the number of transactions from 100 to just 20.

One of the functions of distribution channels is to provide an assortment of products. Because the customers can buy a number of different products at the same location, this reduces the total costs of obtaining a product.

The transportation and storage of goods is another type of physical distribution function. Retailers and other channel members move the goods from the production point to other

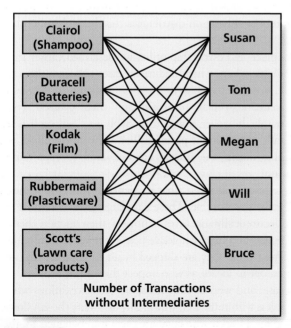
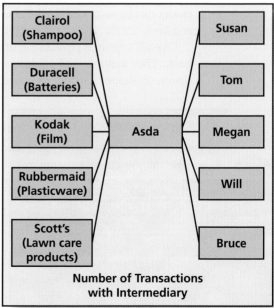

Figure 13.2	Reducing Transactions via Intermediaries

One of the functions of distribution channels is to provide an assortment of products. Because the customers can buy a number of different products at the same location, this reduces the total costs of obtaining a product.

locations where they can be held until they are wanted by consumers. Channel intermediaries also perform a number of *facilitating functions* that make the purchase process easier for customers and manufacturers. For example, intermediaries often provide customer services such as offering credit to buyers. Many of us like to shop in department stores because if we are not happy with the product, we can take it back to the shop, where cheerful customer service personnel may be happy to give us a refund. These same customer services are even more important in business-to-business markets where customers purchase larger quantities of higher priced products.

Some wholesalers and retailers assist the manufacturer by providing repair and maintenance service for products they handle. An appliance, television, hi-fi or computer dealer may serve as an authorised repair centre, provide maintenance contracts, and sell essential supplies to customers. Channel members also perform a risk-taking function. For example, a retailer buys a product from a manufacturer and it just sits on the shelf because no customers want it, they are stuck with the item and must take a loss. Perishable items present an even greater risk of spoilage.

Finally, intermediaries perform a variety of communication and transaction functions. Wholesalers buy products to make them available for retailers and sell products to other channel members. Retailers handle transactions with final consumers. Channel members can provide two-way communication for manufacturers. They may supply the sales force, advertising and other types of marketing communication necessary to inform consumers and persuade them that a product will meet their needs. The channel members can also be invaluable sources of information regarding consumer complaints, changing tastes and new competitors in the market.

The Internet in the Distribution Channel

The internet has become an important place for consumers to shop for everything from Amsterdam tulip bulbs to exotic holidays. By using the internet, even small firms with limited resources enjoy the same market opportunities as their largest competitors in making their products available to customers around the globe.

E-commerce has resulted in radical changes in distribution strategies. Manufacturing firms like Dell and Apple in the personal computer sector rely heavily on internet-driven direct-to-end user distribution strategies, although both have also begun to expand outside this channel. In most cases, though, end users still don't obtain products directly from manufacturers. Rather, goods flow from manufacturers to intermediaries and then on to the final customers. With the web, this need for intermediaries and much of what we assume about the need and benefits of channels is changing. As you saw at the beginning of the book, with Apple iPod's value chain, an increasing number of consumers are buying their music as a download, making retail music shops less necessary. Then too, as more and more consumers have access to faster broadband internet service, downloadable DVDs may replace firms such as Blockbuster as the favoured means of gaining access to films for home viewing.

In the future, channel intermediaries that physically handle the product may become obsolete. Already, many traditional intermediaries are being eliminated as companies question the value added by layers in the distribution channel – a process called **disintermediation**. For marketers, disintermediation reduces costs in many ways: fewer employees, no need to buy or lease expensive retail property in high-traffic locations, and no need to furnish a shop with fancy fixtures and decor. You can also see this process at work when you withdraw cash from an ATM, or when you eat out at self-service restaurants. This reduces or even eliminates the need for an intermediary – in this case the server.

Some companies are using the internet to make coordination among members of a supply chain more effective, and in ways that consumers never see. Such firms are developing better ways to implement **knowledge management**, which refers to a comprehensive approach to collecting, organising, storing and retrieving a firm's information assets. These assets include both databases and company documents and the practical knowledge of employees whose past experience may be relevant to solving a new problem. If a firm tries to share this knowledge with other supply chain members, this can result in a win–win situation for all the partners.

For example, the supply chain in the textile and clothing industry begins with a raw material extraction or production stage (that is, harvesting cotton or developing new synthetic fibres) which supplies the second stage of primary manufacturing. The second stage usually produces a standardised output of commodity material (fibres and fabrics) used to produce commodity products. Progressing downstream, commodity products from the previous stage are used by manufacturers, who apply product development technologies, patents and proprietary features to further add value. The next stage includes marketers of consumer products, followed by distributors and, finally, the retailers who sell to the final consumer.

As technology continues to evolve, some companies are capitalising on the ability of the internet to link partners in the supply chain quickly and easily. The textile and apparel division of DuPont (now a separate company known as Invista) manufactures such products as Lycra that usually goes into active-wear clothing. Invista works closely with companies like Nike and Levi Strauss to develop fibres and fabrics that meet the needs of consumers. Invista's Lycra Assured programme helps to differentiate Invista's 'stretch and recover' Lycra fibre from low-cost competitors that sell the generic version (called Spandex) by providing manufacturers with extensive information they can access online about the performance characteristics of their products.[2] So far, we've learned what a distribution channel is and about some of the functions it performs. Now let's find out about different types of channel intermediaries and channel structures.

Channel Composition: Types of Wholesaling Intermediaries

How can you get your hands on a new Arctic Monkeys T-shirt? You could pick one up at your local music shop, maybe at a trendy clothing shop, or directly over the internet. You might buy an 'official concert T-shirt' from sellers during a live concert. Alternatively, you might acquire an unauthorised copy of the same shirt being sold from a suitcase by a shady character standing *outside* the concert venue. Perhaps you shop online if the group has a website. It might even be possible to catch a deal for one on QVC. Each of these distribution alternatives traces a different path from producer to consumer. Let's look at the different types of wholesaling intermediaries and the different channel structures. We'll hold off focusing on retailers, which are usually the last link in the chain, until later on in this chapter.

Wholesaling intermediaries are firms that handle the flow of products from the manufacturer to the retailer or business user. There are many different types of consumer and business-to-business wholesaling intermediaries. Some of these are independent, but manufacturers and retailers can own them, too. Table 13.1 summarises the important characteristics of each.

Independent Intermediaries   Such companies do business with many different manufacturers and many different customers. Because they are not owned or controlled by any manufacturer, they make it possible for many manufacturers to serve customers throughout the world while keeping prices low.

Wholesalers are independent intermediaries that buy goods from manufacturers and sell to retailers and other business-to-business customers. Because wholesalers take title to the goods (that is, they legally own them), they assume certain risks and can suffer losses if products get damaged, become outdated or obsolete, are stolen, or just don't sell. On the other hand,

Intermediary Type	Description	Advantages
INDEPENDENT INTERMEDIARIES	Do business with many different manufacturers and many different customers	Used by most small- to medium-sized firms
Cash-and-carry wholesalers	Provide products for small-business customers who purchase at wholesaler's location	Distribute low-cost merchandise for small retailers and other business customers
Mail-order wholesalers	Sell through catalogues, telephone, or mail order	Provide reasonable price selling options to small organisational customers
Agents and Brokers	Provide services in exchange for commissions	Maintain legal ownership of product by the seller
Manufacturers' agents	Utilise independent salespeople; carry several lines of non-competing products	Supply sales function for small and new firms
Selling agents, including export/import agents	Handle entire output of one or more products	Handle all marketing functions for small manufacturers
Commission merchants	Receive commission on sales price of product	Provide efficiency primarily in agricultural products
Brokers	Identify likely buyers and bring buyers and sellers together	Enhance efficiency in markets where there are lots of small buyers and sellers
MANUFACTURER-OWNED INTERMEDIARIES	Limit operations to one manufacturer	Create efficiencies for large firms
Sales branches	Maintain some inventory in different geographic areas (similar to wholesalers)	Provide service to customers in different geographic areas
Sales offices	Carry no stock; availability in different geographic areas	Reduce selling costs and provide better customer service
Manufacturers' showrooms	Display products attractively for customers to visit	Facilitate examination of merchandise by customers at a central location

Table 13.1 Types of Intermediaries

because they own the products, they are free to develop their own marketing strategies, including setting the prices they charge their customers.

● *Full-service merchant wholesalers* provide a wide range of services for their customers, including delivery, credit, product-use assistance, repairs, advertising and other promotional support – even market research. Full-service wholesalers often have their own sales force to call on businesses and organisational customers. Some general merchandise wholesalers carry a large variety of different items, whereas speciality wholesalers carry an extensive assortment of a single product line. For example, a confectionery wholesaler would carry pure confectionery goods but stock enough different varieties to give your dentist nightmares for a year.

● In contrast, *limited-service merchant wholesalers* provide fewer services for their customers. Like full-service wholesalers, limited-service wholesalers *take title* to merchandise but are less likely to provide such services as delivery, credit or marketing assistance to retailers. Specific types of limited-service wholesalers include the following:

- *Cash-and-carry wholesalers* who provide low-cost merchandise for retailers and industrial customers that are too small for other wholesalers' sales representatives to call on. Customers pay cash for products and provide their own delivery. Some popular cash-and-carry product categories include groceries, office supplies, and building materials.

- *Mail-order wholesalers* sell products to small retailers and other industrial customers, often located in remote areas, through catalogues rather than a sales force. They usually carry products in inventory and require payment in cash or by credit card before shipment. Mail-order wholesalers supply such products as cosmetics, hardware, and sporting goods.

Agents or brokers are a second major type of independent intermediary. Agents and brokers provide services in exchange for commissions. They may or may not take possession of the product, but they never take title – that is, they do not accept legal ownership of the product. Agents normally represent buyers or sellers on an ongoing basis, whereas brokers are employed by clients for a short period of time.

- *Manufacturers' agents*, also referred to as *manufacturers' reps*, are independent salespeople who carry several lines of non-competing products. They have contractual arrangements with manufacturers that outline territories, selling prices and other specific aspects of the relationship. These agents have little if any supervision and are compensated with commissions based on a percentage of what they sell. Manufacturers' agents often develop strong customer relationships and provide an important sales function for small and new companies.

- *Selling agents*, including export/import agents, market a whole product line or one manufacturer's total output. They are often seen as independent marketing departments because they perform the same functions as full-service wholesalers but do not take title to products. Unlike manufacturers' agents, selling agents often have unlimited territories and control the pricing, promotion and distribution of their products. Selling agents are found in such industries as furniture, clothing and textiles.

- *Commission merchants* are sales agents who receive goods, primarily agricultural products such as grain or livestock, on *consignment*. That is, they take possession of products without taking title. Although sellers may state a minimum price they are willing to take for their products, commission merchants are free to sell the product for the highest price they can get. Commission merchants receive a commission on the sales price of the product.

- *Merchandise brokers*, including export/import brokers, are intermediaries that facilitate transactions in markets such as real estate, food and used equipment in which there are lots of small buyers and sellers. Brokers identify likely buyers and sellers and bring the two together in return for a fee received when the transaction is completed.

Manufacturer-Owned Intermediaries

Sometimes manufacturers set up their own channel intermediaries. In this way, they are able to have separate business units that perform all the functions of independent intermediaries while at the same time maintaining complete control over the channel.

- *Sales branches* are manufacturer-owned facilities that, like independent wholesalers, carry inventory and provide sales and service to customers in a specific geographic area. Sales branches are found in such industries as petroleum products, industrial machinery and equipment, and motor vehicles.

- *Sales offices* are manufacturer-owned facilities that, like agents, do not carry inventory but provide selling functions for the manufacturer in a specific geographic area. Because they allow members of the sales force to be located close to customers, they reduce selling costs and provide better customer service.

- *Manufacturers' showrooms* are manufacturer-owned or leased facilities in which products are permanently displayed for customers to visit. Retailers and the public can visit to see the manufacturer's merchandise and make business-to-business purchases.

Types of Distribution Channels

Objective 2

Describe the types of distribution channels and the steps in planning distribution channel strategies

Firms face many choices when structuring distribution channels. Should they sell directly to consumers and business users? Would they benefit by including wholesalers, retailers, or both in the channel? Would it make sense to sell directly to some customers but use retailers to sell to other customers? Of course, there is no single best channel for all products. The marketing manager must select a channel structure that creates a competitive advantage for the firm and its products based on the size and needs of the target market. Let's consider some of the factors these managers need to think about.

When developing place or distribution strategies, marketers first consider different **channel levels**, or the number of distinct categories of intermediaries that make up a channel of distribution. Many different factors have an impact on this decision. What channel members are available? How large is the market, how frequently do consumers purchase the product, and what services do they require? The producer and the customer are always members, so the shortest channel possible has two levels. Using a retailer adds a third level, a wholesaler adds a fourth level, and so on. Different channel structures exist for both consumer and business-to-business markets.

What is the role of service? As we saw earlier, services are intangible so there is no need to worry about storage, transportation and the other functions of physical distribution. In most cases, the service travels directly from the producer to the customer. However, distribution of some services can be enhanced through the use of an intermediary, often called an *agent*, who helps the parties complete the transaction. Examples include insurance agents, stockbrokers and travel agents.

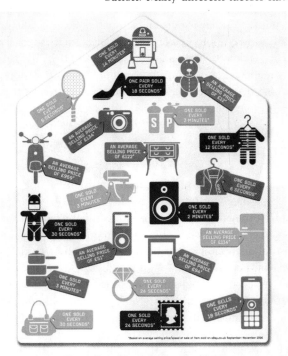

Don't sit on it. Sell it.
You've got dozens of things in your home that millions of buyers on eBay would love to buy. You just need to decide what to sell first. List them. And then watch the bids roll in.

Photo 13.2 eBay has created an entirely new distribution channel that allows consumers to become directly involved in the process on its auction website.
Source: The Advertising Archives

Consumer Channels

As we noted earlier, the simplest channel is a direct channel. Why do some producers sell directly to customers? One reason is that a direct channel may allow the producer to serve its customers better and at a lower price than is possible through using a retailer. By using a direct channel, a strawberry farmer makes sure his customers have fresher strawberries than if he sells them through a local supermarket. Furthermore, if the farmer sells them through a supermarket, the price will be higher because of the supermarket's costs of doing business and required profit. In fact, sometimes this is the *only* way to sell the product, because using channel intermediaries may boost the price above what consumers are willing to pay.

Another reason to use a direct channel is control. When the producer handles distribution, it maintains control of pricing, service and delivery – all the elements of the transaction. Because distributors and dealers carry many products, it can be difficult to get their sales forces to focus on selling one product. In a direct channel, a producer works directly with customers, gaining insights into trends, customer needs and complaints, and the effectiveness of its marketing strategies.

Why do producers choose to use indirect channels to reach consumers? A reason in many cases is that customers are familiar with certain retailers or other intermediaries – it's where they always go to look for what they need. Getting customers to change their normal buying behaviour, for example convincing consumers to buy their washing powder or frozen pizza from a catalogue or over the internet instead of from the supermarket, may prove difficult.

In addition, intermediaries help producers in all the ways described earlier. By creating utility and transaction efficiencies, channel members make producers' lives easier and enhance their ability to reach customers. The *producer–retailer–consumer channel* portrays the shortest indirect channel. Heinz uses this channel when it sells its products through large retailers such as Carrefour or Wal-Mart. Because the retailers buy in large volume, they can buy at a low price which may be passed along to shoppers. The size of these retail giants also means they can provide the physical distribution functions such as transportation and storage that wholesalers handle for smaller retail outlets.

The *producer–wholesaler–retailer–consumer channel* is a common distribution channel in consumer marketing. Take ice cream, for example. A single ice-cream factory supplies, say, four or five regional wholesalers. These wholesalers then sell to 400 or more retailers such as grocery shops. The retailers in turn each sell the ice cream to thousands of customers. In this channel, the regional wholesalers combine many manufacturers' products to supply to grocery shops. Because the grocery shops do business with many wholesalers, this arrangement results in a broad selection of products.

Business-to-Business Channels

Business-to-business distribution channels, as the name suggests, facilitate the flow of goods from a producer to an organisational or business customer. Generally, business-to-business channels parallel consumer channels in that they may be direct or indirect. For example, the simplest indirect channel in industrial markets occurs when the single intermediary – a merchant wholesaler referred to as an industrial distributor rather than a retailer – buys products from a manufacturer and sells them to business customers.

Direct channels are more common in business-to-business markets than business-to-consumer markets. This is because business-to-business marketing often means selling high-priced, high-profit items (a single piece of industrial equipment may cost hundreds of thousands of euros) to a market made up of only a few customers. In such markets, it makes sense financially for a company to develop its own sales force and sell directly to customers – that is, the investment in an in-house sales force pays off.

Dual Distribution Systems

Marketing is not so simple and producers, dealers, wholesalers, retailers and customers alike may actually interact with more than one type of channel. We call these *dual* or *multiple distribution systems*.

The pharmaceutical industry provides a good example of multiple-channel usage. Pharmaceutical companies distribute their products in at least three types of channels. First, they sell to hospitals, clinics, and other organisational customers directly. These customers buy in quantity, purchasing a wide variety of products. Because in hospitals and clinics pills are dispensed one at a time rather than in bottles of 50, hospitals and clinics require different product packaging than when the products are sold to other types of customers. Pharmaceuticals suppliers' second channel is an indirect consumer channel in which the manufacturer sells to large chemist groups that distribute the medicines to their shops across a country.

Alternatively, some of us would rather purchase our prescriptions in a more personal manner from the local independent chemist where we can browse the shelves while we wait. In this version of the indirect consumer channel, the manufacturer sells to wholesalers that in turn supply these independents. Finally, third-party payers such as insurance companies are a third type of channel that pharmaceutical companies may sell to directly.

Hybrid Marketing Systems

Instead of serving a target market with a single channel, some companies have added new channels – direct sales, distributors, retail sales and direct mail. As they add channels and communications methods, they create a **hybrid marketing system**.[3] For example, at one time, you could only buy a Xerox photocopier directly through a Xerox salesperson. Today, unless you are a very large business customer, you will probably purchase a Xerox machine from a local Xerox authorised dealer, or possibly through Xerox On-line. Xerox turned to an enhanced dealer network for distribution because such hybrid marketing systems offer companies certain competitive advantages, including increased coverage of the market, lower marketing costs and a greater potential for customisation of service for local markets.

Now we know what distribution channels and channel intermediaries are and the role of channel members in the distribution of goods and services. We also know that not all channels are alike. Some are direct while others are indirect, and indirect channels can be quite complex. The next section is about how marketers plan channel strategies to meet customer needs better than the competition – that is, seeking the all-important competitive advantage.

Planning a Channel Strategy

Do customers want products in large or small quantities? Do they insist on buying them locally, or will they purchase from a distant supplier? How long are they willing to wait to get the product? As marketers we need to know!

Distribution planning is best accomplished when marketers follow the steps in Figure 13.3. In this section, we will first look at how manufacturers decide on distribution objectives and then examine what influences distribution decisions. Finally, we'll talk about how firms select different distribution strategies and tactics.

Firms that operate within a channel of distribution, i.e. manufacturers, wholesalers and retailers, perform *distribution planning*. In this section, our perspective focuses on distribution planning by producers and manufacturers rather than intermediaries because they, more often than intermediaries, take a leadership role in creating a successful distribution channel.

Step 1: Develop Distribution Objectives

The first step in deciding on a distribution plan is to develop objectives that support the organisation's overall marketing goals. How can distribution work with the other elements of the

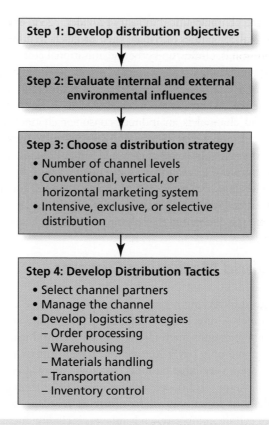

Figure 13.3	Steps in Distribution Planning
	Distribution planning begins with setting channel objectives and includes developing channel strategies and tactics.

marketing mix to increase profits? To increase market share? To increase sales volume? In general, the overall objective of any distribution plan is to make a firm's product available when, where and in the quantities customers want at the minimum cost. More specific distribution objectives, however, depend on the characteristics of the product and the market.

For example, if the product is bulky, a primary distribution objective may be to minimise shipping costs. If the product is fragile, a goal may be to develop a channel that minimises handling. In introducing a new product to a mass market, a channel objective may be to provide maximum product exposure or to make the product available close to where customers live and work. Sometimes marketers make their product available where similar products are sold so that consumers can compare prices.

Step 2: Evaluate Internal and External Environmental Influences

After setting the distribution objectives, marketers must consider their internal and external environments to develop the best channel structure. Should the channel be long or short? Is intensive, selective or exclusive distribution best? Short, often direct, channels may be better suited for business-to-business marketers where customers are geographically concentrated and require high levels of technical know-how and service. Expensive or complex products are frequently sold directly to final customers. Short channels with selective distribution also make more sense with perishable products, since getting the product to the final user quickly is a priority. However, longer channels with more intensive distribution are generally best for inexpensive, standardised consumer goods that need to be distributed broadly and where little technical expertise is required.

The organisation must also examine such issues as its own ability to handle distribution functions, what channel intermediaries are available, the ability of customers to access these intermediaries, and how the competition distributes its products. Should a firm use the same retailers as its competitors? It depends. Sometimes, to ensure customers' undivided attention, a firm sells its products in outlets that don't carry the competitors' products. In other cases, a firm uses the same intermediaries as its competitors because customers expect to find the product there.

Finally, by studying competitors' distribution strategies, marketers can learn from their successes and failures and avoid repeating them. If the biggest complaint of competitors' customers is delivery speed, developing a system that allows same-day delivery can make the competition pale in comparison.

Step 3: Choose a Distribution Strategy

Planning distribution strategies means making at least three decisions. First, distribution planning includes decisions about the number of levels in the distribution channel. The options here were discussed earlier in the section on consumer and business-to-business channels. Beyond the number of levels, distribution strategies also involve decisions about channel relationships – such as whether a conventional system or a highly integrated system will work best, and the distribution intensity or the number of intermediaries at each level of the channel.

Conventional, Vertical, or Horizontal Marketing System? Participants in any distribution channel form an interrelated system. In general, these systems take one of three forms: conventional, vertical and horizontal marketing systems.

A **conventional marketing system** is a multi-level distribution channel in which members work independently of one another. Their relationships are limited to simply buying and selling from one another. Each firm seeks to benefit with little concern for other channel members. Even though channel members work independently, most conventional channels are highly successful. For one thing, all members of the channel are working toward the same goals – to build demand, reduce costs and improve customer satisfaction. Each channel member also knows that it's in everyone's best interest to treat other channel members fairly.[4]

A **vertical marketing system (VMS)** is a channel in which there is formal cooperation among channel members at two or more different levels: manufacturing, wholesaling and retailing. Vertical marketing systems were developed as a way to meet customer needs better by reducing costs incurred in channel activities. Often a vertical marketing system can provide a level of cooperation and efficiency not possible with a conventional channel, maximising the effectiveness of the channel while also maximising efficiency and keeping costs low. Members share information and provide services to other members, recognising that such coordination makes everyone more successful in reaching a desired target market.

There are three types of vertical marketing systems: administered, corporate and contractual:

● In an *administered* VMS, channel members remain independent but voluntarily work together because of the power of a single channel member. Strong brands are able to manage an administered VMS because resellers are eager to work with the manufacturer to carry the product.

● In a *corporate* VMS, a single firm owns manufacturing, wholesaling and retailing operations. Thus, the firm has complete control over all channel operations.

● In a *contractual* VMS, cooperation is enforced by contracts (legal agreements) that spell out each member's rights and responsibilities and how they will cooperate. This arrangement means that the channel members can have more impact as a group than they could alone. In a wholesaler-sponsored VMS, wholesalers get retailers to work together under their leadership in a voluntary chain. Retail members of the chain use a common name, cooperate in advertising and other promotion, and even develop their own private-label products.

In other cases, retailers themselves organise a cooperative marketing channel system. A *retailer cooperative* is a group of retailers that has established a wholesaling operation to help them compete more effectively with the large chains. Each retailer owns shares in the wholesaler operation and is obligated to purchase a certain percentage of inventory from the cooperative operation.

Franchise organisations are a third type of contractual VMS. In these organisations, channel cooperation is explicitly defined and strictly enforced through contractual arrangements in which a franchiser (a manufacturer or a service provider) allows an entrepreneur (the franchisee) to use the franchise name and marketing plan for a fee. In most franchise agreements, the franchiser provides a variety of services for the franchisee, such as helping to train employees, giving access to lower prices for needed materials, and selecting a good location. In return, the franchiser receives a percentage of revenue from the franchisee. Usually the franchisees are obliged to follow the franchiser's business format very closely in order to maintain the franchise. From the manufacturer's perspective, franchising a business is a way to develop widespread product distribution with minimal financial risk while at the same time maintaining control over product quality. From the entrepreneur's perspective, franchises are a popular way to start off in business.

In a **horizontal marketing system**, two or more firms at the same channel level agree to work together to get their product to the customer. Sometimes these agreements are between unrelated businesses. For example, many supermarkets now have formed a horizontal marketing system with banks that maintain a manned branch in the shop. For example in the UK, HSBC branches are sometimes located in Morrisons retail stores, and customers like it because they can do their food shopping and their banking simultaneously.

Most airlines today are members of a horizontal alliance that allows them to cooperate in providing passenger air service. For example, Ireland carrier Aer Lingus is a member of the 'one world' alliance, which also includes American Airlines, British Airways, Cathay Pacific Airways, Finnair, Iberia and Qantas Airways. These alliances increase passenger volume for all airlines because travel agents who book passengers on one of the airline's flights will be more likely to book a connecting flight on the other airline. To increase customer benefits, they also share frequent-flyer programmes and airport lounges.[5]

Intensive, Exclusive, or Selective Distribution?   How many wholesalers and retailers will carry the product within a given market? This may seem like an easy decision: distribute the product through as many intermediaries as possible, but guess again. If the product goes to too many outlets, there may be inefficiency and duplication of efforts. For example, if there are too many Honda dealerships in a particular city, there will be a lot of unsold Hondas sitting on dealer forecourts, and no single dealer will be successful. Alternatively, if there are not enough wholesalers or retailers carrying a product, total sales of the manufacturer's products (and profits) will not be maximised. If customers have to drive hundreds of miles to find a Honda dealer, they may settle for a Ford. Thus, a distribution objective may be to either increase or decrease the level of distribution in the market. The three basic choices are intensive, exclusive and selective distribution. Table 13.2 summarises five decision factors – company, customers, channels, constraints and competition – exploring how they help marketers determine the best fit between distribution system and marketing goals.

Decision Factor	Intensive Distribution	Exclusive Distribution
Company	Oriented towards mass markets	Oriented towards specialised markets
Customers	High customer density	Low customer density
	Price and convenience are priorities	Service and cooperation are priorities
Channels	Overlapping market coverage	Non-overlapping market coverage
Constraints	Cost of serving individual customers is low	Cost of serving individual customers is high
Competition	Based on a strong market presence, often through advertising and promotion	Based on individualised attention to customers, often through relationship marketing

Table 13.2   Characteristics that Favour Intensive Over Exclusive Distribution

Intensive distribution aims to maximise market coverage by selling a product through as many wholesalers or retailers that will stock and sell the product as possible. Marketers use intensive distribution for products such as soft drinks, milk and bread that are quickly consumed and must be frequently replaced. Intensive distribution is necessary for these products because availability is more important than any other consideration in customers' purchase decisions.

In contrast to intensive distribution, **exclusive distribution** means limiting distribution to a single outlet in a particular region. Marketers often sell pianos, cars, executive training programmes, and other products with high price tags through exclusive distribution arrangements. They typically use these strategies with products that are high priced, that have considerable service requirements and when there is a limited number of buyers in any single geographic area. Exclusive distribution enables wholesalers and retailers to better recoup the costs associated with long selling processes for each customer and in some cases extensive after-sales service.

Of course, not every situation neatly fits a category in Table 13.2. Market coverage that is less than intensive distribution but more than exclusive distribution is called **selective distribution**. Selective distribution fits when demand is so large that exclusive distribution is inadequate, but selling costs, service requirements or other factors make intensive distribution a poor fit. Selective distribution strategies are suitable for so-called *shopping products* such as household appliances and electronic equipment for which consumers are willing to spend time visiting different retail outlets to compare alternatives. For producers, selective distribution means freedom to choose only those wholesalers and retailers that have a good credit rating, provide good market coverage, serve customers well and cooperate effectively. Wholesalers and retailers like selective distribution because it results in higher profits than are possible with intensive distribution where sellers often have to compete on price.

Step 4: Develop Distribution Tactics

As with planning for the other marketing Ps, the final step in distribution planning is to develop the distribution tactics necessary to implement the distribution strategy. These decisions are usually about the type of distribution system to use, such as a direct or indirect channel or a conventional or an integrated channel. Distribution tactics relate to the implementation of these strategies, such as selecting individual channel members and managing the channel. These decisions are important because they often have a direct impact on customer satisfaction.

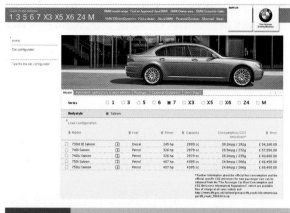

Photo 13.3	BMW's new streamlined distribution strategy lets buyers customise the car online resulting in faster delivery. Source: BMW Group (Germany)

Selecting Channel Partners   When firms agree to work together in a channel relationship, they become partners in what is normally a long-term commitment. Like a marriage, it is important to both manufacturers and intermediaries to select channel partners wisely, or they'll regret the match-up later. In evaluating intermediaries, manufacturers try to answer questions such as these: Will the channel member contribute substantially to our profitability? Does the channel member have the ability to provide the services customers want? What impact will a potential intermediary have on channel control?

For example, which small to medium-sized firm wouldn't jump at the chance to have its products distributed by European retail giant Carrefour? With Carrefour as a channel partner, a small firm could double, triple or quadruple its business. Actually, some firms, recognising that size means power in the channel, have decided against selling to Carrefour because they are not willing to relinquish control of their marketing decision making. There is also a downside to choosing one retailer and selling only through that one retailer. If that retailer stops carrying the product, for example, the company will lose all its customers and it will be back to square one. See the Marketing Ethics box to consider some of the issues surrounding product placement, as suppliers to retail stores grapple to obtain prominent shelf space.

Another consideration in selecting channel members is by analysing a competitors' channel partners. Because people spend time comparing different brands when purchasing a shopping product, firms need to make sure their products are displayed near similar competitors' products. If most competitors distribute their electric drills through mass retailers, a manufacturer has to make sure its brand is there also.

A firm's dedication to social responsibility may also be an important determining factor in the selection of channel partners. Many firms have developed extensive programmes to recruit minority-owned channel members. Starbucks' organisation-wide commitment to good corporate citizenship translates in one way into its supplier diversity programme that works to help minority-owned businesses thrive.[6]

Marketing Ethics

Making the Product Available Ethically

Because their size gives them great bargaining power when negotiating with manufacturers, many large retail chains force manufacturers to pay a **slotting allowance** – a fee paid in exchange for agreeing to place the manufacturer's products on the retailer's valuable shelf space. Although the retailers claim that such fees pay the cost of adding products to their inventory, many manufacturers feel that slotting fees are more akin to highway robbery. Certainly, the practice prevents smaller manufacturers that cannot afford the slotting allowances from getting their products into the hands of consumers.

Debate, Discuss, Disagree

1   Do you think this is ethical?

2   How might you realistically resolve this issue satisfactorily?

Managing the Channel Once a manufacturer develops a channel strategy and aligns channel members, the day-to-day job of managing the channel begins. The **channel leader**, sometimes called a *channel captain*, is the dominant firm that controls the channel. A firm becomes the channel leader because it has power relative to other channel members. This power comes from different sources:

- A firm has *economic power* when it has the ability to control resources.

- A firm such as a franchiser has *legitimate power* if it has legal authority.

- A producer firm has *reward or coercive power* if it engages in exclusive distribution and has the ability to give profitable products and to take them away from the channel intermediaries.

In the past, producers traditionally held the role of channel captain. Anglo-Dutch giant Unilever, for example, developed customer-oriented marketing programmes, tracked market trends and advised retailers on the mix of products most likely to build sales. As large retail chains evolved, the key retailers have begun to assume a leadership role because of the sheer size of their operations. Today it is much more common for such big retailers to dictate their needs to producers instead of producers controlling what product is available to retailers.

Because producers, wholesalers and retailers depend on one another for success, channel cooperation helps everyone. Channel cooperation is also stimulated when the channel leader takes actions that help make its partners more successful. High intermediary profit margins, training programmes, cooperative advertising and expert marketing advice are invisible to end customers but are motivating factors in the eyes of wholesalers and retailers.[7] By improving the speed and accuracy of re-orders, retailers are able to maintain inventory levels necessary to satisfy customers while avoiding ordering errors.

Of course, relations among members in a channel are not always so sweet, particularly as each firm has its own objectives, channel conflict may therefore threaten a manufacturer's distribution strategy. Such conflict most often occurs between firms at different levels of the same distribution channel. Incompatible goals, poor communication and disagreement over roles, responsibilities and functions cause conflict. For example, a producer is likely to feel the firm would enjoy greater success and profitability if intermediaries carry only its brands, but many intermediaries believe they will do better if they carry a variety of brands.

Distribution Channels and the Marketing Mix

How are decisions regarding place related to the other three Ps? For one thing, place decisions affect pricing. Marketers that distribute products through low-priced retailers such as Aldi and Netto will have different pricing objectives and strategies than will those that sell to speciality retailers.

Distribution decisions can sometimes give a product a distinct position in its market. For example, Enterprise Rent-a-Car avoids being overly dependent on the cutthroat airport rental car market by seeking primary locations in residential areas and local business centres. This strategy takes advantage of the preferences of those customers who are not flying and who want short-term use of a rental vehicle, such as when their primary vehicle is in the repair shop. Enterprise built up such a successful following around this business model that loyal customers began to request more Enterprise counters at airports. Now it is a rising competitive threat for traditional airport car rental agencies such as Hertz and Avis.

Of course, the choice of retailers and other intermediaries is also strongly tied to the product itself. Manufacturers select mass retailers to sell mid-price-range products while they distribute top-of-the-line products such as expensive jewellery through high-end department and speciality outlets.

In this section, we've been concerned with the distribution channels firms use to get their products to customers. In the next section, we'll look at the area of logistics – physically moving products through the supply chain.

 ## Logistics: Implementing the Supply Chain

Some marketing textbooks tend to depict the practice of marketing as 90 per cent planning and 10 per cent implementation. In the 'real world', many managers would argue that this ratio should be reversed. Marketing success is very much the art of getting the timing right and delivering on promises – *implementation*. That's why marketers place so much emphasis on efficient **logistics**, the process of designing, managing and improving the movement of products through the supply chain. Logistics covers purchasing, manufacturing, storage and transport. From a company's viewpoint, logistics take place both *inbound* (raw materials, parts, components and supplies) and *outbound* (work-in-progress and finished goods). Logistics is also a relevant consideration regarding product returns, recycling and material re-use, and waste disposal – *reverse logistics*.[8] As we saw in earlier chapters, that's becoming even more important as firms start to consider *sustainability* as a competitive advantage and put more effort into maximising the efficiency of recycling and disposal to save money and the environment at the same time. So you can see, logistics is an important issue across all elements of the supply chain. Let's examine logistics more closely.

Understanding Logistics

Logistics was originally a military term used to describe everything needed to deliver soldiers and equipment to the right place, at the right time and in the right condition. In business, logistics is similar in that its objective is to deliver exactly what the customer wants – at the right time, in the right place and at the right price. The application of logistics is essential to the efficient management of the supply chain. Just as it's said 'an army marches on its stomach' (meaning it can't function without adequate supplies, such as food), a business relies on efficient logistics to be sure it has the resources it needs to successfully compete in the marketplace.

The delivery of goods to customers involves **physical distribution**, which refers to the activities used to move finished goods from manufacturers to final customers. Physical distribution activities include order processing, warehousing, materials handling, transportation and inventory control. This process affects how marketers physically get products where they need to be, when they need to be there and at the lowest possible cost. Effective physical distribution is at the core of successful logistics.

When doing logistics planning, however, the focus is also on the customer. When managers thought of logistics as physical distribution only, the objective was to deliver the product at the lowest cost. Today, firms consider the needs of the customer first. The customer's goals become the logistics provider's goals, and this means that with most logistics decisions, firms must decide on the best trade-off between low costs and high customer service. The appropriate goal is not just to deliver what is needed at the lowest cost but rather to provide the product at the lowest cost possible *so long as the firm meets* delivery requirements. Although it would be nice to transport all goods quickly by air, that is certainly not practical. Sometimes however air transport may be necessary to meet the needs of the customer, no matter what the cost.

Logistics Functions

When developing logistics strategies, marketers must make decisions related to the five functions of logistics: **order processing**, warehousing, materials handling, transportation, and stock control. For each decision, managers must consider how to minimise costs while maintaining the service customers want.

Order Processing   includes the series of activities that occurs between the time an order comes into the organisation and the time a product goes out the door. After an order is received, it is typically sent electronically to an office for record keeping and then on to the warehouse to be filled. When the order reaches the warehouse, personnel there check to see if the item is in stock. If it is not, the order is placed on back-order status. That information is sent to the office and then to the customer. If the item is available, it is located in the warehouse, packaged for shipment, and scheduled for pick-up by either in-house or external shippers.

Fortunately, many firms have automated this process through **enterprise resource planning (ERP) systems**. An ERP system is a software solution that integrates information from across the entire company, including finance, order fulfilment, manufacturing and transportation. Data only need to be entered into the system once, and then the data are automatically shared throughout the organisation and linked to other information. For example, information on the stock of products is tied to sales information so that a sales representative can immediately tell a customer whether the product is available.

Warehousing   Whether we speak of fresh-cut flowers, tinned fruit or computer chips, at some point these goods (unlike services) must be stored. Storing goods allows marketers to match supply with demand. For example, toys and other gift items are big sellers at Christmas, but toy factories operate for 12 months of the year. **Warehousing** – storing goods in anticipation of sale or transfer to another member of the channel of distribution – enables marketers to provide time utility to consumers by holding on to products until consumers need them.

Part of developing effective logistics means deciding how many warehouses a firm needs and where and what type of warehouse each should be. A firm determines the location of its warehouse(s) by the location of customers and access to major motorways, airports or rail transportation. The number of warehouses often depends on the level of service customers require. If customers generally require fast delivery (today or tomorrow at the latest), then it may be necessary to store products in a number of different locations where they can be delivered to the customer quickly.

Firms use private and public warehouses to store goods. Those that use *private warehouses* have a high initial investment, but they also lose less stock due to damage. *Public warehouses* are an alternative, allowing firms to pay for a portion of warehouse space rather than having to own an entire storage facility. Most countries offer public warehouses in all large cities and many smaller cities to support domestic and international trade. A *distribution centre* is a warehouse that stores goods for short periods of time and that provides other functions, such as breaking bulk.

Materials Handling   is the moving of products into, within and out of warehouses. When goods come into the warehouse, they must be physically identified, checked for damage, sorted and labelled. Next they are taken to a location for storage. Finally, they are recovered from the storage area for packaging and shipment. All in all, the goods may be handled over a dozen separate times. Procedures that limit the number of times a product must be handled decrease the likelihood of damage and reduce the cost of **materials handling**.

Transportation   Logistics decisions take into consideration options for **transportation**, the mode by which products move among channel members. Again, making transportation decisions entails a compromise between minimising cost and providing the service customers

Marketing Metrics

Supply chain example

Companies can track a wide range of metrics within the supply chain area. Some of the most common ones are the following:

● On-time delivery

● Forecast accuracy

● Value-added productivity per employee

● Returns processing cost as a percentage of product revenue

● Customer order actual cycle time

● Perfect order measurement.

Let's take a look at the last measure in more detail. The perfect order measure calculates the error-free rate of each stage of a purchase order.[9] This measure helps managers track the steps involved in getting a product from a manufacturer to a customer so that they can pinpoint processes in need of improvement. For example, a company can calculate its error rate at each stage and then combine these rates to create an overall metric of order quality. Suppose the company identifies the following error rates:

● Order entry accuracy: 99.95% correct (5 errors per 10,000 order lines)

● Warehouse pick accuracy: 99.2%

● Delivered on time: 96%

● Shipped without damage: 99%

● Invoiced correctly: 99.8%

The company can then combine these individual rates into an overall perfect order measure by multiplying them together: 99.95% × 99.2% × 96% × 99% × 99.8% = 94.04%.

want. As Table 13.3 shows, modes of transportation, including railroads, water transportation, trucks, airlines, pipelines and the internet, differ in the following ways:

● **Dependability:** The ability of the carrier to deliver goods safely and on time.

● **Cost:** The total transportation costs for moving a product from one location to another, including any charges for loading, unloading, and in-transit storage.

● **Speed of delivery:** The total time for moving a product from one location to another, including loading and unloading.

● **Accessibility:** The number of different locations the carrier serves.

● **Capability:** The ability of the carrier to handle a variety of different products such as large or small, fragile or bulky.

● **Traceability:** The ability of the carrier to locate goods in shipment.

Each mode of transportation has strengths and weaknesses that make it a good choice for different transportation needs. Table 13.3 summarises the pros and cons of each mode.

● **Railroads:** Railroads are best for carrying heavy or bulky items, such as coal and other mining products, over long distances. Railroads are about average in their cost and provide moderate speed of delivery. Although rail transportation provides dependable, low-cost service to many locations, trains can not carry goods to every community.

● **Water:** Ships and barges carry large, bulky goods and are very important in international trade. Water transportation is relatively low in cost but can be slow.

● **Trucks:** Trucks or motor carriers are the most important transportation mode for consumer goods, especially for shorter hauls. Such transport allows flexibility because trucks can travel to locations missed by boats, trains, and planes. Trucks are also able to carry a wide variety of products, including perishable items. Although costs are fairly high for longer distance shipping, they are economical for shorter deliveries. Because trucks provide door-to-door service, product handling is minimal, reducing the chance of product damage.

Transportation Mode	Dependability	Cost	Speed of Delivery	Accessibility	Capability	Traceability	Most Suitable Products
Railroads	Average	Average	Moderate	High	High	Low	Heavy or bulky goods, such as coal and steel
Water	Low	Low	Slow	Low	Moderate	Low	Bulky, non-perishable goods, such as durable components and heavy machine tools
Trucks	High	High for long distances; low for short distances	Fast	High	High	High	A wide variety of products, including those that need refrigeration
Air	High	High	Very fast	Low	Moderate	High	High-value items, such as light electronic goods and fresh flowers
Pipeline	High	Low	Slow	Low	Low	Moderate	Petroleum products and other chemicals
Internet	High	Low	Very fast	Potentially very high	Low	High	Services such as banking, information and entertainment

Table 13.3   A Comparison of Transportation Modes

- **Air:** Air transportation is the fastest and most expensive transportation mode. It is ideal to move high-value items such as certain mail, fresh-cut flowers and live lobsters. Passenger airlines, air-freight carriers and express delivery firms provide such air transportation. Ships remain the major mover of international cargo, but air transportation networks are becoming more important in the development of international markets.

- **Pipeline:** Pipelines are used to carry petroleum products such as oil and natural gas and a few other chemicals. Pipelines flow primarily from oil or gas fields to refineries. They are very low in cost, require little energy, and are not subject to disruption by weather.

- **The internet:** As we discussed earlier in this chapter, marketers of services such as banking, news, and entertainment are taking advantage of distribution opportunities provided by the internet.

Inventory Control: JIT and fast fashion   Another component of logistics is **stock control**, which means developing and implementing a process to ensure that the firm always has sufficient quantities of goods available to meet customers' demands – no more and no less. That explains why firms work so hard to track merchandise so they know where their products are and where they are needed in case a low inventory situation appears imminent.

Some companies are even phasing in a sophisticated technology known as **radio frequency identification (RFID)**. RFID lets firms tag clothes, pharmaceuticals or virtually any kind of product with tiny chips containing information about the item's content, origin and destination. This new technology has the potential to revolutionise inventory control and help marketers ensure that their products are on the shelves when people want to buy them. Great for manufacturers and retailers, but some consumer groups are fighting against RFID, which they refer to as 'spy chips'. Through blogs, boycotts and other anti-company initiatives, these groups proclaim RFID is invading human privacy.

Firms store goods (that is, create stock) for many reasons. For manufacturers, the pace of production may not match seasonal demand, and it may be more economical to produce skis all year round than to produce them only during the winter season. For channel members that purchase goods from manufacturers or other channel intermediaries, it may be economical to order a product in quantities that don't exactly parallel demand. For example, delivery costs make it prohibitive for a petrol station to place daily orders for just the amount of fuel people will use that day. Instead, stations usually order tanker loads and hold fuel in underground tanks. The consequences of running out of fuel may be very bad. Hospitals must keep adequate supplies of blood, certain fluids, drugs and other supplies on hand to meet emergencies, even if some items go to waste.

Inventory control has a major impact on the overall costs of a firm's logistics initiatives. If supplies of products are too low to meet fluctuations in customer demand, a firm may have to make expensive emergency deliveries or lose customers to competitors. If inventories are above demand, unnecessary storage expenses and the possibility of damage or deterioration occur. To balance these two opposing needs, manufacturers are turning to **just in time (JIT)** stock techniques with their suppliers. JIT sets up the delivery of goods just as they are needed on the production floor, minimising the cost of holding stock while ensuring it will be there when it is needed. A supplier's ability to make on-time deliveries is the critical factor in the selection process for firms that have adopted this kind of system. JIT systems reduce stock to very low levels or even zero and ensure consistency by timing deliveries so that they arrive only when a customer needs them. The advantage of JIT systems is the reduced cost of warehousing. For both manufacturers and re-sellers that use JIT systems, the choice of supplier may come down to one whose location is nearest. To win a large customer, a supplier may even have to be willing to set up production facilities close to the customer to guarantee JIT delivery.[10]

Most JIT systems are largely invisible to you as an end consumer. However, if you're a dedicated follower of fashion, you may have encountered this cutting-edge supply chain approach.

Real People, Other Voices

Advice for Jill and Kate

Dr Anthony Willis,
University of Surrey

I would choose option 1. I consider this option feasible, as both Jill and Kate have experience of working with company directors and operating themselves at director level, they both appreciate the importance of good customer service and felt confident that they could tap into this growing market. They recognise that companies were becoming more and more dependent on export and international travel. This segment is lucrative, because business and first class passengers pay significantly more for their flights and the commission per flight reservation would therefore be much greater than for the consumer market.

They would be able to capitalise on the strengths of the Holiday Shop; it's a company which has been established since the 1980s with experience in the retail travel market, it is ABTA accredited. Both Jill and Kate are confident entrepreneurs with trained management skills still on the way up in their careers. With this option they would still have to address a few challenges which are: they are an independent company with limited experience in the corporate business sector, however they do have the experience of dealing with the changes that have taken place over recent years in travel retailing.

The threats that they could encounter will be in the form of competitors and any downturn in the market. They should be able to deal with the competition by concentrating on being able to offer and deliver a coordinated range of activities and benefits and customer service to business customers. The company is part of the distribution channel in hospitality and travel. It is an independent intermediary which will be acting as an agent for airlines, hotel companies and corporate business customers. They are part of a vertical marketing system (VMS) in which I suggest they would be forming partnerships with airlines and hotel groups and corporate businesses to work together in a channel relationship.

This would offer the Holiday Shop a competitive advantage to assist them in operating in this sector in the early stages of what is their retail life cycle. They could promote their new business through *Travel and Trade Gazette*, *Travel Weekly*, and *Selling Longhaul*. They could use word of mouth through the company directors they worked with previously. They would need to establish relationships initially with the local area major employers and offer solutions for their business travellers with company employees required to book travel arrangement through the Holiday Shop.

They need to sign up and use central reservation systems (CRS) and global distribution systems (GDS) such as Amadeus, as part of their channel distribution strategy. This will allow them access to hotel rooms which they can purchase at an advantageous rate which they can use in their pricing strategy as part of gaining entry into this new market. They should grasp the opportunity of this lucrative growing market, selling to corporate businesses while still maintaining a presence in the declining market of selling flights and holidays to the general public.

Christian Grønlund,
a student at Roskilde Business College, Denmark

I would choose option 2. Over the past years we've seen more and more agents giving up. Simply because they're disappearing among the stronger competitors in the industry. And to prevent that from happening changes would have to be made. Being in a market with monopolistic competition makes it very difficult to *stand out from the crowd*. But keeping the personal selling as their niche ensures their competitive advantage. They've been on the business-to-consumer market for almost 30 years. Jill and Kate still have great ambitions for the Holiday Shop, so to maintain that I think it is important to keep at least some degree of independence. Joining Hays Travel also provides opportunities in travelling methods, for instance by choosing to fly with easyJet and stay in an expensive hotel.

Several clothing chains such as H&M and Zara have experienced great success recently because they consistently offer up-to-date styles at affordable prices. Their secret? A concept the industry calls **fast fashion** – which is really another way to say JIT. Zara (from Spain) offers customers a constant supply of new products but only a limited supply of each garment. This means that the shop has to constantly send small batches of new styles through its supply chain. Zara's system depends upon a constant exchange of information among supply chain members so that the company can keep track of which specific styles and colours are selling at which shops in order to replenish stock very quickly. The retailer's fast fashion system has to follow about 300,000 new *stock-keeping units (SKUs)* every year to be sure that its customers continue to get their new fashion fix no matter how many times they visit a shop.[11]

Retailing: Special Delivery

Objective

3

Define retailing and understand how retailing evolves

Shop 'til you drop! For many people, obtaining the product is only half the fun. Others, of course, would rather walk over hot coals than spend time shopping. Marketers need to find ways to deliver products and services that please both types of consumers. **Retailing** is the final stop on the distribution path, the process by which goods and services are sold to consumers for their personal use.

A retail outlet is more than a place to buy something. The retailer adds or subtracts value from the offering with its image, stock, service quality, location and pricing policy. In many cases, the shopping experience *is* what we buy as well as the products we take home.

This section will explore the many different types of retailers, keeping one question in mind: how does a retailer, whether store or non-store (selling via television, phone or computer) manage to entice the consumer? Answering this question isn't getting any easier, as the competition for customers continues to intensify and is fuelled by the explosion of websites selling branded merchandise (or auctioning it like eBay). This, combined with developers continuing to build elaborate shopping centres – and improvements in communications and distribution – make it more and more possible for retailers from around the world to enter local markets.

Retailing: A Mixed (Shopping) Bag

Although we tend to associate huge shops such as Tesco and Carrefour with retailing activity, in reality most retailers are small businesses.[12] Certain retailers are also wholesalers, because they provide goods and services to businesses as well as to end consumers.

As explained earlier, retailers belong to a channel of distribution and as such provide time, place and ownership utility to customers. Some retailers save people time or money by providing an assortment of merchandise under one roof. Others search the world for the most exotic delicacies, allowing shoppers access to goods they would otherwise never see. Still others, such as Borders bookshops with cafés, provide us with interesting environments in which to spend our leisure time and money.

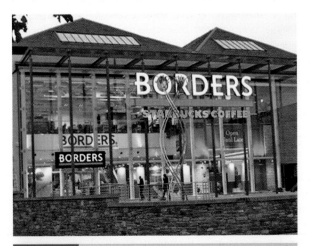

Photo 13.4 | Borders provides a relaxing environment in which you can visit an in-store coffee shop in between browsing the books and magazines.
Source: Borders

The Evolution of Retailing

Retailing has taken many forms over time, including the pedlar who sold his wares from a horse-drawn cart, a majestic urban department store, an intimate boutique and a huge 'hyperstore' that sells everything from snacks to mountain bike tyres. As the economic, social and cultural times change, different types of retailers emerge – often replacing older, outmoded types. How can marketers know what the dominant types of retailing will be tomorrow or 10 years from now?

The Wheel of Retailing

One of the oldest and simplest explanations for these changes is the **wheel of retailing** hypothesis. This hypothesis states that new types of retailers find it easiest to enter the market by offering goods at lower prices than competitors.[13] After they gain a foothold, they gradually trade up, improving their facilities, increasing the quality and assortment of merchandise, and offering amenities such as parking and gift wrapping. This trend results in greater investment and operating costs, so the shop must raise its prices to remain profitable, which then makes it vulnerable to still newer entrants that can afford to charge lower prices – and therefore the wheel turns.

The wheel of retailing helps us explain the development of some but not all forms of retailing. For example, some retailers never trade up; they simply continue to occupy a niche as discounters. Others, such as upmarket speciality shops, start out at the high end. Of course, some retailers move down after experiencing success at the high end. Sometimes they open sister divisions that sell lower priced products, or they develop outlets that sell lower priced versions of their own products.

The Retail Life Cycle

Of course, retailers sell products, but in a way retailers also *are* products because they provide benefits such as convenience or status to consumers, and they must offer a competitive advantage over other retailers to survive. Sometimes where a product is purchased either adds to or takes away from its allure.

From the value chain perspective, a manufacturer's selection of a retail location adds value in two ways: by the utility the retailer provides and by the extent to which the shop enhances the product's image. When a manufacturer makes its product available at Tesco, the value added is primarily the time, place and ownership utility it provides. When a product is available at, say, Marks & Spencer, the value of the product is also increased because the high-end image of the retailer transfers to the product.

Another way to understand how retailers evolve is the **retail life cycle**. Like the product life cycle, this perspective recognises that (like people, soft-drink brands and vacation destinations) retailers are born, they grow and mature, and eventually they die or become obsolete. The life cycle approach allows us to categorise retail stores by the conditions they face at different points in the cycle.[14]

In the *introduction* stage, the new retailer often is an aggressive entrepreneur who takes a unique approach to doing business. This may mean competing on the basis of low price, as the wheel of retailing suggests. However, this newcomer may also enter the market by offering a distinctive assortment or a different way to distribute items, such as through the internet, as Lastminute.com did.

In the introduction stage, profits are low because of high development costs. As the business enters the *growth* stage, the retailer hopefully catches on with shoppers, therefore sales and profits rise. A new idea, however, doesn't stay new for long. Others start to copy and competition increases, so the shop needs to expand what it offers. Often the retailer responds by opening more outlets and develops systems to distribute goods to these new shops – which may in turn cut profits as the firm invests in new buildings and fixtures.

By the time the business reaches the *maturity* stage, many other individual retailers have copied the unique idea of the original entrepreneur to form an entire industry. The industry has over-expanded, and intense competition makes it difficult to maintain customer loyalty. Profits decline as competitors resort to price cutting to keep their customers. We can observe this pattern with fast-food chains like McDonald's.

During the maturity stage, firms seek to increase their share of the market or to attract new customers. McDonald's, having found that many of its customers frequently bought beverages from convenience stores, service stations and other retailers, carried out experiments by adding convenience store-style coolers to its traditional drink dispensers.[15] This would mean McDonald's customers would no longer be limited to a couple of beverages, usually Coke and Sprite, but would have additional beverage choices such as Lucozade, Dr. Pepper and Redbull.

In the *decline* stage, retail businesses, like the general store, become obsolete as newer ways of doing business emerge. Of course, the outdated retailer does not have to fold its tent at this stage. Marketers who anticipate these shifts can avert decline by changing to meet the times. Some retailers such as Starbucks have found growth opportunities in foreign markets. Starbucks now operates over 11,000 coffee shops in America, Latin America, Europe, the Middle East and Pacific Rim. Petrol filling stations had difficulty competing with self-service discount outlets. Many responded by adding variety stores to their retail mix to let drivers buy convenience goods while filling up.

Or, how about a shop that plans to close even as it opens? That's just what happened in Berlin with the launch of a new concept called the Comme des Garçons Guerrilla Store. The shop closed in a year – deliberately! Instead of spending millions to build or renovate a building, Comme des Garçons spent just €2500 to fix up a former bookshop. This 'here today, gone tomorrow' strategy (that insiders call **pop-up retailing**) acknowledges consumers' desires to have different shopping experiences all the time in a unique way.[16]

The Evolution Continues: What's 'In Store' for the Future?

As our world continues to change rapidly, retailers are scrambling to keep up. Three factors motivate and inspire merchants to reinvent the way they do business: demographics, technology and globalisation.

Demographics As we noted earlier in the book, keeping up with changes in population characteristics is at the heart of many marketing efforts. Retailers can no longer afford to stand by and assume that their customer base is the same as it has always been. They must come up with new ways to sell their products to diverse groups.

For example, although many retailers chase after the same set of affluent customers, others are carving out markets by targeting lower income households. Shops like Poundland in the UK have been successful by selling everything in their shops for £1 (about €0.7). By aiming to focus on this particular market segment, this retailer has been quite successful.

Here are some of the ways changing demographics are altering the face of retailing:

- **Convenience for working consumers:** Some retailers are expanding their operating hours because consumers no longer have time to shop during the day. Other retailers, including dry cleaners and pharmacies, are adding drive-up windows. In areas from financial services to interior decorating, enterprising individuals have turned time shortage into a business opportunity by becoming shopping consultants for busy consumers. Many major department stores now offer in-house consultants. Walk-in GP clinics located close to retail stores provide not only convenience but save patients time and money.[17]

- **Recognising cultural diversity:** Although members of different cultural groups can usually find local retailers that cater to their specific needs, larger companies must tailor their strategies to the cultural make-up of specific areas. For example, at Disneyland Paris, the overwhelming majority of employees are able to communicate with 'les guests' in at least two different languages.

Technology In addition to demographics, technology is revolutionising retailing. As we all know, the internet has brought us the age of e-tailing. Whether it's a retailer that purely sells on the web or a traditional UK retailer like Tesco that *also* sells on the web – (its motto is 'you shop, we drop'), we can see that retailing is steadily evolving from bricks to clicks. Our personal computers have turned our homes into virtual shopping centres. There are other technological advances that have little to do with the internet that are also helping to change our shopping experiences.

Photo 13.5	Starbucks is now a household name in Japan. Source: Getty Images/Yoshikazu

Some of the most profound changes are not even visible to shoppers, such as advanced electronic **point-of-sale (POS) systems**, which contain computer chips that collect sales data and are connected directly into the shop's inventory control system. While no longer new, in the 1990s Benetton led in the use of technology with its point-of-sale system. Every day, data was sent from Benetton shops to its corporate headquarters. From there, computer programs analysed patterns of demand for different products and automatically planned to match supply with demand. Such systems make shops efficient. If shoppers in an area are buying a lot of wide-legged jeans, for example, the retailer can make sure there are plenty available.

What about skipping the checkout altogether? At the Extra Future Store in Rheinberg, Germany, shoppers are given a small touch-screen computer with a built-in barcode scanner when they enter. The trolley-top computer also allows shoppers to scan their purchases for payment as they move through the shop. For items like produce that require weighing, the shop has installed scales equipped with digital cameras that use image-recognition software to work out and then price the object they are weighing.[18] Central to the concept are the quarter-size radio-frequency identification (RIFD) tags we discussed earlier. These tags are attached to individual products, tracking their movement from storeroom to shelves to shopping trolley. While only a relatively few products now carry these tags, retailers say eventually they will appear on all items – replacing bar codes.

Globalisation   As we also saw earlier in this book, the world is becoming a much smaller place. Retailers are busy expanding to other countries and bringing with them innovations and new management philosophies. McDonald's, Carrefour and Starbucks are among the global retail success stories. Starbucks has become a household name in Japan (where it's pronounced *STAH-buks-zu*). The coffee shops feature comfortable sofas, hip-hop music and generous servings. These are relatively new concepts in Japan, where café patrons had been accustomed to sitting in dimly lit shops and sipping tea from thimble-size cups.[19]

Of course, understanding global retailing means recognising that the way things are sold differs from country to country. In many developing countries, the retailing industry is made up of small individual retailers who sell cigarettes, soft drinks, snacks, cassette tapes, batteries and just about anything else you can think of.

 ## Family Shops to Hypermarkets: Classifying Retail Stores

We've seen that exciting things are happening in the world of retailing. But the field of retailing covers a lot of ground – from elegant department stores to roadside sellers to websites and trendy café bars. Retail marketers need to understand all the possible ways that they might offer their products in the market, and they also need a way to benchmark their performance to other similar retailers.

Classifying Retailers by What They Sell

One of the most important strategic decisions a retailer makes is *what* to sell – its **merchandise mix**. This choice is similar to settling on a market segment (as discussed earlier): if a shop's merchandise mix is too limited, it may not have enough potential customers, whereas if it is too broad, the retailer runs the risk of being a 'jack of all trades, master of none'. Because what the retailer sells is central to its identity, we will describe some retail types by merchandise mix.

While we learned earlier that a manufacturer's product line consists of product offerings that satisfy a single need, in retailing a *product line* is a set of related products offered by a retailer, such as kitchen appliances or leather goods.

However, a word of caution: as retailers experiment with different merchandise mixes, these direct comparisons are getting harder to make. For example, even though marketers like to distinguish between food and non-food retailers, in reality these lines are blurring. Supermarkets are adding hardware product lines, and some department stores offer gourmet food. In Japan, for example, the major department stores have one floor, which like free-standing supermarkets sells meats, vegetables and other fresh food items, while another entire floor offers store customers a wide range of prepared foods ready for the modern Japanese working woman (or man) to carry home for dinner.

Classifying Retailers by Level of Service

Retailers differ in the amount of service they provide for consumers. Firms recognise that there is a trade-off between service and low prices, so they tailor their strategies to the level of service they offer. Customers who demand higher levels of service must be willing to pay for that service, and those who want lower prices must be willing to give up services. Unfortunately, some consumers don't understand this trade-off and still insist on top-level service while paying low prices!

Retailers like Lidl and Netto which offer low prices are often resourced very efficiently, and tend not to provide so much in-store service. When customers shop here, they make their product selection without any assistance, they often must bring their own bags (or buy them) to transport their goods.

In contrasting that experience to visiting a *full-service retailer*, many of us prefer the likes of Marks & Spencer as it provides supporting services such as gift wrapping, and offers trained retail assistants who can help us select that perfect gift. Other specialised services may be available in such shops. Full-service clothing retailers, for instance, normally provide an alteration service. Bridal consultants may also be useful for helping to plan with the wedding gift process.

Falling in between self-service and full-service retailers are *limited-service retailers*. Stores like Asda/Wal-Mart and Carrefour offer credit and goods return services – but little else. Customers select merchandise without much assistance, preferring to pay a bit less rather than be waited on a bit more.

Classifying Retailers by Merchandise Selection

Another way to classify retailers is in terms of the selection they offer. A retailer's **merchandise assortment**, or selection of products it sells, has two dimensions: breadth and depth. **Merchandise breadth** (or variety) is the number of different product lines available. A *narrow assortment*, such as that found in convenience stores, means that shoppers will find only a limited selection of product lines. A *broad assortment*, such as that in a warehouse store, means there is a wide range of items available.

Merchandise depth is the variety of choices available for each specific product. A *shallow assortment* means that the selection within a product category is limited, so a factory outlet shop may sell men's shirts (all made by the same manufacturer) and only in standard sizes. In contrast, a men's speciality shop may feature a *deep assortment* of shirts in varying shades and in hard-to-find sizes.

Now that we've seen how retailers differ in the breadth and depth of their assortments, let's review some of the major forms these retailers take.

Convenience Stores   Such shops carry a limited number of frequently purchased items, including basic food products, newspapers, etc. They cater for consumers willing to pay a premium for the ease of buying staple items close to home. In other words, convenience stores meet the needs of those who are pressed for time, who buy items in smaller quantities or who shop at irregular hours. But these shops are starting to change, especially in urban areas where many time-pressed shoppers prefer to visit these outlets even for speciality items.

Supermarkets   These are food shops that carry a wide selection of edible and non-edible products. Although large supermarkets and hypermarkets appear as a fixture in some European countries, they have not caught on everywhere. Some Europeans still prefer to walk or cycle to small shops near their homes. In such places, relatively smaller food purchases are made per trip and there is a tendency to shop more frequently. Although wide variety is less important than quality and local ambiance for some Europeans, shopping habits are starting to change as hypermarkets are becoming more popular.

Speciality Shops   Such shops have a relatively narrow and deep stock of goods. They do not sell a lot of product lines, but they offer a good selection of brands within the lines they sell. For many women with less than perfect figures, shopping at a shop that sells only swimsuits means there will be an adequate selection to find a suit that really fits. The same is true for larger, taller men who can't find suits that fit in regular shops but have lots of choices in shops that cater for the big and tall. Speciality shops can tailor their assortment to the specific needs of a targeted consumer, and they often offer a high level of knowledgeable service.

The **factory outlet** is another type of discount retailer. A manufacturer owns these shops. Some factory outlets enable the manufacturer to sell off defective merchandise or excess stock, while others carry items not available at full-price retail outlets and are designed to provide an additional distribution channel for the manufacturer. Although the assortment is not wide because a shop carries only products made by one manufacturer, most factory outlet shops are located on estates where other similar shops are.

Department Stores   These sell a broad range of items and offer a deep selection organised into different sections of the shop. Grand department stores dominated urban centres in the late Victorian era and much of the twentieth century.

In many countries, department stores are thriving and remain consumers' primary place to shop. In Japan, department stores are always crowded with shoppers buying everything from a takeaway sushi dinner to a string of fine pearls. In Spain, a single department store chain, El Corte Engles, dominates retailing. Its branch stores include shop-size departments for electronics, books, music and gourmet foods, and each has a vast supermarket covering one or two floors of the store. Because of increased competition and other retailing options, over recent times department stores have experienced some difficulties. In response, some retail shops have pruned their assortments to concentrate more on *soft goods*, such as clothing and home furnishings, and less on *hard goods*, such as appliances.

Hypermarkets   Such places combine the characteristics of warehouse shops and supermarkets. Originally introduced in Europe, these are huge establishments several times larger than other shops. A supermarket might be 10,000 to 20,000 square metres, whereas a hypermarket takes up 50,000 to 80,000 square metres, or four football pitches. They offer one-stop shopping, often for over 50,000 items, and feature restaurants, beauty salons and children's play areas. Hypermarkets, such as those run by the French firm Carrefour, are popular in Europe, the Middle East and Latin America, where big shops are somewhat of a novelty. More recently, Carrefour has expanded to developing countries such as Egypt, where a burgeoning population and a lack of large retailers provide hyper-opportunities.

Non-shop Retailing

Many products are readily available in places other than shops. Think of the familiar Avon beauty products that are sold to millions of women around the world. Avon allows customers to place orders by phone, fax, catalogue or through a representative.

Avon's success at giving customers alternatives to traditional shop outlets illustrates the increasing importance of **non-shop retailing**, which is any method a firm uses to complete an exchange that does not require a customer visit to a shop. Indeed, many conventional retailers from upmarket fashion retailers like Next to supermarket chain Tesco offer options such as catalogues and websites for customers interested in buying their merchandise.

B2C E-Commerce

Objective

4

Describe B2C E-commerce and its benefits, limitations and future promise

Business-to-consumer (B2C) e-commerce is the online exchange between companies and individual consumers. As more people shop, more retailers will enter the web marketplace, making more types of products available. At the same time, enhanced technology and improvements in delivery and security entice even more consumers to shop online.

Electronic commerce in retailing has enormous potential. The continued success of this non-shop format will depend on the ability of retailers to offer sites that are entertaining and informative and that are worth surfing – even after the novelty wears off.

Benefits of B2C E-Commerce

For both consumers and marketers, B2C e-commerce provides a host of benefits and some limitations. Table 13.4 lists some of these. E-commerce allows consumers and marketers to easily find and make exchanges in a global marketplace. Consumers can choose from hundreds of thousands of sellers worldwide, while marketers can tap into consumer and business markets with virtually no geographic limitations.

From the consumer's perspective, electronic marketing has increased convenience by breaking down many of the time barriers and location issues. You can shop 24 hours a day without leaving home. In less developed countries, the internet lets consumers purchase products that may not be available at all in local markets. Thus, the internet can improve the quality of life without the necessity of developing costly infrastructure, such as opening retail stores in remote locations.

Understanding just what online shoppers really desire and why they are shopping online makes marketers more successful. For some consumers, online shopping provides an additional benefit by fulfilling their experiential needs, that is their need to shop for fun. Consumers who are collectors or who enjoy hobbies are most likely to be **experiential shoppers**. While most online consumers engage in goal-directed behaviour – they wish to satisfy their shopping goal as quickly as possible. Between 20 and 30 per cent of online consumers shop online because they enjoy the thrill as much or more than the actual acquisition of the item. Experiential shoppers linger at sites longer and are motivated by a desire to be entertained. Consequently,

Benefits	Limitations
For the consumer:	**For the consumer:**
Shop 24 hours a day	Lack of security
Less travelling	Fraud
Can receive relevant information in seconds from any location	Can't touch items
More product choices	Exact colours may not reproduce on computer screens
More products available to less-developed countries	Expensive to order and then return
Greater price information	Potential breakdown of human relationships
Lower prices, so less affluent can purchase	**For the marketer:**
Participate in online auctions	Lack of security
Fast delivery	Must maintain website to reap benefits
Electronic communities	Fierce price competition
For the marketer:	Conflicts with shops
The world is your marketplace	Legal issues not resolved
Lower cost of doing business	
Very specialised businesses can be successful	
Real-time pricing	

Table 13.4   Benefits and Limitations of E-Commerce

marketers who wish to attract these customers must design websites that offer surprise, uniqueness and excitement. How well a site satisfies experiential needs might determine how much money consumers will choose to spend at that site.

Marketers realise equally important benefits from e-commerce. Because marketers can reach such a large number of consumers with electronic commerce, it is possible to develop very specialised businesses that could not be profitable if limited by geographic constraints.

As discussed earlier, one of the biggest advantages of e-commerce is that it's easy to get price information. Want to buy a new mountain bike, an MP3 player, or just about anything else you can think of? Instead of going from shop to shop in order to compare prices, many web surfers use search engines that compile and compare prices from suppliers. With readily available pricing information, shoppers can browse brands, features, reviews and information on where to buy a particular product. The benefit being that consumers can find all of this information in one central location, making it easy to spend their money more efficiently.

E-commerce also allows businesses to reduce costs. Compared with bricks-and-mortar retailers, e-tailers' costs are minimal. No expensive retail sites to maintain and no sales assistants to pay. For some products, such as computer software and digitised music, e-commerce provides fast, almost instantaneous delivery.

Marketing Metrics

E-Commerce Conversion Rates

E-commerce marketers often want to measure a metric they call the *conversion rate*, which is the percentage of visitors to an online shop who purchase from it. This is a useful metric, but if this rate is low it doesn't help the retailer understand the possible factors affecting the website's performance. So, in addition to knowing the conversion rate, researchers at IBM compute other metrics called *microconversion rates* that enable them to pinpoint more precisely what may need to be improved in the online shopping process.[20] This technique breaks down the shopping experience into the stages that are involved between visiting a site and actually making a transaction:

- **Product impression:** Viewing a hyperlink to a web page presenting a product.
- **Click-through:** Clicking on the hyperlink and viewing the product's web page.
- **Basket placement:** Placing the item in the 'shopping basket'.
- **Purchase:** Actually buying the item.

These researchers calculate micro-conversion rates for each adjacent pair of measures to come up with additional metrics that can pinpoint specific problems in the shopping process:

- **Look-to-click rate:** How many product impressions are converted to click-throughs? This can help the e-tailer determine if the products featured on the website are the ones that customers want to see.
- **Click-to-basket rate:** How many click-throughs result in a product being placed in the shopping basket? This metric helps to determine if the detailed information provided about the product is appropriate.
- **Basket-to-buy rate:** How many basket placements are converted to purchases? This metric can tell the e-tailer which kinds of products are more likely to be abandoned in the shopping basket instead of being bought. It can also pinpoint problems with the checkout process, such as forcing the shopper to answer too many questions or making them wait too long for their credit card to be approved.

 ## Limitations of B2C E-Commerce

All is not perfect in the virtual world. E-commerce does have its limitations. One drawback relative to shopping in a shop is that customers still must wait a few days to receive most products, which are often sent via private delivery services. So shoppers can't achieve instant gratification by walking out of a shop clutching their latest 'finds'. Many e-commerce sites still suffer from poor design that people find confusing or irritating. One study found that 65 per cent of online shoppers empty their trolleys before they complete their purchase because they find the process hard to follow and there are no real life customer service people available to answer questions. To make matters worse, 30 per cent of online shoppers who have problems with a website say they won't shop there again, and 10 per cent say they won't shop online at all any more.[21]

Security is a concern to both consumers and marketers. We hear horror stories of consumers whose credit cards and other identity information have been stolen. Although an individual's financial liability in most theft cases is limited, because credit card companies usually absorb most or all of the loss, the damage to one's credit rating can last for years.

Consumers also are concerned about internet fraud. Although most of us feel competent to judge a local bricks-and-mortar business by its physical presence, by how long it's been around, and from the reports of friends and neighbours who shop there, we have little or no information on the millions of internet sites offering their products for sale, even though sites like eBay try to address these concerns by posting extensive information about the reliability of individual vendors.

Another problem is that people need 'touch-and-feel' information before buying many products. Although it may be satisfactory to buy a computer or a book on the internet, buying clothing and other items where touching the item or trying it on is essential may be less attractive. As with catalogues, even though most online companies have liberal return policies, consumers can still get stuck with large delivery and return shipping charges for items that don't fit or simply aren't the right colour.

Traditional bricks-and-mortar companies are actually *more* likely to be successful in cyberspace than are internet-only start-ups because they already have established brand names and a base of loyal customers. Traditional retailers are going online, many combining their web retailing with existing shops.

Catalogue companies have had the easiest time making the transition to the web since they have the most experience delivering goods directly to consumers. That explains why almost three-quarters of these firms have profitable e-commerce sites, whereas less than 40 per cent of other web retailers are in the black so far.[22]

We're also seeing movement in the opposite direction. Online travel companies like Expedia.com are adding offline operations and buying traditional travel agencies. These businesses recognise that many shoppers use the web to research their travel options but then actually purchase their tickets offline because of concerns about security and privacy.

Developing countries with primarily cash economies pose yet another obstacle to the success of B2C e-commerce. In these countries, few people use credit cards, so they can't easily pay for items they purchase over the internet. An alternative for payments that may gain popularity in the future is *digital cash*. Currently, digital cash is available on prepaid cards and smart cards such as a prepaid phone card. Another alternative is e-cash, developed by Digicash of Amsterdam. E-cash provides secure payments between computers using e-mail or the internet. You can use e-cash to buy a pizza or to get money from home. To do so, you need e-cash client software and a *digital bank account*, a web-based account that allows you to make payments to internet retailers directly from the account while online. You withdraw money from your bank account, store it on your computer, and spend it when you need to.

As major marketers aim to have a greater presence on the web, they worry that their sales online may *cannibalise* their actual retail store sales.

 ## B2C's Effect on the Future of Retailing

Does the growth of B2C e-commerce mean the death of bricks-and-mortar shops as we know them? Don't plan any funerals for your local shops prematurely. Although some argue that virtual distribution channels will completely replace traditional ones because of their cost advantages, this is unlikely. For example, although a bank saves 80 per cent of its costs when customers do business online from their home computers, not all customers wish to use PC-based banking services. At least in the short term, too many people are accustomed to obtaining goods and services from shops, and of course shopping provides a social outlet that (for now) can't be replaced by solitary surfing. At least in the near future, clicks will have to coexist with bricks.

Shops as we know them will have to continue to evolve to entice shoppers away from their computer screens. In the future, the trend will be *destination retail*. That is, consumers will visit

Marketing Metrics

Abacus

A company called Abacus helps catalogue retailers to measure the shopping habits of their customers. While Abacus relies heavily on the traditional metric of past purchases to determine what people will buy in the future, this database marketer also tracks purchases across countless categories in combination with demographic factors to help retailers, for example, target a single 30-year-old male who likes to surf. Additionally, Abacus keeps track of 'trigger events' such as when a person in its database is getting ready to move, so it can alert a retailer that a consumer may be ready to purchase household items like kitchenware.[23]

retailers not so much to buy a product but for the entertainment provided by the total experience. Many retailers are already developing ways to make the shopping in bricks-and-mortar shops an experience rather than just a place to pick up stuff.

Developing a Shop Positioning Strategy: Retailing as Theatre

Objective

5

Understand the importance of shop image to a retail positioning strategy and explain how a retailer can create a desirable image in the market place

A 'destination retail' strategy reminds us that shopping often is part buying, part entertainment and part social outlet. So far we've seen that shops can be distinguished in several ways, including the types of products they carry and the breadth and depth of their assortments. But recall that a shop is itself a product that adds to or subtracts from the goods the shopper came to buy there.

When we are deciding which shop to buy at, many of us are less likely to say 'I'll go there because their assortment is broad,' or say 'That place is so cool. I really like socialising there.' Shops can entertain us, bore us, make us angry, or even make us sad. In today's competitive marketplace, retailers have to do more than offer good inventory at reasonable prices. They need to position their shops so that they offer a competitive advantage over other shops also fighting for the shopper's attention – not to mention catalogues, websites, and shopping channels that may offer the same or similar merchandise without having to leave the home.

Earlier we discovered that staging a service is much like putting on a play. Similarly, many retailers recognise that much of what they do is theatre. At a time when it is possible to pick up a phone or log on to a computer to buy many items, a customer must have a reason to make a trip to a shop.

Shoppers are an audience to entertain. The 'play' can cleverly employ stage sets (shop design) and actors (retail assistants) that together create a 'scene'. For example, think about buying a pair of trainers. Such retailers that sell these type of goods are far different from the old days, when a tired shop owner waded through box after box of shoes as children ran around the dingy floors. Now retail assistants (actors) are dressed in costumes such as black-striped referee outfits. Shops like Foot Locker are ablaze with neon, with the shoes displayed in clear acrylic walls so that they appear to be floating.[24] All these special effects make the buying occasion less about buying and more about having an experience. As one marketing strategist commented, 'The line between retail and entertainment is blurring.' Even traditional banks are coming on board and re-vamping their buildings to look more like coffee shops and retail boutiques. Some branch banks now offer customers such amenities as comfortable settees, Wi-Fi internet access, and movie screens.[25] In this section, we'll review some of the tools available to the retailing playwright.

Shop Image

When people think of a shop, they often have no trouble portraying it in the same terms they might use in describing a person. They might use words such as *exciting*, *depressed*, *old-fashioned*, *tacky* or *elegant*. **Shop image** is how the target market perceives the shop (its market position relative to the competition). Even shops operated by the same parent company can be quite different from one another. But images don't just happen. Just as brand managers do for products, shop managers work hard to create a distinctive and appealing personality.

To appreciate this idea, consider the dramatic makeover at Selfridges – a well-known British department store chain. At the flagship store in London, shoppers can wander over to a body-piercing salon staffed by teenagers in dreadlocks. In the children's department, giant white plastic blobs hold racks of shocking-pink playsuits. If you need a break from browsing, go to one of the store's 14 restaurants, which often share a theme with the adjacent selling floor. Base Bar, a stripped-down cafeteria full of gleaming aluminium, is next to computers; Lab Cafe is minimalist, next to young designers' clothes. The shop's makeover was publicised by periodic events that screamed cutting edge, including one called 'Body Craze', where thousands of shoppers flocked to see 650 naked people ride the escalators. Do not attempt this at home.[26]

Not every shop can or wants to have naked people running around, but even more modest strategies to enliven the atmosphere make a big difference. In developing a desirable shop image, the resourceful retailer has a number of choices. Ideally, all these elements should work together to create a clear, coherent picture that meets consumers' expectations of what that particular shopping experience should be.

Atmospherics is the use of colour, lighting, scents, furnishings, sounds and other design elements to create a desired setting. Marketers manipulate these elements to create a certain 'feeling' about the retail environment.[27]

Shop Design: Setting the Stage
The elements of shop design should correspond to management's desired image. A bank lobby needs to convey respectability and security because people need to be reassured about the safety of their money. In contrast, a used bookshop might create a disorderly look so that shoppers think treasures lie buried beneath piles of tattered novels.

Here are some other design factors that retailers consider:

- **Shop layout:** This is the arrangement of merchandise in the shop. The placement of fixtures such as shelves, racks and cash registers is important because shop layout determines **traffic flow**; how shoppers will move through the shop and what areas they will pass or avoid. A *grid layout*, usually found in supermarkets, consists of rows of neatly spaced shelves that are at right-angles or parallel to one another. This configuration is useful when management wants to systematically move shoppers down each aisle, being sure that they pass through such high-margin sections as deli and meat.

  A typical strategy is to place staple goods in more remote areas. The designers know that traffic will move to these areas because these are frequently purchased items. They try to place impulse goods in spots shoppers will pass on their way elsewhere. Then they place eye-catching displays to pull people in. In contrast, department and speciality shops typically use a *free-flow layout* because it is more conducive to browsing. A retailer might arrange merchandise in circles or arches or perhaps in separate areas, each with its own distinct image and merchandise mix.

- **Fixture type and merchandise density:** Just as we may form impressions of people from their home decor, our feelings about shops are affected by furnishings, fixtures (shelves and racks that display merchandise), and even how much 'stuff' is packed into the sales area. Generally, clutter conveys a shop with lower priced merchandise. Upmarket shops allocate space for sitting areas, dressing rooms and elaborate displays of merchandise.

- **The sound of music:** An elegant restaurant softly playing Mozart in the background is worlds apart from music venues like the Hard Rock Café, where loud rock-and-roll forms part of the atmosphere. The music playing in a shop has become so central to its personality that many retailers, including Ralph Lauren and Starbucks, have even sold the soundtracks specially designed for them.[28]

- **Colour and lighting:** Marketers use colour and lighting to set a mood. Red, yellow and orange are warm colours. Fast-food chains use a lot of orange to stimulate hunger, whereas blue, green and violet signify elegance and cleanliness. Light colours make one feel more serene, whereas bright colours convey excitement. Fashion designer Norma Kamali replaced fluorescent lights with pink ones after management found that pink lighting was more flattering and made female customers more willing to try on bathing suits.[29]

Shop Personnel   Shop staff (the actors) should complement the image. Each employee has a part to play, complete with props and costumes. Many shops provide employees with scripts to use when they present products to customers.

Although the presence of knowledgeable sales personnel is important to shoppers, they generally rate the quality of service they receive from retail personnel as low, often because shops don't hire enough people to wait on their customers. Retailers are working hard to upgrade service quality, though they often find that the rapid turnover of salespeople makes this a difficult goal to achieve. Perhaps they can learn from Japanese retailers. A visitor to a Japanese shop is greeted by an enthusiastic, cheerful, polite and immaculately dressed employee who, no matter how busy he or she is, tells each new customer they are welcome and bows to them.

Pricing Policy: How Much for a Ticket to the Show?   When consumers form an image of a shop in their minds, the *price points*, or price ranges, of its merchandise often play a role. Discount shops and general merchandisers are likely to compete on a price basis by offering brand names for less.

In recent years, department stores have been hurt by consumers' desires for bargains. The response of many department stores was to run frequent sales, a strategy that often backfired because many consumers would buy *only* when the shop held a sale. Some shops have instead reduced the number of sales they run in favour of lowering prices across the board. As we saw earlier, some shops offer an everyday low pricing (EDLP) strategy; they set prices that are between the list price suggested by the manufacturer and the deeply discounted price offered by shops that compete on price only.

Building the Theatre: Shop Location   Any estate agent will tell you the three most important factors in buying a home are 'location, location and location'. The same is true in retailing and much success is due to not only what type of shop, but also *where* it is. When choosing a site, planners consider such factors as proximity to motorways and major routes. By carefully selecting 'undiscovered' areas, a company may be able to acquire land in towns with expanding populations. In this section we'll review some important aspects of retail locations.

Types of Shop Locations   There are several basic types of retail locations. A shop can be found in a busy city or shopping centre, as a freestanding entity, or in a non-traditional location:

- **Business districts:** A **central business district (CBD)** is the traditional business area found in a town or city centre. Many people are drawn to the area to shop or work, and public transportation is usually available. CBDs have suffered in recent years because of concerns about security, a lack of parking, and the lack of customer traffic at evenings and weekends. To combat these problems, many cities provide incentives such as tax breaks to encourage the opening of shops and entertainment areas.

- **Shopping centres:** A **shopping centre** is a group of commercial establishments owned and managed as a single property. They offer variety and the ability to combine shopping with entertainment. Rents tend to be high in shopping centres, making it difficult for many shops to be profitable. In addition, small speciality shops may find it hard to compete with a shopping centre's key stores, as such major department stores which typically draw many shoppers.

- **Freestanding retailers:** Some shops, usually larger ones such as IKEA or PC World, are freestanding, located by themselves in a separate building. These retailers benefit from lower rents and fewer parking problems. However, the shop must be attractive enough on its own to be a destination point for shoppers because it can't rely on spillover from consumers visiting other shops at the same place.

- **Non-traditional shop locations:** Innovative retailers find new ways to reach consumers. Many entrepreneurs use *carts*, which are small, movable shops that can be set up in many locations including inside shopping centres, in airports or in other public facilities, or *kiosks*, which are slightly larger and offer shop like facilities including telephone points and

Different types of shop locations are best for different types of retailers. Retailers choose from among central business districts, shopping centres, freestanding shops and non-traditional locations.

electricity. Carts and kiosks are relatively inexpensive and a good way for new businesses to get started.

Site Selection: Choosing Where to Build   Long-term population patterns, the location of competitors and the demographic make-up of an area enter into retailers' decisions. The choice of where to open a new shop should reflect the company's overall growth strategy. It should be consistent with long-term goals and be in a place that allows the company to best support the outlet.

Location planners look at many factors when selecting a site. They want to find a place that is convenient to customers in the shop's **trade area**, the geographic zone that accounts for the majority of its sales and customers.[30] A *site evaluation* considers such specific factors as traffic flow; number of parking spaces available; ease of delivery access; visibility from the street; local planning laws that determine the types of buildings, parking, and signage allowed; and such cost factors as the length of the lease and the amount of local taxes.

Planners also consider such population characteristics as age profile and demographic characteristics, as well as mobility – how often are people moving in and out of the area? This type of information is available from a variety of private as well as public sources.

Planners also have to consider the degree of competition they will encounter by locating in one place rather than another. One strategy followed by fast-food outlets is to locate in a *saturated trade area*. This is a site where a sufficient number of shops already exist so that high customer traffic is present but where the retailer believes it can compete successfully by going head to head with the competition. The task, however, is getting harder and harder because at this point many of the good sites are already taken.

Another strategy is to find an *understored trade area*, where too few shops exist to satisfy the needs of the population and the retailer can establish itself as a dominant presence in the community. Over time, these areas may become *overstored* so that too many shops exist to sell the same goods. Those that can't compete are forced to move or close, as has happened to many small family-run shops that can't beat the supermarkets at their sophisticated retailing games.

A shop's targeted consumer segment also determines where it locates. For example, a new, growing community would be appealing for hardware retailers that can supply hammers and saws to homeowners, while upmarket dress shops and travel agencies might find better locations in more established areas because people living there have the income to spend on fashion items and holidays.

Now that you've learned more about retail and distribution, read 'Real People, Real Decisions' to see which strategy Jill and Kate decided upon.

Real People, Real Decisions

How it worked out at the Holiday Shop

Jill and Kate decided to go for option 2. They didn't feel like giving up their independence, not at least without a fight – and wanted to stay in the consumer segment due to their experience of serving this market. However, to become more competitive yet retain their independence Jill and Kate set up a joint venture initiative with Hays Travel, which agreed to pay the Holiday Shop's ABTA bond (around £100,000 each year) in return for 10 per cent of the company's revenue. Hays Travel at the time had around 60 branches and has operational agreements with over 160 independent agents like the one with the Holiday Shop. The business deal provided the same benefits associated with those in option 3, i.e. allowed Hays to negotiate better commission rates with tour operators, airlines, hoteliers and the like – so that the Holiday Shop could pass on better discounts to consumers and compete directly with the online retailers on price. However, importantly Jill and Kate could still retain ownership and operate as independent players.

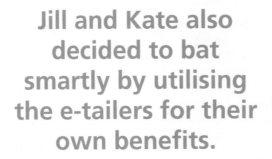

Jill and Kate also decided to bat smartly by utilising the e-tailers for their own benefits.

Jill and Kate also decided to bat smartly by utilising the e-tailers for their own benefits. They recently coined the phrase 'dynamic packaging' to represent the mixing and matching of various e-tailers' services to develop unique offerings for customers. For example it's not unusual today for Holiday Shop employees to package a holiday through using a low-cost airline like easyJet or Jet 2, and then use the Hays reservation system to locate a discount hotel and airport transfer – before adding a mark-up based on the consumer's budget. This type of transaction is particularly attractive to consumers that have a poor credit history, or for those that are concerned about internet fraud (as the Holiday Shop collects payment from the customer and then undertakes the online transaction using its own company credit card). Since making the decision to go down the option 2 route, the business has continued to thrive as an independent operator – and a greater number of customers are returning, knowing that they can still obtain online prices and a holiday with less risk attached.

John Banner Ltd
Attercliffe Road
April 2007

Photo 13.9   Holiday Shop.

Chapter Summary

Now that you have finished reading this chapter, you should be able to answer any of the following potential examination questions:

1. **Explain the concept of the value chain and the key elements in a supply chain.** The value chain consists of five primary activities (inbound logistics, operations, outbound logistics, marketing and sales, and service) and four support activities (procurement, technology development, human resource management, and firm infrastructure). The process is called a value chain because each of these activities adds value to the product or service the customer eventually buys. Whereas the value chain is an overarching concept of how firms create value, the supply chain also encompasses components external to the firm itself, including all activities that are necessary to convert raw materials into a good or service and put it in the hands of the consumer or business customer.

2. **Explain what a distribution channel is and what functions distribution channels perform.** A distribution channel is a series of firms or individuals that facilitates the movement of a product from the producer to the final customer. Channels provide time, place and ownership utility for customers and reduce the number of transactions necessary for goods to flow from many manufacturers to large numbers of customers by breaking bulk and creating assortments. Channel members make the purchasing process easier by providing important customer services. Today the internet is becoming an important player in distribution channels.

3. **Describe the types of wholesaling intermediaries found in distribution channels.** Wholesaling intermediaries are firms that handle the flow of products from the manufacturer to the retailer or business user. Wholesalers are independent intermediaries that take title to a product. Agents and brokers are independent intermediaries that do not take title to products. Manufacturer-owned channel members can include sales branches, sales offices and manufacturers' showrooms.

4. **Describe the types of distribution channels and the steps in planning distribution channel strategies.** Distribution channels vary in length from the simplest two-level channel to longer channels with three or more channel levels. Distribution channels include direct distribution, in which the producer sells directly to consumers, and indirect channels, which may include a retailer, wholesaler or other intermediary. Marketers begin channel planning by developing channel objectives and considering important environmental factors. The next step is to decide a distribution strategy, which involves determining the type of distribution channel that is best. Distribution tactics include the selection of individual channel members and management of the channel.

5. **Explain how logistics is used in the supply chain.** The supply chain includes all the firms that engage in activities that are necessary to turn raw materials into a good or service for a consumer or business customer, including those in the marketing channel of distribution. Every firm occupies a position in a value chain. Companies add value to inputs received from firms upstream. Logistics is the process of designing, managing and improving supply chains, including all those activities that are required to move products through the supply chain. Logistics activities include order processing, warehousing, materials handling, transportation and inventory control.

6. **Define retailing and explain how retailing has evolved.** Retailing is the process by which goods and services are sold to consumers for their personal use. The wheel of retailing hypothesis suggests that new retailers compete on price and over time become more upmarket, leaving room for other new, low-price entrants. The retail life cycle theory suggests retailing institutions are introduced, grow, reach maturity and then decline. Three factors that motivate retailers to evolve are changing demographics, technology and globalisation.

7. **Describe how retailers are classified.** Retailers can be classified by the level of service offered (self-service, full-service and limited-service retailers) and by the merchandise assortment offered. Merchandise assortment is described in terms of breadth and depth, which refer to the number of product lines sold and the amount of variety available for each. Shops can be classified as supermarkets, speciality shops, department stores and hypermarkets.

8. **Describe B2C e-commerce and its benefits, limitations, and future promise.** B2C e-commerce and online exchanges between companies and consumers are growing rapidly. B2C benefits include greater convenience and greater product variety for consumers and opportunities for specialised businesses, lower business costs and instantaneous delivery of some products for marketers. For consumers, the downside of B2C e-commerce includes having to wait to receive products, security issues, and the inability to touch and feel products. For internet-only marketers, success may be difficult to achieve, whereas cannibalisation may be a problem with traditional retailers' online operations.

9. **Explain the importance of shop image to a retail positioning strategy and how a retailer can create an image in the marketplace.** Shop image is how the target market perceives the store relative to the competition. It incorporates the results from many different elements working together to create the most desirable shopping experience, and to ensure that shoppers view a shop favourably relative to the competition. Colour, lighting, scents, furnishings and other design elements – called atmospherics are used to create a 'feel' for a shop environment. Use of atmospherics includes decisions on (1) layout, which determines traffic flow and influences customer behaviour in the shop; (2) the use of fixtures and open space; (3) the use of sound to attract (or repel) certain types of customers; and (4) the use of colour and lighting that can influence customers' moods. The number and type of shop personnel, pricing of products sold in the shop and store location contribute to a shop's image. Major types of retail locations include shopping centres, freestanding retailers and non-traditional locations.

Key Terms

Chapter Review

Marketing Concepts: Testing Your Knowledge

1. What is a value chain?

2. What is a supply chain, and how is it different from a channel of distribution?

3. What is a channel of distribution? What are channel intermediaries?

4. Explain the functions of distribution channels.

5. What factors are important in determining whether a manufacturer should choose a direct or indirect channel? Why do some firms use hybrid marketing systems?

6. What are conventional, vertical and horizontal marketing systems?

7. Explain intensive, exclusive and selective forms of distribution.

8. Explain the steps in distribution planning.

9. What is logistics? Explain the functions of logistics.

10. Define retailing. What is the role of retailing in today's world?

11. How do the wheel of retailing and retail life cycle theories explain the evolution of retailing? How do demo-

graphics, technology and globalisation affect the future of retailing?

12. How are shops classified? Describe the differences in merchandise assortments for supermarkets, speciality shops, discount stores, department stores and hypermarkets.

13. What is B2C e-commerce? What are some benefits of B2C e-commerce for consumers and for marketers? What are the limitations of B2C e-commerce?

14. What are some possible effects of B2C e-commerce on traditional retailing?

15. How is shop positioning strategy like theatre?

16. What is shop image? Why is it important?

17. What is meant by atmospherics? How can the elements of atmospherics be used to increase a shop's success? How are shop personnel a part of shop image?

18. What are some of the different types of locations? What are their advantages and disadvantages?

Marketing Concepts: Discussing Choices

1. The supply chain concept looks at both the inputs of a firm and the means of firms that move the product from the manufacturer to the consumer. Do you think *marketers* should be concerned with the total supply chain concept? Why or why not?

2. You have probably heard someone say, 'The reason products cost so much is because of all the intermediaries'. Do intermediaries increase the cost of products? Would consumers be better off or worse off without intermediaries?

3. Many entrepreneurs choose to start a franchise business rather than 'go it alone'. Do you think franchises offer the

typical business person good opportunities? What are some positive and negative aspects of purchasing a franchise?

4. As universities are looking for better ways to satisfy their customers, an area of increasing interest is the distribution of their service – education. Describe the characteristics of your business school's channel(s) of distribution. What types of innovative distribution might make sense for your school to try?

5. The wheel of retailing theory suggests that the normal path for a retailer is to enter the marketplace with lower priced goods and then to increase quality, services, and

prices. Why do you think this happens? Is it the right path for all retailers? Why or why not?

6. Department stores in the UK appear to be declining in popularity but remain consumers' primary place to shop in other countries such as Japan. Why do you think this is so? Are there ways that department stores can turn this trend around?

Marketing Practice: Applying What You've Learned

1. Assume that you have recently been hired by a firm that manufactures furniture. You feel that marketing should have an input into supplier selection for the firm's products, but the purchasing department says that should not be a concern for marketing. You need to explain to them the importance of the value chain perspective. In a role-playing exercise, explain to the purchasing manager the value chain concept, why it is of concern to marketing, and why the two of you should work together.

2. Assume that you are the director of marketing for a firm that manufactures cleaning chemicals used in industries. You have traditionally sold these products through manufacturer's reps. You are considering adding a direct internet channel to your distribution strategy, but you aren't sure whether this will create channel conflict. Make a list of the pros and cons of this move. What do you think is the best decision?

3. As a one-person marketing department for a confectionery manufacturer (your firm makes high-quality, hand-dipped chocolates using only natural ingredients), you are considering making changes in your distribution strategy. Your products have previously been sold through a network of food brokers that call on speciality food and gift shops. However, you think that perhaps it would be good for your firm to develop a corporate vertical marketing system (that is, vertical integration). In such a plan, a number of company-owned shops would be opened across the country. The chief executive of your company has asked that you present your ideas to the company executives. In a role-playing situation with one of your classmates, present your ideas to your boss, including the advantages and disadvantages of the new plan compared to the current distribution method.

4. Assume that you have recently been given a new marketing assignment by your firm. You are to head up development of a distribution plan for a new product line – a series of do-it-yourself instruction DVDs for home gardeners. These DVDs would show consumers how to plant trees, shrubbery and bulbs; how to care for their plants; how to prune; and so on. You know that in developing a distribution plan, it is essential that you understand and consider a number of internal and external environmental factors. Make a list of the information you will need before you can begin developing the distribution plan. How will you adapt your plan based on each of these factors?

5. Assume you are a business consultant for a chain of traditional department stores. In recent years, the stores have seen declining revenues as speciality shops and hypermarkets have begun to squeeze the department stores out. The chain has asked you for suggestions on how to increase its business. Develop an outline of your recommendations and present your plan to your class.

6. As a university graduate, you and a friend think the career you really would enjoy means being your own boss – you want to start your own business. You feel the future of e-commerce is the place for you to make your fortune. You and your friend are considering two options: (1) a business that sells custom-made jeans based on customers' measurements online and (2) a business that sells gourmet foods from around the world online. In a role-playing exercise, debate with your friend the pros and cons of each of these two online retail businesses and make a decision on which is the best option.

7. All your life you've wanted to be an entrepreneur and to own your own business. Now you're ready to graduate from university, you've decided to open a combination coffee shop and bookshop in a location near your university. You know that to attract both the college student market and other customers from the local community, it will be necessary to design carefully the shop's image. Develop a detailed plan that specifies how you will use atmospherics to create the image you desire.

8. In your job with a marketing consulting firm, you often are asked to make recommendations for shop location. Your current client is a local caterer that is planning to open a new retail outlet for selling take-away gourmet dinners. You are examining the possible types of locations: a shopping centre, a freestanding entity, or some non-traditional location. Outline the advantages and disadvantages of each type of location. Present your recommendations to your client.

9. Assume that you are the director of marketing for a national chain of convenience stores. Your firm has about 200 stores across Europe. The stores are fairly traditional both in design and in the merchandise they carry. Because you want to be proactive in your marketing planning, you are concerned that your firm may need to consider making significant changes because of the current demographic, technological, and global trends in the marketplace. You think it is important to discuss these things with the other executives at your firm. Develop a presentation that includes the following:

   a. A discussion of the demographic changes that will affect your stores.

   b. A discussion of the technological changes that will affect your stores.

c. A discussion of how global changes may provide problems and opportunities for your organisation.

d. Your recommendations for how your firm might meet the challenges faced in each of these areas.

Marketing Miniproject: Learning by Doing

(A) In Europe the distribution of most products is fairly easy. There are lots of independent intermediaries (wholesalers, dealers, distributors and retailers) that are willing to cooperate to get the product to the final customer. State of the art motorway networks often combine with rail, air and water transportation to provide excellent means for moving goods from one part of Europe to another. In many other countries, the means for distribution of products are far less efficient and effective.

For this miniproject, you and one or more of your classmates should first select a consumer product, probably one you normally purchase. Then use either library sources or other people or both (retailers, manufacturers, dealers, classmates, and so on) to gather information to do the following:

1. Describe the path the product takes to get from the producer to you. Draw a model to show each of the steps the product takes. Include as much as you can about transportation, warehousing, materials handling, order processing, stock control, and so on.

2. Select another country in which the same or a similar product is sold. Describe the path the product takes to get from the producer to the customer in that country.

3. Determine if the differences between the two countries cause differences in price, availability or quality of the product.

4. Make a presentation to your class on your findings.

(B) This project is designed to help you understand how atmospherics play a role in consumers' perceptions of a shop.

1. First, select two retail outlets where students at your university are likely to shop. It will be good if you can select two outlets that you feel are quite different in terms of shop image but that sell the same types of products. You might consider two speciality women's clothing shops, two jewellery shops, two department stores or two coffee shops.

2. Visit each of the shops and write down a detailed description of the atmosphere – colours, materials used, types of displays, lighting fixtures, product displays, shop personnel, and so on.

3. Survey some of the students in your university. Develop a brief questionnaire asking about the perceptions of the two shops you are studying. You may want to ask about such things as the quality of merchandise, prices, competence and friendliness of the shop personnel, the attitude of management towards customer service, and so on. What is the 'personality' of each shop?

4. Develop a report of your findings. Compare the description of the shops with the results of the survey. Attempt to explain how the different elements of the shop atmosphere create each shop's unique image.

Real People, Real Surfers

Exploring the Web (A)

Visit the web site for UPS (www.ups.com). UPS has positioned itself as a full service provider of logistics solutions. After reviewing its web site, answer the following questions:

1. What logistics services does UPS offer its customers?

2. What does UPS say to convince prospective customers that its services are better than those of the competition?

▶

Exploring the Web (B)

Many traditional retailers now have websites. Other online retailers do not have actual shops but practise only direct selling. Visit the sites of one or two popular retailers of your choice, then visit the site of a direct-only retailer.

1. Describe each retailer's website. What information is available on each site? How easy was each to navigate? What information did you find interesting and useful on each site? What did you find that you didn't expect to find at a retailer site? What did you find lacking at each site?

2. What differences are there for sites that have traditional bricks-and-mortar shops from those that do not? Does the site encourage consumers to visit the physical shop or just to remain an online shopper?

3. How do the retailers' websites communicate the image or personality of their shops? How are they alike? How are they different? If you had no information except that available on the web, would you know what types of products are sold; whether the products sold are expensive, prestige products, or low-priced products; and what types of consumers each retailer is attempting to attract to its shops? How does each site use graphics or other design elements to represent the 'setting' as retailers do in their shops? How do they communicate the type of consumer they consider their primary market?

4. What recommendations would you make to each retailer to improve its website?

Now, take a look at the website at www.pearsoned.co.uk/solomon to see some videos from YouTube relating to aspects of this chapter.

Also on the website, try some analysis and calculations yourself by looking up the marketing metrics exercise called Distribution and Display to learn how to develop models for selecting the optimal mix of products to display where space is limited.

Marketing Plan Exercise

(A) Dell is a company that has traditionally used one fairly simple supply chain system – direct sales over the internet or by phone to both business and consumer users. In planning for the future, Dell has been exploring potentially making use of other distribution channels and outlets. They are already using kiosks at major airports to demonstrate and sell products. Yet in considering expanding their channels they certainly don't want to damage the backbone of their supply chain process – the direct channel.

1. If you were a marketing executive at Dell, what supply chain options would you suggest in designing a marketing plan beyond the company's traditional distribution model?

2. Can Dell successfully coexist in retail store distribution and in distribution through their traditional direct means? Justify your answer.

3. Assume that your plan recommends Dell become more aggressive in pursuing distribution through shops and other means beyond their traditional direct channel. What intermediaries do you recommend become part of their supply chain? Why?

(B) The wheel of retailing suggests that new retailers enter the marketplace by offering goods at lower prices than competitors and that after they gain a foothold they 'trade up', improving their facilities and their merchandise assortment. Think about a new retail venture, a speciality shop that sells time pieces, such as men's and ladies' watches and clocks.

1. What retailing strategies do you recommend for the new retailer for their first two years in business – what merchandise, what shop image, and what location(s)?

2. What long-term retailing strategies do you recommend?

Marketing in Action Case

Real decisions at IKEA

How would you go about becoming one of the wealthiest people in the world? Ingvar Kamprad did it by flying economy, taking public transport, driving 10-year-old cars, moving from Sweden to Switzerland (for lower taxes) . . . oh, and incidentally, founding IKEA – now the world's largest furniture store.

Kamprad founded IKEA in Sweden in 1943 when he was just 17 years old and while the world was caught up in the Second World War. He began by selling pens, picture frames, wallets and other bargain items out of a catalogue. In 1951 he began selling furniture made by local carpenters and in 1957 opened his first IKEA furniture store in Sweden. Today, the company generates about €15 billion in annual sales from stores located all over the world. By implementing a solid retail strategy, IKEA has become a furniture juggernaut!

IKEA retail locations are gigantic and they focus exclusively on the furniture and home decorating market. IKEA's size and focus limit the breadth of items it offers, but it does provide a great deal of merchandise depth including furniture, decorative accessories and lighting fixtures for all rooms of the house. In designing its store layout, IKEA is responding to consumer interest in one-stop shopping – finding what they want in one shop rather than having to visit numerous places. Also, IKEA makes it easier for customers to shop once they enter the store. Furniture displays are set up in 'lifestyle' themes showing the type of furniture that singles, couples or young families might need. The company also uses vignette displays to suggest how a customer can put together various items to create a certain look. These types of displays are perfect for the

From a promotion standpoint, IKEA has been extremely innovative

generation that is no longer interested in buying furniture to last a lifetime but rather that fits their lifestyle now. And, speaking of lifestyle, IKEA plays to the busy lifestyle of today's consumers by making its products available through its retail locations, in catalogues and on the internet.

For example, in China company representatives decorated the inside of apartment building elevators to illustrate how products available at IKEA can help transform old, stodgy looks into modern, pleasant living spaces. In Singapore the company went after younger age groups by partnering with Nickelodeon for a 'Nick Takes over Your Room' promotion in which IKEA redecorated children's rooms and then Nickelodeon broadcast the kids on TV. In the United States, IKEA has offered gift cards worth up to $4000 to the first customer in the queue on opening day – a promotion that prompts customers to camp out in front of the store for weeks before its grand opening. Finally, before a grand opening at a store in Sacramento, California, IKEA parked a glass-sided tractor trailer around town. The trailer showed two people lounging on IKEA furniture as though they were at home. Such promotions generate much excitement among the target audience that translates into greater awareness of, and more sales for, IKEA.

IKEA has enjoyed great success throughout its history, and that success has not come by accident – IKEA has got to where it is today through great marketing planning. Presently, one of the most important decisions facing IKEA is how and where it should expand. The company has announced its desire to add 50 additional store locations in North America over the next decade and another eight stores in China. Given the heavy expenses that go into building brick-and-mortar retail locations, making the right expansion decision is critical to IKEA's future success.

So far, IKEA has limited its store locations to some of the most heavily populated markets in the countries in which it competes. To continue its growth trends, IKEA may have to begin investigating other (think smaller) communities. IKEA also has to consider how it will respond if and when a lower priced competitor enters its markets. Finally, IKEA must consider that its product assortment and quirky promotions may not appeal to all cultures. As a result, the company will have to adapt its merchandise and promotion to appeal to differing consumer tastes and preferences.

For IKEA, despite the history of success the company has enjoyed thus far, there are no guarantees for the future. One thing about IKEA's future is certain – unless IKEA keeps innovating and makes the right expansion decisions, the company will become increasingly vulnerable to new competitors.

Things to Think About

1. What is the decision facing IKEA?

2. What factors are important in understanding this decision situation?

3. What are the options?

4. What decision(s) do you recommend?

5. What are some ways to implement your recommendation?

Sources: Cora Daniels and Adam Edström, 'Create IKEA, Make Billions, Take Bus', Fortune, 3 May, 2004, 44; Emma Hall and Normandy Madden, 'Ikea Courts Buyers with Offbeat Ideas', *Advertising Age,* 12 April, 2004, 10; Jon Ortiz, 'Customers Drawn to Ikea 'Experience''. *The Sacramento Bee,* 26 February, 2006, D1; Luisa Kroll and Allison Fass, 'The World's Billionaires', Retrieved 19 June, 2006 from website: www.forbes.com/billionaires; Mei Fong, 'Ikea Hits Home in China', *The Wall Street Journal Online,* 3 March, 2006, B1; Mike Duff, 'IKEA Eyes Aggressive Growth', *DSN Retailing Today,* 27 January, 2003, 3, 22.

References

1. Thomas L. Friedman, *The World is Flat: A Brief History of the Twenty-First Century* New York: Farrar, Straus and Giroux, 2006.

2. Paula D. Harveston, Basil G. Englis, Michael R. Solomon and Marla Goldsmith, 'Knowledge Management as Competitive Advantage: Lessons from the Textile and Apparel Value Chain', *Journal of Knowledge Management* 9 (2) (2005), 91–102.

3. Rowland T. Moriarty and Ursula Moran, 'Managing Hybrid Marketing Systems', *Harvard Business Review* (November–December 1990), 2–11.

4. Nirmalya Kumar, 'Living with Channel Conflict', *CMO: The Resource for Marketing Executives*, www.cmomagazine .com/read/100104/channel_conflict.html.

5. www.oneworld.com/home.cfm.

6. www.starbucks.com/aboutus/sup_div.asp.

7. Kumar, 'Living with Channel Conflict'.

8. Toby B. Gooley, 'The Who, What, and Where of Reverse Logistics', *Logistics Management* 42 (February 2003), 38–44; James R. Stock, *Development and Implementation of Reverse Logistics Programs*, Council of Logistics Management (1998), 20.

9. www.supplychainmetric.com/perfect.htm.

10. Faye W. Gilbert, Joyce A. Young and Charles R. O'Neal, 'Buyer – Seller Relationships in Just-in-Time Purchasing Environments', *Journal of Organizational Research* 29 (February 1994), 111–20.

11. Kasra Ferdows, Michael A. Lewis and Jose A.D. Machuca, 'Zara's Secret for Fast Fashion', *Harvard Business Review*, 21 February 2005, http://199.94.20.134/item.jhtml?id= 4652&t=operations.

12. Michael Levy and Barton A. Weitz, *Retailing Management*, 3rd ed. (Boston, MA: Irwin/McGraw-Hill, 1998).

13. Stanley C. Hollander, 'The Wheel of Retailing', *Journal of Retailing* (July 1960), 41.

14. William R. Davidson, Albert D. Bates and Stephen J. Bass, 'The Retail Life Cycle', *Harvard Business Review* (November–December 1976), 89.

15. Lauren Foster and Andrew Ward, 'McDonald's Drinks Menu May Grow', *Food and Beverage*, 19 June 2006, 28.

16. Cathy Horyn, 'A Store Made for Right Now: You Shop until It's Dropped', 17 February 2004, www.nytimes.com.

17. Thomas M. Anderson, 'Checkups on the Run', *Kiplinger Personal Finance* (May 2006), 96.

18. Ian Austen, 'In Germany, Customers Scan as They Shop', 12 May 2003, www.nytimes.com; Annick Moes, 'Technology Rules "Future Store" by Tracking Shoppers and Sales', 19 June 2003, www.wsj.com.

19. Ken Belson, 'As Starbucks Grows, Japan, Too, Is Awash', 21 October 2001, http://query.nytimes.com/search/abstract?res=F50F14FF3B50C728EDDA90994D9404482

20. Joan Raymond, 'Nomore Shoppus Interruptus', *American Demographics* (May 2001), 39.

21. Juhnyoung Lee, Robert Hoch, Mark Podlaseck, Edith Schonberg and Stephen Gomory, 'Analysis and Visualization of Metrics for online Merchandising', www.research.ibm.com/iac/papers/Incs.pdf.

22. Rebecca Quick, 'Hope Springs A new for web Retailers: Study Shows Many are Making Money', 18 April 2000, www.wsj.com; Randy Myers, 'E-Tailers & Space Invaders', e-CFO 47(7) (April 2000).

23. Helen Coster, 'Consumer Spy: Do You Have Quirky Tastes in Mail-Order Shopping? Chances are Abacus Knows All About You', *Forbes* (January 2006), 91.

24. 'A Wide World of Sports Shoes: Fixtures Enhance Appeal of World Foot Locker', *Chain Store Age Executive* (January 1993), 176–81.

25. Jane J. Kim, 'A Latte with Your Loan?', *The Wall Street Journal*, 17 May 2006, D1.

26. Tracie Rozhon, 'High Fashion, from Front Door to the Top Floor', 31 July 2003, www.nytimes.com.

27. L. W. Turley and Ronald E. Milliman, 'Atmospheric Effects on Shopping Behavior: A Review of the Experimental Evidence', *Journal of Business Research* 49 (2000), 193–211.

28. Julie Flaherty, 'Ambient Music Has Moved to Record Store Shelves', 4 July 2001, www.nytimes.com.

29. Deborah Blumenthal, 'Scenic Design for In-Store Try-Ons', *New York Times*, April 1988. 'Service: Retail's No. 1 Problem', *Chain Store Age*, 19 January 1987.

30. Michael Levy and Barton A. Weitz, *Retailing Management*, 3rd ed. (Boston: Irwin/McGraw-Hill, 1998).

Appendix A:
Sample Marketing Plan
The B & V Smoothie Company

Executive Summary

 ### Situation Analysis

B & V Smoothie Company is an entrepreneurial organisation that produces fruit-and-yogurt-based beverages with superior flavour and nutritional content and unique packaging. Within Europe, B & V has targeted a consumer market of younger, health-conscious, upmarket consumers who regularly exercise at gyms and health clubs, and two broad re-seller markets: (1) gyms and health clubs and (2) small upmarket food markets. B & V distributes its products through agents in the EU and via the internet. An analysis of the internal and external environments suggests the firm enjoys important strengths in its product, its employees, and its reputation, while weaknesses are seen in its limited size, financial resources and product capabilities. B & V faces a supportive external environment, highlighted by a growing interest in healthy living, and limited threats, primarily from potential competitive growth.

 ### Marketing Objectives

The B & V marketing objectives are to increase awareness, gross sales (50 per cent) and distribution, and to introduce two new product lines over the next three years:

- a line of low-carbohydrate smoothies
- a line of gourmet flavoured smoothies

Marketing Strategies

To accomplish its growth goals, B & V will direct its marketing activites toward the following strategies:

1. *Target Market Strategy:* B & V will continue to target its existing consumer markets while expanding its business-to-business markets to include hotels and resorts, golf and tennis clubs, and university campuses.

2. *Positioning Strategy:* B & V will continue to position its products as the first-choice smoothie beverage for the serious health-conscious consumer, including those who are seeking to lower their carbohydrate intake.

3. *Product Strategy:* B & V will introduce two new product lines, each identifiable through unique packaging/labelling:

   a. **B & V Smoothie Gold:** a product similar to the original B & V Smoothie beverages but in six unique flavours.

   b. **Low-Carbohydrate B & V Smoothie:** a product with 50 per cent fewer grammes of carbohydrates.

4. *Pricing Strategy:* B & V will maintain the current pricing strategy for existing and new products.

5. *Promotion Strategy:* B & V will augment current personal selling efforts with television and magazine advertising, with sponsorships of key sporting events in major cities and with a sampling programme.

6. *Supply Chain Strategy:* B & V will expand its distribution network to include the business-to-business markets targeted. In addition, to encourage a high level of inventory in larger health clubs, B & V Smoothie will offer free refrigerated display units.

 ## Implementation and Control

The Action Plan details how the marketing strategies will be implemented including the individual(s) responsible, the timing of each activity, and the budget necessary. The measurement and control strategies provide a means of measurement of the success of the plan.

 # Situation Analysis

The B & V Smoothie Company[1] was founded in September 1998 in London with the goal of creating and marketing healthy 'smoothie' beverages for sale to health-conscious consumers. B & V Smoothie expects to take advantage of an increasing desire for healthy foods in Europe – and to ride the wave of consumer interest in low-carbohydrate alternatives. While there are other companies both large and small competing in this market, B & V Smoothie feels it has the expertise to create and market superior products that will appeal to its target market.

[1]B & V Smoothie Company is a fictitious company created to illustrate a sample marketing plan. The market data and statistics are also fictitious to provide a practical scenario for students to follow.

Internal Environment

Mission Statement

The strategic direction and actions of the B & V Smoothie Company are driven by its mission:

> B & V Smoothie seeks to meet the needs of discriminating, health-conscious consumers for high-quality, superior-tasting smoothie beverages and other similar products.

Organisational Structure

As an entrepreneurial company, B & V Smoothie does not have a very sophisticated organisational structure. Key personnel include the following:

- Patrick Bradley, founder and co-director. Bradley is responsible for the creation, design, packaging, and production management of all B & V Smoothie products.
- William Vince, founder and co-director. Vince is responsible for international and domestic distribution and marketing.
- Gayle Humphries, head of finance. Humphries develops the financial strategy and keeps the company's books.
- Alex Johnson, national sales manager. Johnson is responsible for maintaining the sales force of independent sales reps. He also advises on product development.
- Rob LeMay, Pam Sartens and Paul Sartens, shareholders. Next to Patrick Bradley and William Vince, Rob, Pam and Paul own the largest number of shares. They consult and sit on the company's board of directors. Rob is a lawyer and also provides legal services.

Corporate Culture

B & V Smoothie is an entrepreneurial organisation. Thus, a key element of the internal environment is a culture that encourages innovation, risk taking and individual creativity. The company's beginning was based on a desire to provide a unique, superior product, and company decisions have consistently emphasised this mission.

Products

The original B & V Smoothie, introduced in mid-1999, was a fruit-and-yogurt-based beverage that contained only natural ingredients (no additives) and was high in essential nutrients. Table A.1 provides nutritional information for the 340g size B & V Smoothie beverage. Because of the company's patented manufacturing process, B & V Smoothie beverages do not have to be refrigerated and have a shelf life of over a year. Therefore, the product can be shipped and delivered via non-refrigerated carriers. B & V Smoothie currently sells its beverages exclusively through gyms, health clubs, and small upmarket food markets.

At present, the single product line is the B & V Smoothie fruit-and-yogurt beverage. This healthy beverage product has a flavour and nutritional content that makes it superior to competing products. The present product comes in five flavours: strawberry, blueberry, banana, peach and cherry. B & V offers each in a 340g and a 565g size. B & V packages the product in a uniquely shaped, frosted glass bottle with a screw-off cap. The bottle design makes the product easy to hold, even with sweaty hands after workouts. The frosted glass allows the colour of the beverage to be seen but at the same time communicates an upmarket image. The labelling and lid visually denote the flavour with an appropriate colour. Labelling includes complete

Table A.1
Nutritional
Information: B & V
Smoothie Beverage

Serving Size: 340g	Amount per Serving	% Daily Value
Calories	140	
Calories from fat	6	
Total fat	<0.5 g	1
Saturated fat	<0.5 g	2
Cholesterol	6 mg	2
Sodium	70 mg	3
Potassium	100 mg	3
Total carbohydrates	10 g	3
Dietary fibre	5 g	20
Sugar	1 g	
Protein	25 g	50
Vitamin A		50
Vitamin C		50
Calcium		20
Iron		30
Vitamin D		40
Vitamin E		50
Thiamin		50
Riboflavin		50
Niacin		50
Vitamin B_6		50
Vitamin B_{12}		50
Biotin		50
Pantothenic acid		50
Phosphorus		10
Iodine		50
Chromium		50
Zinc		50
Folic acid		50

nutritional information. In the future, B & V Smoothie plans to expand its line of products to increase its market share of the health drink market.

Pricing of B & V Smoothie beverages is as follows:

	340g	565g
Suggested retail price	€4.00	€6.00
Price to retail outlets (health clubs, etc.)	€2.00	€3.00
Price to distributor/discount to sales agent	€1.00	€1.50

Thus, B & V Smoothie receives €1.00 in revenue for each 340g bottle and €1.50 in revenue for each 565g bottle it sells.

At present, B & V Smoothie outsources actual production of the product. Still, the company takes care to oversee the entire production process to ensure consistent quality of its unique product. With this method of production, variable costs for the 340g B & V Smoothie beverages are €0.63, and variable costs for the 565g are €0.71. Current annual fixed costs for B & V Smoothie office space, management salaries and professional services are as follows:

Salaries and employee benefits	€275,000
Office rental, equipment, and supplies	€24,600
Expenses related to sales (travel, etc.)	€32,000
Advertising and other marketing communications	€50,000
Total fixed costs	**€381,600**

Sales of the two sizes of the product are approximately equal; that is, half of sales are for the 340g size and half are for the 565g size. Thus, there is an average contribution margin of €0.58 per bottle. Based on this, to achieve breakeven, B & V Smoothie must sell

$$€381,600/.58 = 657,931 \text{ units}$$

Again, assuming equal sales of the two size products, the break-even point in euros is €822,413.

Previous Sales

Sales of B & V Smoothie products have continued to grow since their introduction to the market in 1999. Actual sales figures for 1999 through to 2006 are shown in Table A.2.

Markets

The consumer market for B & V Smoothie products is made up of anyone who is interested in healthy food and a healthy lifestyle. Although according to published research, nearly 70 per cent of European consumers say they are interested in living a healthy lifestyle, the number of those who actually work to achieve that goal is much smaller. It is estimated that approximately 40 million Europeans actually engage in exercise and/or follow nutritional plans that would be described as healthy. As experts expect the trend toward healthier living to grow globally, the European and international markets for B & V Smoothie products are expected to expand for some time.

Within the European consumer market, B & V Smoothie targets upmarket consumers who regularly work out at gyms and health clubs. While these consumers are primarily younger, there is also a growing older segment that seeks to be physically fit and that also uses health clubs.

Table A.2
Company Sales
Performance

Year	Gross Sales
1999	€87,000
2000	€238,000
2001	€311,000
2002	€436,000
2003	€618,000
2004	€650,000
2005	€710,000
2006	€765,000

Channels

In order to reach its target market, B & V Smoothie places primary emphasis on health clubs and other physical fitness facilities and small, upmarket specialty food markets. The company began developing channel relationships with these outlets through individual contacts by company personnel. As sales developed, the company solicited the services of agents and specialty food distributors. Agents are individuals who sell products for a number of different non-competing manufacturers. By contracting with these agents in various geographic regions, the company can expand its product distribution in a significant number of countries throughout Europe.

The company handles various large accounts for national gym chains. While total sales to these chains are fairly substantial, when considering the large number of facilities within each chain the sales are very small, with much room for growth. The internet is a secondary channel for B & V Smoothie. Online retail outlets currently account for only 5 per cent of B & V Smoothie sales. While this channel is useful for individuals who wish to purchase B & V Smoothie products in larger quantities, B & V does not expect that online sales will become a significant part of the business in the near future.

 # External Environment

Competitive Environment

B & V Smoothie faces several different levels of competition. Direct competitors are companies that also market smoothie-type beverages and include the following:

1. Franchise smoothie retail operations.
2. Online-only smoothie outlets.
3. Other smaller manufacturers.
4. Larger companies such as Nestlé that produce similar products.

Indirect competition comes from the following:

1. Homemade smoothie drinks made from powders sold in retail outlets and over the internet.
2. Homemade smoothie drinks made using a multitude of available recipes.
3. Other healthy beverages, such as juices.

Economic Environment

B & V Smoothie first introduced its products during a period of relative prosperity. The economy in Europe has remained somewhat stable during recent years and sales have grown. Analysts estimate that total gross domestic product (GDP) will increase a little over 2 per cent annually over the next few years in Europe.

Technological Environment

Because B & V Smoothie produces a simple food product, technological advances have minimum impact on the firm's operations. Nevertheless, the use of current technology enables and enhances many of the company's operations. For example, B & V Smoothie uses the internet to enhance its operations in two ways. First, the internet provides an additional outlet for sales. In addition, agents and channel members can keep in contact with the company, allowing for fewer problems with deliveries, orders, and so on.

Political and Legal Environment

Because they are advertised as nutritional products, all B & V Smoothie products must be approved by the appropriate food regulatory body in each European country where the goods are destined. Labelling must also conform to similar regulations. In Europe, there are numerous regulations that are country-specific which the company must constantly remain aware of.

Sociocultural Environment

The social and cultural environment continues to provide an important opportunity for B & V Smoothie. The trend toward healthy foods and a healthier lifestyle has grown dramatically for the past decade or longer. In response to this, the number of health clubs across Europe and the number of independent tourist resorts and spas have also grown. In addition, many travellers demand that hotels offer health club facilities.

During the past three years, consumers around the world have become more aware of the advantages of a low-carbohydrate diet. Analysts project that the target age group of 15- to 44-year-olds will remain stable in the foreseeable future, with an increase of less than 8 per cent projected to 2025. Similarly, their income should neither decrease nor increase significantly in the near future.

 ## SWOT Analysis

The SWOT analysis provides a summary of the strengths, weaknesses, opportunities and threats identified by B & V Smoothie through the analysis of their internal and external environments.

Strengths

The following are the strengths identified by B & V Smoothie:

- A creative and skilled employee team.
- A high-quality product recipe that provides exceptional flavour with high levels of nutrition.
- Because of its entrepreneurial spirit, the ability to remain flexible and to adapt quickly to environmental changes.
- A strong network of European agents and distributors.

- The growth of a reputation of a high-quality product among health clubs, other retail outlets and targeted consumer groups.

Weaknesses

The following are the weaknesses identified by B & V Smoothie:

- Limited financial resources for growth and for advertising and other marketing communications.
- Little flexibility in terms of personnel due to size of the firm.
- Reliance on external production to maintain quality standards and to meet any unanticipated surges in demand for the product.

Opportunities

The following are the opportunities identified by B & V Smoothie:

- A strong and growing interest in healthy living, both among young, upmarket consumers and among older consumers.
- Continuing consumer interest in low-carb alternatives that offer opportunities for additional product lines.

Threats

The following are the threats identified by B & V Smoothie:

- The potential for competitors, especially those with large financial resources who can invest more in promotion, to develop products that consumers may find superior.
- Economic downturn that might affect potential sales.
- Movement away from low-carbohydrate diets, particularly if other forms of dieting gain in popularity.

 ## Marketing Objectives

The following are the marketing objectives set by B & V Smoothie:

- To increase the awareness of B & V Smoothie products among the target market.
- To increase gross sales by 50 per cent over the next two years.
- To introduce two new product lines over the next three years: a line of low-carbohydrate smoothies and a line of gourmet flavoured smoothies.
- To increase distribution of B & V Smoothie products in more countries throughout the EU.

 # Marketing Strategies

 ## Target Markets

Consumer Markets

B & V Smoothies will continue to target its existing consumer markets. The primary consumer target market for B & V Smoothie beverages can be described as follows:

Demographics

- Male and female teens and young adults, ages 15–39
- Household income: €50,000 and above
- Education of head of household: university degree or above
- Primarily located in mid-sized to large European major cities

Psychographics

- Health-conscious, interested in living a healthy lifestyle
- Spend much time and money taking care of their bodies
- Enjoy holidays that include physical activities
- Live very busy lives and need to use time wisely to enjoy all they want to do
- Enjoy spending time with friends

Media Habits

- The target market is more likely to get their news from television or the internet than from newspapers. They are likely to view not only the news channels but also the financial news networks.
- They prefer watching satellite to traditional TV channels.

Business-to-Business Markets

In the past, B & V Smoothie has targeted two categories of re-seller markets: (1) health clubs and gyms and (2) small upmarket specialty food markets. To increase distribution and sales of its products, B & V Smoothie will target the following in the future:

1. Hotels and resorts.
2. Golf and tennis clubs.
3. University campuses.

Upmarket young professionals frequently visit hotels and resorts, and they demand that business travel includes quality accommodation and first-rate health club facilities. The membership of golf and tennis clubs, while including many older consumers, is also an excellent means of providing products conveniently for the targeted groups. University students, probably more than any other consumer group, are interested in health and in their bodies. In fact, many universities have built large, fairly elaborate health and recreational facilities as a means of attracting students. Thus, providing B & V Smoothie beverages on University campuses is an excellent means of meeting the health beverage needs of this group.

 ## Positioning the Product

B & V Smoothie seeks to position its products as the first-choice smoothie beverage for the serious health-conscious consumer, including those who are seeking to lower their carbohydrate intake. The justification for this positioning is as follows. Many smoothie beverages are available. The B & V Smoothie formula provides superior flavour and nutrition in a shelf-stable form. B & V Smoothie has developed its product, packaging, pricing and promotion to communicate a superior, prestige image. This positioning is thus supported by all its marketing strategies.

Product Strategies

To increase its leverage in the market and to meet its sales objectives, B & V Smoothie needs additional products. Two new product lines are planned:

1. *B & V Smoothie Gold:* This product will be similar to the original B & V Smoothie beverages but will come in six unique flavours:

   a. Piña colada

   b. Chocolate banana

   c. Apricot nectarine

   d. Pineapple berry crush

   e. Tropical cherry

   f. Peach delight

   To set the product apart from the original-flavour Smoothie beverages – the labels will include the name of the beverage and the logo in gold lettering, and the bottle cap will be black.

2. *Low-carbohydrate B & V Smoothie:* The low-carbohydrate B & V Smoothie beverage will have approximately 50 per cent fewer grammes of carbohydrates than the original Smoothie beverage or the B & V Smoothie Gold. The low-carbohydrate B & V Smoothie will come in the following four flavours:

   a. Strawberry

   b. Blueberry

   c. Banana

   d. Peach

   Packaging for the low-carbohydrate B & V Smoothie will be similar to other B & V Smoothie beverages but will include the term 'Low Carbohydrate' in large type. The label will state that the beverage has 50 per cent fewer carbohydrates than regular smoothies.

 ## Pricing Strategies

The current pricing strategy will be maintained for the existing and new products. This pricing is appropriate for communicating a high-quality product image for all B & V Smoothie products. The company feels that creating different pricing for the new beverages would be confusing and could create negative attitudes among consumers. Thus, there is no justification for increasing the price of the new products.

 ## Promotion Strategies

In the past, B & V Smoothie has used mainly personal selling to promote its products to the trade channel. To support this effort, signage has been provided for the re-sellers to promote the product at the point of purchase. Posters and stand-alone table cards show appealing photographs of the product in the different flavours and communicate the brand name and the healthy benefits of the product. Similar signage will be developed for use by re-sellers who choose to stock the B & V Smoothie Gold and the Low-Carb Smoothies.

Selling has previously been handled by a team of over 75 agents who sell to re-sellers. In addition, in some markets, an independent distributor does the selling. To support this personal selling approach, B & V Smoothie plans for additional promotional activities to introduce its new products and meet its other marketing objectives. These include the following:

1. *Television advertising:* B & V Smoothie will purchase a limited amount of relatively inexpensive and targeted satellite channel advertising. A small number of commercials will be shown during prime-time programmes with high viewer ratings by the target market. Television advertising can be an important means of not only creating awareness of the product but also enhancing the image of the product. Indeed, consumers are prone to feel that if a product is advertised on prime-time TV, it must be a good product.

2. *Magazine advertising:* Because consumers in the target market are not avid magazine readers, magazine advertising will be limited and will supplement other promotion activities. During next year, B & V Smoothie will experiment with limited advertising in appropriate sporting magazines. The company will also investigate the potential of advertising in university newspapers.

3. *Sponsorships:* B & V Smoothie will attempt to sponsor several key sporting events in major cities. The advantage of sponsorship is it provides visibility for the product while at the same time showing that the company supports activities of interest to the target market.

4. *Sampling:* Sampling of B & V Smoothie beverages at select venues will provide an opportunity for prospective customers to become aware of the product and to taste the flavours. Sampling will include only the two new products being introduced. Venues for sampling will include the following:

   a. marathons

   b. Tour de France (cycling)

   c. gymnastic meetings

   d. student unions on selected campuses

 ## Supply Chain Strategies

As noted earlier, B & V Smoothie distributes its beverages primarily through health clubs and gyms and small upmarket specialty food stores. B & V Smoothie plans to expand its target re-seller market to include the following:

- hotels and resorts
- golf and tennis clubs
- university campuses

To increase leverage in larger health clubs, B & V Smoothie will offer free refrigerated display units. This will encourage the facility to maintain a high level of stock of B & V Smoothie beverages which are ready to consume.

 ## Implementation

The Action Plan details the activities necessary to implement all marketing strategies. In addition, the Action Plan includes the timing for each item, the individual(s) responsible and the budgetary requirements. Table A.3 shows an example of one objective (to increase distribution venues) and the action items B & V Smoothie will use to accomplish it.[2]

[2]Note that the final marketing plan should include objectives, action items, timing information and budget information necessary to accomplish all marketing strategies. We have only one objective in this sample marketing plan.

Table A.3
Action Items for
Accomplishing
Marketing Objective
Regarding Supply
Chain: Objective –
Increase Distribution
Venues

Action Items	Beginning Date	Ending Date	Responsible Party	Cost	Remarks
1. Identify key hotels, resorts, golf clubs and tennis clubs where B & V Smoothies might be sold	1 July	1 September	Wm Vince (consulting firm will be engaged to assist in this effort)	€25,000	Key to this strategy is to selectively choose re-sellers so that maximum results are obtained from sales activities. Because health club use is greater during the months of January to May, effort will be timed to have product in stock no later than 10 January
2. Identify 25 key universities where B & V Smoothies might be sold	1 July	1 August	Wm Vince	0	Information about universities and their health club facilities should be available on the university web pages
3. Make initial contact with larger hotel and resort chains	1 September	1 November	Wm Vince	€10,000	
4. Make initial contact with larger individual (non-chain) facilities	1 September	1 November	Wm Vince	€5000	
5. Make initial contact with universities	15 August	15 September	Agents	0	Agents will be assigned to the 25 universities and required to make an initial contact and report back to Wm Vince on promising prospects
6. Follow up initial contacts with all potential re-sellers and obtain contracts for coming 6 months	15 September	On-going	Wm Vince and agents	€10,000	Although €10,000 is budgeted for this item, actual expenditures will be on an as-needed basis, as follow-up travel cannot be pre-planned

Measurement and Control Strategies

A variety of activities will ensure effective measurement of the success of the marketing plan and allow the firm to make adjustments as necessary. These include market research and trend analysis.

 ## Research

Firms need continuous market research to understand brand awareness and brand attitudes among their target markets. B & V Smoothie will therefore commission exploratory research and descriptive benchmark studies of its target consumer and re-seller markets.

 ## Trend Analysis

B & V Smoothie will carry out a monthly trend analysis to examine sales by re-seller type, country, chain, agent and distributor. This analysis will allow B & V Smoothie to take corrective action when necessary.

Appendix B:
Marketing Maths

To demonstrate the value of marketing, marketers must be detectives, tracking evidence about the marketing value chain. This requires the collection of financial and non-financial data and the application of some basic mathematics.

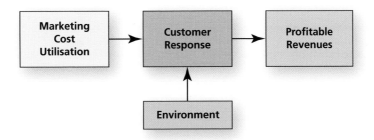

Figure B.1   The marketing value chain

We examine this first by looking at a simple example.

Mail-order Firm

This example is a simplified illustration of the analysis carried out by mail-order businesses. It has been chosen for its simplicity in order to reveal the key pieces of evidence and their relevance to evaluating marketing's contribution.

Demonstrating Value – the Four Steps

1. **Marketing cost allocation**   The marketing department spends money sending direct mail to acquire new customers at a cost of 50p per letter. It can vary the volume of its acquisition mailing and in recent years has annually mailed between 1 million and 3 million letters.

2. **Customer response**   Historical analysis of its mailing discloses a response rate of 2 per cent for annual mail volumes up to 2 million items and then response drops to 1 per cent for volumes above 2 million.

3. **Profitable revenues**   Customer spending activity generates a profit contribution of £15 per customer per annum.

4. **Environment**   After joining, members can continue buying from the wine club for many years. However, most do not continue but become inactive, and the number of active customers remaining from year to year is 70 per cent of the previous year's numbers.

Prediction

On the basis of the evidence in items 1–4 a predictive model (Table B.1) can be constructed to test alternative marketing expenditure decisions. The top section of the model contains a cell

	Units	Year 1	Year 2	Year 3	Year 4	Year 5
Marketing expenditure decision						
Marketing costs – printing, postage and lists	£/year	£ 1,500,000				
Linking expenditure to activity						
Production and postage	£/item	£0.50				
Mail volume = 2m	Mail items	2,000,000				
Mail volume > 2m	Mail items	1,000,000				
Linking our marketing to customer activity						
Response rate at volume = 2m	Per cent	2				
Response rate at volume > 2m	Per cent	1				
New customers	Customers/year	50,000				
Linking other factors to customer activity						
Retention rate	Per cent	70%	70%	70%	70%	70%
Customers – opening balance	Customers	50,000	35,000	24,500	17,150	12,005
Customers – closing balance	Customers	35,000	24,500	17,150	12,005	8,404
Linking customer activity to financial results						
Margin per customer	£/customer	£15	£15	£15	£15	£15
Margin from total customers	£/year	£750,000	£525,000	£367,500	£257,250	£180,075
Contribution after marketing	£/year	(£750,000)	£525,000	£367,500	£257,250	£180,075
Discount Rate (WACC)	%	10%	10%	10%	10%	10%
Discounted cash flow (Years 1–5)		(£750,000)	£472,500	£297,675	£187,535	£118,147
Financial result (NPV 1–5)		£325,857				

Table B.1 Predictive model of mail-order wine club

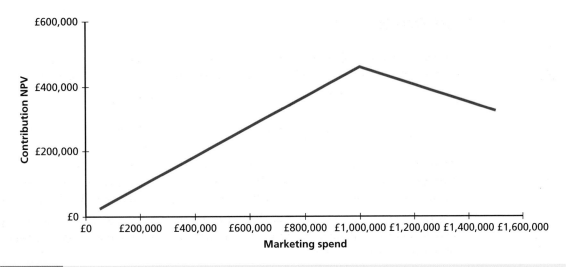

Figure B.2	Investigation of alternative levels of marketing expenditure

for entering the financial expenditure decision to be evaluated. In this example an expenditure of £1.5 million is being evaluated.

The model next follows the links from expenditure to activity, arriving at a mailing volume of 3 million items. These have been split at the 2 million level, because in the next stage of the calculation responses will be calculated. The response to the first 2 million mailing at 2 per cent is 40,000 new customers and to the remaining 1m mailing at 1 per cent is 10,000 new customers, making 50,000 in total. The model then looks at the effect of retention on customer numbers and shows them declining from 50,000 at the start of Year 1 to 8404 at the end of Year 5. Next the model links customer activity to financial results over Years 1–5. The accounting profit is negative in Year 1, as the marketing cost has been attributed to Year 1, but in Years 2, 3, 4 and 5 there are positive contributions. Finally on a Discounted Cash Flow basis, applying the Weighted Average Cost of Capital (WACC) of 10 per cent for the business, the Net Present Value (NPV) of this option is £325,857. Having constructed the model it can be used to investigate alternatives.

 ## Ideas to Increase Value

The model can now be used to investigate alternative levels of marketing expenditure. The results of this investigation are shown in Figure B.2. The analysis finds a maximum financial value of £460,686 to be delivered at an expenditure level of £1 million.

The important lesson from this example is that there is no one magic metric that proves that marketing is doing the best possible job. What this example shows is there is a systematic process that can be followed, involving four kinds of evidence, that can reveal whether marketing resources are being applied with the maximum effectiveness.

 # Four Elements of the Marketing Value Chain

 ## 1. Marketing Cost Allocation

The following questions are important for you to answer.

1.1 Can we accurately assign costs to marketing activity?

1.2 Do we maintain effective records of marketing activity attributes?

1.3 Do we investigate cost-efficiency and drive down waste, scrap and re-work?

1.4 Do we source cost ingredients using effective procurement disciplines?

1.1 Cost accounting
Can we accurately assign costs to all marketing activity?

Marketing has been described as a mixer of ingredients. For example, direct marketing's ingredients are print, postage and address lists; TV advertising's ingredients are TV media spots and film footage. Each activity will have a different mix of ingredients and although these ingredients may be accurately accounted for under cost categories such as print and postage, the cost accounting system may not assign these costs to specific activities. For example, assigning costs to a TV campaign may require digging out information on media spot costs at a greater level of detail than held on the cost accounting system. Gathering this data provides valuable detail that will needed as evidence.

1.2 Marketing activity attributes
Do we maintain effective records of marketing activity attributes?

Marketing activity can be described in many ways and it is important to record details of the activity at or around the time it occurs. Attributes are coding schemes associated with each marketing activity that facilitate evaluation of the value it adds. Three especially important attributes are: audience, offer and creative. Audience attributes are coding schemes for the people who were exposed to the marketing activity. Offer attributes are coding schemes for the product and price including any special deals, discounts etc. Creative attributes are coding schemes for the actual information and imagery to which the audience is exposed (in addition to offer information).

Audience attributes are usually threefold: audience profile, reach and frequency. The audience profile may be defined in terms of demographics (age, sex, income, etc.), geographics (country, region, town, etc.), psychographics (attitudes, interests) and in the case of B2B industry sector (retail, banking, etc.). The reach is the number of individuals exposed to a marketing activity within a given period of time and the frequency is the number of times they were exposed. There is no universal terminology, it is media specific, and related terms in specific media include coverage, penetration, exposure, footfalls, hits, insertions, circulation, readership, opportunities to see and ratings points. These attributes are generally obtained via the media owner and tend to be based on market and audience research. This research data is usually maintained by the media agency but often it is not passed to clients unless specifically requested.

Offer attributes are coding schemes for product and price. Marketing activities may make specific offers and in these cases it is very important to record the specifics of each offer. In other cases, for example corporate image campaigns, no explicit offer is made, and it is important to include codes for these situations too.

Creative attributes define the information and imagery. Sometimes there may be only a few creative executions, for example there may be five variants of a TV advertisement, in which case each one can have its own unique code. For direct marketing too, codifying the envelope, the letter and the enclosure (for example, the brochure) may suffice. For telesales, the script or call guide should be recorded. For pharmaceutical sales, the 'detail' is a scripted discussion of a particular medication.

Note that in other areas of business – such as logistics, back and front office and manufacturing – activity attributes are recorded as a matter of course. Gathering this data in marketing is simply bringing them up to the level of the rest of the business, and will provide detail needed as evidence.

1.3 Waste, scrap and re-work
Do we investigate cost-efficiency and drive down waste, scrap and re-work?

The process of supplying marketing activity (sometimes called the marketing supply chain) is like other manufacturing processes except that the levels of waste, scrap and re-work can be much higher. The chain begins with idea generation and finishes with placement of the finished executed ideas in the channels – this process is iterative, backstepping from time to time, scrapping ideas and material, re-working and polishing material until it achieves sign-off by the client. Studies of the marketing supply chain show it to be unusually inefficient and in need of streamlining. Gathering information of the process efficiency is another important item of evidence.

1.4 Marketing procurement
Do we source cost ingredients using effective procurement disciplines?

Finally, the raw ingredients that are bought to drive marketing activity should be sourced as cost-effectively as all other materials that the firm buys, and it is important therefore that effective procurement disciplines are applied to the marketing supply chain. In particular, where agencies buy materials on behalf of clients, it is important that the costs passed on to clients should be competitive and reasonable. At the same time, the aim is to not to source the cheapest resources and where procurement is involved their role needs to be kept under review to ensure they do an effective job.

 ## 2. Customer Response

The following questions are important:

2.1 Are we collecting data from customers that provides evidence of marketing's value?

2.2 Are we using good practice analysis methods to link marketing activity to customer activity?

2.3 Does our response analysis provide evidence of 'special effects'?

2.1 Customer activity data
Are we collecting data from customers that provides evidence of marketing's value?

Customer data is routinely collected by many businesses, but does its existence necessarily add to the evidence about the value added by marketing? The answer is that only limited parts of the data will provide evidence on this question and the remainder is used for other purposes.

The relevant part of the data needed as evidence concerns customer activity relating to sales revenues. For example, in the specimen evaluation, the relevant data concerned customer membership applications (successful ones). This was linked to revenues in Year 1, but also to Years 2, 3, 4 and beyond.

Much of the customer data collected by your business will not be directly relevant. For example, customer satisfaction data and brand tracking research may not contain evidence directly relevant to estimating the financial value of marketing. We will consider this in more detail later in this paper.

So, it's important to review thoroughly the sources of data and select carefully the ones you need to analyse. Sometimes the data needed may not exist, and in that case it will need to be collected in order to analyse marketing's value.

2.2 Response analysis methods
Are we using good practice analysis methods to link marketing activity to customer activity?

Having gathered data on marketing activity and customer activity it is time to investigate the link between them. It is good practice to apply some method of statistical analysis to the data, as these methods enable the analyst to assess their confidence in the model and the variables in it.

In the vast field of data analysis there are many analytical techniques and their applicability is governed by the number of variables involved which may range from one to many. For example, in the specimen evaluation the analyst found a 'response equation':

New customers = 2% of mailing volume (up to 2m mailing items)

This is known as a *univariate* relationship, as only one variable is needed. For many situations, more than one variable is important, and so *multivariate* methods will be needed. For example, for a consumer product the response equation may have the form:

Sales = function (advertising, price, promotional offer, environmental factors)

Having collected the data, you should plot a graph, and look for patterns that link sales to factors such as advertising, price, promotion, etc. Spreadsheets are the tool of choice for this, and most novices can plot graphs. Even with limited data, there are some patterns that you may notice:

● **Trends** which rise (or fall) steadily over the time period you are examining.

● **Seasonal patterns** which repeat, more or less the same, every 12 months.

● **Short-term peaks** that are the effects of events such as price promotions or important sporting fixtures.

These features are illustrated in Figure B.3.

The analyst would assess their confidence in this model. For example, 90 per cent of the variation in the data might be explained by the model, and also the significance of all the variables is greater than 95 per cent.

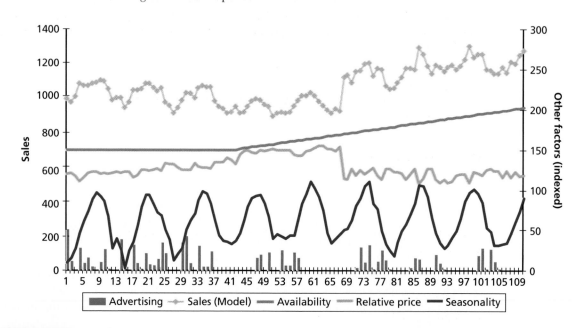

| Figure B.3 | Patterns in time-series data |

Source: R. Shaw and D. Merrick, *Marketing Payback*, FT Prentice Hall, 2005

2.3 Special effects
Does our response analysis provide evidence of "special effects"

Marketing activity has several important effects that are not obvious at first sight and therefore the analyst should be vigilant in investigating them. The most important of these are:

- Persistence of response after marketing activity is finished.
- Synergies between marketing activities.
- Halo effects across products and brands.
- Unintended consequences, such as diminishing returns, stockpiling, cannibalisation and substitution.

Persistence in our specimen evaluation was easily observable: after customers became members of the wine club, they persisted in buying from the club for several years. In the case of TV advertising there are short-term persistence effects (sometimes called 'adstock') which last for a few weeks after the activity, and longer term brand building effects that last for several years.

Synergies between marketing activities can occur. For instance, there is published case evidence of synergy between price changes and advertising: when both occur together the effect is larger than the separate effects. Synergies are used as justification for multi-channel or integrated campaigns.

Halo effects are where the marketing of one thing shines on another. For example, where Product A is advertised then Product B's sales increase. Halo effects are often cited by agencies to help justify their work.

Unintended consequences of marketing are also common and should be investigated. The commonest ones are: diminishing returns, stockpiling, cannibalisation and substitution. Diminishing returns occur when returns decrease as an activity increases. Stockpiling occurs in the case of sales promotions, discounts and offers. Sales peaks can be the visible response, but very often it represents existing customers buying and stockpiling the product, and so a dip in sales may be observed following the peak. Cannibalisation occurs when the peak in sales of one product causes a dip in sales of another. This is often caused by substitution, where customers choose to buy the promoted product by substituting it for a different product that they habitually buy.

3. Environment – Uncontrollable Factors that Affect Results

The key question here is:

3.1 Other factors
Have we gathered evidence of how other factors have impacted our results?

Our results will be affected by other factors than your own marketing. Three such other factors should be investigated:

- Environmental factors such as temperature, the economy, the seasons, day of week.
- Competitor activity.
- Market trends.

Environmental data can usually be found from governmental sources and other agencies. It can be a rich source of insights for the analyst. For example, the model of consumer products cited in section 2.2 (p. 560) might be improved by including average daily temperature in the model.

The reason for this is that the extra variable improves confidence in the overall model without significantly reducing confidence in the individual variables. Note that the parameters in the equation have changed as a result of temperature being included in the equation.

Competitors are frequently cited as causing problems with business results, and are often cited in the financial press. These comments may be based on detailed analysis but may also be based on anecdote and hearsay. To strengthen the evidence it's important to gather key competitor data, and market research firms can often provide the data required. Key competitor data elements to collect can include:

- price changes
- discounts and sales promotions
- distribution changes
- advertising and direct marketing activity

These should be included as factors for the analyst to evaluate and some, but not all, will be significant variables.

Market trends can provide useful evidence for disentangling the effects of our marketing from other factors. Ratio analysis can help differentiate between the behaviour of our firm and the market as a whole:

- Market share refers to the ratio between our revenue and the total for the market.
- Penetration refers to ratio of our customers to the total in the market.
- Share of wallet is used in the context of individual customers and refers to the percentage of their spending that goes to our company.

These may also be included as factors for the analyst to evaluate.

 ## 4. Profitable Revenues

4.1 Do we have good practice financial models linking customer activity to sales and profit figures?

The final step of historical analysis is to link customer activity to financial results and in particular profits. For example, in the specimen evaluation the analyst found that the profit contribution is £15 per customer per year. This example is simple, but in some situations the financial model may be more complex. In particular, not all customer activity will be equally profitable, for example due to:

- product profitability differences
- customer profitability differences

Product profitability differences will be important if different marketing activities drive different product mixes. Some activities may drive high-margin product sales, whereas other activities drive low-margin product sales. For instance, building societies need to ensure their marketing drives the right mix of mortgages and savings. Customer profitability differences need to be taken into account in the same way – for example, high-margin and low-margin customers may need to be distinguished in the analysis.[1]

---

[1]For more detail on these and other techniques, the reader is referred to R. Shaw and D. Merrick, *Marketing Payback*, FT Prentice Hall, 2005.

Glossary

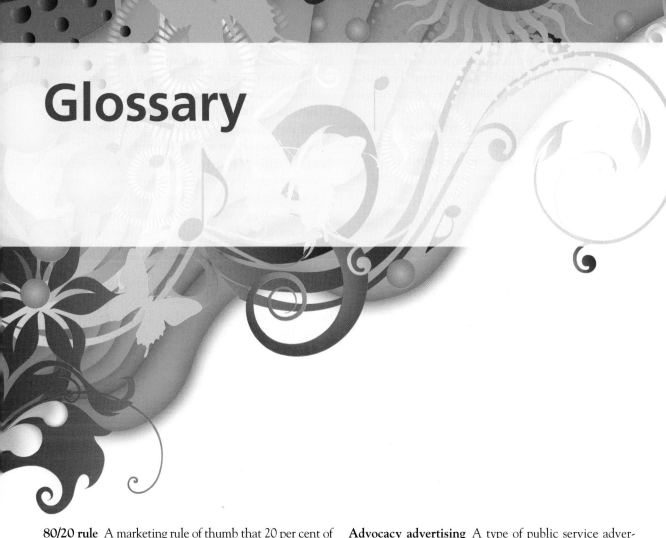

80/20 rule A marketing rule of thumb that 20 per cent of purchasers account for 80 per cent of a product's sales.

A

Action plans Individual support plans included in a marketing plan that provide the guidance for implementation and control of the various marketing strategies within the plan. Action plans are sometimes referred to as marketing programmes.

Advertising Non-personal communication paid for by an identified sponsor using mass media to persuade or inform.

Advertising appeal The central idea or theme of an advertising message.

Advertising campaign A coordinated, comprehensive plan that carries out promotion objectives and results in a series of advertisements placed in media over a period of time.

Advertising exposure The degree to which the target market will see an advertising message placed in a specific vehicle.

Advocacy advertising A type of public service advertising provided by an organisation that is seeking to influence public opinion on an issue because it has some stake in the outcome.

Agents or brokers Channel intermediaries that provide services in exchange for commissions but never take title to the product.

AIDA model The communications goals of attention, interest, desire and action.

Aided recall A research technique that uses clues to prompt answers from people about advertisements they might have seen.

Aperture The best place and time to reach a person in the target market group.

Approach The first step of the actual sales presentation in which the salesperson tries to learn more about the customer's needs, creates a good impression and builds rapport.

Atmospherics The use of colour, lighting, scents, furnishings and other design elements to create a desired shop image.

Attitude A learned predisposition to respond favourably or unfavourably to stimuli on the basis of relatively enduring evaluations of people, objects and issues.

Attitudinal measures A research technique that probes a consumer's beliefs or feelings about a product before and after being exposed to messages about it.

Augmented services The core service plus additional services provided to enhance value.

Average fixed cost The fixed cost per unit produced.

B

Baby boomers The segment of people born between 1946 and 1964.

Back-translation The process of translating material into a foreign language and then back into the original language.

Bait-and-switch An unethical marketing practice in which an advertised special price is used as bait to get customers into the shop with the intention of switching them to a higher-priced item.

Banners Internet advertising in the form of rectangular graphics at the top or bottom of web pages.

Base-point pricing A pricing tactic where customers pay shipping charges from set base point locations whether the goods are actually shipped from these points or not.

BCG growth–market share matrix A portfolio analysis model developed by the Boston Consulting Group that assesses the potential of successful products to generate cash that a firm can then use to invest in new products.

Behavioural learning theories Theories of learning that focus on how consumer behaviour is changed by external events or stimuli.

Behavioural segmentation A technique that divides consumers into segments on the basis of how they act toward, feel about or use a good or service.

Benefit The outcome sought by a customer that motivates buying behaviour – that satisfies a **need or want**.

Born-global firms Companies that try to sell their products in multiple countries from the moment they're created.

Bottom-up budgeting techniques Allocation of the promotion budget based on identifying promotion goals and allocating enough money to accomplish them.

Brand A name, a term, a symbol, or any other unique element of a product that identifies one firm's product(s) and sets them apart from the competition.

Brand competition When firms offering similar goods or services compete on the basis of their brand's reputation or perceived benefits.

Brand equity The value of a brand to an organization.

Brand extensions A new product sold with the same brand name as a strong existing brand.

Brand loyalty A pattern of repeat product purchases, accompanied by an underlying positive attitude toward the brand, that is based on the belief that the brand makes products superior to its competition.

Brand manager An individual who is responsible for developing and implementing the marketing plan for a single brand.

Brand personality A distinctive image that captures a good's or service's character and benefits.

Break-even analysis A method for determining the number of units that a firm must produce and sell at a given price to cover all its costs.

Break-even point The point at which the total revenue and total costs are equal and beyond which the company makes a profit; below that point, the firm will suffer a loss.

Breaking bulk Dividing larger quantities of goods into smaller lots in order to meet the needs of buyers.

Business analysis The step in the product development process in which marketers assess a product's commercial viability.

Business cycle The overall patterns of change in the economy – including periods of prosperity, recession, depression, and recovery – that affect consumer and business purchasing power.

Business plan A plan that includes the decisions that guide the entire organisation.

Business planning An ongoing process of making decisions that guide the firm both in the short term and for the long haul.

Business portfolio The group of different products or brands owned by an organisation and characterised by different income-generating and growth capabilities.

Business-to-business (B2B) e-commerce Internet exchanges between two or more businesses or organisations.

Business-to-business marketing The marketing of those goods and services that business and organisational customers need to produce other goods and services, for resale or to support their operations.

Business-to-business markets The group of customers that include manufacturers, wholesalers, retailers and other organisations.

Business-to-consumer (B2C) e-commerce Online exchanges between companies and individual consumers.

Buttons Small banner-type advertisements that can be placed anywhere on a web page.

Buy class One of three classifications of business buying situations that characterises the degree of time and effort required to make a decision.

Buying centre The group of people in an organisation who participate in a purchasing decision.

Buzz Word-of-mouth communication that is viewed as authentic and generated by customers.

Buzz marketing Using high-profile entertainment or news to get people to talk about your brand.

C

Cannibalisation The loss of sales of an existing brand when a new item in a product line or product family is introduced.

Capacity management The process by which organisations adjust their offerings in an attempt to match demand.

Captive pricing A pricing tactic for two items that must be used together; one item is priced low, and the firm makes its profit on the other, high-margin item essential to the operation of the first item.

Case allowance A discount to the retailer or wholesaler based on the volume of product ordered.

Case study A comprehensive examination of a particular firm or organisation.

Catalogue A collection of products offered for sale in book form, usually consisting of product descriptions accompanied by photos of the items.

Causal research A technique that attempts to understand cause-and-effect relationships.

Channel intermediaries Firms or individuals such as wholesalers, agents, brokers or retailers who help move a product from the producer to the consumer or business user.

Channel leader A firm at one level of distribution that takes a leadership role, establishing operating norms and processes based on its power relative to other channel members.

Channel levels The number of distinct categories of intermediaries that populate a channel of distribution.

Channel of distribution The series of firms or individuals that facilitates the movement of a product from the producer to the final customer.

Classical conditioning The learning that occurs when a stimulus eliciting a response is paired with another stimulus that initially does not elicit a response on its own but will cause a similar response over time because of its association with the first stimulus.

Close The stage of the selling process in which the salesperson actually asks the customer to buy the product.

Cobranding An agreement between two brands to work together in marketing a new product.

Cognitive learning theory Theory of learning that stresses the importance of internal mental processes and that views people as problem solvers who actively use information from the world around them to master their environment.

Collectivist cultures Cultures in which people subordinate their personal goals to those of a stable community.

Commercialisation The final step in the product development process in which a new product is launched into the market.

Communications model The process whereby meaning is transferred from a source to a receiver.

Competitive advantage The ability of a firm to outperform the competition, thereby providing customers with a benefit the competition can't.

Competitive intelligence The process of gathering and analysing publicly available information about rivals.

Competitive-parity method A promotion budgeting method in which an organisation matches whatever competitors are spending.

Component parts Manufactured goods or subassemblies of finished items that organisations need to complete their own products.

Concentrated targeting strategy Focusing a firm's efforts on offering one or more products to a single segment.

Conformity A change in beliefs or actions as a reaction to real or imagined group pressure.

Consumer The ultimate user of a good or service.

Consumer behaviour The process involved when individuals or groups select, purchase, use, and dispose of goods, services, ideas or experiences to satisfy their needs and desires.

Consumer goods The goods purchased by individual consumers for personal or family use.

Consumer interview One-on-one discussion between a consumer and a researcher.

Consumer orientation A management philosophy that focuses on ways to satisfy customers' needs and wants.

Consumer satisfaction/dissatisfaction The overall feelings or attitude a person has about a product after purchasing it.

Consumer-to-consumer (C2C) e-commerce Communications and purchases that occur among individuals without directly involving the manufacturer or retailer.

Continuous innovation A modification of an existing product that sets one brand apart from its competitors.

Contribution per unit The difference between the price the firm charges for a product and the variable costs.

Control A process that entails measuring actual performance, comparing this performance to the established marketing objectives, and then making adjustments to the strategies or objectives on the basis of this analysis.

Convenience product A consumer good or service that is usually low priced, widely available and purchased frequently with a minimum of comparison and effort.

Convenience stores Retailers that carry a limited number of frequently purchased items and cater to consumers willing to pay a premium for the ease of buying close to home.

Conventional marketing system A multiple-level distribution channel in which channel members work independently of one another.

Conventions Norms regarding the conduct of everyday life.

Convergence The coming together of two or more technologies to create a new system with greater benefits than its parts.

Cookie Text file inserted by a web site sponsor into a web surfer's hard drive that allows the site to track the surfer's moves.

Copy testing A marketing research method that seeks to measure the effectiveness of ads by determining whether consumers are receiving, comprehending, and responding to the ad according to plan.

Core service The basic benefit of having a service performed.

Corporate culture The set of values, norms and beliefs that influence the behaviour of everyone in the organisation.

Cost per thousand (CPM) A measure used to compare the relative cost-effectiveness of different media vehicles that have different exposure rates; the cost to deliver a message to 1000 people or homes.

Cost-plus pricing A method of setting prices in which the seller totals all the costs for the product and then adds an amount to arrive at the selling price.

Counter trade A type of trade in which goods are paid for with other items instead of cash.

Creating assortments Providing a variety of products in one location to meet the needs of buyers.

Creative selling process The process of seeking out potential customers, analysing needs, determining how product attributes might provide benefits for the customer, and then communicating that information.

Creative strategy The process that turns a concept into an advertisement.

Credence qualities Product characteristics that are difficult to evaluate even after they have been experienced.

Critical incident technique A method for measuring service quality in which marketers use customer complaints to identify critical incidents – specific face-to-face contacts between consumer and service providers that cause problems and lead to dissatisfaction.

Cross-elasticity of demand When changes in the price of one product affect the demand for another item.

Cross-promotion (cooperative promotion) Two or more products or services combine forces to create interest using a single promotional tool.

Cross-sectional design A type of descriptive technique that involves the systematic collection of quantitative information.

Cultural diversity A management practice that actively seeks to include people of different sexes, races, ethnic groups and religions in an organisation's employees, customers, suppliers and distribution channel partners.

Cultural values A society's deeply held beliefs about right and wrong ways to live.

Culture The values, beliefs, customs, and tastes valued by a group of people.

Custom A norm handed down from the past that controls basic behaviours.

Custom marketing strategy An approach that tailors specific products and the messages about them to individual customers.

Custom research Research conducted for a single firm to provide specific information its managers need.

Customer equity The financial value of a customer relationship throughout the life-time of the relationship.

Customer relationship management (CRM) A philosophy that sees marketing as a process of building long-term relationships with customers to keep them satisfied and to keep them coming back. A concept that involves systematically tracking consumers' preferences and behaviours over time in order to tailor the value proposition as closely as possible to each individual's unique wants and needs.

D

Data mining Sophisticated analysis techniques to take advantage of the massive amount of transaction information now available.

Database marketing The creation of an ongoing relationship with a set of customers who have an identifiable interest in a product or service and whose responses to promotional efforts become part of future communications attempts.

Decline stage The final stage in the product lifecycle in which sales decrease as customer needs change.

Decoding The process by which a receiver assigns meaning to the message.

Demand Customers' desire for products coupled with the resources to obtain them.

Demand-based pricing A price-setting method based on estimates of demand at different prices.

Demographics Statistics that measure observable aspects of a population, including size, age, gender, ethnic group, income, education, occupation and family structure.

Department stores Retailers that sell a broad range of items and offer a good selection within each product line.

Derived demand Demand for business or organisational products derived from demand for consumer goods or services.

Descriptive research A tool that probes more systematically into the problem and bases its conclusions on large numbers of observations.

Developed country A country that boasts sophisticated marketing systems, strong private enterprise, and plenty of market potential for many goods and services.

Developing countries Countries in which the economy is shifting its emphasis from agriculture to industry.

Differential benefit Properties of products that set them apart from competitors' products by providing unique customer benefits.

Differentiated targeting strategy Developing one or more products for each of several distinct customer groups and making sure these offerings are kept separate in the marketplace.

Diffusion The process by which the use of a product spreads throughout a population.

Direct mail A brochure or pamphlet offering a specific product or service at one point in time.

Direct marketing Any direct communication to a consumer or business recipient that is designed to generate a response in the form of an order, a request for further information, and/or a visit to a shop or other place of business for purchase of a product.

Direct-response advertising A direct marketing approach that allows the consumer to respond to a message by immediately contacting the provider to ask questions or order the product

Direct-response TV (DRTV) Advertising on TV that seeks a direct response, including short commercials of less than two minutes, 30-minute or longer infomercials, and home shopping networks.

Discontinuous innovation A totally new product that creates major changes in the way we live.

Disintermediation Eliminating the interaction between customers and salespeople so as to minimise negative service encounters.

Disintermediation (of the channel of distribution) The elimination of some layers of the channel of distribution in order to cut costs and improve the efficiency of the channel.

Disposable income The portion of income people have left over after paying for necessities such as housing, utilities, food and clothing.

Distinctive competency A superior capability of a firm in comparison to its direct competitors.

Diversification strategies Growth strategies that emphasise both new products and new markets.

Dumping A company tries to get a toehold in a foreign market by pricing its products lower than they are offered at home.

Durable goods Consumer products that provide benefits over a long period of time, such as cars, furniture and appliances.

Dynamic pricing A pricing strategy in which the price can easily be adjusted to meet changes in the market place.

Dynamically continuous innovation A change in an existing product that requires a moderate amount of learning or behaviour change.

E

Early adopters Those who adopt an innovation early in the diffusion process but after the innovators.

Early majority Those whose adoption of a new product signals a general acceptance of the innovation.

e-Commerce The buying or selling of goods and services electronically, usually over the Internet.

Economic communities Groups of countries that band together to promote trade among themselves and to make it easier for member nations to compete elsewhere.

Economic infrastructure The quality of a country's distribution, financial, and communications systems.

Economic sanctions Trade prohibitions imposed by one country against another.

Elastic demand Demand in which changes in price have large effects on the amount demanded.

e-Marketers Marketers who use e-commerce in their strategies.

Embargo A quota completely prohibiting specified goods from entering or leaving a country.

Encoding The process of translating an idea into a form of communication that will convey meaning.

Enterprise resource planning (ERP) systems A software system that integrates information from across the entire company. Data need to be entered into the system only once, at one point, and then the data are automatically shared throughout the organisation.

Equipment Expensive goods that an organisation uses in its daily operations that last for a long time.

Ethnocentrism The tendency to prefer products or people of one's own culture.

Ethnographic study A detailed report based on observations of people in their own homes or communities.

European Union (EU) An economic community that now includes most of Europe.

Evaluative criteria The dimensions used by consumers to compare competing product alternatives.

Everyday low pricing (EDLP) See **Value pricing**.

Exchange The process by which some transfer of value occurs between a buyer and a seller.

Exclusive distribution Selling a product only through a single outlet in a particular region.

Experience qualities Product characteristics that customers can determine during or after consumption.

Experiential shoppers Consumers who engage in online shopping because of the experiential benefits they receive.

Experiment Technique that tests prespecified relationships among variables in a controlled environment.

Exploratory research A technique that marketers use to generate insights for future, more rigorous studies.

Export merchants Intermediaries used by a firm to represent them in other countries.

Expropriation A domestic government's seizure of a foreign company's assets without any compensation.

External environment The uncontrollable elements outside an organisation that may affect its performance either positively or negatively.

Extranet A private, corporate computer network that links company departments, employees, and databases to suppliers, customers, and others outside the organisation.

F

Facilitating functions Functions of channel intermediaries that make the purchase process easier for customers and manufacturers.

Family brand A brand that a group of individual products or individual brands share.

Family life cycle A means of characterising consumers within a family structure on the basis of different stages through which people pass as they grow older.

Feedback Receivers' reactions to the message.

Fixed costs Costs of production that do not change with the number of units produced.

FOB delivered pricing A pricing tactic in which the cost of loading and transporting the product to the customer is included in the selling price and is paid by the manufacturer.

FOB origin pricing A pricing tactic in which the cost of transporting the product from the factory to the customer's location is the responsibility of the customer.

Focus group A product-oriented discussion among a small group of consumers led by a trained moderator.

Follow-up Activities after the sale that provide important services to customers.

Franchising A form of licensing involving the right to adapt an entire system of doing business.

Freight absorption pricing A pricing tactic in which the seller absorbs the total cost of transportation.

Frequency The number of times a person in the target group will be exposed to the message.

Frequency programmes Consumer sales promotion programmes that offer a discount or free product for multiple purchases over time; also referred to as loyalty or continuity programmes.

Full-service agency An agency that provides most or all of the services needed to mount a campaign, including research, creation of ad copy and art, media selection and production of the final messages.

Functional planning A decision process that concentrates on developing detailed plans for strategies and tactics for the short term that support an organisation's long-term strategic plan.

G

Gap analysis A marketing research methodology that measures the difference between a customer's expectation of a service quality and what actually occurred.

General Agreement on Tariffs and Trade (GATT) International treaty to reduce import tax levels and trade restrictions.

Generation X The group of consumers born between 1965 and 1976.

Generation Y The group of consumers born between 1977 and 1994.

Geodemography A segmentation technique that combines geography with demographics.

Good A tangible product that we can see, touch, smell, hear or taste.

Government markets The various governmental levels that buy goods and services to carry out public objectives and to support their operations.

Grey market goods Items manufactured outside a country and then imported without the consent of the trademark holder.

Gross domestic product (GDP) The total value of goods and services produced by a nation within its borders in a year.

Gross national product (GNP) The value of all goods and services produced by a country's citizens or organisations, whether located within the country's borders or not.

Gross rating points (GRPs) A measure used for comparing the effectiveness of different media vehicles: average reach × frequency.

Growth stage The second stage in the product life cycle during which the product is accepted and sales rapidly increase.

Guerrilla marketing Marketing activity in which a firm 'ambushes' consumers with promotional content in places they are not expecting to encounter this kind of activity.

H

Heuristics A mental rule of thumb that leads to a speedy decision by simplifying the process.

Hierarchy of effects A series of steps prospective customers move through, from initial awareness of a product to brand loyalty.

Hierarchy of needs An approach that categorises motives according to five levels of importance, the more basic needs being on the bottom of the hierarchy and the higher needs at the top.

Horizontal marketing system An arrangement within a channel of distribution in which two or more firms at the same channel level work together for a common purpose.

Hybrid marketing system A marketing system that uses a number of different channels and communication methods to serve a target market.

Hypermarkets Retailers that are several times larger than supermarkets and offer virtually everything from grocery items to electronics.

I

Idea generation The first step of product development in which marketers brainstorm for products that provide customer benefits and are compatible with the company mission.

Idea marketing Marketing activities that seek to gain market share for a concept, philosophy, belief, or issue by using elements of the marketing mix to create or change a target market's attitude or behaviour.

Import quotas Limitations set by a government on the amount of a product allowed to enter or leave a country.

Impressions The number of people who will be exposed to a message placed in one or more media vehicles.

Impulse purchase A purchase made without any planning or search effort.

Independent intermediaries Channel intermediaries that are not controlled by any manufacturer but instead do business with many different manufacturers and many different customers.

Individualist cultures Cultures in which people tend to attach more importance to personal goals than to those of the larger community.

Industrial goods Goods bought by individuals or organisations for further processing or for use in doing business.

Inelastic demand Demand in which changes in price have little or no effect on the amount demanded.

Information search The process whereby a consumer searches for appropriate information to make a reasonable decision.

Ingredient branding A form of co-branding in which branded materials are used as ingredients or component parts of other branded products.

Innovation A product that consumers perceive to be new and different from existing products.

Innovators The first segment (roughly 2.5 per cent) of a population to adopt a new product.

Inseparability The characteristic of a service that means that it is impossible to separate the production of a service from the consumption of that service.

Institutional advertising An advertising message that promotes the activities, personality, or point of view of an organisation or company.

Intangibility The characteristic of a service that means customers can't see, touch or smell good service.

Intangibles Experience-based products that cannot be touched.

Integrated marketing communications (IMC) A strategic business process that marketers use to plan, develop, execute, and evaluate coordinated, measurable, persuasive brand communication programmes over time to targeted audiences.

Intensive distribution Selling a product through all suitable wholesalers or retailers that are willing to stock and sell the product.

Interactive marketing A promotion practice in which customised marketing communications elicit a measurable response from individual receivers.

Internal environment The controllable elements inside an organisation, including its people, its facilities, and how it does things that influence the operations of the organisation.

Internal reference price A set price or a price range in consumers' minds that they refer to in evaluating a product's price.

Intranet An internal corporate communication network that uses Internet technology to link company departments, employees and databases.

Introduction stage The first stage of the product life-cycle in which slow growth follows the introduction of a new product in the marketplace.

Involvement The relative importance of perceived consequences of the purchase to a consumer.

ISO 14000 Standards of the International Organization for Standardization concerned with 'environmental management' aimed at minimising harmful effects on the environment.

ISO 9000 Criteria developed by the International Organization for Standardization to regulate product quality in Europe.

J

Joint demand Demand for two or more goods that are used together to create a product.

Joint venture A strategic alliance in which a new entity owned by two or more firms is created to allow the partners to pool their resources for common goals.

Just in time (JIT) stock management and purchasing processes that manufacturers and resellers use to reduce stock to very low levels and ensure that deliveries from suppliers arrive only when needed.

K

Kansei engineering A Japanese philosophy that translates customers' feelings into design elements.

Knock-off A new product that copies with slight modification the design of an original product.

Knowledge management A comprehensive approach to collecting, organising, storing and retrieving a firm's information assets.

L

Laggards The last consumers to adopt an innovation.

Late majority The adopters who are willing to try new products when there is little or no risk associated with the purchase, when the purchase becomes an economic necessity, or when there is social pressure to purchase.

Learning A relatively permanent change in behaviour caused by acquired information or experience.

Less developed country (LDC) A country at the lowest stage of economic development.

Licensing An agreement in which one firm sells another firm the right to use a brand name for a specific purpose and for a specific period of time.

Licensing (in foreign markets) An agreement in which one firm gives another firm the right to produce and market its product in a specific country or region in return for royalties.

Lifestyle The pattern of living that determines how people choose to spend their time, money and energy and that reflects their values, tastes and preferences.

Lifetime value of a customer How much profit companies expect to make from a particular customer, including each and every purchase she will make from them now and in the future. To calculate lifetime value, companies estimate the amount the person will spend and then subtract what it will cost the company to maintain this relationship.

Limited-service agency An agency that provides one or more specialised services, such as media buying or creative development.

List price The price the end customer is expected to pay as determined by the manufacturer; also referred to as the suggested retail price or retailers' recommended price (RRP).

Local content rules A form of protectionism stipulating that a certain proportion of a product must consist of components supplied by industries in the host country.

Logistics The process of designing, managing and improving the movement of products through the supply chain. Logistics includes purchasing, manufacturing, storage and transport.

Longitudinal design A technique that tracks the responses of the same sample of respondents over time.

Loss leader pricing The pricing policy of setting prices very low or even below cost to attract customers into a shop.

M

Maintenance, repair, and operating (MRO) products Goods that a business customer consumes in a relatively short time.

Marginal analysis A method that uses cost and demand to identify the price that will maximise profits.

Marginal cost The increase in total cost that results from producing one additional unit of a product.

Marginal revenue The increase in total income or revenue that results from selling one additional unit of a product.

Market All the customers and potential customers who share a common need that can be satisfied by a specific product, who have the resources to exchange for it, who are willing to make the exchange and who have the authority to make the exchange.

Market development strategies Growth strategies that introduce existing products to new markets.

Market fragmentation The creation of many consumer groups due to a diversity of distinct needs and wants in modern society.

Market manager An individual who is responsible for developing and implementing the marketing plans for products sold to a particular customer group.

Market penetration strategies Growth strategies designed to increase sales of existing products to current customers, non-users, and users of competitive brands in served markets.

Market position The way in which the target market perceives the product in comparison to competitors' brands.

Market segment A distinct group of customers within a larger market who are similar to one another in some way and whose needs differ from other customers in the larger market.

Marketing An organisational function and a set of processes for creating, communicating and delivering value to customers and for managing customer relationships in ways that benefit the organisation and its stakeholders.

Marketing concept A management orientation that focuses on identifying and satisfying consumer needs to ensure the organisation's long-term profitability.

Marketing decision support system (MDSS) The data, analysis software and interactive software that allow managers to conduct analyses and find the information they need.

Marketing information system (MkIS) A process that first determines what information marketing managers need and then gathers, sorts, analyses, stores, and distributes relevant and timely marketing information to system users.

Marketing intelligence system A method by which marketers get information about everyday happenings in the marketing environment.

Marketing mix A combination of the product itself, the price of the product, the place where it is made available, and the activities that introduce it to consumers that creates a desired response among a set of predefined consumers.

Marketing plan A document that describes the marketing environment, outlines the marketing objectives and strategy, and identifies who will be responsible for carrying out each part of the marketing strategy.

Marketing research The process of collecting, analysing, and interpreting data about customers, competitors and the business environment in order to improve marketing effectiveness.

Marketplace Any location or medium used to conduct an exchange.

Mass customisation An approach that modifies a basic good or service to meet the needs of an individual.

Mass market All possible customers in a market, regardless of the differences in their specific needs and wants.

Materials handling The moving of products into, within, and out of warehouses.

Maturity stage The third and longest stage in the product life cycle in which sales peak and profit margins narrow.

m-Commerce Promotional and other e-commerce activities transmitted over mobile phones and other mobile devices, such as personal digital assistants (PDAs).

Media planning The process of developing media objectives, strategies and tactics for use in an advertising campaign.

Media schedule The plan that specifies the exact media to use and when.

Medium A communications vehicle through which a message is transmitted to a target audience.

Merchandise assortment The range of products sold.

Merchandise breadth The number of different product lines available.

Merchandise depth The variety of choices available for each specific product line.

Merchandise mix The total set of all products offered for sale by a retailer, including all product lines sold to all consumer groups.

Merchandising allowance Reimburses the retailer for in-store support of the product.

Message The communication in physical form that goes from a sender to a receiver.

Metrosexual A man who is heterosexual, sensitive, educated, and an urban dweller who is in touch with his feminine side.

Mission statement A formal statement in an organisation's strategic plan that describes the overall purpose of the organisation and what it intends to achieve in terms of its customers, products, and resources.

Missionary sales person A sales person who promotes the firm and tries to stimulate demand for a product but does not actually complete a sale.

Modified re-buy A buying situation classification used by business buyers to categorise a previously made purchase that involves some change and requires limited decision making.

Monopolistic competition A market structure in which many firms, each having slightly different products, offer unique consumer benefits.

Monopoly A market situation in which one firm, the only supplier of a particular product, is able to control the price, quality, and supply of that product.

Mores Customs with a strong moral overtone.

Motivation An internal state that drives us to satisfy needs by activating goal-oriented behaviour.

Multiple sourcing The business practice of buying a particular product from many suppliers.

Myths Stories containing symbolic elements that express the shared emotions and ideals of a culture.

N

National or manufacturer brands Brands that the manufacturer of the product owns.

Nationalisation A domestic government's takeover of a foreign company for its assets with some reimbursement, though often not for the full value.

Need The recognition of any difference between a consumer's actual state and some ideal or desired state.

New Era orientation A management philosophy in which marketing means a devotion to excellence in designing and producing products that benefit the customer plus the firm's employees, shareholders and communities.

New-business sales person The person responsible for finding new customers and calling on them to present the company's products or services.

New-task buy A new business-to-business purchase that is complex or risky and requires extensive decision making.

Noise Anything that interferes with effective communication.

Non-durable goods Consumer products that provide benefits for a short time because they are consumed (such as food) or are no longer useful (such as newspapers).

Non-probability sample A sample in which personal judgement is used in selecting respondents.

Non-shop retailing Any method used to complete an exchange with a product end-user that does not require a customer visit to a store.

Norms Specific rules dictating what is right or wrong, acceptable or unacceptable.

North American Free Trade Agreement (NAFTA) An economic community composed of the United States, Canada and Mexico.

Not-for-profit institutions Organisations with charitable, educational, community and other public service goals that buy goods and services to support their functions and to attract and serve their members.

O

Objective-task method A promotion budgeting method in which an organisation first defines the specific communications goals it hopes to achieve and then tries to calculate what kind of promotional efforts it will take to meet these goals.

Oligopoly A market structure in which a relatively small number of sellers, each holding a substantial share of the market, compete in a market with many buyers.

Online auctions e-Commerce that allows shoppers to purchase products through online bidding.

Operant conditioning Learning that occurs as the result of rewards or punishments.

Operational planning A decision process that focuses on developing detailed plans for day-to-day activities that carry out an organisation's functional plans.

Operational plans Plans that focus on the day-to-day execution of the marketing plan. Operational plans include detailed directions for the specific activities to be carried out, who will be responsible for them, and timelines for accomplishing the tasks.

Opinion leader A person who is frequently able to influence others' attitudes or behaviours by virtue of his or her active interest and expertise in one or more product categories.

Order getter A sales person who works to develop long-term relationships with particular customers or to generate new sales.

Order processing The series of activities that occurs between the time an order comes into the organisation and the time a product goes out the door.

Order taker A sales person whose primary function is to facilitate transactions that the customer initiates.

Organisational markets Another name for business-to-business markets.

Out-of-home media A communication medium that reaches people in public places.

Outsourcing The business buying process of obtaining outside vendors to provide goods or services that otherwise might be supplied in-house.

P

Package The covering or container for a product that provides product protection, facilitates product use and storage, and supplies important marketing communication.

Patent Legal documentation granting an individual or firm exclusive rights to produce and sell a particular invention.

Penetration pricing A pricing strategy in which a firm introduces a new product at a very low price to encourage more customers to purchase it.

Perceived risk The belief that choice of a product has potentially negative consequences – financial, physical, or social.

Percentage-of-sales method A method for promotion budgeting that is based on a certain percentage of either last year's sales or on estimates for the present year's sales.

Perception The process by which people select, organise, and interpret information from the outside world.

Perceptual map A vivid way to construct a picture of where products or brands are 'located' in consumers' minds.

Perfect competition A market structure in which many small sellers, all of whom offer similar products, are unable to have an impact on the quality, price or supply of a product.

Perishability The characteristic of a service that makes it impossible to store for later sale or consumption.

Permission marketing E-mail advertising where online consumers have the opportunity to accept or refuse the unsolicited e-mail.

Personal selling Marketing communication by which a company representative interacts directly with a customer or prospective customer to communicate about a good or service.

Personality The psychological characteristics that consistently influence the way a person responds to situations in his or her environment.

Physical distribution The activities used to move finished goods from manufacturers to final customers, including order processing, warehousing, materials handling, transportation and stock control.

Place The availability of the product to the customer at the desired time and location.

Place marketing Marketing activities that seek to attract new businesses, residents or visitors to a town, country or some other site.

Place-based media Advertising media that transmit messages in public places, such as doctors' offices and airports, where certain types of people congregate.

Product mix The total set of all products a firm offers for sale.

Point-of-purchase (POP) promotion In-store displays or signs.

Point-of-sale (POS) systems Retail computer systems that collect sales data and are hooked directly into the shop's inventory control system.

Portfolio analysis A management tool for evaluating a firm's business mix and assessing the potential of an organisation's strategic business units.

Positioning Developing a marketing strategy aimed at influencing how a particular market segment perceives a good or service in comparison to the competition.

Post-testing Research conducted on consumers' responses to actual advertising messages they have seen or heard.

Pre-approach A part of the selling process that includes developing information about prospective customers and planning the sales interview.

Premiums Items offered free to people who have purchased a product.

Press release Information that an organisation distributes to the media, intended to win publicity.

Prestige products Products that have a high price and that appeal to status-conscious consumers.

Pre-testing A research method that seeks to minimise mistakes by getting consumer reactions to ad messages before they appear in the media.

Price The assignment of value, or the amount the consumer must exchange to receive the offering.

Price bundling Selling two or more goods or services as a single package for one price.

Price elasticity of demand The percentage change in unit sales that results from a percentage change in price.

Price fixing The collaboration of two or more firms in setting prices, usually to keep prices high.

Price leadership A pricing strategy in which one firm first sets its price and other firms in the industry follow with the same or very similar prices.

Price lining The practice of setting a limited number of different specific prices, called price points, for items in a product line.

Primary data Data from research conducted to help in making a specific decision.

Private exchanges Systems that link an invited group of suppliers and partners over the web.

Private-label brands Brands that are owned and sold by a certain retailer or distributor.

Probability sample A sample in which each member of the population has some known chance of being included.

Problem recognition The process that occurs whenever the consumer sees a significant difference between his or her current state of affairs and some desired or ideal state; this recognition initiates the decision-making process.

Processed materials Products created when firms transform raw materials from their original state.

Producers The individuals or organisations that purchase products for use in the production of other goods and services.

Product A tangible good, service, idea, or some combination of these that satisfies consumer or business customer needs through the exchange process; a bundle of attributes including features, functions, benefits and uses.

Product adoption The process by which a consumer or business customer begins to buy and use a new good, service or idea.

Product advertising An advertising message that focuses on a specific good or service.

Product category managers Individuals who are responsible for developing and implementing the marketing plan for all the brands and products within a product category.

Product competition When firms offering different products compete to satisfy the same consumer needs and wants.

Product concept development and screening The second step of product development in which marketers test product ideas for technical and commercial success.

Product development strategies Growth strategies that focus on selling new products in served markets.

Product lifecycle A concept that explains how products go through four distinct stages from birth to death: introduction, growth, maturity and decline.

Product line A firm's total product offering designed to satisfy a single need or desire of target customers.

Product specifications A written description of the quality, size, weight, and so forth required of a product purchase.

Production orientation A management philosophy that emphasizes the most efficient ways to produce and distribute products.

Projective technique Test that marketers use to explore people's underlying feelings about a product, especially appropriate when consumers are unable or unwilling to express their true reactions.

Promotion The coordination of a marketer's marketing communications efforts to influence attitudes or behaviour; the coordination of efforts by a marketer to inform or persuade consumers or organisations about goods, services or ideas.

Promotion mix The major elements of marketer-controlled communications, including advertising, sales promotions, public relations and personal selling.

Promotional products Goodies such as coffee mugs, T-shirts and magnets given away to build awareness for a sponsor. Some freebies are distributed directly to consumers and business customers; others are intended for channel partners such as retailers and vendors.

Prospecting A part of the selling process that includes identifying and developing a list of potential or prospective customers.

Protectionism A policy adopted by a government to give domestic companies an advantage.

Prototypes Test versions of a proposed product.

Psychographics The use of psychological, sociological and anthropological factors to construct market segments.

Public relations (PR) Communication function that seeks to build good relationships with an organisation's publics, including consumers, stockholders and legislators.

Public service advertisements (PSAs) Advertising run by the media without charge for not-for-profit organisations or to champion a particular cause.

Publicity Unpaid communication about an organisation appearing in the mass media.

Pull strategy The company tries to move its products through the channel by building desire for the products among consumers, thus convincing retailers to respond to this demand by stocking these items.

Push money A bonus paid by a manufacturer to a sales person, customer, or distributor for selling its product.

Q

Quantity discounts A pricing tactic of charging reduced prices for purchases of larger quantities of a product.

R

Radio frequency identification (RFID) Product tags with tiny chips containing information about the item's content, origin and destination.

Raw materials Products of the fishing, lumber, agricultural and mining industries that organisational customers purchase to use in their finished products.

Reach The percentage of the target market that will be exposed to the media vehicle.

Rebates Sales promotions that allow the customer to recover part of the product's cost from the manufacturer.

Receiver The organisation or individual that intercepts and interprets the message.

Reciprocity A trading partnership in which two firms agree to buy from one another.

Reference group An actual or imaginary individual or group that has a significant effect on an individual's evaluations, aspirations, or behaviour.

Relationship selling A form of personal selling that involves securing, developing, and maintaining long-term relationships with profitable customers.

Reliability The extent to which research measurement techniques are free of errors.

Re-positioning Re-doing a product's position to respond to market place changes.

Representativeness The extent to which consumers in a study are similar to a larger group in which the organisation has an interest.

Research design A plan that specifies what information marketers will collect and what type of study they will do.

Resellers The individuals or organisations that buy finished goods for the purpose of reselling, renting, or leasing to others to make a profit and to maintain their business operations.

Retail lifecycle A theory that focuses on the various stages that retailers pass through from introduction to decline.

Retailing The final stop in the distribution channel by which goods and services are sold to consumers for their personal use.

Return on investment (ROI) The direct financial impact of a firm's expenditure of a resource such as time or money.

Return on marketing investment (ROMI) Quantifying just how an investment in marketing impacts the firm's success, financially and otherwise.

Reverse marketing A business practice in which a buyer firm attempts to identify suppliers who will produce products according to the buyer firm's specifications.

S

Sales management The process of planning, implementing and controlling the personal selling function of an organisation.

Sales presentation The part of the selling process in which the sales person directly communicates the value proposition to the customer, inviting two-way communication.

Sales promotion Programmes designed to build interest in or encourage purchase of a product during a specified time period.

Sales territory A set of customers often defined by geographic boundaries for whom a particular sales person is responsible.

Sampling (1) Distributing free trial-size versions of a product to consumers.

Sampling (2) The process of selecting respondents who statistically represent a larger population of interest.

Scenario Possible future situation that futurists use to assess the likely impact of alternative marketing strategies.

Scrambled merchandising A merchandising strategy that offers consumers a mixture of merchandise items that are not directly related to each other.

Search qualities Product characteristics that the consumer can examine prior to purchase.

Secondary data Data that have been collected for some purpose other than the problem at hand.

Segment profile A description of the 'typical' customer in a segment.

Segmentation The process of dividing a larger market into smaller pieces based on one or more meaningful, shared characteristics.

Segmentation variables Dimensions that divide the total market into fairly homogeneous groups, each with different needs and preferences.

Selective distribution Distribution using fewer outlets than in intensive distribution but more than in exclusive distribution.

Self-concept An individual's self-image that is composed of a mixture of beliefs, observations and feelings about personal attributes.

Selling orientation A managerial view of marketing as a sales function, or a way to move products out of warehouses to reduce inventory.

Service encounter The actual interaction between the customer and the service provider.

Services Intangible products that are exchanged directly from the producer to the customer.

Servicescape The actual physical facility where the service is performed, delivered, and consumed.

SERVQUAL A multiple-item scale used to measure service quality across dimensions of tangibles, reliability, responsiveness, assurance and empathy.

Sex roles Society's expectations regarding the appropriate attitudes, behaviours and appearance for men and women.

Share of customer The percentage of an individual customer's purchase of a product that is a single brand.

Shopping centre A group of commercial establishments owned and managed as a single property.

Shopping product A good or service for which consumers spend considerable time and effort gathering information and comparing alternatives before making a purchase.

Single sourcing The business practice of buying a particular product from only one supplier.

Skimming A very high, premium price that a firm charges for its new, highly desirable product.

Slotting fees Fees a retailer may charge a manufacturer for setting up a new product in inventory and providing it with shelf space.

Social class The overall rank or social standing of groups of people within a society according to the value assigned to such factors as family background, education, occupation and income.

Source An organisation or individual that sends a message.

Specialised services Services purchased from outside suppliers that are essential to the operation of an organisation but are not part of the production of a product.

Specialty product A good or service that has unique characteristics and is important to the buyer and for which the buyer will devote significant effort to acquire.

Specialty shops Retailers that carry only a few product lines but offer good selection within the lines that they sell.

Sponsorships PR activities through which companies provide financial support to help fund an event in return for publicised recognition of the company's contribution.

Stakeholders Buyers, sellers and investors in a company; community residents, and even citizens of the nations where goods and services are made or sold – in other words, any person or organisation that has a 'stake' in the outcomes.

Standard Industrial Classification (SIC) System The numerical coding system commonly used to classify firms into detailed categories according to their business activities.

Standard of living An indicator of the average quality and quantity of goods and services consumed in a country.

Stimulus generalisation Behaviour caused by a reaction to one stimulus occurs in the presence of other, similar stimuli.

Store image The way a retailer is perceived in the marketplace relative to the competition.

Straight re-buy A buying situation in which business buyers make routine purchases that require minimal decision making.

Strategic alliance Relationship developed between a firm seeking a deeper commitment to a foreign market and a domestic firm in the target country.

Strategic business units (SBU) Individual units within the firm that operate like separate businesses, with each having its own mission, business objectives, resources, managers and competitors.

Strategic planning A managerial decision process that matches an organisation's resources and capabilities to its market opportunities for long-term growth and survival.

Subculture A group within a society whose members share a distinctive set of beliefs, characteristics or common experiences.

Supermarkets Food shops that carry a wide selection of edibles and related products.

Supply chain All the firms that engage in activities necessary to turn raw materials into a good or service and put it in the hands of the consumer or business customer.

Supply chain management The management of flows among firms in the supply chain to maximise total profitability.

SWOT analysis An analysis of an organisation's strengths and weaknesses and the opportunities and threats in its external environment.

Syndicated research Research by firms that collect data on a regular basis and sell the reports to multiple firms.

T

Take title To accept legal ownership of a product and the accompanying rights and responsibilities of ownership.

Target costing A process in which firms identify the quality and functionality needed to satisfy customers and what price they are willing to pay before the product is designed. The product is manufactured only if the firm can control costs to meet the required price.

Target market The market segments on which an organisation focuses its marketing plan and toward which it directs its marketing efforts.

Target marketing strategy Dividing the total market into different segments on the basis of customer characteristics, selecting one or more segments, and developing products to meet the needs of those specific segments.

Tariffs Taxes on imported goods.

Team selling The sales function when handled by a team that may consist of a sales person, a technical specialist, and others.

Technical development The step in the product development process in which a new product is refined and perfected by company engineers and the like.

Technical specialist A sales support person with a high level of technical expertise who assists in product demonstrations.

Telemarketing The use of the telephone to sell directly to consumers and business customers.

Test marketing Testing the complete marketing plan in a small geographic area that is similar to the larger market the firm hopes to enter.

Top-down budgeting techniques Allocation of the promotion budget based on the total amount to be devoted to marketing communications.

Total costs The total fixed costs and the variable costs for a set number of units produced.

Total quality management (TQM) A management philosophy that focuses on satisfying customers through empowering employees, from the assembly line onward, to be an active part of continuous quality improvement.

Trade or functional discounts Discounts off list price of products to members of the channel of distribution that perform various marketing functions.

Trade promotions Promotions that focus on members of the 'trade', which include distribution channel members, such as retail sales people or wholesale distributors, that a firm must work with in order to sell its products.

Trade shows Events at which many companies set up elaborate exhibits to show their products, give away samples, distribute product literature, and identify new business contacts.

Trademark The legal term for a brand name, brand mark, or trade character; trademarks legally registered by a government obtain protection for exclusive use in that country.

Traffic flow The direction in which shoppers will move through the shop and what areas they will pass or avoid.

Transactional data An ongoing record of individuals or organisations that buy a product.

Transactional selling A form of personal selling that focuses on making an immediate sale with little or no attempt to develop a relationship with the customer.

Transportation The mode by which products move among channel members.

Trial pricing Pricing a new product low for a limited period of time in order to lower the risk for a customer.

U

Unaided recall A research technique conducted by telephone survey or personal interview that asks whether a person remembers seeing an ad during a specified period of time.

Undifferentiated targeting strategy Appealing to a broad spectrum of people.

Uniform delivered pricing A pricing tactic in which a firm adds a standard shipping charge to the price for all customers regardless of location.

Unique selling proposition (USP) An advertising appeal that focuses on one clear reason why a particular product is superior.

Universal Product Code (UPC) The set of black bars or lines printed on the side or bottom of most items sold in grocery shops and other mass-merchandising outlets. The UPC, readable by scanners, creates a national system of product identification.

Unsought products Goods or services for which a consumer has little awareness or interest until the product or a need for the product is brought to his or her attention.

Usage occasions An indicator used in one type of market segmentation based on when consumers use a product most.

Utility The usefulness or benefit consumers receive from a product.

V

Validity The extent to which research actually measures what it was intended to measure.

Value The benefits a customer receives from buying a product or service.

Value chain Encompasses all the activities in a firm (designing, producing, marketing, delivery and supporting) which create products and services that in turn create value for the consumer and make a profit for the company. Each link in the chain has the potential to either add or remove value from the product the customer eventually buys.

Value pricing A pricing strategy in which a firm sets prices that provide ultimate value to customers.

Value proposition A marketplace offering that fairly and accurately sums up the value that will be realised if the product or service is purchased.

Variability The characteristic of a service that means that even the same service performed by the same individual for the same customer can vary.

Variable costs The costs of production (raw and processed materials, parts and labour) that are tied to and vary depending on the number of units produced.

Venture teams Groups of people within an organisation who work together focusing exclusively on the development of a new product.

Vertical marketing system (VMS) A channel of distribution in which there is formal cooperation among members at the manufacturing, wholesaling and retailing levels.

Viral marketing Creating entertaining or informative messages that are designed to be passed along in an exponential fashion, often electronically or by e-mail.

W

Want The desire to satisfy needs in specific ways that are culturally and socially influenced.

Warehousing Storing goods in anticipation of sale or transfer to another member of the channel of distribution.

Wheel-of-retailing hypothesis A theory that explains how retail firms change, becoming more upscale as they go through their lifecycle.

Wholesalers Intermediaries that buy goods from manufacturers (take title to them) and sell to retailers and other business-to-business customers.

Wholesaling intermediaries Firms that handle the flow of products from the manufacturer to the retailer or business user.

Word-of-mouth The act of consumers providing information to other consumers.

Word-of-mouth marketing Giving people a reason to talk about your products and services, and making it easier for that conversation to take place.

World trade The flow of goods and services among different countries – the value of all the exports and imports of the world's nations.

World Trade Organization (WTO) An organisation that replaced GATT, the WTO sets trade rules for its member nations and mediates disputes between nations.

Y

Yield management pricing A practice of charging different prices to different customers in order to manage capacity while maximising revenues.

Index

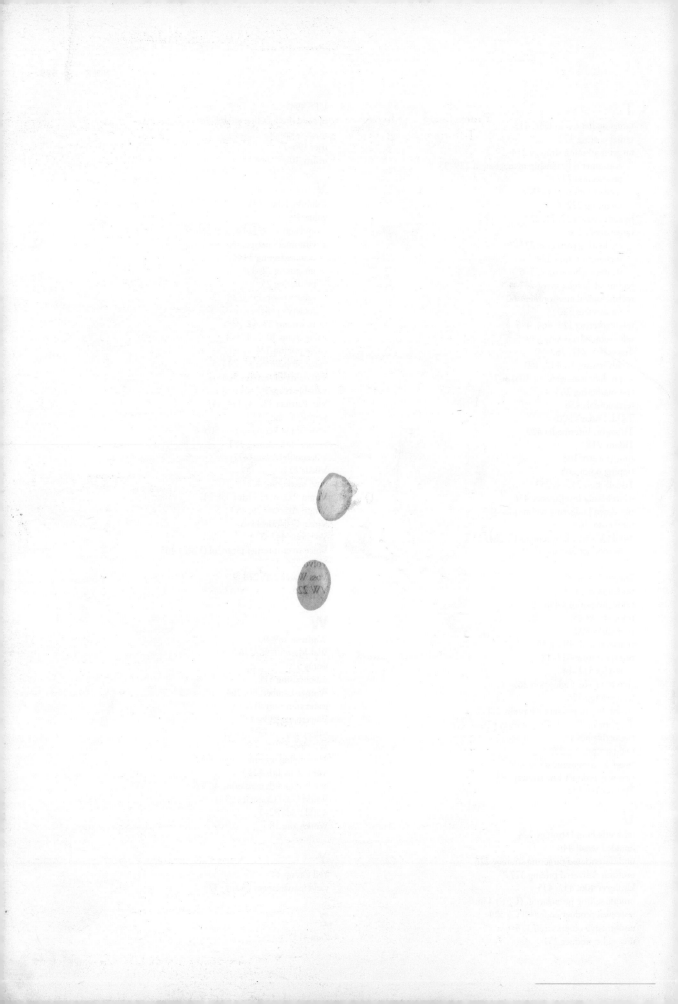